THE
unofficial GUIDE®
ᵀᴼSan Francisco

5TH EDITION

THE *unofficial* GUIDE®
TO San Francisco
5TH EDITION

RICHARD STERLING

Please note that prices fluctuate in the course of time and that travel information changes under the impact of many factors which influence the travel industry. We therefore suggest that you write or call ahead for confirmation when making your travel plans. Every effort has been made to ensure the accuracy of information throughout this book, and the contents of this publication are believed to be correct at the time of printing. Nevertheless, the publishers cannot accept responsibility for errors or omissions, for changes in details given in this guide, or for the consequences of any reliance on the information provided by the same. Assessments of attractions and so forth are based upon the author's own experience; therefore, descriptions given in this guide necessarily contain an element of subjective opinion, which may not reflect the publisher's opinion or dictate a reader's own experience on another occasion. Readers are invited to write the publisher with ideas, comments, and suggestions for future editions.

Published by:
John Wiley & Sons, Inc.
111 River Street
Hoboken, NJ 07030-5774

Produced by Menasha Ridge Press

Cover design by Michael J. Freeland

Interior design by Vertigo Design

For information on our other products and services or to obtain technical support, please contact our Customer Care Department within the United States at 800-762-2974, outside the United States at 317-572-3993, or by fax at 317-572-4002.

John Wiley & Sons, Inc., also publishes its books in a variety of electronic formats. Some content that appears in print may not be available in electronic formats.

ISBN 0-471-77638-6

Manufactured in the United States of America

5 4 3 2 1

CONTENTS

List of Maps vii
About the Author viii

Introduction 1
The City by the Bay: A Metropolitan Mecca 1
About This Guide 3

PART ONE **Planning Your Visit 11**
Understanding the City: A Brief History of San Francisco 11
When to Go: The Sweater Season and the ... Well, Sweater (Wetter) Season 23
How to Get More Information before Your Visit 25
Gays and Lesbians 26
A Calendar of Festivals and Events 29

PART TWO **Accommodations 35**
Deciding Where to Stay 35
Getting a Good Deal on a Room 38
Hotels and Motels: Rated and Ranked 46
Hotel Information Chart 62

PART THREE **Visiting on Business 85**
Not All Visitors Are Headed for Fisherman's Wharf 85

PART FOUR **Arriving and Getting Oriented 91**
Coming into the City 91
A Geographic Overview of San Francisco and the Bay Area 97

Things the Natives Already Know 120
How to Avoid Crime and Keep Safe in Public Places 124

PART FIVE **Getting Around 129**
Driving Your Car 129
Public Transportation 133

PART SIX **Sightseeing, Tours, and Attractions 141**
Touring San Francisco 141
San Francisco for Children 153
Helpful Tips for Tourists 156
San Francisco on Film 160
The Wine Country 161
Napa Valley 167
Sonoma Valley 176
Day Trips in and around the Bay Area 181
Beyond the Bay Area 191
Attraction Profiles 192

PART SEVEN **Dining and Restaurants 235**
The Restaurants 236
Restaurant Profiles 251

PART EIGHT **Entertainment and Nightlife 321**
Performing Arts 321
San Francisco Nightlife 323
Nightclub Profiles 327

PART NINE **Shopping 343**
Top Shopping Neighborhoods 344
The Malls 350
Specialty Shops 352

PART TEN **Exercise and Recreation 365**
The Great Indoors 365
Outdoors, Naturally! 368
Spectator Sports 382

Accommodations Index 387
Restaurant Index 393
Subject Index 397

LIST *of* MAPS

The Bay Area x
San Francisco Neighborhoods 8–9
Accommodations around Town 56–57
Union Square and Nob Hill Accommodations 58
The Civic Center 101
Fisherman's Wharf and Vicinity 106
Golden Gate Park 113
Haight-Ashbury and the Castro 115
The Wine Country 162
Marin County 182
Attractions around Town 194–195
Golden Gate National Recreation Area 196–197
Yerba Buena Gardens and Environs 233
Dining around Town 246–247
Union Square Dining 248
Chinatown Dining 249
San Francisco After Dark 328–329

ABOUT *the* AUTHOR

RICHARD STERLING IS AN AUTHOR of and contributor to numerous cookbooks and guidebooks covering California, Latin America, and Asia. Richard is well known in the Bay Area for his varied and eclectic accomplishments.

THE *unofficial* GUIDE®
ᵀᴼSan Francisco

5TH EDITION

the bay area

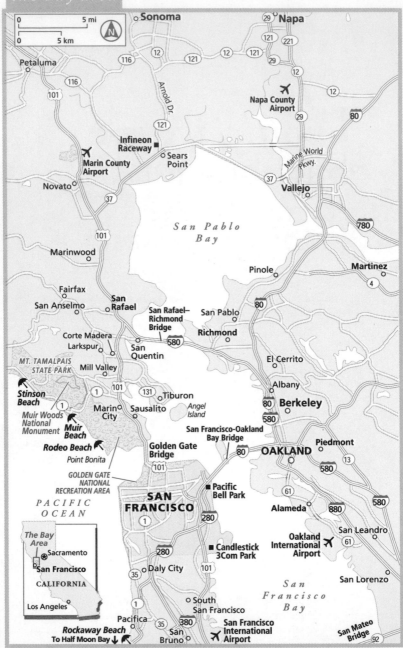

0 — 5 mi
0 — 5 km

Sonoma
Napa
29
121
221
Petaluma
116
12
121
12
121
29
12
101
116
Arnold Dr.
Napa County Airport
12
29
80
Infineon Raceway
Sears Point
121
Marin County Airport
Marine World Pkwy.
37
Vallejo
Novato
37
780
San Pablo Bay
Marinwood
Pinole
Martinez
4
Fairfax
San Anselmo
San Rafael
San Rafael–Richmond Bridge
San Pablo
80
Richmond
Corte Madera
Larkspur
San Quentin
580
El Cerrito
MT. TAMALPAIS STATE PARK
Mill Valley
Albany
Stinson Beach
101
1
131
Tiburon
80
Berkeley
Muir Woods National Monument
Marin City
Sausalito
Angel Island
580
Muir Beach
Rodeo Beach
Point Bonita
Golden Gate Bridge
San Francisco-Oakland Bay Bridge
Piedmont
80
OAKLAND
13
GOLDEN GATE NATIONAL RECREATION AREA
101
580
PACIFIC OCEAN
SAN FRANCISCO
Pacific Bell Park
61
Alameda
880
580
1
280
Oakland International Airport
61
San Leandro
The Bay Area
Sacramento
280
San Francisco
CALIFORNIA
35
Daly City
101
Candlestick 3Com Park
San Francisco Bay
San Lorenzo
Los Angeles
1
South San Francisco
Pacifica
35
380
San Bruno
San Francisco International Airport
San Mateo Bridge
92
Rockaway Beach
To Half Moon Bay ↓

INTRODUCTION

THE CITY *by the* BAY: A METROPOLITAN MECCA

FACE WEST. YES, WEST—TOWARD THAT REVERED and endeared bay city we call San Francisco. Gold diggers armed with little more than a pan and a dream pointed their wagons west to brave the new frontier. Westbound beatniks hitched rides with pockets full of poems, prepared for philosophical face-offs. Hippies happily hitched, carrying all they could possibly want: a joint and a cause. Ivy League graduates hungry for opportunity headed west with an idea and a business plan—and made millions incidentally. East Coasters with a desire for "more" (and better weather) packed up and settled here. And visitors looking for active or relaxing vacations have found everything they are looking for in one city—San Francisco, the Mecca of the West.

You won't find a single bit of bad press on San Francisco (San Fran for short, *never* Frisco). Sure, the boom fizzled and the lights may go dim from time to time, but this Paris of the Pacific, Athens of the West, continues to leave the welcome mat out and the door unlocked for anyone desiring to experience its magical spirit and breadth of opportunity.

The city never fails to live up to expectations. If thick afternoon fog has put a damper on your day, sunny skies await across any bridge. Not used to the towering buildings of downtown? Less than 20 minutes away, across the Golden Gate, are fat-tire trails, blazed hiking trails, cycling paths, romantic hideaways, and some of the best views in the country. There are certain things you can always count on in San Francisco—civic and cultural pride, cool summers, fog horns, hilly streets, mountain vistas and ocean views, and sunny skies across both bridges (the Golden Gate and the Bay Bridge). You will put on and take off a sweater at least three times on any walk, so count on carrying one, as there are distinct pockets of climate in different areas. Maybe that's why visitors come year after year: San Francisco is different, diverse, and easy to love. Even its parameters are easy: 7 by 7 miles, which includes 43 steep hills! A simple formula for a simply enchanting place.

In spite of the gentrification that swept many of San Francisco's neighborhoods during the late 1990s, there still remains a strong mix of culture and cultural identity. The gateway to Asia, San Francisco supports a multicultural population of Chinese, Japanese, and Filipinos. And, lucky you, such cultural diversity brings an amazing assortment of culinary delights. For dim sum or the latest in Chinese herbal medicine, a stroll in Chinatown will cure any craving or cramp. Homemade ravioli is redolent through the streets of North Beach, the city's little Italy. For great Hispanic food, head on over to Cha Cha Cha's after perusing the vibrant art at the Mexican Museum. And what good is a city by a bay if it doesn't boast seafood? Alioto's and Scoma's at Fisherman's Wharf are musts for newbies. Adding to this cosmopolitan bouillabaisse is a gay population that may constitute as much as 25% of the city's total population. The neighborhoods of San Francisco overlap and interrelate, but they maintain distinct identities.

As a result of such strong cultural influences, the arts flourish here. The Mission District is a melting pot of public murals (more than 60 in an eight-block area). More organized venues exist as well: Fort Mason, where you can touch down artistically on three continents; museums showcasing Mexican, Italian-American, and African-American culture; and a world-class opera house, symphony, and ballet company. Contemporary-art lovers will enjoy the renaissance of SoMa, the Soho of San Francisco. The opening of the Museum of Modern Art and the Center for the Arts sparked a gallery boom South of Market (SoMa). Whether you like independent theater, poetry readings, or opera, it is all represented here. And no exploration of the city's arts would be complete without a perusal of Victorians. The houses line the steep hills of the city like trim on a wedding cake. A must do—to really take in the beauty of the homes, hills, and views that the city offers—is a drive down (and I mean down) Divisadero Street. This is just one of a bunch of vantage points that allow you, in one glance, to capture the beauty and enchantment of the city with your camera and your heart.

Europeans love San Francisco because it's the most European of American cities, and Hispanics gravitate to its Spanish-speaking community. San Francisco is home to one of the largest Chinese populations in the United States. Even tough-skinned and proud New Yorkers adore San Francisco, comparing it favorably with the Big Apple.

This book is equally designed for planning a solo getaway, a romantic escape, a visit to a friend or family member, or a family trip.

It's for anyone who wants to see San Francisco's famous vistas, distinct neighborhoods, excellent museums, theater companies, and fabled nightlife; and it is also for business travelers who want to avoid its worst hassles. We show you the best times to visit San Francisco's best-known sights, how to get off the beaten path, and how to avoid the worst crowds and traffic. We suggest the best seasons to visit and offer detailed itineraries and touring strategies for seeing some spectacular destinations beyond the city limits.

In spite of the challenges it presents to first-time visitors, San Francisco never fails to charm. Like the joke says, San Francisco is everyone's favorite city—even people who have never been there. Locals love their city and most of them enjoy sharing its attractions. With their help, and armed with this book, you're ready to discover the incomparable City by the Bay.

ABOUT *this* GUIDE

HOW COME "UNOFFICIAL"?

JUST AS THE CITY OF SAN FRANCISCO INSPIRES unconventional ideas and promotes individuality, so does the goal of the "Unofficial" series. Most "official" guides to San Francisco tout the well-known sights, promote the local restaurants and hotels indiscriminately, and leave out the nitty-gritty. This one is different. We'll be up-front with you. There is more than Fisherman's Wharf, after all. Instead of nabbing you by the ankles in a tourist trap, we'll tell you if it's not worth the wait for the mediocre food served at a well-known restaurant. We'll complain loudly about overpriced hotel rooms that aren't convenient to downtown or the Moscone Convention Center, and we'll guide you away from the crowds and congestion for a break now and then. We'll direct you to little-known local joints and other unique experiences so you can earn bragging rights and satisfy your adrenaline craving.

We sent in a team of evaluators who toured downtown and its outlying neighborhoods and popular attractions, ate in the Bay Area's best and most unique restaurants, performed critical evaluations of the hotels, and visited San Francisco's best and most offbeat nightclubs. If a museum is boring or a major attraction is overrated, we say so—and, in the process, make your visit exactly that: *your* visit.

We got into the guidebook business because we were unhappy with the way travel guides make the reader work to get any usable information. Wouldn't it be nice, we thought, if we made guides that were easy to use?

OTHER GUIDEBOOKS

MOST GUIDEBOOKS ARE COMPILATIONS OF LISTS. This is true regardless of whether the information is presented in list form or artfully distributed through pages of prose. There is insufficient detail in a list, and with prose the presentation can be tedious and contain large helpings of nonessential or marginally useful information. Not enough wheat, so to speak, for nourishment in one instance, and too much chaff in the other. Either way, other guides provide little more than departure points from which readers initiate their own quests.

Sure, many guides are readable and well researched, but they tend to be difficult to use. To select a hotel, for example, a reader must study several pages of descriptions with only the names of the hotels in bold type breaking up the text. Because each description essentially deals with the same variables, it is difficult to recall what was said concerning a particular hotel. Readers generally have no alternative but to work through all the write-ups before beginning to narrow their choices. The presentation of restaurants, clubs, and attractions is similar except that even more reading is usually required. To use such a guide is to undertake an exhaustive research process that requires examining nearly as many options and possibilities as starting from scratch. Recommendations, if any, lack depth and conviction. By failing to narrow travelers' choices down to a thoughtfully considered, well-distilled, and manageable few, these guides compound rather than solve problems.

HOW UNOFFICIAL GUIDES ARE DIFFERENT

WHILE A LOT OF GUIDEBOOKS HAVE BEEN WRITTEN about San Francisco, very little has been evaluative. Most guides come close to regurgitating the hotels' and tourist offices' own promotional material. In preparing this work, however, nothing was taken for granted. Each museum, monument, art gallery, hotel, restaurant, shop, and attraction was visited by a team of trained observers who conducted detailed evaluations and rated each place according to formal criteria. Interviews were conducted to determine what tourists of all ages enjoyed most and least during their visits to San Francisco.

Readers care about the author's opinion. The author, after all, is supposed to know what he is talking about. This, coupled with the fact that the traveler wants quick answers (as opposed to endless alternatives), dictates that authors should be explicit, prescriptive, and, above all, direct. The *Unofficial Guide* tries to do just that. It spells out alternatives and recommends specific courses of action. It simplifies complicated destinations and attractions and allows the traveler to feel in control in the most unfamiliar environments. The objective of the *Unofficial Guide* is not to have the most information or all of the information; it aims to have the most accessible, useful information, unbiased by affiliation with any organization or industry.

An *Unofficial Guide* is a critical reference work that focuses on a travel destination that appears especially complex. Our authors and research team are completely independent from the attractions, restaurants, and hotels we describe. The *Unofficial Guide to San*

Francisco is designed for everyone—couples, women, groups, or individuals traveling for fun, as well as for business travelers and convention-goers, especially those visiting the city for the first time. The guide is directed at value-conscious, consumer-oriented adults who seek a cost-effective, though not Spartan, travel style.

In compiling this guide, we recognize that tourists' age, background, and interests will strongly influence their taste in San Francisco's wide array of activities and attractions and will account for a preference of one over another. Our sole objective is to provide the reader with sufficient description, critical evaluation, and pertinent data to make knowledgeable decisions according to individual tastes.

SPECIAL FEATURES

THE *UNOFFICIAL GUIDE* INCORPORATES THE following special features:

- Friendly introductions to San Francisco's vast array of fascinating neighborhoods
- "Best of" listings giving our qualified opinion on things ranging from bagels to baguettes, five-star hotels to the best views of San Francisco and the Bay Area by night
- Listings keyed to your interests, so you can pick and choose
- Advice to sightseers on how to avoid crowds; advice to business travelers on how to avoid traffic and excessive cost
- A hotel chart that helps narrow your choices fast, according to your needs
- Shorter listings that include only those restaurants, nightclubs, and hotels we think are worth considering
- A detailed index and table of contents to help you find things quickly

HOW THIS GUIDE WAS RESEARCHED AND WRITTEN

WHILE OUR OBSERVERS ARE INDEPENDENT AND impartial, they do not claim to have special expertise. Like you, they visited San Francisco as tourists or business travelers, noting their satisfaction or dissatisfaction.

The primary difference between the average tourist and the trained evaluator is the evaluator's skills in organization, preparation, and observation. The trained evaluator is responsible for much more than simply observing and cataloging. While the average tourist is engrossed when touring Alcatraz, for instance, the professional is rating the attraction in terms of pace, how quickly crowds move, the location of restrooms, and how well children can see through the cellhouse windows to the San Francisco skyline across the Bay. The evaluator also checks out other nearby attractions, alternative places to go if the line at a main attraction is too long, and the best local lunch options. Observer teams used detailed checklists to analyze hotel rooms, restaurants, nightclubs, and attractions. Finally, evaluator ratings and observations were integrated with tourist reactions and the opinions of patrons for a comprehensive profile of each feature and service.

HOW INFORMATION IS ORGANIZED: BY SUBJECT AND BY GEOGRAPHIC AREA

TO GIVE YOU FAST ACCESS TO INFORMATION about the best of San Francisco, we've organized material in several formats.

HOTELS Because most people visiting San Francisco stay in one hotel for the duration of their trip, we have summarized our coverage of hotels in charts, maps, ratings, and rankings that allow you to quickly focus your decision-making process. We do not go on for page after page describing lobbies and rooms that, in the final analysis, sound much the same. Instead we concentrate on the variables that differentiate one hotel from another: location, size, room quality, services, amenities, and cost.

RESTAURANTS We provide a lot of detail when it comes to restaurants. Because you will probably eat a dozen or more restaurant meals during your stay, and because not even you can predict what you might be in the mood for on Saturday night, we provide thorough profiles of the best restaurants in and around San Francisco.

ATTRACTIONS There are those of you who love taking in all the sights and attractions, and those of you who are offended at the thought of taking a cable car to Fisherman's Wharf or Coit tower. OK, OK. We understand the needs of all our selective readers and, as such, have organized much of the city's sites into a handy time-saving chart divided by geographic area. Gonna be in the Marina for dinner? Well, see what's in the area and organize your day accordingly. Saves you time, money, and foot ache!

ENTERTAINMENT AND NIGHTLIFE Visitors frequently try several different clubs or nightspots during their stay. Because clubs and nightspots, like restaurants, are usually selected spontaneously after arriving in San Francisco, we believe detailed descriptions are warranted. The best nightspots and lounges in San Francisco are profiled by category under nightlife in the same section.

GEOGRAPHIC AREA Once you've decided where you're going, getting there becomes the issue. To help you do that, we have divided the San Francisco Bay Area into geographic areas.

CHINATOWN	SOMA/MISSION DISTRICT, INCLUDING NOE
CIVIC CENTER	VALLEY AND POTRERO HILL
UNION SQUARE	RICHMOND/SUNSET DISTRICT
FINANCIAL DISTRICT	TIBURON/SAUSALITO
MARINA DISTRICT	SUBURBAN MARIN
NORTH BEACH	MARIN HEADLANDS TO POINT REYES

LETTERS, COMMENTS, AND QUESTIONS FROM READERS

DO YOU HAVE SOME ISSUES WITH OUR SUGGESTION for the best place to find a scoop of ice cream or cup of joe to go, or did we overlook a well-known San Francisco institution? We want to hear from you! We expect to learn from our mistakes, as well as from the input of our readers, and to improve with each book and edition. Many of those who use the *Unofficial Guide* write to us asking questions, making comments, or sharing their own discoveries and lessons learned in San Francisco. We appreciate your input, both positive and critical, and encourage our readers to continue writing. Readers' comments and observations will be frequently incorporated into revised editions of the *Unofficial Guide* and will contribute immeasurably to its improvement.

How to Write the Author

Richard Sterling
The Unofficial Guide to San Francisco
P.O. Box 43673
Birmingham, AL 35243
UnofficialGuides@menasharidge.com

When you write by mail, be sure to put your return address on your letter as well as on the envelope—sometimes envelopes and letters get separated. And remember, our work takes us out of the office for long periods of time, so please forgive us if our response is delayed.

Our warmest welcome to San Francisco, the City by the Bay.

san francisco neighborhoods

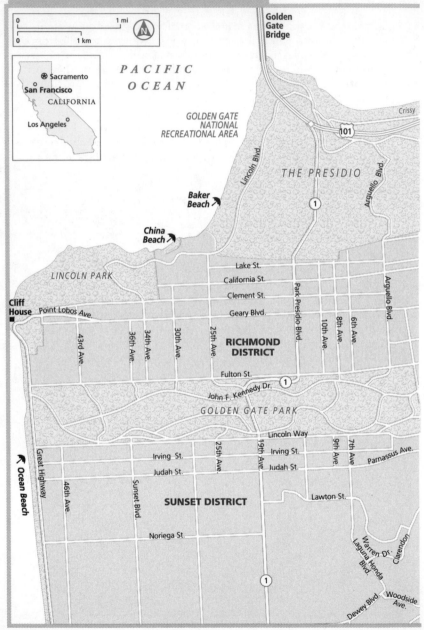

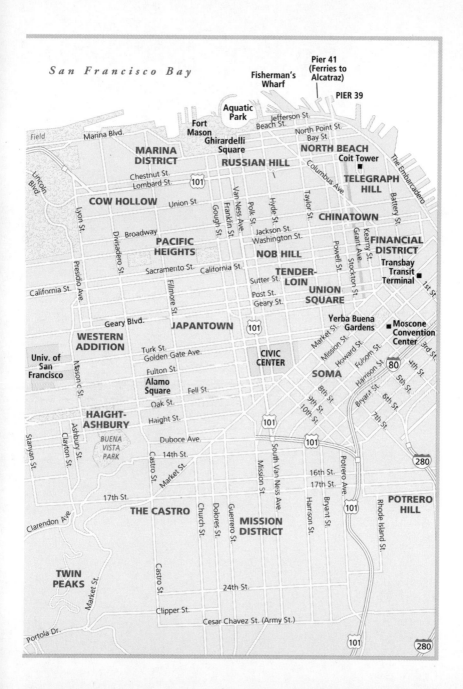

San Francisco Bay

Pier 41
(Ferries to
Alcatraz)

Fisherman's
Wharf

PIER 39

Field

Marina Blvd.

Aquatic
Park

Jefferson St.
Beach St.

Fort
Mason

Ghirardelli
Square

North Point St.
Bay St.

MARINA
DISTRICT

RUSSIAN HILL

NORTH BEACH
Coit Tower

Chestnut St.
Lombard St.

101

COW HOLLOW

Union St.

TELEGRAPH
HILL

Lincoln
Blvd

Lyon St.

Divisadero St.

Broadway

Van Ness Ave.

Franklin St.

Gough St.

Polk St.

Hyde St.

Taylor St.

Columbus Ave.

CHINATOWN

Battery St.

The Embarcadero

PACIFIC
HEIGHTS

Jackson St.
Washington St.

NOB HILL

Grant Ave.

Kearny St.

Stockton St.

FINANCIAL
DISTRICT

Presidio Ave.

Sacramento St.

California St.

Powell St.

Transbay
Transit
Terminal

California St.

Fillmore St.

Sutter St.

TENDER-
LOIN

1st St.

Post St.
Geary St.

UNION
SQUARE

Geary Blvd.

JAPANTOWN

101

Yerba Buena
Gardens

Moscone
Convention
Center

WESTERN
ADDITION

Turk St.
Golden Gate Ave.

CIVIC
CENTER

Market St.

Mission St.

Howard St.

3rd St.

Univ. of
San
Francisco

Mason St.

Fulton St.

SOMA

Folsom St.

80

4th St.

5th St.

Alamo
Square

Fell St.

8th St.

Harrison St.

Bryant St.

6th St.

Oak St.

9th St.

7th St.

HAIGHT-
ASHBURY

Haight St.

10th St.

Stanyan St.

Ashbury St.

Clayton St.

BUENA
VISTA
PARK

Duboce Ave.

14th St.

101

101

280

Castro St.

Market St.

South Van Ness Ave.

Mission St.

16th St.

17th St.

Potrero Ave.

POTRERO
HILL

17th St.

Rhode Island St.

101

Clarendon Ave

THE CASTRO

Church St.

Dolores St.

Guerrero St.

MISSION
DISTRICT

Harrison St.

Bryant St.

TWIN
PEAKS

Market St.

Castro St.

24th St.

Clipper St.

Cesar Chavez St. (Army St.)

Portola Dr.

101

280

PART ONE

PLANNING *your* VISIT

UNDERSTANDING *the* CITY: A BRIEF HISTORY *of* SAN FRANCISCO

AFTER NEW YORK CITY, SAN FRANCISCO IS THE most densely populated city in the United States, with more than 720,000 people crowded on a 49-square-mile peninsula. Understanding why so many people choose to live here is easy: You really never need a down-filled coat or shorts, and the city serves as a backdrop to some of the most beautiful natural landscapes on the planet. The Golden Gate Bridge is photographed widely for its red features towering above the misty fog that engulfs the city predictably every summer and early mornings. Make a turn down Marina Boulevard toward the bridge and you will certainly feel a sense of wonder and peace at the surreal beauty that is within the city and across the bridge. Mountains abound, scenic drives with hairy cliffside drops are everywhere, palm trees and parks punctuate the city . . . it is one of the most beautiful and interesting cities you will ever experience.

THE ORIGINAL NATIVES

THE FIRST SPANISH SETTLERS ARRIVED JUST OVER 200 years ago. But for thousands of years before that, the Bay Area was occupied by Miwok, Ohlone, and Wituk Native American people, who lived across much of Northern California. They formed small villages and survived mainly by hunting and fishing. Not much is known about the earliest San Francisco natives, and the ecologically conscious can only imagine the kinds of lives these Native Americans enjoyed in this beautiful landscape.

One of the first colonists characterized the Indians as "constant in their good friendship and gentle in their manners." But without any political or social organization beyond the tribal level, it did not take long after the first Spanish settlement was built for the local tribes to be wiped out, probably through epidemics brought by the settlers rather than outright genocide. Today, no Bay Area Native Americans survive on their original homelands.

EARLY EXPLORERS

AS YOU DRINK IN THE VIEW FROM FORT POINT OR the visitor center at the southern end of the Golden Gate Bridge, it's hard to imagine that ships cruising up or down the California coast could miss such an impressive sight. But they did. Dozens of European explorers, including heavy hitters such as Juan Cabrillo, Sir Francis Drake, and Sebastian Vizcaino, sailed past for centuries, oblivious of the great harbor beyond. Why? The opening is cloaked in fog for much of the year; even on clear days, the East Bay hills rise behind the opening and disguise the entrance to the point of invisibility.

Sir Francis Drake may have come close. In 1579, while on a mission from Queen Elizabeth I to "annoy" the Spanish provinces, he passed by the bay's entrance. Like so many other explorers, he never saw it. Drake anchored his ship, the *Golden Hind,* just to the north and sent several landing parties ashore. He was met by a band of Miwoks who greeted him with food and drink; in return, Drake claimed their land for Queen Elizabeth and named it Nova Albion (New England).

The first Europeans to cast their eyes on the Bay Area and the site of the future San Francisco were in a company of 60 Spanish soldiers, mule skinners, priests, and Indians led by Gaspar de Portola. The small contingent was the advance party of 300 soldiers and clergy on an overland mission from Mexico in 1769 to secure lands north of the colony for Spain and convert the heathens. Somewhere around Half Moon Bay, south of San Francisco, Portola sent out two scouting parties, one north up the coast and the other east into the mountains. Both groups returned with extraordinary descriptions of the Golden Gate—the entrance from the Pacific into the safe waters of the harbor—and the huge bay. On November 4 the entire party gathered on an exposed ridge, overwhelmed by the incredible view. Father Crespi, the priest, wrote that the bay "could hold not only all the armadas of our Catholic Monarch, but also all those of Europe."

FIRST SETTLEMENT

IT WAS ANOTHER SIX YEARS BEFORE THE SPANISH sent an expedition to explore the bay Portola had discovered. In May 1775, Juan Manuel de Ayala became the first European to sail into San Francisco Bay, when he piloted the *San Carlos* through the Golden Gate. A year later Captain Juan Bautista de Anza came back with 200 soldiers and settlers to establish the Presidio of San Francisco overlooking the Golden Gate. He also established a mission three miles to the southeast along a creek he named Nuestra Señora de Dolores—"Our Lady of Sorrows"—from which comes the mission's name, Mission Dolores. (It's the oldest building in San Francisco.)

Four more missions were established in the Bay Area in the following years. Each was similar, with a church and cloistered residence surrounded by irrigated fields, vineyards, and ranch lands. A contingent of soldiers protected the missions, many of which were attacked by Native Americans. To resist fire, the ubiquitous red-tiled roof replaced the thatched roof. By the end of the 18th century, the Bay Area settlements' population remained less than 1,000. Northern California was still a remote outpost and held little appeal for foreign adventurers. While the garrison was strong enough to resist Indian attacks, it would have easily fallen to attacks from the sea, had there been any.

Small towns, called "pueblos," were established to grow food for the missions and to attract settlers. The first, San Jose, was built in a broad, fertile valley south of Mission Santa Clara. Though the town was considered successful, fewer than 100 inhabitants lived there until well into the 1800s. Another small village, not sanctioned by Spanish authorities, emerged between Mission Dolores and the Presidio around a deepwater landing spot southeast of Telegraph Hill. Called Yerba Buena, or "good grass" (after the sweet-smelling minty herb that grew wild on the nearby hills), it was little more than a collection of shanties and ramshackle jetties. Although not called San Francisco until the late 1840s, this was the beginning of the city.

MEXICAN INDEPENDENCE AND AMERICAN SETTLERS

IN THE 1820s, THE BAY AREA WAS STILL A REMOTE backwater. The mission era ended with the independence of Mexico in 1821; in a few years the missions were secularized, and their lands were handed over to Californios—mostly former soldiers who had settled there after completing their service. The Mexican government hardly exercised any control over distant Yerba Buena and was more willing than the Spanish to let foreigners settle and remain.

In the early part of the decade, a number of Americans and Brits started to arrive in the Bay Area. Many were sailors who jumped ship—even in its toddler years, San Francisco attracted those souls seeking a better life! Other settlers came, started businesses, and influenced the development of San Francisco into a major port town. William Richardson, for example, arrived on a whaling ship in 1822 and stayed for the rest of his life. He married the daughter of the Presidio commander, eventually owned most of southern Marin County, started a profitable shipping company, and ran the only ferry service across the treacherous bay waters.

While the locals were doing well by the 1840s, the Bay Area wasn't viewed as being rich in natural resources, and as a result it wasn't a major factor in international relations. In the 1830s the U.S. government decided to buy all of Mexico north of the Rio Grande, but nothing happened until June 1846, when the Mexican-American War broke out in Texas. U.S. naval forces quickly took over the West Coast—the fulfillment of the United States' "manifest destiny" to cover the continent from coast to coast—and captured San Francisco's Presidio on July 9.

At about the same time, an interesting—although historically insignificant—event occurred north of San Francisco. An ambitious U.S. army captain, John C. Fremont, had been encouraging unhappy settlers to declare independence from Mexico and set him up as their leader. He assembled an unofficial force of about 60 sharpshooting ex-soldiers, spread rumors that war with Mexico was imminent, and persuaded settlers to join him. The result was the Bear Flag Revolt. On June 14, 1846, a force descended on the abandoned Presidio in Sonoma, took the retired commander captive, raised a makeshift flag over the plaza, and declared California independent. The flag, featuring a grizzly bear above the words "California Republic," was eventually adopted as the California state flag.

But the republic was short-lived. Three weeks after the disgruntled settlers hoisted the flag, it was replaced by the Stars and Stripes. California was now U.S. territory. Ironically, on January 24, 1848, just nine days before the U.S. government took formal control at the signing of the Treaty of Guadalupe (which ended the war with Mexico and ceded California to the United States), gold was discovered in the Sierra Nevada foothills 100 miles east of San Francisco. It changed the face of the city—and California—forever.

SUTTER'S SAWMILL AND THE GLEAM OF GOLD!

IT ALL STARTED WITH A SAWMILL. CONTRACTOR James Marshall and a work crew were commissioned to construct a sawmill for John Sutter, a Swiss immigrant whose Sacramento Valley ranch had been granted to him by the Mexican governor of California. On January 24, 1848, along the American River near Sacramento, Marshall uncovered a few tiny gold nuggets. Sutter tried to keep the find under his cap, but word got out. Aided by a notice printed in *The Californian* in San Francisco, as well as by more discoveries of gold by General John Bidwell, the great human migration west began. More than a half-million pioneering spirits from around the world descended upon California in search of instant wealth. By the end of May the editor of *The Californian* announced the suspension of his newspaper because the entire staff had quit. "The whole country from San Francisco to Los Angeles and from the sea shore to the base of the Sierra Nevada," he wrote, "resounds with the sordid cry of gold! GOLD! GOLD!—while the field is left half-planted, the house half-built, and everything neglected but the manufacture of shovels and pickaxes." Before the year was over, more prospectors arrived from neighboring territories, Mexico, and South America.

At the time gold was discovered, the total population of the Bay Area was around 2,000, about a quarter of whom lived in tiny San Francisco (changed from Yerba Buena the year before). Within a year, 100,000 men, known collectively as Forty-Niners (now you'll have one correct answer to a sports trivia question—that's the origin of the modern-day football team's name) had arrived in California; it was one of the most madcap migrations in history. While many of the prospectors passed through San Francisco, few stayed long before moving on to the gold fields. About half made a three-month slog across the continent to get there. And once there, as reflected in an essay written by a gold-hopeful Mr. Chandler, they were "bound to stick awhile longer." The lure of fortune was irresistible. Others arrived by ship in San Francisco, which at that time consisted of a few shoddily constructed buildings, abandoned hulks in the harbor, and rats overrunning filthy streets; there was also a shortage of drinking water. But by the winter of 1850, the shanty-town settlement began to evolve into a proper city. Former miners set up foundries and sawmills to supply prospectors, while traders arrived to cash in on miners' success, selling them clothing, food, drink, and entertainment.

The city where successful miners came to blow their hard-earned cash now boasted luxury hotels and burlesque theaters, some of which featured the semiclad "spider dance" of Lola Montez—the famous femme fatale of the gold rush. Throughout the 1850s, immigrants continued to pour into San Francisco. While many headed on to the mines, enough stuck around to increase the city's population to about 35,000 by the end of 1853. More than half were foreigners, chiefly Mexicans, Germans, Chinese, and Italians.

Lolaland

She may have been a bad dancer—booed and hissed off stage most of her performing life—but she made history with her vicious temper, whip snapping, and bedroom antics. The infamous femme fatale of the Victorian age, Lola Montez stormed the gold rush in California for a fresh start—after many marriages and a decade of seducing kings and czars across Europe—in order to pursue her dream of becoming a respected performer and actress.

She opened a saloon in a boisterous mining town called Grass Valley. Her act included Louis XVI cabinets, ormolu mirrors, priceless jewels from her ex-husbands, a pet bear, a swan bed, gold leaf, and one extra-large deep-red-top billiard table with dragons carved on its legs. With a bosom worth as much as the nuggets of gold and her crazy delusions of capturing California from the United States and becoming the Queen of "Lolaland," she attracted governors, senators, and millionaires.

Early comers to the gold fields made instant fortunes by merely washing nuggets out of streams or scraping gold dust from easily accessible veins in the rock, but it was much more difficult for later arrivals. The real money was being made by merchants, many of whom charged outrageous prices for essentials: $50 for a dozen eggs, $100 for a shovel or pick axe. There were reports of exuberant miners trading a shot glass full of gold dust for an equal amount of whiskey—something like $1,000 a shot.

But the real necessities were buckets, shovels, dippers, and pans. Before long, those who supplied everyday items to prospectors were richer than the miners themselves. Levi Strauss, for instance, arrived from Germany to sell tents but ended up converting his supply of canvas into durable pants. Women, too, were in short supply. Hundreds of prostitutes boarded ships in Mexico and South America, knowing their fares would be paid on arrival by captains selling them to the highest bidder.

THE GOLD BUST

FIVE YEARS AFTER THE DISCOVERY OF GOLD, the easy pickings were gone and the freewheeling mining camps evolved into corporate operations. San Francisco swelled from a frontier outpost to a bustling city with growing industry, a branch of the U.S. Mint, and a few newspapers. But when revenues from the gold fields leveled out in the late 1850s, the speculative base that had made so many fortunes dried up. Building lots that had been advertised at premium rates couldn't be given away, banks went belly-up, and San Francisco declared bankruptcy, following years of political corruption. The freewheeling city descended into near anarchy, and mobs roamed the streets. By the summer of 1856, the Committee of Vigilance was the city's de facto government and hanged petty criminals in front of enthusiastic mobs. Soon, though, cooler heads prevailed and the city was restored to legitimate governance. The rest of the 1850s was relatively uneventful.

BOOM . . .

BUT WHATEVER CHANCE SAN FRANCISCO HAD of becoming placid ended in 1859, when another torrent of riches flowed down the slopes of the Sierras. This time it was silver, not gold. The Comstock Lode, one of the most fantastic deposits ever discovered, was a solid vein of silver mixed with gold, ranging from 10 to more than 100 feet wide and stretching to more than two miles long. It would be an even bigger boom than the gold rush of a decade before.

Most of the silver, however, was buried several hundred feet underground, and mining it would be nothing like the freelance prospecting of the early gold rush. Many of San Francisco's great engineers, including George Hearst, Andrew Hallidie, and Adolf Sutro, put their talents to the formidable task. As the mines went deeper to get at the valuable ore, the mining companies needed larger infusions of capital, which they attracted by issuing shares dealt on the San Francisco Stock Exchange. Speculation was rampant, and the value of shares vacillated wildly, depending on daily rumors and forecasts. Fortunes were made and lost in a day's trading; cagier speculators made millions. By 1863, $40 million in silver had been wrenched from the tunnels around the boomtown of Virginia City, 105 miles from San Francisco, and 2,000 mining companies had traded shares on the city's mining exchange, further pumping up the city's economy.

. . . AND BUST

WHILE SAN FRANCISCO ENJOYED UNSURPASSED prosperity in the 1860s, another major development was taking place: the construction of a transcontinental railroad, completed in 1869. Although the trains opened up California, they also brought problems. The Southern Pacific ensnared San Francisco in its web, creating a monopoly over transportation in the Bay Area. Besides controlling long-distance railroads, the firm also owned the city's streetcar system, the network of ferry boats that crisscrossed the bay, and even the cable-car line that lifted rich San Franciscans up California Street to their Nob Hill palaces.

The coming of the railroad usurped San Francisco's role as the West Coast's primary supply point, and products began to flood in from the East well under prices that local industry could meet. At about the time the Comstock mines began to taper off, a depression set in. A series of droughts wiped out agricultural harvests, followed by the arrival of thousands of now-unwanted Chinese workers who had built the railroads. As unemployment rose through the late 1870s, frustrated workers took out their aggression on the city's substantial Chinese population. At mass demonstrations, thousands rallied behind the slogan, "The Chinese Must Go!" For much of the late 19th century, San Francisco wrestled with problems of racism; the need to build a varied, stable economy; and corruption in city politics.

A GOLDEN AGE

AT THE BEGINNING OF THE EARLY 20TH CENTURY, San Francisco was entering a golden age. The city now boasted a population of some 400,000 inhabitants—about 45% of the population of California (today it's about 4%). Political corruption was still a problem, but the economy was expanding—due in equal parts to the Spanish-American War and the Klondike Gold Rush in Alaska. Both events increased ship traffic in the port, where dockworkers were beginning to organize themselves into unions on an unprecedented scale.

THE GREAT EARTHQUAKE

CIVIC REFORMERS' EFFORTS TO REVERSE MUNICIPAL abuses were well under way when one of San Francisco's most defining events occurred: the Great Earthquake of 1906. On April 18, the city was awakened by violent earth tremors. At 8.1 on the Richter scale, it was the worst earthquake to hit the United States before or since (over ten times as strong as the 1989 quake). While the earthquake, which lasted 48 seconds, destroyed hundreds of buildings, the postquake conflagration caused the most damage. Ruptured natural gas mains exploded and chimneys toppled, starting fires across the city that destroyed 28,000 buildings. Looting was rampant, forcing the mayor to post a "Shoot to Kill" order. The fire raged for three days and all but leveled the entire area from the waterfront north to south of Market Street and west to Van Ness Avenue (where mansions were dynamited to form a fire break). Five hundred people were killed in the immense disaster and 100,000 were left homeless. Those who didn't flee the city made camp in what is now Golden Gate Park, where soldiers from the Presidio set up a tent city for about 20,000 displaced San Franciscans. Today you can pay tribute to one of the allies of the fight against total devastation—one fire hydrant that saved the Mission District from burning to the ground. The 1906 earthquake fire hydrant is on the corner of 20th and Church Streets.

RECOVERY

RESTORATION OF THE RUINED CITY BEGAN almost immediately. Financial assistance flooded in from around the world, $8 million in a few weeks. Even the hated Southern Pacific railroad pitched in, freighting in supplies without charge, offering free passage out of the city, and putting heavy equipment and cranes to work on clearing up rubble.

Much of the reconstruction was completed by 1912, and an era of political reform and economic restructuring was ushered in when James Rolph was elected mayor. The opening of the Panama Canal in 1914, which made the long sea journey around Cape Horn obsolete, and the first transcontinental phone call later that year (from Alexander Graham Bell himself) held great significance for San Francisco. The completion of the Civic Center and the opening of the Panama Pacific International Exhibition (which attracted 19 million visitors) were icing on the cake. The distant war in Europe had few repercussions in San Francisco beyond boosting the economy.

THE ROARING TWENTIES AND THE DEPRESSION

LIKE MOST AMERICAN CITIES, SAN FRANCISCO prospered through the 1920s after recovering from a steep drop in employment after World War I. Financiers and industrialists erected the city's first skyscrapers, and the jazz clubs and speakeasies of the Barbary Coast District were in full swing. San Francisco, now completely recovered from the 1906 quake, was the West Coast's premier art and culture center—a role that it passed to Los Angeles in the next decade. It was also a major banking center: the Bank of America, headquartered here, became the largest bank in the world.

After the stock market crash of 1929, San Francisco bore the full brunt of a recession that hit the city's port activities particularly hard. In 1934, one of the most severe strikes in its history broke out. On July 5—Bloody Thursday—police protecting strike-breakers from angry picketers fired into the crowd, wounding 30 and killing 2. The army was sent in to restore order; in retaliation, unions called a strike, and 125,000 workers put down their tools, halting San Francisco's economy for four days.

It was also an era that saw some of the city's finest monuments take form—for example, Coit Tower. In 1933, Alcatraz Island became the site of America's notorious federal prison. But most importantly, two great structures over San Francisco Bay, the Golden Gate Bridge and the San Francisco–Oakland Bay Bridge, were built. Before the bridges opened, the Bay Area was served by an impressive number of ferry boats; in 1935, their peak year, 100,000 commuters crossed San Francisco Bay by boat each day. Just five years later, the last of the ferries was withdrawn from service, unable to compete with the new bridges.

WORLD WAR II

FOLLOWING JAPAN'S ATTACK ON PEARL HARBOR and the advent of World War II, San Francisco became the main military port on the Pacific; more than 1.5 million servicemen were shipped to the South Pacific from Fort Mason. New shipyards sprang up within months, the number of factories tripled, and the Bay Area was transformed into a massive war machine. The Kaiser Shipyards in Richmond, the largest shipbuilding facility, employed more than 100,000 workers on round-the-clock shifts.

Men and women poured into the region from all over the country for jobs in the plants. Today, Hunters Point, one of the most economically distressed neighborhoods in San Francisco, and Marin City, one of its most affluent suburbs, are remnants of cities built to house the influx of workers who moved to the Bay Area during the war.

THE 1950s: EMERGENCE OF THE BEAT GENERATION

FOLLOWING THE WAR, THOUSANDS OF GIS RETURNING from the South Pacific passed through San Francisco and many decided to stay. New neighborhoods such as Sunset, with massive tracts of lookalike housing, were formed, and huge highways were built. The postwar years brought prosperity but also created a backlash. As the middle class moved out of the inner city, many of their offspring moved back in. North Beach bars and cafés incubated a wellspring of iconoclastic, antiestablishment youth in what was to become the Greenwich Village of the West Coast. Leading this movement was writer Jack Kerouac, who, after the publication of the movement-defining book *On the Road*, was asked by reporters to define the term "beat." He first heard the term a decade before his writing, from a rough-and-tumble 42nd Street–hustler who used the term to describe a state of exalted exhaustion. The novel was a classic story that broke open conformist 1950s America. The Beat Generation was news, and Kerouac had been officially dubbed its chief incarnation. Tired of conventional America, this tribe was searching—on a quest for spiritual identity and vision—and many of them found clarity in San Francisco.

The Beat Generation rebelled against the empty materialism of the 1950s; many lost themselves in orgies of jazz, drugs, and Buddhism. The new counterculture also fostered a highly personal, expressive blend of prose and poetry. City Lights Bookstore in North Beach became the focal point for the new literary movement, which included poets Lawrence Ferlinghetti (the shop's owner, who you can still spot in between book shelves—usually the poetry section) and the late Allen Ginsberg.

PSYCHEDELIC 1960s

BY THE EARLY 1960s THE STEAM WAS GONE from the Beat movement. Shortly thereafter, though, an offshoot of the antiestablishment trend surfaced—the hippies. Originally the term was a Beat putdown for the inexperienced, enthusiastic young people following in the footsteps of their countercultural elders. The first hippies appeared on college campuses around San Francisco.

There was a difference, though. Hippies were experimenting with a new hallucinogenic drug called LSD (better known by its street name, acid). Around 1965, hippies began moving into communes in low-rent Victorian houses in the Haight-Ashbury District, west of the city's center. It was the beginning of flower power and would culminate in 1967's "Summer of Love," when 100,000 young people converged on the area.

REVOLUTIONARY POLITICS

WHILE HIPPIES TUNED INTO PSYCHEDELIC MUSIC by bands such as Jefferson Airplane, Big Brother and the Holding Company, and the Grateful Dead, across the bay, in Berkeley and Oakland, it was politics, not acid and acid rock, that topped the agenda. The Free Speech Movement began at the University of California, Berkeley campus, in 1964 and laid the ground for passionate protests against the Vietnam War in the Bay Area and around the country later in the decade.

The most famous protest took place in Berkeley's People's Park, a plot of university-owned land that local activists took over as a community open space. Four days later, an army of police under the command of Edwin Meese (later attorney general under President Ronald Reagan) tear-gassed demonstrators and stormed the park, accidentally killing one bystander and seriously injuring more than 100 others.

In a response to the era's overt racism, the Black Panthers emerged in the impoverished flatlands of Oakland. Formed in 1966 by Bobby Seale, Huey Newton, and Eldridge Cleaver, the Panthers were a heavily armed but outnumbered band of activists who wanted self-determination for blacks. A nationwide organization sprung from the Oakland headquarters; 30 members across the country died in gun battles with police and the FBI.

MAKING HEADLINES: THE 1970s AND 1980s

STUDENT UNREST, ANTIWAR PROTESTS, AND FLOWER power spilled over into the early 1970s, though at a less-fevered pitch. One headline-grabbing event was the 1974 kidnapping of Patty Hearst, who was snatched from her Berkeley apartment by the Symbionese Liberation Army, a small, hardcore group of revolutionaries demanding free food for Oakland's poor in exchange for the rich heiress. Later on, during her captivity, Hearst helped the SLA and was photographed wielding a submachine gun in the robbery of a San Francisco bank.

Compared to the 1960s, most of the decade was quiet. The Bay Area Rapid Transit (BART) finally opened, and the Golden Gate National Recreation Area was established to protect 75,000 acres of incredibly scenic open areas on both ends of the Golden Gate Bridge. In 1973, the Transamerica Pyramid was completed, receiving mixed reviews from San Francisco critics; today it's a beloved piece of the city's skyline.

New battle lines were being drawn. The city's homosexuals, inspired by the 1969 Stonewall Riots in New York City, began to organize, demanding equal status with heterosexuals. Just as important, gays and lesbians "came out," refusing to hide their sexuality and giving rise to the gay liberation movement. One leader, Harvey Milk, won a seat on the city Board of Supervisors, becoming the first openly gay man to win public office in San Francisco. When he was assassinated in 1978 along with Mayor George Moscone, the entire city was shaken. A riot ensued when Milk's killer, former Supervisor Dan White, was found guilty of manslaughter and not murder.

In the 1980s, San Francisco's gay community retreated somewhat, hit by a staggering AIDS epidemic that toned down a notoriously promiscuous scene. The gay community, in conjunction with City Hall, continues to fight the disease.

During Mayor (now Senator) Diane Feinstein's term, San Francisco added millions of square feet of office towers to downtown's Financial District as some bemoaned the Manhattanization of the city.

There were also setbacks. A hundred million people watched on national TV as a 7.1 magnitude earthquake shook San Francisco during the third game of the 1989 World Series between Bay Area rivals, the San Francisco Giants and the Oakland As; freeways collapsed, power was out for three days, and dozens were killed. Two years later a horrific fire in the Oakland hills killed 26 people and destroyed 3,000 homes. In the early 1990s, most of the problems San Francisco faced were similar to those in other American cities: urban poverty, drug abuse, homelessness, and AIDS. An ongoing economic turndown in California was amplified by post–Cold War military cutbacks, which saw the closure of military bases in the Bay Area and the loss of 35,000 civilian jobs. But things were brewing about 30 miles south of San Francisco that would send the city into a mass of hysterics reminiscent of the flash and fortune during the gold rush era.

THE DOT: RIP

NOTHING DEFINES THE ECONOMIC AND SOCIAL climate in San Francisco in the mid-1990s more than a dot. The "dot com," as the Internet industry became known, redefined the global economy and sent investors running like dogs to a bone. In this case, the apparent billion-dollar bone would prove in the end to be bare for most investors and entrepreneurs alike.

The Nasdaq was at an all-time high, jobs were plentiful, and San Francisco more than any other city was riding high on the dot-com coattails, thanks to the technological revolution pouring out of neighboring Silicon Valley. Industrial SoMa District became the hub of Internet companies, trendy bars, and elaborate bashes. Rents soared, neighborhoods became gentrified, and stock options landed in the laps of everyone from landlords to graduating nieces. It seemed that retiring at the ripe old age of 30 wasn't just a pipe dream, and a million dollars could be earned by anyone from the mail clerk to the janitor. Hopes were high, bank accounts overflowing, and Mercedes and BMW dealerships quite busy.

Then in April 2000, there was a crash that sent heads spinning, horses galloping, and doors slamming in the Internet industry. As hard as it tried, the dot-com empire couldn't keep out profit loss, market devaluation, and downsizing. Pioneering fortune seekers were left in the rubble, sharing casualty stories at pink-slip parties. Their inflated titles and salaries faced judgment day in front of a more frugal post–dot com market. Jobs were hard to come by, and as a result most returned from where they came, with their tails between their legs.

Today, the city is in a state of transition. The transition comes with mixed feelings, however. Some native San Franciscans are happy to see the hype and prices fall, while others mourn the loss of the boom. In any case, vacancy signs in a once impossible real-estate market are swinging on chains outside buildings, rents are lowering, and the artistic community is seeing a revival. The face of technology is changing also, and it is a matter of time before recovery comes full circle and a new trend surfaces.

WHEN *to* GO: THE SWEATER SEASON *and the* . . . WELL, SWEATER (WETTER) SEASON

MAYBE YOU HAVEN'T HEARD, BUT SAN FRANCISCO isn't very warm—and summer is its coolest time. So right now you are probably staring at your suitcase packed with tanks, shorts, and swimsuits, thinking, "What the heck do I pack?" The answer is simple. Pack the fleece *and* the tank. The City by the Bay is in fact just that—a city by a bay—and it is regularly swept by winds from the water that surrounds it on three sides. Yet it boasts one of the most stable climates in the world. Temperatures during the day rarely venture more than 5°F from the average 60°F. Temperatures at night rarely drop lower than 40°F, and snow is virtually unheard of. This stable weather, however, can be frustrating. It is impossible to predict. With sunny rays beaming through your window, you'll wake up anticipating a bright, warm day, and by the time you've showered and tied your shoes, the fog is thick enough to cut with a knife and the temperature has turned chilly. We don't mean to sound like a nagging old grandmother, but dress in layers!

Now for the tank. Take a drive across any bridge and you'll feel a heat resurrection. The toes will start to uncurl and the hairs will flatten as all things simmer under the sun and heat that await in the East Bay, South Bay, and Marin County. Almost everywhere else in the Bay Area is warmer than San Francisco, especially in the summer, when Berkeley and Oakland bask in sunshine, and the wine country and surrounding valleys shrivel like prunes under the intense heat.

THE DRY SEASON

SORRY-I'M-NOT-THAT-WARM SAN FRANCISCO HAS two kinds of weather: wet and dry. The dry season starts in April and usually lasts through October (and sometimes into November). If the virtually dry months of July and August sound too good to be true, you're right. It is too good to be true. There's a catch—the city's fabled fog envelops the city mornings and evenings during much of the summer, hovering over the Golden Gate and obscuring the bridge. But the fog usually burns off by early afternoon—just in time for you to burn off that burrito by jogging, biking, or kayaking.

Summer is also the most crowded. If you're visiting in the summer, don't be like the rest of the shivering shorts-clad tourists at Fisherman's Wharf—bring the sweater! The city can be decidedly unsummerlike, even in July and August,

unofficial **TIP**
A final note: When dense afternoon fogs roll in during the summer months, the temperature can drop as much as 20°F in less than an hour.

especially at waterside locales such as the Wharf, Fort Point, the ocean beaches, and the Golden Gate Bridge.

THE WET SEASON

WINTER BRINGS MOST OF SAN FRANCISCO'S rainfall, usually starting sometime in November and continuing through March. Often the rain is quite torrential, especially in December and January. Yet daytime highs rarely plunge far below 60°F, and the lows hover in the mid-40s. Two days in a row without rain are rare on a winter trip to the city, but crowds are nonexistent and finding a convenient and reasonably priced hotel room is less of a hassle. And again, bring the sweaters.

THE SHOULDER SEASONS

IF YOU WANT TO ENJOY SAN FRANCISCO WHEN the weather is on its best behavior and you want to avoid large crowds, you have two options: spring and fall. These are the favorite seasons of *Unofficial Guide* researchers. In May and June the hills are at their greenest and are covered with wildflowers. Yet rainfall is nearly nil and daytime highs average in the mid-60s. Crowds at major tourist attractions usually don't pick up until later in the summer, when families with children begin to arrive. September and October are San Francisco's warmest months. They're popular months with visitors, but they lack the big crowds that pack the city's attractions during the height of the summer season. Warm, cloudless days are the norm. As a bonus, it's grape-harvesting season in the wine country, making a one- or two-day excursion to Napa or Sonoma imperative.

unofficial **TIP**
September and October are the city's least foggy months (although many visitors don't seem to mind the fog).

AVOIDING CROWDS

IN GENERAL, POPULAR TOURIST SITES ARE BUSIER on weekends, and Saturdays are busier than Sundays. The summer season by far is the busiest time of year at most attractions. If Alcatraz is on your itinerary (and if you're a first-time visitor to San Francisco, it should be), call in advance for tickets on a weekday, and hit attractions at Fisherman's Wharf on the same day. On summer weekends, the wharf is jammed with visitors.

Driving in San Francisco's rush-hour traffic is a true bite-your-nails experience. The major arteries and bridges are very congested during rush hour. If you're driving to the city on a weekday, avoid hitting town between 7 a.m. and 9 a.m. and between 4 p.m. and 6 p.m. If you're driving in on a weekend, you're still not off the hook. Traffic in and around San Francisco on Saturday and Sunday afternoons sometimes exceeds weekday rush-hour intensity. One theory is that frisky San Franciscans like to head to playgrounds outside of the city.

Evidence of this is seen as cars toting surfboards, snow'
kayaks, and ropes venture across the bridges. Another
the region around the city, the fifth-largest in the country, re
population of six million. On weekends, residents of San Jose, Be
ley, Oakland, and other towns nearby do what you would if you lived
here—they drive to San Francisco. Try to arrive before noon on
weekends and you'll miss the worst of the weekend crush.

HOW *to* GET MORE INFORMA-TION *before* YOUR VISIT

FOR ADDITIONAL INFORMATION ON ENTERTAINMENT, sightseeing, maps, shopping, dining, and lodging in San Francisco, call or
write:

San Francisco Convention and Visitors Bureau
Hallidie Plaza, 900 Market Street
San Francisco, CA 94102-2804
☎ 415-391-2000 or fax 415-362-7323
www.sfvisitor.org

The Convention and Visitors Bureau's Visitor Information Center
is in the Benjamin Swig Pavilion on the lower level of Hallidie Plaza
at Market and Powell Streets. It's easy to find, and the center's multilingual staff can help answer any questions you may have. Hours are
8:30 a.m. to 5 p.m. The center is closed Easter, Thanksgiving, Christmas, and New Year's Day.

There are great Web sites that can help in your preparation. A few
to check out include:

- **www.sfstation.com** provides up-to-the-minute events and insider information.
- **www.sfarts.org** will give you the scoop on everything indy, controversial, and artistic that's happening in all forms of art.
- **www.sfchamber.com** is your run-of-the-mill tourist information put out by the chamber of commerce. It's handy for maps and mainstream attractions.
- **www.sfgate.com** is a branch of the newspaper, the *Chronicle*. Great place for current events and activities, as well as jobs (if the city inspires you enough to move!).
- **www.sfvisitor.org** is valuable for a rundown of neighborhoods and maps.
- **www.bayarea.citysearch.com** is the San Francisco leg of the popular "what to do and where to go" nationwide city guide.
- **www.sonoma.com** is your guide to everything wine in Sonoma County, including current info on Napa lodgings, dining, and tours.

GAYS *and* LESBIANS

IN SAN FRANCISCO, "THE LOVE THAT DARE NOT speak its name" is expressed more freely than in any other U.S. city. San Francisco boasts the largest gay and lesbian population of any city in America, with some reports estimating that one quarter of its total population of 723,000 is gay. Hundreds of restaurants, hotels, shops, and other businesses and services are owned and operated by gays, who enjoy a high level of visibility, acceptance, and political clout in the community at large.

HISTORY

THE ROOTS OF THE CITY'S LARGE GAY POPULATION and its live-and-let-live ambience go back to the waning days of World War II, when the United States military began purging its ranks of homosexuals and suspected homosexuals, booting them out at the point of embarkation. This was often San Francisco, the major military stepping-off point. Many of the men, officially stigmatized, stayed in the Bay Area. Another migration occurred in the McCarthy era of the early 1950s, when the federal government dismissed thousands of homosexuals from their jobs. Persecution by the U.S. military and local police was common in the postwar years; in the early 1960s, gays began organizing for their civil rights.

By the 1970s, an estimated one in four San Francisco voters was gay, and homosexuals were an influential minority group. It didn't hurt that gays tended to vote in larger numbers and contributed to political candidates who supported issues important to gays. As gays of the flower-power generation began moving in and restoring Victorian town houses, Castro Street (formerly an Irish-American neighborhood going to seed) became a flourishing enclave and the embodiment of the gay drive for acceptance.

In 1977, the Castro District elected Harvey Milk to the city Board of Supervisors. Milk, a gay activist who organized the district's merchants group, became the first openly gay city official elected in the United States. The drama of gay liberation heightened when former Supervisor Dan White, a former cop and the city's most anti-gay politician, assassinated Milk and pro-gay mayor George Moscone in City Hall in 1978. Six months later, after White was sentenced to only five years for the double murder, a mob marched on City Hall, drawing worldwide attention and headlines. (White, paroled in 1985, eventually committed suicide.)

In the 1970s, San Francisco became notorious for its bar-and-bathhouse culture and its anonymous promiscuity. But the reputation toned down after AIDS struck in the early 1980s, causing more than 11,000 deaths in San Francisco. Socially, the city's gay scene mellowed in the 1990s, although gay bars, parades, and street fairs are still prevalent.

The 1980s also saw a flowering of the city's lesbian culture that parallels the male upswing of the 1970s. Today, as in most American cities, the lesbian community is more subtle and less visible than the gay scene (but it's just as powerful politically). Much smaller than the Castro, the main lesbian community is concentrated around 16th and Valencia Streets in the Mission District, while larger lesbian communities are across the bay in Oakland and Berkeley.

In the late 1990s, the city's gays and lesbians escaped the moral backlash provoked by AIDS in other parts of the country, thanks to San Francisco's tolerance and the gay community's support of people with AIDS and their survivors. Gays have, by and large, melded into the mainstream. Gay life is less ghettoized, and gay bars and clubs are scattered all over town. For years the city has had gay and lesbian political leaders, police officers, bureaucrats, and judges. It can be argued that one of the major aims of the gay liberation movement has been met here—the acceptance of people regardless of whether they're gay or straight.

GAY VISITORS

WHAT DOES ALL THIS MEAN FOR GAY AND LESBIAN visitors to the city? By and large, you needn't concern yourself with fitting in during a visit to San Francisco. Take, for example, getting a room. While many hotels are gay-owned and cater to a gay clientele, the Bay Area's level of tolerance just about guarantees that a visitor's sexual orientation—and the roommate's gender—isn't going to be an issue at any hotel in or around San Francisco.

BEFORE YOU GO

FOR INFORMATION ON THE CITY'S GAY SCENE, check out **www. timeout.com/sanfrancisco/gay**. A good site for tours is **www.sfgay tours.com**.

GAY AND LESBIAN PUBLICATIONS AND COMMUNITY BULLETIN BOARDS

NUMEROUS NEWSPAPERS AND MAGAZINES in San Francisco cater to the gay and lesbian community. The largest and best-known are the *San Francisco Bay Times* (distributed every other Thursday; ☎ 415-626-0260; **www.sfbaytimes.com**) and the weekly *Bay Area Reporter* (distributed on Thursdays; ☎ 415-861-5019; **www.ebar.com**). Both are free and are distributed to bookstores, bars, and street vending boxes. The newspapers provide complete event calendars and resource listings for gays and lesbians.

Other publications include *Drummer* (a gay leather and S/M webzine; **www.drummer.com**), *Girlfriends* (a monthly magazine for lesbians; ☎ 415-648-9464; **www.girlfriendsmag.com**), and *Odyssey* (a gay nightclub and listing guide published every other Friday;

☎ 415-621-6514). The *Gay Guide* and *Betty and Pansy's Severe Queer Review* are more underground papers found at cafés throughout the Castro and the Mission. An excellent place to find these publications and others under one roof is the bookstore **A Different Light** (489 Castro Street; ☎ 415-431-0891).

The San Francisco gay and lesbian community has several information resources. One of the more popular is the **Women's Building of the Bay Area** in the Mission District (☎ 415-431-1180; **www.womensbuilding.org**). It's a clearinghouse for feminist and lesbian art, entertainment, and resource information; call from 9 a.m. to 5 p.m. weekdays.

CELEBRATE GAY TIMES: TOP GAY ATTRACTIONS

- **AIDS Memorial Chapel** and the **Keith Haring Altarpiece** in Grace Cathedral off of California Street, ☎ 415-749-6300.
- **The Names Project Visitor Center** on Market Street is perhaps the most well known of all AIDS memorials. You can watch the panels being created, and there are tons of informational videos on the making of the quilt and the meaning of the project. The national headquarter's number in Atlanta is ☎ 404-688-5500.
- **Gay, Lesbian, and Transgender Pride Parade** (☎ 415-864-3733; **www.sfpride.org**) every June follows Market Street from the Civic Center to the Embarcadero. The parade is for the flamboyant, shy, family, couple . . . anybody wanting to express themselves for a day! Dykes on Bikes kicks off the celebration; $3 donation requested.
- **Castro Street Fair** in October is a scaled-down version of the Pride Parade. Costumes, shopping, and munching are all part of the festivities (☎ 415-841-1824; **www.castrostreetfair.org**).
- **A Different Light Bookshop** (489 Castro Street; ☎ 415-431-0891; **www.adlbooks.com**) stocks its shelves with mostly gay and lesbian literature by gay and lesbian authors.
- **Theatre Rhinoceros** (2926 16th Street, in the Mission at South Van Ness; ☎ 415-861-5079; **www.therhino.org**) is the place to come for gay performance art.
- **Bay to Breakers Race** (☎ 415-359-2800; **www.baytobreakers.com**) held in May is not just the largest footrace in the world, it's also the most fun you'll ever have on a Sunday afternoon! Come dressed up (although clothes are optional), bring the beer or margarita, and race your way from Fremont Street to Ocean Beach.
- **Cruisin' the Castro Tour** on Tuesdays through Saturdays (☎ 415-255-1821) takes you on a walking tour to all the sights of the Castro, highlighting history along the way.

GAY NEIGHBORHOODS

THE TRADITIONAL NEIGHBORHOOD FOR GAY MEN has been the sprawling Castro, now more typified by prepped-up, well-heeled yuppies than the disheveled leftists and ex-hippies that symbolized the early days of the gay liberation movement. SoMa, the city's emerging art-and-nightlife district, features a gay enclave around Folsom Street; the look tends toward black leather and chains. Polk Street and the edges of the Tenderloin District is the tight-blue-jeans-and-pimps zone of young gay transients; it's not the safest part of town at 2 a.m. (or anytime—see below). An enclave of successful gay business executives resides in posh and proper Pacific Heights. Noe's 24th Street, Bernal Heights, and Hayes Valley are San Francisco's newest lesbian/gay-oriented neighborhoods. Just take a look inside Bernal's dyke bar Wild Side West—the oldest women's bar in the city.

While San Francisco is hands-down the most tolerant city in the country, gay bashing is still alive. Avoid displays of affection in the Mission District, the largely Hispanic neighborhood where street gangs have attacked gay men. While the Polk Street area has a long gay history, it's now primarily a hustling scene with many bars and porn shops; it's a dangerous area, and more gay bashing is reported here than in any other part of the city.

A CALENDAR *of* FESTIVALS *and* EVENTS

SAN FRANCISCO HOSTS A VARIETY OF ANNUAL special events throughout the year, including films, jazz and blues festivals, craft fairs, art festivals, street fairs, and ethnic festivals. Exact dates are subject to change, so be sure to call the number indicated if you are interested in attending.

unofficial **TIP**
We've highlighted some not-to-be-missed events that are true showcases of the city's vibrant arts, funk, and soul (look for the ★).

January

CHINESE NEW YEAR CELEBRATION The city's largest festival with a parade from Market and Second streets to Columbus Avenue. ☎ 415-982-3000; **www.chineseparade.com.**

MACWORLD EXPO Where better to see the latest in chips, bytes, and megahertz than San Francisco! Moscone Center. ☎ 415-974-4000; **www.macworldexpo.com.**

MARTIN LUTHER KING JR.'S BIRTHDAY CELEBRATION A host of festivities highlight the city's commemoration of Dr. King's life. San Francisco Exploratorium. ☎ 415-561-0360; **www.exploratorium.edu.**

SAN FRANCISCO INDEPENDENT FILM FESTIVAL Showcases the best of indie films from the Bay Area and beyond. Various locations. ☎ 415-820-3907; **www.sfindie.com.**

SAN FRANCISCO SPORTS AND BOAT SHOW Boats, fishing tackle, camping gear, and hunting equipment on display. Cow Palace. ☎ 415-931-2500; **www.sfboatshow.com.**

SEA LION'S ANNUAL ARRIVAL AT PIER 39 Spectators can see, hear, and enjoy hundreds of sea lions in close proximity. ☎ 415-705-5500; www.pier39.com.

February

★ **CALIFORNIA INTERNATIONAL ANTIQUARIAN BOOK FAIR** World's largest rare book fair. Concourse Exhibition Center. ☎ 415-551-5190; www.californiabookfair.com.

SAN FRANCISCO ARTS OF PACIFIC ASIA SHOW Exhibitors from around the world offer antiques and art from the Pacific Asia region. Fort Mason. ☎ 310-455-2886; www.asianart.org.

SAN FRANCISCO ORCHID SOCIETY'S PACIFIC ORCHID EXPOSITION An annual expo featuring dozens of floral collections. Fort Mason. ☎ 415-665-2468; www.orchidsanfrancisco.org.

SAN FRANCISCO TRIBAL, FOLK, AND TEXTILE ARTS SHOW More than 80 folk and ethnic art dealers sell North American pottery, basketry, textiles, and jewelry. Fort Mason. ☎ 310-455-2886; www.caskeylees.com.

★ **TULIPMANIA** View more than 40,000 brilliantly colored tulips from around the world. Pier 39, Fisherman's Wharf. ☎ 415-705-5500; www.pier39.com.

March

ACROSS THE BAY 12K RACE The largest run ever to cross the Golden Gate Bridge. It ends with a bang, at the post-race party at Fisherman's Wharf. 8 a.m. start time. Sausalito to Fisherman's Wharf. ☎ 415-759-2690; www.rhodyco.com/across12k.html.

BOUQUETS TO ART Works by 100 floral designers, lectures by horticultural experts, luncheons, and tea service. California Palace of the Legion of Honor. ☎ 415-750-3600; www.famsf.org.

★ **ST. PATRICK'S DAY PARADE DOWNTOWN** The Irish have an annual march from Fifth and Market streets to the Embarcadero. ☎ 415-675-9885; www.sfstpatricksdayparade.com.

SAN FRANCISCO FLOWER AND GARDEN SHOW 27 gardens, 300 market booths, orchid show, and 75 free seminars. Cow Palace. ☎ 415-771-6909; www.gardenshow.com/sf.

SAN FRANCISCO INTERNATIONAL ASIAN-AMERICAN FILM FESTIVAL The biggest ever in North America dedicated to the exhibition of Asian-American and Asian cinema. AMC Kabuki Theaters. ☎ 415-225-4299; www.naatanet.org/festival.

April

CHERRY BLOSSOM FESTIVAL Taiko drumming, martial arts, Japanese food. A parade from Civic Center to Japantown. Japantown. ☎ 415-563-2313; www.nccbf.org.

★ **SAN FRANCISCO INTERNATIONAL FILM FESTIVAL** (April th
May) More than 100 films and videos from around the world. Various locations but mostly at the AMC Kabuki and Castro Theaters.
☎ 415-561-5000; **www.sffs.org.**

May

CINCO DE MAYO CELEBRATION Arts, crafts, and food, as well as a
parade to celebrate Mexican independence. Mission District. ☎ 415-
256-3005; **www.cincodemayosf.com.**

SAN FRANCISCO DECORATOR SHOWCASE Top Bay Area designers display the latest design innovations at luxurious San Francisco homes.
Pacific Heights. ☎ 415-447-3115; **www.decoratorshowcase.org.**

★ *SAN FRANCISCO EXAMINER BAY TO BREAKERS FOOTRACE* Come
sporting your birthday suit or whatever other costume you can
muster up and take part in the world's largest footrace. Clothes
optional, beer mandatory. The Embarcadero to the Great Highway.
☎ 415-359-2800; **www.baytobreakers.com.**

SAN FRANCISCO YOUTH ARTS FESTIVAL Area students display
their works. Golden Gate Park. ☎ 415-750-8630; **www.sfyoutharts
festival.org.**

June

★ **HAIGHT STREET FAIR** Bring out the tie dye and lava lamps—the
Haight celebrates its roots with arts, crafts, and entertainment.
Haight Street. ☎ 415-863-3489; **www.haightstreetfair.org.**

JUNETEENTH FESTIVAL An annual outdoor event celebrating African-
American culture. Fillmore Street. ☎ 415-931-2729; **www.sfjune
teenth.org.**

★ **LESBIAN, GAY, BISEXUAL, TRANSGENDER PRIDE CELEBRATION FESTI-
VAL AND PARADE** San Francisco's celebration of lesbian and gay
pride. Castro District. ☎ 415-864-3733; **www.sfpride.org.**

NORTH BEACH FESTIVAL San Francisco's oldest street fair offers arts,
crafts, and live entertainment. Grant Avenue and Green Street. ☎ 415-
989-2220; **www.sfnorthbeach.org.**

SAN FRANCISCO INTERNATIONAL LESBIAN AND GAY FILM FESTIVAL
The second-largest film festival in California showcases more than
100 films and videos from around the world. Castro Theatre and
other locations. ☎ 415-703-8650; **www.frameline.org/festival.**

★ **UNION STREET SPRING FESTIVAL ARTS AND CRAFTS FAIR** Arts and
crafts, wine, food, a waiter's race, tea dancing, a fashion show, street
performers, and a swing dance contest. Union Street. ☎ 800-310-
6563; **www.unionstreetfestival.com.**

July

CABLE CAR BELL-RINGING COMPETITION Where the cars come to belt out their favorite tune—operators clang out melodies on the cars' bells and compete for top bell-ringer. Fisherman's Wharf. ☎ 415-474-1887; www.cablecarmuseum.org.

FILLMORE STREET JAZZ FESTIVAL Three stages of continuous jazz performances, more than 300 artists' booths, and an international food court. Free. Fillmore Street. ☎ 800-731-0003; www.fillmorejazzfestival.com.

FOURTH OF JULY CELEBRATION It's that childhood favorite, fireworks! Entertainment, food, arts and crafts. Fisherman's Wharf. ☎ 415-705-5500; www.pier39.com.

JEWISH FILM FESTIVAL Films from American and international filmmakers showcase Jewish culture. Castro. ☎ 415-621-0556; www.sfjff.org.

August

ACC CRAFT FAIR The largest juried craft fair on the West Coast features necklaces, stoneware, silk scarves, and quilts. Fort Mason. ☎ 800-836-3470; www.craftcouncil.org.

AFRO SOLO ARTS FESTIVAL Festival commemorating the African-American experience through solo performances. Yerba Center of Arts and other locations. ☎ 415-771-2370; www.afrosolo.org/events.html.

GOLDEN GATEWAY TO GEMS Minerals, crystals, and jewelry from all over the world. San Francisco County Fair Building. ☎ 415-564-4230; www.sfgms.org.

NIHONMACHI STREET FAIR Lion dancers, taiko drummers, Japanese arts and crafts, music, food, and children's events. Japantown and Japan Center. ☎ 415-771-9861; www.nihonmachistreetfair.org.

September

★ **À LA CARTE, À LA PARK** Bring an empty stomach and an adventurous gastronomic appetite for this outdoor smorgasbord. Outdoor dining with over 40 restaurants and chefs, wineries and microbreweries, celebrity chefs, and music. Golden Gate Park. ☎ 415-478-2277.

AUTUMN MOON FESTIVAL Multicultural entertainment, traditional lion and dragon dances, Chinese costumes, and children's activities. Grant Avenue between California and Pacific Streets. ☎ 415-982-6306; www.moonfestival.org.

FOLSOM STREET FAIR A popular fair with arts and crafts, kinky collectibles, entertainment, and food. For obvious reasons, it's for adults only! Folsom Street. ☎ 415-861-3247; www.folsomstreetfair.com.

GHIRARDELLI SQUARE CHOCOLATE FESTIVAL A chocolate lover's dream! Sample chocolate treats and more. Ghirardelli Square. ☎ 415-775-5500; **www.ghirardellisq.com.**

★ **SAN FRANCISCO BLUES FESTIVAL** The oldest blues festival in the country. Great Meadow, Fort Mason. ☎ 415-979-5588; **www.sfblues.com.**

SAN FRANCISCO FRINGE FESTIVAL Marathon of 260 performances by 50 theater companies in various venues. Downtown. ☎ 415-931-1094; **www.sffringe.org.**

SAN FRANCISCO GRAND PRIX Top international bicycle racers compete through the streets of San Francisco. ☎ 415-705-6000; **www.sanfrangrandprix.com.**

SAN FRANCISCO INTERNATIONAL ART EXPOSITION Galleries exhibit their collections of more than 1,500 artists, ranging from painting to drawing to sculpture to prints and video. Fort Mason. ☎ 312-587-3300; **www.sfiae.com.**

SAN FRANCISCO SHAKESPEARE FESTIVAL All of Shakespeare's classics. Pack a picnic lunch and your *Cliffs Notes* and enjoy Saturdays and Sundays on several weekends throughout the summer; locals arrive by noon for a seat. Golden Gate Park. ☎ 415-865-4434; **www.sfshakes.org.**

SAUSALITO ART FESTIVAL A fine-arts festival with more than 20,000 original works of art from around the world. Sausalito. ☎ 415-332-3555; **www.sausalitoartfestival.org.**

October

INTERNATIONAL VINTAGE POSTER FAIR The oldest and largest vintage poster fair in the world. Fort Mason Center. ☎ 650-548-6700; **www.posterfair.com.**

ITALIAN HERITAGE PARADE AND FESTIVAL A commemoration of the city's Italian heritage with a parade through North Beach. North Beach, Fisherman's Wharf. ☎ 415-703-9888; **www.sfcolumbusday.org/parade.**

SAN FRANCISCO JAZZ FESTIVAL Features local, national, and international jazz artists at locations throughout the city. ☎ 800-850-7353; **www.sfjazz.org.**

November/December

CHRISTMAS AT SEA Caroling, storytelling, hot cider, cookies, children's crafts, and Santa. Hyde Street Pier. ☎ 415-561-6662.

GHIRARDELLI SQUARE ANNUAL TREE LIGHTING CEREMONY Deck the 35-foot Christmas tree with cheer and good tidings. Ghirardelli Square. ☎ 415-775-5500; **www.ghirardellisq.com.**

ORIGINALS HOLIDAY GIFT SHOW An arts-and-crafts fair for the holiday season. Concourse Exhibition Center. ☎ 707-778-6300; www.originalsartandcraftshow.com.

SAN FRANCISCO BALLET'S *NUTCRACKER* America's oldest ballet company, regarded as one of its finest, presents Tchaikovsky's beloved family classic every December. War Memorial Opera House. ☎ 415-865-2000; www.sfballet.org.

SAN FRANCISCO INTERNATIONAL AUTO SHOW The latest and greatest in automobiles. Moscone Center. ☎ 415-331-4406; www.sfauto show.com.

PART TWO

ACCOMMODATIONS

▌ DECIDING WHERE *to* STAY

SAN FRANCISCO HOTELS GENERALLY OFFER GOOD values, inter-esting Pacific urban architecture and décor, and remarkably diverse amenities. As a generalization, service at San Francisco hotels, if not quirky, is somewhat differently defined. At the bar your drinks may not come any faster than they would at home, and your room-service breakfast may arrive cold. But ask the bartender or food server, "What should I do next?" and you're in for a spirited and opinion-ated discourse on the city.

The idea that information is the most valuable service a hotel can offer is novel in most cities. In San Francisco, however, hotels that don't even have room service or a bar may publish their own guide-books and pamphlets on attractions, or they may have 24-hour concierge service. With 32% of San Francisco guest rooms scoring four stars or higher, the quality of guest rooms is exceptionally high. Plus, guest rooms in the Bay Area are reasonably priced. On average, rooms here are less expensive than rooms in New York City, Wash-ington, D.C., Chicago, and other comparable destinations. This combination of high-quality rooms and reasonable rates makes San Francisco attractive for both leisure and business travelers.

Hotels dot the San Francisco peninsula and Bay Area suburbs, so you need not be more than ten minutes from tourist attractions or businesses. As in most cities, guest-room rates are higher in more desirable areas. The steepest rates are generally found within walking distance of Union Square, and some of the best hotel bargains are located in less fashionable neighborhoods. Of these, many have excellent on-premises security and may be of particular interest to those who plan to tour by car.

A distinctive characteristic of San Francisco's hotel scene is an artful marriage of historic architecture with modern interior design. Some of the city's hotels are modern, but the vast majority are housed in older buildings. Historic hotel buildings include some of the world's oldest skyscrapers and quaint Victorian and Edwardian mansions.

Step inside the nicer San Francisco hotels and you'll find some of the more inventive interior design you'll encounter in this country. Though palatial room size is not characteristic of San Francisco hotels, utilizing square footage wisely is. In both common areas and guest rooms, the *Unofficial Guide* hotel inspectors were impressed by how creatively form and function are blended. Several of San Francisco's nicest hotels have such ergonomically exact guest rooms that we were reminded of Tokyo. The comfortable integration of modern technology such as in-room fax machines, microwaves, and coffeemakers is noteworthy in guest rooms that are sometimes smaller than 200 square feet.

In San Francisco, you are more likely to find a guest room suited to your individual needs than in destinations where hotel homogeneity rules. The **Nob Hill Lambourne,** for example, offers a state-of-the-art, in-room treadmill and an honor bar with healthy foods for quite reasonable rates. Similarly, the **Hotel Triton** boasts 24 environmentally sensitive guest rooms and suites designed by Jerry Garcia and nature artist Wyland.

The décor runs the gamut of historical and modern styles. Classic opulence, signaled by airplane hangar–sized lobbies, chandeliers the size of canoes, and richly textured upholstery can be found at hotels such as the **Fairmont** and the **Westin Saint Francis.** There is also an emphasis on modern interior decorating. Using elements of art deco, art nouveau, and modern art, the finished interior in the modern design style contains whimsically curved lines, bold patterns, and metallic and bright colors. You can see one of the best examples of this style at the **Hotel Diva,** where black and primary colors accent the theme of brushed chrome. Another is the newly renovated **Hotel Monaco,** which uses lush textures such as velvet and deep colors, including eggplant and ruby, to create a look of futuristic affluence.

San Francisco hotels market and cater to diverse groups, and their amenities and ambience reflect this trend. While some properties target business or leisure travelers, others have more specific markets. These include opera fans at the **Inn at the Opera,** wine lovers at many Bay Area hotels, and spa junkies at others. Aspiring actors and film buffs will want to check out the **Hotel Bijou,** which offers a small movie theater and a 24-hour hotline to current San Francisco film shoots and casting-call opportunities.

A FEW NOTEWORTHY PROPERTIES

SAN FRANCISCO IS HOME TO A FEW NOTEWORTHY properties that we have not ranked and rated because their clientele is so narrowly defined.

Those wishing to relive the Summer of Love may want to stay at the **Red Victorian Bed, Breakfast, and Art Center.** Owned and run by veteran flower child Sami Sunchild, the bed-and-breakfast is in the heart of the historic Haight-Ashbury neighborhood. Each of its 18 rooms is decorated with a different theme, ranging from the Summer of Love room and the Rainbow room to the Japanese Tea Garden room and the Butterfly room.

Guests of the "Red Vic" are encouraged to socialize at the breakfast table, and reclusive types may find this aspect of the bed-and-breakfast overwhelming if not downright annoying. Outgoing folks will probably have a lot of fun, as Ms. Sunchild conducts breakfast like a love-in; each guest is encouraged to tell the others where they are from and what they do for a living. Tip: If you make your living working for a right-wing political organization, conducting experiments that include vivisection, or designing weapons, you'll want to lie. When one guest told the group he was a social worker from New Zealand, Ms. Sunchild almost squealed with delight as she exclaimed, "See, we take care of the people who take care of the world!" Room rates at the Red Victorian Bed, Breakfast, and Art Center range from $96 to $200. For more information, call ☎ 415-864-1978 or visit **www.redvic.com.**

If you're looking for a bed-and-breakfast that touts itself as "welcoming diversity," you might try the **Hayes Valley Inn,** located in the Civic Center area at Gough and Hayes Streets. The owners pride themselves on catering to alternative lifestyles and making gay travelers feel at ease. Special rooms are provided for guests traveling with pets. Rates range from $73 to $105, all rooms having shared baths in the hall. Contact ☎ 415-431-9131 or visit **www.hayesvalleyinn.com** for information and reservations.

House O' Chicks is a women's bed-and-breakfast in the Castro District. Two guest rooms share a bathroom; one guest room has a TV and VCR, the other has a stereo, and both have a homey atmosphere. Innkeeper Dorie Lane tells prospective guests that "it's like coming to a friend's house and she has a room all made up for you." Common areas include the living room, dining room, library, and kitchen, and all rooms contain original women's artwork. The innkeeper prefers to set room rates at the time of booking. Call ☎ 510-658-1719 or visit **www.houseochicks.com** for information and reservations.

Most of the other hotels and bed-and-breakfasts in the Castro District are places where everyone will feel comfortable, though they are particularly convenient for gay travelers wishing to explore shops and clubs in the Castro area.

Edward II Inn and Suites offers three guest rooms with private entrances in a 1906 Edwardian mansion and has a strict nonsmoking policy. Call ☎ 415-922-3000 or visit **www.edwardii.com.**

The **Castillo Inn** has four guest rooms that share one bathroom, and a two-bedroom suite at another location. This bed-and-breakfast on Henry Street in the heart of the Castro District is also strictly nonsmoking. Call ☎ 800-865-5112.

By now you may be wondering, "Can't I just get a normal room in San Francisco?" The answer, of course, is yes. For conservative tastes, traditional hotel rooms are easy to find. But you will need to ask for what you want. In San Francisco, the difference between name-brand corporate hotels and freestanding, proprietary, or "boutique" hotels is not clearly delineated. This is because many of the corporate hotels in San Francisco occupy older buildings that once housed freestanding and family-owned hotels. Don't expect cookie-cutter guest rooms just because you're staying at your favorite name-brand hotel. If you prefer to stay in a rectangular room with the bathroom adjacent to the front door, two double beds, and a picture window opposite the front door, be sure to shop around.

GETTING *a* GOOD DEAL
on a ROOM

MONEY-SAVING TIPS

TO SAY THAT YOU RECEIVE GOOD VALUE FOR your lodging dollar in San Francisco doesn't mean that San Francisco is cheap. If you are looking for ways to save money beyond getting a discount on the price of a room, consider the following.

1. Stay in a less-than-fashionable neighborhood. San Francisco is made up of many distinct neighborhoods, and this emphasis on address reflects itself in pricing. Unless you need to be there for convenience, it may not be worth it to stay on Nob Hill when the same level of room in North Beach may be half the cost. The most expensive areas are Union Square and Nob Hill.

2. Seek a suite that includes a kitchen. Several hotels offer this option; suites can accommodate four or more people and help save on restaurant bills.

3. Stay at the worst room at a good hotel instead of the best one at a lesser hotel. Ask for the smallest room, lowest floor, worst view. The cost differential can be considerable, although the rest of the hotel services, amenities, and public rooms remain the same. You're getting the biggest bang for your buck.

4. Avoid room service and minibars. Bring food up from groceries, delis, or convenience stores. Or make like a resident and have a restaurant deliver (allowed at some hotels, frowned on at others—check first). Neighborhood restaurants, especially the "ethnics," are good and reasonable. If you eat like a local rather than a tourist, you will save money.

5. Skip the in-house movies. Bring a book. Better yet, walk down the street to see dramatic stories and sights beyond fiction.

6. Try a bed-and-breakfast. They are plentiful in the Bay Area and range from accommodations in houseboats and Victorian mansions to Junior's room when he's away at college. For information and options contact Bed *&* Breakfast California at **www.bedandbreakfast.com.**

GETTING A DISCOUNTED RATE

BECAUSE SAN FRANCISCO IS POPULAR YEAR-ROUND, room rates tend not to fluctuate much. Even so, the market is highly competitive and there are deals for the smart shopper. Check out deals through ads, agents, special events, and openings. These include weekend and convention deals, frequent-mileage clubs, automobile or other travel clubs, senior rates (some with age requirements as low as 50 years), military or government discounts, corporate or shareholder rates, packages, long-stay rates (usually at least five nights), and travel industry rates. Some hotels might even give lower rates if you are visiting because of bereavement or medical problems. You can also try some of the following.

Surf the Net

Check out the Internet. Last-minute bargains are now available online. You can judge comparative value by seeing a listing of hotels—what they offer, where they are located, and what they charge.

Special Weekend Rates

Most hotels that cater to business, government, and convention travelers offer special weekend discount rates that range from 15% to 40% below normal weekday rates. Find out about weekend specials by calling individual hotels or consulting your travel agent.

Getting Corporate Rates

Many hotels offer discounted corporate rates (5–20% off rack rate). Usually you do not need to work for a large company or have a special relationship with the hotel to obtain these rates. Simply call the hotel of your choice and ask for their corporate rates. Many hotels will guarantee you the discounted rate on the phone when you make your reservation. Others may make the rate conditional on your providing some sort of verification, for instance a fax on your company's letterhead requesting the rate, or a company credit card or business card upon check-in. Generally the screening is not rigorous.

Preferred Rates

If you cannot book the hotel of your choice through a half-price program (see below), you and your travel agent may have to search for a smaller discount, often called a preferred rate. A preferred rate might be a discount available to travel agents to stimulate their booking activity or a discount initiated to attract a certain class of traveler. Most preferred rates are promoted through travel industry publications and are accessible only through an agent.

We recommend sounding out your travel agent about possible deals. Be aware, however, that the rates shown on agents' computerized reservations systems are not always the lowest rates obtainable. Zero in on a couple of hotels that fill your needs in terms of location and quality of accommodations, and then have your agent call the hotel for the latest rates and specials. Hotel reps are almost always more responsive to travel agents because agents represent a source of additional business. Again, there are certain specials that hotel reps will disclose only to agents. Travel agents also come in handy when the hotel you want is supposedly booked. A personal appeal from your agent to the hotel's director of sales and marketing will get you a room more than half the time.

Half-Price Programs

Larger discounts on rooms (35–60%) in San Francisco or anywhere else are available through half-price hotel programs, often called travel clubs. Program operators contract with an individual hotel to provide rooms at deep discounts, usually 50% off, on a "space available" basis. Space available in practice means that you can reserve a room at the discounted rate whenever the hotel expects to be at less than 80% occupancy. A little calendar sleuthing to help you avoid special events and citywide conventions will increase your chances of choosing a time when these discounts are available.

Most half-price programs charge an annual membership fee or directory subscription rate of $25–$125. Once you're enrolled, you'll receive a membership card and a directory listing participating hotels. You will notice immediately that there are many restrictions and exceptions. Some hotels, for instance, "black out" certain dates or times of year. Others may offer the discount only on certain days of the week or require you to stay a certain number of nights. Still others may offer a much smaller discount than 50% off the rack rate.

Programs specialize in domestic travel, international travel, or both. More established operators offer members between 1,000 and 4,000 hotels in the United States to choose from. All of the programs have a heavy concentration of hotels in California and Florida, and most have a very limited selection of participating properties in New York or Boston. Offerings in other cities and regions of the United States vary considerably. The programs with the largest selections of San Francisco hotels are Encore, ITC-50, Great American Traveler, Quest, Privilege International, and Entertainment Publications. Each of these programs lists between 25 (Great American Traveler) and more than 60 (Encore) hotels in the greater San Francisco area.

Encore	☎ 800-444-9800; www.preferredtraveller.com
Entertainment Publications	☎ 800-445-4137; www.entertainment.com
ITC-50	☎ 800-513-7000; www.itc50online.com
Great American Traveler	☎ 800-548-2812
Privilege Card International	☎ 800-236-9732; www.privilegecard.com
Quest	☎ 800-742-3543; www.questprograms.com

One problem with half-price programs is that not all hotels offer a full 50% discount. Another slippery problem is the base rate against which the discount is applied. Some hotels figure the discount on an exaggerated rack rate that nobody would ever have to pay. A few participating hotels may deduct the discount from a supposed "superior" or "upgraded" room rate, even though the room you get is the hotel's standard accommodation. Though hard to pin down, the majority of participating properties base discounts on the rate published in the *Hotel & Travel Index* (a quarterly reference work used by travel agents) and work within the spirit of their agreement with the program operator. As a rule, if you travel several times a year, your room-rate savings will easily compensate you for program membership fees.

A noteworthy addendum: deeply discounted rooms through half-price programs are not commissionable to travel agents. In practical terms this means that you must ordinarily make your own inquiry calls and reservations. If you travel frequently, however, and run a lot of business through your agent, he or she will probably do your legwork, lack of commission notwithstanding.

Wholesalers, Consolidators, and Reservation Services

If you do not want to join a program or buy a discount directory, you can take advantage of the services of a wholesaler or consolidator. Wholesalers and consolidators buy rooms or options on rooms (room blocks) from hotels at a low, negotiated rate. Then they resell the rooms at a profit through travel agents or tour operators, or directly to the public. Most wholesalers and consolidators have a provision for returning unsold rooms to participating hotels, but they are not inclined to do so. The wholesaler's or consolidator's relationship with any hotel is predicated on volume. If they return rooms unsold, the hotel may not make as many rooms available to them the next time around. Thus wholesalers and consolidators often offer rooms at bargain rates, anywhere from 15% to 50% off rack, occasionally sacrificing their profit margins in the process, to avoid returning the rooms to the hotel unsold.

When wholesalers and consolidators deal directly with the public, they frequently represent themselves as "reservation services." When you call, you can ask for a rate quote for a particular hotel or ask for their best available deal in the area you prefer. If there is a maximum amount you are willing to pay, say so. Chances are the service will find something that will work for you, even if they have to shave a dollar or two off their own profit. A list of services that sell rooms in San Francisco follows.

Accommodations Express	☎ 800-444-7666; www.accommodationsexpress.com
Hotel Locators	☎ 800-576-0003; www.hotellocators.com
Central Reservations Service	☎ 800-548-3311; www.crshotels.com
Hotel Reservations Network	☎ 800-964-6835; www.hoteldiscounts.com

Quikbook	☎ 800-789-9887; www.quikbook.com
San Francisco Reservations	☎ 800-677-1550

The discount available (if any) from a reservation service depends on whether the service functions as a consolidator or a wholesaler. Consolidators are strictly sales agents who do not own or control the room inventory they are trying to sell. Their discounts are determined by the hotels with rooms to fill and vary enormously, depending on how desperate the hotel is to unload the rooms. When you deal with a room reservation service that operates as a consolidator, you pay for your room as usual when you check out of the hotel.

Wholesalers have longstanding contracts with hotels; this allows the wholesaler to purchase rooms at an established deep discount. Some wholesalers hold purchase options on blocks of rooms, while others actually pay for rooms and own the inventory. Because a wholesaler controls the room inventory, it can offer whatever discount it pleases consistent with current demand. In practice, most wholesaler reservice discounts fall in the 10% to 40% range. When you reserve a room with a reservation service that operates as a wholesaler, you must usually pay for your entire stay in advance with your credit card. The service then sends you a written confirmation and usually a voucher (indicating prepayment) for you to present at the hotel.

Our experience has been that the reservation services are more useful for finding rooms when availability is scarce than for obtaining deep discounts. When we called the hotels ourselves, we were often able to beat the reservation services' rates when rooms were generally available. When the city was booked, however, and we could not find a room by calling the hotels ourselves, the reservation services could almost always get us a room at a fair price.

HOW TO EVALUATE A TRAVEL PACKAGE

HUNDREDS OF SAN FRANCISCO PACKAGE VACATIONS are offered to the public each year. Packages should be a win-win proposition for both the buyer and the seller. The buyer has to make only one phone call and deal with a single salesperson to set up the whole vacation—transportation, rental car, lodging, meals, attraction admissions, and even golf and tennis. The seller, likewise, has to deal with the buyer only once, eliminating the need for separate sales, confirmations, and billing. In addition to streamlining sales, processing, and administration, some packagers also buy airfares in bulk on contract like a broker playing the commodities market. Buying a large number of airfares in advance allows the packager to buy them at a significant savings from posted fares. The same practice is applied to hotel rooms. Because selling vacation packages is an efficient way of doing business, and because the packager can often buy individual package components (airfare, lodging, etc.) in bulk at a discount, savings in operating expenses realized by the seller are sometimes passed on to the buyer. This means that, in addition to convenience, the package is an exceptional value. In any event, that's the way it is supposed to work.

In practice, all too often the seller cashes in on discounts and passes none on to the buyer. In some instances, packages are loaded with extras that cost the packager next to nothing but inflate the retail price sky-high. As you would expect, the savings to be passed along to customers do not materialize.

When considering a package, you should choose one that includes features you are sure to use; whether you use all the features or not, you will most certainly pay for them. Second, if cost is of greater concern than convenience, make a few phone calls and see what the package would cost if you booked its individual components (airfare, rental car, lodging, etc.) on your own. If the package price is less than the à la carte cost, the package is a good deal. If the costs are about the same, the package is probably worth buying just for the convenience.

If your package includes a choice of rental car or airport transfers (transportation to and from the airport), take the car if your hotel offers free (or at least affordable) parking. Take the transfers if you plan to spend your time in the area from Nob Hill and Union Square down to the San Francisco Bay. If you want to run around town or go on excursions outside the city, take the car. And if you take the car, be sure to ask if the package includes free parking at your hotel.

Tour operators, of course, prefer to sell you a whole vacation package. When business is slow, however, they will often agree to sell you just the lodging component of the package, usually at a nicely discounted rate.

Hotel-Sponsored Packages

In addition to tour operators, packages are frequently offered by hotels. Usually "land only" (i.e., no airfare included), the hotel packages are sometimes exceptional deals. Promotion of hotel specials tends to be limited to the hotel's primary markets, which for most properties is California, Washington, Oregon, Arizona, Hawaii, Nevada, Texas, Illinois, and New York. If you live in other parts of the country, you can take advantage of the packages but probably will not see them advertised in your local newspaper. An important point regarding hotel specials is that the hotel reservationists do not usually inform you of existing specials or offer them to you. In other words, you have to ask.

HELPING YOUR TRAVEL AGENT HELP YOU

WHEN YOU CALL YOUR TRAVEL AGENT, ASK IF HE or she has been to San Francisco. If the answer is no, be prepared to give your travel agent some direction. Do not accept any recommendations at face value. Check out the location and rates of each suggested hotel and make sure the hotel is suited to your itinerary.

Because some travel agents are unfamiliar with San Francisco, your agent may try to plug you into a tour operator's preset package. This essentially allows the travel agent to set up your whole trip with a single phone call and still collect an 8–10% commission. The problem with this scenario is that most agents will place 90% of their San Francisco business with only one or two wholesalers or tour operators. In other words, it's the line of least resistance for them and leaves you with very little choice.

Travel agents will often use wholesalers who run packages in conjunction with airlines, such as Delta Vacations or American Airlines' Fly-Away Vacations. Because of the wholesaler's exclusive relationship with the carrier, these trips are easy for travel agents to book. However, they will probably be more expensive than a package offered by a high-volume wholesaler who works with a number of airlines in a primary San Francisco market.

To help your travel agent get you the best possible deal, do the following:

1. Determine where you want to stay in San Francisco, and if possible choose a specific hotel. This can be accomplished by reviewing the hotel information in this guide and by writing or calling hotels that interest you.

2. Check out the hotel deals and package vacations advertised in the Sunday travel sections of the *Los Angeles Times, San Francisco Examiner*, or *Dallas Morning News* newspapers. Often you will be able to find deals that beat the socks off anything offered in your local paper. See if you can find specials that fit your plans and include a hotel you like.

3. Call the hotels or tour operators whose ads you have collected. Ask any questions you have about their packages, but do not book your trip with them directly.

4. Tell your travel agent about the deals you find and ask if he or she can get you something better. The deals in the paper will serve as a benchmark against which to compare alternatives your agent proposes.

5. Choose from the options that you and your travel agent uncover. No matter which option you select, have your agent book it. Even if you go with one of the packages in the newspaper, it will probably be commissionable (at no additional cost to you) and will provide the agent some return on the time invested on your behalf. Also, as a travel professional, your agent should be able to verify the quality and integrity of the deal.

IF YOU MAKE YOUR OWN RESERVATION

AS YOU POKE AROUND TRYING TO FIND A GOOD DEAL, there are several things you should know. First, always call the specific hotel rather than the hotel chain's national, toll-free number. Quite often, the reservationists at the national number are unaware of local specials. Always ask about specials before you inquire about corporate rates. Do not be reluctant to bargain. If you are buying a hotel's weekend package, for example, and want to extend your stay into the

Hotel and Motel Toll-Free Numbers

Best Western	☎ 800-528-1234 U.S. and Canada ☎ 800-528-2222 TDD
Comfort Inn	☎ 800-228-5150 U.S. and Canada ☎ 800-228-3323 TDD
Courtyard by Marriott	☎ 888-236-2427 U.S. ☎ 800-228-7014 TDD
Days Inn	☎ 800-325-2525 U.S. ☎ 800-329-7155 TDD
Doubletree Hotels	☎ 800-222-8733 U.S. and Canada ☎ 800-451-4833 TDD
Econo Lodge	☎ 877-424-6423 U.S. ☎ 800-228-3323 TDD
Embassy Suites	☎ 800-362-2779 U.S. and Canada ☎ 800-528-9898 TDD
Hampton Inn	☎ 800-426-7866 U.S. and Canada ☎ 800-451-4833 TDD
Hilton	☎ 800-445-8667 U.S. and Canada ☎ 800-368-1133 TDD
Holiday Inn	☎ 800-465-4329 U.S. and Canada ☎ 800-238-5544 TDD
Howard Johnson	☎ 800-654-2000 U.S. and Canada
Hyatt	☎ 800-233-1234 U.S. and Canada ☎ 800-228-9548 TDD
Marriott	☎ 888-236-2427 U.S. and Canada ☎ 800-228-7014 TDD
Quality Inn	☎ 800-228-5151 U.S. and Canada ☎ 800-228-3323 TDD
Radisson	☎ 800-333-3333 U.S. and Canada ☎ 800-906-2200 TDD
Ramada Inn	☎ 800-272-6232 U.S. ☎ 800-228-3232 TDD
Renaissance Hotels and Resorts	☎ 800-468-3571 U.S. and Canada
Ritz-Carlton	☎ 800-241-3333 U.S.
Sheraton	☎ 800-325-3535 U.S. and Canada ☎ 800-329-7155 TDD
Wyndham	☎ 800-996-3426 U.S.

following week, you can often obtain at least the corporate rate for the extra days. Do your bargaining, however, before you check in, preferably when you make your reservations. Use our list of hotel and motel naional toll-free numbers to find the local numbers, or to investigate chain-wide promotions.

HOTELS *and* MOTELS: RATED *and* RANKED

WHAT'S IN A ROOM?

EXCEPT FOR CLEANLINESS, STATE OF REPAIR, AND décor, most travelers do not pay much attention to hotel rooms. There is, of course, a discernible standard of quality and luxury that differentiates Motel 6 from Holiday Inn, Holiday Inn from Marriott, and so on. In general, however, hotel guests fail to appreciate the fact that some rooms are better engineered than others.

Contrary to what you might suppose, designing a hotel room is (or should be) more complex than picking a bedspread to match the carpet and drapes. Making the room usable to its occupants is an art, a planning discipline that combines form and function.

Décor and taste are important, certainly. No one wants to spend several days in a room that is dated, garish, or even ugly. But beyond the décor, several variables determine how livable a hotel room is. In San Francisco, for example, we have seen some beautifully appointed rooms that are simply not well designed for human habitation. The next time you stay in a hotel, pay attention to the details and design elements of your room. Even more than décor, these will make you feel comfortable and at home.

It takes the *Unofficial Guide* researchers quite a while to inspect a hotel room. Here are a few of the things we check and suggest you check, too.

ROOM SIZE While some smaller rooms are cozy and well designed, a large and uncluttered room is generally preferable, especially for a stay of more than three days.

TEMPERATURE CONTROL, VENTILATION, AND ODOR The guest should be able to control the temperature of the room. The best system, because it's so quiet, is central heating and air-conditioning controlled by the room's own thermostat. The next best system is a room module heater and air-conditioner, preferably controlled by an automatic thermostat but usually by manually operated button controls. The worst system is central heating and air without any sort of room thermostat or guest control.

The vast majority of hotel rooms have windows or balcony doors that have been permanently sealed. Though there are some legitimate safety and liability issues involved, we prefer windows and balcony doors that can be opened to admit fresh air. Hotel rooms should be odor free and smoke free, and they should not feel stuffy or damp.

ROOM SECURITY Better rooms have locks that require a plastic card instead of the traditional lock and key. Card and slot systems allow the hotel to change the combination or entry code of the lock with each new guest. A burglar who has somehow acquired a conventional room key can afford to wait until the situation is right before using the key to gain access. Not so with a card-and-slot system. Though larger hotels and hotel chains with lock-and-key systems usually rotate their locks once each year, they remain vulnerable to hotel thieves much of the time. Many smaller or independent properties rarely rotate their locks.

In addition to the entry lock system, the door should have a deadbolt and preferably a chain that can be locked from the inside as well. A chain by itself is not sufficient. Doors should also have a peephole. Windows and balcony doors should have secure locks.

SAFETY Every room should have a fire or smoke alarm, clear fire instructions, and preferably a sprinkler system. Bathtubs should have a nonskid surface, and shower stalls should have doors that open outward or slide side to side. Bathroom electrical outlets should be high on the wall and not too close to the sink. Balconies should have sturdy, high rails.

NOISE Most travelers have been kept awake by the television, partying, or amorous activities of people in the next room, or by traffic on the street outside. Better hotels are designed with noise control in mind. Wall and ceiling constructions are substantial, effectively screening routine noise. Carpets and drapes, in addition to being decorative, also absorb and muffle sounds. Mattresses mounted on stable platforms or sturdy bed frames do not squeak even when challenged by the most acrobatic lovers. Televisions are enclosed in cabinets and have volume governors so that they rarely disturb guests in adjacent rooms.

In better hotels, the air-conditioning and heating system is well maintained and operates without noise or vibration. Likewise, plumbing is quiet and positioned away from the sleeping area. Doors to the hall and adjoining rooms are thick and well fitted to better block out noise.

If you are easily disturbed by noise, ask for a room on a higher floor, off main thoroughfares, and away from elevators and vending machines.

DARKNESS CONTROL Ever been in a hotel room where the curtains would not quite meet in the middle? Thick, lined curtains that close completely in the center and extend beyond the edges of the window or door frame are required. In a well-planned room, the curtains, shades, or blinds should almost totally block light at any time of day.

LIGHTING Poor lighting is a common problem in American hotel rooms. The lighting is usually adequate for dressing, relaxing, or watching television, but not for reading or working. Lighting needs to be bright over tables and desks, and beside couches and easy chairs. Since so many people read in bed, there should be a separate light for each person. A room with two queen beds should have individual lights for four people. Better bedside reading lights illuminate a small area, so if one person wants to sleep and another wants to read, the sleeper will not be bothered by the light. The worst situation by far is a single lamp on a table between beds. In each bed, only the person next to the lamp has sufficient light to read. This deficiency is often compounded by weak lightbulbs.

In addition, closet areas should be well lit, and there should be a switch near the door that turns on room lights when you enter. A desirable but seldom-seen feature is a bedside console that allows a guest to control all or most lights in the room from bed.

FURNISHINGS At a bare minimum, the bed(s) should be firm. Pillows should be made with nonallergenic fillers, and a blanket should be provided in addition to the sheets and a spread. Bedclothes should be laundered with fabric softener and changed daily. Better hotels usually provide extra blankets and pillows in the room or on request, and they sometimes place a second top sheet between the blanket and spread.

There should be a dresser large enough to hold clothes for two people during a five-day stay. A small table with two chairs, or a desk with a chair, should be provided. The room should be equipped with a luggage rack and a three-quarter- to full-length mirror.

The television should be color and cable-connected; ideally, it should have a volume governor and a remote control. It should be mounted on a swivel base and preferably enclosed in a cabinet. Local channels should be posted on the set, and a local TV program guide should be supplied. The telephone should be touch-tone and conveniently situated for bedside use, and it should have on or near it clear dialing instructions and a rate card. Local white and Yellow Pages should be provided. Better hotels install phones in the bathroom and equip room phones with long cords.

Well-designed hotel rooms usually have a plush armchair or a sleeper sofa for lounging and reading. Better headboards are padded for comfortable reading in bed, and there should be a nightstand or table on each side of the bed(s). Nice extras in any hotel room include a small refrigerator, a digital alarm clock, and a coffeemaker.

BATHROOM Two sinks are better than one, and you cannot have too much counter space. A sink outside the bath is a great convenience when one person bathes as another dresses. Sinks should have drains with plugs.

Better bathrooms have a tub and shower with a nonslip bottom. Tub and shower controls should be easy to operate. Adjustable shower heads are preferred. The bath needs to be well lit and should have an exhaust fan and a guest-controlled bathroom heater. Towels and washcloths should be large, soft, fluffy, and generously supplied. There should be an electrical outlet for each sink, conveniently and safely placed.

Complimentary shampoo, conditioner, and lotion are a plus, as are robes and bathmats. Better hotels supply tissues and extra toilet paper in the bathrooms. Luxurious baths feature a phone, a hair dryer, and sometimes a small television or even a Jacuzzi.

VENDING Complimentary ice and a drink machine should be located on each floor. Welcome additions include a snack machine and a sundries (combs, toothpaste) machine. The latter are seldom found in large hotels that have restaurants and shops.

ROOM RATINGS

TO DISTINGUISH PROPERTIES ACCORDING TO QUALITY, tastefulness, state of repair, cleanliness, and size of standard rooms, we have grouped the hotels and motels into classifications denoted by stars. Star ratings in this guide apply to San Francisco–area properties only and do not necessarily correspond to ratings awarded by Mobil, AAA, or other travel critics. Because stars carry little weight when awarded in the absence of commonly recognized standards of comparison, we have linked our ratings to expected levels of quality established by specific American hotel corporations.

★★★★★	Superior	Tasteful and luxurious by any standard
★★★★	Extremely Nice	What you would expect at a Hyatt Regency or Marriott
★★★	Nice	Holiday Inn or comparable quality
★★	Adequate	Clean, comfortable, and functional without frills (like a Motel 6)
★	Budget	Spartan, not aesthetically pleasing, but clean

Star ratings apply to room quality only and describe the property's standard accommodations. For most hotels and motels, a "standard accommodation" is a hotel room with either one king bed or two queen beds. In an all-suite property, the standard accommodation is either a one- or two-room suite. In addition to standard accommodations, many hotels offer luxury rooms and special suites that are not rated in this guide. Star ratings for rooms are assigned without regard to whether a property has restaurant(s), recreational facilities, entertainment, or other extras.

In addition to stars (which delineate broad categories), we also employ a numerical rating system. Our rating scale is 0–100, with 100 as the best possible rating. Numerical ratings are presented to show the difference we perceive between one property and another. For instance, rooms at the **Fairmont Hotel,** the **Hotel Monaco,** and the

San Francisco Hotels by Neighborhood

CIVIC CENTER

Archbishop's Mansion

Cathedral Hill Hotel

Hotel Carlton

Hotel Majestic

Inn at the Opera

The Jackson Court

Phoenix Hotel

Queen Anne Hotel

Radisson Miyako Hotel

UNION SQUARE

Andrews Hotel

Beresford Arms

Campton Place Hotel

Cartwright Hotel

Clift Hotel

The Commodore Hotel

Crowne Plaza Union Square

The Donatello

Fitzgerald Hotel

Galleria Park Hotel

Grand Hyatt San Francisco

Grant Plaza

Handlery Union Square Hotel

Hilton San Francisco

Hotel Adagio

Hotel Beresford

Hotel Bijou

Hotel Diva

Hotel Monaco

Hotel Nikko

Hotel Rex

Hotel Triton

Hotel Union Square

Hotel Vintage Court

Inn at Union Square

Kensington Park Hotel

King George Hotel

Maxwell Hotel

Monticello Inn

Nob Hill Lambourne

Pan Pacific Hotel

Petite Auberge

Prescott Hotel

Renaissance Parc Fifty Five

Savoy Hotel

Serrano Hotel

Sir Francis Drake Hotel

Villa Florence

Warwick Regis Hotel

Westin Saint Francis are all rated as four-and-a-half stars (★★★★½). In the supplemental numerical ratings, the Fairmont Hotel is rated a 95, the Hotel Monaco is rated a 94, and the Westin Saint Francis is a 91. This means that within the four-and-a-half-star category, the Fairmont Hotel and Hotel Monaco are comparable, and both have slightly nicer rooms than the Westin Saint Francis.

The location column identifies the greater San Francisco area where you will find a particular property.

UNION SQUARE (CONTINUED)

Westin St. Francis

White Swan Inn

FINANCIAL DISTRICT

Hotel Vitale

Hyatt Regency San Francisco

Mandarin Oriental

MARINA DISTRICT

Buena Vista Motor Inn

Comfort Inn by the Bay

Cow Hollow Motor Inn and Suites

Days Inn Fisherman's Wharf

Edward II Inn and Suites

Hotel del Sol

Marina Motel

Motel Capri

Pacific Heights Inn

Star Motel

Super 8 Motel

Town House Motel

Travelodge by the Bay

Travelodge Golden Gate

Union Street Inn

NOB HILL

Fairmont Hotel

Huntington Hotel

Mark Hopkins Inter-Continental

Renaissance Stanford Court Hotel

Ritz-Carlton

NORTH BEACH

Courtyard by Marriott Fisherman's Wharf

Hyatt Fisherman's Wharf

Marriott Fisherman's Wharf

Radisson Fisherman's Wharf

Sheraton at Fisherman's Wharf

SOMA/MISSION DISTRICT

Argent Hotel San Francisco

Four Seasons Hotel

Harbor Court Hotel

Hotel Milano

Hotel Palomar

San Francisco Marriott

Sheraton Palace Hotel

W Hotel San Francisco

RICHMOND/SUNSET DISTRICT

Days Inn at the Beach

Hotel Drisco

Laurel Inn

Seal Rock Inn

Stanyan Park Hotel

HOW THE HOTELS COMPARE

COST ESTIMATES ARE BASED ON THE HOTEL'S published rack rates for standard rooms. Each "$" represents $50. Thus a cost symbol of "$$$" means that a room (or suite) at that hotel will cost about $150 a night.

Below is a hit parade of the nicest rooms in town. We've focused strictly on room quality and have excluded any consideration of location, services, recreation, or amenities. In some instances, a one- or

How the Hotels Compare in San Francisco

HOTEL	OVERALL RATING	QUALITY RATING	COST ($=$50)
Four Seasons Hotel	★★★★★	98	$$$$$$$$$
Mandarin Oriental	★★★★★	98	$$$$$$$$$$$–
W Hotel San Francisco	★★★★★	98	$$$$$$$–
Campton Place Hotel	★★★★★	97	$$$$$$$+
Hotel Nikko	★★★★★	96	$$$$$$$+
Ritz-Carlton	★★★★★	96	$$$$$$$$$–
Cathedral Hill Hotel	★★★★½	95	$$$
Fairmont Hotel	★★★★½	95	$$$$$
Argent Hotel San Francisco	★★★★½	94	$$$$$$$
Hotel Monaco	★★★★½	94	$$$$$
Archbishop's Mansion	★★★★½	93	$$$$–
Nob Hill Lambourne	★★★★½	92	$$$
Prescott Hotel	★★★★½	92	$$$$+
Clift Hotel	★★★★½	91	$$$$$$$–
Westin St. Francis	★★★★½	91	$$$$$–
Hotel Carlton	★★★★½	90	$$
Hotel Diva	★★★★½	90	$$$–
Hotel Vitale	★★★★½	90	$$$$$
Huntington Hotel	★★★★½	90	$$$$$$$
Inn at the Opera	★★★★½	90	$$$$–
The Jackson Court	★★★★½	90	$$$+
Pan Pacific Hotel	★★★★½	90	$$$$$
Renaissance Stanford Court Hotel	★★★★½	90	$$$$–
White Swan Inn	★★★★½	90	$$$$
Hotel Majestic	★★★★	89	$$$–
Hotel Palomar	★★★★	89	$$$$$

two-room suite can be had for the same price or less than that of a hotel room.

If you use subsequent editions of this guide, you will notice that many of the ratings and rankings change. In addition to the inclusion of new properties, these changes also consider renovations or improved maintenance and housekeeping. A failure to properly

HOTEL	OVERALL RATING	QUALITY RATING	COST ($=$50)
Sheraton Palace Hotel	★★★★	89	$$$$$$$–
Hyatt Fisherman's Wharf	★★★★	88	$$$$$
Hyatt Regency San Francisco	★★★★	88	$$$$$
Grand Hyatt San Francisco	★★★★	87	$$$$$–
The Donatello	★★★★	86	$$$$$
Hilton San Francisco	★★★★	86	$$$$$
Hotel Triton	★★★★	86	$$$$$–
San Francisco Marriott	★★★★	86	$$$$
Fitzgerald Hotel	★★★★	85	$$–
Harbor Court Hotel	★★★★	85	$$$$
Hotel Drisco	★★★★	85	$$$$
Hotel Milano	★★★★	85	$$$$–
Hotel Rex	★★★★	85	$$$$
Renaissance Parc Fifty Five	★★★★	85	$$$$–
Galleria Park Hotel	★★★★	84	$$$$–
Hotel Union Square	★★★★	84	$$
Mark Hopkins Inter-Continental	★★★★	84	$$$$$
Kensington Park Hotel	★★★★	83	$$$–
Serrano Hotel	★★★★	83	$$$$
Warwick Regis Hotel	★★★★	83	$$$
The Commodore Hotel	★★★½	82	$$+
Hotel Bijou	★★★½	82	$$$
Sheraton at Fisherman's Wharf	★★★½	82	$$$$
Sir Francis Drake Hotel	★★★½	82	$$$$
Union Street Inn	★★★½	82	$$$$–
Hotel Adagio	★★★½	80	$$$$$+

maintain guest rooms or a lapse in housekeeping standards can affect the ratings negatively.

Finally, before you begin to shop for a hotel, take a hard look at this letter we received from a couple in Hot Springs, Arkansas:

> *We cancelled our room reservations to follow the advice in your book [and reserved a hotel room highly ranked by the* Unofficial

How the Hotels Compare in San Francisco (continued)

HOTEL	OVERALL RATING	QUALITY RATING	COST ($=$50)
Hotel del Sol	★★★½	80	$$$
Inn at Union Square	★★★½	80	$$$$–
Laurel Inn	★★★½	80	$$$$–
Marriott Fisherman's Wharf	★★★½	80	$$$$
Maxwell Hotel	★★★½	80	$$$
Monticello Inn	★★★½	80	$$$$+
Queen Anne Hotel	★★★½	80	$$$–
Villa Florence	★★★½	80	$$$$
Crowne Plaza Union Square	★★★½	76	$$$$+
Radisson Miyako Hotel	★★★½	76	$$$–
Beresford Arms	★★★½	75	$$$
Buena Vista Motor Inn	★★★½	75	$$
Cartwright Hotel	★★★½	75	$$$+
Petite Auberge	★★★½	75	$$$
Phoenix Hotel	★★★½	75	$$$–
Savoy Hotel	★★★½	75	$$$–
Seal Rock Inn	★★★½	75	$$$–
Stanyan Park Hotel	★★★½	75	$$$–
Edward II Inn	★★★	74	$$
Courtyard Marriott Fisherman's Wharf	★★★	73	$$$+

Guide. *We wanted inexpensive, but clean and cheerful. We got inexpensive, but [also] dirty, grim, and depressing. I really felt disappointed in your advice and the room. It was the pits. That was the one real piece of information I needed from your book! The room spoiled the holiday for me aside from our touring.*

Needless to say, this letter was as unsettling to us as the bad room was to our reader. Our integrity as travel journalists, after all, is based on the quality of the information we give our readers. Even with the best of intentions and the most conscientious research, however, we cannot inspect every room in every hotel. What we do, in statistical terms, is take a sample. We check out several rooms selected at random in each hotel and base our ratings and rankings on those rooms. The inspections are conducted anonymously and without the knowledge of the management. Although unusual, it is

accommodations around town

1. The Abigail Hotel
2. Archbishop's Mansion
3. Argent Hotel San Francisco
4. Buena Vista Motor Inn
5. The Carlton
6. Cathedral Hill Hotel
7. Comfort Inn by the Bay
8. Courtyard Fisherman's Wharf
9. Cow Hollow Motor Inn and Suites
10. Days Inn at the Beach
11. Days Inn Fisherman's Wharf
12. Edward II Inn
13. Four Seasons Hotel and Residences
14. Harbor Court Hotel
15. Holiday Inn Financial District
16. Hotel del Sol
17. Hotel Drisco
18. Hotel Majestic
19. Hotel Milano
20. Hotel Palomar
21. Hotel Vitale
22. Hyatt Fisherman's Wharf
23. Hyatt Regency San Francisco
24. Inn at the Opera
25. The Jackson Court
26. Laurel Inn
27. Mandarin Oriental
28. Marina Motel
29. Marriott Fisherman's Wharf
30. Motel Capri
31. Pacific Heights Inn
32. Pacific Motor Inn
33. The Phoenix Hotel
34. Queen Anne Hotel
35. Radisson Fisherman's Wharf
36. Radisson Miyako Hotel
37. San Francisco Marriott
38. Seal Rock Inn
39. Sheraton at Fisherman's Wharf

40. Sheraton Palace Hotel
41. Stanyan Park Hotel
42. Star Motel
43. Super 8 Motel
44. Town House Motel
45. Travelodge by the Bay
46. Travelodge Golden Gate
47. Union Street Inn
48. W Hotel San Francisco

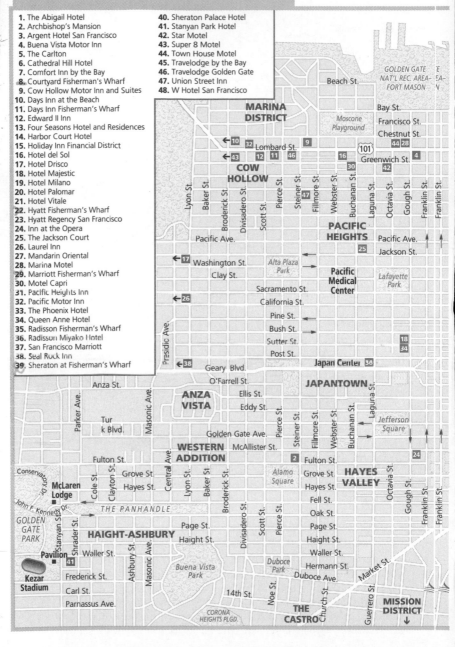

HOTEL	OVERALL RATING	QUALITY RATING	COST ($=$50)
Andrews Hotel	★★★	72	$$
Handlery Union Square Hotel	★★★	72	$$$$
Cow Hollow Motor Inn and Suites	★★★	70	$$
Grant Plaza	★★★	70	$$–
Motel Capri	★★★	70	$$–
Pacific Heights Inn	★★★	70	$$–
Radisson Fisherman's Wharf	★★★	70	$$$$–
Hotel Vintage Court	★★★	68	$$$$
King George Hotel	★★★	65	$$$–
Marina Motel	★★★	65	$$
Days Inn at the Beach	★★½	64	$$
Super 8 Motel	★★½	62	$$–
Travelodge by the Bay	★★½	62	$$+
Comfort Inn by the Bay	★★½	60	$$$
Hotel Beresford	★★½	60	$$$–
Town House Motel	★★½	60	$$–
Travelodge Golden Gate	★★½	60	$$+
Days Inn Fisherman's Wharf	★★	55	$$–
Star Motel	★★	53	$$

certainly possible that the rooms we randomly inspect are not representative of the majority of rooms at a particular hotel. Another possibility is that the rooms we inspect in a given hotel are representative, but that by bad luck a reader is assigned a room that is inferior. When we rechecked the hotel our reader disliked, we discovered our rating was correctly representative, but that he and his wife had unfortunately been assigned to one of a small number of threadbare rooms scheduled for renovation.

The key to avoiding disappointment is to snoop around in advance. We recommend that you ask for a photo of a hotel's standard guest room before you book, or at least get a copy of the hotel's promotional brochure. Be forewarned, however, that some hotel chains use the same guest-room photo in their promotional literature for all hotels in the chain; a specific guest room may not resemble the

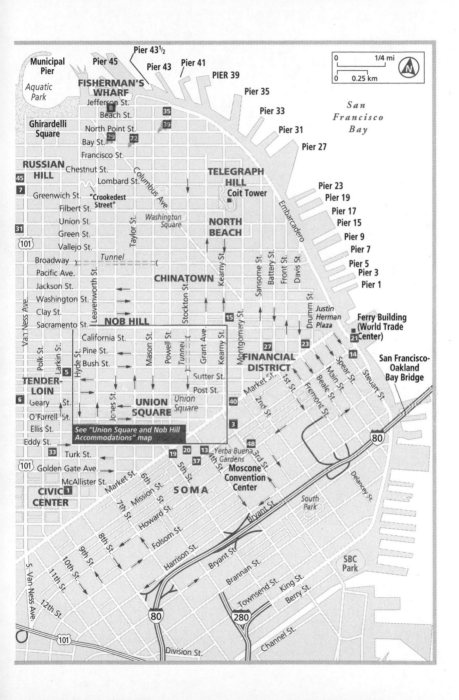

union square and nob hill accommodations

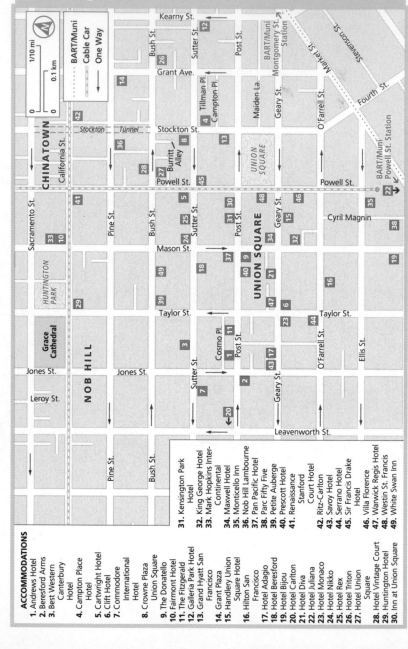

ACCOMMODATIONS

1. Andrews Hotel
2. Beresford Arms
3. Best Western Canterbury Hotel
4. Campton Place Hotel
5. Cartwright Hotel
6. Clift Hotel
7. Commodore International Hotel
8. Crowne Plaza Union Square
9. The Donatello
10. Fairmont Hotel
11. The Fitzgerald
12. Galleria Park Hotel
13. Grand Hyatt San Francisco
14. Grant Plaza
15. Handlery Union Square Hotel
16. Hilton San Francisco
17. Hotel Adagio
18. Hotel Beresford
19. Hotel Bijou
20. Hotel Carlton
21. Hotel Diva
22. Hotel Juliana
23. Hotel Monaco
24. Hotel Nikko
25. Hotel Rex
26. Hotel Triton
27. Hotel Union Square
28. Hotel Vintage Court
29. Huntington Hotel
30. Inn at Union Square

31. Kensington Park Hotel
32. King George Hotel
33. Mark Hopkins Inter-Continental
34. Maxwell Hotel
35. Monticello Inn
36. Nob Hill Lambourne
37. Pan Pacific Hotel
38. Parc Fifty Five
39. Petite Auberge
40. Prescott Hotel
41. Renaissance Stanford Court Hotel
42. Ritz-Carlton
43. Savoy Hotel
44. Serrano Hotel
45. Sir Francis Drake Hotel
46. Villa Florence
47. Warwick Regis Hotel
48. Westin St. Francis
49. White Swan Inn

brochure photo. When you or your travel agent call, ask how old the property is and when your guest room was last renovated. If you arrive and are assigned a room inferior to that which you had been led to expect, demand to be moved to another room.

How the Hotels Compare in Outside Areas

HOTEL	OVERALL RATING	QUALITY RATING	COST ($=$50)
MARIN COUNTY			
Mill Valley Inn	★★★★½	95	$$$$–
Inn Above Tide	★★★★½	93	$$$$$+
Casa Madrona	★★★★½	90	$$$$$–
Embassy Suites Hotel	★★★★	83	$$$$
Acqua Hotel	★★★½	80	$$$$
Villa Inn	★★½	56	$$–
BERKELEY			
Claremont Resort	★★★★½	92	$$$$$$
Doubletree Hotel Berkeley Marina	★★★★	83	$$$+
Hotel Durant	★★★½	75	$$$
OAKLAND			
Oakland Airport Hilton	★★★½	80	$$
Waterfront Plaza Hotel	★★★½	80	$$$$
La Quinta Inn Oakland Airport	★★★½	75	$$–
Oakland Marriott City Center	★★★	74	$$$
SOUTH BAY			
Ritz-Carlton Half Moon Bay	★★★★★	97	$$$$$$$$–
SAN FRANCISCO AIRPORT			
Hyatt Regency San Francisco Airport	★★★★	86	$$$–
Embassy Suites San Francisco Airport	★★★★	85	$$$
Westin Hotel San Francisco Airport	★★★★	84	$$+
San Francisco Airport Marriott	★★★★	83	$$+
Sheraton Gateway Hotel	★★★½	82	$$$–
Doubletree Hotel San Francisco Airport	★★★½	80	$$
Best Western Grosvenor Hotel	★★★	70	$$+
Travelodge San Francisco Airport North	★★★	70	$$–
Red Roof Inn San Francisco Airport	★★½	60	$+
Vagabond Inn Airport	★★½	58	$$–

How the Hotels Compare in the Wine Country

HOTEL	OVERALL RATING	QUALITY RATING	COST ($=$50)
Auberge du Soleil	★★★★★	99	$$$$$$$$$$$$$$$$$
Inn at Southbridge	★★★★½	92	$$$$$$$$
Vintage Inn	★★★★½	91	$$$$$$$$$–
Napa Valley Lodge	★★★★½	90	$$$$$$–
Sonoma Mission Inn and Spa	★★★★½	90	$$$$$$$$$
Rancho Caymus	★★★★	87	$$$$$
Cedar Gables Inn	★★★★	85	$$$$
El Dorado Hotel	★★★★	85	$$$$–
Silverado Country Club and Resort	★★★★	85	$$$+
Sonoma Hotel	★★★★	85	$$+
Harvest Inn	★★★★	84	$$$$$$$$+
Napa Valley Marriott Hotel	★★★★	84	$$$$–
Mount View Hotel	★★★½	81	$$$$–
Best Western Sonoma Valley Inn	★★★½	80	$$$$$–
El Bonita Motel	★★★½	80	$$$$–
Dr. Wilkinson's Hot Springs Resort	★★★½	75	$$$$–
El Pueblo Inn	★★★½	75	$$$
Napa Valley Railway Inn	★★★½	75	$$+
Hotel St. Helena	★★★	74	$$$+
John Muir Inn	★★★	65	$$$

The Top 30 Best Deals in San Francisco

HOTEL	OVERALL RATING	QUALITY RATING	COST ($=$50)
1. Fitzgerald Hotel	★★★★	85	$$–
2. Hotel Carlton	★★★★½	90	$$
3. Hotel Union Square	★★★★	84	$$
4. Hotel Diva	★★★★½	90	$$$–
5. Cathedral Hill Hotel	★★★★½	95	$$$
6. Grant Plaza	★★★	70	$$–
7. Pacific Heights Inn	★★★	70	$$–
8. Kensington Park Hotel	★★★★	83	$$$–
9. Buena Vista Motor Inn	★★★½	75	$$
10. Hotel Majestic	★★★★	89	$$$–

The Top 30 Best Deals in San Francisco (continued)

HOTEL	OVERALL RATING	QUALITY RATING	COST ($=$50)
11. Nob Hill Lambourne	★★★★½	92	$$$
12. The Jackson Court	★★★★½	90	$$$+
13. The Commodore Hotel	★★★½	82	$$+
14. Motel Capri	★★★	70	$$−
15. Archbishop's Mansion	★★★★½	93	$$$$−
16. Inn at the Opera	★★★★½	90	$$$$−
17. Renaissance Stanford Court Hotel	★★★★½	90	$$$$−
18. Edward II Inn	★★★	74	$$
19. Cow Hollow Motor Inn and Suites	★★★	70	$$
20. Andrews Hotel	★★★	72	$$
21. Warwick Regis Hotel	★★★★	83	$$$
22. Queen Anne Hotel	★★★½	80	$$$−
23. Radisson Miyako Hotel	★★★½	76	$$$−
24. White Swan Inn	★★★★½	90	$$$$
25. Savoy Hotel	★★★¼	75	$$$−
26. Stanyan Park Hotel	★★★½	75	$$$−
27. Seal Rock Inn	★★★½	75	$$$−
28. Renaissance Parc Fifty Five	★★★★	85	$$$$−
29. Prescott Hotel	★★★★½	92	$$$$+
30. Phoenix Hotel	★★★½	75	$$$−

The Top 10 Best Deals in the Wine Country

HOTEL	OVERALL RATING	QUALITY RATING	COST ($=$50)
1. Sonoma Hotel	★★★★	85	$$+
2. Napa Valley Railway Inn	★★★½	75	$$+
3. Silverado Country Club and Resort	★★★★	85	$$$+
4. El Dorado Hotel	★★★★	85	$$$$−
5. Napa Valley Marriott Hotel	★★★★	84	$$$$−
6. El Pueblo Inn	★★★½	75	$$$
7. Cedar Gables Inn	★★★★	85	$$$$
8. El Bonita Motel	★★★½	80	$$$$−
9. Mount View Hotel	★★★½	81	$$$$−
10. Dr. Wilkinson's Hot Springs Resort	★★★½	75	$$$$−

Hotel Information Chart

Acqua Hotel ★★★½
555 Redwood Highway
Mill Valley, CA 94941
☎ 415-380-0400
FAX 415-380-9696
TOLL-FREE 888-662-9555
www.acquahotel.com

QUALITY	80
COST	$$$$
LOCATION	MARIN COUNTY
DISCOUNTS AVAILABLE	AAA, AARP, SENIOR, GOVT.
NO. OF ROOMS	50
ON-SITE DINING	–
ROOM SERVICE	–
BAR	–
PARKING PER DAY	FREE
MEETING FACILITIES	–
EXTRA AMENITIES	FREE BREAKFAST, PM TEA AND WINE, ROBES, MINIBAR
BUSINESS AMENITIES	DATAPORT, 2-LINE PHONE, BUSINESS CENTER, VOICEMAIL, SECRETRIAL SERVICES
DÉCOR	PACIFIC RIM
POOL/SAUNA	–
EXERCISE FACILITIES	FITNESS ROOM

Andrews Hotel ★★★
624 Post Street
San Francisco, CA 94109
☎ 415-563-6877
FAX 415-928-6919
TOLL-FREE 800-926-3739
www.andrewshotel.com

QUALITY	72
COST	$$
LOCATION	UNION SQUARE
DISCOUNTS AVAILABLE	AAA, AARP, SENIOR, GOVT., MILITARY
NO. OF ROOMS	48
ON-SITE DINING	–
ROOM SERVICE	–
BAR	–
PARKING PER DAY	$25
MEETING FACILITIES	–
EXTRA AMENITIES	FREE BREAKFAST, FREE WINE
BUSINESS AMENITIES	DATAPORT, 2-LINE PHONE, VOICEMAIL
DÉCOR	QUEEN ANNE/ VICTORIAN
POOL/SAUNA	–
EXERCISE FACILITIES	–

Archbishop's Mansion ★★★★½
1000 Fulton Street
San Francisco, CA 94117
☎ 415-563-7872
FAX 415-885-3193
TOLL-FREE 800-543-5820
www.thearchbishopsmansion.com

QUALITY	93
COST	$$$$–
LOCATION	CIVIC CENTER
NO. OF ROOMS	15
ON-SITE DINING	–
ROOM SERVICE	LIMITED
BAR	–
PARKING PER DAY	FREE
MEETING FACILITIES	–
EXTRA AMENITIES	FREE BREAKFAST, NEWSPAPER, FREE WINE HOUR, MINI-BAR, VCR
BUSINESS AMENITIES	DATAPORT, BUSINESS CENTER,
DÉCOR	FRENCH CHATEAU
POOL/SAUNA	–
EXERCISE FACILITIES	FITNESS ROOM

Best Western Grosvenor Hotel ★★★
380 S. Airport Boulevard
South San Francisco, CA 94080
☎ 650-873-3200
FAX 650-589-3495
TOLL-FREE 800-722-7141
www.grosvenorsfo.com

QUALITY	70
COST	$$+
LOCATION	SAN FRANCISCO INT'L AIRPORT
DISCOUNTS AVAILABLE	AAA, AARP, GOVT., SENIOR
NO. OF ROOMS	207
ON-SITE DINING	●
ROOM SERVICE	●
BAR	●
PARKING PER DAY	FREE
MEETING FACILITIES	●
EXTRA AMENITIES	FREE BREAKFAST, AIRPORT SHUTTLE, COFFEEMAKER
BUSINESS AMENITIES	DATAPORT, VOICEMAIL
DÉCOR	EUROPEAN
POOL/SAUNA	POOL, SAUNA, WHIRLPOOL
EXERCISE FACILITIES	FITNESS ROOM

Best Western Sonoma Valley Inn ★★★½
520 Second Street West
Sonoma, CA 95476
☎ 707-938-9200
FAX 707-938-0935
TOLL-FREE 800-334-5784
www.sonomavalleyinn.com

QUALITY	80
COST	$$$$$–
LOCATION	WINE COUNTRY
DISCOUNTS AVAILABLE	AAA, AARP
NO. OF ROOMS	78
ON-SITE DINING	–
ROOM SERVICE	–
BAR	–
PARKING PER DAY	FREE
MEETING FACILITIES	●
EXTRA AMENITIES	FREE BREAKFAST, WINE IN ROOM, PET FRIENDLY, COFFEEMAKER, FRIDGE, SOME FIREPLACES
BUSINESS AMENITIES	DATAPORT
DÉCOR	MODERN CALIFORNIAN
POOL/SAUNA	POOL, WHIRLPOOL
EXERCISE FACILITIES	PRIVILEGES (FEE)

Buena Vista Motor Inn ★★★½
1599 Lombard Street
San Francisco, CA 94123
☎ 415-923-9600
FAX 415-441-4775
TOLL-FREE 800-835-4980
www.buenavistamotorinn.com

QUALITY	75
COST	$$
LOCATION	MARINA
DISCOUNTS AVAILABLE	AAA, AARP
NO. OF ROOMS	50
ON-SITE DINING	–
ROOM SERVICE	–
BAR	–
PARKING PER DAY	FREE
MEETING FACILITIES	–
EXTRA AMENITIES	ROOFTOP SUN DECK, TEA/ COFFEEMAKER, TOURS
BUSINESS AMENITIES	DATAPORT, FAX, COPIER
DÉCOR	MOTEL
POOL/SAUNA	–
EXERCISE FACILITIES	–

Argent Hotel
San Francisco ★★★★½
50 Third Street
San Francisco, CA 94103
☎ 415-974-6400
FAX 415-543-8268
TOLL-FREE 877-222-6699
www.argenthotel.com

QUALITY	94
COST	$$$$$$$
LOCATION	SOMA/ MISSION DISTRICT
DISCOUNTS AVAILABLE	AAA
NO. OF ROOMS	667
ON-SITE DINING	•
ROOM SERVICE	–
BAR	•
PARKING PER DAY	$42
MEETING FACILITIES	•
EXTRA AMENITIES	GIFT SHOP
BUSINESS AMENITIES	DATAPORT, VOICEMAIL
DÉCOR	ART DECO
POOL/SAUNA	SAUNA
EXERCISE FACILITIES	–

Auberge du Soleil ★★★★★
180 Rutherford Hill Road
Rutherford, CA 94573
☎ 707-963-1211
FAX 707-963-8764
TOLL-FREE 800-348-5406
www.aubergedusoleil.com

QUALITY	99
COST	$$$$$$$$$$$$$$$$$
LOCATION	WINE COUNTRY
NO. OF ROOMS	50
ON-SITE DINING	•
ROOM SERVICE	•
BAR	•
PARKING PER DAY	FREE
MEETING FACILITIES	•
EXTRA AMENITIES	SAFE, DVD PLAYER, FRUIT, MASSAGE, ROBE, SLIPPERS, MINIBAR, COFFEEMAKER, TOASTER
BUSINESS AMENITIES	DATAPORT, VOICEMAIL
DÉCOR	SOUTHWESTERN
POOL/SAUNA	POOL, STEAM ROOM, SPA, WHIRLPOOL
EXERCISE FACILITIES	–

Beresford Arms ★★★½
701 Post Street
San Francisco, CA 94109
☎ 415-673-2600
FAX 415-929-1535
TOLL-FREE 800-533-6533
www.beresford.com

QUALITY	75
COST	$$$
LOCATION	UNION SQUARE
DISCOUNTS AVAILABLE	AAA, AARP, GOVT.
NO. OF ROOMS	95
ON-SITE DINING	–
ROOM SERVICE	–
BAR	•
PARKING PER DAY	$22
MEETING FACILITIES	–
EXTRA AMENITIES	FREE BREAKFAST, VCR, WET BAR, PM TEA AND WINE
BUSINESS AMENITIES	DATAPORT, 2-LINE PHONE, FAX
DÉCOR	EUROPEAN
POOL/SAUNA	WHIRLPOOL
EXERCISE FACILITIES	–

Campton Place Hotel ★★★★★
340 Stockton Street
San Francisco, CA 94108
☎ 415-781-5555
FAX 415-955-5536
TOLL-FREE 800-235-4300
www.camptonplace.com

QUALITY	97
COST	$$$$$$$+
LOCATION	UNION SQUARE
DISCOUNTS AVAILABLE	AAA
NO. OF ROOMS	110
ON-SITE DINING	•
ROOM SERVICE	–
BAR	•
PARKING PER DAY	$38
MEETING FACILITIES	•
EXTRA AMENITIES	FITNESS TERRACE, SAFE, MINIBAR, BOSE STEREO, VCR, SLIPPERS
BUSINESS AMENITIES	DATAPORT, 2-LINE PHONE, FAX
DÉCOR	EUROPEAN
POOL/SAUNA	–
EXERCISE FACILITIES	–

Cartwright Hotel ★★★½
524 Sutter Street
San Francisco, CA 94102
☎ 415-421-2865
FAX 415-398-6343
TOLL-FREE 800-919-9779
www.cartwrighthotel.com

QUALITY	75
COST	$$$+
LOCATION	UNION SQUARE
DISCOUNTS AVAILABLE	AAA, AARP
NO. OF ROOMS	114
ON-SITE DINING	–
ROOM SERVICE	–
BAR	–
PARKING PER DAY	$25
MEETING FACILITIES	•
EXTRA AMENITIES	FREE BREAKFAST, WINE/TEA HOUR, COFFEEMAKER, PET FRIENDLY, NEWSPAPER
BUSINESS AMENITIES	DATAPORT, 2-LINE PHONE, VOICEMAIL
DÉCOR	EUROPEAN BOUTIQUE
POOL/SAUNA	PRIVILEGES
EXERCISE FACILITIES	PRIVILEGES

Casa Madrona ★★★★½
801 Bridgeway
Sausalito, CA 94965
☎ 415-332-0502
FAX 415-332-2537
TOLL-FREE 800-288-0502
www.casamadrona.com

QUALITY	90
COST	$$$$$–
LOCATION	MARIN COUNTY
NO. OF ROOMS	63
ON-SITE DINING	•
ROOM SERVICE	•
BAR	•
PARKING PER DAY	$20
MEETING FACILITIES	•
EXTRA AMENITIES	FREE BREAKFAST, PM WINE/CHEESE, MINIBAR, COFFEEMAKER
BUSINESS AMENITIES	DATAPORT, VOICEMAIL
DÉCOR	EACH ROOM IS DIFFERENT
POOL/SAUNA	SPA
EXERCISE FACILITIES	–

Hotel Information Chart (continued)

Cathedral Hill Hotel ★★★★½
1101 Van Ness Avenue
San Francisco, CA 94109
☎ 415-776-8200
FAX 415-441-2841
TOLL-FREE 800-622-0855
www.cathedralhillhotel.com

QUALITY	95
COST	$$$
LOCATION	CIVIC CENTER
DISCOUNTS AVAILABLE	GROUP
NO. OF ROOMS	400
ON-SITE DINING	•
ROOM SERVICE	•
BAR	•
PARKING PER DAY	$20
MEETING FACILITIES	•
EXTRA AMENITIES	HAIR SALON, GIFT SHOP, CAR RENTAL, TOURS, VIDEO GAMES, COFFEE-MAKER
BUSINESS AMENITIES	DATAPORT
DÉCOR	CONTEMPORARY
POOL/SAUNA	POOL
EXERCISE FACILITIES	FITNESS ROOM

Cedar Gables Inn ★★★★
486 Coombs Street
Napa, CA 94559
☎ 707-224-7969
FAX 707-224-4838
TOLL-FREE 800-309-7969
www.cedargablesinn.com

QUALITY	85
COST	$$$$
LOCATION	WINE COUNTRY
DISCOUNTS AVAILABLE	AAA, AARP
NO. OF ROOMS	9
ON-SITE DINING	–
ROOM SERVICE	–
BAR	–
PARKING PER DAY	FREE
MEETING FACILITIES	–
EXTRA AMENITIES	BREAKFAST, WINE, HORS D'OEUVRES
BUSINESS AMENITIES	–
DÉCOR	ENGLISH COUNTRY MANOR
POOL/SAUNA	–
EXERCISE FACILITIES	–

Claremont Resort ★★★★½
41 Tunnel Road
Berkeley, CA 94705
☎ 510-843-3000
FAX 510-848-6208
TOLL-FREE 800-551-7266
www.claremontresort.com

QUALITY	92
COST	$$$$$$
LOCATION	BERKELEY
DISCOUNTS AVAILABLE	AAA, AARP
NO. OF ROOMS	279
ON-SITE DINING	•
ROOM SERVICE	•
BAR	•
PARKING PER DAY	$19
MEETING FACILITIES	•
EXTRA AMENITIES	FULL SPA, TENNIS COURTS
BUSINESS AMENITIES	DOUBLE DATAPORTS, 2-LINE PHONE, VOICEMAIL
DÉCOR	TRADITIONAL
POOL/SAUNA	POOL, SAUNA, WHIRLPOOL
EXERCISE FACILITIES	FITNESS CLASSES (YOGA, PILATES, TAI CHI)

Courtyard Marriott Fisherman's Wharf ★★★
580 Beach Street
San Francisco, CA 94133
☎ 415-775-3800
FAX 415-441-7307
TOLL-FREE 800-645-9258
www.marriott.com

QUALITY	73
COST	$$$+
LOCATION	NORTH BEACH
DISCOUNTS AVAILABLE	AAA, AARP, GOVT.
NO. OF ROOMS	132
ON-SITE DINING	•
ROOM SERVICE	–
BAR	–
PARKING PER DAY	$15
MEETING FACILITIES	–
EXTRA AMENITIES	BREAKFAST
BUSINESS AMENITIES	DATAPORT
DÉCOR	MODERN
POOL/SAUNA	–
EXERCISE FACILITIES	FITNESS ROOM

Cow Hollow Motor Inn and Suites ★★★
2190 Lombard Street
San Francisco, CA 94123
☎ 415-921-5800
FAX 415-922-8515
www.cowhollowmotorinn.com

QUALITY	70
COST	$$
LOCATION	MARINA
NO. OF ROOMS	129
ON-SITE DINING	•
ROOM SERVICE	–
BAR	–
PARKING PER DAY	FREE
MEETING FACILITIES	–
EXTRA AMENITIES	COFFEEMAKER
BUSINESS AMENITIES	–
DÉCOR	MOERN
POOL/SAUNA	–
EXERCISE FACILITIES	–

Crowne Plaza Union Square ★★★½
480 Sutter Street
San Francisco, CA 94108
☎ 415-398-8900
FAX 415-989-8823
TOLL-FREE 800-243-1135
http://cpsanfrancisco-union-square.felcor.com

QUALITY	76
COST	$$$$+
LOCATION	UNION SQUARE
DISCOUNTS AVAILABLE	AAA, AARP, GOVT., MILITARY
NO. OF ROOMS	404
ON-SITE DINING	•
ROOM SERVICE	•
BAR	•
PARKING PER DAY	$38
MEETING FACILITIES	•
EXTRA AMENITIES	NEWSSTAND, CD PLAYER, PET FRIENDLY, SAFE, MULTILINGUAL STAFF
BUSINESS AMENITIES	DATAPORT, 2-LINE PHONE, VOICEMAIL
DÉCOR	MODERN
POOL/SAUNA	–
EXERCISE FACILITIES	FITNESS ROOM

Clift Hotel ★★★★½
495 Geary Street
San Francisco, CA 94102
☎ 415-775-4700
FAX 415-441-4621
TOLL-FREE 800-697-1791
www.clifthotel.com

QUALITY	91
COST	$$$$$$–
LOCATION	UNION SQUARE
DISCOUNTS AVAILABLE	AAA, CORP.
NO. OF ROOMS	374
ON-SITE DINING	•
ROOM SERVICE	•
BAR	•
PARKING PER DAY	$45
MEETING FACILITIES	•
EXTRA AMENITIES	BABYSITTING, DVD, CD, VIDEO GAME LIBRARY, BOARD GAMES, MASSAGE
BUSINESS AMENITIES	DATAPORT, FAX, 2-LINE PHONE, VOICEMAIL, BUSINESS CENTER
DÉCOR	EUROPEAN
POOL/SAUNA	–
EXERCISE FACILITIES	FITNESS ROOM

Comfort Inn by the Bay ★★½
2775 Van Ness Avenue
San Francisco, CA 94109
☎ 415-928-5000
FAX 415-441-3990
TOLL-FREE 800-228-5150
www.hotelchoice.com

QUALITY	60
COST	$$$
LOCATION	MARINA
DISCOUNTS AVAILABLE	AAA, AARP, MILITARY
NO. OF ROOMS	138
ON-SITE DINING	–
ROOM SERVICE	–
BAR	–
PARKING PER DAY	$25
MEETING FACILITIES	–
EXTRA AMENITIES	BREAKFAST, COFFEE-MAKER, NEWSPAPER, TENNIS COURTS, SAFE, TOURS
BUSINESS AMENITIES	DATAPORT, FAX, COPIER, VOICEMAIL
DÉCOR	MODERN
POOL/SAUNA	–
EXERCISE FACILITIES	TENNIS COURT

The Commodore Hotel ★★★½
825 Sutter Street
San Francisco, CA 94109
☎ 415-923-6800
FAX 415-923-6804
TOLL-FREE 800-338-6848
www.thecommodorehotel.com

QUALITY	82
COST	$$+
LOCATION	UNION SQUARE
DISCOUNTS AVAILABLE	AAA, AARP, GOVT.
NO. OF ROOMS	110
ON-SITE DINING	•
ROOM SERVICE	–
BAR	•
PARKING PER DAY	$26
MEETING FACILITIES	•
EXTRA AMENITIES	TOURS, FRIDGE, COFFEEMAKER, AIRPORT SHUTTLE
BUSINESS AMENITIES	DATAPORT, VOICEMAIL, FAX
DÉCOR	NEO-DEC•
POOL/SAUNA	–
EXERCISE FACILITIES	PRIVILEGES

Days Inn at the Beach ★★½
2600 Sloat Boulevard
San Francisco, CA 94116
☎ 415-665-9000
FAX 415-665-5440
TOLL-FREE 800-329-7466
www.daysinn.com

QUALITY	64
COST	$$
LOCATION	RICHMOND/SUNSET DISTRICT
DISCOUNTS AVAILABLE	AAA, AARP, GOVT.
NO. OF ROOMS	33
ON-SITE DINING	–
ROOM SERVICE	–
BAR	–
PARKING PER DAY	FREE
MEETING FACILITIES	–
EXTRA AMENITIES	FREE BREAKFAST, MICROWAVE
BUSINESS AMENITIES	–
DÉCOR	MODERN
POOL/SAUNA	–
EXERCISE FACILITIES	–

Days Inn Fisherman's Wharf ★★
2358 Lombard Street
San Francisco, CA 94123
☎ 415-922-2010
FAX 415-931-0603
TOLL-FREE 800-329-7466
www.daysinn.com

QUALITY	55
COST	$$–
LOCATION	MARINA
DISCOUNTS AVAILABLE	AAA, AARP, GOVT.
NO. OF ROOMS	22
ON-SITE DINING	–
ROOM SERVICE	–
BAR	–
PARKING PER DAY	FREE
MEETING FACILITIES	–
EXTRA AMENITIES	FREE BREAKFAST, TENNIS
BUSINESS AMENITIES	–
DÉCOR	MODERN
POOL/SAUNA	–
EXERCISE FACILITIES	TENNIS COURT

The Donatello ★★★★
501 Post Street
San Francisco, CA 94102
☎ 415-441-7100
FAX 415-885-8842
TOLL-FREE 800-227-3184
www.thedonatellosf.com

QUALITY	86
COST	$$$$$
LOCATION	UNION SQUARE
DISCOUNTS AVAILABLE	AAA, AARP, GOVT.
NO. OF ROOMS	943
ON-SITE DINING	•
ROOM SERVICE	•
BAR	•
PARKING PER DAY	$28
MEETING FACILITIES	•
EXTRA AMENITIES	LOUNGE MUSIC, SPA SERVICES, SOUND-PROOFING, SAFE, TENNIS, MICRO-WAVE, SAFE, FRIDGE, BABYSITTING, NEWSPAPER
BUSINESS AMENITIES	DATAPORT, 2-LINE PHONE, VOICEMAIL
DÉCOR	EUROPEAN BOUTIQUE
POOL/SAUNA	SAUNA, WHIRLPOOL
EXERCISE FACILITIES	FITNESS ROOM

Hotel Information Chart (continued)

Doubletree Hotel
Berkeley Marina ★★★★
200 Marina Boulevard
Berkeley, CA 94710
☎ 510-548-7920
FAX 510-548-7944
TOLL-FREE 800-222-TREE
www.doubletree.com

QUALITY	83
COST	$$$+
LOCATION	BERKELEY
DISCOUNTS AVAILABLE	AAA, AARP, GOVT., MILITARY
NO. OF ROOMS	376
ON-SITE DINING	•
ROOM SERVICE	•
BAR	•
PARKING PER DAY	FREE
MEETING FACILITIES	•
EXTRA AMENITIES	MARINA, COFFEE-MAKER, NEWSPAPER, COOK-IES, PET FRIENDLY
BUSINESS AMENITIES	DATAPORT, 2-LINE PHONE, VOICEMAIL
DÉCOR	CONTEMPORARY
POOL/SAUNA	POOL, SAUNA, WHIRLPOOL
EXERCISE FACILITIES	–

Doubletree Hotel
San Francisco Airport ★★★½
835 Airport Boulevard
Burlingame, CA 94010
☎ 415-344-5500
FAX 650-340-8851
TOLL-FREE 800-222-TREE
www.doubletree.com

QUALITY	80
COST	$$
LOCATION	SAN FRANCICO INT'L AIRPORT
DISCOUNTS AVAILABLE	AAA, AARP, GOVT., MILITARY
NO. OF ROOMS	400
ON-SITE DINING	•
ROOM SERVICE	•
BAR	•
PARKING PER DAY	$13
MEETING FACILITIES	•
EXTRA AMENITIES	AIRPORT SHUTTLE, PET FRIENDLY, GIFT SHOP, SAFE
BUSINESS AMENITIES	DATAPOR, NOTARY PUBLIC, FAX, AUDIOVISUAL, VIDEO CONFERENCE
DÉCOR	EUROPEAN
POOL/SAUNA	–
EXERCISE FACILITIES	FITNESS ROOM

Dr. Wilkinson's
Hot Springs Resort ★★★½
1507 Lincoln Avenue
Calistoga, CA 94515
☎ 707-942-4102
www.drwilkinson.com

QUALITY	75
COST	$$$$–
LOCATION	WINE COUNTRY
NO. OF ROOMS	42
ON-SITE DINING	–
ROOM SERVICE	–
BAR	–
PARKING PER DAY	FREE
MEETING FACILITIES	•
EXTRA AMENITIES	SPA, MASSAGE, WINE TOURS, TEA/COFFEEMAKER, HOT CHOCOLATE
BUSINESS AMENITIES	DATAPORT, VOICE-MAIL
DÉCOR	VICTORIAN, NEO-DEC•
POOL/SAUNA	POOL, WHIRLPOOL, STEAM ROOM
EXERCISE FACILITIES	–

El Pueblo Inn ★★★½
896 W. Napa Street
Sonoma, CA 95476
☎ 707-996-3651
FAX 707-935-5988
TOLL-FREE 800-900-8844
www.elpuebloinn.com

QUALITY	75
COST	$$$
LOCATION	WINE COUNTRY
DISCOUNTS AVAILABLE	AAA, AARP
NO. OF ROOMS	38
ON-SITE DINING	–
ROOM SERVICE	–
BAR	–
PARKING PER DAY	FREE
MEETING FACILITIES	–
EXTRA AMENITIES	COFFEEMAKER, BIS-COTTI, TEA, HOT CHOCOLATE, FRIDGE, MASSAGE
BUSINESS AMENITIES	DATAPORT, VOICE-MAIL
DÉCOR	EARLY CALIFORNIA
POOL/SAUNA	POOL, WHIRLPOOL
EXERCISE FACILITIES	–

Embassy Suites Hotel ★★★★
101 McInnis Parkway
San Rafael, CA 94903
☎ 415-499-9222; FAX 415-499-9268; TOLL-FREE 800-EMBASSY
www.embassymarin.com

QUALITY	83
COST	$$$$
LOCATION	MARIN COUNTY
DISCOUNTS AVAILABLE	AAA, AARP, GOVT.
NO. OF ROOMS	235
ON-SITE DINING	•
ROOM SERVICE	•
BAR	•
PARKING PER DAY	FREE
MEETING FACILITIES	•
EXTRA AMENITIES	FREE BREAKFAST, PM RECEPTION, SALON, GIFT SHOP, ATM, SAFE, NEWSSTAND, MULTILINGUAL STAFF, FRIDGE,
BUSINESS AMENITIES	DATAPORT, 2-LINE PHONE, FAX, BUSI-NESS CENTER, AUDIOVISUAL, VIDEO CONFERENCE
DÉCOR	CONTEMPORARY
POOL/SAUNA	POOL, WHIRLPOOL
EXERCISE FACILITIES	FITNESS ROOM, WALKING/JOGGING TRACK

Embassy Suites SFO ★★★★
150 Anza Boulevard
Burlingame, CA 94010
☎ 415-342-4600; FAX 650-343-8137; TOLL-FREE 800-EMBASSY
www.embassysuites.com

QUALITY	85
COST	$$$
LOCATION	SAN FRANCICO INT'L AIRPORT
DISCOUNTS AVAILABLE	AAA, AARP, GOVT., MILITARY
NO. OF ROOMS	344
ON-SITE DINING	•
ROOM SERVICE	•
BAR	•
PARKING PER DAY	FREE
MEETING FACILITIES	•
EXTRA AMENITIES	FREE BREAKFAST, PM RECEPTION, MICRO-WAVE, ATM, SAFE, COFFEEMAKER, SAFE, PET FRIENDLY,
BUSINESS AMENITIES	DATAPORT, 2-LINE PHONE, FAX, BUSI-NESS CENTER, AUDIOVISUAL, VIDEO CONFERENCE
DÉCOR	ATRIUM HOTEL
POOL/SAUNA	POOL, SAUNA, STEAM ROOM
EXERCISE FACILITIES	FITNESS ROOM

Edward II Inn ★★★
3155 Scott Street
San Francisco, CA 94123
☎ 415-922-3000
FAX 415-931-5784
TOLL-FREE 800-473-2846
www.edwardii.com

QUALITY	74
COST	$$
LOCATION	MARINA
DISCOUNTS AVAILABLE	AAA
NO. OF ROOMS	30
ON-SITE DINING	•
ROOM SERVICE	•
BAR	•
PARKING PER DAY	$12
MEETING FACILITIES	–
EXTRA AMENITIES	FREE BREAKFAST, BATHROBES, NEWSPAPER, COFFEE, TEA, HOT CHOCOLATE, MANICURE, PEDICURE, PM REFRESHMENTS AT THE PUB
BUSINESS AMENITIES	FAX
DÉCOR	ENGLISH COUNTRY
POOL/SAUNA	SPA NEARBY
EXERCISE FACILITIES	FITNESS ROOM, MEDITATION ROOM

El Bonita Motel ★★★½
195 Main Street
St. Helena, CA 94574
☎ 707-963-3216
FAX 707-963-8838
TOLL-FREE 800-541-3284
www.elbonita.com

QUALITY	80
COST	$$$$–
LOCATION	WINE COUNTRY
DISCOUNTS AVAILABLE	AAA, AARP
NO. OF ROOMS	41
ON-SITE DINING	–
ROOM SERVICE	–
BAR	–
PARKING PER DAY	FREE
MEETING FACILITIES	–
EXTRA AMENITIES	FREE BREAKFAST, COFFEEMAKER, FRIDGE, MICROWAVE, PET FRIENDLY
BUSINESS AMENITIES	BUSINESS CENTER
DÉCOR	1950S
POOL/SAUNA	WHIRLPOOL, POOL, SAUNA
EXERCISE FACILITIES	–

El Dorado Hotel ★★★★
405 First Street West
Sonoma, CA 95476
☎ 707-996-3030
FAX 707-996-3148
TOLL-FREE 800-289-3031
www.eldoradosonoma.com

QUALITY	85
COST	$$$$–
LOCATION	WINE COUNTRY
NO. OF ROOMS	27
ON-SITE DINING	•
ROOM SERVICE	•
BAR	•
PARKING PER DAY	FREE
MEETING FACILITIES	–
EXTRA AMENITIES	FREE BREAKFAST, COFFEE, TEA, DVD/CD PLAYER, FRIDGE, NEWSPAPER
BUSINESS AMENITIES	DATAPORT, VOICEMAIL, FAX, COPIER
DÉCOR	OLD WORLD
POOL/SAUNA	POOL
EXERCISE FACILITIES	–

Fairmont Hotel ★★★★½
950 Mason Street
San Francisco, CA 94108
☎ 415-772-5000
FAX 415-772-5013
TOLL-FREE 800-678-8946
www.historichotels.org

QUALITY	95
COST	$$$$$
LOCATION	NOB HILL
DISCOUNTS AVAILABLE	AAA, AARP, GOVT.
NO. OF ROOMS	591
ON-SITE DINING	•
ROOM SERVICE	–
BAR	–
PARKING PER DAY	$49
MEETING FACILITIES	•
EXTRA AMENITIES	MASSAGE, SAFE, ROBES, FRIDGE, SALON, SPA
BUSINESS AMENITIES	DATAPORT, 2-LINE PHONE, FAX, BUSINESS CENTER, AUDIOVISUAL, VIDEO CONFERENCE, VOICEMAIL
DÉCOR	GRAND HOTEL
POOL/SAUNA	SAUNA, WHIRLPOOL
EXERCISE FACILITIES	–

Fitzgerald Hotel ★★★★
620 Post Street
San Francisco, CA 94109
☎ 415-775-8100
FAX 415-775-1278
TOLL-FREE 800-334-6835
www.fitzgeraldhotel.com

QUALITY	85
COST	$$–
LOCATION	UNION SQUARE
DISCOUNTS AVAILABLE	AAA, AARP, GOVT.
NO. OF ROOMS	46
ON-SITE DINING	–
ROOM SERVICE	–
BAR	–
PARKING PER DAY	$24
MEETING FACILITIES	–
EXTRA AMENITIES	FREE BREAKFAST, FRIDGE, MICROWAVE, COFFEEMAKER
BUSINESS AMENITIES	DATAPORT, 2-LINE PHONE
DÉCOR	EUROPEAN
POOL/SAUNA	PRIVILEGES
EXERCISE FACILITIES	PRIVILEGES

Four Seasons Hotel ★★★★★
757 Market Street
San Francisco, CA 94103
☎ 415-633-3000; FAX 415-633-3009; TOLL-FREE 800-332-3442
www.fourseasons.com

QUALITY	98
COST	$$$$$$$$$
LOCATION	SOMA/ MISSION DISTRICT
NO. OF ROOMS	277
ON-SITE DINING	•
ROOM SERVICE	•
BAR	•
PARKING PER DAY	$44
MEETING FACILITIES	•
EXTRA AMENITIES	TECHNOLOGY CENTER, FREE BREAKFAST
BUSINESS AMENITIES	24-HOUR FACILITIES, FAX, DELIVERY, COMPUTER CENTER, MULTI-LINE PHONE, AUDIOVISUAL EQUIPMENT
DÉCOR	CONTEMPORARY
POOL/SAUNA	POOL
EXERCISE FACILITIES	HEALTH CLUB, BASKETBALL, GOLF COURSE

Hotel Information Chart (continued)

Galleria Park Hotel ★★★★
191 Sutter Street
San Francisco, CA 94104
☎ 415-781-3060
FAX 415-433-4409
TOLL-FREE 866-756-3036
www.galleriapark.com

QUALITY	84
COST	$$$$–
LOCATION	UNION SQUARE
DISCOUNTS AVAILABLE	AAA, AARP, GOVT.
NO. OF ROOMS	177
ON-SITE DINING	•
ROOM SERVICE	•
BAR	•
PARKING PER DAY	$33
MEETING FACILITIES	•
EXTRA AMENITIES	ROOFTOP TRACK, PARK
BUSINESS AMENITIES	DATAPORT, 2-LINE PHONE, 24-HOUR BUSINESS CENTER
DÉCOR	ART NOUVEAU
POOL/SAUNA	–
EXERCISE FACILITIES	FITNESS ROOM

Grand Hyatt San Francisco ★★★★
345 Stockton Street
San Francisco, CA 94108
☎ 415-398-1234
FAX 415-391-1780
TOLL-FREE 800-233-1234
www.hyatt.com

QUALITY	87
COST	$$$$$–
LOCATION	UNION SQUARE
DISCOUNTS AVAILABLE	AAA, SENIOR, GOVT.
NO. OF ROOMS	685
ON-SITE DINING	•
ROOM SERVICE	•
BAR	•
PARKING PER DAY	$41
MEETING FACILITIES	•
EXTRA AMENITIES	BABYSITTING, PILLOW-TOP MATTRESSES, COFFEEMAKER, MINIBAR, WINE RECEPTION, SAFE
BUSINESS AMENITIES	DATAPORT, 2-LINE PHONE
DÉCOR	EUROPEAN WITH ORIENTAL ACCENTS
POOL/SAUNA	–
EXERCISE FACILITIES	FITNESS ROOM

Grant Plaza ★★★
465 Grant Avenue
San Francisco, CA 94108
☎ 415-434-3883
FAX 415-434-3886
TOLL-FREE 800-472-6899
www.grantplaza.com

QUALITY	70
COST	$$–
LOCATION	UNION SQUARE
DISCOUNTS AVAILABLE	AAA, AARP, GOVT.
NO. OF ROOMS	72
ON-SITE DINING	–
ROOM SERVICE	–
BAR	–
PARKING PER DAY	$20
MEETING FACILITIES	–
EXTRA AMENITIES	–
BUSINESS AMENITIES	DATAPORT, VOICE-MAIL
DÉCOR	CONTEMPORARY
POOL/SAUNA	–
EXERCISE FACILITIES	PRIVILEGES (FEE)

Hilton San Francisco ★★★★
333 O'Farrell Street
San Francisco, CA 94102
☎ 415-771-1400
FAX 415-771-6807
TOLL-FREE 800-HILTONS
www.hilton.com

QUALITY	86
COST	$$$$$
LOCATION	UNION SQUARE
DISCOUNTS AVAILABLE	AAA, AARP, GOVT.
NO. OF ROOMS	1,896
ON-SITE DINING	•
ROOM SERVICE	•
BAR	•
PARKING PER DAY	$36
MEETING FACILITIES	•
EXTRA AMENITIES	GIFT SHOP, BABYSIT-TING
BUSINESS AMENITIES	DATAPORT, 2-LINE PHONE
DÉCOR	MODERN
POOL/SAUNA	POOL, SAUNA, WHIRLPOOL
EXERCISE FACILITIES	FITNESS ROOM

Hotel Adagio ★★★½
550 Geary Street
San Francisco, CA 94102
☎ 415-775-5000
FAX 415-775-9388
TOLL-FREE 800-228-8830
www.thehoteladagio.com

QUALITY	80
COST	$$$$$+
LOCATION	UNION SQUARE
DISCOUNTS AVAILABLE	AAA, AARP, GOVT., SENIOR
NO. OF ROOMS	171
ON-SITE DINING	•
ROOM SERVICE	•
BAR	•
PARKING PER DAY	$33
MEETING FACILITIES	•
EXTRA AMENITIES	INTERNET, IN-ROOM DINING
BUSINESS AMENITIES	DATAPORT, 2-LINE PHONE, BUSINESS CENTER, VOICEMAIL, SECRETRIAL SERVICES
DÉCOR	TRADITIONAL EURO-PEAN
POOL/SAUNA	–
EXERCISE FACILITIES	FITNESS ROOM

Hotel Beresford ★★½
635 Sutter Street
San Francisco, CA 94102
☎ 415-673-9900
FAX 415-474-0449
TOLL-FREE 800-533-6533
www.beresford.com

QUALITY	60
COST	$$$–
LOCATION	UNION SQUARE
DISCOUNTS AVAILABLE	AAA, AARP, GOVT., SENIOR
NO. OF ROOMS	114
ON-SITE DINING	•
ROOM SERVICE	–
BAR	•
PARKING PER DAY	$20 STANDARD, $35 OVERSIZED
MEETING FACILITIES	–
EXTRA AMENITIES	FREE BREAKFAST, SATELLITE TV
BUSINESS AMENITIES	DATAPORT, COPIER, FAX
DÉCOR	VICTORIAN
POOL/SAUNA	–
EXERCISE FACILITIES	–

Handlery
Union Square Hotel ★★★
351 Geary Street
San Francisco, CA 94102
☎ 415-781-7800
FAX 415-781-0216
TOLL-FREE 800-843-4343
www.handlery.com

QUALITY	72
COST	$$$$
LOCATION	UNION SQUARE
DISCOUNTS AVAILABLE	AAA, AARP
NO. OF ROOMS	284
ON-SITE DINING	•
ROOM SERVICE	•
BAR	–
PARKING PER DAY	$32
MEETING FACILITIES	•
EXTRA AMENITIES	BARBER SHOP, BABYSITTING, VIDEO GAMES, NEWSPAPER
BUSINESS AMENITIES	DATAPORT, MODEM, MULTI-LINE PHONE
DÉCOR	TRADITIONAL EUROPEAN
POOL/SAUNA	POOL, SAUNA
EXERCISE FACILITIES	PRIVILEGES (FEE)

Harbor Court Hotel ★★★★
165 Steuart Street
San Francisco, CA 94105
☎ 415-882-1300
FAX 415-882-1313
TOLL-FREE 800-346-0555
www.harborcourthotel.com

QUALITY	85
COST	$$$$
LOCATION	SOMA/ MISSION DISTRICT
DISCOUNTS AVAILABLE	AAA, AARP, GOVT., MILITARY
NO. OF ROOMS	131
ON-SITE DINING	–
ROOM SERVICE	•
BAR	•
PARKING PER DAY	$35
MEETING FACILITIES	•
EXTRA AMENITIES	WINE RECEPTION
BUSINESS AMENITIES	DATAPORT, 2-LINE PHONE
DÉCOR	1907 LANDMARK BUILDING
POOL/SAUNA	PRIVILEGES
EXERCISE FACILITIES	PRIVILEGES

Harvest Inn ★★★★
1 Main Street
St. Helena, CA 94574
☎ 707-963-9463
FAX 707-963-4402
TOLL-FREE 800-950-8466
www.harvestinn.com

QUALITY	84
COST	$$$$$$$$+
LOCATION	WINE COUNTRY
DISCOUNTS AVAILABLE	AAA
NO. OF ROOMS	54
ON-SITE DINING	•
ROOM SERVICE	–
BAR	•
PARKING PER DAY	FREE
MEETING FACILITIES	•
EXTRA AMENITIES	FREE BREAKFAST, VCR, VOICE MAIL, IN-ROOM SPA TREATMENTS
BUSINESS AMENITIES	DATAPORT, 2-LINE PHONE
DÉCOR	ENGLISH TUDOR
POOL/SAUNA	POOL, WHIRLPOOL
EXERCISE FACILITIES	–

Hotel Bijou ★★★½
111 Mason Street
San Francisco , CA 94102
☎ 415-771-1200
FAX 415-346-3196
TOLL-FREE 800-771-1022
www.hotelbijou.com

QUALITY	82
COST	$$$
LOCATION	UNION SQUARE
DISCOUNTS AVAILABLE	AAA, AARP, GOVT., SENIOR
NO. OF ROOMS	65
ON-SITE DINING	–
ROOM SERVICE	•
BAR	–
PARKING PER DAY	$25
MEETING FACILITIES	•
EXTRA AMENITIES	BREAKFAST, THEATER, FILM, TOURS, CASTING CALLS
BUSINESS AMENITIES	DATAPORT, 2-LINE PHONE, VOICEMAIL
DÉCOR	SAN FRANCISCO CINEMA
POOL/SAUNA	–
EXERCISE FACILITIES	–

Hotel Carlton ★★★★½
1075 Sutter Street
San Francisco, CA 94109
☎ 415-673-0242
FAX 415-673-4904
TOLL-FREE 800-922-7586
www.carltonhotel.com

QUALITY	90
COST	$$
LOCATION	CIVIC CENTER
DISCOUNTS AVAILABLE	AAA, AARP
NO. OF ROOMS	163
ON-SITE DINING	•
ROOM SERVICE	•
BAR	–
PARKING PER DAY	$25 SELF, $30 VALET
MEETING FACILITIES	•
EXTRA AMENITIES	WINE BAR
BUSINESS AMENITIES	DATAPORT
DÉCOR	EARLY SAN FRANCISCO ESTATE
POOL/SAUNA	–
EXERCISE FACILITIES	–

Hotel del Sol ★★★½
3100 Webster Street
San Francisco, CA 94123
☎ 415-921-5520
FAX 415-931-4137
TOLL-FREE 877-433-5765
www.thehoteldelsol.com

QUALITY	80
COST	$$$
LOCATION	MARINA
NO. OF ROOMS	57
ON-SITE DINING	–
ROOM SERVICE	–
BAR	–
PARKING PER DAY	FREE
MEETING FACILITIES	–
EXTRA AMENITIES	BREAKFAST, VCR, TOURS
BUSINESS AMENITIES	DATAPORT, 2-LINE PHONE, VOICEMAIL
DÉCOR	EUROPEAN
POOL/SAUNA	POOL
EXERCISE FACILITIES	–

Hotel Information Chart *(continued)*

Hotel Diva ★★★★½
440 Geary Street
San Francisco, CA 94102
☎ 415-885-0200
FAX 415-346-6613
TOLL-FREE 800-553-1900
www.hoteldiva.com

QUALITY	90
COST	$$$–
LOCATION	UNION SQUARE
NO. OF ROOMS	1,102
ON-SITE DINING	–
ROOM SERVICE	–
BAR	–
PARKING PER DAY	$30
MEETING FACILITIES	•
EXTRA AMENITIES	CD PLAYER, IPOD RENTAL
BUSINESS AMENITIES	DATAPORT, VOICE-MAIL, 24-HOUR BUSINESS CENTER
DÉCOR	CONTEMPORARY
POOL/SAUNA	–
EXERCISE FACILITIES	FITNESS ROOM

Hotel Drisco ★★★★
2901 Pacific Avenue
San Francisco, CA 94115
☎ 415-346-2880
FAX 415-567-5537
TOLL-FREE 800-634-7277
www.hoteldrisco.com

QUALITY	85
COST	$$$$
LOCATION	RICHMOND/SUNSET DISTRICT
NO. OF ROOMS	48
ON-SITE DINING	•
ROOM SERVICE	•
BAR	•
PARKING PER DAY	PARKING ON STREET ONLY
MEETING FACILITIES	•
EXTRA AMENITIES	BREAKFAST, ROBE, SLIPPERS, MINIBAR, PM WINE, TOURS, NEWSPAPER, COFFEE/TEA, VCR
BUSINESS AMENITIES	DATAPORT, 2-LINE PHONE, SPEAKER PHONE, VOICEMAIL, BUSINESS CENTER
DÉCOR	TRADITIONAL
POOL/SAUNA	–
EXERCISE FACILITIES	FITNESS ROOM AND YMCA PRIVILEGES

Hotel Durant ★★★½
2600 Durant Avenue
Berkeley, CA 94704
☎ 510-845-8981
FAX 510-486-8336
TOLL-FREE 800-2-DURANT
www.hoteldurant.com

QUALITY	75
COST	$$$
LOCATION	BERKELEY
DISCOUNTS AVAILABLE	AAA, AARP, GOVT.
NO. OF ROOMS	144
ON-SITE DINING	•
ROOM SERVICE	LIMITED
BAR	•
PARKING PER DAY	$10 LOW SEASON, $20 HIGH SEASON
MEETING FACILITIES	•
EXTRA AMENITIES	–
BUSINESS AMENITIES	DATAPORT, VOICE-MAIL, BUSINESS CENTER, POSTAL SERVICE
DÉCOR	OLD EUROPE
POOL/SAUNA	–
EXERCISE FACILITIES	–

Hotel Nikko ★★★★★
222 Mason Street
San Francisco, CA 94102
☎ 415-394-1111; FAX 415-394-1106; TOLL-FREE 800-NIKKO-US
www.hotelnikkosf.com

QUALITY	96
COST	$$$$$$$+
LOCATION	UNION SQUARE
DISCOUNTS AVAILABLE	AAA, GOVT., SENIOR
NO. OF ROOMS	532
ON-SITE DINING	•
ROOM SERVICE	–
BAR	•
PARKING PER DAY	$39 STANDARD, $43 LARGE SUV
MEETING FACILITIES	•
EXTRA AMENITIES	HAIR SALON, ART GALLERY, STAR-BUCK'S
BUSINESS AMENITIES	DATAPORT, 2-LINE PHONE, VOICEMAIL, BUSINESS CENTER, COLOR COPIERS, BINDING, FAXING, PACKING, SHIPPING
DÉCOR	MODERN
POOL/SAUNA	POOL, WHIRLPOOL, SAUNA
EXERCISE FACILITIES	HEALTH CLUB

Hotel Palomar ★★★★
12 Fourth Street
San Francisco, CA 94103
☎ 415-348-1111
FAX 415-348-0302
TOLL-FREE 866-373-4941
www.hotelpalomar.com

QUALITY	89
COST	$$$$$
LOCATION	SOMA/MISSION DISTRICT
DISCOUNTS AVAILABLE	AAA, AARP, CORP., GOVT., MILITARY
NO. OF ROOMS	214
ON-SITE DINING	•
ROOM SERVICE	•
BAR	•
PARKING PER DAY	$41
MEETING FACILITIES	•
EXTRA AMENITIES	PET FRIENDLY, NEWS-PAPER, AVEDA BATH PRODUCTS, IN-ROOM SPA TREATMENTS, SAFE
BUSINESS AMENITIES	DATAPORT, FAX, 2-LINE PHONE
DÉCOR	MODERN
POOL/SAUNA	WHIRLPOOL IN SOME ROOMS
EXERCISE FACILITIES	FITNESS ROOM

Hotel Rex ★★★★
562 Sutter Street
San Francisco, CA 94102
☎ 415-433-4434
FAX 415-433-3695
TOLL-FREE 800-433-4434
www.thehotelrex.com

QUALITY	85
COST	$$$$
LOCATION	UNION SQUARE
DISCOUNTS AVAILABLE	AAA, AARP, GOVT.
NO. OF ROOMS	94
ON-SITE DINING	•
ROOM SERVICE	•
BAR	•
PARKING PER DAY	$34
MEETING FACILITIES	•
EXTRA AMENITIES	PM WINE, NEWSPAPER
BUSINESS AMENITIES	DATAPORT, 2-LINE PHONE, VOICEMAIL
DÉCOR	1920S–1940S LITERARY SALON
POOL/SAUNA	–
EXERCISE FACILITIES	PRIVILEGES

Hotel Majestic ★★★★
1500 Sutter Street
San Francisco, CA 94109
☎ 415-441-1100
FAX 415-673-7331
TOLL-FREE 800-869-8966
www.thehotelmajestic.com

QUALITY	89
COST	$$$–
LOCATION	CIVIC CENTER
DISCOUNTS AVAILABLE	AAA, AARP, GOVT.
NO. OF ROOMS	57
ON-SITE DINING	•
ROOM SERVICE	•
BAR	•
PARKING PER DAY	$20
MEETING FACILITIES	•
EXTRA AMENITIES	IN-ROOM DINING, FREE BREAKFAST
BUSINESS AMENITIES	DATAPORT, 2-LINE PHONE
DÉCOR	VICTORIAN BOUTIQUE
POOL/SAUNA	–
EXERCISE FACILITIES	–

Hotel Milano ★★★★
55 Fifth Street
San Francisco, CA 94103
☎ 415-543-8555
FAX 415-543-5885
TOLL-FREE 800-398-7555
www.hotelmilanosf.com

QUALITY	85
COST	$$$$–
LOCATION	SOMA/ MISSION DISTRICT
DISCOUNTS AVAILABLE	AAA, AARP, GOVT.
NO. OF ROOMS	108
ON-SITE DINING	–
ROOM SERVICE	–
BAR	–
PARKING PER DAY	$30
MEETING FACILITIES	–
EXTRA AMENITIES	VIDEO GAMES, SAFE, NEWSPAPER
BUSINESS AMENITIES	DATAPORT, VOICE-MAIL, FAX
DÉCOR	MODERN ITALIAN
POOL/SAUNA	SAUNA, STEAM ROOM, WHIRLPOOL
EXERCISE FACILITIES	FITNESS ROOM

Hotel Monaco ★★★★½
501 Geary Street
San Francisco, CA 94102
☎ 415-292-0100
FAX 415-292-0111
TOLL-FREE 866-622-5284
www.monaco-sf.com

QUALITY	94
COST	$$$$$
LOCATION	UNION SQUARE
DISCOUNTS AVAILABLE	AAA, AARP, GOVT., SENIOR
NO. OF ROOMS	201
ON-SITE DINING	–
ROOM SERVICE	–
BAR	–
PARKING PER DAY	$39
MEETING FACILITIES	•
EXTRA AMENITIES	MASSAGE, WINE, PET FRIENDLY, AVEDA BATH PRODUCTS, NEWSPAPER, SAFE
BUSINESS AMENITIES	DATAPORT, 2-LINE PHONE, VOICEMAIL
DÉCOR	BEAUX ARTS/ MODERN ECLECTIC
POOL/SAUNA	WHIRLPOOL, STEAM ROOM, SAUNA
EXERCISE FACILITIES	FITNESS ROOM

Hotel St. Helena ★★★
1309 Main Street
St. Helena, CA 94574
☎ 707-963-4388
FAX 707-963-5402
TOLL-FREE 888-478-4355
www.hotelsthelena.com

QUALITY	74
COST	$$$+
LOCATION	WINE COUNTRY
DISCOUNTS AVAILABLE	MID-WEEK
NO. OF ROOMS	18
ON-SITE DINING	–
ROOM SERVICE	–
BAR	–
PARKING PER DAY	FREE
MEETING FACILITIES	–
EXTRA AMENITIES	FREE BREAKFAST
BUSINESS AMENITIES	–
DÉCOR	VICTORIAN
POOL/SAUNA	–
EXERCISE FACILITIES	–

Hotel Triton ★★★★
342 Grant Avenue
San Francisco, CA 94108
☎ 415-394-0500
FAX 415-394-0555
TOLL-FREE 800-800-1299
www.hoteltriton.com

QUALITY	86
COST	$$$$$–
LOCATION	UNION SQUARE
DISCOUNTS AVAILABLE	AAA, AARP, GOVT.
NO. OF ROOMS	140
ON-SITE DINING	–
ROOM SERVICE	•
BAR	–
PARKING PER DAY	$37
MEETING FACILITIES	•
EXTRA AMENITIES	PM WINE, TAROT CARD READER, YOGA, ART GALLERY, DJ ON FRIDAYS, MASSAGES
BUSINESS AMENITIES	DATAPORT, BUSI-NESS CENTER
DÉCOR	ULTRA MODERN
POOL/SAUNA	–
EXERCISE FACILITIES	FITNESS ROOM

Hotel Union Square ★★★★
114 Powell Street
San Francisco, CA 94108
☎ 415-397-3000
FAX 415-399-1874
TOLL-FREE 800-553-1900
www.hotelunionsquare.com

QUALITY	84
COST	$$
LOCATION	UNION SQUARE
DISCOUNTS AVAILABLE	CORP., GOVT., MILITARY
NO. OF ROOMS	131
ON-SITE DINING	–
ROOM SERVICE	–
BAR	–
PARKING PER DAY	$29
MEETING FACILITIES	•
EXTRA AMENITIES	BREAKFAST, BOUTIQUE, NINTENDO
BUSINESS AMENITIES	DATAPORT, VOICE-MAIL, 24-HOUR BUSINESS CENTER
DÉCOR	TRADITIONAL EURO-PEAN
POOL/SAUNA	PRIVILEGES
EXERCISE FACILITIES	PRIVILEGES

Hotel Information Chart (continued)

Hotel Vintage Court ★★★
650 Bush Street
San Francisco, CA 94108
☎ 415-392-4666
FAX 415-433-4065
TOLL-FREE 800-654-1100
www.vintagecourt.com

QUALITY	68
COST	$$$$
LOCATION	UNION SQUARE
DISCOUNTS AVAILABLE	AAA, AARP, GOVT., SENIOR
NO. OF ROOMS	107
ON-SITE DINING	–
ROOM SERVICE	–
BAR	–
PARKING PER DAY	$24 SELF, $32 VALET
MEETING FACILITIES	•
EXTRA AMENITIES	PM WINE, NINTENDO
BUSINESS AMENITIES	DATAPORT, 2-LINE PHONE, VOICEMAIL
DÉCOR	EUROPEAN BOUTIQUE
POOL/SAUNA	–
EXERCISE FACILITIES	PRIVILEGES

Hotel Vitale ★★★★½
8 Mission Street
San Francisco, CA 94105
☎ 415-278-3700
FAX 415-278-3750
TOLL-FREE 888-890-8688
www.hotelvitale.com

QUALITY	90
COST	$$$$$
LOCATION	FINANCIAL DISTRICT
NO. OF ROOMS	199
ON-SITE DINING	–
ROOM SERVICE	–
BAR	–
PARKING PER DAY	$42
MEETING FACILITIES	–
EXTRA AMENITIES	NEWSPAPER, SLIPPERS, ROBE, SAFE, SPA
BUSINESS AMENITIES	DATAPORT, VOICEMAIL, BUSINESS CENTER
DÉCOR	MODERN
POOL/SAUNA	WHIRLPOOL
EXERCISE FACILITIES	FITNESS ROOM

Huntington Hotel ★★★★½
1075 California Street
San Francisco, CA 94108
☎ 415-474-5400
FAX 415-474-6227
TOLL-FREE 800-227-4683
www.huntingtonhotel.com

QUALITY	90
COST	$$$$$$$
LOCATION	NOB HILL
DISCOUNTS AVAILABLE	GOVERNMENT
NO. OF ROOMS	135
ON-SITE DINING	•
ROOM SERVICE	•
BAR	•
PARKING PER DAY	$29
MEETING FACILITIES	•
EXTRA AMENITIES	LIMO SERVICE, SHERRY, SAFE, NEWSPAPER, NOB HILL SPA
BUSINESS AMENITIES	DATAPORT, 2-LINE PHONE, VOICEMAIL, BUSINESS CENTER
DÉCOR	EUROPEAN
POOL/SAUNA	POOL, JACUZZI, SAUNA
EXERCISE FACILITIES	SPA AND FITNESS CENTER

Inn Above Tide ★★★★½
30 El Portal
Sausalito, CA 94965
☎ 415-332-9535
FAX 415-332-6714
TOLL-FREE 800-893-8433
www.innabovetide.com

QUALITY	93
COST	$$$$$+
LOCATION	MARIN COUNTY
NO. OF ROOMS	29
ON-SITE DINING	–
ROOM SERVICE	•
BAR	–
PARKING PER DAY	$12
MEETING FACILITIES	–
EXTRA AMENITIES	BREAKFAST, WINE AND CHEESE, NEWSPAPER, IN-ROOM DINING
BUSINESS AMENITIES	DATAPORT, 2-LINE PHONE, INTERNET, 24-HOUR FAX AND COPY SERVICE
DÉCOR	NAUTICAL
POOL/SAUNA	SPA SERVICES
EXERCISE FACILITIES	–

Inn at Southbridge ★★★★½
1020 Main Street
St. Helena, CA 94574
☎ 707-967-9400
FAX 707-967-9486
TOLL-FREE 800-520-6800
www.innatsouthbridge.com

QUALITY	92
COST	$$$$$$$$
LOCATION	WINE COUNTRY
DISCOUNTS AVAILABLE	AARP
NO. OF ROOMS	21
ON-SITE DINING	–
ROOM SERVICE	•
BAR	•
PARKING PER DAY	FREE
MEETING FACILITIES	•
EXTRA AMENITIES	FULL SPA, WINE BAR, BREAKFAST, SAFE
BUSINESS AMENITIES	DATAPORT, 2-LINE PHONE
DÉCOR	EUROPEAN
POOL/SAUNA	–
EXERCISE FACILITIES	PRIVILEGES (FEE)

Inn at the Opera ★★★★½
333 Fulton Street
San Francisco, CA 94102
☎ 415-863-8400
FAX 415-861-0821
TOLL-FREE 800-590-0157
www.innattheopera.com

QUALITY	90
COST	$$$$–
LOCATION	CIVIC CENTER
DISCOUNTS AVAILABLE	AAA, GOVT., CORP.
NO. OF ROOMS	46
ON-SITE DINING	•
ROOM SERVICE	•
BAR	•
PARKING PER DAY	$25
MEETING FACILITIES	–
EXTRA AMENITIES	BREAKFAST
BUSINESS AMENITIES	DATAPORT, BUSINESS CENTER
DÉCOR	CLASSIC EUROPEAN
POOL/SAUNA	–
EXERCISE FACILITIES	–

Hyatt Fisherman's Wharf ★★★★
555 North Point Street
San Francisco, CA 94133
☎ 415-563-1234
FAX 415-749-6122
TOLL-FREE 800-233-1234
www.hyatt.com

QUALITY	88
COST	$$$$$
LOCATION	NORTH BEACH
DISCOUNTS AVAILABLE	AAA, GOVT., SENIOR
NO. OF ROOMS	313
ON-SITE DINING	•
ROOM SERVICE	•
BAR	•
PARKING PER DAY	$12 DAY USE, $36 OVERNIGHT
MEETING FACILITIES	•
EXTRA AMENITIES	BREAKFAST, NEWSPAPER, PILLOW-TOP MATTRESSES, SAFE
BUSINESS AMENITIES	DATAPORT, 2-LINE PHONE, VOICEMAIL
DÉCOR	WHARF/VICTORIAN
POOL/SAUNA	POOL, WHIRLPOOL
EXERCISE FACILITIES	FITNESS ROOM

Hyatt Regency San Francisco ★★★★
5 Embarcadero Center
San francisco, CA 94111
☎ 415-788-1234
FAX 415-398-2567
TOLL-FREE 800-233-1234
www.hyatt.com

QUALITY	88
COST	$$$$$
LOCATION	FINANCIAL DISTRICT
DISCOUNTS AVAILABLE	AAA, GOVT., SENIOR
NO. OF ROOMS	805
ON-SITE DINING	•
ROOM SERVICE	•
BAR	•
PARKING PER DAY	$27 SELF, $41 VALET
MEETING FACILITIES	•
EXTRA AMENITIES	SAFE, NEWSPAPER, COFFEEMAKER, MINIBAR
BUSINESS AMENITIES	DATAPORT, 2-LINE PHONE, VOICEMAIL, SPEAKER PHONE
DÉCOR	MODERN ATRIUM HIGH-RISE
POOL/SAUNA	PRIVILEGES
EXERCISE FACILITIES	PRIVILEGES AND FITNESS ROOM

Hyatt Regency San Francisco Airport ★★★★
1333 Bayshore Highway
Burlingame, CA 94010
☎ 415-347-1234
FAX 650-696-2669
TOLL-FREE 800-233-1234
www.hyatt.com

QUALITY	86
COST	$$$–
LOCATION	SAN FRANCICO INT'L AIRPORT
DISCOUNTS AVAILABLE	AAA, AARP, GOVT., SENIOR
NO. OF ROOMS	793
ON-SITE DINING	•
ROOM SERVICE	•
BAR	•
PARKING PER DAY	$15 SELF, $20 VALET
MEETING FACILITIES	•
EXTRA AMENITIES	NEWSPAPER, COFFEEMAKER
BUSINESS AMENITIES	DATAPORT, 2-LINE PHONE, BUSINESS CENTER
DÉCOR	MODERN
POOL/SAUNA	POOL, WHIRLPOOL
EXERCISE FACILITIES	FITNESS ROOM

Inn at Union Square ★★★½
440 Post Street
San Francisco, CA 94102
☎ 415-397-3510
FAX 415-989-0529
TOLL-FREE 800-288-4346
www.unionsquare.com

QUALITY	80
COST	$$$$–
LOCATION	UNION SQUARE
DISCOUNTS AVAILABLE	SENIOR
NO. OF ROOMS	30
ON-SITE DINING	–
ROOM SERVICE	–
BAR	–
PARKING PER DAY	$23 SELF, $35 VALET STANDARD, $40 VALET OVERSIZED
MEETING FACILITIES	•
EXTRA AMENITIES	BREAKFAST, PM WINE AND APPETIZERS
BUSINESS AMENITIES	DATAPORT, 2-LINE PHONE, VOICEMAIL
DÉCOR	BOUTIQUE
POOL/SAUNA	PRIVILEGES
EXERCISE FACILITIES	PRIVILEGES

The Jackson Court ★★★★½
2198 Jackson Street
San Francisco, CA 94115
☎ 415-929-7670
FAX 415-929-1405
www.jacksoncourt.com

QUALITY	90
COST	$$$+
LOCATION	CIVIC CENTER
NO. OF ROOMS	10
ON-SITE DINING	–
ROOM SERVICE	–
BAR	–
PARKING PER DAY	$20
MEETING FACILITIES	–
EXTRA AMENITIES	BREAKFAST, TEA AND COOKIES, TOURS, NEWSPAPER, GAME ROOM, DRY CLEANING
BUSINESS AMENITIES	–
DÉCOR	CONTEMPORARY
POOL/SAUNA	–
EXERCISE FACILITIES	–

John Muir Inn ★★★
1998 Trower Avenue
Napa, CA 94558
☎ 707-257-7220
FAX 707-258-0943
TOLL-FREE 800-522-8999
www.johnmuirnapa.com

QUALITY	65
COST	$$$
LOCATION	WINE COUNTRY
DISCOUNTS AVAILABLE	AAA, AARP, GOVT., SENIOR
NO. OF ROOMS	60
ON-SITE DINING	–
ROOM SERVICE	–
BAR	–
PARKING PER DAY	FREE
MEETING FACILITIES	•
EXTRA AMENITIES	BREAKFAST
BUSINESS AMENITIES	DATAPORT
DÉCOR	TRADITIONAL
POOL/SAUNA	POOL, WHIRLPOOL
EXERCISE FACILITIES	–

Hotel Information Chart (continued)

Kensington Park Hotel ★★★★
450 Post Street
San Francisco, CA 94102
☎ 415-788-6400
FAX 415-399-9484
TOLL-FREE 800-553-1900
www.kensingtonparkhotel.com

QUALITY	83
COST	$$$–
LOCATION	UNION SQUARE
DISCOUNTS AVAILABLE	AAA, AARP, GOVT.
NO. OF ROOMS	88
ON-SITE DINING	•
ROOM SERVICE	–
BAR	•
PARKING PER DAY	$30
MEETING FACILITIES	•
EXTRA AMENITIES	PM SHERRY AND TEA
BUSINESS AMENITIES	DATAPORT, BUSINESS CENTER
DÉCOR	QUEEN ANNE
POOL/SAUNA	PRIVILEGES
EXERCISE FACILITIES	–

King George Hotel ★★★
334 Mason Street
San Francisco, CA 94102
☎ 415-781-5050
FAX 415-391-6976
TOLL-FREE 800-288-6005
www.kinggeorge.com

QUALITY	65
COST	$$$–
LOCATION	UNION SQUARE
DISCOUNTS AVAILABLE	AAA, AARP, GOVT.
NO. OF ROOMS	153
ON-SITE DINING	•
ROOM SERVICE	•
BAR	•
PARKING PER DAY	$26 SELF, $32 VALET
MEETING FACILITIES	•
EXTRA AMENITIES	APPLES, NEWSPAPER, SAFE
BUSINESS AMENITIES	DATAPORT, VOICE-MAIL, 24-HOUR BUSINESS CENTER
DÉCOR	ENGLISH BOUTIQUE
POOL/SAUNA	PRIVILEGES
EXERCISE FACILITIES	PRIVILEGES

**La Quinta Inn
Oakland Airport** ★★★½
8465 Enterprise Way
Oakland, CA 94621
☎ 510-632-8900
FAX 510-632-4713
TOLL-FREE 866-725-1661
www.lq.com

QUALITY	75
COST	$$–
LOCATION	OAKLAND
DISCOUNTS AVAILABLE	AAA, AARP, GOVT.
NO. OF ROOMS	152
ON-SITE DINING	–
ROOM SERVICE	–
BAR	–
PARKING PER DAY	$119 FOR 14 DAYS
MEETING FACILITIES	–
EXTRA AMENITIES	BREAKFAST, AIRPORT SHUTTLE, COFFEEMAKER, PET FRIENDLY
BUSINESS AMENITIES	–
DÉCOR	MODERN
POOL/SAUNA	POOL
EXERCISE FACILITIES	PRIVILEGES

**Mark Hopkins
Inter-Continental** ★★★★
1 Nob Hill
San Francisco, CA 94108
☎ 415-392-3434
FAX 415-421-3302
TOLL-FREE 800-327-0200
www.ichotelsgroup.com

QUALITY	84
COST	$$$$$
LOCATION	NOB HILL
DISCOUNTS AVAILABLE	AAA, AARP, GOVT., MILITARY
NO. OF ROOMS	422
ON-SITE DINING	•
ROOM SERVICE	–
BAR	•
PARKING PER DAY	$51
MEETING FACILITIES	•
EXTRA AMENITIES	LOUNGE MUSIC, CAR RENTAL, ROBES, NEWSPAPER, SAFE
BUSINESS AMENITIES	DATAPORT, 2-LINE PHONE, VOICEMAIL, BUSINESS CENTER
DÉCOR	GRAND HOTEL
POOL/SAUNA	–
EXERCISE FACILITIES	–

**Marriott
Fisherman's Wharf** ★★★½
1250 Columbus Avenue
San Francisco, CA 94133
☎ 415-775-7555
FAX 415-474-2099
TOLL-FREE 800-228-9290
www.marriott.com

QUALITY	80
COST	$$$$
LOCATION	NORTH BEACH
DISCOUNTS AVAILABLE	AAA, AARP, GOVT, SENIOR, MILITARY
NO. OF ROOMS	285
ON-SITE DINING	•
ROOM SERVICE	•
BAR	•
PARKING PER DAY	$38
MEETING FACILITIES	•
EXTRA AMENITIES	MINIBAR, PET FRIENDLY, NEWSPAPER
BUSINESS AMENITIES	DATAPORT, 2-LINE PHONE, VOICEMAIL
DÉCOR	MODERN
POOL/SAUNA	SAUNA, WHIRLPOOL
EXERCISE FACILITIES	FITNESS ROOM

Maxwell Hotel ★★★½
386 Geary Street
San Francisco, CA 94102
☎ 415-986-2000
FAX 415-397-2447
TOLL-FREE 888-734-6299
www.maxwellhotel.com

QUALITY	80
COST	$$$
LOCATION	UNION SQUARE
DISCOUNTS AVAILABLE	AAA, AARP
NO. OF ROOMS	153
ON-SITE DINING	–
ROOM SERVICE	•
BAR	–
PARKING PER DAY	$26 SELF, $32 VALET
MEETING FACILITIES	•
EXTRA AMENITIES	SAFE, NEWSPAPER, TOURS
BUSINESS AMENITIES	DATAPORT, 2-LINE PHONE, VOICEMAIL
DÉCOR	ART DECO
POOL/SAUNA	–
EXERCISE FACILITIES	PRIVILEGES

Laurel Inn ★★★½
444 Presidio Avenue
San Francisco, CA 94115
☎ 415-567-8467
FAX 415-928-1866
TOLL-FREE 800-552-8735
www.thelaurelinn.com

QUALITY	80
COST	$$$$–
LOCATION	RICHMOND/SUNSET DISTRICT
DISCOUNTS AVAILABLE	AAA, AARP, GOVT., SENIOR, MILITARY, CORP.
NO. OF ROOMS	49
ON-SITE DINING	–
ROOM SERVICE	–
BAR	–
PARKING PER DAY	FREE
MEETING FACILITIES	–
EXTRA AMENITIES	BREAKFAST, KITCHENETTES, VCR
BUSINESS AMENITIES	DATAPORT, VOICE-MAIL, 2-LINE PHONE
DÉCOR	MODERN
POOL/SAUNA	–
EXERCISE FACILITIES	PRIVILEGES

Mandarin Oriental ★★★★★
222 Sansome Street
San Francisco, CA 94104
☎ 415-276-9888
FAX 415-433-0289
TOLL-FREE 800-622-0404
www.mandarinoriental.com/
sanfrancisco

QUALITY	98
COST	$$$$$$$$$$–
LOCATION	FINANCIAL DISTRICT
DISCOUNTS AVAILABLE	GOVERNMENT
NO. OF ROOMS	158
ON-SITE DINING	•
ROOM SERVICE	•
BAR	•
PARKING PER DAY	$46
MEETING FACILITIES	•
EXTRA AMENITIES	NINTENDO, SAFE, PET FRIENDLY, NEWS-PAPER, ROBES, TEA, COOKIES, BINOCU-LARS
BUSINESS AMENITIES	DATAPORT, VOICE-MAIL, 2-LINE PHONE, FAX, COPYING
DÉCOR	MODERN
POOL/SAUNA	–
EXERCISE FACILITIES	FITNESS ROOM

Marina Motel ★★★
2576 Lombard Street
San Francisco, CA 94123
☎ 415-921-9406
FAX 415-921-0364
TOLL-FREE 800-346-6118
www.marinamotel.com

QUALITY	65
COST	$$
LOCATION	MARINA
NO. OF ROOMS	38
ON-SITE DINING	–
ROOM SERVICE	–
BAR	–
PARKING PER DAY	FREE
MEETING FACILITIES	–
EXTRA AMENITIES	KITCHENETTES, BREAKFAST COUPONS
BUSINESS AMENITIES	–
POOL/SAUNA	–
EXERCISE FACILITIES	–

Mill Valley Inn ★★★★½
165 Throckmorton Avenue
Mill Valley, CA 94941
☎ 415-389-6608
FAX 415-389-5051
TOLL-FREE 800-595-2100
www.marinhotels.com/mill_
guestrooms.html

QUALITY	95
COST	$$$$–
LOCATION	MARIN COUNTY
NO. OF ROOMS	25
ON-SITE DINING	–
ROOM SERVICE	•
BAR	–
PARKING PER DAY	FREE
MEETING FACILITIES	•
EXTRA AMENITIES	BREAKFAST, ROBES, NEWSPAPER
BUSINESS AMENITIES	DATAPORT, VOICE-MAIL, FAX
DÉCOR	EUROPEAN TRADI-TIONAL
POOL/SAUNA	–
EXERCISE FACILITIES	–

Monticello Inn ★★★½
127 Ellis Street
San Francisco, CA 94102
☎ 415-392-8800
FAX 415-398-2650
TOLL-FREE 866-778-6169
www.monticelloinn.com

QUALITY	80
COST	$$$$+
LOCATION	UNION SQUARE
DISCOUNTS AVAILABLE	AAA, AARP, GOVT., SENIOR
NO. OF ROOMS	91
ON-SITE DINING	–
ROOM SERVICE	–
BAR	–
PARKING PER DAY	$30
MEETING FACILITIES	–
EXTRA AMENITIES	BREAKFAST, PM WINE, PET FRIENDLY, IN-ROOM SPA SERVICES
BUSINESS AMENITIES	DATAPORT, FAX, 2-LINE PHONE, VOICEMAIL
DÉCOR	CONTEMPORARY COLONIAL
POOL/SAUNA	PRIVILEGES (FEE)
EXERCISE FACILITIES	PRIVILEGES (FEE)

Motel Capri ★★★
2015 Greenwich Street
San Francisco, CA 94123
☎ 415-346-4667
FAX 415-346-3256

QUALITY	70
COST	$$–
LOCATION	MARINA
DISCOUNTS AVAILABLE	AAA
NO. OF ROOMS	46
ON-SITE DINING	–
ROOM SERVICE	–
BAR	–
PARKING PER DAY	FREE
MEETING FACILITIES	–
EXTRA AMENITIES	–
BUSINESS AMENITIES	–
POOL/SAUNA	–
EXERCISE FACILITIES	–

Hotel Information Chart (continued)

Mount View Hotel ★★★½
1457 Lincoln Avenue
Calistoga, CA 94515
☎ 707-942-6877
FAX 707-942-6904
TOLL-FREE 800-816-6877
www.mountviewhotel.com

QUALITY	81
COST	$$$$–
LOCATION	WINE COUNTRY
DISCOUNTS AVAILABLE	AAA
NO. OF ROOMS	32
ON-SITE DINING	•
ROOM SERVICE	–
BAR	•
PARKING PER DAY	FREE
MEETING FACILITIES	–
EXTRA AMENITIES	BREAKFAST, FULL SPA, DVD PLAYERS, AVEDA BATH PRODUCTS
BUSINESS AMENITIES	DATAPORT, FAX, VOICEMAIL
DÉCOR	CALIFORNIA SPA
POOL/SAUNA	WHIRLPOOL, SPA, SAUNA
EXERCISE FACILITIES	–

Napa Valley Lodge ★★★★½
2230 Madison Street
Yountville, CA 94599
☎ 707-944-2468
FAX 707-944-9362
TOLL-FREE 800-368-2468
www.woodsidehotels.com

QUALITY	90
COST	$$$$$$–
LOCATION	WINE COUNTRY
DISCOUNTS AVAILABLE	AAA, AARP
NO. OF ROOMS	55
ON-SITE DINING	–
ROOM SERVICE	–
BAR	–
PARKING PER DAY	FREE
MEETING FACILITIES	•
EXTRA AMENITIES	FREE CHAMPAGNE, BREAKFAST, WINE TASTING
BUSINESS AMENITIES	DATAPORT
DÉCOR	CALIFORNIA
POOL/SAUNA	POOL, SAUNA, WHIRLPOOL
EXERCISE FACILITIES	FITNESS ROOM

Napa Valley Marriott Hotel ★★★★
3425 Solano Avenue
Napa, CA 94558
☎ 707-253-7433
FAX 707-258-1320
TOLL-FREE 800-228-9290
www.napavalleymarriott.com

QUALITY	84
COST	$$$$–
LOCATION	WINE COUNTRY
DISCOUNTS AVAILABLE	AAA, AARP, GOVT., SENIOR
NO. OF ROOMS	272
ON-SITE DINING	•
ROOM SERVICE	•
BAR	•
PARKING PER DAY	FREE
MEETING FACILITIES	•
EXTRA AMENITIES	BASKETBALL AND TENNIS COURTS, SALON
BUSINESS AMENITIES	DATAPORT
DÉCOR	MODERN
POOL/SAUNA	POOL, WHIRLPOOL, SPA
EXERCISE FACILITIES	FITNESS ROOM

Oakland Marriott City Center ★★★
1001 Broadway
Oakland, CA 94607
☎ 510-451-4000
FAX 510-835-3466
TOLL-FREE 800-228-9290
www.marriott.com

QUALITY	74
COST	$$$
LOCATION	OAKLAND
DISCOUNTS AVAILABLE	AAA, AARP, GOVT., MILITARY, SENIOR
NO. OF ROOMS	484
ON-SITE DINING	•
ROOM SERVICE	•
BAR	•
PARKING PER DAY	$15 SELF, $26 VALET
MEETING FACILITIES	•
EXTRA AMENITIES	MASSAGE SERVICE, NEWSPAPER
BUSINESS AMENITIES	DATAPORT, 2-LINE PHONE, VOICEMAIL, 24-HOUR BUSINESS CENTER, AUDIO-VISUAL EQUIPMENT
DÉCOR	MODERN
POOL/SAUNA	POOL
EXERCISE FACILITIES	FITNESS ROOM

Pacific Heights Inn ★★★
1555 Union Street
San Francisco, CA 94123
☎ 415-776-3310
FAX 415-776-8176
TOLL-FREE 800-523-1801
www.pacificheightsinn.com

QUALITY	70
COST	$$–
LOCATION	MARINA
DISCOUNTS AVAILABLE	AAA, AARP, GOVT.
NO. OF ROOMS	40
ON-SITE DINING	–
ROOM SERVICE	–
BAR	–
PARKING PER DAY	FREE
MEETING FACILITIES	–
EXTRA AMENITIES	BREAKFAST, NEWSPAPER, SOME KITCHENETTES
BUSINESS AMENITIES	–
DÉCOR	MODERN
POOL/SAUNA	WHIRLPOOL IN SOME ROOMS
EXERCISE FACILITIES	–

Pan Pacific Hotel ★★★★½
500 Post Street
San Francisco, CA 94102
☎ 415-771-8600
FAX 415-398-0267
TOLL-FREE 800-533-6465
www.panpacific.com

QUALITY	90
COST	$$$$$
LOCATION	UNION SQUARE
DISCOUNTS AVAILABLE	AAA, AARP, GOVT.
NO. OF ROOMS	338
ON-SITE DINING	•
ROOM SERVICE	•
BAR	•
PARKING PER DAY	$42
MEETING FACILITIES	•
EXTRA AMENITIES	LIMO SERVICE, PILLOW PREFERENCE, SAFE, NEWSPAPER, LUXURY LOCKER STORAGE SPACE
BUSINESS AMENITIES	DATAPORT, FAX, BUSINESS CENTER
DÉCOR	MODERN
POOL/SAUNA	–
EXERCISE FACILITIES	FITNESS ROOM

Napa Valley Railway Inn ★★★½
6503 Washington Street
Yountville, CA 94599
☎ 707-944-2000

QUALITY	75
COST	$$+
LOCATION	WINE COUNTRY
DISCOUNTS AVAILABLE	AAA, AARP, MILITARY
NO. OF ROOMS	9
ON-SITE DINING	—
ROOM SERVICE	—
BAR	—
PARKING PER DAY	FREE
MEETING FACILITIES	—
EXTRA AMENITIES	NO TELEPHONES, TRAIN CARS ARE SUITES
BUSINESS AMENITIES	—
DÉCOR	ROOMS IN ANTIQUE
POOL/SAUNA	—
EXERCISE FACILITIES	—

Nob Hill Lambourne ★★★★½
725 Pine Street
San Francisco, CA 94108
☎ 415-433-2287
FAX 415-433-0975
TOLL-FREE 800-274-8466
www.nobhilllambourne.com

QUALITY	92
COST	$$$
LOCATION	UNION SQUARE
DISCOUNTS AVAILABLE	AAA, AARP
NO. OF ROOMS	20
ON-SITE DINING	—
ROOM SERVICE	—
BAR	—
PARKING PER DAY	$34
MEETING FACILITIES	•
EXTRA AMENITIES	BREAKFAST, PM WINE, KITCH- ENETTES, VCR, ROBES
BUSINESS AMENITIES	DATAPORT, FAX, 2-LINE PHONE, VOICEMAIL
DÉCOR	BUSINESS & WELLNESS BOUTIQUE
POOL/SAUNA	—
EXERCISE FACILITIES	—

Oakland Airport Hilton ★★★½
1 Hegenberger Road
Oakland, CA 94621
☎ 510-635-5000
FAX 510-383-4062
TOLL-FREE 800-HILTONS
www.hilton.com

QUALITY	80
COST	$$
LOCATION	OAKLAND
DISCOUNTS AVAILABLE	AAA, AARP, GOVT., MILITARY
NO. OF ROOMS	365
ON-SITE DINING	•
ROOM SERVICE	•
BAR	•
PARKING PER DAY	$10
MEETING FACILITIES	•
EXTRA AMENITIES	AIRPORT SHUTTLE, PET FRIENDLY, NEWS- PAPER
BUSINESS AMENITIES	DATAPORT, 2-LINE PHONE, VOICEMAIL, PRINTER, COPIER, FAX, NOTARY PUBLIC, AUDIO- VISUAL EQUIPMENT
DÉCOR	MODERN
POOL/SAUNA	POOL
EXERCISE FACILITIES	FITNESS ROOM

Petite Auberge ★★★½
863 Bush Street
San Francisco, CA 94108
☎ 415-928-6000
FAX 415-673-7214
TOLL-FREE 800-365-3004
www.petiteaubergesf.com

QUALITY	75
COST	$$$
LOCATION	UNION SQUARE
NO. OF ROOMS	26
ON-SITE DINING	—
ROOM SERVICE	—
BAR	—
PARKING PER DAY	$30
MEETING FACILITIES	—
EXTRA AMENITIES	BREAKFAST, PM WINE AND HORS D'OEUVRES, TOURS
BUSINESS AMENITIES	DATAPORT, VOICEMAIL
DÉCOR	FRENCH COUNTRY INN
POOL/SAUNA	—
EXERCISE FACILITIES	—

Phoenix Hotel ★ ★ ★ ½
601 Eddy Street
San Francisco, CA 94109
☎ 415-776-1380
FAX 415-885-3109
TOLL-FREE 800-248-9466
www.thephoenixhotel.com

QUALITY	75
COST	$$$–
LOCATION	CIVIC CENTER
DISCOUNTS AVAILABLE	AAA, GOVT.
NO. OF ROOMS	44
ON-SITE DINING	•
ROOM SERVICE	•
BAR	•
PARKING PER DAY	FREE
MEETING FACILITIES	—
EXTRA AMENITIES	BREAKFAST
BUSINESS AMENITIES	DATAPORT, VOICE- MAIL
DÉCOR	ARTSY 1950S COURT- YARD HOTEL
POOL/SAUNA	POOL
EXERCISE FACILITIES	—

Prescott Hotel ★★★★½
545 Post Street
San Francisco, CA 94102
☎ 415-563-0303
FAX 415-563-6831
TOLL-FREE 866-271-3632
www.prescotthotel.com

QUALITY	92
COST	$$$$+
LOCATION	UNION SQUARE
DISCOUNTS AVAILABLE	AAA, AARP, GOVT., MILITARY
NO. OF ROOMS	164
ON-SITE DINING	•
ROOM SERVICE	•
BAR	•
PARKING PER DAY	$38 STANDARD, $50 OVERSIZED
MEETING FACILITIES	—
EXTRA AMENITIES	PM WINE, NEWSPA- PER, SAFETY DEPOSIT BOXES, PET FRIENDLY
BUSINESS AMENITIES	DATAPORT, FAX, 2-LINE PHONE
DÉCOR	EARLY CALIFORNIA
POOL/SAUNA	—
EXERCISE FACILITIES	FITNESS ROOM

Hotel Information Chart (continued)

Queen Anne Hotel ★★★½
1590 Sutter Street
San Francisco, CA 94109
☎ 415-441-2828
FAX 415-775-5212
TOLL-FREE 800-227-3970
www.queenanne.com

QUALITY	80
COST	$$$–
LOCATION	CIVIC CENTER
DISCOUNTS AVAILABLE	AAA, AARP, GOVT.
NO. OF ROOMS	48
ON-SITE DINING	–
ROOM SERVICE	•
BAR	–
PARKING PER DAY	$20 SELF, $30 VALET
MEETING FACILITIES	•
EXTRA AMENITIES	FREE BREAKFAST, PM TEA AND SHERRY
BUSINESS AMENITIES	DATAPORT, VOICE-MAIL
DÉCOR	VICTORIAN
POOL/SAUNA	PRIVILEGES
EXERCISE FACILITIES	PRIVILEGES

Radisson Fisherman's Wharf ★★★
250 Beach Street
San Francisco, CA 94133
☎ 415-392-6700
FAX 415-986-7853
TOLL-FREE 800-333-3333
www.radisson.com

QUALITY	70
COST	$$$$–
LOCATION	NORTH BEACH
DISCOUNTS AVAILABLE	AAA, AARP, GOVT.
NO. OF ROOMS	355
ON-SITE DINING	–
ROOM SERVICE	–
BAR	–
PARKING PER DAY	$28
MEETING FACILITIES	•
EXTRA AMENITIES	BAY VIEWS, IN-ROOM SAFE
BUSINESS AMENITIES	DATAPORT, VOICE-MAIL, 2-LINE PHONE
DÉCOR	CONTEMPORARY
POOL/SAUNA	POOL
EXERCISE FACILITIES	FITNESS ROOM

Radisson Miyako Hotel ★★★½
1625 Post Street
San Francisco, CA 94115
☎ 415-922-3200
FAX 415-921-0417
TOLL-FREE 800-333-3333
www.radisson.com

QUALITY	76
COST	$$$–
LOCATION	CIVIC CENTER
DISCOUNTS AVAILABLE	AAA, AARP, GOVT.
NO. OF ROOMS	218
ON-SITE DINING	•
ROOM SERVICE	•
BAR	•
PARKING PER DAY	$20
MEETING FACILITIES	•
EXTRA AMENITIES	JAPANESE ROOMS AVAILABLE, IN-ROOM MASSAGE
BUSINESS AMENITIES	DATAPORT, VOICE-MAIL, 2-LINE PHONE, BUSINESS CENTER
DÉCOR	CONTEMPORARY JAPANESE
POOL/SAUNA	–
EXERCISE FACILITIES	FITNESS ROOM

Renaissance Stanford Court Hotel ★★★★½
905 California Street
San Francisco, CA 94108
☎ 415-989-3500
FAX 415-391-0513
TOLL-FREE 800-468-3571
www.marriott.com

QUALITY	90
COST	$$$$–
LOCATION	NOB HILL
DISCOUNTS AVAILABLE	AAA, AARP, GOVT., MILITARY, SENIOR
NO. OF ROOMS	393
ON-SITE DINING	•
ROOM SERVICE	–
BAR	•
PARKING PER DAY	$41
MEETING FACILITIES	•
EXTRA AMENITIES	PET FRIENDLY, ROBE, VCR, VIDEO GAMES
BUSINESS AMENITIES	DATAPORT, 2-LINE PHONE, BUSINESS CENTER
DÉCOR	MODERN
POOL/SAUNA	–
EXERCISE FACILITIES	FITNESS ROOM

Ritz-Carlton ★★★★★
600 Stockton Street
San Francisco, CA 94108
☎ 415-296-7465
FAX 415-291-0288
TOLL-FREE 800-241-3333
www.ritzcarlton.com

QUALITY	96
COST	$$$$$$$$–
LOCATION	NOB HILL
NO. OF ROOMS	336
ON-SITE DINING	•
ROOM SERVICE	–
BAR	•
PARKING PER DAY	$55
MEETING FACILITIES	•
EXTRA AMENITIES	MASSAGE SERVICE
BUSINESS AMENITIES	DATAPORT, 2-LINE PHONE, VOICEMAIL
DÉCOR	TRADITIONAL
POOL/SAUNA	POOL, SAUNA, WHIRLPOOL
EXERCISE FACILITIES	FITNESS ROOM

Ritz-Carlton Half Moon Bay ★★★★★
1 Miramontes Point Road
Half Moon Bay, CA 94019
☎ 650-712-7000
FAX 650-712-7070
TOLL-FREE 800-241-3333
www.ritzcarlton.com

QUALITY	97
COST	$$$$$$$$–
LOCATION	SOUTH BAY
NO. OF ROOMS	261
ON-SITE DINING	•
ROOM SERVICE	–
BAR	•
PARKING PER DAY	$35
MEETING FACILITIES	•
EXTRA AMENITIES	GOLF, SPA, SHUTTLE, ROBES, FRIDGE, SAFE
BUSINESS AMENITIES	DATAPORT, 2-LINE PHONE, VOICEMAIL
DÉCOR	TRADITIONAL
POOL/SAUNA	WHIRLPOOL, SAUNA, STEAM ROOM, SPA
EXERCISE FACILITIES	FITNESS ROOM, YOGA STUDIO

Rancho Caymus ★★★★
1140 Rutherford Road
Rutherford, CA 94573
☎ 707-963-1777
FAX 707-963-5387
TOLL-FREE 800-845-1777
www.ranchocaymus.com

QUALITY	87
COST	$$$$$
LOCATION	WINE COUNTRY
DISCOUNTS AVAILABLE	AAA, AARP
NO. OF ROOMS	26
ON-SITE DINING	•
ROOM SERVICE	–
BAR	•
PARKING PER DAY	FREE
MEETING FACILITIES	–
EXTRA AMENITIES	BREAKFAST, FRIDGE
BUSINESS AMENITIES	–
DÉCOR	CALIFORNIA MISSION
POOL/SAUNA	–
EXERCISE FACILITIES	–

Red Roof Inn
San Francisco Airport ★★½
777 Airport Boulevard
Burlingame, CA 94010
☎ 415-342-7772
FAX 650-342-2635
TOLL-FREE 800-RED-ROOF
www.redroof.com

QUALITY	60
COST	$+
LOCATION	SAN FRANCICO INT'L AIRPORT
DISCOUNTS AVAILABLE	AAA, SENIOR
NO. OF ROOMS	200
ON-SITE DINING	•
ROOM SERVICE	–
BAR	–
PARKING PER DAY	FREE
MEETING FACILITIES	–
EXTRA AMENITIES	FREE SHUTTLE, PARK, STAY, AND FLY, PET FRIENDLY
BUSINESS AMENITIES	DATAPORT, FAX, COPIER
DÉCOR	MODERN
POOL/SAUNA	POOL
EXERCISE FACILITIES	PRIVILEGES

Renaissance
Parc Fifty Five ★★★★
55 Cyril Magnin Market
San Francisco, CA 94102
☎ 415-392-8000
FAX 415-403-6602
TOLL-FREE 800-650-7272
www.marriott.com

QUALITY	85
COST	$$$$–
LOCATION	UNION SQUARE
DISCOUNTS AVAILABLE	AAA, AARP, GOVT.
NO. OF ROOMS	1,010
ON-SITE DINING	•
ROOM SERVICE	•
BAR	•
PARKING PER DAY	$38
MEETING FACILITIES	•
EXTRA AMENITIES	VIDEO GAMES, VCR, BAY WINDOWS, NEWSPAPER, FRIDGE, SAFETY DEPOSIT BOXES
BUSINESS AMENITIES	DATAPORT, 2-LINE PHONE, BUSINESS CENTER
DÉCOR	MODERN
POOL/SAUNA	SAUNA
EXERCISE FACILITIES	FITNESS ROOM

San Francisco
Airport Marriott ★★★★
1800 Old Bayshore Highway
Burlingame, CA 94010
☎ 415-692-9100
FAX 650-692-8016
TOLL-FREE 800-228-9290
www.marriott.com

QUALITY	83
COST	$$+
LOCATION	SAN FRANCICO INT'L AIRPORT
DISCOUNTS AVAILABLE	AAA, AARP, GOVT., MILITARY, SENIOR
NO. OF ROOMS	686
ON-SITE DINING	•
ROOM SERVICE	–
BAR	•
PARKING PER DAY	$17 SELF, $20 VALET
MEETING FACILITIES	•
EXTRA AMENITIES	VIDEO GAMES, RUNNING PATH, PET FRIENDLY
BUSINESS AMENITIES	DATAPORT, 2-LINE PHONE, VOICEMAIL
DÉCOR	TRADITIONAL
POOL/SAUNA	POOL, SAUNA, WHIRLPOOL
EXERCISE FACILITIES	FITNESS ROOM

San Francisco Marriott ★★★★
55 Fourth Street
San Francisco, CA 94103
☎ 415-896-1600; FAX 415-486-8101; TOLL-FREE 800-228-9290
www.sfmarriott.com

QUALITY	86
COST	$$$$
LOCATION	SOMA/ MISSION DISTRICT
DISCOUNTS AVAILABLE	AAA, AARP, GOVT., MILITARY, SENIOR
NO. OF ROOMS	1,498
ON-SITE DINING	•
ROOM SERVICE	•
BAR	•
PARKING PER DAY	$48
MEETING FACILITIES	•
EXTRA AMENITIES	NEWSPAPER, SHOE SHINE, RENTAL CARS, SAFETY DEPOSIT BOXES
BUSINESS AMENITIES	DATAPORT, 2-LINE PHONE, BUSINESS CENTER, VOICEMAIL, AUDIOVISUAL EQUIPMENT, NOTARY PUBLIC
DÉCOR	MODERN
POOL/SAUNA	POOL, SAUNA, WHIRLPOOL
EXERCISE FACILITIES	FITNESS ROOM

Savoy Hotel ★★★½
580 Geary Street
San Francisco, CA 94102
☎ 415-441-2700
FAX 415-441-0124
TOLL-FREE 800-227-4223
www.thesavoyhotel.com

QUALITY	75
COST	$$$–
LOCATION	UNION SQUARE
DISCOUNTS AVAILABLE	GOVERNMENT
NO. OF ROOMS	83
ON-SITE DINING	
ROOM SERVICE	BREAKFAST
BAR	•
PARKING PER DAY	$29
MEETING FACILITIES	–
EXTRA AMENITIES	SAFE, MINIBAR, PM WINE
BUSINESS AMENITIES	DATAPORT, 2-LINE PHONE
DÉCOR	EUROPEAN BOUTIQUE
POOL/SAUNA	–
EXERCISE FACILITIES	PRIVILEGES

Hotel Information Chart (continued)

Seal Rock Inn ★★★½
545 Point Lobos Avenue
San Francisco , CA 94121
☎ 415-752-8000
FAX 415-752-6034
TOLL-FREE 888-732-5762
www.sealrockinn.com

QUALITY	75
COST	$$$–
LOCATION	RICHMOND/SUNSET DISTRICT
NO. OF ROOMS	27
ON-SITE DINING	•
ROOM SERVICE	–
BAR	–
PARKING PER DAY	FREE
MEETING FACILITIES	–
EXTRA AMENITIES	KITCHENETTES, FIRE-PLACE
BUSINESS AMENITIES	DATAPORT, 2-LINE PHONE
DÉCOR	MODERN
POOL/SAUNA	POOL
EXERCISE FACILITIES	PING PONG, BADMITTON

Serrano Hotel ★★★★
405 Taylor Street
San Francisco, CA 94102
☎ 415-885-2500
FAX 415-474-4879
TOLL-FREE 866-289-6561
www.serranohotel.com

QUALITY	83
COST	$$$$
LOCATION	UNION SQUARE
DISCOUNTS AVAILABLE	AAA, CORP., GOVT., MILITARY, SENIOR
NO. OF ROOMS	236
ON-SITE DINING	•
ROOM SERVICE	•
BAR	•
PARKING PER DAY	$39
MEETING FACILITIES	•
EXTRA AMENITIES	PM WINE, PET FRIENDLY, VIDEO GAMES, INTERNET
BUSINESS AMENITIES	DATAPORT, FAX, 2-LINE PHONE, VOICEMAIL, AUDIO-VISUAL, BUSINESS CENTER
DÉCOR	ECLECTIC CALIFOR-NIAN
POOL/SAUNA	SAUNA
EXERCISE FACILITIES	FITNESS ROOM

Sheraton at Fisherman's Wharf ★★★½
2500 Mason Street
San Francisco, CA 94133
☎ 415-362-5500
FAX 415-956-5275
TOLL-FREE 800-325-3535
www.sheratonatthewharf.com

QUALITY	82
COST	$$$$
LOCATION	NORTH BEACH
DISCOUNTS AVAILABLE	AAA, GOVT.
NO. OF ROOMS	529
ON-SITE DINING	•
ROOM SERVICE	•
BAR	•
PARKING PER DAY	$36
MEETING FACILITIES	•
EXTRA AMENITIES	VIDEO GAMES, TEA/COFFEE MAK-ERS, CAR RENTAL, NEWSPAPER, SAFETY DEPOSIT BOXES
BUSINESS AMENITIES	DATAPORT, 24-HOUR BUSINESS CENTER AND CURRENCY EXCHANGE, VOICE-MAIL, 2-LINE PHONE
DÉCOR	CONTEMPORARY
POOL/SAUNA	POOL
EXERCISE FACILITIES	FITNESS ROOM

Sir Francis Drake Hotel ★★★½
450 Powell Street
San Francisco, CA 94102
☎ 415-392-7755
FAX 415-391-8719
TOLL-FREE 800-795-7129
www.sirfrancisdrake.com

QUALITY	82
COST	$$$$
LOCATION	UNION SQUARE
DISCOUNTS AVAILABLE	AAA, AARP, GOVT., SENIOR
NO. OF ROOMS	417
ON-SITE DINING	•
ROOM SERVICE	•
BAR	•
PARKING PER DAY	$38 STANDARD, $47 OVERSIZED
MEETING FACILITIES	•
EXTRA AMENITIES	PET FRIENDLY, MINI-BAR, FRIDGE, SAFETY DEPOSIT BOXES
BUSINESS AMENITIES	2-LINE PHONE, VOICEMAIL, BUSINESS CENTER
DÉCOR	CALIFORNIA COLONIAL
POOL/SAUNA	–
EXERCISE FACILITIES	FITNESS ROOM

Sonoma Hotel ★★★★
110 W. Spain Street
Sonoma, CA 95476
☎ 707-996-2996
FAX 707-996-7014
TOLL-FREE 800-468-6016
www.sonomahotel.com

QUALITY	85
COST	$$+
LOCATION	WINE COUNTRY
DISCOUNTS AVAILABLE	GROUP
NO. OF ROOMS	16
ON-SITE DINING	•
ROOM SERVICE	–
BAR	•
PARKING PER DAY	FREE
MEETING FACILITIES	–
EXTRA AMENITIES	BREAKFAST, WINE TASTING, HANDMADE SOAPS
BUSINESS AMENITIES	DATAPORT
DÉCOR	FRENCH PROVENÇAL
POOL/SAUNA	–
EXERCISE FACILITIES	–

Sonoma Mission Inn and Spa ★★★★½
100 Boyes Boulevard
Boyes Hot Springs, CA 95476
☎ 707-938-9000; FAX 707-938-4250; TOLL-FREE 800-862-4945
www.fairmont.com/sonoma

QUALITY	90
COST	$$$$$$$$$
LOCATION	WINE COUNTRY
NO. OF ROOMS	228
ON-SITE DINING	•
ROOM SERVICE	•
BAR	•
PARKING PER DAY	$18
MEETING FACILITIES	•
EXTRA AMENITIES	FULL SPA, MASSAGE, GOLF COURSE, BABYSITTING, ROBES, SAFE
BUSINESS AMENITIES	DATAPORT, VOICE-MAIL, 24-HOUR BUSINESS CENTER
DÉCOR	VARIETY
POOL/SAUNA	POOL, SAUNA, STEAM ROOM
EXERCISE FACILITIES	FITNESS ROOM, GOLF, YOGA, PILATES, AQUATIC CLASSES

Sheraton Gateway Hotel ★★★½
600 Airport Boulevard
Burlingame, CA 94010
☎ 415-340-8500; FAX 650-343-1546; TOLL-FREE 888-627-8323
www.sheratonsfo.com

QUALITY	82
COST	$$$–
LOCATION	SAN FRANCICO INT'L AIRPORT
DISCOUNTS AVAILABLE	AAA, AARP, GOVT.
NO. OF ROOMS	404
ON-SITE DINING	•
ROOM SERVICE	–
BAR	•
PARKING PER DAY	$13
MEETING FACILITIES	•
EXTRA AMENITIES	COFFEEMAKER, ATM, PET FRIENDLY, MULTI-LINGUAL STAFF, SAFETY DEPOSIT BOXES
BUSINESS AMENITIES	DATAPORT, 2-LINE PHONE, 24-HOUR BUSINESS CENTER, VOICEMAIL
DÉCOR	TRADITIONAL
POOL/SAUNA	POOL, SAUNA, WHIRLPOOL
EXERCISE FACILITIES	FITNESS ROOM, JOGGING PATH

Sheraton Palace Hotel ★★★★
2 New Montgomery Street
San Francisco, CA 94105
☎ 415-512-1111
FAX 415-543-0671
TOLL-FREE 800-325-3535
www.starwoodhotels.com

QUALITY	89
COST	$$$$$$$–
LOCATION	SOMA/ MISSION DISTRICT
DISCOUNTS AVAILABLE	AAA, GOVT.
NO. OF ROOMS	550
ON-SITE DINING	•
ROOM SERVICE	–
BAR	•
PARKING PER DAY	$40
MEETING FACILITIES	•
EXTRA AMENITIES	MASSAGE, SAFE, ROBES, FRIDGE, PET FRIENDLY
BUSINESS AMENITIES	DATAPORT, 2-LINE PHONE, VOICEMAIL
DÉCOR	GRAND HOTEL
POOL/SAUNA	POOL, SAUNA, WHIRLPOOL
EXERCISE FACILITIES	FITNESS ROOM

Silverado Country Club and Resort ★★★★
1600 Atlas Peak Road
Napa, CA 94558
☎ 707-257-0200
FAX 707-257-2867
TOLL-FREE 800-532-0500
www.silveradoresort.com

QUALITY	85
COST	$$$+
LOCATION	WINE COUNTRY
DISCOUNTS AVAILABLE	AAA, AARP
NO. OF ROOMS	281
ON-SITE DINING	•
ROOM SERVICE	–
BAR	•
PARKING PER DAY	FREE
MEETING FACILITIES	•
EXTRA AMENITIES	GOLF COURSE, SPA, TENNIS, MASSAGE
BUSINESS AMENITIES	DATAPORT, 2-LINE PHONE, AUDIOVI-SUAL EQUIPMENT
DÉCOR	CONTEMPORARY
POOL/SAUNA	POOL, SAUNA, WHIRLPOOL
EXERCISE FACILITIES	FITNESS ROOM, YOGA AND AQUATIC CLASSES, GOLF, TENNIS

Stanyan Park Hotel ★★★½
750 Stanyon Street
San Francisco, CA 94117
☎ 415-751-1000
FAX 415-668-5454
www.stanyanpark.com

QUALITY	75
COST	$$$–
LOCATION	RICHMOND/SUNSET DISTRICT
DISCOUNTS AVAILABLE	AAA
NO. OF ROOMS	36
ON-SITE DINING	•
ROOM SERVICE	–
BAR	–
PARKING PER DAY	$14
MEETING FACILITIES	–
EXTRA AMENITIES	BREAKFAST, PM TEA AND COFFEE
BUSINESS AMENITIES	DATAPORT, VOICEMAIL
DÉCOR	VICTORIAN
POOL/SAUNA	–
EXERCISE FACILITIES	–

Star Motel ★★
1727 Lombard Street
San Francisco, CA 94123
☎ 415-346-8250
FAX 415-441-4469
TOLL-FREE 800-835-8143
www.starmotel.com

QUALITY	53
COST	$$
LOCATION	MARINA
DISCOUNTS AVAILABLE	AAA, AARP, GOVT.
NO. OF ROOMS	52
ON-SITE DINING	–
ROOM SERVICE	–
BAR	–
PARKING PER DAY	FREE
MEETING FACILITIES	–
EXTRA AMENITIES	BREAKFAST, COFFEE AND TEA
BUSINESS AMENITIES	
DÉCOR	MOTEL
POOL/SAUNA	–
EXERCISE FACILITIES	–

Super 8 Motel ★★½
2440 Lombard Street
San Francisco, CA 94123
☎ 415-922-0244
FAX 415-922-8887
TOLL-FREE 800-800-8000
www.super8.com

QUALITY	62
COST	$$–
LOCATION	MARINA
DISCOUNTS AVAILABLE	AAA, AARP, GOVT., SENIOR
NO. OF ROOMS	32
ON-SITE DINING	–
ROOM SERVICE	–
BAR	–
PARKING PER DAY	FREE
MEETING FACILITIES	–
EXTRA AMENITIES	VCR, MICROWAVE, FRIDGE, JACUZZI, DVD PLAYER AND RENTALS
BUSINESS AMENITIES	
DÉCOR	MOTEL
POOL/SAUNA	–
EXERCISE FACILITIES	–

Hotel Information Chart (continued)

Town House Motel ★★½
1650 Lombard Street
San Francisco, CA 94123
☎ 415-885-5163
FAX 415-771-9889
TOLL-FREE 800-255-1516
www.sftownhousemotel.com

QUALITY	60
COST	$$–
LOCATION	MARINA
DISCOUNTS AVAILABLE	AARP, GOVT.
NO. OF ROOMS	23
ON-SITE DINING	–
ROOM SERVICE	–
BAR	–
PARKING PER DAY	FREE
MEETING FACILITIES	–
EXTRA AMENITIES	BREAKFAST, FRIDGE
BUSINESS AMENITIES	–
DÉCOR	MODERN
POOL/SAUNA	–
EXERCISE FACILITIES	–

Travelodge by the Bay ★★½
1450 Lombard Street
San Francisco, CA 94123
☎ 415-673-0691
FAX 415-673-3232
TOLL-FREE 800-578-7878
www.travelodgebythebay.com

QUALITY	62
COST	$$+
LOCATION	MARINA
DISCOUNTS AVAILABLE	AAA, AARP, GOVT., SENIOR
NO. OF ROOMS	72
ON-SITE DINING	•
ROOM SERVICE	–
BAR	•
PARKING PER DAY	$12
MEETING FACILITIES	–
EXTRA AMENITIES	BREAKFAST, COFFEE-MAKER, NEWSPAPER, SAFE, PET FRIENDLY
BUSINESS AMENITIES	DATAPORT, FAX
DÉCOR	MOTEL
POOL/SAUNA	–
EXERCISE FACILITIES	NEARBY

Travelodge Golden Gate ★★½
2230 Lombard Street
San Francisco, CA 94123
☎ 415-922-3900
FAX 415-921-4795
TOLL-FREE 800-578-7878
www.travelodge.com

QUALITY	60
COST	$$+
LOCATION	MARINA
DISCOUNTS AVAILABLE	AAA, AARP, GOVT., SENIOR
NO. OF ROOMS	29
ON-SITE DINING	–
ROOM SERVICE	•
BAR	–
PARKING PER DAY	FREE
MEETING FACILITIES	–
EXTRA AMENITIES	NEWSPAPER, SAFE, COFFEEMAKER, TOURS
BUSINESS AMENITIES	DATAPORT, FAX
DÉCOR	MOTEL
POOL/SAUNA	–
EXERCISE FACILITIES	NEARBY

Villa Florence ★★★½
225 Powell Street
San Francisco, CA 94102
☎ 415-397-7700
FAX 415-397-1006
TOLL-FREE 800-553-4411
www.villaflorence.com

QUALITY	80
COST	$$$$
LOCATION	UNION SQUARE
DISCOUNTS AVAILABLE	AAA, AARP, GOVT., SENIOR
NO. OF ROOMS	183
ON-SITE DINING	•
ROOM SERVICE	–
BAR	•
PARKING PER DAY	$38
MEETING FACILITIES	•
EXTRA AMENITIES	PM WINE, NINTENDO, NEWSPAPER, PET FRIENDLY, IN-ROOM SPA SERVICES
BUSINESS AMENITIES	DATAPORT, VOICE-MAIL, COPIER, FAX, PRINTER
DÉCOR	ITALIAN RENAISSANCE
POOL/SAUNA	–
EXERCISE FACILITIES	PRIVILEGES (FEE)

Villa Inn ★★½
1600 Lincoln Avenue
San Rafael, CA 94901
☎ 415-456-4975
FAX 415-456-1520
TOLL-FREE 800-424-4777

QUALITY	56
COST	$$–
LOCATION	MARIN COUNTY
DISCOUNTS AVAILABLE	AAA, AARP, GOVT.
NO. OF ROOMS	60
ON-SITE DINING	–
ROOM SERVICE	•
BAR	–
PARKING PER DAY	FREE
MEETING FACILITIES	–
EXTRA AMENITIES	BREAKFAST, FRIDGE, KITCHENETTE
BUSINESS AMENITIES	2-LINE PHONE
POOL/SAUNA	POOL, WHIRLPOOL
EXERCISE FACILITIES	–

Vintage Inn ★★★★½
6541 Washington Street
Yountville, CA 94599
☎ 707-944-1112
FAX 707-944-1617
TOLL-FREE 800-351-1133
www.vintageinn.com

QUALITY	91
COST	$$$$$$$$–
LOCATION	WINE COUNTRY
DISCOUNTS AVAILABLE	AAA, AARP
NO. OF ROOMS	80
ON-SITE DINING	–
ROOM SERVICE	–
BAR	–
PARKING PER DAY	FREE
MEETING FACILITIES	•
EXTRA AMENITIES	WINE, SPA, FREE BREAKFAST
BUSINESS AMENITIES	DATAPORT, 2-LINE PHONE, BUSINESS CENTER, AUDIO-VISUAL EQUIPMENT
DÉCOR	CALIFORNIA
POOL/SAUNA	POOL, SAUNA, WHIRLPOOL
EXERCISE FACILITIES	CYCLING, TENNIS, GOLF

Travelodge San Francisco Airport North ★★★
326 S. Airport Boulevard
San Francisco, CA 94080
☎ 650-583-9600
FAX 650-873-9392
TOLL-FREE 800-578-7878
www.travelodge.com

QUALITY	70
COST	$$–
LOCATION	SAN FRANCICO INT'L AIRPORT
DISCOUNTS AVAILABLE	AAA, AARP, GOVT., SENIOR
NO. OF ROOMS	199
ON-SITE DINING	•
ROOM SERVICE	–
BAR	–
PARKING PER DAY	FREE
MEETING FACILITIES	•
EXTRA AMENITIES	COFFEE, SAFE, FRIDGE, MICROWAVE, SOFA BED, ATM
BUSINESS AMENITIES	DATAPORT, VOICE-MAIL, FAX
DÉCOR	MODERN TROPICAL
POOL/SAUNA	POOL
EXERCISE FACILITIES	–

Union Street Inn ★★★½
2229 Union Street
San Francisco, CA 94123
☎ 415-346-0424
FAX 415-922-8046
www.unionstreetinn.com

QUALITY	82
COST	$$$$–
LOCATION	MARINA
NO. OF ROOMS	6
ON-SITE DINING	–
ROOM SERVICE	–
BAR	–
PARKING PER DAY	$15
MEETING FACILITIES	–
EXTRA AMENITIES	FULL BREAKFAST, PM WINE
BUSINESS AMENITIES	–
DÉCOR	VICTORIAN
POOL/SAUNA	–
EXERCISE FACILITIES	–

Vagabond Inn Airport ★★½
1640 Bayshore Highway
Burlingame, CA 94010
☎ 415-692-4040
FAX 650-692-5314
TOLL-FREE 800-522-1555
www.vagabondinn.com

QUALITY	58
COST	$$–
LOCATION	SAN FRANCICO INT'L AIRPORT
DISCOUNTS AVAILABLE	AAA, AARP, GOVT., SENIOR
NO. OF ROOMS	91
ON-SITE DINING	–
ROOM SERVICE	–
BAR	–
PARKING PER DAY	FREE
MEETING FACILITIES	•
EXTRA AMENITIES	BREAKFAST, NEWSPAPER, PET FRIENDLY, FRIDGE, MICROWAVE, TEA/COFFEE MAKER, SHUTTLE SERVICE
BUSINESS AMENITIES	DATAPORT, 2-LINE PHONE, FAX, VOICEMAIL
POOL/SAUNA	–
EXERCISE FACILITIES	–

W Hotel San Francisco ★★★★★
181 Third Street
San Francisco, CA 94103
☎ 415-777-5300
FAX 415-817-7823
TOLL-FREE 877-WHOTELS
www.whotel.com

QUALITY	98
COST	$$$$$$–
LOCATION	SOMA/MISSION DISTRICT
DISCOUNTS AVAILABLE	AAA, GOVT., SENIOR
NO. OF ROOMS	423
ON-SITE DINING	•
ROOM SERVICE	•
BAR	•
PARKING PER DAY	$46
MEETING FACILITIES	•
EXTRA AMENITIES	STEREO, VIDEOS, NEWSPAPER, ROBES, SAFE, MINIBAR, COFFEEMAKER, VCR/DVD PLAYERS, PET FRIENDLY
BUSINESS AMENITIES	DATAPORT, FAX, 2-LINE PHONE
DÉCOR	ULTRAMODERN
POOL/SAUNA	POOL, STEAM, WHIRLPOOL
EXERCISE FACILITIES	FITNESS ROOM, YOGA

Warwick Regis Hotel ★★★★
490 Geary Street
San Francisco, CA 94102
☎ 415-928-7900
FAX 415-441-8788
TOLL-FREE 800-203-3232
www.warwicksf.com

QUALITY	83
COST	$$$
LOCATION	UNION SQUARE
DISCOUNTS AVAILABLE	AAA, AARP, GOVT.
NO. OF ROOMS	74
ON-SITE DINING	•
ROOM SERVICE	•
BAR	•
PARKING PER DAY	$29
MEETING FACILITIES	•
EXTRA AMENITIES	SAFE, ROBES, VIDEO GAMES, UMBRELLAS
BUSINESS AMENITIES	DATAPORT, 2-LINE PHONE, VOICEMAIL
DÉCOR	EUROPEAN BOUTIQUE
POOL/SAUNA	PRIVILEGES
EXERCISE FACILITIES	PRIVILEGES

Waterfront Plaza Hotel ★★★½
10 Washington Street
Oakland, CA 94607
☎ 510-836-3800
FAX 510-832-5695
TOLL-FREE 800-729-3638
www.waterfrontplaza.com

QUALITY	80
COST	$$$$
LOCATION	OAKLAND
DISCOUNTS AVAILABLE	AAA, AARP
NO. OF ROOMS	145
ON-SITE DINING	•
ROOM SERVICE	–
BAR	•
PARKING PER DAY	$12 DAY USE, $20 OVERNIGHT
MEETING FACILITIES	•
EXTRA AMENITIES	FERRY TO SAN FRANCISCO, VIDEO GAMES, SAFE, MINI-BAR, COFFEE/TEA MAKER
BUSINESS AMENITIES	DATAPORT, VOICEMAIL
DÉCOR	NAUTICAL
POOL/SAUNA	POOL, SAUNA
EXERCISE FACILITIES	FITNESS ROOM

Hotel Information Chart *(continued)*

	Westin Hotel San Francisco Airport ★★★★	**Westin St. Francis** ★★★★½	**White Swan Inn** ★★★★½
	1 Old Bayshore Highway Milbrae, CA 94030 ☎ 650-692-3500 FAX 650-872-8111 TOLL-FREE 800-228-3000 www.starwoodhotels.com	335 Powell Street San Francisco, CA 94102 ☎ 415-397-7000 FAX 415-774-0124 TOLL-FREE 800-937-8461 www.westinstfrancis.com	845 Bush Street San Francisco, CA 94108 ☎ 415-775-1755 FAX 415-775-5717 TOLL-FREE 800-999-9570 www.whiteswaninnsf.com
QUALITY	84	91	90
COST	$$+	$$$$$–	$$$$
LOCATION	SAN FRANCICO INT'L AIRPORT	UNION SQUARE	UNION SQUARE
DISCOUNTS AVAILABLE	AAA, SENIOR, GOVT.	AAA, AARP, GOVT.	
NO. OF ROOMS	396	1,195	26
ON-SITE DINING	•	•	–
ROOM SERVICE	•	•	–
BAR	•	•	–
PARKING PER DAY	$15 SELF, $20 VALET	$39	$30
MEETING FACILITIES	•	•	•
EXTRA AMENITIES	AIRPORT SHUTTLE, SOUNDPROOF ROOMS, COFFEE/TEA MAKER, SAFE, REFRESHMENT CENTER	TOURS, IN-ROOM MASSAGES, SAFE, MINIBAR	BREAKFAST, TEA AND COOKIES, FIREPLACE, WET BAR, ROBES, COFFEEMAKER, NEWSPAPER, PM WINE AND HORS D'OEUVRES, CHOCOLATES
BUSINESS AMENITIES	DATAPORT, BUSINESS CENTER, VOICEMAIL, 2-LINE PHONE	DATAPORT, CORDLESS PHONE, AUDIOVISUAL EQUIPMENT	DATAPORT, VOICEMAIL, COMPUTER STATION, AUDIOVISUAL EQUIPMENT
DÉCOR	MODERN	GRAND HOTEL	ENGLISH GARDEN INN
POOL/SAUNA	POOL, WHIRLPOOL	SPA	PRIVILEGES
EXERCISE FACILITIES	FITNESS ROOM	–	FITNESS ROOM

PART THREE

VISITING
on BUSINESS

NOT ALL VISITORS *are* HEADED *for* FISHERMAN'S WHARF

WHILE SOME PEOPLE MAKE IT THEIR BUSINESS to vacation in San Francisco, others have no choice. Whether or not those lucky few who are getting forced to visit this wonderful city know it or not, San Francisco is a business traveler's dream. The city is compact enough to allow you to make deals in the afternoon, catch some of the city's natural wonders as the sun is setting, and go to dinner by evening.

In case you haven't noticed, Silicon Valley, about 50 miles south of San Francisco, is a global center for high-technology business and manufacturing. Headquarters of major corporations that make their home here: Chevron, Hewlett-Packard, Bank of America, Intel, Apple Computer, Sun Microsystems, Wells Fargo, Seagate Technology, and Gap.

The city is also a major center for higher education. It's the home of San Francisco State University, the University of San Francisco, Hastings College of Law (University of California), the University of California Medical Center, the San Francisco Art Institute, and other public and private colleges. Across the bay is the University of California, Berkeley, one of the world's great research institutions. As a result, San Francisco hosts many visiting academics, college administrators, and students and their families.

In many ways, the problems facing business visitors on their first trip to San Francisco don't differ much from the problems of folks in town intent on seeing its best-known tourist attractions and breathtaking scenery. Business visitors need to stay in a convenient hotel, avoid the worst of the city's traffic, get around in an unfamiliar city, and know the locations of San Francisco's best restaurants. For the most part, though, business visitors aren't nearly as flexible about the timing of their visit as folks who pick San Francisco as a vacation destination. While we advise that the best times to visit are the shoulder seasons between winter and summer, the necessities of business may dictate that August, when the city is often shrouded in fog, or January, the rainiest month, is when you pull into town. No matter the time of year, you should certainly find the time to squeeze a morning or afternoon out of your busy schedule and spend a few hours exploring some of the places that draw millions of visitors to San Francisco each year.

THE MOSCONE CENTER

SAN FRANCISCO IS HOME TO ONE MAJOR CONVENTION center, the 1.6-million-square-foot Moscone Center (747 Howard Street, San Francisco, CA 94103; ☎ 415-974-4000; **www.moscone.com**). The facility is actually three convention venues (Moscone North, Moscone West, and Moscone South) on adjacent 11-acre blocks bounded by Mission, Folsom, Third, and Fourth streets near the heart of downtown. Named for San Francisco Mayor George R. Moscone (murdered in 1978 along with Supervisor Harvey Milk), this modern, $420 million convention center is located in the booming SoMa District (South of Market) four blocks south of Union Square.

Within walking distance are 20,000 hotel rooms, the city's main shopping district, the Powell Street cable cars to Chinatown, Nob Hill, Fisherman's Wharf, and San Francisco's best restaurants. Next door is the San Francisco Museum of Modern Art (SFMOMA), and across the street is the Yerba Buena Center, with a park, art gallery, theaters, cafes, ice skating and bowling, and The Rooftop children's area. Nearby is Metreon, the Sony entertainment center with four stories and 350,000 square feet offering 15 movie theaters, an IMAX theater, eight restaurants, and shopping. Without a doubt, San Francisco and the Moscone Center add up to one of the best convention destinations in the world.

But there's more to come. Already home to the San Francisco Museum of Modern Art, the California Historical Society, the Cartoon Art Museum, and several art galleries, SoMa will also become home to two other established San Francisco museums—the Mexican Museum and the Jewish Museum; both should be in new digs near the Moscone Center in the next few years.

The Layout

Moscone South offers 260,560 square feet of primary exhibit area in a column-free space that can be divided into three halls. (The distinctive arches that make the hall column-free also reduce usable floor space by about 40%.) Forty-one flexible meeting rooms provide more than 60,000 square feet of meeting space. The lobby-level, 42,675-square-foot Esplanade Ballroom accommodates more than 5,000 delegates and is surrounded by terraced patios.

Across the street and connected to Moscone South by an underground concourse and a pedestrian sky bridge is the smaller Moscone North, which opened in 1992 and contains 181,440 square feet of exhibit space in two halls and up to 53,410 square feet of flexible meeting space in 17 rooms. The lobby provides a striking entrance to the exhibit level; delegates descend on escalators and stairs illuminated by skylights.

The freestanding Moscone West, a 300,000-square-foot, three-story convention hall that opened in 2003, is on the corner of Fourth and Howard Streets, just a few steps away from Moscone North and South. Designed to snag smaller conventions when the big shows at its sister facilities are setting up and breaking down, Moscone West provides nearly 100,000 square feet of dedicated function space per floor. Using the latest technology such as its second-floor "air curtains"—suspended panels that allow the floor to be configured into meeting rooms—Moscone West is designed to handle a wide range of meetings and shows. The entrance to Moscone West's nine underground loading docks is on Howard Street.

The buildings are modern, bright, and airy, featuring extensive use of skylights and large expanses of glass that admit ample light to the mostly underground site. Outside, the buildings are enhanced by landscaped walkways, gardens, patios, sculptures, and a walk-through fountain. The meeting rooms on the mezzanine level in Moscone South have windows that overlook the main hall, while the second- and third-floor lobbies in Moscone West provide good views of the city.

All major exhibit areas and most meeting rooms are on one underground level linked by the underground concourse; additional meeting rooms are located on Moscone South's mezzanine level. Twenty completely enclosed loading docks are located on the same level as the main halls, providing direct drive-in access to Moscone North and South.

unofficial **TIP**
A note to exhibitors: All installation and dismantling of exhibits, and all handling of materials require union labor, including signs and carpet laying. But union labor isn't required for the unpacking and placement of exhibitors' merchandise in the booth, or if the display is installed by one person in less than 30 minutes without the use of tools.

Services

Two business centers, one each in the lower lobbies of Moscone North and Moscone South, provide access to photocopying services, transparencies, fax, overnight mail, UPS, office supplies, and cellular phone rental. The centers are open during event hours, and major credit cards are accepted for purchases and services.

Nursing services are on site during events at first-aid stations in Moscone North, Moscone South, and the esplanade level. A gift shop in the Moscone South lower lobby sells souvenirs. Hungry? Each convention group works with the Moscone Center to set up food service, so food availability differs with each convention. However, the neighborhood is full of places to eat, ranging from fast food and cafes to gourmet fare. The closest places to grab a quick bite to eat are the two cafes located in Yerba Buena Center (Mission at Third Street; ☎ 415-978-2787) and the Museum of Modern Art Café (151 Third Street; ☎ 415-357-4000), which offers reasonably priced sandwiches, salads, desserts, beer, and wine (closed Wednesdays).

Parking and Public Transportation

The Moscone Center has no on-site parking. But 5,000 parking spaces can be found within walking distance in garages and parking lots and on the street. Still, dealing with a car in this dense city scene is a hassle. With so many hotels, restaurants, museums, art galleries, and public transportation within walking distance of the convention center, why bother with a car?

Consider using San Francisco's public transportation systems instead. Powell Street Station, only two blocks from the convention center, provides access to BART (Bay Area Rapid Transit) and Muni Metro (streetcars); adjacent are the Powell Street cable-car lines to Nob Hill and Fisherman's Wharf (although the wait in line to board a cable car can be lengthy during peak tourist seasons).

Muni Metro will get you to the Financial District and the city's outlying neighborhoods, while BART can whisk you beyond the city to Oakland and Berkeley. Muni buses and cable cars will get you just about everywhere else. Plus, there are cabs.

Lodging within Walking Distance of the Moscone Center

A couple of hotels are within an easy stroll of the Moscone Center: the San Francisco Marriott (55 Fourth Street; ☎ 415-896-1600) offers 1,500 rooms; the Sheraton Palace (2 New Montgomery Street; ☎ 415-512-1111) has 550 rooms; the Argent Hotel San Francisco (50 Third Street; ☎ 415-974-6400) has 667 rooms; and the Galleria Park Hotel (191 Sutter Street; ☎ 415-781-3060) offers 177 rooms.

unofficial **TIP**
Because the convention sponsor brings big business to San Francisco, it usually can negotiate volume discounts substantially below rack rate. Some conventions and trade shows have more bargaining clout and negotiating skill than others, and your convention sponsor may not be one of them.

Convention Rates: How They Work and How to Do Better

If you're attending a major convention or trade show, the meeting's sponsoring organization has probably negotiated "convention rates" with a number of hotels. Under this arrangement, hotels agree to "block" a certain number

Executive Amusement

BEST HOTEL FOR FITNESS FREAKS Nob Hill Lambourne (725 Pine Street; ☎ 415-433-2287; **www.nobhilllambourne.com**). Each room comes with stationary bike, treadmill, or rowing machine and the option of private yoga classes.

CLIMBING THE LADDER If you're feeling stuck at the mid-management level, consider climbing to new heights at the world's largest indoor climbing gym, **Mission Cliffs** (2295 Harrison Street; ☎ 415-550-0515; **www.touchstoneclimbing.com/mc.html**). You'll find that clinging onto that left handhold is about as tricky as holding onto a dot com position.

SAVVY SPIN DOCTORS Looking for the best in dry cleaning? If it's the top choice for fashion designers, celebrities, and models, it's good enough for you. **Buchanan Cleaners** (2137 Buchanan Street; ☎ 415-923-9251).

PRESIDENTIAL PUTTING GREENS Lincoln Park (34th Avenue and Clement Street) has one of the most amazing panoramic vistas of downtown San Francisco anywhere. And it's close to home!

BEST TOUR TEMPTATION Feeling trapped by the confines of corporate America? Head to Alcatraz—not just the run-of-the-mill tour—but the **Alcatraz After Dark Tour.** It's amazing what is revealed when the lights go out in "The Rock." For information on this tour, call ☎ 415-705-5555.

BETTER THAN A PUNCHING BAG Feeling the urge to stalk and shoot after a rather stressful day of meetings? Instead head to **Pacific Rod and Gun Club** (520 Muir Drive; ☎ 415-586-8349; **www.prgc.net**). You know the cue "pull," and BAM!–shoot that skeet!

MA AND PA CAR RENTAL If you are tired of dealing with big rental-car agencies that simply ask for a corporate number, head to **City Rent-A-Car** (1748 Folsom Street; ☎ 415-861-1312 or 1433 Bush Street; ☎ 415-359-1331; **www.cityrentacar.com**). You get small-town service by the two brothers that own it, and the rates are cheaper than those of the big guns.

of rooms at an agreed-upon price for conventioneers. In the case of a small meeting, only one hotel may be involved; but city-wide conventions may involve almost all downtown and airport hotels.

Once a convention or trade show sponsor completes negotiations with participating hotels, it sends its attendees a housing list that includes all the hotels serving the convention, along with the special convention rate for each. Using the strategies covered in the previous section, you then can compare these convention rates with the rack rates.

If the negotiated convention rate doesn't sound like a good deal, try to reserve a room using a half-price club, a consolidator, or a tour operator. Remember, however, that many of the deep discounts are available only when the hotel expects to be at less than 80% occupancy, a rarity when a big convention is in town.

Strategies for Beating Convention Rates

- Reserve early. Most big conventions and trade shows announce meeting sites one to three years in advance. Get your reservation booked as far in advance as possible using a half-price club. If you book well ahead of the time the convention sponsor sends out the housing list, chances are good that the hotel will accept your discounted reservation.
- Compare your convention's housing list with the list of hotels presented in this guide. You may be able to find a suitable hotel not on the housing list.
- Use a local reservations agency or consolidator. This is also a good strategy if you need to make reservations at the last minute. Local reservations agencies and consolidators almost always control some rooms, even in the midst of a huge convention or trade show.

The Moscone Center can have a considerable impact on San Francisco when, say, 65,000 exhibitors and trade-show attendees come into town and snatch up almost every hotel room in the city. Luckily, though, the large conventions and trade shows register no discernible effect on the availability of restaurant tables or traffic congestion; it's just hotel rooms that get scarce.

unofficial **TIP**
Check the Moscone Center's Web site at **www.moscone.com** for a complete and up-to-date list of 2006 and 2007 conventions and trade shows scheduled. It can help when planning your trip if you are crowd weary.

PART FOUR

ARRIVING *and* GETTING ORIENTED

 COMING *into the* **CITY**

BY CAR

SAN FRANCISCO IS LOCATED ON THE TIP OF A peninsula linked to the mainland by two bridges. As a result, visitors arriving by car enter the city by one of three routes: from the south on US 101, from the east on I-80 (via the San Francisco–Oakland Bay Bridge), or from the north on US 101 (on the Golden Gate Bridge).

US 101 and a parallel highway, I-280, link the city to the rest of the peninsula to the south, including Palo Alto, Santa Clara, and San Jose, located at the southern end of San Francisco Bay. US 101 is also the coastal highway that continues farther south to Gilroy, Salinas, San Luis Obispo, Santa Barbara, and Los Angeles, 400 miles away. A more scenic—and significantly slower—option that hugs the coast is California Route 1, which leads directly to Santa Cruz, Carmel, Big Sur, and Morro Bay.

Travelers coming from the east on I-80 (which goes through Sacramento, Reno, Salt Lake City, Omaha, Chicago, and other points east before reaching New York City) pass through Oakland before crossing San Francisco Bay on the Bay Bridge and entering downtown San Francisco. It's also the route for people coming to the Bay Area on I-5, the north-south interstate through California's Central Valley (and the fastest driving route from Los Angeles).

Drivers coming through Oakland are confronted with a maze of interstate highways that link to form a kind of beltway around San Francisco. In addition to the San Francisco–Oakland Bay Bridge, San Francisco Bay is crossed by two more bridges to the south (these connect with the San Francisco peninsula well south of the city). I-580 crosses San Pablo Bay north of San Francisco, where it connects the East Bay city of Richmond with San Rafael. US 101 to the north, via the Golden Gate Bridge, links San Francisco to Marin County and the rest of Northern California, including San Rafael, Petaluma, Healdsburg, and Eureka. Again, California Route 1 is the slow and scenic option; the two-lane road follows the coast north.

BY PLANE

MOST DOMESTIC AND FOREIGN VISITORS WHO fly to San Francisco land at the San Francisco International Airport, 14 miles south of downtown directly on US 101. It's the fifth-busiest airport in the United States, and it's undergoing a major expansion. Luckily, many domestic fliers have a choice: Oakland International Airport, a smaller, more distant facility, is worth considering, especially if you can get a direct flight from your hometown. Oakland International is located five miles south of downtown Oakland, across San Francisco Bay (about 24 miles from downtown San Francisco).

San Francisco International Airport (SFO)

Seventy-four percent of visitors arrive by air, most of them through the San Francisco International Airport (SFO); **www.flysfo.com.** A $2.4 billion construction project is nearing completion to ready the airport for a projected volume of 51 million passengers in 2006. Plans include an international terminal, an airport rail-transit system (called AirTrain), a BART (Bay Area Rapid Transit) station, and elevated roadways. The centerpiece of the program is a two-million-square-foot international terminal that was completed in the spring of 2000.

THE LAYOUT SFO handles an average of 109,000 passengers a day on 71 passenger airlines. It's shaped somewhat like a ship's wheel with the spokes radiating out. There are four terminals, numbers 1, 2, 3, and the International terminal. At press time, terminal 2 was closed for renovation. The terminals surround a parking garage and are linked by indoor corridors featuring changing art exhibits (nice to know if you've got time to kill) and the AirTrain, an automated light-rail system that connects the terminals, parking garages, rental-car station, and Bart station. Each terminal features shops, restaurants, and newsstands, and the International Terminal has a small boutique shopping mall and some excellent restaurants at its two food courts. Five airport information booths, open from 8 a.m. to midnight, are located in the baggage-claim areas; multilingual agents can provide information on ground transportation, Bay Area lodging, and cultural events.

ARRIVING From your gate, follow the signs down to the baggage area on the lower level. After getting your luggage, step outside to the center island to catch a door-to-door or hotel shuttle van, or a cab or limo. Short-term parking is across the street. To reach the central parking garage or the BART station (the cheap way to San Francisco, but only recommended if you don't have a lot of luggage), follow the signs down another level to the AirTrain (where you take an elevator up to the automated light rail line). The Blue Line goes to the rental-car facility, while the Red Line links the terminals and parking garages.

unofficial **TIP**
If you've got time to kill, give AirTrain a spin. It's free and the views are good.

AIRPORT SECURITY Airport security at SFO has been upgraded since the terrorist attacks of September 11. Passengers are advised:

- Carry-on and checked luggage will be screened;
- Arrive two hours prior to departure for domestic flights and three hours prior to departure for international flights;
- Unattended vehicles left in front of the terminal will be ticketed and towed;
- Government-issued identification is required. You will be asked to show your ID at several points in the pre-flight/boarding process.
- Only passengers with airline tickets are allowed beyond screening checkpoints;
- Passengers must remove coats, jackets, blazers, but not shoes unless specifically instructed to do so.
- Electronic devices are subject to screening at checkpoints;
- Laptops and video cams must be removed from their cases;
- Passengers are limited to one carry-on bag plus one personal carry-on item;
- Knives of any length must be placed in checked baggage;
- Cutting and puncturing instruments and athletic equipment that can be used as a weapon must be placed in checked baggage.

For the latest information on security procedures at SFO, visit its Web site at **www.flysfo.com.**

Getting Downtown

DRIVING If you're renting a car, take the AirTrain Blue Line to the central rental-car facility. After picking up your car keys, get explicit directions to US 101, which goes to downtown San Francisco.

unofficial **TIP**
It's a good idea to call ahead to your hotel for turn-by-turn driving directions.

To reach Market Street near Union Square (the main downtown hotel district), take US 101 to I-280 north; then take the Sixth Street exit. Market Street is about six blocks from the end of the exit; across Market Street, Sixth Street becomes Taylor Street, a one-way street heading north toward Fisherman's Wharf. It's about a 25-minute drive to downtown from the airport (longer during rush hour).

CABS AND SHUTTLES Cabs are available outside the baggage area near the yellow column at all terminals. Typical fares to downtown San Francisco are about $29–$44; up to five riders can split the cost.

Door-to-door shared van service to downtown San Francisco, available outside the doors of the arrival level on the center island, is priced at around $14–$17 per person ($7–$14 for children). The vans leave every 15 to 20 minutes between 6 a.m. and 11 p.m. and every 30 minutes during late-night hours.

Major shuttle services include **Bay Shuttle** (☎ 415-564-3400) and **Supershuttle** (☎ 415-558-8500; or **www.super.shuttle.com**), which allows you to make back-to-the-airport reservations on their Web site. You can also reserve by phone a return trip with any of the shuttle services. For more information, contact one of the van services or the SFO ground transportation hotline (call ☎ 511 within the San Francisco Bay Area, ☎ 510-817-1717 outside the San Francisco Bay Area, or visit **www.511.org**).

Shuttle Savvy: Tips for a Smooth Ride

1. Generally shuttles to and from both SFO and Oakland are similar in service and price—you can expect to pay around $35–$45 per person from Oakland and about $17 from SFO.

2. The trip downtown from SFO generally takes about 30 minutes, although traffic can sometimes make it up to an hour. Oakland is farther away and the Bay Bridge traffic can be relentless; expect about an hour commute into downtown.

3. If there are three or more in your party it might be cheaper to split the cost of a taxi (no waiting). Be sure to check with the shuttle for departure times. Often, the shuttle waits for a few flights to land to fill up before heading out. So if you are first, be prepared to wait. There seems to be a rule, however, that the ground transportation center enforces that states shuttles must leave within ten minutes of its first customer.

4. If there are numerous people in the shuttle, check to see where on the drop-off list you fit. If you are last to be dropped off you're in for a torturously long trip.

PUBLIC TRANSPORTATION The easiest way into the city is via BART, whose trains run right up to the International terminal. For only $5.15 one-way, travelers are now whisked to downtown San Francisco in a half hour. To reach the BART station, follow signs to AirTrain, the airport's light rail system. When you arrive at the station, be ready to fumble with the automated ticket machine. Luggage is permitted on the trains in two open-space areas on each car (small luggage will fit under the seats). The trains run every 15 minutes during regular business hours and every 20 minutes in the evenings and on weekends. Hours of operation are 4 a.m. to midnight weekdays, 6 a.m. to midnight on Saturdays, and 8 a.m. to midnight on Sundays.

Oakland International Airport (OAK)

Smaller is better at Oakland International Airport (**www.flyoakland.com**), across the bay from San Francisco and five miles south of downtown Oakland. With only two terminals on one level, Oakland is a lot less confusing to weary travelers.

THE LAYOUT Terminal 1 handles all domestic and international airlines, with the exception of Southwest Airlines, which claims all of Terminal 2. From your gate, follow signs to the baggage area near the entrance and to the right. Ground transportation is outside the door, including shuttle vans to downtown San Francisco (to the left of Terminal 1 under the covered walkway). Most rental-car agencies are across the street; no need to take a shuttle bus to a remote lot. Shuttles to the BART station in Oakland and bus service are located outside the terminals.

unofficial T

While Oakland is the obvious airport choice if your destination is in the East Bay area, it's also a hassle-free alternative for San Francisco–bound travelers—at least, the ones who can book a direct flight from their hometowns.

Getting Downtown

DRIVING To reach downtown San Francisco from Oakland International, exit the airport and take Hegenberger Road to I-880 north. Follow signs for I-80, which takes you across the double-decker San Francisco–Oakland Bay Bridge ($3 toll for westbound). The first two exits after the bridge take you downtown. It's about a 30-minute drive (longer during rush hour).

CABS AND SHUTTLES Cabs are usually outside the baggage areas between Terminals 1 and 2; fare to downtown San Francisco is about $50. Door-to-door shuttle services to downtown (about $35–$45) include **City Express** (☎ 888-874-8885 or 510-638-8830), **Air Transit Shuttle** (☎ 510-568-3434), and **Citywide Shuttle Service** (☎ 510-336-0090).

PUBLIC TRANSPORTATION Shuttle service via AirBART to the BART Oakland Coliseum station is $2 one way (50 cents for children under age 11, disabled, and seniors). Ticket machines for AirBART are in Terminals 1 and 2. To purchase a BART ticket at the station, you'll need $1, $5, $10, or $20 bills for the ticket machines. (Note that the machines will not dispense more than $4.95 in change for any one transaction.) The ride should take about 15 minutes. Once you arrive at coliseum station, take a BART train to one of four downtown San Francisco stations on Market Street ($3.15 one way). For BART info, call ☎ 510-465-2278 or visit **www.bart.gov.** AC Transit's Line 58 bus connects the airport with the Alameda/Oakland Ferry and downtown Oakland's Jack London Square. One-way fare is $1.75 (85 cents for children ages 5–17, disabled and seniors); exact fare is required. The ferry also provides a scenic trip across San Francisco Bay to the city's Ferry Terminal and Pier 39 in Fisherman's Wharf. One-way fares are $5.50 for adults,

ages 5–12, and $3.25 for seniors, disabled, and active
el. For ferry schedules, call ☎ 510-522-3300 or look up
ry.com.

TAFFED TICKET OFFICE, WAITING ROOM, and baggage check is located in the Ferry Building at the foot of Market Street. Motor coaches transport passengers to the Amtrak station in Emeryville, near Oakland, and to three other downtown San Francisco points: Pier 39 in Fisherman's Wharf, the Hyatt Regency in the Financial District, and Macy's near Union Square.

The motor-coach trip from Emeryville takes about ten minutes; your luggage is checked through to your final stop downtown (or, for departing passengers, to your train). Cities with daily round-trip service to San Francisco are Los Angeles and San Diego (five trips a day), Sacramento (four trips a day), Seattle and Portland (one trip a day), and Chicago (one trip a day). For exact schedule and fare information, check **www.amtrak.com** or call ☎ 800-USA-RAIL.

WHERE TO FIND TOURIST INFORMATION IN SAN FRANCISCO

IF YOU'RE SHORT ON MAPS OR NEED MORE information on sightseeing, restaurants, hotels, shopping, or things to do in San Francisco and the Bay Area, there are several places to stop and pick up maps and brochures.

- Berkeley Convention and Visitor Bureau, 2015 Center Street, Berkeley, CA 94704; ☎ 800-847-4823 or 510-549-7040; **www.visitberkeley.com.**

- Downtown San Francisco: San Francisco Convention and Visitors Bureau, Hallidie Plaza at Powell and Market streets (lower level); ☎ 415-283-0177, fax 415-362-7323; **www.sfvisitor.org.** Weekdays 9 a.m.–5 p.m.; weekends 9 a.m.–3 p.m.; closed Easter, Thanksgiving, Christmas, and New Year's days.

- Marin County: Marin County Convention and Visitors Bureau, 1013 Larkspur Landing Circle, Larkspur; ☎ 415-925-2060; **www.visit marin.org.** Weekdays 9 a.m. to 5 p.m.; closed Thanksgiving, Christmas, and New Year's days.

- Napa Valley wine country: Napa Valley Conference and Visitors Bureau, 1310 Napa Town Center. ☎ 707-226-7459, fax 707-255-2066; **www.napavalley.com.** Daily 9 a.m.–5 p.m.; closed Thanksgiving, Christmas, and New Year's days.

- Sonoma wine country: Sonoma Valley Visitors Bureau, 453 First Street East; ☎ 707-996-1090; **www.sonomavalley.com.** Daily 9 a.m.–5 p.m.

A GEOGRAPHIC OVERVIEW
of SAN FRANCISCO *and*
THE BAY AREA

SAN FRANCISCO, WITH MORE THAN 750,000 residents, is the second most densely populated city in the country (after New York). The city, on the West Coast of the United States about halfway between the northern and southern ends of California, is situated on the tip of a hilly peninsula jutting into San Francisco Bay and, to the west, overlooking the Pacific Ocean. San Francisco is the epicenter of a larger metropolitan area with a total population of about six million, making it the fifth-largest urban area in the United States.

California, the most populous state in the Union (and its third largest), is bordered to the east by Arizona and Nevada. To the north is Oregon and the Pacific Northwest; to the south is the international border with Mexico. Along California's nearly 800-mile coastline, which forms the western edge of the state, is the Pacific Ocean. The largest city in California is Los Angeles, 400 miles to the south; the state capital is Sacramento, about 90 miles northeast of San Francisco.

THE BIG ONE!

WE'VE ALL HEARD STORIES AS KIDS THAT "the Big One" is going to rock California and forever knock it off our map, sending the state to find restful solitude in the Pacific Ocean. And the culprit of such a sinking fate? The San Andreas Fault, of course. The San Andreas Fault, the active frontier between the Pacific and North American tectonic plates, runs vertically through California. And like a nose on a dangerous face, San Francisco is smack dab in the center, which allows the fault to create violent tremors and devastating earthquakes as it readjusts itself in the earth below. She is temperamental, as evidenced by the quakes of 1906 and 1989, as well as the impending granddaddy of them all predicted for sometime in the future.

Seismologists are unable to predict when tremors or earthquakes will occur or how severe they'll be. The actual shifting of the plates doesn't cause the damage; instead, the resulting collapses, fires, and landslides can kill hundreds. Since the 1989 quake, many San Francisco buildings have been strengthened to withstand tremors, and shelters (such as the one at the Moscone Convention Center) are stocked as emergency relief sites. In addition, most hotels have their own evacuation procedures.

unofficial **TIP**
For more detailed information on what to do in the event of a tremor while you're in San Francisco, check the local phone directory, which has pages full of detailed advice.

YOU OUGHTTA BE IN PICTURES!

VISITORS LOVE SAN FRANCISCO, IN LARGE PART because of its breathtaking beauty and sense of care and compassion of its inhabitants. It is an easy place to live in, visit, navigate, and fall in love with. If you are not convinced at first glimpse of the Golden Gate Bridge, just look beyond at the Marin Headlands, the carpet of mountains that in the spring become covered with flowers and chaparral. Year-round, the Headlands harbor secret playgrounds for adrenaline junkies of all ages. Further away from the Headlands is Mount Tamalpais, or Mount Tam as it is affectionately called. Hike, bike, drive . . . you name it and the Mountain will provide it. It also has one of the best views of the city and the surrounding Bay area—on a clear day you can see across to the Sierra Nevada range. If you survive the hike or winding drive to the top, you can head south to Stinson Beach or toward Muir Woods, where you can drive your car through one of the giant redwoods that tower in the forest. Both ends of the Golden Gate Bridge are anchored in the Golden Gate National Recreation Area, more than 75,000 acres of parkland managed by the National Park Service; it's a recreational playground to San Franciscans.

North of the Marin Headlands is Point Reyes National Seashore, a windswept peninsula on the Pacific Coast covered with woodlands, prairies, and marshes. A geologic "island" cut off from the mainland by the San Andreas fault, Point Reyes was discovered by Sir Francis Drake in 1579. Today it is a carefully preserved sanctuary for more than 350 species of birds and a paradise for botanists and nature lovers, who, with a little luck, can spot elk, lynx, coyotes, and falcons. Winter visitors can watch migrating whales at an overlook near the 1870 Point Reyes Lighthouse.

Closer to home within the bay (one of the greatest natural harbors in the world) is Angel Island, only reachable by ferry from Tiburon, Oakland, and San Francisco. No motorized vehicles are allowed in this state park, which is chock full of trails for hiking or biking. Throughout the island are picnic tables, and there are even spooky ruins of a military garrison, known as the "Ellis Island of the West," that served as a quarantine station for Asian immigrants until November 1940. And nearby Alcatraz is becoming a place that you don't want to escape—it's now making a comeback as a nature and wildlife habitat.

Heaven exists south, also. Just follow the number "1"—Route 1, that is. Its narrow road winds along the crashing waves of the Pacific Ocean. You'll be so close to the edge and the water that you may even feel the salty spray from below. It's a high like no other. Along the way are villages and towns like Half Moon Bay, and the occasional nude beach. The Santa Cruz Mountains, running down the spine of the San Francisco peninsula, provide a dramatic backdrop to crashing ocean waves and offer fantastic views of the ocean and bay along Skyline Boulevard, which follows the mountain ridges.

SAN FRANCISCO NEIGHBORHOODS

HILLS OR NO HILLS, THE FIRST DEVELOPERS OF the city decided on a grid system. It was a convenient way of organizing neighborhoods and streets, but they did not have to consider the stick-shift vehicle back then! San Francisco's hills, more than anything else, thrill visitors with astounding vistas. Surrounded by the shimmering waters of the bay and the Pacific Ocean, the city's land mass is packed on and around nearly four dozen hills—steep markers that delineate San Francisco's shifting moods and economic prosperity—the higher you get, the higher the real estate. The Financial District is the granddaddy of commercial square footage, while the rest of the city remains charming in its residential—almost suburban—nature. "It's a city you can actually live in," is the catch phrase most use when explaining the benefits of this urban bliss.

Armed with a good map, comfortable walking shoes, and ankle weights (if you are so inclined) to take advantage of the quad workout while pounding the hills, you'll find that the best way to absorb the city's aura is to walk. You can hit most of downtown San Francisco's major sights and neighborhoods in a day. The city is compact, and thanks to that grid layout, well organized. It's easy to foot the city, and the bus maps are free and easy to read.

unofficial **TIP**
You'll be amazed at the cleanliness as well as the differing architecture and personality that each neighborhood boasts.

Chinatown

North along Grant Avenue and through the flamboyant, green-and-ocher imperial Dragon Gate is bustling Chinatown, a dense warren of restaurants and tacky tourist shops that's the second-largest Chinese community outside of Asia (New York's is number one). Since gold rush days, 24-square-block Chinatown has served as the hub for San Francisco's Chinese population. It's a city within a city, crowded with retail outlets and sidewalk displays jammed with silk, porcelain, teak furniture, handmade jewelry, and the usual tourist gewgaws (the farther you walk up Grant Avenue, the cheaper the postcards get). Walk a little farther to Chinatown's open-air markets, glitzy emporiums, and herbalists' shops filled with exotic herbs and spices. At Grant Avenue and Stockton Street is the main Chinese food-shopping district, crowded with displays of unfamiliar fruits (you have to try the infamous Durian fruit—"smells like hell but tastes like heaven") and fish stores with tanks of live eels, fish, frogs, and turtles waiting to be killed on the spot for customers.

If you have only one experience in Chinatown, make it dim sum. The delicious tidbits, generally served for brunch, are a local institution. Most dim sum houses open at 10 a.m. and close by mid- or late afternoon. Typically, waiters circle the restaurant's dining room, pushing carts stacked with covered bamboo or stainless-steel containers filled with steamed or fried dumplings, shrimp balls, spring rolls, steamed buns, and Chinese pastries. Just point to what looks appealing; the waiters usually don't speak English and ordering is done by gestures. It's cheap, too—you have to order an awful lot of food to spend more than $10 a person. One of the oldest dim sum institutions in Chinatown is Hang Ah Tea Room on Pagoda Place, off Sacramento and Stockton Streets. Keeping in tune with 24-hour breakfasts, it is open until 9 p.m. Dim sum at dusk? Why not!

unofficial TIP
For a feel of the real, non-touristy Chinatown, duck into a side alley (such as Waverly Street, which parallels Grant Avenue between Clay and Washington streets), where you'll see stores that sell lychee wine, Chinese newspapers, dried lotus, and powdered antlers (reputed to restore male virility).

Ross Alley, which runs above Grant Avenue between Washington and Jackson streets, houses small garment shops, laundries, florists, and one-chair barber shops. At the Golden Gate Fortune Cookie Company at 56 Ross Alley, visitors can watch little old women fold bits of wisdom into that oh-so-familiar shape. Early morning, when shopkeepers are busy setting out their wares, is a good time to get a feel for the real Chinatown. Late January is the Chinese New Year's fest and parade. Slithering giant snakes and dragons, lanterns, and floats march down Grant Avenue in celebration. It is definitely a sight to see, especially if you are traveling with children. For an abbreviated version of the Chinese New Year celebrations, the weekly Lion Dance, held every Sunday, snaps, crackles, and pops its way down Grant Avenue.

Civic Center and the Tenderloin

Eight blocks west of Union Square on Geary Boulevard is Van Ness Avenue, a broad north-south boulevard and the main thoroughfare of the Civic Center District, acclaimed by critics as one of the finest collections of beaux arts buildings in the country. **City Hall,** built in 1914, is widely considered one of the most beautiful public buildings in America; on a historical note, it's the building in which Dan White shot Mayor George Moscone and Supervisor Harvey Milk in 1978.

Across the plaza from City Hall is the stately former public library, now the home of the **Asian Art Museum,** the largest collection of Asian art in the West. The south end of the plaza contains the **Civic Auditorium** (built in 1913), and on the north side is the **State Office Building** (1926). Also in the neighborhood are a few other distinguished buildings, including the **Veterans Auditorium Building** (1932), the **Opera House,** and the **Louise M. Davies Symphony Hall.** Two blocks away is the contemporary **San Francisco Public Library** (1996), a modern interpretation of the classic beaux arts style.

Surrounding the area is a diverse collection of restaurants, antiques shops, and galleries. But Civic Center and its fine collection of buildings (and the adjacent Tenderloin, on the north side of Market Street between the theater district and Civic Center) have become

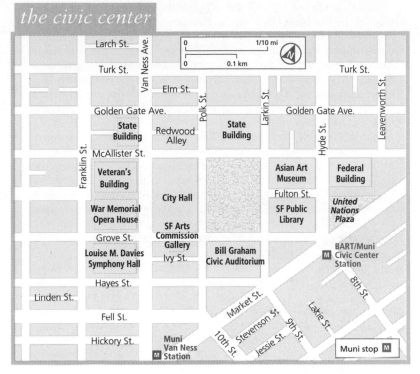

the civic center

the focal point for San Francisco's most glaring problem, the homeless. Periodically police evict hundreds of street people who converge on the plaza opposite City Hall and its lawns. With suited and gowned San Franciscans heading in and out of the ballet, opera, and symphony, it's not a problem easily disguised. Civic Center and the Tenderloin remain one of the last down-and-out sections of town.

Nob Hill/Russian Hill

In a city renowned for its hills, Nob Hill heads the list. As California novelist and journalist Joan Didion wrote, Nob Hill is "the symbolic nexus of all old California money and power." Its mansions, exclusive hotels, and posh restaurants tower over the rest of the city. While early San Franciscans of wealth preferred lower sections of town, the installation of cable cars in the 1870s turned Nob Hill into a valuable piece of real estate. The generally accepted borders of Nob Hill are Bush Street and Pacific Avenue, and Stockton and Larkin Streets.

unofficial **TIP**
For visitors, Nob Hill doesn't offer much in the way of sights—unless it's the fantastic views from the top of the hill, which is 376 feet above sea level. Your best bet is to wander, gaze at the exteriors of exclusive clubs (such as the Pacific Union Club at 1000 California Street), stop at a hotel bar for a drink, and bask in the aura of privilege and luxury that distinguishes this most famous of San Francisco locales.

You won't find a better hotel bar than one of the grande dames of Nob Hill—the **Mark Hopkins,** the **Fairmont,** or the **Huntington.** Perhaps Nob Hill's most famous landmark is the Mark Hopkins Inter-Continental San Francisco, a 380-room hotel at California and Mason Streets; great views open at the **Top O' the Mark** lounge, which dates from 1939 and is a charming place to watch the setting sun. You may recognize the Fairmont from its TV stint as the hotel in the show *Hotel* (its penthouse suite goes for $10,000 a day; butler, maid, and limo included).

More Nob Hill treasures include Huntington Park, a flowered square where visitors can see nannies pushing trendy baby joggers and walking well-groomed poodles. The great, gray eminence atop Nob Hill on California Street is **Grace Cathedral,** the largest Gothic structure in the West. Among its many splendors is the cast of the gilded bronze doors created by Lorenzo Ghiberti for the Baptistry in Florence; their ten rectangular reliefs depict scenes from the Old Testament. They stand at the top of the steps to the cathedral's east entrance.

unofficial **TIP**
Russian Hill, named for a graveyard (long since removed) for Russian seamen, is also where Armistead Maupin's fictional crew in *Tales of the City* made their home.

Russian Hill, next door, manages to be both expensive and Bohemian. Home to many rich and famous people, it also has a fair share of artists, struggling writers, and students from the nearby **San Francisco Art Institute.** Again, there's not much here in the way of sights—except for great views, wooded open spaces, picturesque cul-de-sacs, and "the crookedest street in the world" (Lombard Street, with eight turns in one block at its eastern end). Russian Hill, within walking distance of Union Square, is bordered by Broadway and Chestnut, Taylor, and Larkin streets.

Union Square

unofficial **TIP**
Union Square is safe during the day, but it's best to avoid the area after dark.

Perhaps the nearest thing to a city center in San Francisco is the refurbished Union Square, its liveliest urban space. A few acres of concrete and greenery surrounded by huge department stores, swank hotels, and expensive shops, its adjacent streets are jammed with cars and tour buses, upscale shoppers, befuddled tourists, street musicians, beggars and street people bumming quarters, and businesspeople late for appointments. It's all here, from the sleazy to the sublime.

In addition to giving credit cards a workout at Neiman-Marcus, Saks Fifth Avenue, or Macy's, you can catch a cable car on Powell Street for a ride up Nob Hill or board a motorized trolley for a city tour. Maiden Lane, an elegant, tree-lined alley that extends two blocks east of Union Square from Stockton to Kearny Streets, features exclusive shops and restaurants. Union Square is also the focal point for the city's main hotel district, so for a lot of visitors it's the obvious place to start a walking tour.

Union Square is also San Francisco's primary theater district. **The American Conservatory Theater** (ACT) at the Geary Theater (415 Geary Boulevard) offers both classic and contemporary works (and a penchant for Moliere) in a restored landmark theater that reopened in 1996. The city's premier African-American theater company calls the **Lorraine Hansberry Theater** (620 Sutter Street) home, while the **Curran Theatre** (445 Geary Boulevard) and the **Marine's Memorial** (609 Sutter Street) present Broadway musicals from New York. Pick up half-price tickets at the TIX kiosk for performances that day; cash only.

The Financial District

Frequently called "the Wall Street of the West," the Financial District lies northeast of Union Square in an area bordered by Embarcadero and Market, Third, Kearny, and Washington streets. Among the towering skyscrapers are several corporate headquarters and the Pacific Coast Stock Exchange, along with lots of elaborate corporate architecture (including the city's tallest landmark, the Transamerica Pyramid).

Brokers, bankers, and insurance agents pursue wealth during the week on several acres of landfill on and around Montgomery Street; unlike most cities' financial areas, the Financial District remains lively on evenings and weekends, thanks to its many restaurants and nightclubs. What motivates these financial movers and shakers can be studied at the **Wells Fargo History Museum** (420 Montgomery Street), which offers insights into the city's rich history.

The Marina District and Pacific Heights

So what if the Marina District is snubbed by many anti-yuppies as the Mecca for all things moneyed? And so what if it is built on earthquake-friendly landfill? Filled with Mediterranean-style houses painted in lollipop colors, the Marina District is one of the most beautiful districts in the city, which is why most of its inhabitants are young 20- and 30-something professionals or families. Prices are high and some would argue that so are the egos. With the Presidio to the west and Fort Mason to the east, the Marina is also one of the city's greenest neighborhoods. Yacht clubs, kite fliers, and joggers make the district feel somewhat like a resort. Ironically, the Marina, built to celebrate the rebirth of the city after the 1906 quake, was the city's worst casualty in the 1989 disaster. Tremors tore through the unstable landfill on which the district is built, and many homes collapsed into smoldering ruins. Rebuilding occurred almost immediately, though, and many of the shimmering new homes are just that—new houses built after the last major earthquake. Nor was the disaster enough to bring rents down; the Marina continues to attract a very well-heeled and smart set.

unofficial **TIP**
Fort Mason and Municipal Pier are great spots to escape the congestion of nearby Fisherman's Wharf.

The Marina's main commercial drag is Chestnut Street, an urban thoroughfare with a swinging-singles reputation; the local Safeway has been dubbed "the Body Shop" for the inordinate amount of cruising that goes on there. A long stretch of turf at Marina Green is popular with the fit, the Lycra-clad, and Frisbee-catching dogs.

A bit east of the Marina is Fort Mason, located on the other side of Aquatic Park and the 1,800-foot curving Municipal Pier. Millions of GIs shipped out to the South Pacific in World War II from Fort Mason, but today it's a public park. Some locals call it "Fort Culture"—here you'll find in old, shed-like buildings a variety of nonprofit arts organizations, museums, and galleries.

Although mainly a daytime destination, Fort Mason attracts crowds at night for performances of its acclaimed Magic Theatre, one of the oldest and largest theater companies on the West Coast. At night, the fort's pretty bluff is one of the most romantic spots in the city. Fort Mason is also the start of the Golden Gate Promenade, a three-and-a-half-mile paved walkway along San Francisco Bay that ends at Fort Point National Historical Site, directly under the Golden Gate Bridge. A park along this promenade introduced in 2001 is Crissy Field. The park is the result of restoring approximately 100 acres of the neglected "backyard" of the Presidio. It was transformed from asphalt, chain-link fences, and deteriorating buildings to a vibrant new park that follows along the sands of the bay.

At the westernmost edge of the Marina is its most notable landmark, the **Palace of Fine Arts** (at Baker and Beach streets). An interpretation of a classical ruin complete with manicured lawns, ponds, and ducks, it's all that's left of the 1915 Panama Pacific Exhibition. Next door is the **Exploratorium,** a unique science museum with more than 700 hands-on science exhibits for youngsters and adults.

When a cable-car line opened in the Pacific Heights District in 1878, this neighborhood south of Fort Mason and west of Van Ness Avenue quickly evolved into an enclave for San Francisco's nouveaux riches. Attempting to outdo the wooden castles on Nob Hill with mansions featuring Gothic arches, Byzantine domes, and stained-glass windows, the denizens of Pacific Heights created monuments to the bonanza era of the late 19th century. But the opulence and magnificence was short-lived. The earthquake of 1906 reduced the exquisite homes to shambles and the district never fully recovered. Much of the area was rebuilt with luxury apartment houses, but many original Victorian houses remain, including the city's most photographed group of dainty "painted ladies."

Today, Pacific Heights, along with the adjacent Cow Hollow and Presidio Heights districts, are home to more college graduates, professionals, and high-income families than any other city district. A fine collection of Victorian houses on Union Street has evolved into a premiere shopping area with more than 300 boutiques, restaurants, antique shops, and coffeehouses.

Fisherman's Wharf

Although visitors are hard-pressed to find vestiges of its once-busy shipbuilding, fishing, and industrial might, Fisherman's Wharf was once an active fishing port. Then, about 30 years ago, the area was transformed into a tourist circus, and that's what it remains today. Here your tourist dollar is pursued with a vengeance at T-shirt shops, fast-food joints, stalls selling sweatshirts and baseball caps, and piers transformed into souvenir complexes, overpriced restaurants, and places to take a cruise on the bay.

In spite of the lamentable statistic that more than 10 million visitors a year come to Fisherman's Wharf, it's tempting to say that, unless you've got restless children in tow, stay away. And while by and large that's good advice, there remain a few good reasons to come (aside from the view, which is great).

Probably the best is **Alcatraz,** 12 minutes away by ferry in San Francisco Bay; it's one of the best places to go in San Francisco and shouldn't be missed. (The ferry leaves from Pier 41; advance reservations are a good idea.) Other worthwhile activities at the wharf include taking a cruise on the bay, renting a bike, or strolling down the **Golden Gate Promenade,** a three-and-a-half-mile paved path by the bay leading to the bridge of the same name. Last but not least, walk out on Pier 41 and wave at the collection of barking sea lions just offshore.

For those restless kids, a cluster of pricey attractions should do the trick. **Aquarium of the Bay** is a commercial aquarium where visitors walk through a submerged transparent tunnel and view Pacific Coast marine creatures. Along Jefferson Street are two rainy-day places: the **Wax Museum** and **Ripley's Believe It or Not.** Things get better at the **Hyde Street Pier,** where the National Park Service has berthed a collection of real 19th century ships open to the public. Another block west is the **Maritime Museum,** a gorgeous art deco building full of nautical treasures.

The wharf also has two refurbished shopping complexes. **The Cannery,** a former fruit-packing factory on Jefferson Street at Leavenworth Street, has three levels of shops and restaurants. **Ghirardelli Square** at 900 North Point Street (at the western end of Fisherman's Wharf) is a boutique mall that's come a long way since its days as a chocolate factory. Its handsome redbrick facade and red neon sign are San Francisco landmarks.

North Beach

The Italians moved the Irish out in the late 19th century, causing quite a fury. In the 1960s, the beatniks stomped the area, causing everyone to

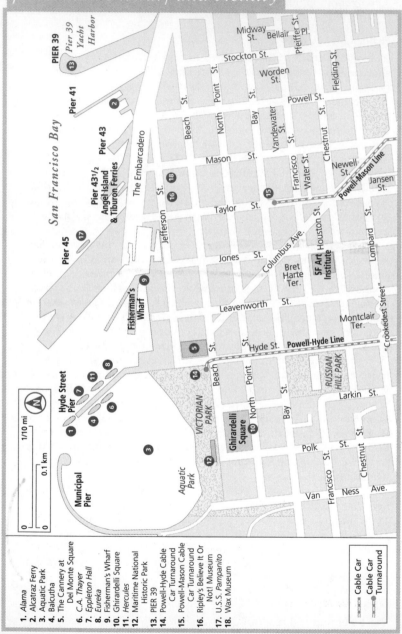

fisherman's wharf and vicinity

1. Alama
2. Alcatraz Ferry
3. Aquatic Park
4. Balcutha
5. The Cannery at Del Monte Square
6. C.A. Thayer
7. Eppleton Hall
8. Eureka
9. Fisherman's Wharf
10. Ghirardelli Square
11. Hercules
12. Maritime National Historic Park
13. PIER 39
14. Powell-Hyde Cable Car Turnaround
15. Powell-Mason Cable Car Turnaround
16. Ripley's Believe It Or Not! Museum
17. U.S.S. Pampanito
18. Wax Museum

Cable Car
Cable Car Turnaround

complain. And now that the neighborhood is becoming increasingly Chinese thanks to its Chinatown borders, the Italians are ready to fling
fettuccini. But despite such changing of the guard
over the decades, North Beach remains one of the
city's most interesting districts—thanks to the diverse cultural invasions. It was once San Francisco's original waterfront, and years later landfill

unofficial **TIP**
North Beach is a great
place for lounging around
in cafés and bars, casual
shopping and browsing,
and exploring side streets
on foot.

extended the waterfront farther north. One of the city's oldest neighborhoods, North Beach still has the well-worn feel of a pair of old,
comfortable shoes.

To get a feel for the neighborhood's melting-pot ethnic mix, stop by
Washington Square, where you'll see elderly Italians playing bocci ball
and Chinese gracefully slicing through the air in the early morning doing
their Tai Chi routines. Kick off the shoes, lay in the park, and gaze up at
spires of the Church of St. Peter and Paul, where Joe DiMaggio married
Marilyn Monroe. Or get up early one morning and head to Molinari's
Deli, which opened in 1896. Leave through the swinging salami and pick
up a cannoli and cappuccino at Liguria bakery on the northeast corner
of the park. When the caffeine kicks in, consider walking up **Telegraph
Hill** to Coit Tower for a great vista of San Francisco (see below).

The corner of Grant and Columbus avenues in North Beach was
the crossroads of the Beat world of the 1950s. "It was a good time to
be in San Francisco," wrote journalist Hunter S. Thompson. "Anybody with half a talent could wander around North Beach and pass
himself off as a 'comer' in the new era. I know, because I was doing
it . . . It was a time for breaking loose from the old codes, for digging
new sounds and new ideas, and for doing everything possible to
unnerve the Establishment."

For a taste of North Beach's literary and beatnik past, stop in **City
Lights Bookstore** (at Columbus Avenue and Broadway), ground zero
for the Beat Generation; the small alley that runs down the side of the
shop is now called Jack Kerouac Street after the most famous of the
Beat writers. Also at Columbus and Broadway, poetry meets porn on
a block of declining strip joints and rock clubs; the most famous is
the Condor Club, former home of Carol Doda and her silicone-
enhanced breasts.

Telegraph Hill

Bordering North Beach is Telegraph Hill, noted for its great views of
the bay, vine-covered lanes, quaint cottages, pastel clapboard homes,
and lousy parking. Once the home of struggling writers and artists,
Telegraph Hill is now occupied by a wealthier class of people. At the
top is **Coit Tower,** named for Lillie Hitchcock Coit, who bequeathed
the funds to build this popular tourist landmark.

Getting there, though, can be a chore. Many of the houses dangle
precipitously over the steep inclines, and the sidewalks turn to steps

as you near the top. An easier option is to take the No. 39 bus to the tower and then walk down the **Greenwich Steps,** a brick staircase lined with ivy and roses that descends steeply to Montgomery Street. Near the base of the steps is an all-glass-brick art-deco apartment house used in the Humphrey Bogart film *Dark Passage.*

The Castro District

One of the most fascinating, social, and educational gay-oriented parts of the city is the Castro District. The lesbian and gay community that makes its home in the Castro has contributed significantly to every aspect of the city's life, from economics and the arts to politics. (It's said that no San Francisco politician can win citywide election without the backing of the gay community.)

Some say that the Castro is still the wildest neighborhood in town, and others say that it's merely a shadow of its former self. It's a good guess that much of the Castro's energy and unabashed hedonism has been channeled into AIDS support groups, care for the sick, and city politics. In the 1970s, the gay community transformed the neighborhood into a fashionable, upscale enclave of shops, restaurants, bars, and restored homes.

Probably the best way to explore the Castro is by taking a walking tour. One of the best we have found is Cruisin' the Castro Tour, which meets Tuesday through Saturday mornings at 10 a.m. at the Rainbow Flag at the corner of Castro and Market streets above the Castro Muni subway station (☎ 415-255-1821; **www.cruisinthecastro.com**). On this tour you will learn about gay history in the district from 1849 to present. The tour includes America's only "Pink Triangle Park;" Harvey Milk's residence and camera shop; the legendary Castro Theatre, which specializes in foreign, repertory, and art films; the Human Rights Campaign Action Center; unique shops; and lunch at the delicious Firewood Café. If you get hungry, you must visit a few Castro institutions like Café Flore or Red Dora's Bearded Lady Dyke Café.

The Mission District

For culture vultures craving salsa or an authentic taqueria, the Mission is the place to come. This mostly Latino neighborhood is hip, happening, and historical, made up of Mexican, Central American and, increasingly, a wave of New Bohemia. Named for Mission Dolores, San Francisco's oldest building and the sixth in a chain of Spanish settlements that stretched for 650 miles, the district is one of the cheaper districts to live in, which explains the Bohemian appeal.

Positioned way south of downtown, the Mission, as it is simply called, is blanketed in sun and warmth most of the summer while the rest of the city suffocates in the rolling afternoon fog. The district is large, also, and is serviced by two BART stations, one at each end.

The Mission is an international hodgepodge, with large numbers of South Americans, Samoans, Vietnamese, Koreans, and Native

Americans moving in; it's considered San Francisco's most diverse neighborhood. The district's main drag, Mission Street, is a bustling commercial avenue filled with discount shops, used-clothing stores, pawnbrokers, cafés, cheap ethnic restaurants, bars, clubs, produce stands, and pool rooms. Salsa and Mexican music blast from bars, and the air is redolent with the aroma of Hispanic cooking.

Mission Street is also a good place to start a tour of the Mission's 200-odd murals, painted as a result of a City Hall scheme to channel the energy of the district's poor youth; the biggest concentration is along 24th Street between Mission Street and South Van Ness Avenue. More Latino culture is on display at the **Mission Cultural Center** (2868 Mission Street), where visitors can enjoy temporary art exhibits, theatrical productions, and poetry readings.

unofficial **TIP**
While the neighborhood is safe during the day, visitors should use extra caution at night when visiting clubs and restaurants in the district.

Noe Valley

One of the more hip neighborhoods bordering the Mission is Noe Valley. This is *the* place to live these days. A walk up Valencia Street to 24th Street will take you to the heart of this beloved and sunny neighborhood. It is the land of organic produce, smoothies, New Age music, and paint-it-yourself pottery stores. Trendy cafes and bookstores and funky boutiques are everywhere, and it seems that many Mission weary have migrated here for its quaint village feel. The neighborhood has a large lesbian population, but more noticeable are the new moms, dads, and babies that crawl, stroll, and toddle the streets in Noe. It is safer and quieter than nearby Mission, and up until recently quite cheap to rent. **Dolores Park** is nearby and is one of the best features of Noe, with views of downtown that will knock your socks off! The sprawling greenery lined with palm trees, friendly frolicking dogs, and pairs of lounging lovers make the park one of the best vantage points near the Mission.

Potrero Hill

Tucked away from the hustle and bustle of city life, Potrero Hill is probably San Francisco's newest trend in neighborhood. Quiet streets, funky houses that seem right out of the movie *Edward Scissorhands,* and unobstructed views of downtown from every vantage point qualify Potrero as a fortified funky hood. Everything has a homegrown feel to it—you won't find any Barnes and Noble or Starbucks here. Its recent revitalization in art, theater, healing arts, and loft and warehouse spaces makes Potrero prime real estate. And for those in the know, the crookedest street doesn't reside on Lombard but at Vermont and 20th

unofficial **TIP**
Even though it might not seem like there's much going on, you'll be surprised to find some very popular cafés, bars, and restaurants located on Potrero Hill's 17th and 18th Streets, like **Bottom of Hill, Farley's, Lilo Lounge,** and **Thanya & Salee.**

Street. The end of Vermont Street packs more thrilling twists and turns into its eight switchbacks than Lombard; plus, the views are almost as good, and you get the added bonus of landing in the Mission district, home of the best burritos this side of Tijuana!

South of Market (SoMa)

Over the last 15 years or so, this dreary area of old factory spaces has been spruced up into galleries, a convention center, trendy restaurants, museums, gay bars, and nightclubs. SoMa is becoming the West Coast version of New York's SoHo in a big way. The **San Francisco Museum of Modern Art** (151 Third Street) is housed in a $62 million structure that some critics say is more beautiful than any of the art inside.

Whether you are purveying Picasso or pump-up-the-music VIP clubs, SoMa is where it's happening. The district can be divided roughly into four regions: the increasingly developed area around the art museum, including the Moscone Convention Center and the futuristic Metreon entertainment center; the nightclub region around 11th and Folsom Streets; the blocks between Third and Fourth streets, where you'll find the new Yerba Buena Center; and the still undeveloped dock areas of Mission Rock and China Basin. Artists, dancers, and musicians like SoMa for the relatively low rents (by San Francisco standards) for huge spaces they can convert into studios and living quarters.

By day, SoMa remains an oddly colorless and semi-industrial neighborhood of warehouses and factory outlets. That's no surprise, considering that the area has always been home to industry. Several foundries were located in SoMa in the 1850s, along with rows of prefabricated housing imported from the East, making the neighborhood San Francisco's first industrial population. But in the late 1990s, the city's denizens, including artists, trendsetters, and hipsters of all kinds, descended on a formerly gray landscape lit up by the neon facades of bars and clubs.

If you've already hit the Top O' the Mark (see Nob Hill, above), you can continue your high-altitude buzz at the Saul Steinberg-esque **San Francisco Marriott Hotel** and its 39th-floor bar, the **View Lounge.** Located near Fourth and Market streets south of Union Square near the edge of SoMa, the bar features concentric parabolic windows that slope backward to form a kind of half dome, creating the illusion that you're floating over the city in the nose of a helicopter. Drink prices surpass the bar's altitude but absorbing the cool attitude of the place is an experience worth the price. On your way out pay tribute to the sole surviving martini glass forever enshrined in the bar—it stood the test of the 1989 earthquake that rocked the hotel's walls on opening night!

The Presidio, Fort Point, and the Golden Gate Bridge

After hundreds of years of sporadic military occupation by Spain, Mexico, and the United States, this northwestern tip of the San Francisco peninsula was handed over to the National Park Service in 1994. Now the former army base is in the slow process of evolving into a national park. Blissfully free of developed attractions, the **Presidio** offers miles of eucalyptus-scented roadways, trails, ancient gun fortifications, and incredible views from its sandy buffs. Almost 30 of its 1,500 acres are part of the **San Francisco National Military Cemetery.**

The Presidio's main entrance is on Lombard Street, west of Pacific Heights and the Marina District. Small military buildings remain scattered across the former army post. The Presidio's dramatic location (and maybe the most impressive view in the city) is **Fort Point,** the ruins of an old brick fortress overlooking the impossibly scenic Golden Gate, with breathtaking vistas that include the San Francisco skyline on one side and the Marin Headlands across the strait.

unofficial **TIP**
Visitors should consider both driving and walking across the bridge; the drive is thrilling as you pass under the huge towers, and the half-hour walk allows the bridge's enormous size and spectacular views to sink in.

Overhead at Fort Point, traffic roars on the **Golden Gate Bridge,** probably the most famous bridge in the world. Formerly thought unbridgeable, the mile-wide Golden Gate between the tip of the San Francisco peninsula and Marin County was finally spanned in 1937, and until 1959 it ranked as the world's longest suspension bridge (4,200 feet). A sobering note: about seven people a month commit suicide by jumping off the bridge to the water 260 feet below.

There's a viewing area off the northbound lanes of US 101, with parking and access to trails and the bridge's walkways. (There's no need to cross the bridge by car to return to US 101 southbound.) If you drive across to Marin County, a $3 toll for cars is collected at the southern end of the bridge.

The Beaches, Lands End, the Palace of the Legion of Honor, and Cliff House

South of the Golden Gate Bridge along the Pacific coastline are some of the city's finest beaches. Former military installations hidden among trees and behind sand dunes provide protection from the wind for picnickers. The sandy shoreline of **Baker Beach** faces the entrance of Golden Gate, a scenic backdrop for hiking, fishing, and sunbathing; swimming in these treacherous waters, alas, is dangerous. Behind Baker Beach, **Battery Chamberlain** points a 95,000-pound cannon ominously to sea.

unofficial **TIP**
A bit farther south, **China Beach** provides an intimate atmosphere on a small beach nestled on a steep shoreline—perfect for family outings and picnics. It's also San Francisco's safest swimming beach (although not as popular as the more accessible Baker Beach).

Hikers are attracted to **Lands End,** a shoreline noted for its absence of cars and abundance of birds, trees, and scenic vistas. Hallmarks are the sound of the ocean, the smell of pine and cypress, and views of coastal scenery. At low tide, the wrecks of ships that fell victim to the treacherous water are visible. You can also follow the route of an abandoned 19th-century railroad that once led to Cliff House; stay on the main trail because the cliffs are steep and dangerous. Visitors can also explore defense batteries at **West Fort Miley.**

At the south end of Lands End is the **Palace of the Legion of Honor,** a white-pillared twin of the famous Legion d'Honneur in Paris. Some say it's the city's best art museum, but there's no argument about its spectacularly scenic setting overlooking the Pacific Ocean. And with Rodin's "Thinker" in the courtyard, this art museum makes an elegant impression.

Cliff House, a mainstay of San Francisco tourism for more than a century, still attracts plenty of visitors, sometimes by the busload. Just offshore from the restaurant and gift shop are **Seal Rocks,** home base for sea lions and marine birds. Next door are the ruins of the once-elaborate **Sutro Baths,** a 19th-century swimming emporium that could hold 24,000 people in its heyday; it burned to the ground in the 1960s. Come just before sunset for cocktails and a view of Seal Rocks and the setting sun from the restaurant; it's a San Francisco tradition.

Cliff House also marks the northern terminus of **Ocean Beach,** a four-mile stretch of sand and crashing surf that's always windy and wavy. You won't find much in the way of frills or stunning scenery, but the beach is a great place for jogging, walking, and people-watching. Don't go in the water, though. The ocean is always dangerous, even when it looks calm.

Farther down the coast are two more notable San Francisco locales. The **San Francisco Zoo** (at Great Highway and Sloat Boulevard) is Northern California's largest animal emporium and features animals in grassy enclosures behind moats, not pacing in cages. Next is **Fort Funston,** with easy hiking trails, great views of the ocean and coastal scenery, and hang gliders floating overhead. Locals call this place Fort Fun.

Golden Gate Park

In a city awash in greenery, Golden Gate Park is San Francisco's biggest open space; in fact, it's the largest man-made urban park in the world. The park dazzles visitors with a nearly endless succession of sandy beaches, urban vistas, rolling coastal hills, and the wide expanse of the Pacific Ocean. Exploration of the 1,040-acre park, which stretches from Haight-Ashbury in the east for 52 blocks to the Pacific coast in the west, could take days. Ideally, the best way to discover Golden Gate Park is to wander aimlessly. That, unfortunately, isn't an option for most visitors. The park slopes gently from east to west and is roughly divided into two parts. The easternmost part

*un*official **TIP**
Overall Golden Gate Park is safe, but it's a good idea to stay on well-populated paths and avoid the park entirely on foot after dark.

golden gate park

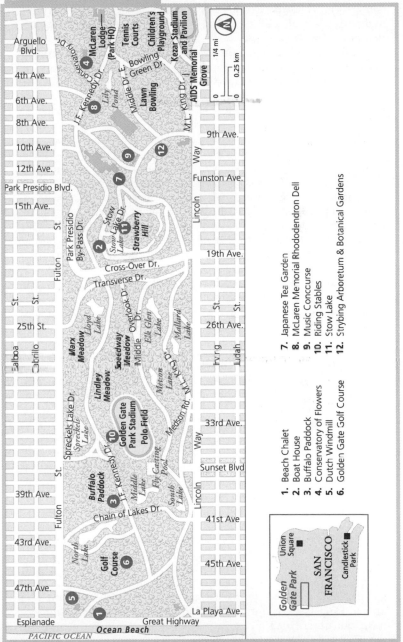

Arguello Blvd.
4th Ave.
6th Ave.
8th Ave.
10th Ave.
12th Ave.
Park Presidio Blvd.
15th Ave.

McLaren Lodge (Park HQ)
Tennis Courts
Children's Playground
Kezar Stadium and Pavilion
AIDS Memorial Grove
E. Bowling Green Dr.
Lawn Bowling
Lily Pond
Conservatory Dr.
J.F. Kennedy Dr.
Middle Dr.
M.L. King Dr.

9th Ave.
Funston Ave.
19th Ave.
26th Ave.

Stow Lake Dr.
Strawberry Hill
Stow Lake
Park Presidio By-Pass Dr.
Cross-Over Dr.
Transverse Dr.

Fulton St.
Balboa St.
Cabrillo St.
25th St.

Marx Meadow
Lloyd Lake
Speedway Meadow
Overlook Dr.
Middle Dr.
Elk Glen Lake
Mallard Lake
Metson Dr.
Meteor Lane Dr.
M.L. King Dr.

Irving St.
Judah St.
33rd Ave.

Lindley Meadow
Golden Gate Park Stadium Polo Field
Spreckels Lake Dr.
Spreckels Lake
Buffalo Paddock
J.F. Kennedy Dr.
Middle Lake
Fly Casting Pool
South Lake
Chain of Lakes Dr.

Sunset Blvd
Lincoln Way
41st Ave.
45th Ave.
47th Ave.

39th Ave.
43rd Ave.
Fulton St.
North Lake
Golf Course

Esplanade
Great Highway
La Playa Ave.
Ocean Beach
PACIFIC OCEAN

1/4 mi
0.25 km
0

1. Beach Chalet
2. Boat House
3. Buffalo Paddock
4. Conservatory of Flowers
5. Dutch Windmill
6. Golden Gate Golf Course
7. Japanese Tea Garden
8. McLaren Memorial Rhododendron Dell
9. Music Concourse
10. Riding Stables
11. Stow Lake
12. Strybing Arboretum & Botanical Gardens

Golden Gate Park
Union Square
SAN FRANCISCO
Candlestick Park

contains all the main attractions—art and science museums, horti-cultural gardens, bandstands, and the Japanese Tea Garden. The western end is less developed, contains more open space and trails, and has a less-sculpted look. It's also where you'll find a herd of buf-falo and a Dutch windmill.

Golden Gate Park's major attraction is the **de Young Memorial Museum,** a gallery of mostly American art, which was closed for ren-ovation until late 2005 (it was still closed at presstime). Across the Music Concourse is the **California Academy of Sciences,** a popular des-tination for families that includes a planetarium and an aquarium; kids love the place. (Too bad it's closed for renovation until 2008.)

The **Japanese Tea Garden** shows how trees, landscape, rocks, and buildings can be arranged into a work of art; you can also get tea and cookies served by kimono-clad waitresses. The **Strybing Arboretum** is 70 gorgeous acres of lawns and trees illustrating the diversity of plant life that thrives in San Francisco's Mediterranean-style climate.

While most people head to the western end of the park to do noth-ing whatsoever, **Stow Lake** can also feed the urge to loaf. Boats of all types—including the nonrowing kind—are available for rent by the hour, as are bicycles for riding on the nearly flat paths that honeycomb the park. You'll also find restrooms, drinking water, and a snack bar.

A herd of buffalo roam inside the **Bison Paddock** off JFK Drive at 38th Avenue. You can get close to the shaggy (and once nearly extinct) beasts at their feeding area near the western end. At the edge of the park near the ocean is a tulip garden and a Dutch windmill (a can't-be-missed landmark).

Haight-Ashbury

Hippies and the Haight. You can't have one without the other. The Haight was once the free-love zone and although the era of free sex, love, drugs, and the Grateful Dead has found restful solitude in the hearts of its followers and present-day wannabes, the Haight remains true to its tie-dye roots. Just take a stroll and you'll see for yourself—from Mama's tattoo parlor, leather and vintage shops, to the flowers and candles left at 710 Ashbury Street, the one-time home of the Grateful Dead. The biggest flashback of the year occurs during the Haight Street Fair in June—a must-see for all!

About eight blocks long, the area is surrounded by gorgeous restored Edwardian and Victorian houses. Today, though, there are more home-less than hippies on the blocks around the district's epicenter at Haight and Ashbury Streets. A neighborhood of more than 1,000 Victorian houses in decline in the 1950s, the Haight was reborn with the hippie movement of the late 1960s. The big houses were subdivided into flats, and the flower children disseminated the values of the counterculture all around Haight Street. But idealism mixed with drugs and unemploy-ment didn't prove to be an effective formula for social improvement. In the 1970s and 1980s the neighborhood devolved into a place only street-wise natives could navigate safely. With the rise of real-estate prices

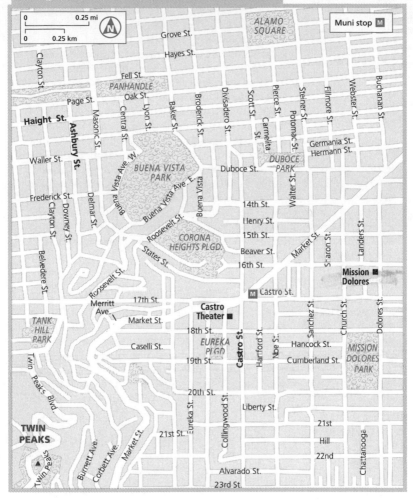

haight-ashbury and the castro

around the city, gentrification has set in—although the drug-dazed, backpack-toting drifters asking for change are still common. Today young execs and upper-middle-class professionals rub shoulders with the homeless remnants of the hippie era. The result is a tense bustle of eclectic eccentrics, perfect for people-watchers.

Japantown

Bounded by Geary Boulevard and California Street, Octavia, and Fillmore streets, Japantown is called home by only about 4% of San Francisco's Japanese-American residents. Most, though, return regularly for shopping and social and religious activities. The construction of

unofficial **TIP**
For a taste of ethnicity, visit Japantown on weekends, especially in spring and summer, when many Japanese cultural events, from tea ceremonies to martial arts demonstrations and musical performances, take place.

Japan Center in 1968 was the inspiration for a community renewal effort, with residents and merchants pitching in to beautify the surrounding blocks. The block-long Buchanan Mall, landscaped with flowering trees and fountains, marks the center's northern entrance.

Full of restaurants and stores, **Japan Center** is also the home of the **Japanese Consulate** and the **Kabuki Complex,** an eight-screen, ultramodern movie complex that hosts the Independent Film Festival annually. The other highlight at Japan Center is the **Kabuki Hot Springs,** genuine Japanese baths that offer shiatsu massage, steam baths, and other luxuriating facilities.

Compared to Chinatown, Japantown looks bland, well tended, and new. Places of interest include the Buddhist Church of San Francisco (Pine Street and Octavia Street), a sumptuous temple filled with what are claimed to be relics of Buddha, and St. Mary's Cathedral (where Geary Boulevard meets Gough Street), the city's newest Roman Catholic cathedral (1971). Walk inside and gaze at the cathedral's 190-foot dome.

Twin Peaks

Ah yes, the Jekyll and Hyde temperament of Twin Peaks. It is at once the granddaddy of inspiration points and one of San Francisco's most distinctive landmarks and, at the same time, the foggiest, most mist-filled part of town. You love it for the views but hate it for the behind-a-waterfall, bring-the-raincoat, and need-some-Prozac kinda weather.

Why is the district called Twin Peaks? There are two hills that make up the area, and Spanish explorers first called them "breasts of the Indian girl," but prudish Americans settled on the less-descriptive Twin Peaks. The peaks' slopes contain curving roads that feature some of the most expensive homes in San Francisco, a testament to the theory that the better the view, the higher the price of real estate. And what a view! The 360-degree overlook, on a clear evening, is magical.

unofficial **TIP**
Both the Golden Gate and Bay bridges are visible, as is all of downtown and its surrounding districts. A hot date spot for sure!

Luckily, Twin Peaks is one of a few hills in the city spared from development, making a walk, bike ride, or drive to the top doable. (It's also on the itinerary of almost every tour bus in town, so keep that in mind.)

Richmond and the Sunset

Don't let the name fool you. The Sunset is not very sunny. Due to the heavy fog that blankets the area through most of the year, much of the Sunset District has developed a distinctly quiet and residential character. The vast size of the district, however, has fostered the development of several varied and vibrant neighborhoods. The west end of the Sunset (abutting the Pacific Ocean) bears a closer resemblance to a beach town than a suburb; surfers and nature lovers brave the cool sea spray to combine the convenience of city living with a raw outdoor lifestyle. The San Francisco Zoo borders the Sunset to the south, as does the Stonestown Galleria, a large mall complex. Along the northeastern border, the Upper Haight meets the Sunset to produce a quieter and more upscale neighborhood with a 1960s-influenced mindset, including the requisite cafes and poetry readings. The southeastern corner runs up to the western side of Twin Peaks and the neighborhoods of Forest Hill and West Portal. This area around Eighth Avenue and Irving Street is filled with local but city-wide favorite food stops such as The House (Asian fusion) and Café For All Seasons (French Bistro), in addition to a wide array of Chinese restaurants and Japanese noodle parlors and sushi bars.

ACROSS TWO BRIDGES:
THE BAY AREA AND NEARBY CITIES

THE EAST BAY, AS YOU WILL HEAR IT REFERRED, consists of Berkeley and Oakland and is connected to San Francisco via the double-decker Bay Bridge. The red pillars of the Golden Gate Bridge connect the city to points north, including Marin County, Sausalito, Tiburon, Marin City, and Mill Valley. North of these points on US 101 above Marin County are Petaluma and Santa Rosa (57 miles away), and, slightly to the east, country valleys Napa and Sonoma (about 60 miles away). About 125 miles north along the rugged coastline is Mendocino, a small picturesque town that was once a logging village and then became a haven for artists in the 1950s. The Oregon state line is almost 400 miles to the north.

The Sierra Nevada Mountains and the Nevada state line are about 200 miles east of the city. Yosemite National Park, southeast of San Francisco in the Sierra Nevada range, is 184 miles away. Fifty miles south along the peninsula (below the southern end of San Francisco Bay) are San Jose and Silicon Valley. South along the coast are the cities of Santa Cruz (80 miles), Monterey (115 miles), Santa Barbara (320 miles), Los Angeles (400 miles), and San Diego (550 miles).

THE MAJOR HIGHWAYS

SAN FRANCISCO'S MAJOR HIGHWAY, US 101, LINKS Seattle and San Diego along the Pacific Coast. The freeway threads its way through the city on Van Ness Avenue after crossing the Golden Gate Bridge at the northwestern tip of the city and continues south along the peninsula to San Jose and beyond.

I-80 crosses the San Francisco–Oakland Bay Bridge and continues northeasterly to Sacramento. I-80 also intersects with I-580 and I-880 in Oakland. I-580 (the Eastshore Freeway) heads north toward Richmond and then swings west across San Pablo Bay to San Rafael and

US 101, north of San Francisco. To the south, I-880 follows the eastern shore of San Francisco Bay south toward San Jose, while I-580 swings east toward Stockton and an intersection with I-5, the inland interstate link that runs from Vancouver to San Diego.

Below San Francisco, I-280 begins south of the city and parallels US 101 toward Redwood City, Stanford, and Sunnyvale; its northern end is one of the most beautiful stretches of interstate highway in the country. US 101 (here called the Bayshore Freeway) follows the western shore of San Francisco Bay on a more direct route to the cities of Palo Alto, Santa Clara, and San Jose.

The Layout

Someone back in the day had the idea to lay the city out on a grid. A nice concept when considering flat terrain like New York City, but when you are negotiating a stick shift up steep Divisadero, Lombard, or Filbert streets, you'll be sweating bricks and cursing the wise guy! Admittedly the city is easy to navigate as a result of this checkerboard pattern. The city's 42 hills, like stones beneath a checked tablecloth, divide the city into areas that are the foundation for distinctive neighborhoods. If you know the cross street when searching for an address, the task is fairly simple. The major east/west axis is Geary Boulevard, which runs from downtown to the Pacific Ocean. The major north/south streets are Van Ness Avenue, Divisadero Street, and Park Presidio Boulevard. The exception is Market Street, which cuts diagonally across the city from the Embarcadero to the Castro.

unofficial **TIP**
It would be nice if street addresses along Market, Mission, and other streets in the SoMa District had street numbers that corresponded with the intersecting numerical streets, but they don't.

Most of San Francisco's streets are very long, with numbers typically ranging from 1 to 4000. Street numbers get higher going from east to west and from south to north. Distances are measured in blocks, with numbers rising by 100 from block to block. South of Market Street the streets are numbered (beginning with First Street and continuing through 30th Street). Do not confuse these streets with the numbered avenues that begin three miles west of downtown and run from Second Avenue to 48th Avenue at the ocean.

Throughout the northwest sector of the city (downtown to Fisherman's Wharf) and in the cookie-cutter neighborhood of Sunset, streets are one-way, with the exceptions of Columbus Avenue, Market Street, and Van Ness Avenue. When traffic on a street goes only one way, the traffic in the two streets on either side of it move in the opposite direction.

MAJOR ARTERIES AND STREETS

MARKET STREET IS SAN FRANCISCO'S MAIN DRAG. Many of the city's buses and streetcars follow this route from the outlying suburbs past the Castro and Mission districts, Civic Center, SoMa, and Union

Square to the downtown Financial District. Underground subways operated by BART and light-rail trains operated by Muni Metro load and disgorge passengers at seven underground stations located along Market Street.

The tall office buildings clustered downtown are at the northeast end of Market Street; one block beyond lie the Embarcadero and the bay. The building with the tall tower at the end of the street is the Ferry Building, one of a few major structures to survive the 1906 earthquake and fire (and now a recently refurbished food and produce market). The Embarcadero curves along San Francisco Bay from south of the Bay Bridge to the northeast perimeter of the city and ends at Fisherman's Wharf, San Francisco's famous cluster of piers and tourist attractions. (The elevated freeway used to continue along the bay west of the wharf but was almost completely removed after the 1989 earthquake, much to the relief of many San Franciscans, who can now enjoy unimpeded views of the bay.) Beyond Fisherman's Wharf are Aquatic Park, Fort Mason, the Presidio, and Golden Gate National Recreation Area, all linked by the Golden Gate Promenade, a three-and-a-half-mile pedestrian walkway.

From the eastern perimeter of Fort Mason, Van Ness Avenue runs due south back to Market Street; it's also US 101 south of the Golden Gate Bridge. The rough triangle formed by these three major thoroughfares—Market Street to the southeast, the Embarcadero and the waterfront to the north, and Van Ness Avenue to the west—contains most of the city's major tourist attractions and neighborhoods of interest to visitors.

OTHER MAJOR STREETS

A FEW OTHER MAJOR THOROUGHFARES THAT visitors are bound to encounter include Mission Street, which parallels Market Street to the south in SoMa; it's also the main street in the Mission District south of downtown. Montgomery Street in the Financial District links to Columbus Avenue in North Beach, while Bay, Jefferson, and Beach streets are major east-west arteries in and around Fisherman's Wharf.

Grant Avenue is Chinatown's touristy main street, while Powell Street runs north-south from Market Street to the bay past Union Square; it's also a major cable-car route, as the street climbs Nob Hill. Lincoln Boulevard is the major road through the Presidio, a former army base at the northwest corner of the city that's now part of Golden Gate National Recreation Area.

Geary Boulevard, California Street, and Broadway are major east-west streets downtown; Geary goes the distance to the Pacific Ocean, where it merges with Point Lobos Avenue just before reaching Cliff House, a major tourist landmark. Visitors following signs for US 101 on Van Ness Avenue to reach the Golden Gate Bridge will make a left onto Lombard Street, then zoom past the Palace of Fine Arts as they approach the famous span.

At the southern end of Market Street (just past Twin Peaks) the name changes to Portola Drive; turn right on Sloat Boulevard to reach the San Francisco Zoo and Ocean Beach. There you'll find Great Highway, which parallels the ocean. Turn right on Great Highway and head north to reach the western end of Golden Gate Park (look for the Dutch windmill). The park's main drag is John F. Kennedy Drive, which is closed to traffic on Sundays. At the eastern end of Golden Gate Park are Fell and Oak streets, which head east to Van Ness Avenue and Market Street.

THINGS *the* NATIVES *already* KNOW

TIPPING

EVERYBODY NEEDS A REFRESHER COURSE ON THE tipping protocol. To start, tipping is not a question. Do tip, it's as simple as that. You'll find service to be outstanding at restaurants, hotels, and even in taxis. Here are some guidelines for those sticky moments when you are left wondering if the hotel or restaurant is spitting in your food or naming their first born after you.

PORTERS AND SKYCAPS $2 a bag.

CAB DRIVERS A lot depends on service and courtesy. If the fare is less than $8, give the driver the change and $1. Example: If the fare is $4.50, give the cabbie fifty cents and a buck for tip. If the fare is more than $8, give the driver the change and $2. If you ask the cabbie to take you only a block or two, the fare will be small, but your tip should be large ($2–$3) to make up for his or her wait in line and to partially compensate him or her for missing a better-paying fare. Add an extra dollar to your tip if the driver handles a lot of luggage.

unofficial TIP
You'll find the cab drivers in San Francisco the most amusing and interesting of most major cities. Strike up a conversation and learn what makes them tick!

PARKING VALETS $2 is correct if the valet is courteous and demonstrates some hustle. $1 will do if the service is just OK. Pay only when you check your car out, not when you leave it.

BELLMEN AND DOORMEN When a bellman greets you at your car with a rolling luggage cart and handles all of your bags, $5 is about right. The more luggage you carry yourself, of course, the less you should tip. Add another $1 or $2 if the bellman opens your room. For calling a taxi, tip the doorman $1–$2.

WAITERS Whether in a coffee shop, an upscale eatery, or room service from the hotel kitchen, the standard gratuity range is 15–20% of the tab, before sales tax. At a buffet or brunch where you serve yourself, leave a dollar or two for the person who brings your drinks. Some restaurants, however, are adopting the European custom of automatically adding a 15% gratuity to the bill, so check before leaving a cash tip.

COCKTAIL WAITERS AND BARTENDERS Here you tip by the round. For two people, $1 a round; for more than two people, $2 a round. For a large group, use your judgment: Is everyone drinking beer, or is the order long and complicated? Tip accordingly.

HOTEL MAIDS When you check out, leave $1–$3 per day for each day of your stay, provided service was good.

HOW TO LOOK AND SOUND LIKE A NATIVE

YOU MAY FEEL THE PRESSURE TO POLISH UP on beatnik literature, pull out those old bell-bottoms, or read the latest version of Windows in order to fit in San Francisco. Home to artists, performers, intellectuals, and folks of every describable (and sometimes indescribable) sexual bent, the city is where most of America's new personal, technical, and social trends materialize. If it's important to you not to look like a visitor on holiday, disguise the camera and adhere to the following advice.

1. If you do the Fishermen's Wharf thing, don't wear shorts and a T-shirt; freezing, underdressed tourists huddling for warmth at the wharf is an enduring San Francisco cliché.
2. Don't call cable cars "trolleys."
3. Don't pronounce Ghirardelli with a soft "g"; the square's name is pronounced "GEAR-ar-delly."
4. Never utter the two-syllable "Frisco." We are not responsible for what could happen should you get caught saying this.
5. Carry a sweater when it's 75° outside, 'cause chances are the temp will drop.
6. Rice-A-Roni originated on Madison Avenue. Nobody here eats it.

LOCAL PUBLICATIONS

SAN FRANCISCO HAS ONE OF THE LARGEST DAILY newspapers in the country, the *San Francisco Chronicle,* **www.sfgate.com,** published in the morning. The Sunday edition "pink section," so called because, hold onto your hats, it's pink, is the Bay Area's bible of arts, leisure, entertainment and all other social goings-on.

Free weekly tabloid papers include the *San Francisco Bay Guardian,* **www.sfbg.com,** and the *SF Weekly,* **www.sfweekly.com.** Both offer coverage on everything from art to politics and generally provide more detailed information on local nightlife and entertainment than the dailies. *Where San Francisco* is a free monthly magazine for tourists, offering information on shopping, dining, and entertainment, as well as maps and listings of things to do while in town; look for a copy in your hotel room. *Bay City Guide,* **www.bay cityguide.com,** found in many museums and shops, is a free monthly magazine; it provides maps and listings of things to do for visitors.

San Francisco Magazine, **www.sanfran.com,** is the city's leading glossy magazine, and it focuses on dining, the arts, entertainment, and ten-best lists. A city magazine in direct competition with *San Francisco Magazine* is *7 x 7,* **www.7x7mag.com**—named for the city's square area. It aims to provide more in-depth, investigative pieces as opposed to the cookie-cutter top-ten lists and such that *San Francisco Magazine* produces. *San Francisco Arts Monthly,* **www.sfarts.org,** is a tabloid listing the city's visual and performing arts calendars. *Street Sheet,* sold by homeless and formerly homeless people on the city's streets for a buck, provides a street-level view of homelessness and helps the homeless earn money. The *Bay Area Reporter,* **www.ebar.com,** distributed free on Thursdays, covers the gay community, including in-depth news, information, and a weekly calendar of goings-on for gays and lesbians.

LIVE FROM WKR–SAN FRANCISCO

ASIDE FROM THE BABBLE OF FORMAT ROCK, easy listening, and country music stations, San Francisco is home to radio stations that really stand out for high-quality broadcasting. Tune in to what hip San Franciscans listen to:

SAN FRANCISCO'S HIGH-QUALITY RADIO STATIONS		
FORMAT	FREQUENCY	STATION
Jazz	91.1 FM	KCSM
NPR	91.7 FM	KQED
Talk, classical, community affairs	94.1 FM	KPFA
Classical	102.1 FM	KDFC
Rock	104.5 FM	KFOG
Rock	105.3 FM	KTIS

A good Saturday-morning outing is to NPR's taping of "West Coast Live" radio show, hosted by Sedge Thomson at Fort Mason. For $15–$18 you can be part of the audience of fascinating interviews with musicians, authors, poets, comics, and so on. Bring your best sound effects because the audience is usually called upon to create some together. (Contact at ☎ 415-664-9500 or **www.wcl.org.**)

ACCESS FOR THE DISABLED

STEEP HILLS ASIDE, TRAVELERS WITH MOBILITY problems are likely to find San Francisco more in tune with their needs than other

U.S. cities; it's considered one of the most barrier-free towns around. Nearly all buildings and public transportation are equipped for easy access. In compliance with the Americans with Disabilities Act, direction signs, toilets, and entrances are adapted for blind and disabled visitors. Many theaters (both movie and stage) offer special audio equipment for hearing-impaired people.

Parking spaces reserved for people with disabled permits are marked by a blue-and-white sign and a blue curb; frequently a wheelchair outline is painted on the pavement. Disabled persons may pay a $6 fee and present a state-of-origin permit or plaque with photo I.D. to get a temporary permit at the Department of Motor Vehicles (1377 Fell Street; ☎ 415-557-1170); there's a service window reserved for the disabled.

Most street corners downtown have dropped curbs and most city buses have wheelchair lifts. Major museums throughout the Bay Area are fitted with wheelchair ramps, and many hotels offer special accommodations and services for wheelchair-bound visitors.

All Muni Metro and BART stations are wheelchair accessible. Wheelchair-boarding platforms are located at many stops, including some islands on Market Street. In addition, Muni operates more than 30 accessible bus lines. For a complete listing of transit lines, including a chart indicating which lines offer disabled access, pick up a copy of the *Official San Francisco Street and Transit Map,* available at most newsstands for $3. Call ☎ 415-923-6336 (touch-tone only) to get recorded schedule information. For more information on disabled access to public transportation or a *Muni Access Guide,* write to the Accessible Services Program, 949 Presidio, San Francisco, CA 94115, call ☎ 415-673-6864 or 415-923-6366 (TDD), or visit **www.sfmuni.com/rider.**

A Paratransit Taxi Service provides discount taxi service to qualified disabled persons unable to use fixed Muni lines; to get a certificate, call the San Francisco Paratransit Broker at ☎ 415-351-7000. Golden Gate Transit, which operates buses between the city and Marin County, publishes a handbook on accessible equipment and procedures; to get a copy of *Welcome Aboard,* call ☎ 415-923-2000 or 415-257-4554 (TDD).

TIME ZONE

SAN FRANCISCO IS IN THE PACIFIC TIME ZONE, which puts it three hours behind New York, two hours behind Chicago, one hour behind the Rocky Mountains, and eight hours behind Greenwich Mean Time.

PHONES

THE SAN FRANCISCO AREA IS SERVED BY THREE area codes: 415 inside the city and Marin County, 510 in Alameda and Contra Costa counties in the East Bay (including Oakland and Berkeley), and 650 to the south in San Mateo County and around San Francisco International Airport. Calls from pay phones range from 35 to 50 cents (depending on which carrier owns the pay phone); if you talk for more than three minutes, additional payments may be requested. To call outside the 415 area code, dial 1 plus the appropriate area code and the seven-digit number.

LIQUOR, TAXES, AND SMOKING

LIQUOR AND GROCERY STORES AND SOME DRUGSTORES sell packaged alcohol from 6 a.m. to 2 a.m. daily. Most restaurants, bars, and nightclubs are licensed to serve a full line of alcoholic beverages during these hours, although some have permits to sell beer and wine only. The legal drinking age is 21.

An 8.5% sales tax is added to purchases in San Francisco. If your purchases are shipped to a destination outside of California, they're exempt from the sales tax. An 8.5% tax is added to restaurant bills, and most hotels tack on a 14% room tax to the bill.

Before you light up, think twice in San Francisco. The city has stiff antismoking laws, making it illegal to light up in offices, public buildings, banks, lobbies, stores, sports arenas, stadiums, public transportation, and theaters. This extends into bars and restaurants. The no-smoking-in-bars law gets cheers and jeers. Nonsmokers, you won't come home smelling like the Marlboro man, but you may find yourself solo at the bar while your compadres escape to the front for a drag every 15 minutes.

HOW *to* AVOID CRIME *and* KEEP SAFE *in* PUBLIC PLACES

CRIME IN SAN FRANCISCO

SAN FRANCISCO, LIKE ANY LARGE CITY, HAS ITS share of violent crime, drug abuse, and poverty. But the good news for visitors is that by and large the city is safe. San Francisco ranks low among U.S. cities for serious crime.

Downtown San Francisco, where tourists and business visitors spend most of their time, is unusually safe for a large city. "One good thing is that we've got a very lively downtown with lots of different things going on at all hours of the day. It's never completely dead," notes Dewayne Tully, a police service aid with the San Francisco Police Department. "Even the Financial District, an area usually dead at night in most cities, has lots of clubs and restaurants." Because of crowds and 24-hour foot, horse, motorcycle, and car patrols by San Francisco's finest, few visitors to San Francisco are victims of street crime.

EXERCISING CAUTION: SOME HOT SPOTS

CERTAIN NEIGHBORHOODS REQUIRE DIFFERENT behaviors. The Tenderloin area, on the downtown side of the Civic Center, is a rather seedy part of town. Interesting culturally, this area, as well as the Mission District, houses most of the city's diminishing minority populations. Both districts have resisted the gentrification that has swept most of the city's neighborhoods. But after dark the Tenderloin and the Mission get suspect. There are usually always people hanging around. If you come from other big cities, like New York, Miami, or Chicago, it will be nothing you aren't used to. Just take a few precautions. Women should leave purses at home. Put money in your bras, and leave the noticeably sparkling carats in the jewelry boxes at home. Checking over your shoulder constantly will only bring attention to your wary wanderings. Be cautious but look confident and secure, and you should be fine. South of downtown, Market Street also gets seedy and is a haven for vagrants from about Fifth Street west to Gough Street. If you head out to any of these areas at night, simply take a taxi to your destination. If you have to walk a few blocks you will most likely be fine. Some of San Francisco's hottest neighborhoods for nightlife, including Mission, SoMa, and Haight-Ashbury, also require some extra caution at night.

If you are the victim of a crime or witness one, you can get immediate police, fire, or medical assistance by dialing 911 from any pay phone without inserting money. For nonemergency help (for instance, to report a car break-in), dial the San Francisco Police Department at ☎ 415-553-0123. For more information on personal safety in San Francisco, call San Francisco SAFE, Inc. (SAFE stands for Safety Awareness for Everyone) at ☎ 415-673-SAFE; **www.sfsafe.org.**

unofficial **TIP**
Men can carry two wallets. Carry an inexpensive wallet in your hip pocket with about $20 in cash and some expired credit cards. This is the one you hand over if you're accosted. Your real credit cards and the bulk of whatever cash you have should be in a money clip or a second wallet hidden elsewhere on your person. Women can carry a fake wallet in their purse and keep the real one in a pocket or money belt.

THE DOS AND DON'TS

1. Have a plan: Random violence and street crime are facts of life in any large city. Be cautious and alert, and plan ahead. When you're out and about, know your route and have your agenda somewhat outlined; that way you appear to know what you are doing and where you are going.

2. Confirm your route or transportation with your hotel.

3. Leave all valuables in a safe deposit box in your hotel or at home.

4. Leave identification on your children indicating a phone number or hotel where you are staying in case they become lost or separated from you.

5. Write down all traveler's check numbers and leave them at home or at the hotel.

6. Girls, the bra is still a viable option for money! Guys, a money belt below the pants is a convenient way to carry wallet and money.

7. At night—women, keep your purses tucked under your arm; if you're wearing a coat, put it on over your shoulder-bag strap. If you're wearing rings, turn the setting palm-in.

8. Be discreet: don't wave money around.

IF YOU'RE APPROACHED OR ACCOSTED

IN PUBLIC TRANSPORT Transportation in the city is quite organized and generally safe. It becomes questionable late at night when riders are few. If you find yourself riding the bus or train at night, it is best to take a seat close to the conductor or bus driver. These people have a phone and can summon help in the event of trouble.

IN CABS At night, it's best to go to one of the hotel stands or phone for a cab. If you suspect foul play on the cab driver's part, check the driver's certificate, which by law must be posted on the dashboard. Address the cabbie by his last name or mention the number of his cab. This alerts the driver to the fact that you are going to remember him and/or his cab. Not only will this contribute to your safety, it will keep your cabbie from trying to run up the fare. Generally, though, the cabs in the city are safe and the drivers can be quite interesting to talk with!

If you need to catch a cab at the train stations, bus terminals, or airports, always use the taxi queue. Taxis in the official queue are properly licensed and regulated. Never accept an offer for a cab or limo made by a stranger in the terminal or baggage claim. At best, you may be significantly overcharged for the ride. At worst, you may be abducted.

SELF-DEFENSE

IN A SITUATION WHERE IT IS IMPOSSIBLE TO RUN, you'll need to be prepared to defend yourself. Most police insist that a gun or knife is not much use to the average person. More often than not, they say, the weapon will be turned against the victim. The best self-defense device for the average person is Mace. Not only is it legal in most states, it's nonlethal and easy to use.

When you shop for Mace, look for two things. The dispenser should be able to fire about eight feet, and it should have a protector cap so it won't go off by mistake in your purse or pocket. Carefully read the directions that come with your device, paying particular attention to how it should be carried and stored and how long the active ingredients will remain potent. Wear a rubber glove and test-fire your Mace, making sure you fire downwind.

When you are out about town, make sure your Mace is easily accessible, say, attached to your keychain. If you are a woman and you keep your Mace on a keychain, avoid the habit of dropping your keys (and the Mace) into the depths of your purse when you leave your hotel room or car. The Mace will not do you any good if you have to dig for it. Keep your keys and your Mace in your hand until you safely reach your destination.

CARJACKINGS AND HIGHWAY ROBBERY

WITH THE RECENT SURGE IN CARJACKINGS, DRIVERS also need to take special precautions. "Keep alert when you're driving in traffic," one police official warns. "Keep your doors locked, with the windows rolled up and the air-conditioning or heat on. In traffic, leave enough space in front of you so that you can make a U-turn and aren't blocked in. That way, if someone approaches your car and starts beating on your windshield, you can drive off." Store your purse or briefcase under your knees when you are driving, not on the seat beside you.

Also be aware of other drivers bumping you from the rear or driving alongside you and gesturing that something is wrong with your car. In either case, do not stop or get out of your car. Continue until you reach a very public and well-lit place where you can check things out and, if necessary, get help.

RIPOFFS AND SCAMS

A LIVELY STREET SCENE IS AN INCUBATOR FOR RIPOFFS and scams. Although pickpockets, scam artists, and tricksters work throughout San Francisco, they are particularly thick in Union Square, along the Embarcadero and Fisherman's Wharf, and at BART stations. While some scams are relatively harmless, others can be costly and dangerous.

Pickpockets work in teams, sometimes using children. One person creates a diversion, such as dropping coins, spilling ice cream on you, or trying to sell you something, and a second person deftly picks your pocket. In most cases your stolen wallet is almost instantaneously passed to a third team member walking by. Even if you realize immediately that your wallet has been lifted, the pickpocket will have unburdened the evidence.

Because pickpockets come in all sizes and shapes, be especially wary of any encounter with a stranger. Anyone from a man in a nice suit asking directions or a six-year-old wobbling toward you on in-line skates could be creating a diversion for a pickpocket. The primary tip-off to a con or scam is someone approaching you. If you ask help of somebody in a store or restaurant, you are doing the approaching and the chances of being the victim of a scam are quite small. When a stranger approaches you, however, regardless of the reason, beware.

Most travelers carry a lot more cash, credit cards, and other stuff in their wallet than they need. If you plan to walk in San Francisco or anywhere else, transfer exactly what you think you will need to a very small, low-profile wallet or pouch. When the *Unofficial Guide* authors are on the street, they carry one American Express card, one VISA card, and a minimum amount of cash. Think about it. You do not need your gas credit cards if you're walking, and you don't need all those hometown department store credit cards if you're away from home.

Don't carry your wallet and valuables in a fanny pack. Thieves and pickpockets can easily snip the belt and disappear into the crowd with the pack before you realize what's happened. As far as pockets are concerned, front pockets are safer than back pockets or suitcoat pockets, though pickpockets (with a little extra effort) can get at front pockets, too. The safest place to carry valuables is under your arm in a holster-style shoulder pouch. Lightweight, comfortable, and especially accessible when worn under a coat or vest, shoulder pouches are available from catalogs and most good travel stores. Incidentally, avoid pouches that are worn on your chest and suspended by a cord around your neck. Like the fanny pack, they can be easily cut off or removed by pickpockets.

THE HOMELESS

IF YOU'RE NOT FROM A BIG CITY OR HAVEN'T visited one in a while, you're in for a shock when you come to San Francisco, where there is a large homeless population. The homeless are more evident in some areas than others, but you're likely to bump into them just about anywhere. Take a drive down Van Ness Avenue and you will see one perched at almost every street corner with the most amusing signs. "No lies. It's for beer," reads one. They definitely are most creative in their approach.

Most homeless people are harmless and are simply looking for a little help here and there. Don't be afraid of them. And if you feel the urge to give, keep a little pocket change handy. If you are approached for money and don't want to or can't give anything, the best method is to say, "Sorry, I don't have anything." A simple acknowledgment goes a long way and they most likely will part your company with a "Have a nice day," or "God bless you." There is a notion, perhaps valid in some instances, that money given to a homeless person generally goes toward the purchase of alcohol or drugs. If this bothers you, carry granola bars for distribution or buy some inexpensive gift coupons that can be redeemed at a McDonald's or other fast-food restaurant for coffee or a sandwich.

Those moved to get more involved in the nationwide problem of homelessness can send inquiries—or a check—to the National Coalition for the Homeless, 1612 K Street, NW, Suite 1004, Washington, D.C. 20006; **www.nationalhomeless.org.**

PART FIVE

GETTING AROUND

DRIVING *your* CAR

YOU'LL HAVE A LOVE/HATE RELATIONSHIP WITH DRIVING in San Francisco. In one sense, the city's best sites and scenery are most easily explored in a car (mix one convertible and a sunny day for an unforgettable experience). From Route 1 along the Pacific Coast, driving across the Golden Gate Bridge to the Headlands or Mount Tamalpais, to driving through rolling vineyards of Napa or Sonoma, the Bay Area offers the best of scenic drives. And the hills . . . Filbert between Hyde and Leavenworth, Hill Street at 22nd, or Divisadero from Broadway to the Marina . . . white knuckled and gasping, you'll plunge over the edge maniacally laughing, yodeling, screaming . . . whatever inspires you! Stick-shift novices need not apply. The city is compact enough to get in a good bit of sights on your own time, too.

Here's where the hate parts come in. Finding parking, legal parking that is (many innovative parking-blazers have initiated rather creative solutions to the crunch), is frustrating. And to add insult to injury, traffic is a nightmare. There are even Web sites devoted to the highway horror (for example **www.sfbaytraffic.info**), or you can call ☎ 511 for up-to-date info on bridges and freeways. Downtown, near the financial center, is usually crowded throughout the day, but during peak rush hours of about 8 a.m. to 10 a.m. and 4:30 p.m. to 6:30 p.m., you'll feel about as slow-moving and cramped as the Tin Man without a lube job. Most of the traffic frustration comes into play when approaching either of the two bridges. The same goes for North Beach, Chinatown, and Telegraph Hill, areas infamous for traffic congestion and scarce parking.

Our advice is to keep your car in your hotel's garage and use it sparingly for excursions away from downtown and beyond the city or in the

unofficial **TIP**
Keep your car in your hotel's garage and use it only for excursions beyond the city or in the evenings after rush hour.

unofficial **TIP**
Before heading out of the
city by car, call California
Road Conditions for
information on haz-
ardous conditions.

evenings after rush hour. If you are planning to
go outside of the city, especially during winter
months, it is best to call California Road Conditions before heading out. They can inform you
of any mudslides, construction, or hazardous
weather conditions. Call ☎ 800-427-ROAD
(7623) if calling from within California or
☎ 916-445-ROAD (7623) if calling from outside California.

RENTAL CARS

ALL THE MAJOR CAR-RENTAL AGENCIES OPERATE in the city and
have desks at the airports. Take your pick from the national agencies of
Alamo, Avis, Budget, Dollar, Hertz, National, and Thrifty. There are also
some homegrown places to rent a car, like City Rent-A-Car (☎ 415-861-
1312), Fox Rent-A-Car (☎ 800-225-4369), or Specialty Car Rental
(☎ 800-400-8412), for your chance at that convertible or dream BMW 323i.

unofficial **TIP**
When renting a car in San
Francisco, purchase an insurance plan—the city is notorious for fender benders
and scrapes on vehicles.

All car-rental agencies usually require a
minimum age of 25, and fares range depending on class of car, length of rental, where and
when you pick up and drop off, and mileage
plans. Usually you can find good deals online
(**expedia.com** or **travelocity.com**). If you are an
uninsured driver, you may want to buy an insurance plan for the
duration of your rental. The city is notorious for fender benders and
nicks and scrapes on vehicles, so protect yourself—purchase the
insurance. Keep in mind also that some credit cards offer protection
as well. Inquire with the credit card company, or if you do have car
insurance, call to verify your plan.

unofficial **TIP**
Weekday rush hour is
from 6 a.m. to 10 a.m.
and from 3 p.m. to 7 p.m.

TIME OF DAY

SAN FRANCISCO'S WEEKDAY RUSH HOUR
starts as early as 6 a.m. and lasts until around
10 a.m.; it picks up again around 3 p.m. and
goes to as late as about 7 p.m. In between, traffic is congested but usually flows—at least beyond downtown and
Fisherman's Wharf.

Weekends, on the other hand, can be just as bad as weekday rush
hours—and often worse. While traffic on Saturday and Sunday mornings is usually light, it picks up around noon and doesn't let up until
well into the evening. Remember, about 6 million people live in the Bay
Area, and on weekends many of them jump in their cars and head to
San Francisco or to surrounding playgrounds across either bridge.

A PRAYER BEFORE PARKING

PARKING IS ONE OF THE MAIN REASONS *not* to explore San Francisco by car. In some areas you will drive around blocks for more than

an hour finding a vacant spot. Often, the meter is timed to allow only a half hour of parking (not a lot of time to go sightseeing or attend a business meeting) or if it's a nonmetered street you have only two hours without a color-coded neighborhood permit. Rules, rules, rules. Traffic cops and meter maids on their minimobiles uphold those rules diligently, and the meters, unless posted otherwise, are in effect Monday through Saturday, usually from 8 a.m. to 6 p.m. (Meter rates: downtown, $3 for one hour; Fisherman's Wharf, $2.50 for one hour; rest of the city, $1.50 for one hour.)

Colored curbs in San Francisco indicate reserved parking zones. Red means no stopping or parking; yellow indicates a half-hour loading limit for vehicles with commercial plates, yellow and black means a half-hour loading limit for trucks with commercial plates; green, yellow, and black indicates a taxi zone; and blue is for vehicles marked with a California-issued disabled placard or plate. Green is a ten-minute parking zone for all vehicles, and white is a five-minute limit for all vehicles.

San Francisco cops don't take parking regulations lightly, and any improperly used spot can become a tow-away zone. The number one source of citations in the city is failing to recognize street cleaning, which requires one side of the street to be vacated on particular days, usually during morning hours. Be aware of street-cleaning signs and stay out of parking lanes opened up for rush-hour traffic. Many residential neighborhoods have permit parking, and a parking ticket can cost you more than $50, plus $100 for towing and additional charges for storage. Parking in a bus zone or wheelchair-access space can set you back $250, while parking in a space marked handicapped or blocking access to a wheelchair ramp costs $275. If you get towed, go to the nearest district police department for a release and then pick up your car at the towing company.

From meters, color-coded permits and curbs, and the task of parallel parking—and, let's face it, there are some of you who haven't done it since driver's ed—you may wonder how to survive your trip without parking citations taking up half your scrapbook. You can opt for one of many city parking garages throughout the city's neighborhoods. They cost anywhere from $20 to $30 a day. Check with your

unofficial **TIP**
Check with your hotel to see if you can get a reduced rate at a nearby garage.

hotel to see if you can get a reduced rate at a nearby garage that allows unlimited access to your car. Or, take advantage of the city's convenient and reliable public transportation, or our favorite, foot it. Not for naught do we call this the "walking city."

When you're parking on San Francisco's steep hills, there is only one way to rest easy: curb your wheels. Turn the front tires away from the curb when your car is facing uphill so that if the brake fails, the car rolls back into the curb. If facing downhill, turn your wheels toward the curb so that the car can roll forward into the curb, effectively using it as a block. Because even the best brakes can fail, curbing your wheels is the law in San Francisco (and you'll see plenty of street signs to remind you).

THE "YOU DIDN'T KNOW TO ASK" Q & A:

- Should I park in the middle turning lane when I see others doing it? What you'll see sometimes in and around the Mission and SoMa, especially on busy weekend evenings, is that middle turning lanes become a row of parked cars. *Do not* follow the leader here—the city will dispatch tow trucks faster than you can say "Hold the anchovies."

- Where can I leave the car for a few days if I don't want to pay for a parking garage? This is just between you and us—one of the best-kept secrets of the Bay Area—the Presidio! Enter from Lombard Street in the Marina, or Park Presidio in the Richmond, and you'll enter parking paradise. No meters, and no permits necessary! The only threats to this parking nirvana are the leaves, pollen, and bird poop that come from tree-lined streets.

- What time in the morning should I move my car if it's parked in a two-hour permit zone? Usually the permit zones are enforced from 8 a.m. to 6 p.m. If you have left your car overnight you have until 10 a.m. (two hours past 8 a.m.).

- How do the traffic cops know that my car has exceeded the meter or permit limit? Remember kindergarten? Chalk! They chalk tires and check back to see if the car has or hasn't moved. One way around this is to check for chalk marks on your tires. If there are none, you might be good for another two hours. Or simply roll your car back and forth to get rid of it.

- Which areas are easiest for parking? The Marina is fairly easy but *do not* even come an inch over someone's driveway. They are sticklers about that sort of thing. Bernal Heights, Potrero Hill, and parts of Noe Valley are all pretty stress-free. What constitutes stress free, you might ask? Less than a 15-minute search.

- Where should I worry about theft or vandalism? The Mission, Chinatown, Financial, and Tenderloin districts are hot spots for broken windows, car break-ins, and keying. Never leave purses or CDs where they are visible from the window. Store them in the trunk.

- Why do I sometimes see cars parked on the sidewalks outside a house or apartment building? There is something fun about pulling up the curb onto the sidewalk and parking your vehicle! The thrill of trespassing is sweet indeed. There is a level of understanding between parking officials and residents. Usually it is tolerated during late hours (after midnight). But be ready for an early morning wake-up call to move it before anybody complains, or worse, you get busted!

PUBLIC TRANSPORTATION

SAN FRANCISCO MUNICIPAL RAILWAY (**www.sfmuni.com**), commonly called Muni, is a citywide transportation system that consists of all cable cars, streetcars (called Muni Metro), conventional buses, and electric buses. All fares are $1.50 for adults and 50 cents for seniors, disabled passengers (with a valid Regional Transit Connection Discount Card), and children ages 5–17; children ages 4 and under ride free. Cable-car fare is $5 per person (kids ages 4 and under ride free). One-dollar bills are accepted on most buses, but the drivers don't give change. If you need a transfer, ask for one when you board; it's free and valid for two hours and a maximum of two rides in any direction.

Many San Franciscans feel a fierce devotion to the system; some affectionately call it "Joe Muni." No wonder; it's a European-style transportation system that gets people around the city cheaply and efficiently. You're never more than a couple of blocks from a bus stop or train station. Not that it's without some drawbacks—buses can be jam-packed, especially at rush hour and on weekends, and occasionally you may have to wait for a bus while fully loaded buses pass you by. Yet despite its problems, riding Muni is interesting. You can learn more about the city from the friendly bus drivers and helpful passengers than from any guidebook.

PASSPORT TO SAVINGS

MUNI PASSPORTS ALLOW UNLIMITED USE OF all buses, cable cars, and Muni Metro streetcars in San Francisco. It's a great money-saving deal that makes it even easier and more convenient to use San Francisco's public transportation. In addition, Muni passports provide discounts at dozens of city attractions, including museums, theaters, and bay tours.

Muni passports come in three versions: one-day ($11), three-day ($18), and seven-day ($24). Pocket-sized and easy to use, the passports are available at locations throughout the city, including the San Francisco Convention and Visitors Bureau Visitor Information Center (in Hallidie Plaza at Powell and Market streets), TIX Bay Area (Powell Street on Union Square), and Muni (949 Presidio, room 239). Be sure to pick up a copy of the *Official San Francisco Street and Transit Map* for $3. To use a passport, scratch off the dates of the day (or days) you're using the pass and simply show it to the driver, who will wave you aboard.

unofficial **TIP**
Muni passports allow unlimited use of the entire public transportation system and provide discounts at many city attractions and tours.

BUSES

YOU'LL NEVER SEE A MORE CLEAN, QUIET, AND pollutant-free (thanks to some of the electric buses) or friendly bus service in any other city. Bus service in San Francisco reaches into all parts of the city

and beyond. Numbers are placed on the top of the bus with their destinations on the front. Along the streets, bus stops are indicated by signs
displaying the Muni logo; the route numbers of the buses serving the
stop are listed below the sign. Some stops are merely marked on light
posts with a yellow sign and the bus number spray painted in black.
Usually stops along a route are every three or four blocks. Some bus
stops have three-sided glass shelters, with route numbers painted on the
exterior and route maps posted inside. Along Market Street, some
buses stop at the curb while others stop at islands in the street.

When you board, give the driver $1.25 or flash your Muni pass-
port; if you need a transfer, get it as soon as you board. The driver
will rip off a transfer ticket and it is usually good for two hours. You
are only supposed to use the transfer for one
other bus ride, but if the bus driver doesn't take
it or you don't throw it away, you can keep
using it! It's one of those little treasures of public transportation. If you're not sure about
where to get off, ask the driver to let you know
when you're near your destination. Drivers are
usually considerate and glad to help. The buses
get very crowded at times. Often you will be
standing in the aisle and you may not be aware that your stop has
arrived. Fellow passengers are quite cordial and helpful and you'll be
pleased when "back door please" is yelled out in your favor, or "wait"
as the driver pulls away too soon. Rush hour is obviously busy, but
also consider the after-school rush between 2 p.m. and 3 p.m. Kids
talking Britney, boys, and basketball snap their gum and fling their
backpacks as they load onto the buses on their way home.

unofficial **TIP**
The transfer ticket is usually good for two hours,
but if the bus driver
doesn't take it or you
don't throw it away, you
can keep using it.

Most bus lines operate from 6 a.m. to midnight, after which there is
an infrequent Night Owl service; for safety's sake, take a cab at those
late hours. Popular tourist bus routes include numbers 5, 7, and 71,
which go to Golden Gate Park; numbers 41 and 45, which go up and
down Union Street; and number 30, which runs through Union Square,
Ghirardelli Square, and the Marina. If you need help figuring out
which bus or buses to take to reach a specific destination, call Muni at
☎ 415-673-MUNI (6864). The large maps have all routes marked, making it easy to plan your path and see where different routes intersect.

MUNI METRO STREETCARS

MUNI METRO STREETCARS OPERATE UNDERGROUND downtown
and on the streets in the outer neighborhoods. At four underground
stations along Market Street downtown, Muni shares quarters with
BART, the Bay Area's commuter train system. Orange, yellow, and
white illuminated signs mark the station entrances; when you get
inside the terminal, look for the separate Muni entrance.

Pay or show your Muni passport and go down to the platform. To
go west, choose the outbound side of the platform; to go east, choose

the downtown side. Electronic signs with the name of the next train begin to flash as it approaches. The doors open automatically; stand aside to let arriving passengers depart before you step aboard. To open the doors and exit at your stop, push on the low bar next to the door.

Five of Muni Metro's six streetcar lines are designated J, K, L, M, and N, and these share tracks downtown beneath Market Street but diverge below the Civic Center into the outer neighborhoods. The J line goes to Mission Dolores; the K, L, and M lines go to Castro Street; and the N line parallels Golden Gate Park. The sleek trains run about every 15 minutes and more frequently during rush hours. Service is offered daily from 5 a.m. to 12:30 a.m., Saturday from 6 a.m. to 12:30 a.m., and Sunday from 8 a.m. to 12:20 a.m.

An addition to the streetcar system (and its sixth route) is the F-Market line, beautiful green and cream–colored, 1930s-era streetcars that run along Market Street from downtown to the Castro District and back. The historic cars are charming, and they're a hassle-free alternative to crowded buses and underground terminals.

BART

BART (**www.bart.gov**), AN ACRONYM FOR Bay Area Rapid Transit, is a 103-mile system of high-speed trains that connects San Francisco with the East Bay cities of Berkeley, Oakland, Richmond, Concord, and Fremont, and to the south, with San Francisco International Airport. Four stations are located underground along Market Street (these also provide access to Muni Metro streetcars). Fares vary depending on distance; tickets are dispensed from self-service machines in the station lobbies. The trains run every 10 to 20 minutes on weekdays from 4 a.m. to midnight, on Saturday from 6 a.m. to midnight, and on Sunday from 8 a.m. to midnight.

BART is mostly used by commuters from the East Bay and is not a very useful means of traveling in the city for visitors. The stop in Berkeley, however, is close enough to the campus and other sites of interest. One other exception is the BART extension to San Francisco International Airport.

CABLE CARS

AFTER THE RED CROWN OF THE GOLDEN Gate Bridge atop fluffy clouds, cable cars are probably San Francisco's most famous symbol. And they are the nation's only mobile historical monuments. Ride one just to say you've personally experienced its ringing bells on Powell Street. Cynical natives will snub their noses at such a thing—it's as if they are being asked to eat a bowl full of Rice-A-Roni. But get them alone and they'll swear by it, especially the California Street line, the one that tourists tend to miss. It's a fun thing to bring the kids to do—and anybody can appreciate the Willy Wonka-esque Cable Car Barn and Museum on Mason Street ☎ 415-474-1887; there you can stand at an observation platform and watch the cable wind around the giant wheels. The cars, pulled by cables buried underneath the streets, operate on three lines from 6:30 a.m. to 12:30 a.m. daily at about 15-minute intervals.

The first San Francisco cable car made its maiden voyage in 1873. By 1906, just before the earthquake, the system hit its peak, with 600 cars on a 110-mile route. But the system was heavily damaged by the quake and fire, and many lines weren't rebuilt. Electric trolleys took over some routes, and the number of cable cars dwindled over the years. In the 1950s and '60s there was talk of scrapping the system entirely, but once it was declared a historical monument it had to be saved. In 1984, the city spent more than $60 million on a two-year renovation of the system, including new track and cable vaults, renovation of the Cable Car Barn, and restoration of the cars, which were given a new coat of shiny maroon, blue, and gold paint, as well as new brakes, seats, and wheels. Today there are 44 cable cars in all, with 27 in use at peak times. An average of 13 million people travel on the 17 miles of tracks each year—more than 35,000 people a day.

Three Lines

There are three cable-car lines in San Francisco. The most popular route for tourists is the Powell-Hyde line, which starts at the Powell and Market Street turntable south of Union Square. The line skirts Union Square, climbs Nob Hill (with good views of Chinatown), goes past the Cable Car Barn, crosses Lombard Street, and descends to Hyde Street to the turntable near Aquatic Park and Fisherman's Wharf. The Powell-Mason line starts at the same place, but after the Cable Car Barn it passes by North Beach and ends at Bay Street. For the best views on either line, try to face east.

The California line runs from California and Market Streets to Van Ness Avenue, passing through the Financial District and Chinatown; it's used more by commuters than tourists (a tourist attraction in itself). At Nob Hill the Powell lines cross over the California line, so passengers can transfer between lines (but they have to pay again). At the end of all lines, all passengers must get off.

For each of the three lines, the return journey follows the outward route, so riders can catch different views from the other side of the car. If you'd rather sit than stand, try boarding at the end of the line. During peak tourist seasons and on weekends, lines are long to board the cars at the turntables where the cars get turned around, and boarding at cable-car stops along the routes can be impossible as the cars rumble by, full of smiling, camera-toting tourists.

Safety Tips

As much fun as the cable cars are to ride, it's important to keep safety in mind when you're on one. If it's not crowded—not likely in the summer or fall after 9 a.m. or so—you can choose to sit or stand inside, sit outside on a bench, or stand at the end of the car. Adventurous types and some cable-car purists prefer hanging on to a pole while standing on a side running board. But wherever you decide to ride, hang on tight.

Try not to get in the way of the gripman, who operates the grip lever that holds and releases the cable pulling the car; he needs a lot of room. A yellow stripe on the floor marks an off-limits area, and passengers should stay out of it. Be extra cautious while the car is moving. Passing other cable cars is exciting because they pass so close, but be careful not to lean out too far. And be careful getting on and off. Often cable cars stop in the middle of busy intersections; you don't want to step in front of a moving car or truck.

FERRIES

IN THE DAYS BEFORE THE GOLDEN GATE AND BAY bridges were built, Bay Area commuters relied on hundreds of ferries to transport them to and from the northern counties and the East Bay. Although no longer a necessity, ferries continue to operate in smaller numbers, transporting suburban commuters who prefer a tension-free boat ride across the bay to the headache of rush-hour traffic. The ferries are also favorite ways for local residents and visitors to enjoy San Francisco's incredible scenery. On weekends, many suburban families leave their cars at home and take the ferries for fun and relaxation.

One person's commute can be another's excursion. Although the ferries don't offer the narrated audio tours of the commercial sight-seeing cruises offered at Fisherman's Wharf, they're less expensive. Food and bar service is offered on board, but the modern ferries only transport foot traffic and bicycles, not cars.

The Ferry Building at the foot of Market Street is the terminus for ferries to Sausalito and Larkspur. For prices and schedules, call Golden Gate Transit at ☎ 415-923-2000. Private ferry service to Sausalito, Tiburon, and Angel Island operates from Pier 41 at Fisherman's Wharf. For more information, call the Blue & Gold Fleet at ☎ 415-705-5555, or visit **www.blueandgoldfleet.com.**

TAXIS

UNLIKE NEW YORK AND CHICAGO, CABS IN San Francisco tend to be expensive and scarce. However, if you're in the center of town, no ride will be longer than about three miles. You can usually hail a moving taxi downtown, but in general it's better to call and make arrangements for pickup, if you're not actually on the street at the time. The dispatch will call your number to alert you of the taxi's arrival. Another option is to head toward a cab stand at a major hotel, but the wait can be long during rush hour and in bad weather.

San Francisco taxis have rooftop signs that are illuminated when the cab is empty. Rates are $2.85 for the first mile and increase 45 cents each additional fifth of a mile (this is subject to change, especially due

To Cross or not to Cross?

San Francisco ranks among the top pedestrian fatality rates in the country, though in recent years this rate has been coming down. But be constantly aware that red-light runners are a bit of a plague here, especially on the wide open streets such as Howard and 19th Avenue. Whether walking or driving, be sure you've got the green light, and look both ways to be sure no one is screaming down the road in your direction. Another thing to be aware of when crossing the street or aggressively pursuing a yellow light in a car: the traffic lights in San Francisco, unlike pedestrian-heavy cities like New York or D.C., don't have delayed timing. As soon as one side turns red, the other instantly turns green.

to the fluctuating price of oil). Major cab companies include Veteran's Cab ☎ 415-552-1300; Yellow Cab ☎ 415-626-2345; DeSoto Cab ☎ 415-970-1300; and Luxor Cab ☎ 415-282-4141.

WALKING

FORGET THE GYM. YOU HAVE A LEG PRESS ON almost every street in San Francisco. Pump your quads as you tread the hills—some so steep that stairs have been cut to make the trek easier, and your spirit will be fed dessert as the brightly colored Victorians and backdrop of blue ocean surprise at every corner. It's a walker's nirvana. What separates this city from others is its compact size and well-laid streets. Major tourist areas are within a half hour or less of one another. Another nice feature to footing the city is the surprising green spaces still firmly rooted within the city. Duck under a tree or sit in one of the many parks for a picnic as you glare at the glass-covered skyscrapers of downtown.

unofficial **TIP**
Be aware that the traffic lights don't have delayed timing. As soon as one side turns red, the other instantly turns green.

You don't have to ask the Scarecrow for directions here—most street intersections are marked with green-and-white signs bearing the name of the cross street; this can get confusing along Market Street, where street names are different on each side of the thoroughfare. Street names are also frequently imprinted in the pavement at corners. Often, electronic "walk" signs indicate when it's safe (and legal) to cross the street.

A Walk for Any Mood

Even if walks have never been a highlight for you, you will find inspiration in San Francisco to lace up and put feet to the path. One of the most active and exhilarating walks is The Golden Gate Promenade's three-and-a-half-mile path. Along its trail are joggers, and views of Alcatraz and those cold-blooded souls braving the frigid Pacific as they windsurf or kite-surf. All along the way are pit stops—Aquatic Park, Fort Mason, Marina Green, to the newly renovated Crissy Field. For a more romantic stroll, the Presidio is one of the most valued green spaces in the city. And the fact that there is a spot called Lover's Lane should be indicative enough. The whole trail takes only about 15 minutes. Another killer spot within the Presidio is Inspiration Point, which looks out toward the Palace of Fine Arts and the Golden Gate. A mandatory walk that would fit in nicely if you are already strolling The Golden Gate Promenade is to walk across the Golden Gate Bridge. You'll be humming Tony Bennett's classic in no time! If you are a foodie and love to walk, stop, eat, walk, stop, eat, then a stroll down Union Street or Chestnut in the Marina or almost any street in the Mission will satisfy your craving. Bernal Heights is one neighborhood being resurrected with community gardens and green spaces and an all-out funky vibe. A walk down Cortland Avenue, the main drag here, will take you to Good Prospect Community Garden, and further along on Eugenia Street, you climb hidden stairways past bizarre and brightly colored Victorians and bungalows to Bernal Community Gardens. The cherry on top of this walk is the short hike to the bald top of Bernal Hill, which offers views of Mount Diablo and the Golden Gate. It's really one of the best vantage points to watch the foggy fingers move in and choke the bridge and surrounding neighborhoods. There are great walks even for bargain shoppers. The secondhand stores on Upper Fillmore Street are chock full of great deals on hot brand-name items.

PART SIX

SIGHTSEEING, TOURS, *and* ATTRACTIONS

TOURING SAN FRANCISCO

THE BEAUTY OF TOURING SAN FRANCISCO IS that Grandma can feel right at home sitting on a bench next to Dolores Park in the Mission while the college grad can sit on the grass in the same park and feel a compatible vibe. It's a friendly city for anybody who wants to experience its spectrum of offerings. There is much to see, yet the city is compact and manageable when taken in neighborhood by neighborhood. And like the consummate Californian, San Francisco is continually reinventing itself, working on self-improvement, getting in shape. The Marina District, devastated by the 1989 earthquake, is thriving with new and rebuilt Mediterranean-style houses in lollipop colors. The waterfront is reawakening; the Presidio is transforming into a national park; and major projects such as the Yerba Buena Gardens are changing the face of the city.

Half the fun of discovering this town is simply wandering around and stumbling on great views, interesting shops, a location used in a favorite movie, and things that even the locals may not be aware of. While metropolitan, San Francisco is small; if you get disoriented, just remember that downtown is east, and the Golden Gate Bridge is north. And if you do get lost, you can't go too far because the city is surrounded by water on three sides. Here are some hints for first-time visitors.

TAKING AN ORIENTATION TOUR

VISITORS TO SAN FRANCISCO CAN'T HELP BUT NOTICE the regular procession of open-air tour buses—"motorized cable cars" is probably a more accurate term—that prowl Union Square, Fisherman's Wharf, North Beach, and major tourist spots. Not to be confused with real cable cars (the rubber tires are a dead giveaway), the vehicles operated by Gray Lines offer regularly scheduled shuttle

unofficial **TIP**
If this is your first visit, take one of the tours early in your trip, even on the first day. The narrated tours are a no-brainer for exhausted visitors who want spoon-fed details of San Francisco's major sights while learning the lay of the land. Think of the tours as an educational system that not only gets you to the most well-known attractions but also provides a timely education on the city's history and scope.

buses along regular routes that include the city's top attractions. Between stops, a tour guide discusses the city's cataclysmic fire of 1906, Barbary Coast days during the gold rush, and the flower-power era of the 1960s.

The guides also suggest good places to eat and drop tidbits of interesting and often funny San Francisco trivia. On Gray Line motorized "cable cars," your ticket allows unlimited re-boarding for that day, so you can get off at any scheduled stop to tour, eat, shop, or explore. That helps determine which sights warrant another day of exploration. Tour buses run about every 30 minutes (every hour in the winter), and boarding locations include some of the city's most popular attractions.

Gray Line

Both of the guided tours that operate a regular route in and around downtown San Francisco are good values. **Gray Line** features San Francisco-style motorized cable cars and a tour guide for trips lasting two-and-a-half hours. On the two-and-a-half-hour tour, passengers board at Union Square or Pier 39 in Fisherman's Wharf. On the on/off tour, visitors can get off and reboard at Pier 39, the Palace of Fine Arts, Fort Point, the Golden Gate Bridge, the Presidio, and Union Square. If it rains, tours may be canceled or an enclosed vehicle may be substituted.

The cost for the two-and-a-half-hour tour is $28 for adults; $14 for children ages 5–11; and $26 for seniors ages 60 and over. Departures begin at 10 a.m. daily and continue about every 45 minutes until 4 p.m.; during the winter, the tours depart hourly. Passengers can pay an additional $17 and go on a bay cruise departing from Fisherman's Wharf. Tickets for both tours can be purchased at booths in Union Square or at Pier 39 in Fisherman's Wharf. For more information, call ☎ 888-428-6937, or visit **www.graylinesanfrancisco.com.**

SPECIALIZED TOURS

GRAY LINE OFFERS SEVERAL GENERAL-INTEREST tours around the city and special tours to destinations beyond San Francisco. A four-hour deluxe city tour via motor coach takes visitors to the city's major attractions, including the Civic Center, Mission Dolores, Twin Peaks, Golden Gate Park, and Cliff House. Reservations are required for the tour, which departs daily at 9:15 a.m., 11:15 a.m., and 2:15 p.m. The price is $40 for adults and $38 for seniors ages 60 and over.

Gray Line offers tours to Muir Woods and Sausalito daily; the three-and-a-half-hour tours leave at 9:15 a.m. and 11:15 a.m. The cost is $42 for adults, $20 for children ages 5–11, and $40 for seniors ages 60 and over. Gray Line also offers day tours to Yosemite, the wine country, and Monterey, as well as airplane and helicopter tours. Coach tours from San Francisco include pick-up and drop-off at your hotel. For more information or reservations, call ☎ 888-428-6937 or 415-558-9400, or visit **www.graylinesanfrancisco.com.**

Tower Tours leads a deluxe city tour to Chinatown, North Beach, Telegraph Hill and Coit Tower, the Marina District, the Presidio, Cliff House and Seal Rocks, and Golden Gate Park. Scheduled stops on the tour (which uses minibuses with large windows, not motor coaches) are Vista Point at the Golden Gate Bridge, Cliff House above Seal Rocks, the Japanese Tea Garden in Golden Gate Park (small admission fee not included), and Twin Peaks (weather permitting).

Three-and-a-half-hour tours depart daily at 9 a.m., 11 a.m., and 2 p.m.; $44 for adults, $19 for children ages 5–11. Tower Tours also offers day trips to Muir Woods and Sausalito, Yosemite, Alcatraz, and Monterey and Carmel. All tours include pick-up and return to your hotel; meals aren't included. For more information, call ☎ 888-657-4520 or visit **www.towertours.net.**

Off-the-beaten-track tours of San Francisco architecture and the city's best sights are offered by **Quality Tours.** A seven-passenger Chevy Suburban provides more comfort and greater visibility than a bus, and it can handle Lombard Street, "the crookedest street in the world." Rates are $80 an hour and the tour guide is a former University of California at Berkeley architecture professor. Pick-up and drop-off at your hotel is included. In addition, custom tours are available. For more information and reservations (required), call ☎ 650-994-5054 or visit **www.qualitytours.com.**

BAY CRUISES

VISITORS CAN ENJOY SPECTACULAR VIEWS OF the city skyline, the Golden Gate and Bay bridges, and Alcatraz Island on narrated cruises around San Francisco Bay. **Red & White Fleet** offers a Golden Gate Bridge cruise that passes Fort Mason, the Presidio, and Fort Point before going under the famous bridge. The hour-long cruises depart from Pier 43 in Fisherman's Wharf every 45 minutes, from 10 a.m. to 6 p.m. in the summer and from 10 a.m. to 4:45 p.m. in the winter. The price is $21 for adults, $17 for seniors and children ages 12–17, and $13 for children ages 5–11. For more information, call ☎ 415-673-2900 or visit **www.redandwhite.com.**

Blue & Gold Fleet offers one-hour cruises in San Francisco Bay departing from Pier 39 in Fisherman's Wharf every day except Christmas. The boats leave every half hour from 10 a.m. to 6:45 p.m. spring through fall, and every 45 minutes from 10 a.m. to 4 p.m. in the winter. The price is $21 for adults, $17 for seniors and children ages 12–17, and $13 for children ages 5–11. Blue & Gold also offers ferry service to Sausalito and Tiburon from Pier 41, a Muir Woods tour, and a Napa-Sonoma wine-country tour. For more information, call ☎ 415-773-1188; to make advance reservations, call ☎ 415-705-5555 or visit **www.blueandgoldfleet.com.**

The **Angel Island–Tiburon Ferry** operates daily in summer and on weekends in winter. Round-trip fares are $10 for adults and $7.50 for children ages 5–11. A $1 fee is charged for bicycles. For schedule information and directions, call ☎ 415-435-2131, or visit **www.angel islandferry.com.**

AIR TOURS

FOR 50 YEARS **San Francisco Seaplane Tours** HAS WHISKED visitors aloft from the waters of the San Francisco Bay on flights over the city and its famous landmarks. Thirty-minute sightseeing rides from Pier 39 in Fisherman's Wharf leave daily at 10:30 a.m., noon, 1:30 p.m., 3 p.m., and 4:30 p.m.; the price is $129 for adults and $99 for children (minimum of two passengers). Flights are also offered from Sausalito, including a 30-minute city and bay tour ($129 for adults, $99 for children). Champagne sunset tours leave 30 minutes before sundown and take passengers over San Francisco at dusk; the ride lasts 35 to 40 minutes and costs $169 a person. Reservations are recommended for all tours and required for the sunset tour; call toll-free ☎ 888-SEA-PLANE or look up **www.seaplane.com** for more information.

San Francisco Helicopter Tours and Charters offers jet helicopter flights daily from San Francisco International Airport, about a half-hour south of downtown. Thirty-minute flights are $130 for adults and $95 for children. Hotel pick-up and return is included in the price; the maximum number of passengers is between four and six. For more information and reservations (required), call ☎ 800-400-2404 or visit **www.sfhelicoptertours.com.**

WALKING TOURS

unofficial **TIP**
San Francisco is best seen up close, and the best way to do that is on a walking tour.

CITY GUIDES WALKING TOURS, presented by the San Francisco Friends of the Library, provides more than 200 trained volunteers who conduct about 20 different history walks each month. The one- to two-hour tours are led daily year-round, rain or shine. And here's the good part: The guided walks are free. An expanded schedule, offered in May and October, provides more than 40 different walks, with more than 125 free tours available. Walking tours are offered of San Francisco's most famous (and, in some cases, infamous) districts, as well as hidden neighborhoods most tourists miss.

No reservations are required; just meet at the place and time designated in the current tour schedule. Wear comfortable shoes (although tours are not strenuous unless so listed) and look for the City Guide, who should be wearing a badge. For a recorded schedule of walks, call ☎ 415-557-4266 or visit **www.sfcityguides.org.** You can pick up a printed walk schedule at the San Francisco Convention and Visitors Bureau, Hallidie Plaza at Powell and Market Streets, or at any city library.

Victorian Home Walk takes visitors on tours of the city's famed Victorian houses, with an emphasis on exploring neighborhoods off the beaten tourist path. Tours depart daily at 11 a.m. from the lobby of the Westin St. Francis Hotel at 335 Powell Street; rates are $20 a person (no credit cards accepted). The walk lasts about two-and-a-half hours, and transportation is included. For more information or to make reservations (required), call ☎ 415-252-9485 or visit **www.victorianwalk.com.**

Feel like a native on **Helen's Walk Tour,** a three-and-a-half-hour exploration of Union Square, Chinatown, and North Beach offered Monday through Thursday. The walk begins at 9 a.m. "under the clock" in the lobby of the Westin St. Francis Hotel on Union Square. The cost is $50 per person; family and group rates are available. For more information and to make reservations (required), call ☎ 888-808-6505 or 510-524-4544 or visit **www.ollin.com/hwt.html.**

Relive the 1960s on the two-hour **Haight-Ashbury Flower Power** walking tour. Learn about the Summer of Love and the Diggers and see shrines to the late Jerry Garcia (of the Grateful Dead). The tours depart at 9:30 a.m. on Tuesdays and Saturdays at the corner of Stanyan and Waller streets in the Haight; the cost is $15 per person. Reservations are required; call ahead at ☎ 415-863-1621.

For free, in-depth walking tours of Golden Gate Park, call **Friends of Recreation & Parks** at ☎ 415-263-0991 or visit **www.frp.org.** A variety of guided walks are offered throughout the week, including tours of the Japanese Tea Garden and Stern Grove. **Cruisin' the Castro** is an award-winning tour with an emphasis on the neighborhood's history; sights include Harvey Milk's camera shop and the AIDS quilt museum. The walk, offered Tuesday through Saturday, starts at 10 a.m. and lasts three hours; lunch is included. The cost is $45 per person. For reservations, contact at ☎ 415-550-8110 or **www.cruisinthecastro.com.**

All About Chinatown takes visitors on a behind-the-scenes walk of this colorful neighborhood, covering its history, culture, and traditions. Tours leave daily at 10 a.m. from Old St. Mary's Cathedral, 660 California (corner of California and Grant Avenue). The three-hour walk finishes with a dim sum lunch (two hours without lunch). The cost is $40 a person with lunch, $25 without lunch; children ages 6–11, $25 with lunch, $10 without; children ages 12–17, $30 with lunch, $15 without; under age 6 is free. For more information and reservations (required), call ☎ 415-982-8839 or visit **www.allaboutchinatown.com.**

TOURING ON YOUR OWN: OUR FAVORITE ITINERARIES

IF YOUR TIME IS LIMITED AND YOU WANT TO experience the best of San Francisco in a day or two, here are some suggested itineraries.

The schedules assume you're staying at a downtown hotel, have already eaten breakfast, and are ready to go around 9 a.m. If you've got two days, make reservations for a morning ferry ride to Alcatraz Island and for *Beach Blanket Babylon* (Wednesday through Sunday evenings at Club Fugazi in North Beach) before you hit town.

Day One

1. Walk to Union Square or Fisherman's Wharf and tour San Francisco's major sights on one of the open-air, motorized "cable car" services; Gray Line offers unlimited reboarding privileges for the day. You can also pay an additional $17 for a one-hour narrated cruise of San Francisco Bay.

2. At Fisherman's Wharf, skip touristy Pier 39 and walk west to the Hyde Street Pier, where you can explore real 19th-century ships; or walk another block or two to the National Maritime Museum, which is free and chock-full of nautical goodies. Or, if it's a nice day, take a bay cruise.

3. For lunch, try the clam chowder served in a bowl of sourdough bread at Boudin's Bakery in Fisherman's Wharf; it's fast and cheap ($6.50).

4. On the "cable car" tour, stop at the Golden Gate Bridge. Don't just gaze at the scenery from the overlook near the visitor center; walk onto the bridge for even better views. Take a jacket (it gets very windy).

5. Back at Union Square after your circuit on the "cable car," walk up Grant Avenue to Chinatown; to get the real flavor of this exotic neighborhood, walk a block west to Stockton Street, which is less touristy.

6. Continue walking north through Chinatown to Columbus Avenue; now you're in North Beach. Settle in at a nice sidewalk cafe for a latte and primo people-watching; then browse at City Lights Bookstore, a North Beach landmark.

7. For a spectacular view of San Francisco, hike up Telegraph Hill to Coit Tower; if your legs and feet aren't up for the steep walk, take the No. 39 bus (board near Washington Square). After savoring the view (best around sunset), walk down the Greenwich Steps, a brick staircase lined with ivy and roses that descends steeply to Montgomery Street. Near the base of the steps is a glass-brick, art-deco apartment house used in the Humphrey Bogart film *Dark Passage*.

8. Have dinner at Enrico's (504 Broadway; ☎ 415-982-6223), an Italian-inspired California restaurant. This place, popular with locals as well as tourists, opened in 1886 as an Italian restaurant, then in the 1950s morphed into a beatnik coffee house patronized by Ginsberg, Kerouac, and friends, and finally became the jazz supper club it is today.

Day Two

1. Get to Fisherman's Wharf for a morning ferry ride to Alcatraz. Allow at least two hours to explore the prison ruins and island.

2. Have lunch at Greens (in Building A at Fort Mason), with a full view of the Golden Gate Bridge and the Marin Headlands. It's an outstanding

vegetarian restaurant (not just sprouts and tofu) in a former enclosed pier with polished wood floors and a serene atmosphere. Call ahead for reservations: ☎ 415-771-6222.

3. Take a stroll along the Marina Green where kite fliers, happy joggers, and prancing dogs converge. You can continue toward Crissy Field (closer to the Golden Gate Bridge) or turn on Broderick or Divisidero, and then explore the Marina District and its beautiful waterside houses. If you've got time, stroll the parklike grounds of the Palace of Fine Arts. Right off of the Marina Green is a simple snack stand that serves hot chili (great on cool afternoons), hot dogs, veggie sandwiches, ice cream, Gatorade, and other hunger-curbing snacks. It's convenient if you want to picnic near the Palace of Fine Arts.

4. Take the cable car from the Beach and Hyde streets turnaround (Powell-Mason line) or the turnaround near Taylor and Bay streets (Powell-Hyde line); both head toward Union Square as they pass through Nob Hill. If it's a nice day, hop off and explore Nob Hill and Russian Hill. At sunset, order cocktails at the Top O' the Mark lounge in the Mark Hopkins Inter-Continental San Francisco, a 380-room hotel at California and Mason streets.

5. Have dinner at John's Grill (63 Ellis Street near Union Square), where you can pay homage to Dashiell Hammett and Sam Spade while enjoying 1930s dining at its best.

6. Enjoy an evening of zany entertainment at *Beach Blanket Babylon* (at Club Fugazi in North Beach), San Francisco's long-running musical revue famous for its excellent singers, enormous hats, and stunning costumes; advance reservations are required.

If You've Got More Time

If you're spending more than two days in town or if this is not your first visit, consider some of these options.

1. Drive or take a bus up Van Ness Avenue to Union Street and Pacific Heights, where you'll find some of the best examples of San Francisco's famed Victorian houses. The Union Street shops are an upscale retail experience, with more than 300 boutiques, restaurants, antiques shops, and coffeehouses.

2. Visit the California Palace of the Legion of Honor, a world-class European art museum in Lincoln Park with a spectacular view of the Pacific and the Marin Headlands. It's also a location used in Hitchcock's classic thriller *Vertigo*. Drive or take the No. 38 bus from Union Square.

3. Spend at least half a day in Golden Gate Park. The Japanese Tea Garden is a work of art; families should head to the California Academy of Sciences. Other options include renting a bike or rowboat.

4. Go to Sausalito or Tiburon for lunch and an afternoon. You can drive, but taking the ferry from Fisherman's Wharf is a better way to reach these two upscale, bayside communities across from San Francisco.

5. Serious shoppers will want to exercise their credit cards around Union Square, where they'll find the city's major department stores and many high-end specialty shops. Discount shoppers should head to SoMa, which is loaded with warehouse retail spaces. On-the-edge fashion victims and vintage-clothes browsers should head to Haight-Ashbury.

6. If you've got a car, make the trip across the Golden Gate Bridge to Muir Woods (giant redwoods) and Mount Tamalpais (a knock-your-socks-off view of San Francisco Bay and the Pacific). You can do both in half a day.

7. Drive up Twin Peaks for its stunning view of the city (from its highest location). *Hint:* Go at night (and take a jacket or sweater).

8. The San Francisco Museum of Modern Art is the city's newest art emporium, and even if you're not a big fan of modern art, the building alone is worth the price of admission. It's a knockout.

9. Don't miss Fort Point. While the Civil War–era brick fortress isn't much to get excited about, the view, framed by the Golden Gate Bridge, is. It's got our vote as the most scenic spot in the city (and not just because it's the place where Jimmy Stewart pulls Kim Novak out of the water in Hitchcock's *Vertigo*).

10. Take a drive along the city's western edge south of the Golden Gate Bridge, and you'll see yet another reason why San Franciscans love living here. The views of the Pacific and the coast are spectacular. Good places to explore include Seal Rocks, Cliff House, Ocean Beach, and Fort Funston.

THE MANGIA! TOUR

THERE ARE TWO THINGS EVERYONE RAVES ABOUT IN San Francisco—the weather and the food. Here's an agenda for you foodies out there who want to take in the diverse flavor of the city. A word on planning: definitely make a reservation for dinner. Eating is the main event for most on weekends and even weekdays for top restaurants. It's just the way—so call ahead.

Day 1

BREAKFAST We're going to start this day's gastronomic adventures in Berkeley. As the T-shirt boasts, you get "friendly service and good food" at one of the most loved breakfast joints in the Bay Area, **Bette's Ocean-view Diner** (1807 Fourth Street, Berkeley; ☎ 510-644-3230). You'll come for the pancakes, as most people do, and want to endure the never-ending lines for the fat omelettes. Or are you a scrapple fan? They've got that, too! The lines are extraordinarily long with people coming from all over, so be sure to get there early if you want to be seated in a timely manner. If you get there late, don't fret. Stroll along Fourth Street shops and you'll hear your name yelled over the loudspeaker.

LUNCH While you are in Berkeley, after shopping or taking in the hippies on Telegraph near campus, a must-stop is **Viks Distributors Inc.** (726 Allston Way, Berkeley; ☎ 510-644-4412). International cuisine in San

Francisco is fantastic, evidenced by the publicity their sushi and Chinese food get. But Viks is probably one of the best Indian food restaurants anywhere! Don't expect frills here. It resembles a warehouse with folding chairs and tables and you have to order at the counter and wait for your name to be announced when it is ready. What makes this place stand out from the rest is the freshness and hard-to-find Indian dishes you may never have tried before.

unofficial **TIP**
At Viks, order from the *chaat*—the snack bar. Portions are small, so you can sample more of the menu (a billboard on the wall).

DINNER After eating such a heavy Indian meal, we're going to take it down a notch and direct you to **Millennium Restaurant** (580 Geary Street; ☎ 415-345-3900) for the most creative and innovative vegetarian meals. You can't leave San Francisco without trying things their way. It's probably the one place where vegetarians equal the omnivores. You'll be amazed at the many different uses for tofu. This restaurant is in constant competition with another top vegetarian haunt—Greens. But the atmosphere (and the food) here is heartier.

AFTER DINNER CAFE So you had a long day touring Berkeley, survived the Bay Bridge traffic getting back into the city, settled your insides with some avocado and tomato salad, and now what? Head to North Beach to the popular Beat Generation watering hole, **Caffe Trieste** (609 Vallejo Street; ☎ 415-392-6739), for the best coffee in town. Its imported Italian coffee is sold by the cup or by the bean. Snacks like pizza and sandwiches are available, and on Saturday afternoons, musicians and opera singers take over the existential vibe and perform.

Or you'll scream for **Mitchell's Ice Cream** (688 San Jose Avenue; ☎ 415-648-2300), unarguably the best ice cream in town, as evidenced by the lines of people waiting for their number to be called. You'll be craving this family-owned treasure months after returning from San Francisco. The range of unique flavors—Chicago Cheesecake, Avocado, and Halo-Halo (a popular East Asian–style mélange) to name a few, are true representations of the diverse cultural population and dining experiences in San Francisco. Unexplainably delicious.

SUBDUED LATE NIGHT Unlike New York, San Francisco isn't open all night. It's hard to find a place open at midnight to grab a bite to eat—not just a bite but a big slab of hearty meat if you are up for it! One neighborhood late-night favorite is **Brazen Head** (3166 Buchanan Street; ☎ 415-921-7600) in Cow Hollow. It's open until 2 a.m., and the atmosphere is mellow, publike but with a down-home, cozy feeling.

PIANO BAR LATE NIGHT If you are just coming from a showing of *Beach Blanket Babylon* or are heading to the latest top club in town, then **Lefty O'Doul's** at Union Square (333 Geary Boulevard) is in order. The music is mirthful, though the singers are often off-key, and the steam table is one of the most popular in town. It's pure comfort food, so don't eat too much if you're going dancing afterward.

Day 2

BREAKFAST For more than 90 years, **Sears Fine Foods Restaurant** in the heart of Union Square (439 Powell Street; ☎ 415-986-1160) has been flipping more than 16 varieties of pancakes for locals and tourists alike who have made this a city landmark. Lines can form on weekends at this eatery, resembling an old-style diner from the 1940s, so be sure to get an early jump on the day. If flapjacks aren't your thing, then try their hard-to-beat corned beef with hash, or varieties of eggs and omelets.

BRUNCH If you do get a late start to your day, you may want to consider participating in a citywide tradition—brunch. Fresh flowers at each table, thoughtful place settings, and the open kitchen attract locals to **Ella's Restaurant** (500 Presidio Avenue; ☎ 415-441-5669). Attentive to every detail, right down to the lemon-and-ginger oatmeal pancakes. Her menus change weekly, but expect eclectic lunches and creative soups. The restaurant also serves dinner, but it is an obligatory brunch destination on weekends. The pastries are also tops.

Option Two: dim sum! **Ton Kiang Restaurant** is one of San Francisco's best Chinese restaurants (5821 Geary Boulevard; ☎ 415-386-8530). It is hectic and seems chaotic but the restaurant is used to it. The dishes get so-so reviews, but people come for the fun of dim sum. Be sure to grab a table by the kitchen doors so you can be the first to take your pick off the dim sum trays as they come out fresh and hot.

DINNER There are two things you can't leave the city without trying—sushi and burritos. We've got your bases covered. Decide on what you crave first. You can't go wrong with most of the sushi restaurants in town, but **Ebisu Sushi** in the Sunset (1283 Ninth Avenue; ☎ 415-566-1770) is voted as one of the best. The sushi chefs at this lively place will become your closest friends after one sitting of their spicy tuna rolls. Don't be surprised with little freebies that the chefs divvy up among guests. It's their way of introducing you to new sushi creations. The fish is the freshest, and rolls are very creative. It's also along the main strip in the sunset, so an after-meal stroll to see other restaurants or stores is possible.

Or if the idea of raw fish isn't to your liking, **La Taqueria** (2889 Mission Street; ☎ 415-285-7117) will roll you the best burrito in town. It's a rather rundown place in the Mission, but looks are deceiving. It's fresh, cheap, and filling. There are tons of Mexican taco stands in this part of town, so keep an eye out for the bright red electric sign.

THE ADRENALINE TOUR

YOU'LL NEVER FIND A PLACE SO CHOCK-FULL OF outdoor activity as San Francisco. Its never-break-a-sweat weather and bay breezes, not to mention mountains and proximity to national parks and the ocean, make it a prime destination for outdoor enthusiasts.

Day 1. Close to Home

TO START YOUR DAY Pick up a smoothie with a wheat-grass booster at **Jambo Juice** on Chestnut and Pierce streets and take an early morning misty walk along the Marina Green. You have two choices—you can walk along the water toward the bridge and then over the bridge toward the **Marin Headlands,** or you can drive across the bridge. Either way, hiking the Headlands is a must-do while in San Francisco. It's so close to the city, offers dramatic views, and it's a great way to get the heart rate and spirit escalated. Any hiker of any ability can do the Headlands. You can begin shortly after exiting the Golden Gate Bridge at the Bay Area Ridge Trail, also known as the Coastal Trail. The trail can get narrow and steep but the effort is worthwhile. The trail loops around, and about midway don't forget to look back—you will see clear across the famous Golden Gate out to sea, and if it's a clear day you can see the jagged silhouette of the Farallon Islands 22 miles away. You can get trail maps and more information on the Headlands by stopping at the **Visitor Center,** which is to the right off the exit ramp onto Alexander Avenue. Turn left on Bunker Road and you'll see signs. A trek in the Headlands is completely self-led and vast—great for couples and power hikers. Their Web site is **www.nps.gov/goga/mahe.**

If you want something a bit more confined and subdued, particularly if you have children with you, give **Angel Island** your morning attention. Ferries leave from Fisherman's Wharf every half hour or so and deposit you at the car-free island in the middle of the Bay. You will be dropped at Perimeter Trailhead, which takes you around the island along well-groomed, wide trails passing shops for bicycle rentals, tram tours, kayak rentals, and the Cove Café. For more information, call ☎ 415-435-1915.

A BREATHER ... Return from your hike and deposit yourself along the beach at Crissy Field near the Marina District. You can sit and watch the kite fliers and the wind or kite surfers in the water circle the pillars of the Golden Gate Bridge. There is a snack bar nearby if you need to rehydrate yourself or get a sandwich.

OR NOT ... If you haven't had enough, you can rent a bike at **Blazing Saddles** (1095 Columbus Avenue; ☎ 415-202-8888; **www.blazing saddles.com**). The obligatory bike route for those who want the best scenery and burn for their body is taking the Great Highway bike path. The path leads you right into Fort Funston and Lake Merced—which takes you into late afternoon.

A GREAT FINISH Lake Merced off the Great Highway to Skyline Boulevard offers you the chance to jog, rollerblade, bike, or hike. If you've never tried it (and the wind is right), the lake offers windsurfing lessons, including all equipment. You can pick up a bite to eat and rehydrate yourself with a thick malt beer or the pure H2O at the Boat

House. On the drive or pedal back toward the city you can watch the sunset and decompress at **Fort Funston** off of the Great Highway. Pick a perch—benches conveniently offered—and watch the hangliders soar weightlessly off a cliff and over the crashing waves below. A great finish to the day.

Day 2: Farther Afield

TO START THE DAY What rollerblading was in the 1990s, mountain biking is today. And **Mount Tamalpais,** or Mount Tam for those in the know, is supposedly the place where it originated. Tons of bike trails crisscross the mountain and most lead to the popular **Old Railroad Grade.** Which portion to take depends on how far you want to go. You could choose to start your fat-tire tryst from quaint Mill Valley off West Blithedale Avenue, or you could drive up Summit Avenue if you are feeling less ambitious. If you need bike rentals, you can get them before taking off at Blazing Saddles (1095 Columbus Avenue; ☎ 415-202-8888).

A BREATHER . . . Your butt will most definitely be in need of a break. There is no better place on that side of the bridge to take lunch or brunch than **Sam's Anchor Cafe** (27 Main Street; ☎ 415-435-4527) in Tiburon. You could choose to bike it or drive, but it is one of the most popular brunch places in the city, because of its relaxed seaside mood and excellent views. Grab a cold one.

OR NOT . . . Close to Tiburon is the savvy town of Sausalito. Here you will find **Sea Trek Ocean Kayaking Center,** an all-inclusive rental service. They offer classes, guided trips, and kayaks for newbies and pros alike. Their prices are reasonable and service top notch. You'll slice through the water starting out at Sausalito's Schoonmaker Point Marina, and there's a good chance of meeting face to face with seals, pelicans, and even the occasional whale in Richardson Bay. For more information, call ☎ 415-488-1000, or check out **www.seatrekkayak.com.** The currents in the bay are very strong and with the occasional huge cargo ship coming through the Golden Gate from an overseas journey, so expect to battle waves. You will sweat! Just remain calm and stick close to your party or a guide if that makes you more comfortable. Life jackets are provided for everyone. You'll be too exhausted for anything else, so spend the evening at a movie or soaking in a hot bath!

Or, if rumors of great white sharks lurking 22 miles away at the Farallon Islands deter you from sticking an inch of your toe in the bay (although according to locals, they *never* enter the bay), we have another plan. Instead of heading to Sausalito from Mount Tam, continue your adrenaline journey along Highway 1 down toward **Stinson Beach.** The drive is winding, twisting, and at some points nail-biting, but the heights of the pavement will prepare you for the heights of the cliff face that you can scale just south of Stinson Beach at **Red Rock Beach,** also known by locals as Mickey's. You'll climb your way up a cliff overlooking the Pacific below. The route is pretty challenging and only those who are seasoned climbers should attempt it. For more information, call ☎ 415-388-2070.

SAN FRANCISCO *for* CHILDREN

FITTING ANY VACATION AND TOUR AROUND diaper changes, feeding times, and cranky kids is about as challenging as getting a tan during San Francisco summers. So what do you do? San Francisco offers plenty of fun-filled places and things to do that will satisfy the most curious—and fidgety—kids. But the beauty is that you will love it, too.

The *Unofficial Guide* rating system for attractions includes an "appeal to different age groups" category with a range of appeal from one star (★), don't bother, to five stars (★★★★★), not to be missed. Before we get you started on specific attractions that will keep you and the little ones occupied, here are some tips to smooth over any sticky situations that may arise, and prevent further gray hairs.

There is a reason that the mats came out at noon during kindergarten. And there is a reason that parents are droopy-eyed at 6 a.m. while their kids are bright-eyed and bushy-tailed. Kids are morning people—and it seems that energy fades around mid-afternoon. Try to plan the bulk of the activities in the early morning, when their attention is easily harnessed. There are plenty of mellow activities to plan after lunch—like sitting in a park, watching the boats in the bay . . .

If you have babies with you, make sure that you are allowed to bring them in to certain "grown up" places. Life would be much different for many if the final words of *Gone with the Wind* were interrupted by a howling screech.

SOME SUGGESTIONS

SAN FRANCISCO HAS MORE FOR KIDS TO enjoy than museums, a zoo, and vistas of the bay. A **cable-car ride** never fails to delight—let's face it, even a ride on BART could be a fun experience for kids. The icing on the cake is a stop at the **Cable Car Museum** (☎ 415-474-1887) near Chinatown (it's free). And while you are near **Chinatown,** take a stroll. All the trinkets and barking toys that the shops have on display will amuse—and thankfully, if ripping that fuzzy eraser from the hand causes a tantrum, almost everything here is cheap!

unofficial **TIP**
Any parent-survival manual will tell you this, but it is our responsibility to remind you, too: pack a bag of "goodies" for the kids. Buses can take longer than expected, and lines can be frustratingly long even for the grown-ups. Their favorite coloring book with some crayons, action figures, a portable radio, Teddy Grahams, diced peaches . . . whatever it will take to make things less traumatic for you, them, and those around you.

Another kid pleaser raved about by native parents is the **Basic Brown Bear** (The Cannery, 2801 Leavenworth Street; ☎ 415-409-2806; **www.basicbrownbear.com**). This is where teddy is conceived—albeit in a G-rated kinda way. Kids can select a teddy bear from among dozens of styles and then stuff it themselves. Tours of the factory are offered daily from 10 a.m. to 5 p.m.

A PARK FOR EVERY SUE, SAM, AND SPOT

SO THE EXPLORATORIUM SENT THE KIDS SPINNING in orbit. What to do with all that energy? A great cool-down option for you, and a place for them to release their energy in a vast open space, is to visit one of the many parks found within the city. **Golden Gate Park** is your best option. It is huge and has the **Children's Playground,** with a carousel that's fun for toddlers. You can also rent a boat on Stow Lake; bicycles, in-line skates, and roller skates are also available for rent. Call ☎ 415-752-0347 for boat rentals, ☎ 415-668-6699 for bike rentals.

Another bizarre kid-pleasing attraction in the giant park is the **Bison Paddock** at the western end. You won't be able to get close enough to pet them but it is an oddly amusing sight to see bisons roaming freely in the prairie of a city park. Near the paddock is **Spreckels Lake,** where remote-control boats cruise up and down. It's fun to sit and watch the miniboats go by. **The Presidio** is second runner-up. It's big, green, has a children's playground, a pretty cheap and uncrowded bowling alley, cannons to climb on, and there is even a Burger King. There is plenty of free parking here, too. Near the Presidio is the **Marina Green,** a strip of green that runs along the bay by the Marina. It is kite-flying heaven—and a great place for a picnic. While you are in the Marina, be sure to visit the **wave organ**—a funky creation of granite pipes that are nestled at different depths within the breaking water. The "organ" creates different tones when the waves hit the pipes. Expect sounds of orchestral proportions at high tide.

If you happen to catch a hot, sunny day in the city, a good idea might be to head to **China Beach,** one of the most kid-friendly beaches in our view. It's located in the posh Sea Cliff neighborhood and the beach is small enough to keep your eye on the kids as they run free. The facilities here are spotless and the surf is calm, thanks to the protective cliffs and coves that surround the beach. Along the Great Highway 1, right after the San Francisco Zoo, is **Fort Funston.** This isn't so much a play park but rather a park for sitting and watching the humans with wings soar off cliffs. Fort Funston is one of the only places to watch hang gliders 1-2-3-jump off a cliff right next to your bench and soar above the crashing Pacific Ocean.

unofficial **TIP**
Great places to walk include the **Golden Gate Promenade** (a three-and-a-half-mile paved walkway that starts near Fisherman's Wharf and follows the bay shore west to the bridge of the same name) and Ocean Beach, a four-mile stretch of sand beginning just south of Cliff House.

Most kids will like the view of the Pacific Ocean and the Golden Gate Bridge from atop 200-foot cliffs near the California Palace of the Legion of Honor in Lincoln Park. The kids might also enjoy taking a bay cruise and seeing

San Francisco from the water. And don't forget another place popular with both children and adults: **Lombard Street,** "the crookedest street in the world," so steep that the road has to zigzag to make the descent (between Hyde and Leavenworth streets).

RAINY-DAY BLUES

KIDS CLIMBING THE HOTEL WALLS? Let them work it off at **Mission Cliffs,** the world's largest indoor climbing gym (2295 Harrison Street at 19th Street; ☎ 415-550-0515; **www.mission-cliffs.com**).

Another option is a movie. The **AMC Kabuki 8** (1881 Post Street; ☎ 415-922-4262) in Japantown is an eight-screen theater complex that's sure to be playing something the kids will enjoy. **Metreon Center** (101 Fourth Street at Mission Street; ☎ 415-369-6000), featuring 15 movie theaters, a Sony IMAX theater, eight restaurants, shopping, and interactive, Disneyland-style attractions geared to families, is located three blocks south of Union Square. Speaking of Disney, check out the **Disney Store** at Pier 39. Shopping excursions could include a stop at Union Square and the **Virgin Records** store.

KID-FRIENDLY MENUS

IF YOU ARE TIRED OF MAKING STOPS AT THE GOLDEN ARCHES or Pizza Hut, there are several options that will please your palate as well as satisfy the picky taste of your little ones. **The Garden Terrace** in the Downtown Marriott has kids in mind for sure. They offer a half-price kids' buffet, and drinks are served with a straw straight from the crookedest street in San Fran. The menu was also designed by kids. Other dining spots children enjoy include the **Hard Rock Café,** featuring great burgers, rock memorabilia, and yet another deafening sound level (Pier 39; ☎ 415-956-2013); and **Mel's Drive-In,** straight out of *American Graffiti* and as American as it gets, with greasy fries, frothy milk shakes, and Patsy Cline crooning on the tabletop jukeboxes (2165 Lombard Street; ☎ 415-921-3039; or 3355 Geary Boulevard; ☎ 415-387-2244). **Johnny Rockets** is open late and has burgers, fries, shakes (short walk from the Marina Green, at 2201 Chestnut Street; ☎ 415-931-6258) and is right next to **Mrs. Field's Cookies** (☎ 415-441-1978). **Barney's Hamburgers** (3344 Steiner Street; ☎ 415-563-0307 or 4138 24th Street; ☎ 415-282-7770) has no relation to the purple beast that frolics on the boob tube. It has a wide selection of beef burgers but also could be the kids' first introduction to alternatives, like tofu burgers and garden burgers.

unofficial **TIP**
There is no better place to have your first sushi experience than San Francisco. Give it a go—if anything, it will be fun to see the kids' faces when you tell them it is raw fish.

PRO SPORTS AND OTHER AMUSEMENTS

DEPENDING ON THE SEASON AND TICKET availability, take the gang to a 49ers, Giants, Golden State Warriors, Oakland As, or Oakland

Raiders game. If you are visiting in the sports off-season you might want to try visiting the **Potrero Hill Recreation Center** (801 Arkansas Street at 22nd Street; ☎ 415-695-5009) where, every summer, college basketball players and pros play in a Pro-Am League. Games are usually scheduled Monday through Thursday evenings at 8 p.m. And it's free!

The kids will enjoy sailing on **Lake Merritt** or taking a ride on the Merritt Queen, a miniature Mississippi sternwheeler that plies the lake on weekends. Youngsters enjoy **Children's Fairyland** on the north shore of Lake Merritt; it's one of the most imaginative children's parks in the country (☎ 510-452-2259; **www.fairyland.org**). Admission is $6 (only adults accompanied by a child or children accompanied by an adult are admitted).

Farther afield are some kid-pleasing attractions that are still near San Francisco. **Six Flags Marine World** is a 160-acre theme park with wildlife of all kinds, including butterflies, elephants, seals, and giraffes. Admission also includes a variety of shows. The park is a 45-minute drive northeast of the city in Vallejo and is open March through September. You can also take a ferry from Fisherman's Wharf; ☎ 707-643-6722.

Paramount's Great America is a giant amusement park filled with rides such as the *Top Gun* Jetcoaster and the *Days of Thunder* Racetrack, both based on Paramount movies; it's just the place for the roller-coaster crowd. The park is a one-hour drive south of San Francisco in Santa Clara; just drive south on US 101 until you see the signs. The park is open April through September; ☎ 408-988-1776. Something to combine with a scenic drive down Route 1 along the Pacific Coast is a stop at **Monterey Bay Aquarium** (886 Cannery Row, Monterey; ☎ 831-648-4888.) The neon jellyfish tank and the walk-through tour of the Monterey Bay that starts underwater make this one of the best aquariums in the country. A little less ambitious than roller coasters and glow-in-the-dark fish is the age-old backup plan—bowling. How long has it been since you stuck your fingers in a black ball and kicked back the leg, sending pins crashing (or cleaning the gutter over and over)?

HELPFUL TIPS *for* TOURISTS

SAVE 50% WHEN YOU VISIT SAN FRANCISCO'S most popular museums and attractions with a **CityPass.** Participating attractions are the California Academy of Sciences, California Palace of the Legion of Honor, Exploratorium, Steinhart Aquarium, San Francisco Bay Cruise, and the San Francisco Museum of Modern Art. Passes cost $42 for adults and $34 for children ages 5–17. Children ages 4 and under pay the regular reduced fare at each attraction. Ticket books are sold at participating attractions and are good for nine days, beginning with the first day you use them. Don't remove the individual tickets from the booklet; just present the CityPass at each attraction, the clerk at the site removes the ticket, and you walk in. Also included is a seven-day Muni Passport valid for unlimited rides on cable cars, light rail, and buses (☎ 888-330-5008; **www.citypass.com/city/sanfrancisco.html**).

WHEN ADMISSION IS FREE

Many San Francisco museums that usually charge admission open their doors for free one day a month. If you'd like to save a few bucks during your visit, use the following list when planning your touring itinerary. And don't forget that summer is the season of free events and outdoor concerts.

- Asian Art Museum (first Tuesday of the month)
- Berkeley Art Museum (first Thursday of the month)
- California Academy of Sciences (first Wednesday of the month)
- California Palace of the Legion of Honor (first Tuesday of the month)
- Center for the Arts at Yerba Buena Gardens (first Thursday of the month)
- de Young Museum (first Tuesday of the month)
- Exploratorium (first Wednesday of the month)
- Hearst Museum of Anthropology (every Thursday)
- Oakland Museum of California (second Sunday of the month), special exhibits not included
- San Francisco Museum of Modern Art (first Tuesday of the month)
- San Francisco Zoo (first Wednesday of the month)
- Yerba Buena Gallery (first Tuesday of the month)

In addition, a few worthy attractions around town are free to the public all the time. Here's the list.

- Berkeley Rose Gardens
- Cable Car Museum
- Chinese Cultural Center of San Francisco
- Fort Point National Historic Site
- Golden Gate Band Concerts (Sundays at 1 p.m., April–October)
- Golden Gate Bridge (pedestrians and bicyclists)
- Hyde Street Pier
- Midsummer Music Festival (Stern Grove, Sloat Avenue at 19th Street, Sunday afternoons at 2 p.m., June–August)
- Musee Mecanique at Pier 45
- Museum of Money of the American West
- National Maritime Museum
- The Randall Museum
- San Francisco Fire Museum
- San Francisco Shakespeare Festival (Golden Gate Park, Sundays in September)
- Strybing Arboretum
- Wells Fargo History Museum

GET A "VIRTUAL FRIEND"

THE BEST WAY TO EXPLORE SAN FRANCISCO and find the stuff most tourists never see is to talk to a local, right? Now you can, sort of: Joie de Vivre Hospitality, a chain of boutique hotels in the Bay Area, provides "virtual friends" on its Web site (**www.jdvhospital ity.com;** click on "meet the locals"). "Friends" will describe a perfect day in the city. Ranging from Donald, "a hip San Francisco doctor with an appetite for eclectic restaurants" to Teri, "a helicopter pilot who loves baseball, dinner with friends, and flying under the Golden Gate Bridge," these real San Franciscans offer insider advice for visitors. You can even take a test on the Web site that matches you to two of the personalities most similar to yours. The Web site also provides many pages of insider info (click "Things to Do"), including favorite restaurants, visual arts, romantic hideouts and peaceful retreats, hidden places, great walking tours, and more. And it's all free.

BREATHTAKING VIEWS

WE ARE ALL DRAWN TO *THE VIEW*—A GLIMPSE of something larger, majestic, something that can breathe new life in us or suck it out if it so chooses. Breathtaking. Whether it's nature at its most expansive, or the sparkling twilight of a sky filled with stars, or a cityscape bright with energy—everyone requests a view. You don't have to know the manager of the Fairmont Hotel to get compelling views in San Francisco. Simply take a stroll and use our list of some of the best views in the city as your guide.

1. **Fort Point.** Ideally, you should be blindfolded and brought to this Civil War–era fortress. You should remove the blind as you face the Marin Headlands across the Golden Gate. Overhead is the massive Golden Gate Bridge, perhaps the most beautiful suspension bridge in the world. It's a view to die for.

2. Although it's better at night, the view from **Twin Peaks** is good whenever the weather is clear. It's a stupendous, 360° view of San Francisco.

3. The best view of the city's skyline is from **Treasure Island.** To get there, take the Treasure Island Exit from the Bay Bridge and drive to the parking area just outside the naval station.

4. For the best view of the waterfront, hike up **Telegraph Hill** to Coit Tower. Don't drive, though; parking is scarce. Either walk or take the No. 39 bus.

5. Drive across the **Golden Gate Bridge,** get off in Sausalito, and follow signs to Mount Tamalpais, where you can drive to the 2,800-foot summit (well, almost) for a heart-stopping view of San Francisco Bay, the city, the Golden Gate and Bay bridges, and the Pacific Ocean.

6. For a view of the bay that's almost as good as the one from Mount Tam, go to Berkeley, through the University of California Berkeley campus, and find Grizzly Peak Boulevard. Then drive up the winding road to

the **Lawrence Hall of Science.** Park in the lot and enjoy the vista from the plaza of the Children's Science Museum.

7. The view from the **Golden Gate Bridge** is best at sunset, when the slanting sun casts shadowy patterns on the lofty bridge towers and on the sea below—and the tour buses have left for the day. The pedestrian walkway is open until 9 p.m.

8. For an even better view of **Seal Rocks** than the one you get at Cliff House, walk up to Sutro Heights Park, which overlooks the Pacific from a lofty vantage point. Park in the lot just north of Cliff House (on the other side of the Great Highway).

9. Drive across the Golden Gate Bridge to **Vista Point,** which offers superb views of the bridge and the San Francisco skyline. It's beautiful on a sunny day, but it might be even better when the fog rolls over the hills or at night when the city glimmers beyond the Golden Gate. **The Headlands** offer postcard-perfect views of the city and the approaching fog just knocking at the gate.

10. The neighborhood of Potrero Hill, at 19th and Texas streets, makes the city skyline appear like a pop-up book. Honorable mention goes to **Dolores Park.**

SECRET STAIRCASES

SCATTERED THROUGHOUT SAN FRANCISCO'S many hills are pocket parks, restful benches, and many stairways—about 350 of them, mostly in residential neighborhoods and often adorned with flowers planted by neighbors. The stairways are used by residents to allow direct vertical access from one street to another; because most streets wind around the hills, people frequently use staircases as shortcuts.

A walk centered around an exploration of the city's staircases is cheaper than a fitness center and frequently offers views that rival what you'll find on the Golden Gate Bridge. Put on your walking shoes, grab your camera, and explore some of the city's oldest, most scenic hidden attractions—its stairways. For a comprehensive guide to the city's stairways, pick up a copy of *Stairway Walks in San Francisco, 5th ed.* by Adah Bakalinsky, available in bookstores or directly from the Wilderness Press (☎ 510-558-1666), or on **amazon.com.** Here's a sampling of some of San Francisco's best stairways.

1. The carefully landscaped stairs found near the famous Lombard Street (between Hyde and Leavenworth streets).

2. At Broadway and Lyon Street, more than ten flights of majestic stone steps surrounded by well-kept greenery and regal views of the Palace of Fine Arts, the bay, and the Marin Headlands.

3. The Greenwich Street Steps at the base of Coit Tower on Telegraph Hill; more than three separate flights of stairs that climb through tall trees and past hillside gardens and stunning views (see Part 10, Exercise and Recreation, for more specifics).

4. The Fort Mason/Aquatic Park Steps overlooking Alcatraz; the small clearing at the top features tranquility and picnic tables.

5. Pemberton Stairway in the Twin Peaks neighborhood, newly renovated with terra-cotta concrete stairs and just-planted gardens.

6. Filbert Street Steps, between Sansome Street and Telegraph Hill, a 377-step climb through verdant flower gardens and charming 19th-century cottages.

SAN FRANCISCO *on* FILM

SOME OF YOU MAY REMEMBER THAT SCENE in the classic *It Came From Beneath the Sea* circa 1955, in which a giant octopus attacks the Golden Gate Bridge and tears it in half. If you don't, it's a sure rental before you set out seeing the sights of the city. If you are a movie junkie and love to relive favorite scenes, then San Francisco is just the fix. Before renting any flicks, pick up a copy of *The San Francisco Movie Map*, sold at the California Historical Society gift shop and other locations around town. Some other notable movies that feature San Francisco include:

- *Sweet November* (2000), starring Keanu Reeves and Charlize Theron, was a flop at the box office, but it showcased the best of San Francisco as the goo-goo-eyed couple pranced around Potrero Hill and Noe Valley.
- *The Rock* (1996), starring Sean Connery, Nicolas Cage, and Ed Harris, was another Alcatraz action adventure.
- *Interview with the Vampire* (1994) The devilish leader of the vampires played by Tom Cruise offers Christian Slater "the choice" in a night-time drive across the Golden Gate Bridge.
- *The Joy Luck Club* (1993), noted for its realistic depiction of Chinese Americans, was made in Chinatown.
- *Basic Instinct* (1992) You know the shot—that crossing-the-legs-with-no-panties-shot that made the movie famous. The entire movie was shot in San Fran, evidenced by the car-chase scenes through town.
- *Escape from Alcatraz* (1979), a true story starring Clint Eastwood as the leader of a trio of escapees who actually made it off the Rock.
- *Birdman of Alcatraz* (1962) with Burt Lancaster as Robert Stroud, the convict turned ornithologist.
- *What's Up, Doc?* (1972), a screwball comedy starring Barbra Streisand and Ryan O'Neal, was filmed at the San Francisco Hilton (33 O'Farrell Street), called Hotel Bristol in the film. While we are on hotels: the lobby of the Fairmont Hotel on Nob Hill was featured in that 1980s television series *Hotel*.
- *Vertigo* (1958) It's not a place, it's a classic thriller directed by Alfred Hitchcock. The British director loved San Francisco and he shows the town at its best in this 1958 film starring James Stewart and Kim Novak. Locations in the movie include Mission Dolores, the California

Palace of the Legion of Honor (the movie's scenes were filmed in Gallery 6), the Palace of Fine Arts, and Fort Point (where Stewart dives into San Francisco Bay to save Novak).

▌▌ THE WINE COUNTRY

AFTER A FEW DAYS OF TOURING HECTIC San Francisco, what could be better than relaxing in a setting of pastoral splendor only an hour from Union Square? The wine country is a region of wooded hills and luxuriant valleys where tilled fields create geometric patterns across the landscape and narrow lanes wind among the hills. Quaint country inns and designer restaurants with massive wine lists are abundant and pamper the well-heeled visitors who flock to these valleys, defined by low oak-and-chaparral-covered ridges.

For most folks, the visual grandeur is secondary to the lure of the fruit of the land. The wines produced in the Napa and Sonoma valleys rival the best vintages of France—and everybody wants to see where the magic is made. Wineries are everywhere in the two neighboring valleys, located north of San Francisco and inland of the Pacific Coast. They are so numerous that it's easy to think this is the wine-making capital of California. In fact, only about five percent of the state's total production comes from the region. But far and away the best wines produced in the country come from here. The reason is the region's Mediterranean climate: hot, dry summers and cool, wet winters result in stressed-out grapevines that produce small, thick-skinned fruit. Because most of a wine's flavor and character comes from the skin rather than the pulp, the grapes that grow in these valleys result in premium vintages that impress wine snobs around the world.

Wine has been made in the valleys since the 18th century, when clerics in Spanish missions planted vineyards to produce black grapes for sacramental wines. After centuries of ups and downs, the wine business began booming in the 1960s. Wine has evolved into an increasingly popular national drink, and the valleys have recovered from the last slump caused by Prohibition, when many vineyards were converted into orchards.

Today's renaissance is extraordinary; acreage has expanded exponentially and big business has moved in, most notably Coca-Cola and Nestlé. Even the French, formerly aloof, have formed partnerships with local growers. Napa Valley boasts more than 250 wineries, while Sonoma Valley has about 35. Winemaking in the valleys is now a multibillion-dollar business, and millions of folks tour the wine country each year.

WHICH VALLEY?

DAYTRIPPERS ON A SELF-GUIDED DAY TOUR of the wine country are faced with a choice: **Napa** or **Sonoma?** Alas, touring both valleys

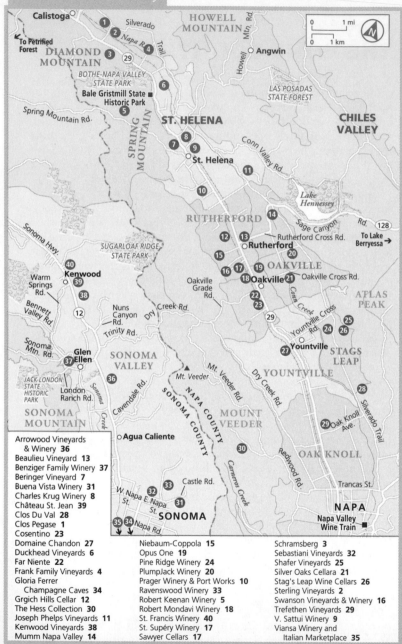

the wine country

Arrowood Vineyards
& Winery **36**
Beaulieu Vineyard **13**
Benziger Family Winery **37**
Beringer Vineyard **7**
Buena Vista Winery **31**
Charles Krug Winery **8**
Château St. Jean **39**
Clos Du Val **28**
Clos Pegase **1**
Cosentino **23**
Domaine Chandon **27**
Duckhead Vineyards **6**
Far Niente **22**
Frank Family Vineyards **4**
Gloria Ferrer
Champagne Caves **34**
Grgich Hills Cellar **12**
The Hess Collection **30**
Joseph Phelps Vineyards **11**
Kenwood Vineyards **38**
Mumm Napa Valley **14**

Niebaum-Coppola **15**
Opus One **19**
Pine Ridge Winery **24**
PlumpJack Winery **20**
Prager Winery & Port Works **10**
Ravenswood Winery **33**
Robert Keenan Winery **5**
Robert Mondavi Winery **18**
St. Francis Winery **40**
St. Supéry Winery **17**
Sawyer Cellars **17**

Schramsberg **3**
Sebastiani Vineyards **32**
Shafer Vineyards **25**
Silver Oaks Cellara **21**
Stag's Leap Wine Cellars **26**
Sterling Vineyards **2**
Swanson Vineyards & Winery **16**
Trefethen Vineyards **29**
V. Sattui Winery **9**
Viansa Winery and
Italian Marketplace **35**

in one day just isn't practical. Napa, the easternmost valley, is by far the best known of the two. It stretches for 35 miles from the town of Napa north to the resort town of Calistoga. In the long, narrow valley, grape arbors alternate with wild grasses, and the rich bottomland gives way to forested slopes of the surrounding ridges. Once past the congested and unexciting town of Napa, the beautiful valley looks more like southern France than Northern California.

Yet Napa is fashionable beyond belief and attracts millionaires the way a magnet draws iron filings. The valley also seems to draw more than its fair share of pinch-faced connoisseurs who mutter in mangled French as they swirl and sniff premium vintages in the tasting rooms of the wineries. Thankfully, the wine snobs are vastly outnumbered. Napa Valley has been discovered and hordes of tourists have made it one of California's most popular attractions. Many of the wineries along CA 29 are huge, with massive parking lots that contain special areas reserved for tour buses. While the countryside is pretty (increasingly so the farther north you go), very little in Napa Valley is small-scale or intimate.

Sonoma Valley, on the other hand, has fewer wineries. Most are relatively small, still family-run, and tucked away on side roads. They don't line the highway like designer discount outlets (also found in Napa). There's also notably less pretension in the wine-tasting rooms. In addition, Sonoma has more to offer than wineries, including a Spanish mission and the former estate of Jack London, one of America's greatest writers. As you've probably guessed by now, *Unofficial Guide* researchers, who loathe crowds and tourist hype, give the edge to Sonoma over its eastern neighbor. Another plus: It's closer to San Francisco (though not by much).

We prefer less-touristy Sonoma, but that doesn't mean you should rule out Napa. If one of your favorite wines is produced by, say, the Robert Mondavi Winery, head to Napa, where that well-known firm provides a variety of tours and tastings (call ☎ 888-766-6328 extension 2000 for reservations). You'll have a great time. Plus, the crowds and oversized wineries decrease the farther north you go in Napa. Calistoga, at the top of the valley, offers a lot for visitors to see and do. Another solution to the "Which valley?" conundrum is to make your visit an overnight affair and tour both valleys. We suggest a two-day tour later in this chapter.

TOURING STRATEGIES

VISITING THE WINE COUNTRY SHOULDN'T BE about following a strict itinerary and seeing how much you can do in one day of hectic touring. It's quite the opposite, a joie-de-vivre kind of thing: a celebration of the good things in life, such as wonderful scenery, great food, and good friends. These are all complimented by fine wine—thus the popularity of touring the wine country.

Don't schedule too rigidly your visit to Napa or Sonoma. Still, a little judicious planning can go a long way to ensuring that a visit is pleasant, even memorable. Whether you decide to visit Napa, Sonoma, or both valleys, we'll provide you with specific advice that will allow you to get the most enjoyment from a one- or two-day excursion.

PLANNING

ALTHOUGH SEVERAL TOUR COMPANIES IN San Francisco provide bus tours to the wine country, we think the best way to enjoy a visit is to rent a car, giving you the flexibility for a relaxing, fun-filled trip. You'll get more from a wine-country excursion if you can give it some focus. For example, plan on visiting one or two wineries that produce wines you enjoy at home. Or structure your day around a bike ride or something else not wine-related (we provide suggestions below). Then leave some time for a spontaneous stop at one or two other wineries, a picnic in a park, a museum visit, or shopping in one of the many towns.

unofficial **TIP**
If at all possible, don't visit the wine country on a weekend; the best time to visit is early in the week. Plan on leaving San Francisco around 9 a.m. to get past the worst of morning rush-hour traffic and into the wine country by midmorning. Be sure to eat a good breakfast before leaving; you'll appreciate it later in the morning when you've sampled your first glass or two of wine.

Don't plan on visiting more than two or three wineries in a day. Otherwise the day becomes a blur of wine-tasting rooms that run together in your memory and your palate—not to mention the problem of too much alcohol consumption. One advantage of a two-day wine-country tour is that you can trade off driving; that way, there's always someone who can taste the wine and someone who can safely navigate the car.

Many folks pack a picnic lunch, visit a winery, buy a bottle of wine, and enjoy an outdoor meal in a picnic area provided at many wineries. (Most of the picnic areas are in fabulously beautiful settings surrounded by forests and vineyards.) You can buy sandwiches or fixings at local delicatessens and groceries; don't forget to bring a corkscrew. Keep in mind that the whole point of visiting the wine country is to relax and have a good time.

WINERY TOURS

WITH ABOUT 400 WINERIES IN AND AROUND the Napa and Sonoma valleys, picking a few to visit can be tough. You can just wander around and stop in wineries on a whim, but we think it pays to be selective. Visit a winery that makes a wine you like or, if you need some help, consult the list of wineries on pages 170 and 176.

Virtually all of the wineries are open to the public from about 10 a.m. to 4 p.m. daily (and an hour to two later in the summer). Most have tasting rooms and maybe a picnic area outside. While many firms offer free wine tastings, increasingly some wineries (especially in Napa) are charging a few dollars for the opportunity to sample the fruits of their vineyards.

Larger winemaking concerns, for example Mondavi in Napa and Sebastiani in Sonoma, offer guided tours of the premises (some for a small fee). Visitors tour in groups of about 30; the tours last a half hour or so, ending with a visit to a tasting room. These are usually large, comfortable, and well-appointed rooms where visitors sample the wares; they can also purchase wine here or in a nearby sales room. Smaller wineries, by and large, require reservations at least a day in advance (even earlier in the summer and fall) for a tour with a smaller group that may last two hours.

So Which Tour Is Right for You?

NONRESERVATION TOURS If your interest in wine is casual, a non-reservation tour at one of the larger wineries should do the trick. You'll gain insight into the wine country's unusual climate, which is the main reason the area produces such good wine. You'll also get a glimpse of the winemaking process, from the huge stainless-steel vats where the grapes are fermented to the large warehouses where the new wine ages in oak barrels. Tour guides provide a good overview of the fascinating and complex operation of a winery; tours usually depart on the hour or half-hour throughout the day. The icing on the cake, of course, is the end of the tour, when you arrive in the tasting room and sample different wines made on the premises; often you can help yourself to hors d'oeuvres as you sample different vintages.

RESERVATION-ONLY TOURS Reservation-only guided tours, some of them free, are longer and best appreciated by wine-savvy folks who know the basics of winemaking and want to learn more. And they will as they're led around the winery by their tour guide, often an employee who really knows and appreciates good wine. On many tours, visitors spend a lot of time in the aging rooms, which are stacked to the ceiling with oak barrels. The guide may not only discuss, say, how American versus French oak barrels affect the tannin content in red wines; he or she may also tap barrels at various stages of aging and let you taste the difference. With the exception of the actual quaffing of the grape, this can be either utterly fascinating or excruciatingly boring, depending on your level of interest.

On a reservation-only tour, you'll also get from-the-hip insights into the winemaking business (such as how much of the winery's grape production comes from leased vineyards—and why). You may also pick up some valuable tips, such as which vintages are best for particular wines.

unofficial **TIP**
1995 gets rave reviews for virtually all wines produced in the wine country; warm winds from the Central Valley swept through just before the harvest, making the grapes smaller and thickening their skins.

WINE TASTING: TO SWIRL OR TO SNIFF? The ancient Greeks had it wrong: The nectar of the gods isn't sweet ambrosia, it's wine. Yet deciding which wine is the best can be like trying to determine the one true religion. That's OK. A trip to the wine country can be the start of a lifetime enjoyment of the fermented grape as you begin an education on how to savor this mysterious beverage.

Keep in mind that there are two types of California wines: varietals, made primarily from a particular kind of grape, such as cabernet sauvignon or zinfandel, and the lower-quality generics, wines blended from several different grapes and often named for a European wine region such as Burgundy.

To learn more about wines, you need to taste them. Unfortunately, folks who are unversed in the liturgy of wine tasting can feel awfully uncomfortable as a nearby wine snob swirls and sniffs a glass of wine. Don't be intimidated. You're on vacation. Why let a self-styled connoisseur ruin your fun?

Here are some things that will provide the start to the education of your palate. First, the look or appearance is important. Wine should be clear and brilliant, not cloudy. Consider the smell, or "nose" of the vintage, which includes the aroma or scent of the grapes themselves, and the "bouquet," the smell from fermentation and aging. Finally, consider the taste. Let the wine wash around your mouth for a moment and determine if it's sweet or dry, light-bodied (watery) or full-bodied (like milk), rough or mellow. But mainly, enjoy. Chat it up with the winery employees behind the counter and you'll gain more insight (and maybe they'll pour some reserve vintages for your tasting enjoyment).

WHEN TO GO

THE BEST TIME TO VISIT THE WINE COUNTRY IS IN the fall, when the harvest occurs and the air is redolent with the aroma of fermenting wine. Depending on the weather, this can be anytime in September or October. Street fairs and festivals are the norm, and it's the season of golf tournaments, wine auctions, and art and food fairs. The countryside is beautiful, with trees turning brilliant gold and red. And the weather usually cooperates, too. It can get hot, and there's not much chance of rain. Yet there are drawbacks to visiting at harvest time: traffic clogging the major roads in both valleys and a decrease in attention from winery employees, who are justifiably consumed with getting the grapes in.

unofficial **TIP**
If you do plan to visit the wine country in the fall, try to go during the week, not on weekends, to avoid the worst of the tourist crush. It's also a good idea to make lodging and dinner reservations weeks in advance.

Spring and summer are also prime times for visiting the wine country. And it shows—CA 29 in Napa Valley is often backed up on weekends. (You'll encounter a bit less traffic in Sonoma on spring and summer weekends.) Summer in the wine country is notoriously hot and dry, so be sure to pack a sun hat and try to get an early start.

PURCHASING WINE AT A WINERY

QUESTION: CAN YOU GET GREAT DEALS on wine sold at wineries? The answer, by and large, is no. The sales rooms in the wineries aren't there to compete with retail liquor outlets in your hometown. As a result, the prices are pretty much what you would pay at home, give or take a couple of bucks a bottle. Of course, the selec-

unofficial **TIP**
Winter, the rainy season, is a good time to visit; although the landscape isn't as colorful, there's a stark beauty to the valleys and mountains and a more laid-back atmosphere in the wineries. And the crowds are minimal.

tion is usually a lot better, and you'll also find special vintages available only at the winery. So while the sales rooms do a brisk business, nobody is getting great bargains.

Wine is also sold by the case at the wineries. Depending on the state you live in, you can have your purchase shipped home (you pay the shipping cost). States that allow shipments from the wineries are California, Colorado, Idaho, Illinois, Iowa, Maine, Minnesota, Missouri, Nebraska, Nevada, New Mexico, North Dakota, Oregon, Washington, Washington, D.C., West Virginia, Wisconsin, and Wyoming. If you don't live in one of these states, you're not completely out of luck. Make your purchase and ship it home yourself (tax laws limit shipments by wineries to the states listed above). The cost is about $40 a case, and the folks at the winery can suggest where to take your purchase and have it shipped.

GETTING THERE

THE WINE COUNTRY SPREADS NORTH FROM the top of San Francisco Bay in two parallel valleys, Napa and Sonoma; in between are the oak-covered Mayacamas Mountains. To get there by car, cross the Golden Gate Bridge on US 101 to CA 37 east. Then bear left onto CA 121; next, turn left onto CA 12 for Sonoma Valley or drive a few miles more and turn left onto CA 29, Napa Valley's main drag. In nonrush-hour traffic, it's about an hour's drive from downtown San Francisco to the southern entrances of the valleys.

NAPA VALLEY

THE HEART OF AMERICA'S WINE CULTURE is found in Napa Valley, a region with roots going back to the mid-19th century. The valley is defined by two rough-hewn mountain ranges, and vestiges of its tumultuous geologic past still bubble to the surface of the earth at hot springs in Calistoga and at (the other) Old Faithful Geyser.

Compared to the natural features, the wineries in Napa Valley are recent interlopers. Virtually the entire California wine industry was

unofficial **TIP**
You can make a drive in the valley more interesting by heading south from Calistoga on the more scenic Silverado Trail, which creates a circuit instead of an out-and-back excursion. While not nearly as commercial, this pleasant two-lane highway passes plenty of wineries. The crossroads between the two parallel roads are also scenic and worth exploring.

killed by Prohibition; only a few wineries survived. This means most of the players in the valley today are relative newcomers—a diverse collection of wealthy doctors, lawyers, actors, filmmakers, artists, and business executives all motivated to outdo their neighbors in creating memorable vintages. The joke used to be that they were all going broke creating wine—and loving it. Today, not all of them are going broke.

Napa Valley is anchored in the south by the town of the same name, and visitors on a one-day outing should pass it by. Continue up CA 29 toward the villages of Yountville, Oakville, and Rutherford, where things start to get more interesting (and scenic). Saint Helena, the next town, is considered the heart of Napa's wine-growing region, while Calistoga, a resort town for more than 100 years, is its northern anchor.

NAPA VALLEY DINING AND LODGING

WHETHER YOU ARE PLANNING A MARRIAGE proposal, a solo retreat, or a gathering of friends, there are top-rated dining and lodging options in all areas of the wine country. Be advised that many, perhaps most, lodging places in the valley require a two-night minimum, especially on weekends and in high season. Here are a few we recommend:

Napa Dining

- **NV Restaurant** (1106 First Street; ☎ 707-265-6400; open Monday–Saturday for dinner, 5–10 p.m.).
  This classic California kitchen relies on local, seasonal ingredients. One could make a satisfying meal on the appetizers, and the dessert menu is especially creative.
- **Julia's Kitchen** (500 First Street; ☎ 707-265-5700; open daily for lunch and dinner).
  Julia Child donated much of her kitchen and part of her spirit to this Copia operation. Look for California cooking using local ingredients, some grown on the premises.

Napa Lodging

- **The Napa Inn Bed and Breakfast** (1137 Warren Street; ☎ 707-257-1444; about $120–$295 per night).
  Candlelight breakfasts and fireplaces make this a very romantic spot within the valley.
- **Blue Violet Mansion** (443 Brown Street; ☎ 707-253-2583; about $200–$359 per night).
  Won an award for best bed-and-breakfast in North America.

- **Cedar Gables Inn** (486 Combs Street; ☎ 707-224-7969; about $190–$319 per night).
  A historic B&B centrally located within the heart of Napa.

Yountville Dining

- **Brix Restaurant** (7377 Saint Helena Highway; ☎ 707-944-2749).
  Watch the renowned chef in the exhibition kitchen that is the center-piece of the beautifully decorated space. The menu is cutting-edge.
- **The French Laundry** (6640 Washington Street; ☎ 707-944-2380).
  Redolent of roses and pure culinary artistry atop the porcelain plate— your palate will experience its very first . . . well, you know.
- **Wine Garden Restaurant** (6476 Washington Street; ☎ 707-945-1002).
  Housed in a former diner, this chic little California-style gem still man-ages to maintain a friendly neighborhood diner feel.

Yountville Lodging

- **Bordeaux House** (6600 Washington Street; ☎ 707-944-2855; about $120–$230 per night).
  Centrally located B&B. Perfect for those who like to stroll around.
- **Castle in the Clouds** (7400 Saint Helena Highway; ☎ 707-944-2785; about $255–$365 per night).
  High on the hill overlooking Napa, as the name suggests. Amazing views!
- **Villagio Inn & Spa** (6481 Washington Street; ☎ 707-944-8877; about $230–$1,165 per night).
  Tuscan-inspired countryside inn and spa. Gardens and trickling water outside ease any tension away; a great weekend getaway.

Saint Helena Dining

- **Martini House** (1245 Spring Street; ☎ 707-963-2233).
  The service, food, and wine are all world-class and the décor is stun-ningly gorgeous. And yet it never intimidates. The staff is just too good at what they do to let that happen.
- **Wine Spectator Greystone Restaurant** (2555 Main Street; ☎ 707-967-1010).
  Their "today's temptations," a selection of the chef's daily creations, is a big table pleaser. Fresh herbs from their garden accompany all French dishes.
- **La Toque** (1140 Rutherford Cross Road; ☎ 707-963-9770; www.latoque.com).
  Not in Saint Helena proper, but in nearby Rutherford, about five min-utes south. At this French-inspired California restaurant, the fixed-price menu changes daily and features superb creations by one of the valley's finest chefs.

Saint Helena Lodging

- **Harvest Inn** (One Main Street; ☎ 707-963-9463; about $270–$550 per night).
  Private terraces look out onto eight acres of beautiful landscape and vineyards. One of the most serene places in the valley, this is a great place to do nothing.
- **The Inn at Southbridge** (1020 Main Street; ☎ 707-967-9400; about $275–$535 per night).
  You'll feel like you're on a European holiday. This is a cozy inn, complete with down comforters, fireplaces, and private balconies overlooking Napa.

Calistoga Dining

- **Brannan's Grill** (1374 Lincoln Avenue; ☎ 707-942-2233; www.brannansgrill.com).
  It looks like a classic steakhouse, but the fare here is "seasonal new American." The Liberty duck is a signature dish, as is the triple cream cheeseburger.
- **Calistoga Inn** (1250 Lincoln Avenue; ☎ 707-942-4104; www.calistogainn.com).
  One of the happiest dining rooms in the valley, specializing in comfort food. When you've had it with the high-toned eating common in Napa, come here for meat and potatoes perfectly rendered.

Calistoga Lodging

- **The Pink Mansion** (1415 Foothill Boulevard; ☎ 707-942-0558; www.pinkmansion.com; about $175–$345 per night).
  Elegance at its best; built in 1875, this bed-and-breakfast is a historic landmark.
- **Safari West Wildlife Preserve and Tent Camp** (3115 Porter Creek Road; ☎ 707-579-2551; www.safariwest.com; about $225 per night).
  African animals in this luxury safari tent camp create a unique experience.
- **Silver Rose Resort Winery** (351 Rosedale Road; ☎ 800-995-9381; www.silverrose.com; about $165–$305 per night).
  A romantic hideaway nestled among vineyards, and equipped with its own winery and spa. Each room is uniquely decorated and you'll be reluctant to leave yours. But do go to the daily barrel tasting in the winery.

NAPA VALLEY WINERIES

WITH SOMETHING LIKE 240 WINERIES IN Napa Valley (most of which are open to the public), it's just not possible to provide a comprehensive listing. Plus, part of the fun is touring on your own without a rigid itinerary, and making your own discoveries. First-time visitors will have no trouble finding wineries; both of the valley's two major routes (CA 29 and, to the east, the Silverado Trail) pass dozens of estates. To get you on your way, here's a sampling of Napa wineries well worth a visit.

- **Robert Mondavi Winery** (on CA 29, Oakville; ☎ 888-766-6328; www.robertmondaviwinery.com).

This is wine central for the Napa wine industry. The winery was founded in 1966, when there were only about six wineries in the valley with national distribution. Today Mondavi offers one of the best tours in the valley, and its Spanish mission–style architecture is a knockout. A retail area sells wines, T-shirts, and books. There is a tasting room where reserve wine is sold by the glass. Tours are offered on the hour, and it's a good idea to make reservations.

- **Niebaum-Coppola Estate** (1991 Saint Helena Highway; ☎ 707-968-1100; www.niebaumcoppola.com).

Up the road in Rutherford, this is a huge operation with a fountain-enhanced plaza and a small museum highlighting the career of its owner, film director Francis Ford Coppola. The entire place is unmatched for sheer panache. The museum is free and fun; on display are old movie projectors, film props from *The Godfather* movies, and a real Tucker automobile (from *Tucker: A Man and His Dream*). Of course, you'll also find a tasting room and a retail sales room. Winery tours are by appointment only.

- **Frog's Leap** (8815 Conn Creek Road; ☎ 707-963-4704; www.frogleap.com).

Also in Rutherford, Frog's Leap was once a deserted "ghost winery." But today it sits beside 40 acres of organically grown Merlot and Sauvignon Blanc vines. Originally built in 1884, the winery features a big red, wooden barn with period photos dotting the interior. Winery tours are by reservation only.

- **Sterling Vineyards** (1111 Dunaweal Lane; ☎ 707-942-3300; www.sterlingvineyards.com).

At the top of the valley in Calistoga, Sterling was built with tourists in mind. An aerial tram leads to a white cluster of Mediterranean monastic stucco buildings that rise from a bluff south of town. The 300-foot knoll features a visitor center, tasting room, self-guided winery tour, gift shop, and retail room.

- **Silverado Vineyards** (6121 Silverado Trail; ☎ 707-257-1770; www.silveradovineyards.com).

On the Silverado Trail in Napa, Silverado Vineyards has spectacular views across the valley—and excellent wines. Owned by the family of the late Walt Disney, the winery has a stunning setting and an interior display of original art by American naturalist painters John James Audubon and Thomas Hill. Winery tours are by appointment only.

- **Vincent Arroyo Winery** (just north of Calistoga off CA 29 at 2361 Glenwood Avenue; ☎ 707-942-6995; www.vincentarroyo.com).

For a low-key, off-the-beaten-path and virtually noncommercial winery experience, stop by Vincent Arroyo Winery. Joy, the resident canine, has a wine named after her—and the Petite Sirah is superb. Call for directions.

NAPA VALLEY ATTRACTIONS

- **Bale Grist Mill State Historic Park** (north of Saint Helena on CA 29; ☎ 707-963-2236).

  This is a flour mill operation that predates California statehood. Built in 1846 and restored to operating condition, the mill features a 36-foot wooden waterwheel and large millstones. On weekends, a miller grinds grain and visitors can see baking demonstrations. You can also purchase flour from the mill.

- **Copia, the American Institute for Wine Food and the Arts** (500 First Street, Napa; ☎ 707-259-1600; open Wednesday–Sunday, 10 a.m.–5 p.m.; www.copia.org).

  Copia is like the Smithsonian of gastronomy. An institute dedicated to the role of food, wine, and art in American life, it's part museum, part school, part restaurant, and part theater. The core exhibit in the museum is called "Forks in the Road: Food, Wine and the American Table." It explores not only the physical, but the emotional and spiritual aspects of food and wine in American life. You can come here for the museum, then have lunch in either Julia's Kitchen (☎ 707-265-5700) or The American Market Café (☎ 707-265-5701). Or you can visit the tasting room and explore the wines of California and beyond. Attend the lectures and the cooking classes, shop in the bookstore, or do it all and stay on in the evening for the Friday Night Flick. Admission is $12.50.

- **kids** • **Old Faithful Geyser** (☎ 707-942-6463; www.oldfaithfulgeyser.com).

  Outside of Calistoga (not to be confused with a similar geothermal phenomena at Yellowstone National Park in Wyoming), Old Faithful offers a spectacular show by nature as 350° water shoots 60 feet in the air for three or four minutes. The cycle repeats about every 45 minutes, and kids love it. The setting is breathtakingly scenic, with Mount Saint Helena and the craggy Palisades Mountains in the background. The cost is a pricey $8 for adults, $7 for seniors, and $3 for children ages 6–12 (free for ages 5 and under); and no, you can't see this natural performance from the parking lot—tall bamboo blocks the view.

- **Petrified Forest** (☎ 707-942-6667; www.petrifiedforest.org).

  West of Calistoga, the Petrified Forest offers a pleasant walk in the woods past 3.5-million-year-old fallen giants—fossilized redwoods, some of them eight feet in diameter. Alas, they're not upright and some of the specimens were buried and now lie in pits. It's a pleasant and scenic place to walk off that second (or third, or fourth) glass of wine. Admission is $6 adults; $5 seniors and children ages 12–17; $3 children ages 3–11.

- **The Sharpsteen Museum** (1311 Washington Street, Calistoga; ☎ 707-942-5911; www.sharpsteen-museum.org).

  Revisit the early days of Calistoga and Napa Valley at the Sharpsteen Museum. Built by a retired Walt Disney animator, this one-room museum highlights the resort's history with dioramas, old photographs, doll houses, re-creations of Victorian interiors, gold-panning displays, and a horse carriage. It's an eclectic mix of historical items that's worth a peek. Admission is $3; children under age 12 free; the museum is open daily (except Christmas and Thanksgiving) from 11 a.m. to 4 p.m.

- **Silverado Museum** (1490 Library Lane, Saint Helena; ☎ 707-963-3757; www.silveradomuseum.org).

This museum is dedicated to the life and works of Robert Louis Stevenson, author of classic works of literature such as *Treasure Island* and *Dr. Jekyll and Mr. Hyde*. The Scottish writer lived in the area in 1880 with his bride and regained his health in the mountain air and sunshine. The two-room museum includes memorabilia, manuscripts, childhood letters, paintings, and the desk used by the writer. Located near the public library in Saint Helena (from CA 29, go east on Adams Street to Library Lane), the museum is open from noon to 4 p.m. daily, except Mondays and holidays; admission is free.

OUTDOOR FUN IN NAPA VALLEY

NAPA VALLEY IS FAMOUS FOR BICYCLING, with gentle hills, wide shoulders on the main roads, low traffic on the side roads, and great scenery. **Saint Helena Cyclery** (1156 Main Street, Saint Helena; ☎ 707-963-7736) rents bikes, and the town is a good, centrally located starting point to enjoy a ride. The hourly rate is $10 for high-quality hybrid (city) bikes; included are a lock, water bottle, rear rack, and bag to carry your picnic supplies. The daily rate is $30. The shop also provides maps and tour information. No reservations are accepted; the shop is open daily.

Getaway Adventures (1117 Lincoln Avenue; ☎ 800-499-2453; www.getawayadventures.com) in Calistoga has been leading bicycling, hiking, kayaking, and other outdoor tours since 1992. Offering both bike rentals and van-supported, single-day and multiday trips in the wine country, Getaway specializes in what owner Randy Johnson calls a "stop and smell the Zinfandel pace."

Try horseback riding in Napa Valley. **Napa Valley Trail Rides** (☎ 707-996-8566 or www.napa sonomatrailrides.com) provides horses and guides April through October at Skyline Wilderness Park. Rates start at $90 for a two-hour ride. There's an additional $5 park entrance fee.

Napa's dry, southerly breezes create optimal conditions for all kinds of aerial sports. **Balloons Above the Valley** (5091 Solano Avenue, Napa; ☎ 800-464-6824; www.balloonrides.com) launches hot-air balloons with 8 to 16 passengers. Liftoff is around 6:30 a.m., when the cool morning air is best for ballooning (making a stay in the valley the night before almost mandatory). The flight

unofficial **TIP**
Randy Johnson, owner of **Getaway Adventures**, advises bicycle enthusiasts who want to explore the fabled back roads of Napa and nearby Sonoma on their own to ship their own bikes to the wine country. "I don't recommend bringing it on the plane, because it's liable to get lost. Most shops will reassemble your bike for little or no cost. If you're in the wine country for more than a few days and cycling is your main focus, there's no way you'll duplicate the experience on a rental bike."

lasts about an hour to an hour and a half depending on the weather, and ends with a champagne breakfast. Daily flights (weather permitting) cost $210 a person; reservations are required.

SHOPPING IN NAPA VALLEY

Napa Premium Outlets (☎ 707-226-9876; **www.premiumoutlets.com**) in Napa features 50 stores specializing in discounted designer fashions and name-brand merchandise, ranging from Brooks Brothers to Tommy Hilfiger. To reach the outlet mall, take CA 29 to the First Street Exit. Saint Helena, generally recognized as Napa Valley's main hub, is also Grand Central for shoppers. Main Street, noted for its arching sycamore trees, is lined with upscale gift shops, boutiques, clothing stores, jewelers, and wine shops.

unofficial **TIP**
The best place in the county to buy wine is probably the **Safeway** (1026 Hunt Avenue, Saint Helena; ☎ 707-963-3833). Probably no outlet has a larger selection at better prices. But **Dean and Deluca** (607 Saint Helena Highway; ☎ 707-967-9980) is also a good supplier.

In Calistoga, there are specialized retailers, including antiques stores, clothing shops, and a bookstore. The historic **Calistoga Depot** (1458 Lincoln Avenue) a former railway station, has been converted into a mall; the **Calistoga Wine Stop** (1458 Lincoln Avenue, #2; ☎ 707-942-5556) is housed in an antique railroad car. The wine shop at **All Seasons Café** (1400 Lincoln Avenue; ☎ 707-942-9111) offers a wide selection of hard-to-find Napa wines.

HEALTH SPAS IN NAPA VALLEY

FOR FOLKS WHO PREFER THEIR ENTERTAINMENT closer to the ground, Calistoga is home to about a dozen health spas featuring hot mineral springs, heated pools, mud baths, steam baths, and massages. At **Calistoga Spa Hot Springs** (1006 Washington Street; ☎ 707-942-6269; **www.calistogaspa.com**) guests can steep in four different mineral pools (starting at $25) or indulge in a volcanic-ash mud bath with steam rinse ($58). The spa also has 57 rooms, ranging from $127 to $185 a night.

Dr. Wilkinson's Hot Springs Resort (1507 Lincoln Avenue, Calistoga; ☎ 707-942-4102; **www.drwilkinson.com**) offers a full range of soothing treatments, including mud baths, mineral whirlpool baths, blanket wraps, therapeutic massage, facials, acupressure face-lifts, and salt-glow scrubs. The Works, a two-hour spa treatment, is $109; facials start at $89. The resort is open daily, and appointments are recommended.

NAPA VALLEY WINE TRAIN

ENJOY A RELAXING GOURMET DINING EXCURSION on one of several restored 1915 Pullman railroad cars that run between Napa and

Saint Helena year-round. The **Napa Valley Wine Train** (☎ 800-427-4124 or 707-253-2111; **www.winetrain.com**) offers a three-hour, 36-mile excursion through Napa Valley. You won't stop at any wineries but you can enjoy classic European cuisine with California overtones prepared on board. There are two seatings for lunch and dinner; passengers spend half the trip in a dining car and half in a lounge car.

The train ride plus a three- or four-course lunch or dinner ($90–$110 a person; more for paired wines) includes a glass of wine; train fare and tips are included. A trip without a meal in the Silverado Deli Car, where there's an à la carte menu, costs $47.50. Reservations are required.

AMERICAN SAFARI CRUISES

TAKE A TRIP UP THE NAPA AND PETALUMA RIVERS, slip beneath the Golden Gate Bridge, nose around the north bay shore, all in dreamy comfort with a glass of Merlot in hand. Boarding in San Francisco, American Safari operates multiday/night cruises through the northern bay and the wine country. The vessels are luxurious without being ostentatious, the service staff truly aim to please, and the cooks are first-rate. During the day on-board guides lead informative tours to wineries, galleries, and historical sites. At night passengers cruise and dine and, if you like, party! The bar and kitchen are open as long as you are awake. You can go on the day tours, or stay on board and soak in the hot tub or watch movies in the lounge or just veg out. Call ☎ 888-862-8881 or visit **www.am safari.com/california.html**.

VISITOR INFORMATION

YOU CAN GET MORE INFORMATION ON WINERIES, accommodation, dining, and attractions by contacting the **Napa Valley Conference and Visitors Bureau** (1310 Napa Town Center, Napa, CA 94559; ☎ 707-226-7459; **www.napavalley.org**). Other visitor contacts in Napa Valley include the **Calistoga Chamber of Commerce** (1458 Lincoln Avenue, #9, Calistoga, CA 94515: ☎ 707-942-6333; 9 a.m.–5 p.m., Monday–Friday; **www.calistogafun.com**) and the **Saint Helena Chamber of Commerce** (1010 Main Street, Suite A, Saint Helena, CA 94574; ☎ 800-799-6456 or 707-963-4456; **www.sthelena.com**).

For help finding a room, especially in the harvest season when this can be challenging, try these free reservation services: **Napa Valley Reservations Unlimited** (☎ 800-251-6272; **www.napavalley reservations.com**) and **Wine Country Concierge** (☎ 888-946-3289 or 707-252-4472; 9 a.m.–5:30 p.m., Monday–Friday; **www.winetrip.com**). Both keep a list of available rooms at bed-and-breakfast accommodations and other lodging.

unofficial **TIP**
In the spring, summer, or fall, remember that traffic along CA 29 is relentless. Make it a point to request sleeping quarters that face the vineyards, not the highway.

SONOMA VALLEY

WHILE NAPA VALLEY IS UPSCALE AND ELEGANT, its next-door neighbor, Sonoma Valley, is overalls and corduroy. Unlike the eye-catching architecture in the wineries of Napa, the wineries here tend to be understated converted barns. Smaller producers whose families have grown grapes for generations still make wine in rustic buildings that are often beautiful in their simplicity. Here, family-run wineries are more apt to treat visitors like friends, and tastings are usually free.

Sonoma Valley is home to Northern California's earliest wine-making, with stunning old vineyards planted on rolling hills. The Spanish-era town of Sonoma is the cultural hub for Sonoma Valley, one of four major wine regions found in Sonoma County (the others are Alexander Valley, Russian River Valley, and Dry Creek Valley). A charming eight-acre plaza green in Sonoma built by General Mariano Guadalupe Vallejo in 1834 is a rural oasis surrounded by the area's best shops and restaurants.

Crescent-shaped Sonoma Valley curves between oak-covered mountain ranges and, most folks say, beats its neighbor hands-down on looks. (The scenery attracted writer Jack London, who owned a ranch in Glen Ellen; now it's a state park.) The valley presents a criss-cross pattern of vineyards; unlike the nearly endless procession of megawineries lining the highway at Napa, most wineries are tucked away on winding back roads.

SONOMA VALLEY WINERIES

ABOUT A HALF-DOZEN WINERIES ARE LOCATED a mile east of Sonoma Plaza, down East Napa Street. You could combine a visit to a few of these wineries with a tour of the Sonoma Mission, lunch on the plaza, and a side trip to an attraction outside of town. The result would be a day with a minimum amount of driving and maximum time for fun.

Wineries outside town are often on small back roads, so get a map from the tourist office on the plaza; also, keep your eyes peeled for sign-posts leading to the vineyards (otherwise it's easy to miss a turn).

- **Sebastiani Winery** (☎ 707-933-3200; www.sebastiani.com).
  For sheer convenience, Sebastiani can't be beat. Free shuttle buses whisk visitors from Sonoma Plaza to the stone winery about a mile away. Professional guides lead tours throughout the day, and visitors learn about winemaking, see a large collection of hand-carved casks, and view a display of antique winemaking equipment.

- **Buena Vista Carneros Winery** (☎ 800-678-8504; www.buenavistawinery.com).
  Not as convenient to reach but a must-see is this winery east of Sonoma. Set among towering trees and fountains, this is the birth-place of California's premium wine industry. Prior to its founding in

1857, California wine was made with lesser grapes, such as the black mission. BV is also the first winery to grow the zinfandel grape. It's also drop-dead gorgeous, with huge stone buildings, a mezzanine art gallery, and historical exhibits. History tours are given at 11 a.m and 2 p.m. daily ($15 per person); free self-guided tours are available 10 a.m.–5 p.m; there's also a beautiful, terraced picnic area.

- **Bartholomew Park Winery** (☎ 707-935-9511; www.bartpark.com). This winery is almost as beautiful, and not far from Buena Vista. Surrounded by vineyards, the winery features an attractive museum that highlights winemaking, the history of the area, and the winery's previous owners. In addition, there are hiking trails, a picnic area, and a "wine garden" (a picnic area with a pavilion).

- **Ravenswood Winery** (☎ 888-669-4629; www.ravenswood-wine.com). Ravenswood, also east of Sonoma, is a small winery in a gorgeous hillside setting. Best known for its hearty zinfandels and its anti wine-snob attitude, the winery offers reservation-only tours led by knowledgeable and enthusiastic employees. Winery tours start daily at 10:30 a.m. ($10 per person).

- **Benziger Family Winery** (☎ 707-935-4046 or 888-490-2739; www.benziger.com). Head up CA 12 a few miles to reach this winery in Glen Ellen. The winery specializes in premium estate and Sonoma County wines, they're also well known for their labels designed by famous artists. Guided ($10 per person) and self-guided tours are offered daily, and there's a picnic area where you can have lunch.

- **Kunde Estate Winery** (☎ 707-833-5501; www.kunde.com). You can enjoy a tour of caves at Kunde Estate Winery in Kenwood, north of Glen Ellen. A winery and visitor center is located at the foot of a stunning mountain of grapes. The family owns 2,000 acres, with 800 acres under vine. Rustic grounds at Kenwood Vineyards complement the attractive tasting room and the winery's artistic bottle labels. Group tours are by appointment only; free guided tours of aging caves are available Friday and Saturday, 10:30 a.m.–4:30 p.m.

SONOMA VALLEY ATTRACTIONS

THE TOWN OF SONOMA IS THE SITE OF THE last and the northernmost of the 21 missions established by Spain and Mexico, called El Camino Real ("the king's highway"). Popularly called **Sonoma Mission,** El Camino Real was founded in 1823 and features a stark white facade and, inside, a small museum. Across the street is the **Sonoma Barracks,** built with Native American labor in the 1830s to house Mexican troops. It's a two-story adobe structure with sweeping balconies and a museum dedicated to California history.

Next door, the **Toscano Hotel** is furnished as it was in the 19th century, with wood-burning stoves, brocade armchairs, and gambling tables. These and other antique buildings around Sonoma Plaza are part of **Sonoma State Historic Park** (☎ 707-938-1519; **www.napanet. net/~sshpa**). The admission is $2 for adults and $1 for children and gets you into all of the historic buildings. In the oak-studded plaza across the street is a monument to the Bear Flag Revolt, located on the spot where California was declared an independent republic in 1846 (and remained so for 25 days).

Another excellent pit stop before heading to sights farther in Sonoma is the **Sonoma Cheese Factory** (2 Spain Street on Sonoma Plaza, Sonoma; ☎ 707-996-1000; **www.sonomajack.com**). You can choose to picnic here on the cute benches that are scattered nearby, or simply browse inside and watch them slap, drain, and drag clumps of Jack and Cheddar through cheesecloth. There are plenty of samples on hand for you to try.

kids **Traintown** (☎ 707-938-3912; **www.traintown.com**) a mile south of Sonoma Plaza, offers a 20-minute train ride through 10 acres of landscaped park. There's also a petting zoo, an antique carousel, and cabooses. Train fare is $3.75 for all ages. Open daily, 10 a.m.–5 p.m., June through September, and Friday through Sunday the rest of the year.

If Napa Valley is Robert Louis Stevenson country, then Sonoma belongs to Jack London. A world adventurer and the most famous American writer of his time (he died in 1916 at age 40), London bought a 1,400-acre ranch a few miles northwest of Glen Ellen; today it's **Jack London State Historic Park** (☎ 707-938-5216). Attractions include a museum with memorabilia, a reconstruction of London's office, and exhibits on the fascinating life of the author of *The Call of the Wild*. There's also a continuously running video of a film made about the writer just days before his death; silent, grainy, and shaky, the short home movie is haunting.

Almost as spooky are the ruins of London's mansion, **Wolf House** (☎ 707-938-5216; **www.parks.sonoma.net/jlpark**), which mysteriously burned to the ground in 1913 before the author could move in. It's a half-mile stroll through gorgeous woods to the stone ruins; you can also detour to visit the writer's simple grave. For fans of American literature, the park is a real find. Admission is $6 a car.

OUTDOOR FUN IN SONOMA VALLEY

SONOMA VALLEY IS 7 MILES WIDE AND 17 MILES long, and with its rolling hills, 13,000 acres of vineyards, and forested mountains on either side, the valley offers much to do outdoors. **Goodtime Touring Company** (18503 Sonoma Highway, Sonoma; ☎ 888-525-0453; **www.goodtimetouring.com**) rents bikes for exploring the valley's miles of paved, low-traffic back roads. Rentals are $25 a day, including a helmet, lock, cable, maps, and road service and repair during regular business hours. The shop also offers lunch rides, including food, for $125 a person (reservations required three days in advance.

The **Sonoma Cattle Company** (☎ 707-996-8566; **www.napasonoma trailrides.com**) offers trail rides at Skyline Wilderness Park. The guided tours last for approximately two hours in the Skyline Wilderness. Reservations are required, and rates start at $90 per person.

Combine a scenic view from the air, the nostalgia of a bygone era, and the excitement of a roller coaster at **Aeroschellville Biplane and Glider Rides** (☎ 707-938-2444; **www.vintageaircraftco.com**). The firm offers a variety of rides in its fleet of 1940 Boeing Stearman biplanes and a North American–built, World War II Navy, SNJ-4 pilot trainer. All pilots are certified by the Federal Aviation Administration. Twenty-minute one-passenger rides are $130; two-passenger rides are $190. Aerobatic rides lasting 20 minutes are $170 for one passenger and $230 for two. War-plane rides range from $250 to $550.

SHOPPING IN SONOMA VALLEY

THE CENTRAL PLAZA IN THE OLD SPANISH TOWN of Sonoma is where you'll find the best shops, including gourmet stores, boutiques, a designer lingerie shop, antiques stores, and a brass shop. The **Sonoma Cheese Factory** (2 Spain Street; ☎ 707-996-1931; **www.sonoma jack.com**) on the square is the place to go for picnic supplies, a bottle of wine, or sandwiches for that winery picnic; you can also eat on the premises and watch cheese being made. The **Mercado,** a small shopping center just east of the plaza, houses several stores with unusual items. **Baksheesh** (423 First Street West; ☎ 707-939-2847) features handmade gifts crafted by Third World artisans. **Milagros** (414 First Street East; ☎ 707-935-8566) sells Mexican folk art, home furnishings, masks, and wood carvings.

Seven miles north of Sonoma off CA 12 in Glen Ellen is **Jack London Village** (14301 Arnold Drive), located on the banks of Sonoma Creek. It's a collection of shops, art studios, craft shops, cafés, a wine shop, and a music shop in a bucolic setting. There's also the **Glen Ellen Winery** (☎ 707-935-4046) and, across the street, the **Jack London Bookstore** (☎ 707-996-2888), an important resource center for the writer's fans.

DINING IN SONOMA VALLEY

AS IT IS THROUGHOUT THE WINE COUNTRY, dining is serious business in Sonoma Valley. Dinner reservations should be made at least two weeks in advance in summer and fall. Top-rated dining establishments include:

- **Doce Lunas** (8910 Sonoma Highway, Kenwood; ☎ 707-833-4000). Entrees include lamb shank with garlic and rosemary, osso bucco, and pork spareribs. Try the sticky toffee pudding for dessert.
- **Saddles Steakhouse** (29 East MacArthur Street, Sonoma; ☎ 707-933-3191). Boots and saddles are the main features of the décor. The crispy red cornmeal onion rings are a mighty fine prelude to a steak or prime rib.

A Two-day Excursion in the Wine Country

The ideal way for visitors to tour the wine country is to spend a night. That way you can visit Napa and Sonoma valleys, share the driving (you'll need a car), split wine-imbibing chores with a friend, and have a more relaxed trip.

After touring Napa Valley, head to Calistoga, where your room at one of the hot-springs resorts awaits you—say, Dr. Wilkinson's Hot Springs or Calistoga Spa Hot Springs (see Health Spas in Napa Valley on page 174). Rooms range from basic motel-style and cheap (think Janet Leigh in *Psycho*) to Victorian and expensive (including **Hideaway Cottages;** ☎ 707-942-4108), all with kitchens and some with living rooms. Take a mud bath in a composition of local volcanic ash, imported peat, and naturally boiling mineral hot-springs water. Folks have been coming to Calistoga for about 150 years to experience this; now it's your turn. For about 90 minutes, you will simmer at a temperature of about 104°, and your body will love you for it. A full treatment costs about $75.

The next day, drive to Sonoma Valley. Get there either by heading south through Napa Valley on the Silverado Trail to CA 121 and west to CA 12, or by taking a back road. If you go the back-road route, you can spend the second day of your wine-country visit driving south through the valley. When you get to the southern end of Sonoma Valley at the end of the day, you're less than an hour from San Francisco.

- **Saffron** (13648 Arnold Drive, Glen Ellen; ☎ 707-938-4844). Chef-owner Christopher Dever, a grad of California Culinary Academy, changes menus frequently, and features local produce, seafood, and a touch of saffron.

TOP-RATED ACCOMMODATIONS IN SONOMA VALLEY

- **The Fairmont Sonoma Mission Inn** (18140 Sonoma Highway, Boyes Hot Springs; ☎ 800-257-7544; www.sonomamissioninn.com). Rates are $329–$700. This resort and spa in Sonoma County has a superb bar and restaurant.
- **The Lodge at Sonoma** (1325 Broadway, Sonoma; ☎ 707-935-6600; www.thelodgeatsonoma.com). Rates are $229–$299. The Lodge is a resort that offers a full spa in the heart of wine country.
- **MacArthur Place** (29 East MacArthur Street, Sonoma; ☎ 707-938-2929; www.macarthurplace.com). Rates are $299–$475. This historic inn and spa is situated on a corner of what was a sprawling ranch, but is now a getaway villa of cottages and lawns with a spa and restaurant.

- **Sonoma Creek Inn** (239 Boyes Boulevard, Boyes Hot Springs; ☎ 888-712-1289; www.sonomacreekinn.com). Rates are $79–$169. This charming little place was designed to recall the days of the great American Road Trip via roads like Route 66.

VISITOR INFORMATION

FOR MORE INFORMATION ON Sonoma Valley, contact the **Sonoma County Tourism Program** (420 Aviation Boulevard, Suite 106; ☎ 707-565-5384; **www.sonomacounty.com**); ask for a free visitors' guide. Maps and brochures are available at the small visitor center on the east side of Sonoma Plaza. For help locating a room, especially in the busy summer and fall, contact **Wine Country Concierge** (☎ 888-946-3289 or 707-252-4472; **www.wine trip.com**), which has a list of available rooms at B&Bs and other lodging.

> *un*official **TIP**
> If you've got a room in San Francisco and you're heading to the wine country, don't check out; the hassle of repeatedly packing and unpacking is too time consuming. Reserve a room at a hot-springs resort in Calistoga at the north end of the valley, pack the minimum, and get out of town. It's definitely hedonistic—and expensive—and totally in character with this vacation within a vacation.

DAY TRIPS IN *and* AROUND *the* BAY AREA

IF YOU'VE GOT THE TIME OR IF YOUR VISIT to San Francisco is a repeat trip, consider exploring some places outside the city. Northern California is spectacularly scenic, and a trip to the area really isn't complete unless you take at least one day to venture beyond town limits.

From Marin County, Point Reyes, and the wine country to the north; to the East Bay cities of Oakland and Berkeley; to the villages, mountains, and coastal scenery to the south, there's plenty to see and do. A trip beyond hectic San Francisco can be a welcome respite from the heavy traffic and round-the-clock activity in the city's livelier neighborhoods. Here are a few suggestions for day trips beyond the city's limits.

> *un*official **TIP**
> For a locals' feel, try the **The No Name Bar** (757 Bridgeway; ☎ 415-332-1392), a no-frills Sausalito institution. It's smoky, small, and funky, with great Irish coffee and decent martinis. But don't try to order any foo-foo drinks here. The regulars have been known to heckle those who do.

MARIN COUNTY
Sausalito and Tiburon

For folks on a tight schedule or without a car, these two bay-side villages across from San Francisco are destinations well worth visiting. And with ferry service available from Fisherman's Wharf, it's a short trip that combines a refreshing boat ride with spectacular scenery. Neither destination requires a full day; a sunny afternoon is just about perfect.

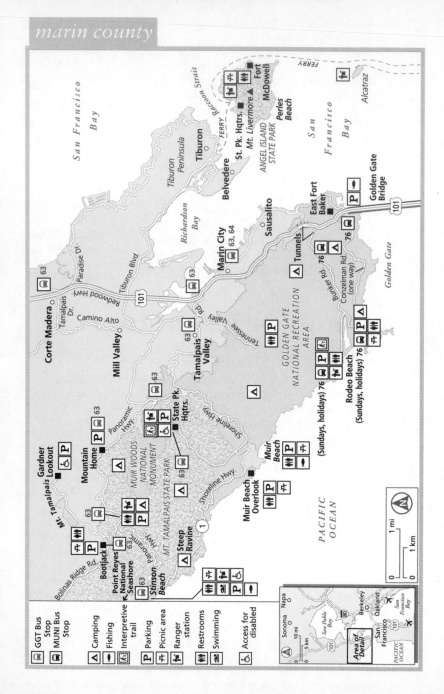

marin county

SAUSALITO Once a gritty little fishing village full of bars and bordellos, Sausalito today is decidedly more upscale. Think French Riviera, not Barbary Coast. With approximately 7500 residents (not all of them cash-flush yuppies), the town still manages to hang on to a faintly Bohemian air, although most of its attractions are upscale boutiques and restaurants. The main drag is Bridgeway, where sleek, Lycra-clad bicyclists, in-line skaters, and joggers flash by along the waterfront.

Caledonia Street, one block inland, has a wider selection of cafés and shops. Half a mile north of town, the tourist onslaught is less evident and visitors can see the town's well-known ad-hoc community of houseboats and barges. But most folks come just to exercise their credit cards or hang out in a bar or waterfront restaurant. And that's not a bad idea: the views of the bay and the San Francisco skyline are great.

unofficial **TIP**
For a more scenic trip to Tiburon, take the ferry.

The **Blue & Gold Fleet** provides ferry service to Sausalito, a 30-minute boat ride from Pier 41 in Fisherman's Wharf. One-way tickets are $8.50 for adults and $4.50 for children ages 5–11. For departure times and information, call ☎ 415-773-1188. Golden Gate Ferries depart from the Ferry Building at the foot of Market Street. One-way tickets are $6.45 for adults, $3.20 for seniors and the physically disabled, and $2.65 for children ages 6–18. For schedules, call ☎ 415-923-2000. If you're driving, take US 101 north across the Golden Gate Bridge; then take the first right, the Alexander Avenue exit. Alexander becomes Bridgeway in Sausalito. For more information, visit **www.blueandgoldfleet.com**.

TIBURON Less touristy but more upscale is the best way to describe Tiburon, which is frequently compared to a New England fishing village. (Maybe so, if the New Englanders are wealthy and commute to high-rise offices by ferry every day.) Visitors can soak up this heady ambience in pricey waterfront restaurants and bars, then stroll the gorgeous promenade. Tiburon is also the most convenient stepping-off point to nearby Angel Island, where you can hike or bike on 12 miles of trails in the state park. A good lunch or dinner destination in Tiburon is **Guaymas** (5 Main Street; ☎ 415-435-6300), with authentic Mexican cuisine and a panoramic view of San Francisco and the bay.

Ferry service to Tiburon is provided by the **Blue & Gold Fleet** from Pier 41 in Fisherman's Wharf; one-way tickets are $8.50 for adults and $4.50 for children. For departure times and information, call ☎ 415-773-1188 or visit **www.blueandgoldfleet. com**. By car, take US 101 north across the Golden Gate Bridge to the Tiburon/CA 131 Exit, then follow Tiburon Boulevard all the way to downtown. It's about a 40-minute drive from San Francisco.

unofficial **TIP**
Tram tours and bike and kayak rentals are closed from late-November to mid-March.

Angel Island

Over the years Angel Island has been a prison, a notorious quarantine station for immigrants, a missile base, and a favorite site for duels. Today the largest island in San Francisco Bay is a state park; it's a terrific destination for a picnic, stroll, hike, or mountain-bike ride, or simply a place to get away from traffic, phones, and television.

unofficial **TIP**
To save money, rent a bike in San Francisco and bring it on the ferry.

Angel Island, located across Raccoon Strait from Tiburon, is accessible only by ferry. Visitors arrive at a small marina abutting a huge lawn area equipped with picnic tables, benches, barbecue pits, and restrooms. There's also a small store, cafe, gift shop, and mountain bike rental concession. Tram tours highlight the island's history. You can also rent a stable, two-person sea kayak and see the island from the water. There are 12 miles of trails on the wooded island, and cyclists and hikers can explore the spooky ruins of the former immigration center (called the "Ellis Island of the West").

unofficial **TIP**
Always use caution when walking on the rocky coastline, where unwary hikers can be swept away by large waves or trapped by the incoming tide.

Blue & Gold Fleet ferries to Angel Island depart from Pier 41 in Fisherman's Wharf daily in the summer and on weekends in the winter. The round-trip fare is $13.50 for adults, $8 for children ages 6–12; free for children age 5 and under. For departure times and information, call ☎ 415-773-1188. The **Angel Island–Tiburon Ferry** operates daily in summer and on weekends in winter. Round-trip fares are $10 for adults and $7.50 for children ages 5–11. A $1 fee is charged for bicycles. For schedule information and directions, call ☎ 415-435-2131, or visit **www.angelislandferry.com.**

Marin Headlands

Aside from offering the postcard views of San Francisco, the **Headlands,** as they are affectionately called, is *the* playground for San Franciscans—particularly those who live in the Marina District. The fact that it is anchored to the city by the walkable Golden Gate Bridge makes it one of the most prized places to play on weekends. With minimal hassle—except bridge traffic—you can park for free and within ten minutes of leaving your hotel or home, you can put boot to the dirt on tons of hiking trails. Or if you prefer fat-tire skirmishes, there are also plenty of mountain-biking opportunities—you would expect nothing less from the place that is said to be the origination of mountain biking as we know it. The Headlands, largely undeveloped terrain, are dominated by 2,800-foot Mount Tamalpais. The coastline here is more rugged than on the San Francisco side of the bridge, and it's a Mecca for nature lovers. Visitors are treated to great views of the city, ocean, and bay; hiking trails and rugged beaches; and the concrete remains of old forts and gun emplacements standing guard over the Golden Gate (no shots were ever fired in anger).

While physically close to San Francisco, the Headlands seem a world apart. Windswept ridges, protected valleys, and beaches offer the best of nature, but they're less than an hour's drive from the hectic city. The hillsides near the Golden Gate provide magnificent views of the entrance of the bay. The Marin Headlands Visitor Center (☎ 415-331-1540) is open daily from 9:30 a.m. to 4:30 p.m. and offers detailed information on enjoying the rugged countryside.

The Headlands offer a vast expanse of wild and open terrain; rolling hills covered with shrubs, grasses, and wildflowers; small coves, large beaches, and rocky coastal cliffs; and forested ridges and redwood valleys. The park, part of Golden Gate National Recreation Area, has abundant wildlife—deer, hawks, and seabirds are common, and bobcats and whales are sometimes sighted. Fog is heaviest in the summer in areas closer to the Golden Gate, and ocean swimming is always dangerous.

unofficial **TIP**
Rugged and steep trails crisscross the Headlands; remember to bring drinking water and stay off the cliffs, which are prone to landslides and covered with poison oak.

Major attractions include the Point Bonita Lighthouse (open spring through fall on weekends), Muir and Stinson beaches, Muir Woods, Mount Tamalpais, and Olema Valley. Hikers, cyclists, and equestrians can pick up detailed trail maps and information at the visitor center. And don't forget to bring your lunch: there are few places to eat in the Headlands.

To reach the Marin Headlands and the visitor center, drive north on US 101 across the Golden Gate Bridge, take the first exit (Alexander Avenue), bear left, and follow the road up the hill. Go through the one-way tunnel (there's a traffic light), which puts you on Bunker Road and leads to the visitor center, Rodeo Beach, and the Point Bonita Lighthouse.

unofficial **TIP**
A good lunch option on Telegraph Avenue is **Cafe Intermezzo** (2442 Telegraph Avenue; ☎ 510-849-4592), a crowded self-serve sandwich, salad, and soup place that serves great oversized sandwiches on homemade bread. Cheap, too.

THE EAST BAY

ACROSS THE BAY BRIDGE FROM SAN FRANCISCO, two cities offer startling contrasts to the chic town on the peninsula. Oakland is a gritty, blue-collar city that earns its livelihood with shipping and transportation to and from the Port of Oakland, dominated by huge cranes. The city spreads north toward Berkeley, a college town that's home to a campus of the University of California and a fascinating cross-section of aging hippies and radicals, hustling young Republicans, students, and Nobel Prize laureates. The two towns blend together so that they're physically indistinguishable, although Oakland's lowbrow reputation stands in stark contrast to Berkeley, a self-consciously hip, intellectual hotbed. However, Oakland lays claim to some impressive historical and literary associations of its own. Gertrude Stein and Jack London both grew up in the city at about the same time, albeit at different ends of the social spectrum.

Oakland

Located just over the Bay Bridge, or via BART, Oakland is the workhorse of the Bay Area, with one of the busiest ports on the West Coast. Yet in spite of its blue-collar reputation and Ms. Stein's oft-quoted withering reference to her hometown ("There is no there there"), Oakland has a few tricks up its sleeve that make the town worth a visit. Not the least of its attributes is the weather, often mild and sunny, while San Francisco is draped in chilly fog.

Leading the list is the **Oakland Museum of California** (1000 Oak Street; ☎ 510-238-2200, **www.museumca.org;** adults $8, seniors and students $5, children free, second Sunday of month free; open Wednesday–Friday, 10 a.m.–5 p.m.; Saturday, 10 a.m.–8 p.m.; Sunday, noon–6 p.m. It focuses on the history, geography, and culture of California. The museum also possesses a superb collection of the works of Californian photographers such as Ansel Adams and Dorothea Lange. Other things to do in Oakland include riding a genuine Italian gondola on downtown **Lake Merritt,** taking the kids to **Children's Fairyland** (on the north shore of Lake Merritt), or ogling the restored art deco interior of the **Oakland Paramount Theatre** (2025 Broadway; ☎ 510-893-2300). Tours of the beautiful theater are offered on the first and third Saturdays of the month (excluding holidays), starting at 10 a.m. and lasting two hours. The cost is $1 a person and no reservations are necessary. Children must be 10 years of age and accompanied by an adult.

Jack London Square is Oakland's version of Fisherman's Wharf and shamelessly plays up the city's connection with the writer, who grew up along the city's waterfront. The complex of boutiques and eateries is just about as tacky as its cousin across the bay—and about as far from "the call of the wild" as you can get. However, Jack London's favorite watering hole is still pouring whiskey and gin and the famous local "steam beer." Find it at the south end of the square, Heinholds First and Last Chance Saloon, ☎ 510-839-6761. Some better eating options include **Bay Wolf** (3853 Piedmont Avenue; ☎ 510-655-6004), the city's most venerable and revered restaurant, serving Mediterranean-inspired California cuisine; and Oliveto (5655 College Avenue; ☎ 510-547-5356), owned by an alumnus of the famous Chez Pannise, serving the rustic fare of northern Italy.

To reach Oakland's Jack London Square by car, take the Bay Bridge to I-880 to Broadway, turn south, and go to the end. You'll find ample parking in the underground garage. On BART, get off at the 12th Street station and walk south along Broadway about a half mile (or grab the No. 51A bus to the foot of Broadway). To get to Lake Merritt, cross the Bay Bridge and follow signs to downtown Oakland and exit at Grand Avenue South. To get to the Oakland Museum, take I-580 to I-980 and exit at Jackson Street. Via BART, get off at the Lake Merritt station, a block south of the museum.

Berkeley

Probably more than any other town in the country, Berkeley conjures up images of the rebellious 1960s, when students of the University of California, Berkeley, led the protests against the Vietnam War. At times, virtual full-scale battles were fought almost daily between protestors and cops, both on campus and in the streets of the surrounding town (most notably in People's Park, off of Telegraph Avenue).

These days, things are more sedate in this college town, although admirers and detractors still refer to it as "Berzerkley" and the "People's Republic of Berkeley." While student angst is down, the progressive impulse lingers and is best experienced on **Telegraph Avenue,** south of the campus. On the four blocks or so closest to the university, it's a regular street fair filled with vendors selling handmade jewelry, tie-dyed T-shirts, and bumper stickers promoting leftist causes and lifestyles. The sidewalks on both sides of Telegraph Avenue are usually jammed with students, tourists, bearded academics, homeless people, and gray-haired hippies. Coffeehouses, restaurants, art and crafts boutiques, head shops, and excellent used-book-and-record stores line the street; order a latte and enjoy the endless procession of interesting people who throng the street most afternoons and evenings.

*uno*ffi*cial* **TIP**
The view of San Francisco Bay from the Lawrence Hall of Science is stupendous.

The selection of restaurants is truly intimidating in Berkeley; every ethnic cuisine in the world, it seems, is represented. The only thing you won't find is a steak house. And you'll find only three fast-food restaurants in the whole city.

The 31,000-student **University of California** campus is noted for its academic excellence and its 15 Nobel Prize winners. There are several museums on campus worth exploring, including the **Berkeley Art Museum** and, for kids, the **Lawrence Hall of Science** (easiest to reach if you've got a car).

To reach Berkeley, about ten miles northeast of San Francisco, take the Bay Bridge, follow I-80 east to the University Avenue exit, and follow the wide street until you hit the campus. To get to Telegraph Avenue, turn right on Oxford and drive three blocks to Durant. Turn left and drive three blocks and make a right onto Telegraph.

Parking close to campus is notoriously difficult, so try to arrive early on weekends and get a space in one of the many private parking lots located just off campus. Try **Center Street Garage** (2025 Center Street; ☎ 510-843-1788) or the **Allston Parking Facility** (2061

Allston Way; ☎ 510-981-9443). Another option is **BART,** which has a Berkeley station one block from the campus.

POINT REYES NATIONAL SEASHORE

THIS 85,000-ACRE PARK OF SANDY BEACH and scrubland is on a geologic "island" located about an hour's drive north of San Francisco. Windswept and ruggedly beautiful, Point Reyes is a wildlife paradise. Shorebirds, seabirds, invertebrates, and marine mammals thrive on this peninsula, which juts into the cold waters of the Pacific just west of the San Andreas fault. Folks who love scenic beauty and wildlife should put this scenic destination on their "A-list" of places to go on an excursion from San Francisco.

In 1579, English explorer Sir Francis Drake is said to have anchored his ship, the *Golden Hind,* in Drakes Bay, on the southern coast of the wing-shaped peninsula. There's evidence he careened his ship to make repairs and stayed about five weeks before sailing westward across the Pacific on his round-the-world voyage of discovery. Nearly 200 years passed before settlers arrived. After the United States' conquest of California, the land was broken into dozens of dairy ranches, and beef and dairy cattle have roamed the brushy flatlands of Point Reyes ever since.

unofficial **TIP**
A better bet for whale-watching on Point Reyes is to come early on a weekday to avoid the crowds. Dress warmly—it's usually cold and windy—and bring binoculars and a camera with a telephoto lens.

Touring Suggestions

The best place to begin a visit is the **Bear Valley Visitor Center** and its extensive collection of exhibits, specimens, and artifacts. The center is open from 9 a.m. to 5 p.m. on weekdays and 8 a.m. to 5 p.m. on weekends and holidays. You can pick up maps and tide tables and get advice from a ranger on places to hike, picnic, and view wildlife. Ranger-led tours are also offered on a varying schedule, and several hiking trails are accessible from the visitor center. For more information, call ☎ 415-464-5100, or visit **www.nps.gov/pore.**

From December through March, **gray whales** make their 10,000-mile migration between the Bering Sea and Baja California, swimming past Point Reyes. The best spot to view the whales is from

unofficial **TIP**
If you want to make a weekend of your visit to Point Reyes, consider camping. Backcountry camping is limited to four areas maintained by the park service: Coast, Sky, Glenn, and Wildcat camps.

Point Reyes Lighthouse, which has limited parking. Because of the popularity of whale-watching on weekends, the park provides shuttles to the lighthouse from Bear Valley.

Nearly 500 tule elk roam Point Reyes (reintroduced following an absence of more than 100 years). The **Tule Elk Preserve** is at the northern tip of the park, and you're apt to spot some elk on a walk down the moderately difficult **Tomales Point Trail.** Other good places to view wildlife include **Fivebrooks Pond** (waterfowl), the wetlands of Limantour (ducks), and the promontory overlooking Chimney Rock (sea lions, harbor seals, and seabirds).

A Car Tour

Point Reyes is worth a full day or more of exploration. But if your time is limited, you can get a good sampling of what Point Reyes has to offer in about half a day—mostly through the windows of your car. From the visitor center, continue on Bear Valley Road to Sir Francis Drake Boulevard, pass through the village of Inverness, and follow signs for the Point Reyes Lighthouse. For a spectacular view of the entire peninsula, turn right on Mount Vision Road, a steep and twisty paved lane that rises to almost 1,300 feet before it dead-ends.

Return to Sir Francis Drake Boulevard and turn left to continue toward the lighthouse. On the right are two beaches ripe for exploration (but not swimming; the waters are cold and dangerous) before you reach the **Lighthouse Visitor Center.** The lighthouse offers a spectacularly scenic view of the ocean and the tip of the peninsula; it's just under a half-mile walk from the parking area, followed by a 300-step descent down the cliff to the lighthouse. The visitor center is open daily, 10 a.m.–4:30 p.m., closed Tuesday and Wednesday (call ☎ 415-669-1534 or visit **www.ptreyeslight.com/lthouse.html**).

After you visit the lighthouse, backtrack by car to the turn to **Chimney Rock** (a good place to view wildlife) or continue driving to the mainland. To reach the elk reserve, turn left about two miles past Mount Vision Road, and then turn left on Pierce Point Road and drive to **Pierce Point Ranch,** a renovated dairy ranch with a self-guided trail through the historic complex. Then hike down the **Tomales Point Trail,** and you may spot some elk.

unofficial **TIP**
When visiting Point Reyes, wear hiking boots and be prepared for changes in the weather.

Food, Lodging, and Directions

You'll find restaurants, cafes, delicatessens, general stores, and bakeries in the nearby villages of Olema, Point Reyes Station, Inverness, and Marshall; a café is located at Drakes Beach inside the park at the Kenneth C. Patrick visitor center, (☎ 415-669-1250). Inns and bed-and-breakfasts are also nearby. **Point Reyes Lodging** (call ☎ 800-539-1872 or visit **www.ptreyes.com**) specializes in booking cottages and small inns in the Point Reyes area.

To reach Point Reyes from San Francisco, cross the Golden Gate Bridge and stay on US 101 north. Exit at Sir Francis Drake Boulevard and head west; it's about a 20-mile drive (much of it through congested Marin County, although the scenery improves dramatically around Taylor State Park) to CA 1 at Olema. From here it's about a one-minute drive to the Bear Valley Visitor Center. A longer and more scenic route is CA 1, reached from US 101 in Sausalito.

SOUTH OF SAN FRANCISCO

CA 1 IS A SPECTACULARLY SCENIC ROAD THAT stretches south of San Francisco to Carmel, winding past cliffs and coves, pocket beaches, lighthouses, and old historic towns and villages. Visitors to San Francisco can enjoy driving along the coast for about 75 miles to Santa Cruz. From there, turn inland and north to return along the crest of the Santa Cruz Mountains for scenery from a higher perspective.

A Scenic Car Tour

For a full day of scenic car touring, get started around 9 a.m. and head to the Great Highway (south of Cliff House and at the western end of Golden Gate Park) and drive south. Bring picnic supplies or grab a bite in one of the many towns along the way. You'll have time to get out and enjoy many of the attractions, but don't linger too long if you want to get back before evening. And don't forget to bring a state highway map (in case of detours or in case you want to devise your own circuit route).

The coastline of the San Francisco peninsula south of the city is largely undeveloped. Bluffs protect the many nudist beaches from prying eyes and make excellent launching points for hang gliders, as you can see at Fort Funston, about a mile south of the San Francisco Zoo. Skyline Boulevard follows the coast past Daly City, a community of ticky-tacky housing that's probably the ugliest thing most folks will see on a visit to San Francisco.

But things improve after you reach CA 1. San Pedro Beach marks the end of San Francisco's suburban sprawl and is a popular surfing beach. Continually eroding cliffs offer great scenery from the road but don't handle the presence of the highway well, and the road is washed away regularly in winter storms. Gray Whale Cove State Beach is clothing-optional and, in spite of its name, isn't an especially good place for whale-watching.

Half Moon Bay and a Scenic Side Trip

Main Street in Half Moon Bay features a shopping area with gift shops, bookstores, a saddlery, jewelry stores, bars, restaurants, and art galleries. There's also a full-size grocery store that sells sandwiches and picnic supplies. For a view of the town's eponymous bay, go to **Half Moon Bay State Beach** (Kelly Avenue from CA 1; ☎ 650-726-8819). Parking is $2–$4.

For a contrast to the surf, continue south on CA 1 and turn right onto Higgins-Purisima Creek Road. The narrow paved road winds and climbs for eight miles through ranch country before returning to CA 1. Turn left to continue south. **Pigeon Point Lighthouse** (☎ 650-879-2120; **www.parksca.gov**) is in a spectacular coastal setting, and free guided half-hour historical tours of the lighthouse grounds are available from 10 a.m. to 4 p.m., Friday through Sunday, except on rainy days. Children under age 8 must be chaperoned by an adult; reservations are requested.

Elephant Seals

For sightings of some unusual wildlife, stop at **Año Nuevo State Reserve** just south of Pigeon Point. Huge northern elephant seals come ashore from early December through March to give birth and mate. Bull seals often engage in battles for breeding access to the females.

Popular guided walks to view the wildlife activity are offered by trained naturalists from December 15 through March 31. Advance reservations are recommended for the two-hour, three-mile (round-trip) hike. The cost is $5 per person, plus $3 for parking. Call ☎ 800-444-7275 between 8 a.m. and 5 p.m. to reserve a spot; for additional information, call ☎ 650-879-2025. Juvenile seals are present year-round, and you can walk the trail unescorted to see them; in the winter, when 300 to 400 adults appear, visitors must be on guided tours.

Just north of Santa Cruz is **Wilder Ranch State Park,** a cultural preserve with adobe farm buildings from the Spanish Mission era and buildings from the late 19th century. Docent-led tours are offered on weekends; there are also 28 miles of trails for hiking.

Mountain Scenery and Giant Redwoods

Grab something to eat in Santa Cruz, but on a one-day outing there isn't enough time to explore this resort city, famous for its boardwalk and roller coaster. It's a good turnaround point; you can head back to San Francisco through the mountains. Follow signs to CA 9 north, a scenic road that twists and turns through mountains, forests, and the towns of Felton and Boulder Creek, where you turn left onto CA 236.

At **Big Basin Redwoods State Park** you don't need to get out of the car to be overwhelmed by the huge trees. This forest of giant redwoods is more impressive than the stand at Muir Woods in Marin. But get out of the car anyway to explore the park headquarters and a small museum. Then continue toward San Francisco, 67 miles away. CA 236 gets narrow and twisty before returning to CA 9; turn left to continue north.

Next, turn left on CA 35 (Skyline Drive) for more incredible scenery; views are of the Pacific on the left and San Francisco Bay on the right. There are plenty of overlooks where you can stop and enjoy the vistas. Next, take CA 92/35 (a right turn) and then turn left onto CA 35, which leads to I-80, a 20-mile stretch of some of the most scenic interstate highway in the country—and, in a few minutes, San Francisco.

BEYOND *the* BAY AREA

MANY OUTSTANDING DESTINATIONS ARE TOO FAR from San Francisco for a day trip but close enough to consider for an overnight trek. Leading the list is **Yosemite National Park** (☎ 209-372-0200; **www.nps.gov/yose**), a wilderness of evergreen forests, alpine meadows, and sheer walls of granite. Spectacular Yosemite Valley features soaring cliffs, plunging waterfalls, gigantic trees, and rugged canyons.

The park is about 200 miles from San Francisco, or about a five-hour drive. World-famous Yosemite attracts about 4 million visitors a year. Peak tourist season is June to August, and crowds diminish in the fall. Advance lodging reservations are essential year-round.

Lake Tahoe (**Lake Tahoe Visitors Authority,** ☎ 800-288-2463 or 530-544-5050; **www.bluelaketahoe.com**), about 200 miles from the city, is rated one of the most beautiful bodies of water in the world. It lies in an alpine bowl on the border between Nevada and California and is surrounded by forested peaks. Tahoe features resorts, gambling, hiking trails, lakeside cabins, historic architecture, and special events such as golf tournaments.

South of the city down the Pacific coast is **Monterey Bay,** with Santa Cruz at its northern end and Monterey at its southern end. The first capital of California, Monterey was established by the Spanish in 1770; many Spanish, Mexican, and early American buildings still stand. South of Monterey is **Carmel-by-the-Sea,** a pretty hillside town founded as an artists' colony in the early 20th century. The **Monterey Peninsula** (**Monterey Peninsula Visitors and Convention Bureau,** ☎ 831-649-1770) is about a two-hour drive from San Francisco.

North of San Francisco along the rugged coastline is **Mendocino** (**Mendocino Coast Chamber of Commerce,** ☎ 707-961-6300), a small picturesque town that was once a logging village. In the 1950s it became a haven for artists and was so well restored that the town was declared a historic monument. Inland from town are forests of giant redwood trees. The town itself is tucked away on a rocky promontory above the Pacific and retains the charm of its logging days; it's largely unspoiled by tourism. Mendocino is about 125 miles from San Francisco; a leisurely drive up the spectacular coast can take as long as ten hours one way.

■ ATTRACTION PROFILES

FISHERMAN'S WHARF AND BEYOND

LET'S FACE IT, THERE ARE JUST SOME PLACES THAT you need to see when you visit San Francisco. You'll want to show off those obligatory shots of you in the "I escaped Alcatraz" T-shirt, or standing next to the barking sea lions at Pier 39 near Fisherman's Wharf. But the beauty of this city is that the untourist track is just as interesting, and colors a vivid picture of San Francisco's creative, innovative, and quaint spirit. The streets of San Francisco offer even the cheapskate, satisfied with a brisk walk up a hill and a good view of the bridge, something for his money. And at the end of the day the tourist, the untourist, the cheapskate, and even the splurger will be smiling on the bus as the sun sets behind another San Francisco day.

Each neighborhood has its own cluster of attractions to see. This book provides you with a comprehensive guide to San Francisco's top attractions, including some "coulda left San Fran without it" sights. We give you enough information so that you can choose the places you want to see based on your own interests. Each attraction is organized by neighborhood so you can plan your visit logically, without spending valuable time crisscrossing the city.

A TIME-SAVING CHART

BECAUSE OF THE WIDE RANGE OF ATTRACTIONS in and around San Francisco—from a hall filled with sculptures by Rodin at the Legion of Honor, to historic ships that you can explore at Hyde Street Pier in Fisherman's Wharf—we've provided the chart on pages 198 and 199 to help you prioritize your touring. In it, you'll find the location, authors' rating from one star (skip it) to five stars (not to be missed), and a brief description of the attraction. Each attraction is individually profiled later in this section.

 ### Alcatraz Island

APPEAL BY AGE	PRESCHOOL ★★★★	GRADE SCHOOL ★★★★★	TEENS ★★★★★
YOUNG ADULTS ★★★★★		OVER 30 ★★★★★	SENIORS ★★★★★

In San Francisco Bay, North Beach; to get there, take a 12-minute (one-way) ferry trip from Pier 41 (in Fisherman's Wharf, at the foot of Powell Street); ☎ 415-705-1042; Blue & Gold Fleet ☎ 415-705-5555; www.nps.gov/alcatraz; or for ticket and ferry information, ☎ 415-773-1188; www.blueandgoldfleet.com.

Type of attraction The island in San Francisco Bay is best known for its maximum-security, minimum-privilege federal penitentiary: a cellhouse tour, trails, museum exhibits, wildflowers, wildlife, and spectacular views of the San Francisco skyline. Self-guided, audio, and guided tours. **Admission** With audio tour: $16.50 for adults; $14.75 for seniors (ages 62 and over); and $10.75 for children ages 5–11. Tickets can be purchased without the audio tour: $11.50 adults; $9.75 seniors (ages 62 and over); and $8.25 for children ages 5–11. Self-guided tour maps and guides are available on the island in English, Spanish, German, and Japanese for $1. To purchase tickets in advance by phone, call ☎ 415-705-5555. **Hours** Ferries leave about every half hour throughout the day, beginning at 9:30 a.m. Alcatraz closes at 6:30 p.m. in the summer and 4:30 p.m. the rest of the year. Closed on Christmas and New Year's Day. Special evening tours called "Alcatraz After Dark" are also available. **When to go** Try to make the first ferry of the day; it's less crowded, and the weather is generally better and less windy. **Special comments** Weather in the middle of San Francisco Bay is unpredictable; it's also frequently different from mainland weather. The best advice is to be prepared and dress in layers; shorts and T-shirts are not a good idea. You have to hike steep grades to get to the cellhouse; wear sturdy shoes. There's no food service on the island, but you can buy a snack on the ferry. Restrooms, telephones, drinking water, and soft-drink vending machines are available on the island. **Authors' rating** A San Francisco and U.S. landmark that shouldn't be missed; the audio tour of

attractions around town

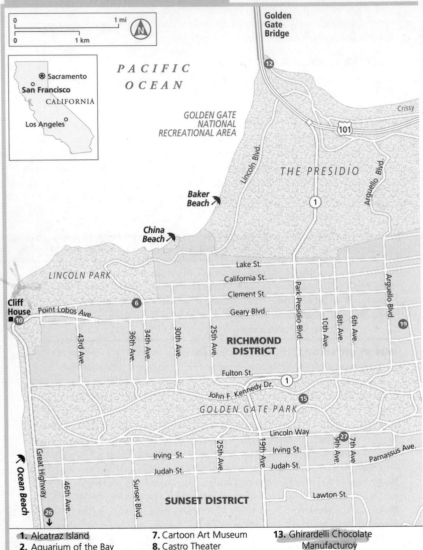

1. Alcatraz Island
2. Aquarium of the Bay
3. Asian Art Museum
4. Cable Car Museum
5. California Historical Society
6. California Palace of the
    Legion of Honor
7. Cartoon Art Museum
8. Castro Theater
9. City Lights Bookstore
10. Cliff House
11. Coit Tower
12. Fort Point National
    Historic Site
13. Ghirardelli Chocolate
    Manufacturoy
14. Haas-Lilienthal House
15. Japanese Tea Garden
16. Mission Dolores
17. Museum of Money of the
    American West

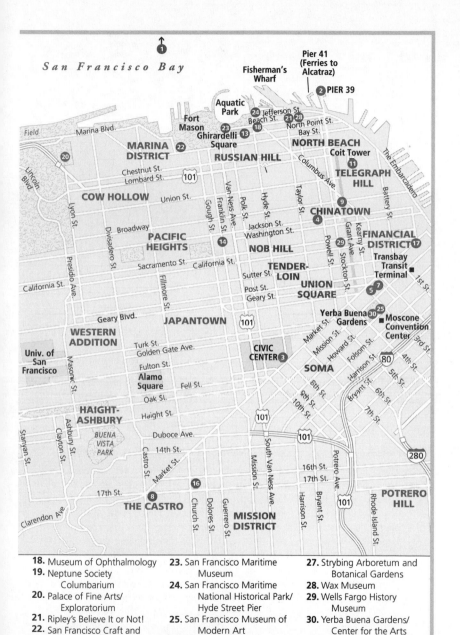

18. Museum of Ophthalmology
19. Neptune Society Columbarium
20. Palace of Fine Arts/ Exploratorium
21. Ripley's Believe It or Not!
22. San Francisco Craft and Folk Art Museum

23. San Francisco Maritime Museum
24. San Francisco Maritime National Historical Park/ Hyde Street Pier
25. San Francisco Museum of Modern Art
26. San Francisco Zoo

27. Strybing Arboretum and Botanical Gardens
28. Wax Museum
29. Wells Fargo History Museum
30. Yerba Buena Gardens/ Center for the Arts

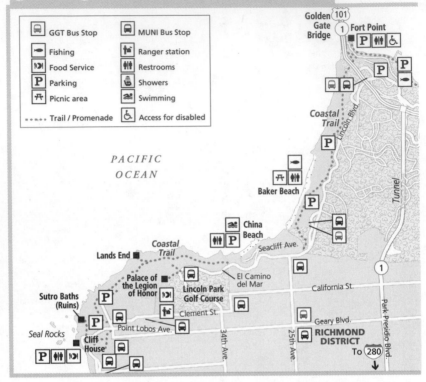

golden gate national recreation area

🚌	GGT Bus Stop	🚏	MUNI Bus Stop
➤	Fishing	👫	Ranger station
▶	Food Service	👫	Restrooms
P	Parking	🚿	Showers
☂	Picnic area	≈	Swimming
•••••	Trail / Promenade	♿	Access for disabled

the cellhouse is outstanding. ★★★★★. **How much time to allow** At least 2 hours; bring a lunch and you can easily spend half a day on the Rock. You can catch any returning ferry back to Fisherman's Wharf; a schedule is posted at the dock.

DESCRIPTION AND COMMENTS   One of Golden Gate National Recreation Area's most popular destinations, Alcatraz Island offers a close-up look at a federal prison long off limits to the public. The island is best known for its sinister reputation. It was called the Rock, Hell-catraz, and Uncle Sam's Devil Island by the hardened criminals who lived there during its federal penitentiary years (1934–63). Only a handful were truly notorious; the list includes Al Capone, Doc Barker, Alvin "Creepy" Karpis, George "Machine Gun" Kelly, and Robert Stroud, the Birdman of Alcatraz.

On the cellhouse tour you'll see why a sentence to Alcatraz was rated hard time by prisoners. The cells are tiny (inmates were confined 23 hours a day), and extreme precautions were taken to control the prisoners, prevent escapes, and quell riots. In the dining room, considered potentially the most dangerous place in the prison, tear-gas canisters are visible in the ceiling. Some cells are also furnished as they were when Alcatraz was a working prison, with cots, personal items (such as packets of Bugler

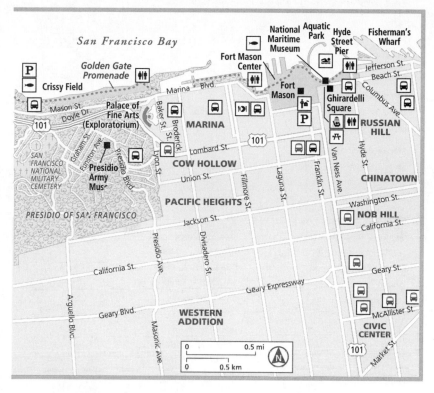

cigarette tobacco, brushes, and books), and a few pictures.

In stark contrast to the deteriorating prison, Alcatraz (Spanish for "pelican") is a place of natural beauty. On trails around the island, visitors can see flowers such as fuchsias, geraniums, jade trees, agave, and periwinkles, as well as outstanding views of San Francisco and Oakland. Tidepools teem with marine life, including crabs and sea stars.

TOURING TIPS Make advance reservations; Alcatraz is very popular. During peak summer and holiday periods, ferry rides to the island are booked as much as a week in advance. The down side to advance reservations is that no refunds are given if the weather is lousy. But Alcatraz in bad weather is better than no Alcatraz at all.

After disembarking and listening to a park ranger's introductory remarks, go inside for the 13-minute video presentation that gives a good overview of the island's history. Make note of the schedule of outdoor ranger walks offered daily. The guided walks highlight a variety of topics, including the island's military history, famous inmates, escapes, natural history, and the Native American occupation. Try to catch the first ferry of the day (strongly recommended). Take the audio

San Francisco Attractions

NAME	TYPE	AUTHORS' RATING
CHINATOWN		
Cable Car Museum	History and real machinery	★★½
CIVIC CENTER		
Asian Art Museum	Largest collection in West	★★½
Haas-Lilienthal House	Furnished Victorian mansion	★★½
FINANCIAL DISTRICT		
Museum of Money of the American West	History of the West	★★
Wells Fargo History Museum	Pony Express and more	★★½
MARINA DISTRICT		
Ghirardelli Chocolate Manufactory and Soda Fountain	Demonstrates how chocolate is made	★★★
Palace of Fine Arts / Exploratorium	Classical Roman rotunda with hands-on museum	★★★½
San Francisco Craft and Folk Art Museum	Small gallery	NA
San Francisco Maritime Museum	Seafaring exhibits	★★★½
San Francisco Maritime National Historical Park / Hyde Street Pier	19th-century ships that visitors can board	★★★★
NORTH BEACH		
Alcatraz Island	Island prison and wildlife destination	★★★★★
Aquarium of the Bay	Commercial aquarium	★★★★
City Lights Bookstore	Beat bookstore	★★★★
Coit Tower	View from Telegraph Hill	★★½
Museum of Ophthalmology	Museum of all things eyes	★★
Ripley's Believe It or Not! Museum	Museum of the odd and unusual	★
Wax Museum	250 wax figures at Fisherman's Wharf	★
SOMA/MISSION DISTRICT		
California Historical Society	History exhibits	★★
Cartoon Art Museum	Gallery of cartoons	★★★★
Castro Theater	Landmark	★★★★
Mission Dolores	City's oldest building	★★★

NAME	TYPE	AUTHORS' RATING
SOMA/MISSION DISTRICT		
San Francisco Museum of Modern Art	Huge modern art gallery	★★★★½
Yerba Buena Gardens/ Center for the Arts	Art complex and gardens	★★★★
RICHMOND/SUNSET DISTRICT		
California Palace of the Legion of Honor	Museum of ancient and European art in scenic setting	★★★★
Cliff House	Oceanside tourist landmark	★★½
Fort Point National Historic Site	Civil War–era fort, great views	★★★★★
Japanese Tea Garden	Stroll-style garden	★★★★
Neptune Society Columbarium	Cemetery housed in copper-domed neoclassical structure	★★★
San Francisco Zoo	Largest zoo in northern California	★★★½
Strybing Arboretum and Botanical Gardens	70 acres of gardens	★★★
MARIN HEADLANDS TO POINT REYES		
Marin French Cheese Company	Oldest cheese makers in America	★★★
Marine Mammal Center	Rehabilitation and education center	★★★★
Mount Tamalpais/East Peak	Scenic hike with stunning view of city	★★★½
Muir Woods National Monument	Grove of majestic, coastal redwoods	★★★★
BERKELEY		
Berkeley Art Museum and Pacific Film Archive	Eclectic art on UC Berkeley campus	★★★
Berkeley Rose Gardens	Landmark with terraced gardens	★★★
Lawrence Hall of Science	Hands-on children's science museum	★
Phoebe Hearts Museum of Anthropology	Native American artifacts	★½
OAKLAND		
Oakland Museum of California	Museum of state's ecology	★★★½

cellhouse tour while it's not too crowded; after the video ends, walk up to the cellhouse for the 35-minute audio tour narrated by guards and inmates. Their recounting of daily life is vivid, blunt, and often scary. It's not to be missed. After the tour, don't be in a hurry to leave. Go on a ranger-led tour or hike some of the trails to discover the natural beauty and abundant wildlife (hawks, ravens, geese, finches, and humming-birds) that thrive on this evolving ecological preserve.

OTHER THINGS TO DO NEARBY Fisherman's Wharf, where ferries to and from Alcatraz embark and arrive, is Tourist Central. Major attractions worth your time include UnderWater World, the San Francisco Maritime Museum, and historic ships at Hyde Pier. You can also take ferries to Angel Island and Tiburon or a cruise on San Francisco Bay. Or rent a bike and ride the Golden Gate Promenade to the famous bridge with the same name; it's three-and-a-half miles one way. Mediocre restaurants abound in Fisherman's Wharf. A good, less expensive option is clam chowder in a bowl of sourdough bread (about $6.50) from Boudin's Bakery.

kids   Aquarium of the Bay

APPEAL BY AGE	PRESCHOOL ★★★★	GRADE SCHOOL ★★★★★	TEENS ★★★★
YOUNG ADULTS ★★★★		OVER 30 ★★★	SENIORS ★★★

Pier 39, San Francisco; in Fisherman's Wharf, North Beach;
☎ **415-623-5300; www.aquariumofthebay.com**

Type of attraction An aquarium where visitors are transported on a moving walkway through a clear tunnel to view thousands of marine animals. A self-guided audio tour. **Admission** $13.95 for adults, $7 for seniors ages 65 and over and children ages 3–11. Free for kids ages 2 and younger. Family rate for two adults and either one or two children is $29.95. **Hours** Monday–Thursday, 10 a.m.–6 p.m.; Friday–Sunday, 10 a.m.–7 p.m.; summer hours, 9 a.m.–8 p.m. Closed on Christmas Day. **When to go** Anytime. **Special comments** Don't refuse the audio-tour gizmo handed out before the tour begins—it will make a lot more sense. Not for claustrophobics or folks who get sweaty hands in highway tunnels. **Author's rating** While it's great to see a shark or ray glide overhead, this is a small attraction—and too expensive. ★★. **How much time to allow** 40 minutes to 1 hour.

DESCRIPTION AND COMMENTS Aquarium of the Bay offers a different take on the massive fish emporiums that are sprouting like mushrooms across America's urban landscape. Instead of walking past windows and peering into large tanks, you'll find yourself transported on a moving walkway through tanks in clear tunnels where you look at fish and other marine creatures on both sides and overhead. Sharks pass directly over you—only inches away. The emphasis is on the marine life of northern California; the audio tour provides a commentary as you're transported (or walk—you can step off the moving sidewalk at any time) through the aquarium. After the tank tour, visitors walk through a couple of small exhibits on California nonmarine habitats and a "touch tank" for the kids. These pale in comparison, though, to the underwater experience and inadvertently emphasize the brevity of the tour.

TOURING TIPS On weekends and holidays, the line for the audio tour contraption and the elevator can get long. But once under way, the line moves briskly. If a tour bus pulls in front of you and disgorges 40 tourists, go window-shopping on Pier 39 to kill some time until the line goes down (it won't take long).

OTHER THINGS TO DO NEARBY Walk on Pier 41 (where the Alcatraz ferry departs) and wave at the barking sea lions that congregate just offshore. If you bought tickets in advance, take the ferry to Alcatraz. You can also shop for overpriced tourist gewgaws on Pier 39 or eat in one of many overpriced seafood restaurants. Better bets in this tourist-crazed section of town are the San Francisco Maritime Museum and the Museum of the City of San Francisco (in the Cannery).

Asian Art Museum

APPEAL BY AGE	PRESCHOOL ★	GRADE SCHOOL ★★	TEENS ★★
YOUNG ADULTS ★★★	OVER 30 ★★★		SENIORS ★★★½

200 Larkin Street, Civic Center Plaza (in San Francisco's former main library, across from City Hall); ☎ 415-581-3500; www.asianart.org

Type of attraction One of the largest museums in the Western world devoted exclusively to Asian art. A self-guided tour. **Admission** $10 for adults, $7 for seniors, and $6 for college students with ID and children ages 13–17; children ages 12 and under free; $5 after 5 p.m. Thursdays; free to everyone on the first Tuesday of the month. **Hours** Tuesday–Sunday, 10 a.m.–5 p.m.; until 9 p.m. on Thursdays; closed on Mondays. **When to go** Anytime. **Special comments** Go on Thursday nights when admission is $5 after 5 p.m. and check out the latest special exhibition, or browse through 2,500 treasures in the galleries with performances, demonstrations, and special lectures showcasing the art and culture from all corners of Asia. **Author's rating** Fabulous and exotic art—but a little cold. ★★½. **How much time to allow** 2 hours (or longer, if Asian art is your thing).

DESCRIPTION AND COMMENTS The Asian Art Museum's collection is built around art donated by industrialist Avery Brundage. Today its holdings include nearly 2,500 art objects spanning 6,000 years of history and representing more than 40 Asian countries.

There are 29,000 square feet of gallery space enhanced with state-of-the-art displays and programs. The museum's three floors include exhibits of furniture, jade, scrolls, ceramics, tapestry, Buddhist temple bells, jewelry, folding screens, books and manuscripts, armor, swords, knives, and baskets. The first floor features temporary exhibition space and an excellent cafe.

TOURING TIPS Take the escalator to the third floor to a series of small exhibit rooms that start with Indian art, progress to art from the Persian world, and finish with West Asian art. On the second floor, walk across the enclosed bridge for spectacular Samsung Hall. Free docent-led tours are offered at 11 a.m. and 1 p.m. daily; a Highlights of China tour at 11:30 a.m. daily; and architectural tours of the building at noon and 2:30 p.m. daily (with an additional tour at 6 p.m. on Thursday).

OTHER THINGS TO DO NEARBY   Not much; Civic Center Plaza is located at the edge of the Tenderloin, San Francisco's skid row. Across the plaza is City Hall, which boasts a spectacular rotunda that's worth a look. Take the elevator to the fourth floor for the best view.

Berkeley Art Museum/Pacific Film Archive

APPEAL BY AGE	PRESCHOOL ★	GRADE SCHOOL ★★	TEENS ★★★
YOUNG ADULTS ★★★	OVER 30 ★★★		SENIORS ★★★

2626 Bancroft Way, Berkeley (on the University of California at Berkeley campus); ☎ 510-642-0808; www.bampfa.berkeley.edu

Type of attraction One of the largest university art museums in the world. A self-guided tour. Admission $8 for adults; $5 for seniors and children ages 13–17, non–UC Berkeley students, and disabled persons; free for Berkeley students and children ages 12 and under. Free to everyone on the first Thursday of the month. Hours Wednesday, Friday–Sunday, 11 a.m.–5 p.m; Thursday, 11 a.m.–7 p.m. Closed Monday, Tuesday, and major holidays. When to go Anytime. Special comments The museum's seven galleries are linked by carpeted ramps and stairs, and an elevator is available. Author's rating It's not on par with the Legion of Honor or the de Young Museum across the bay, but it's still a major collection in a visually striking building. ★★★. How much time to allow 1–2 hours.

DESCRIPTION AND COMMENTS   In seven linked, spiraling galleries, the Berkeley Art Museum displays its collections of Asian art, Western art from the Renaissance to the present, and the work of 20th-century painter Hans Hoffmann. The other four galleries are devoted to exhibitions that change about four times a year.

TOURING TIPS   Parking in Berkeley is notoriously bad; arrive as early as possible to find a space in one of the public lots near the campus. A better bet from San Francisco is BART; the Berkeley station is located at Center and Shattuck streets, and it's a short walk east to the campus. The Museum Store offers a wide range of books and periodicals on art and film, as well as posters, cards, and jewelry. Café Muse features better-than-average museum dining indoors or in the sculpture garden.

OTHER THINGS TO DO NEARBY   The Hearst Museum of Anthropology is across Bancroft Way on the ground floor of Kroeber Hall. Museum of Paleontology houses one of the largest and oldest collections of fossils in North America. It's free and open Monday through Friday, noon to 4 p.m., and it's located in the Valley Life Sciences Building on campus. The Lawrence Hall of Science, a hands-on science museum, has a spectacular view of the Bay Area. Drive or take a University Hill Service Shuttle to get there. Telegraph Avenue, in the heart of the People's Republic of Berkeley, features a diverse selection of restaurants, gift shops, street vendors, street musicians, street people, and gray-haired hippies; it's as if the 1960s never ended.

Berkeley Rose Gardens

APPEAL BY AGE	PRESCHOOL ★★	GRADE SCHOOL ★★	TEENS ★★★
YOUNG ADULTS ★★★		OVER 30 ★★★	SENIORS ★★

At Euclid and Eunice streets, in Berkeley;
www.bpfp.org/adoptaparkgroups/rosegarden

Type of attraction A 3.6-acre Berkeley landmark with terraces of roses. **Admission** Free. **Hours** From dawn to dusk. **When to go** Late spring and early summer are the best times to catch the roses in full bloom. **Author's rating ★★★. How much time to allow** A half hour would be sufficient, but stay longer if you are looking for a quiet place to relax.

DESCRIPTION AND COMMENTS A terraced amphitheater redolent with the smell of roses—hundreds of different types of roses—that color the terraces overlooking the San Francisco Bay and skyline. The Garden was built between 1933 and 1937 and has been maintained by a volunteer group, the Friends of the Berkeley Gardens. It is no wonder that it's a popular wedding place—it is truly an inspiration and romantic stop. There is a tennis court right next door.

TOURING TIPS Come when the sun is setting. The views of the city skyline and the sparkling bay are breathtaking. Park your car along the side of the street and get out and walk. There is no formal place to park.

OTHER THINGS TO DO NEARBY Had your fill of flowers? How about a bug show at the Essig Museum of Entomology? Located on the Berkeley campus, room 211 of Wellman Hall, ☎ 510-643-0804.

Cable Car Museum

APPEAL BY AGE	PRESCHOOL ★★½	GRADE SCHOOL ★★★	TEENS ★★
YOUNG ADULTS ★★½		OVER 30 ★★½	SENIORS ★★★

1201 Mason Street (at Washington Street), San Francisco (Nob Hill);
☎ 415-474-1887; www.cablecarmuseum.org

Type of attraction A building housing the machinery that moves the city's famed cable cars; museum features photographs, old cable cars, signposts, mechanical devices, and a video explaining the system. A self-guided tour. **Admission** Free. **Hours** April–September, daily, 10 a.m.–6 p.m.; rest of the year, daily, 10 a.m.– 5 p.m. Closed on major holidays. **When to go** Anytime. **Special comments** Go up to the mezzanine viewing area or down to an enclosed area where you can see inside the system. **Author's rating** It's fun to watch the machinery that pulls San Francisco's famed cable cars, and the price is right. **★★½. How much time to allow** 30 minutes to 1 hour.

DESCRIPTION AND COMMENTS When you try to envision what makes San Francisco's cable cars go, think horizontal elevator. Here you can see the machinery that moves the cables pulling the cars on the four lines of the only cable-car operation in the world. You'll also see an old cable car, 19th-century photos, some of the machinery that grips and releases the cable running under the streets, and a video. It's noisy and smells like a factory. A must for railroad buffs and most children.

TOURING TIPS If you're frustrated in your attempts to board the jam-packed cable cars, you can at least stop in to satisfy your curiosity about how it works. It's also a place to pick up a one-day or multiday Muni pass for unlimited rides on the city's buses, subways, and—if you're lucky or have the patience to wait in line—cable cars.

OTHER THINGS TO DO NEARBY Chinatown is only two blocks away. Three blocks south at California and Mason Streets is the Mark Hopkins Inter-Continental Hotel, famous for its Top O' the Mark lounge. Nob Hill, which overlooks Union Square, is home to many of the city's elite and some of its finest hotels.

California Academy of Sciences

Closed until 2008. A temporary exhibit featuring aquatic animals, a naturalist center, and prototypes of new exhibits is now at 875 Howard Street (near the Moscone Center). Open daily from 10 a.m.–5 p.m.; **www.cal academy.org.**

California Historical Society

APPEAL BY AGE	PRESCHOOL ★	GRADE SCHOOL ★	TEENS ★★
YOUNG ADULTS ★★	OVER 30 ★★		SENIORS ★★★

678 Mission Street, San Francisco; in SoMa near Third Street;
☎ **415-357-1848; www.calhist.org**

Type of attraction A gallery displaying temporary exhibitions from the society's collection of paintings, watercolors, drawings, lithographs, photographs, and artifacts. A self-guided tour. **Admission** $3 for adults, $1 for seniors and students, free for children ages 6 and under with an adult. Free on the first Tuesday of the month. **Hours** Wednesday–Friday, noon–4:30 p.m. Closed Saturday–Tuesday and major holidays. **When to go** Anytime. **Special comments** The gallery is all on one level. **Author's rating** The airy, sky-lit central gallery is beautiful, but its small size relegates this museum to the fill-in category. ★★. **How much time to allow** 1 hour.

DESCRIPTION AND COMMENTS Founded in 1871, the California Historical Society moved to this location in 1995. Items from the society's vast collection rotate about four times a year, so what you see on your visit won't be what we saw on ours. But it's a very attractive gallery and worth a stop, especially for first-time visitors to California looking for insight into the state's fascinating history.

TOURING TIPS Don't miss the storefront bookstore, which features books by California authors ranging from Jack London to Joan Didion. You'll also find unusual postcards and a map showing places around San Francisco used as locations in Hollywood films.

OTHER THINGS TO DO NEARBY Yerba Buena Gardens is a block away, and just beyond that is the San Francisco Museum of Modern Art.

California Palace of the Legion of Honor

APPEAL BY AGE	PRESCHOOL ★★	GRADE SCHOOL ★★★	TEENS ★★★
YOUNG ADULTS ★★★★	OVER 30 ★★★★		SENIORS ★★★★

In the northwest corner of San Francisco at 34th Avenue and Clement Street, in Lincoln Park; ☎ 415-863-3330 (recorded information); ☎ 415-750-3600 (main switchboard); www.legionofhonor.org

Type of attraction A recently renovated museum of ancient and European art housed in a reproduction of an 18th-century French palace; a spectacularly scenic setting. A self-guided tour. **Admission** $10 for adults, $7 for seniors, $5 for children ages 12–17; children ages 11 and under, free. A $2 discount is given to holders of Muni bus transfers; free to all the first Tuesday of the month. **Hours** Tuesday–Sunday, 9:30 a.m.–5 p.m.; first Tuesday of the month, 9:30 a.m.–8:45 p.m. Closed Monday and Thanksgiving, Christmas, and New Year's Day. **When to go** Anytime. **Special comments** Admission to the Legion of Honor also gives you free, same-day admission to the de Young Museum in Golden Gate Park. **Author's rating** Rather highbrow in tone, but the building and much of the art and physical location are spectacular. ★★★★. **How much time to allow** 2 hours.

DESCRIPTION AND COMMENTS Built in the 1920s and dedicated to the thousands of California servicemen who died in France in World War I, the Legion of Honor is visually stunning. Visitors enter through a magnificent courtyard dominated by an original cast of Auguste Rodin's "The Thinker." The building is in an eye-popping location overlooking the Golden Gate Bridge and the Marin Headlands; its design was inspired by the Palais de la Legion d'Honneur in Paris, built in 1786. If it all looks vaguely familiar, that's because you've watched Vertigo too many times on late-night TV; it's where Kim Novak went to gaze upon the portrait of Carlotta (a movie prop you won't find in the museum).

Inside is an impressive collection of ancient and European art covering 4,000 years. Heavy hitters include Rodin, Monet, Manet, Degas, Gainsborough, Reynolds, Rubens, Rembrandt, Van Gogh, Dalí, Picasso, Renoir, and Seurat. Additional artwork is on display in sumptuous galleries, which feature soaring ceilings, blond hardwood floors, and natural light. You'll also find extensive collections of furniture, silver, and ceramics.

TOURING TIPS Most of the art is on the main level, and ancient art and ceramics are on the lower-level terrace. Probably the most popular galleries are the two dedicated to Rodin; these stunning rooms are just past the central rotunda on the main level. Galleries 1–9 (to the left as you face the entrance) feature medieval, Renaissance, and 18th-century art; galleries 11–19 (to the right) contain art from the 18th through the early 20th centuries. Special exhibits are held in Rosekrans Court, housed under a glass structure that floods the galleries with natural light.

Parking is abundant around the museum, but the convenient lot across from the entrance is small and fills quickly; leaving your car parked on a nearby side street may result in a stiff, uphill hike to the museum entrance. A good option is public transportation; from Union Square, take the No. 38 bus to 33rd and Clement Streets; transfer to the No. 18 bus (and save $2 on admission) or walk uphill to the museum.

OTHER THINGS TO DO NEARBY Cliff House, a mile or so south on the coast, provides fantastic views of the Marin coast and Seal Rocks, home base for sea lions and a variety of marine birds; bring binoculars. There's also a restaurant and a visitor center. To the north are Fort Point and the Golden Gate Bridge; to the south are Ocean Beach (the water is cold and dangerous) and Golden Gate Park. A couple of miles down the coast are the San Francisco Zoo and Fort Funston, with great views, easy trails, and hang gliders doing their thing on the strong ocean air currents.

Cartoon Art Museum

APPEAL BY AGE	PRESCHOOL ★★	GRADE SCHOOL ★★★	TEENS ★★★
YOUNG ADULTS ★★★	OVER 30 ★★★★		SENIORS ★★★

655 Mission Street, between New Montgomery and Third Street in SoMa; ☎ 415-CARTOON or 415-227-8666; www.cartoonart.org

Type of attraction The only museum west of the Mississippi dedicated to the preservation, collection, and exhibition of original cartoon art. A self-guided tour. **Admission** $6 adults, $4 students and seniors, $2 children ages 6–12. First Tuesday of the month is "pay what you wish" day. **Hours** Tuesday–Sunday, 11 a.m.– 5 p.m.; closed Mondays and all major holidays. **When to go** Anytime. **Special comments** While there's lots here to delight children, cartoons of an explicitly adult nature are placed in rooms restricted to ages 18 and older. Cartoons are displayed at adult eye level. Call ahead to make sure the museum isn't closed due to installation of a new exhibit. **Author's rating** How can you resist a cartoon art museum? ★★★★. **How much time to allow** 1–2 hours.

DESCRIPTION AND COMMENTS From at least the turn of the 20th century, the Bay Area has been home to a healthy population of professional cartoonists. (Maybe it's a combination of great vistas and San Francisco's relaxed atmosphere.) Well-known cartoonists spotlighted in this small museum over the years include Scott Adams ("Dilbert"), Bill Griffith ("Zippy the Pinhead"), Morrie Turner ("Wee Pals"), Phil Frank ("Farley"), and Paul Mavrides ("The Fabulous Furry Freak Brothers"). Many of the cartoons hail from San Francisco's underground "comix" movement of the late 1960s and early 1970s. Needless to say, most of the art is satirical, scathingly funny, and often risqué. Wonderful, in other words.

TOURING TIPS The new space is larger than the previous space, so exhibits have been expanded. There are more than three major shows a year.

OTHER THINGS TO DO NEARBY Yerba Buena Gardens and Center for the Arts is a block down Mission Street, and the Museum of Modern Art is on Third Street on the other side of Yerba Buena Gardens. The California Historical Society has a small gallery at 678 Mission Street.

Castro Theatre

APPEAL BY AGE	PRESCHOOL ★	GRADE SCHOOL ★	TEENS ★
YOUNG ADULTS ★★	OVER 30 ★★★★		SENIORS ★★★★

429 Castro Street, San Francisco; in the Mission District; ☎ 415-621-6120 is the information line with a recording of current movies; to reach the box office directly call 415-621-6350; www.thecastrotheatre.com

Type of attraction A city landmark that stands as an icon to one of the world's most prominent gay neighborhoods. **Admission** Movie tickets unless otherwise noted are $8.50. Matinee tickets and tickets for senior citizens and children under 12 are $5.50. **Hours** The box office opens an hour before the first movie of the day and only sells tickets for the current day. **When to go** Anytime. **Special comments** The theater is easily spotted; just look for the massive marquee on Castro Street—easily becoming as recognizable as the Transamerica Building. **Author's rating** From classic movies like *Funny Girl* to its interesting architecture, it's a nice way to either see the inside of a neighborhood icon or step in for a night at the movies. ★★★★. **How much time to allow** If you are stopping to glimpse the exterior, only allow a few minutes. Movies usually run about 2 hours.

DESCRIPTION AND COMMENTS This elaborate landmark on Castro Street can't make up its mind whether its motif is Roman, Asian, Arabic, or that Miami style—art deco. After a major renovation, the theater still boasts an interior and exterior that remain true to its 1920s and 1930s heyday and the vision of designer Timothy Pflueger (the same guy who gave the city the Paramount Theater in Oakland, the former I. Magnin building on Union Square, 450 Sutter, and the Pacific Telephone Building on New Montgomery.)

The ceiling and light fixtures are elaborate, as is most of the interior. Be sure to get to the theater early to take in the splendor of this classic space. The small theater feels a bit like an opera house, with the help of the huge Wurlitzer organ that begins each movie. It rises out of the theater pit just before show time, leading the audience in a series of classic show tunes followed by "San Francisco."

TOURING TIPS The hooting and hollering and sing-alongs of the audience bring down the house! Loads of fun, especially if they are showing such campy classics as *My Fair Lady* or *Return of the Body Snatchers*.

 ## City Lights Bookstore

APPEAL BY AGE	PRESCHOOL —	GRADE SCHOOL —	TEENS —
YOUNG ADULTS ★★	OVER 30 ★★★★		SENIORS ★★★

261 Columbus Avenue (off Broadway in North Beach), San Francisco;
☎ **415-362-8193; www.citylights.com**

Type of attraction A Beat bookstore made famous by its Beat inhabitants such as Jack Kerouac, Allen Ginsberg, and owner/artist Lawrence Ferlinghetti. **Admission** Free (all new poetry welcome!). **Hours** Daily, 10 a.m.–midnight. **When to go** Anytime. **Special comments** If you see a gray-haired and bearded man standing in the aisles, chances are it is the Beat owner and poet laureate himself—Lawrence Ferlinghetti. **Author's rating** You'll feel a sudden surge of creative energy just by reading the titles of the new releases from independent literary forces. The Beat Generation held such a spell over the city, and this bookstore is one of the few landmarks left. A definite stop. ★★★★. **How much time to allow** Anywhere from a few minutes to purchase a postcard to all day, browsing the poetry and literature stacked on the wooden shelves.

DESCRIPTION AND COMMENTS Founded in 1953 by poet Lawrence Ferlinghetti and Peter D. Martin, City Lights is one of the few truly great independent bookstores or alternative literary scenes in the United States. Famed the world over for unique "finds" and rare first editions, it is made even more famous by the icons of a generation—those beatniks—who nurtured their creative restlessness here.

TOURING TIPS Often the bookstore hosts readings and book signings. Contact them directly for a schedule of guest authors and poets. Aisles and shelves are often overflowing and it is difficult to find a specific title. Don't hesitate to ask for help.

OTHER THINGS TO DO NEARBY Stop by Vesuvio Café across the street, the famous bar and literary hangout that was once the favorite watering hole of Jack Kerouac. Coit Tower is also in North Beach. Pick up a good read and head to the top!

  Cliff House

APPEAL BY AGE	PRESCHOOL ★★★★	GRADE SCHOOL ★★★★	TEENS ★★★★
YOUNG ADULTS ★★★		OVER 30 ★★★	SENIORS ★★★

1090 Point Lobos Avenue (at the Great Highway), San Francisco;
Cliff House Restaurant ☎ 415-386-3330;
visitor center ☎ 415-556-8642; www.cliffhouse.com

Type of attraction A San Francisco oceanside tourist landmark with spectacular views and a restaurant. Self-guided tour. **Admission** Free. **Hours** Visitor center: daily, 10 a.m.–5 p.m.; restaurant: Monday–Thursday, 9 a.m.–9 p.m.; Friday and Saturday, 9 a.m.–10 p.m.; Sunday, 8:30 a.m.–9 p.m. **When to go** When the coast isn't socked in by fog. Cocktails at sunset in the restaurant are a San Francisco tradition. **Special comments** Lots of stairs if you opt to explore Sutro Heights Park and the ruins of Sutro Baths. There's also a steep set of stairs down to the visitor center. **Author's rating** A bizarre blend of spectacular scenery, an overpriced seafood restaurant with a view, San Francisco history, and tourist schlock. Probably not to be missed, but it's no tragedy if you do. ★★★. **How much time to allow** 30 minutes to 1 hour (longer if you dine).

DESCRIPTION AND COMMENTS A San Francisco tourist landmark for more than 100 years, Cliff House still packs them in—often by the busload. The attraction? Dining with a magnificent view of the Pacific, with Seal Rocks in the foreground just offshore. But there's more here than the opportunity to drop big bucks for an expensive lunch or dinner while you watch waves crash against the rocks—or there will be, after renovations are completed (the restaurant remains open). The whole place is owned by the National Park Service (it's part of the Golden Gate National Recreation Area). Just offshore from the restaurant and the temporarily closed visitor center is Seal Rocks. Next door (so to speak) are the concrete ruins of Sutro Baths, a three-acre swimming emporium that once held 1.6 million gallons of water and rented 20,000 bathing suits and 40,000 towels a day. Musee Mechanique, an unworldly collection of antique penny arcade amusements that will still eat up your quarters, has moved temporarily to a location at Pier 45 in Fisherman's Wharf. The Giant Camera, a huge camera obscura you walk into to see an image of Seal Rocks magnified on a huge parabolic screen, is temporarily closed.

TOURING TIPS Across the Great Highway and just up the hill is Sutro Heights Park, where you walk up a short, steep path to a great view overlooking Cliff House, Seal Rocks, the ruins, and the Pacific.

OTHER THINGS TO DO NEARBY Drive a few miles south to Fort Funston and watch hang gliders calmly jump off cliffs and swoop and soar along the shore. You can take a walk along Ocean Beach, which starts just below Cliff House, and view actual native San Franciscans. Golden Gate Park, with museums, trails, and a lake with rowboats for rent, is to the south. You can't miss the entrance; look for the Dutch windmill.

 Coit Tower

APPEAL BY AGE	PRESCHOOL ★★★	GRADE SCHOOL ★★★	TEENS ★★★
YOUNG ADULTS ★★★		OVER 30 ★★★	SENIORS ★★★

At the top of Telegraph Hill Boulevard, near North Beach in San Francisco; ☎ 415-362-0808; www.coittower.org

Type of attraction A landmark tower with an observation deck atop Telegraph Hill. A self-guided tour. **Admission** The elevator ride to the top is $3 per person. Admission to the murals and the ground-floor gift shop is free. Murals on the second floor are available only on tour at 11 a.m. on Saturday or by special arrangement. **Hours** Daily, 10 a.m.–5 p.m. **When to go** Anytime. **Special comments** The elevator doesn't go all the way to the top; you must negotiate a set of steep, winding stairs to the observation deck. Small children will need a lift to see the outstanding 360° view. Skip it in lousy weather. **Author's rating** A great view, but it's almost as good from the parking lot at the base of the tower. ★★½. **How much time to allow** 30 minutes to 1 hour.

DESCRIPTION AND COMMENTS Built as a monument to San Francisco's volunteer firefighters with funds left by renowned eccentric Lillie Hitchcock Coit, this landmark provides a breathtaking view of the city, San Francisco Bay, the Oakland and Golden Gate bridges—the works. Some say the tower is shaped to resemble a firehose nozzle, but others disagree. There's no doubt about Ms. Coit's dedication to firefighters. Early in the gold rush, she is said to have deserted a wedding party and chased after her favorite fire engine. Lillie died in 1929 at age 86, leaving the city $125,000 to "expend in an appropriate manner . . . to the beauty of San Francisco." Coit Tower is the result. In the lobby of the tower base are 19 WPA-era murals depicting labor-union workers.

TOURING TIPS Don't drive; the parking lot at the base of Coit Tower is small, and the wait for a space can be long. Walk the steep hill or take the No. 39 Coit bus at Washington Square Park (board at Columbus Avenue and Union Street), which will take you up Telegraph Hill.

OTHER THINGS TO DO NEARBY   Walk down steep Telegraph Hill to Washington Square and North Beach, the city's Bohemian district of bars, Italian restaurants, coffee houses, and City Lights Bookstore, the former hangout of Jack Kerouac, Allen Ginsberg, and other Beatnik greats.

de Young Memorial Museum

Golden Gate Park, 50 Hagiwara Tea Garden Drive, San Francisco;
☎ **415-863-3330; www.thinker.org/deyoung/visiting**

After a major demolition and renovation, this institution reopened at press time. San Francisco's oldest art museum in Golden Gate Park features American paintings, sculpture, and decorative arts from colonial times to the 20th century.

Fort Point National Historic Site

APPEAL BY AGE	PRESCHOOL ★★★	GRADE SCHOOL ★★★★	TEENS ★★★
YOUNG ADULTS ★★★★	OVER 30 ★★★★★	SENIORS ★★★★★	

In the Presidio at the end of Marine Drive (at the southern end of the Golden Gate Bridge), San Francisco; ☎ **415-556-1693; www.nps.gov/fopo**

Type of attraction A Civil War–era brick coastal fortification beneath Golden Gate Bridge; superb vistas of San Francisco's key topographical features. Guided and self-guided tours. **Admission** Free; donation requested. **Hours** Friday–Sunday, 10 a.m.–5 p.m. Closed Thanksgiving, Christmas, and New Year's Day. **When to go** In July and August come before noon if you're driving; the small parking lot fills fast. A better option in these busy months (or whenever the weather is nice) is to bike or walk along the Golden Gate Promenade to the fort and its dramatic setting. **Special comments** Lots of steep, narrow stairs, tricky footing, and a scarcity of handrails in the fort. Portable restrooms are located outside the entrance of the fort, and flush toilets are near the wharf on Marine Drive. Bring a jacket or sweater; Fort Point can be very windy and cool. **Author's rating** Come just for the view. Put this on your "must see" list. ★★★★★. **How much time to allow** 1 hour; longer for a guided tour and a demonstration.

DESCRIPTION AND COMMENTS   This fort, built between 1853 and 1861 by the U.S. Army Corps of Engineers, was designed to prevent the entrance of a foreign fleet into San Francisco Bay. The setting—the Golden Gate Bridge overhead, the San Francisco skyline to the east, the rugged Marin Headlands across the straight, and the Pacific Ocean stretching to the horizon—is breathtaking.

History buffs will enjoy exploring the fort, which symbolizes the commercial and strategic military importance of San Francisco. But most visitors will simply want to hoof it to the fourth (and highest) level for an even better view of the dramatic panorama (with Golden Gate Bridge traffic pounding overhead). The interior of the fort is bare bones, but some of the rooms on upper levels contain photo exhibits about its past. Film buffs will recognize the spot where James Stewart fished Kim Novak out of San Francisco Bay in Alfred Hitchcock's classic thriller, *Vertigo*. A final note: the fort's impressive muzzle-loading cannons (rendered obsolete by rifled cannons during the Civil War and removed by 1900) were never fired in anger.

TOURING TIPS Go to the gift shop on the ground level for a free 17-minute video introduction to the fort. You can sign up here for a free guided tour, pick up a self-guided tour booklet, and see a schedule of demonstrations (such as gun-loading by costumed personnel). You can also rent a 40-minute audio tour of the fort ($2.50 for adults, $1 for children). Be sure to walk around the sea wall to the chain-link fence for a full view of the Pacific Ocean. You may also see die-hard surfers and swimmers in wetsuits negotiating the surf and ships passing under the bridge.

OTHER THINGS TO DO NEARBY At the southern end of the Golden Gate Bridge on Lincoln Boulevard is a scenic overlook, visitor center, parking lot, and starting point for a walk on the bridge or along paths overlooking the Pacific. The best bet for getting there is to drive, although you can walk up the very steep path. The Presidio, a former U.S. Army base that's now part of Golden Gate National Recreation Area, is filled with old buildings, a museum, a military cemetery, a golf course, trails, and stands of eucalyptus trees planted with military precision.

Drive south along the Pacific for more great views, magnificent private residences, the California Palace of the Legion of Honor (a classy art museum also used in *Vertigo*), Cliff House, and Ocean Beach. On the way back downtown from Fort Point are the Palace of Fine Arts and the Exploratorium (a hands-on science museum) and Fort Mason (with museums, restaurants, fishing piers, marinas, and picnic areas).

 kids ## Ghirardelli Chocolate Manufactory and Soda Fountain

APPEAL BY AGE	PRESCHOOL ★★★	GRADE SCHOOL ★★★★	TEENS ★★★★★
YOUNG ADULTS ★★★★★		OVER 30 ★★★★	SENIORS ★★★

Ghirardelli Square Clock Tower, 900 North Point Street, San Francisco; near the Marina District; ☎ 415-474-3938; www.ghirardelli.com

Type of attraction Come and see how the chocolate is made. An excellent excursion for the little ones. Self-guided tour. **Admission** Free. **Hours** Weekdays, 9 a.m.–11:30 a.m.; weekends, 9 a.m.–midnight. **When to go** Anytime, great for dessert. **Special comments** Start at the soda fountain. **Author's rating** It's probably going to be a major hit with the kids. But who outgrows chocolate? ★★★. **How much time to allow** 1 hour or more, depending on cravings!

DESCRIPTION AND COMMENTS It's the garden of delectable chocolates, from truffles to their world-famous hot fudge sundaes and the ever-popular Alcatraz Rock (rocky road ice cream in a shell of hard chocolate). It's interactive tasting while you see the machinery that pumps out delicious treats.

TOURING TIPS Foggy or rainy days and weekends create swamps of chocolate lovers. If you want to avoid crowds, come on a weekday, preferably in the morning. That's when the goodies are fresh anyway.

OTHER THINGS TO DO NEARBY Of course, Fisherman's Wharf is a hop, skip, and a jump away, and Pier 39 is close also.

Haas-Lilienthal House

APPEAL BY AGE	PRESCHOOL ★	GRADE SCHOOL ★★	TEENS ★★
YOUNG ADULTS ★★	OVER 30 ★★★		SENIORS ★★★

2007 Franklin Street, San Francisco; near Washington Street in Pacific Heights; ☎ 415-441-3000; www.sfheritage.org

Type of attraction The only fully furnished Victorian house in San Francisco open to the public. A guided tour. **Admission** $8 per person; $5 for seniors and under 12. **Hours** Wednesday, noon–3 p.m.; Sunday, 11 a.m.–4 p.m. **When to go** Anytime. **Special comments** Two flights of stairs on the tour. **Author's rating** A fascinating glimpse into the life of an upper-middle-class San Francisco family of the late 19th century. ★★½. **How much time to allow** 1 hour.

DESCRIPTION AND COMMENTS This exquisite 1886 high Victorian mansion has been maintained in nearly original condition since the last descendant of the builders to live in the house died in 1972. The hour-long, docent-led tour reveals a wealth of details on the house (one of a very few to survive the 1906 earthquake and fire) and the life of a rich (but not fabulously so) Jewish merchant family. The distinctive Queen Anne, third-floor tower is strictly decorative; the windows are nine feet above the floor, while the sliding doors on the recessed front entrance were only open when the family was receiving visitors.

Inside, the formal front parlor was used for receiving important guests, and the family parlor behind it was used for guests lower on the social scale. More fascinating details include the small dining room off the main dining room used by children and servants; what appears to be a window at the back is in fact a jib door that slides up and may have been built so that coffins could be passed in and out of the house when a family member died.

TOURING TIPS Don't walk up the stairs to the main entrance; you'll get to do this later. Instead, walk to the right (as you face the house) and down the sidewalk to the tour entrance.

OTHER THINGS TO DO NEARBY Two other impressive Victorian houses are nearby. You can't go in, but they're worth a look: the Edward Coleman House at Franklin and California Streets; and the Bransten House at 1735 Franklin Street. Pacific Heights is home to some of the city's most expensive and dramatic real estate, with some mansions and town houses selling for prices starting at $1 million.

Stroll the neighborhood, or down the hill toward the Marina and take lunch on either Union or Chestnut streets.

Japanese Tea Garden

APPEAL BY AGE	PRESCHOOL ★★	GRADE SCHOOL ★★	TEENS ★★
YOUNG ADULTS ★★★★	OVER 30 ★★★★		SENIORS ★★★★

In Golden Gate Park; ☎ 415-752-4227

Type of attraction A stroll-style garden with a harmonious blend of architecture, landscape, bridges, footpaths, shrines, and gates; tea house serves tea, soft drinks, juices, and cookies. **Admission** $3.50 per person; children ages 5 and under, free. Free tours are offered Wednesday and Sunday at 1 p.m (inside the main gate). Scheduled events have a separate admission charge. **Hours** Daily, 8:30 a.m.–6:30 p.m. Open every day of the year. **When to go** In nice weather. In April, the cherry trees are in bloom. **Special comments** Some mild uphills and uneven footing. **Author's rating** Beautiful and fascinating. ★★★★. **How much time to allow** 1–2 hours.

DESCRIPTION AND COMMENTS In Japan, a garden is considered one of the highest art forms, and after a visit to the Japanese Tea Garden, you'll understand why. On winding paths visitors encounter carp pools, a pagoda, a bronze Buddha, dwarf trees, flowers, cherry trees, footbridges, and a Zen garden. Even when it's packed with hordes of visitors, this artfully designed garden imparts a sense of tranquility.

The garden was part of the Japanese Village exhibit of the California Midwinter International Exposition of 1894, which was held in what is now the Music Concourse in Golden Gate Park. It was built by Japanese artisans, and in the decades after the exposition closed, the garden was expanded from one acre to five acres. In that limited amount of space, the garden expresses the essence of nature by the use of specially selected plants and stones arranged in harmony with the landscape.

TOURING TIPS Come in nice weather and take your time. The atmosphere in the garden is extremely soothing—a perfect stop on a harried touring schedule. Tea service by a kimono-clad waitress in the Tea House is $3.50. The fortune cookies were originally introduced here in 1914. (Ironically, they're called Chinese fortune cookies now.) Stop in the gift shop to see a wide array of Japanese gifts and toys, including kites and fans.

OTHER THINGS TO DO NEARBY The Asian Art Museum, where you can find more Japanese art, is next door. Across Martin Luther King Jr. Drive is the Strybing Arboretum, 70 acres of gardens. If it's a nice day, drive or walk to Stow Lake and rent a rowboat ($13 an hour) or a paddleboat ($17 an hour), with a $1 deposit; Stow Lake Boat Rentals (☎ 415-752-0347).

kids Lawrence Hall of Science

APPEAL BY AGE	PRESCHOOL ★★★★★	GRADE SCHOOL ★★★★★	TEENS ★★★
YOUNG ADULTS ★★		OVER 30 ★★	SENIORS ★★

Centennial Drive, Berkeley (below Grizzly Peak Boulevard, overlooking the University of California, Berkeley campus);
☎ **510-642-5132 for 24-hour information; www.lhs.berkeley.edu or www.lawrencehallofscience.org**

Type of attraction A hands-on science museum for youngsters. A self-guided tour. **Admission** $9.50 for adults; $7.50 for seniors, students, and children ages 5–18; $5.50 for children ages 3–4. Planetarium shows on Saturday and Sunday at 1 p.m., 2:15 p.m., and 3:30 p.m; $3 adults and $2.50 children ages 18 and under (with museum admission price). **Hours** Daily, 10 a.m.–5 p.m.; closed on major holidays. **When to go** When the weather is clear for the spectacular view. **Special comments** Parking is very tight on this hilltop setting, so try to arrive early. Visitors must pay 50 cents per half hour to park. If you're not driving, take BART to the downtown Berkeley station and catch the Local Shuttle at Center Street and Shattuck Avenue. Then transfer to the Hill Service Shuttle at the Hearst Mining Circle on campus. Call Transportation Services at ☎ 510-642-5132 for info. **Author's rating** A great view of the bay but otherwise strictly for youngsters. ★. **How much time to allow** At least half a day for kids; you'll have to drag them away.

DESCRIPTION AND COMMENTS Named after Ernest O. Lawrence, one of the University of California at Berkeley's best-known Nobel Prize laureates, this hands-on science museum enthralls tots through grade-schoolers. It's hard to list a sampling of the many activities available, but they include a gravity wall, earthquake exhibits, play areas, and math and chemistry exhibits (where kids play scientific sleuths and use real chemical and forensic tests to solve a whodunit). Hour-long planetarium shows suitable for children 8 and up are offered on weekend and holiday afternoons; children under age 6 aren't admitted except for "Flying High" at 1 p.m., which is suitable for children ages 4 and up. The Lawrence Memorial Room, probably the only exhibit in the museum that's not hands-on and geared toward children, features artifacts, an explanation of how a cyclotron works, and awards given to Ernest O. Lawrence (including his Nobel Prize in physics).

TOURING TIPS Outside, youngsters can clamber on Pheena—a 50-foot, 3,000-pound replica of a fin whale—and a 60-foot long, scientifically accurate model of a double-helix DNA molecule. Adults can keep one eye on the kids and the other on the drop-dead view. A cafeteria on the lower level offers school lunch–style fare and a panoramic view, while the museum store sells books, games, puzzles, and science-oriented gift items.

OTHER THINGS TO DO NEARBY The university's Botanical Garden is located in Strawberry Canyon on the winding road below the Lawrence Hall of Science and above the campus stadium; it includes a redwood grove, a large selection of native plants, plant species from around the world, and picnic tables. The Museum of Paleontology houses one of the largest and oldest collections of fossils in North America. It's open Monday through Friday, noon to 4 p.m.; it's located in the Valley Life Sciences Building on campus and admission is free. The Berkeley Art Museum, also on campus, is an excellent art museum. Telegraph Avenue is a hopping street scene with an diverse selection of restaurants, gift shops, street vendors, street musicians, street people, and gray-haired hippies.

Marin French Cheese Company

APPEAL BY AGE	PRESCHOOL ★★	GRADE SCHOOL ★★★	TEENS ★★★
YOUNG ADULTS ★★★★		OVER 30 ★★★★	SENIORS ★★★★

7500 Red Hill Road, Petaluma; ☎ 800-292-6001;
www.marinfrenchcheese.com

Type of attraction The oldest continuously operating cheese producer in the United States, set amidst an ancient farm in the Marin countryside. Guided tours daily. Admission Free. Hours Sales room: daily, 8:30 a.m.–5 p.m.; tours: daily, 10 a.m.–4 p.m. When to go Anytime. Special comments: Visit the Web site for directions and a map. Author's rating ★★★. How much time to allow 1–3 hours, depending on whether or not you picnic.

DESCRIPTION AND COMMENTS This is a great getaway from the hustle and bustle of the big bad city. As soon as you turn off Highway 101, you know you're in a different environment. The sprawling farmstead by itself is lovely for a short hike, a quiet sit by the pond, or a game of Frisbee. The cheese-making operation is fun to watch, and the guides know a lot of local history as well as "cheeseology." The store on premises has all you need to outfit a picnic, including their own wine label. Also on premises is an art gallery with regular exhibits, mostly of modern art. Check the Web site for schedules.

TOURING TIPS The weather is always milder here than in the city, so be prepared for sunshine.

OTHER THINGS TO DO NEARBY Here you're about halfway to Sonoma Valley, so you can make this a stop along the way.

Marine Mammal Center

APPEAL BY AGE	PRESCHOOL ★★★★	GRADE SCHOOL ★★★★	TEENS ★★★★
YOUNG ADULTS ★★★★		OVER 30 ★★★	SENIORS ★★★

Fort Cronkite near Rodeo Lagoon in the Marin Headlands;
☎ **415-289-7325; www.marinemammalcenter.org**

Type of attraction A rehabilitation and education center that nurtures orphaned or injured sea lions, seals, and any other marine mammal. Admission Free, but donations welcome. Hours Daily, 10 a.m.–4 p.m. except Thanksgiving, Christmas, and New Year's days. When to go The best time to visit depends on the season. Winter is usually inactive—they don't get many mammals in at that time. Spring, however, is pupping season when young pups are abundant in the waters—thus making the center busy. Winter and spring, there are more northern elephant seals and harbor seals. The summer and fall months see more California sea lions. Call the center to check on the number of "residents" they have that particular day. Special comments The organization receives funding from grants and loans. Although it's free to get in, donations would be a nice gesture. Author's rating When people have you going in circles (especially after Fisherman's Wharf), this is a nice escape. You truly get an understanding of the marine life in and around the bay. ★★★★. How much time to allow 1–2 hours.

DESCRIPTION AND COMMENTS This hospital in the headlands is one of the main organizations devoted to the welfare of the seals and sea lion population off of the Bay Area. Every year they get orphaned or injured pups and adult seals or sea lions. The facility is open to visitors to generate donations and educational awareness on the impact the environment and human handling can have on the populations. Volunteers are on hand at the center to answer any questions about patients at the center or involving marine life in the bay in general, including whales. You can see the pups get bottle-fed, and read about the successful release of past patients.

TOURING TIPS Call to check on patients' availability. The health of the animals is their first priority, so sometimes the biologists keep many of the animals out of public viewing. Be respectful of the animals!

OTHER THINGS TO DO NEARBY The Headlands offer much in the way of outdoor recreation or scenic drives. Since you probably would drive to the center, consider driving to Mount Tamalpais for amazing views, or down along CA 1 to Stinson Beach, for vertigo-inducing cliffside roads, and R&R.

Mexican Museum

Fort Mason Center, Building D, Marina Boulevard and Buchanan Street, San Francisco; ☎ 415-202-9700; www.mexicanmuseum.org

Special comments At press time, the gallery was closed for relocation to Mission Street between Third and Fourth streets. It does conduct a regular Diego Rivera mural tour. See Web site for details.

Mission Dolores

APPEAL BY AGE	PRESCHOOL ★	GRADE SCHOOL ★★	TEENS ★★
YOUNG ADULTS ★★	OVER 30 ★★★		SENIORS ★★★

3321 16th Street in the Mission District, San Francisco; ☎ 415-621-8203; www.missiondolores.org

Type of attraction San Francisco's oldest building (1791) and the 6th of 21 missions built by Franciscan priests along El Camino Real, the Spanish road linking the missions from Mexico to Sonoma. Self-guided and audio tours. **Admission** $5 for adults and teenagers, $4 for children ages 5–12. **Hours** Summer, daily, 9 a.m.–4:30 p.m.; other times of year, 9 a.m.–4 p.m. Closes at noon on Good Friday and at 2 p.m. on Easter. Closed Thanksgiving and Christmas. **When to go** Try to go when it's not raining; the cemetery, probably the most interesting part, is out in the open. **Special comments** Restrooms are near the cemetery entrance. **Author's rating** Surprisingly small, but worth visiting for an authentic taste of San Francisco's Spanish heritage. ★★. **How much time to allow** 30 minutes to 1 hour.

DESCRIPTION AND COMMENTS With adobe walls four feet thick and the original redwood logs supporting the roof, Mission Dolores has survived four major earthquakes and is the only one of the original missions along the El Camino Real (the Royal Way) that has not been rebuilt. Mass is still celebrated in the building, which is 114 feet long and 22 feet wide. The repainted ceiling depicts original Ohlone Indian designs done with vegetable dyes. The decorative altar came from Mexico in 1796, as did the two side altars (in 1810).

Outside the mission, a diorama shows how it appeared in 1791. Peek inside the basilica, completed in 1918, to view beautiful stained-glass windows. The small museum displays artifacts such as lithographs of the California missions and a revolving tabernacle from the Philippines. You can also see the adobe walls, which were formed and sun-dried nearby.

The highlight (for us anyway) is the cemetery—really a lush garden with headstones. Most of the markers are dated in the years following the California gold rush and many of the family names are Irish.

TOURING TIPS Film buffs won't find the headstone of Carlotta Valdes in the mission's cemetery. It was a prop in Alfred Hitchcock's *Vertigo,* part of which was filmed here.

OTHER THINGS TO DO NEARBY Walk a couple of blocks down 16th Street for a selection of ethnic restaurants. Dolores Street, with an aisle of palm trees up and down the center, is fun and funky. The Mission District is full of the good and the bad—homeless people, taquerias, a thriving alternative scene, organic cafés, hash houses . . . you name it and the Mission's got it. Both 16th Street and Mission Street show off the Mission District's diverse flavors, including offbeat bookstores, Asian restaurants, and interesting shops. Good Vibrations (603 Valencia Street; ☎ 415-522-5460) features everything you wanted to know about sex, and then some. The Mission Cultural Center at 2868 Mission Street (Tuesday–Saturday, 10 a.m.–4 p.m.; ☎ 415-821-1155) has a large second-floor gallery with changing art exhibitions, usually with a Hispanic flavor; it's free.

Mount Tamalpais—East Peak

APPEAL BY AGE	PRESCHOOL ★★	GRADE SCHOOL ★★★	TEENS ★★★
YOUNG ADULTS ★★★		OVER 30 ★★★	SENIORS ★★

Mount Tamalpais State Park, 12 miles north of the Golden Gate Bridge in Marin County; exit US 101 at Sausalito and follow signs to the park; ☎ 415-388-2070; www.parks.ca.gov

Type of attraction A half-mile hike to the summit of Mount Tamalpais and a stunning view of San Francisco, the bay, the Golden Gate Bridge, and the Pacific Ocean. A self-guided tour. Admission Free. Parking in the lot below the summit is $6 per car; $5 for seniors. Hours Daily, sunrise–sunset. When to go In clear weather. Special comments Locals call it "Mount Tam." Wear sturdy shoes if you opt for the steep hike to the summit. Author's rating May be the best view of San Francisco. ★★★½. How much time to allow 1 hour.

DESCRIPTION AND COMMENTS The incredible vistas you see on the drive up to the top of Tamalpais are a trip in themselves. *Warning:* Anyone afraid of heights and falling off narrow, cliff-clinging curved roads with a thousand-foot drop should either pass on the drive up or go blindfolded. Until 1930, tourists rode the Mount Tamalpais and Muir Woods Railway to the top, where a tavern and dance pavilion were located near the present parking lot. From the summit, the view is spectacular—including 3,890-foot Mount Diablo to the east and, on a clear day, the snow-capped Sierras 140 miles to the east. Any soaring birds you see are probably turkey vultures. If you're not up for the half-mile, 220-foot-elevation-gain hike to the summit, you can opt for a self-guided tour around the peak or just enjoy the view from the overlook near the restrooms.

TOURING TIPS Unless you're wearing hiking boots and are used to narrow foot trails, don't take the plank trail to the summit. Although it looks easy, it quickly gets very steep, with treacherous footing. Instead, take the Verna Dunshee Trail, a self-guided tour just over a half-mile long that goes counterclockwise around the peak; pick up a brochure in the gift shop. The trail starts to the right of the restrooms. A snack bar, phones, and drinking water are available near the parking lot.

OTHER THINGS TO DO NEARBY Hikers of all abilities will find plenty of scenic trails in the state park. Muir Woods National Monument is a grove of majestic coastal redwoods, the tallest trees in the world. Stinson Beach, located beneath steep hills rising to Mount Tam, offers vistas of the sea and hills, while Muir Beach, further south down Route 1, has a semicircular cove where you can relax and enjoy the scenery. To the north, Point Reyes National Seashore provides more stunning scenery, hiking trails, miles of undisturbed beaches, and, December through April, whale-watching. In Sausalito, you'll find restaurants, shopping, and yacht- and people-watching opportunities galore. Tiburon is where really wealthy San Franciscans live; stroll the path along the waterfront and shop in the town's upscale retail stores.

 Muir Woods National Monument

APPEAL BY AGE	PRESCHOOL ★★★	GRADE SCHOOL ★★★★	TEENS ★★★★
YOUNG ADULTS ★★★★	OVER 30 ★★★★	SENIORS ★★★★

12 miles north of the Golden Gate Bridge in Marin County. Exit US 101 at Sausalito and follow the signs; ☎ 415-388-2595; www.visitmuirwoods.com or www.nps.gov/muwo

Type of attraction A grove of majestic coastal redwoods, the tallest trees in the world. A self-guided tour. **Admission** $3 per person ages 17 and up. **Hours** Daily, 8 a.m.–7 p.m.; visitor center is open daily, 9 a.m.–4:30 p.m. **When to go** When it's not raining. To avoid crowds, arrive before 10 a.m. or after 4 p.m. **Special comments** Roads leading to the park are steep and winding; vehicles more than 35 feet long are prohibited. No picnicking is allowed in Muir Woods. **Author's rating** Go ahead and hug a tree—if you are the Jolly Green Giant! These huge trees are truly awesome. ★★★★. **How much time to allow** 30 minutes to 1 hour to stroll the paved loops in Redwood Canyon; avid hikers can spend several hours or the entire day hiking unpaved trails leading to Mount Tamalpais State Park.

DESCRIPTION AND COMMENTS No trip to Northern California would be complete without a glimpse of these world-famous giant redwood trees, which are much like the trees that covered much of the Northern Hemisphere 140 million years ago. Today, redwoods are only found in a narrow, 500-mile discontinuous strip of Pacific coast from southern Oregon to below Monterey, California. The huge specimens in the Cathedral and Bohemian groves are the largest redwoods in Muir Woods. The tallest is 252 feet; the thickest is 14 feet across. The oldest is at least 1,000 years old, but most of the mature trees here are 500 to

800 years old. The towering trees, the fallen giants, and the canyon ferns impart awe and tranquility—even when the paved paths are clogged with visitors.

TOURING TIPS Take the time and the modest effort to walk the paved path to Cathedral Grove; you'll encounter fewer people, and there are more fallen trees. Try walking the paths in a figure 8 by crossing footbridges over Redwood Creek. Avoid visiting on weekends and holidays; parking is usually a real hassle. The best time to come is early or late in the day; you'll encounter fewer people, and there's a better chance of seeing wildlife. The park's 560 acres include six miles of walking trails; except for the mostly level and paved main trail, the footpaths are unpaved. Wear sturdy hiking boots and a jacket. If you plan to venture beyond the main trail, bring rain gear. A gift shop, snack bar, restrooms, drinking water, and telephones are located near the main entrance.

OTHER THINGS TO DO NEARBY You can drive almost to the summit of Mount Tamalpais for yet another incredible view of San Francisco, the Golden Gate Bridge, and the Pacific Ocean. On a scenic drive through Marin County, stop at Stinson Beach (where you can relax and enjoy the coastal scenery) and take the white-knuckle curves along Route 1, which follows the Pacific coast. Drive north to Point Reyes National Seashore to enjoy windswept terrain, miles of undisturbed beaches, hiking trails, and whale-watching (December through April). Plenty of places to eat and drink in Mill Valley and Sausalito.

Museum of Money of the American West

APPEAL BY AGE	PRESCHOOL ★	GRADE SCHOOL ★★	TEENS ★★
YOUNG ADULTS ★★	OVER 30 ★★		SENIORS ★★

Basement of the Union Bank of California, 400 California Street, San Francisco; in the Financial District; ☎ 415-291-4653

Type of attraction A small museum highlighting the gold rush, gold mining, and the development of money in California's history. A self-guided tour. **Admission** Free. **Hours** Monday–Friday, 9 a.m.–5 p.m. Closed weekends and bank holidays. **When to go** Anytime. **Special comments** One set of stairs to climb and descend; restrooms are next to the museum entrance. **Author's rating** An interesting but narrow slice of California history that's worth a peek. ★★. **How much time to allow** 30 minutes.

DESCRIPTION AND COMMENTS California history and gold are the focus of this one-room museum in the basement of the huge Bank of California building. On display are gold nuggets, coins, old banknotes, diagrams of the Comstock mines (the source of the fortune that founded this bank and many civic projects in San Francisco), a set of dueling pistols, and plenty of 19th-century photos of the gold rush era that put California on the map.

TOURING TIPS Check out the huge vault at the bottom of the stairs outside the entrance to the museum. You can't miss the stunning bank lobby in this colonnaded building, which was completed in 1908.

OTHER THINGS TO DO NEARBY The Wells Fargo History Museum is around the corner on Montgomery Street. Although its 27th-floor observation deck is now closed, the Transamerica Pyramid on Montgomery Street has a lobby observatory that lets you control cameras on the roof for TV-monitor views of the city; not nearly as exciting as seeing it with your own eyes, but it's free. Transamerica Redwood Park is next to the distinctive landmark; its fountains, greenery, and whimsical sculptures make for a nice place for a brown-bag lunch.

Museum of Ophthalmology

APPEAL BY AGE	PRESCHOOL ★★★	GRADE SCHOOL ★★★★	TEENS ★★★
YOUNG ADULTS ★★★	OVER 30 ★★★		SENIORS ★★★

655 Beach Street, third floor (at Hayes Street), near Fisherman's Wharf; ☎ 415-561-8502

Type of attraction A zany, offbeat stop after hitting the more conventional museums. It's a showcase of all things eyes. **Admission** Free. **Hours** Monday–Friday, 9 a.m.–5 p.m., by appointment only. **When to go** Anytime. Fun close to Halloween. **Special comments** Some of the preserved eyes may make you want to take lunch a bit late. But the kids will certainly get a kick out of it. **Author's rating** A small but interesting stop if you are so inclined to watch what watches! ★★. **How much time to allow** 1 hour.

DESCRIPTION AND COMMENTS On display are diseased eyeballs that have found rest in a jar of formaldahyde, as well as glass eyes, old surgical instruments, and rare books. It's a historical medical museum, so lectures are often given.

TOURING TIPS Information tours can be given if you choose not to be self-guided.

OTHER THINGS TO DO NEARBY Fisherman's Wharf is around the corner.

Neptune Society Columbarium

APPEAL BY AGE	PRESCHOOL ★	GRADE SCHOOL ★	TEENS ★★
YOUNG ADULTS ★★	OVER 30 ★★★		SENIORS ★★★

1 Loraine Court, off Anza and Stanyan streets; ☎ 415-771-0717; www.neptune-society.com

Type of attraction A cemetery of sorts—a beautiful copper-domed neoclassical work of Victorian architecture that serves as a repository for the ashes of some of San Francisco's famed and upper crust. **Admission** Free. **Hours** Weekdays, 10 a.m.–4 p.m.; weekends, 10 a.m.–2 p.m. **When to go** Anytime—especially when the tourists are flocking to other well-known sites in the city. **Special comments** Beautiful gardens to stroll through. **Author's rating** The architecture and the gardens are excellent; it's also a non-touristy and unique place. ★★★. **How much time to allow** 1 hour.

DESCRIPTION AND COMMENTS In the early 20th century, cemeteries were banned from San Francisco, so those wealthy few who were laid to rest in Odd Fellows' Cemetery in the Richmond had to be placed indoors.

Thus the Columbarium. Those unlucky souls who didn't have the money to "move on up" still remain below. The Columbarium houses the ashes, tombstones, and interesting family memorabilia of the deceased. Most of them are wealthy aristocrats who made their stamp on the city. Among them are the remains of the Folgers of coffee fame, the Magnins, Kaisers, Eddys, Shattucks, Hayeses, and Brannans. You'll see fancy urns of alabaster, copper, and some more offbeat ones as well.

TOURING TIPS Emmit Smith, the eccentric caretaker, also leads guided tours. His storytelling is worth the visit!

OTHER THINGS TO DO NEARBY Across the street is a park, and the Coronet Movie Theater is on Geary. There are also lots of shops to explore on Arguello and Clement streets.

Oakland Museum of California

APPEAL BY AGE	PRESCHOOL ★★★	GRADE SCHOOL ★★★★	TEENS ★★★
YOUNG ADULTS ★★★	OVER 30 ★★★★		SENIORS ★★★★

1000 Oak Street, Oakland. The museum is one block from the Lake Merritt BART station. If you're driving from San Francisco, cross the Oakland Bridge and get on I-880 south; exit at Jackson Street. The museum parking garage has entrances on Oak Street and 12th Street; ☎ 510-238-2200; www.museumca.org

Type of attraction A museum showcasing California's ecology, history, and art. A self-guided tour. Admission $8 for adults, $5 for seniors and students, free to children ages 5 and under. Free on the second Sunday of the month. Hours Wednesday–Friday, 10 a.m.–5 p.m.; Saturday, 10 a.m.–8 p.m; Sunday, noon–5 p.m. Closed Mondays and Tuesdays, and July Fourth, Thanksgiving, Christmas, and New Year's Day. Open until 9 p.m. on the first Friday of the month. When to go Anytime. Special comments Free tours are available on request most weekdays and at 1:30 p.m. on weekends. Check with the information desk at the entrance of each gallery. Author's rating Everyone should find something to like in this large, attractive, and diversified museum. ★★★½. How much time to allow Depending on your interests in things Californian, anywhere from 2 hours to half a day.

DESCRIPTION AND COMMENTS The Oakland Museum is actually three museums in one. The first level features beautiful displays and dioramas of California's various ecosystems, ranging from coast to mountains to deserts. Level two focuses on history, culture, and technology from pre-Colonial days through the 20th century. In the exhibits focusing on modern life, you'll find displays and artifacts that touch on Hollywood, mountain bikes, Harley-Davidson choppers, the Beat movement, surfboards, political and labor strife, and most of the things we associate with the frenetic, hedonistic California lifestyle; a confusing jumble, but fascinating. Level three is a large art gallery highlighting California artists and art ranging from huge landscapes to off-the-wall modern work. It's a gorgeous, airy, and light-filled space.

TOURING TIPS Plan to linger on the second level's exhibits on history, technology, and culture. California's muticultural past is on display in all its diversity, with stories of Native American weavers and hunters, Spanish missionaries, vaqueros, gold miners, railroad builders, factory workers, union organizers, and immigrants—virtually everyone who sought the California dream. Outside—integrated with the graceful, three-tiered building erected in 1969—are seven and a half acres of gardens that give the museum the look of an old, overgrown villa. Evergreens around the perimeter provide a tall screen, while regular rows of small trees mark elevations inside the complex; flowers and fragrant plants line the walkways.

OTHER THINGS TO DO NEARBY The historic Paramount Theater (at 21st Street and Broadway) is a spectacular example of Art Deco architecture; the old movie palace has been converted to a general entertainment complex. Oakland's waterfront Jack London Square is the city's version of Fisherman's Wharf—and just as contrived. At Lake Merritt, a beautiful outdoor wildlife sanctuary, you can rent a boat, take a lakeside stroll, and view wildlife. Kids will enjoy Children's Fairyland on the north side of the lake. Fairy tales come alive at old Gepetto's workshop and other settings from children's stories. The Oakland Museum's café serves salads, sandwiches, snacks, and desserts; for more upscale dining, the Bay Wolf (3853 Piedmont Avenue) is known for its California and Mediterranean cuisine; it's open for lunch and dinner.

kids Palace of Fine Arts/Exploratorium

APPEAL BY AGE	PRESCHOOL ★★★★	GRADE SCHOOL ★★★★★	TEENS ★★★★
YOUNG ADULTS ★★★★		OVER 30 ★★★★	SENIORS ★★★

3601 Lyon Street, San Francisco; in the Marina District just off US 101 near the Golden Gate Bridge; Exploratorium: ☎ 415-561-0360 (recorded information), ☎ 415-561-0399 (recorded directions), or ☎ 415-563-7337 (further information); www.exploratorium.edu

Type of attraction A landmark classical Roman rotunda originally built for the Panama-Pacific Exposition of 1915; a hands-on science museum for children and adults. A self-guided tour. **Admission** Palace of Fine Arts and grounds, free. Exploratorium, $13 for adults, $10 for seniors and students, $10 for people with disabilities and children ages 13–17, and $8 for children ages 4–12. Free to all on the first Wednesday of the month. The Tactile Dome is $16 per person and includes admission to the museum; advance reservations are required. **Hours** Palace: always open. Exploratorium: Tuesday–Sunday, 10 a.m.–5 p.m. Closed Mondays, except holidays. **When to go** Palace of Fine Arts: in nice weather, although the fake ruins are lovely in a light rain; just make sure you bring an umbrella. Exploratorium: avoid weekday mornings during the school year, when school field trips are scheduled. Weekends and holidays are almost always busy, but lines at exhibits are rare. **Special comments** The Palace of Fine Arts is outdoors; dress accordingly. Ample free parking is available for both attractions. **Author's rating** A restored recreation of a Roman ruin and a hands-on science museum are an odd coupling, but both succeed. ★★★½. **How much time to allow** 2–4 hours for the Exploratorium; 30 minutes for the Palace of Fine Arts, although it's a scenic and peaceful setting that will tempt most visitors to linger.

DESCRIPTION AND COMMENTS Originally built in 1915 and restored in the late 1960s, the Palace of Fine Arts is a colossal fake Roman ruin with beautifully manicured greenery, an artificial lake, and waterfowl. The gorgeous setting is a great place to stroll, eat a picnic lunch, or take a break from a hectic touring schedule. The palace was so popular that after the 1915 Panama-Pacific Exhibition (which drew more than 18 million visitors), it was retained and later completely rebuilt (after decaying into real ruins). It's a San Francisco landmark and a favorite stop for tour buses.

Inside the adjacent exhibition shed is the Exploratorium, a hands-on science museum with more than 600 exhibits dedicated to the principle that one learns by doing. Exhibits range from a protein production line (where you chain together metal "molecules" to form DNA in a kind of jigsaw puzzle) to gyroscopes, a pendulum, AIDS exhibits, optical illusions, and a video-enhanced bobsled run—not to be missed for the 6- to 12-year-old set. Another major attraction is the Tactile Dome, a geodesic dome that visitors explore in the dark—crawling, climbing, sliding, and exploring different textures in 13 chambers. (Some reports say private groups have experienced it in the nude.) Advanced reservations are required, and an extra fee is charged; call ☎ 415-561-0362 weekdays between 10 a.m. and 4 p.m. Not recommended for people in casts, women in the last trimester of pregnancy, or the claustrophobic.

TOURING TIPS Neither attraction lends itself to strategic touring. The palace, with its towering, curved colonnades and rotunda, is stunningly gorgeous—and otherwise empty (a great place for a brown-bag lunch). The Exploratorium is best approached with an open mind and some strong preferences for specific branches of science and technology; otherwise you run the risk of wandering until something strikes your fancy.

OTHER THINGS TO DO NEARBY The residences of the nearby Marina District reflect the Mediterranean-revival architecture popular in the 1920s, with pastel town houses on curving streets. Head toward Chestnut Street to find neighborhood restaurants and shops. The Presidio, a former army base now managed by the National Park Service, has hiking and biking trails and hundreds of historical buildings. On the shores of San Francisco Bay, Marina Green is often full of kite fliers, sunbathers, joggers, and yachters. The Golden Gate Promenade, a three-and-a-half-mile path stretching between Fisherman's Wharf and the Golden Gate Bridge, offers fine views, and you're near the halfway point.

Phoebe A. Hearst Museum of Anthropology

APPEAL BY AGE	PRESCHOOL ★★	GRADE SCHOOL ★★	TEENS ★★
YOUNG ADULTS ★★		OVER 30 ★★	SENIORS ★★

University of California at Berkeley, 103 Kroeber Hall, Berkeley (Bancroft Way at College Avenue on the University of California Berkeley campus); ☎ 510-643-7648; hearstmuseum.berkeley.edu

Type of attraction A small museum highlighting California cultural anthropology, ethnography, and archaeology. A self-guided tour. Admission $4 for adults,

$3 for seniors, and $1 for students with ID. Free to children ages 12 and under. Free for everyone on Thursday. **Hours** Wednesday–Saturday, 10 a.m.–4:30 p.m.; Sunday, noon to 4 p.m. Closed Monday, Tuesday, and major holidays. **When to go** Anytime. **Special comments** The gift shop offers a good selection of hand-made crafts. **Author's rating** Ho-hum. Unless you have a strong interest in anthropology, think of this small gallery of static exhibits as a fill-in spot. ★½. **How much time to allow** 30 minutes.

DESCRIPTION AND COMMENTS In this one-room gallery you'll find tools and implements of California's Native Americans, including food-preparation utensils, baskets, brushes, trays, paddles, bowls, fishing gear, and hunting tools such as slings, traps, and bows and arrows.

TOURING TIPS The most interesting display is a very small exhibit about Ishi, the last Yahi Indian of Northern California who lived and worked in the museum from 1911 until his death in 1916.

OTHER THINGS TO DO NEARBY The Berkeley Art Museum is across the street. Fossil hunters will like the Museum of Paleontology, housing one of the largest and oldest collections of fossils in North America. It's open Monday through Friday, noon to 4 p.m.; it's located in the Valley Life Sciences Building on campus and admission is free. Youngsters will love the Lawrence Hall of Science, a hands-on science museum with a spectacular view of the Bay Area. Drive or take a university Hill Service Shuttle to get there. Telegraph Avenue features a lively street scene with an incredibly diverse selection of restaurants, gift shops, street vendors, street musicians, street people, and gray-haired hippies.

Ripley's Believe It or Not! Museum

APPEAL BY AGE	PRESCHOOL ★★★	GRADE SCHOOL ★★★★	TEENS ★★★★
YOUNG ADULTS ★★		OVER 30 ★★	SENIORS ★

175 Jefferson Street (at Taylor), San Francisco; across from Fisherman's Wharf; ☎ 415-771-6188; www.ripleysf.com

Type of attraction 250 exhibits of the odd and unusual based on the comic strip by Robert Ripley, "the modern Marco Polo." A self-guided tour. **Admission** $12 for adults and older children, $7 for seniors and children ages 5–12. **Hours** Sunday–Thursday, 10 a.m.–10 p.m.; Friday and Saturday, 10 a.m.–midnight. **When to go** Anytime. **Special comments** Anyone nervous about earthquakes should skip the simulated event. **Author's rating** Silliness aimed at 11-year-old boys and not much on hand that has anything to do with San Francisco. ★. **How much time to allow** 1 hour.

DESCRIPTION AND COMMENTS Here's where you come to gawk at displays of human oddities such as Unicorn Man (with a 13-inch spike growing out of the back of his head), the world's tallest man, and grainy films of restless natives chowing down on baked crocodile. For minor titillation, a few sexy teasers are thrown in, such as the optical illusion of the naked lady on the beach who's not there when you walk back for a better look.

While the overwhelming majority of exhibits have nothing to do with San Francisco (and are repeated at other Ripley museums from Australia to Key West), there are a couple of exceptions: the scale model of a cable car made of matches and a simulated earthquake, along with pictures of the 1989 event. Neither is worth the price of admission.

TOURING TIPS Only come in lousy weather and in the company of adolescents. Better yet, send the youngsters in while you check out better options around Fisherman's Wharf.

OTHER THINGS TO DO NEARBY The San Francisco Maritime Museum is close, as is Aquarium of the Bay, a fish emporium that gives visitors a different perspective from the other large aquariums sprouting up around the nation. A good and relatively cheap lunch alternative is the clam chowder in a bowl of sourdough bread, served across the street at Boudin's Bakery.

San Francisco Craft and Folk Art Museum
51 Yerba Buena Lane (at Mission between Third and Fourth), San Francisco; ☎ 415-227-4888; www.mocfa.org

Type of attraction Temporary exhibitions of contemporary crafts, American folk art, and traditional ethnic art. A self-guided tour. **Admission** $5, $4 seniors, free for children under age 18. **Hours** Tuesday–Friday, 11 a.m.–6 p.m.; Saturday and Sunday, 11 a.m.–5 p.m. **When to go** Anytime. **Special comments** Fomerly in Fort Mason, the museum is now housed in a new SoMa building. **Author's rating** The museum only features temporary shows, so it's not possible to give it a rating. **How much time to allow** 30 minutes to an hour.

DESCRIPTION AND COMMENTS It isn't just about basket weaving and throwing pots. Exhibits are both American and international. At press time, a future exhibit will feature furniture designs of the Scandanavian modernist movement of the mid-20th century.

TOURING TIPS Be careful of red light runners in this area.

OTHER THINGS TO DO NEARBY It's not far from SFMOMA, so if you've had your fill of fine art this will make for a welcome break.

San Francisco Maritime Museum

APPEAL BY AGE	PRESCHOOL ★★★	GRADE SCHOOL ★★★	TEENS ★★★
YOUNG ADULTS ★★★		OVER 30 ★★★	SENIORS ★★★★

900 Beach Street, San Francisco; a few blocks west of Fisherman's Wharf; ☎ 415-556-3002; www.nps.gov/safr/local

Type of attraction Maritime art, ship figureheads, intricate models, and thematic exhibits echoing San Francisco's maritime past. A self-guided tour. **Admission** Free. Hyde Street Pier, $4 adults, $2 seniors and children ages 12–17. **Hours** Daily, 10 a.m.–5 p.m. **When to go** Anytime. **Special comments** One set of stairs; restrooms, drinking water, and telephones are available. **Author's rating** After exploring real ships at Hyde Street Pier, this museum is icing on the cake for folks fascinated by San Francisco's colorful seafaring past; an excellent, nontouristy destination at Fisherman's Wharf. ★★★½. **How much time to allow** 1–2 hours.

DESCRIPTION AND COMMENTS Located in a gorgeous art deco building at the foot of Polk Street, this small museum is jam-packed with an amazing array of maritime artifacts. While the exhibits are heavy on exquisitely detailed ship models (including the battleship U.S.S. *California* and a German five-masted schooner), also on hand are scrimshaw, carved nautilus shells, a ship's medicine box, a seagoing doll once owned by a sea captain's daughter (from the days when skippers took their families on long voyages), an exploding harpoon used to hunt whales, 19th-century photographs, and some small boats (not models). Not to be missed if you're fascinated by ships, nautical lore, and seafaring.

TOURING TIPS   A great destination on a rainy day. If it's not foggy, the view of San Francisco Bay from the second-floor balcony is terrific. If looking at all those models makes you yearn for the real thing, walk a few blocks east to the Hyde Street Pier, where you can board and explore ships built in the 19th century.

OTHER THINGS TO DO NEARBY   Aquatic Park features plenty of greenery and seating, a sandy shoreline, and great views. The Golden Gate Promenade is a scenic, usually windy, three-and-a-half-mile path to the bridge of the same name; walk or rent a bike, pack a lunch, and have a picnic at a quiet spot along the way. Aquatic Park surrounds the Hyde Street cable-car turnaround; if the line's not too long, hop on board. Ghirardelli Square and the Cannery are both only a credit card's throw away. Walk a few blocks east to Fisherman's Wharf and the heart of the tourist hubbub, where you can rent a bike, buy a T-shirt, eat clam chowder out of a bowl made of sourdough bread (at Boudin's Bakery), take a ferry to Alcatraz (with advance reservations), or walk across the bottom of a giant fish tank (at Aquarium of the Bay).

kids San Francisco Maritime National Historical Park— Hyde Street Pier

APPEAL BY AGE	PRESCHOOL ★★★★	GRADE SCHOOL ★★★	TEENS ★★★
YOUNG ADULTS ★★★½	OVER 30 ★★★★		SENIORS ★★★½

At the foot of Hyde Street in San Francisco near Fisherman's Wharf; ☎ 415-556-0859 for tickets and info; www.nps.gov/safr

Type of attraction A collection of real 19th-century ships that visitors can board. Self-guided and guided tours. **Admission** $5. **Hours** Daily, 9:30 a.m.–5:30 p.m. **When to go** When the weather is good. Wind or rain can make for potentially perilous conditions on ship decks—and because the pier juts into San Francisco Bay, it can get cold. **Author's rating** Step aboard one of these great old ships and enter the long-gone world of Cape Horn passages and coastal runs under sail. Fabulous. ★★★★. **How much time to allow** 1 hour to half a day, depending on your interest.

DESCRIPTION AND COMMENTS   While you stroll the decks and explore the passageways in these ships, it's easy to make a mental trip back in time. On the *C. A. Thayer,* a three-masted schooner that once carried lumber and fished for cod in the Bering Sea, you can peer inside the captain's cabin and, below deck, watch a video of the ship's final voyage in 1950, narrated by her last skipper. This is nirvana for anyone who has fantasized about a sea voyage under sail.

Other ships to explore include the *Eureka,* a sidewheel ferry built in 1890 and the world's largest passenger ferry in her day. The *Alma* is the last San Francisco Bay scow schooner still afloat, and the *Balclutha* is a square-rigged Cape Horn sailing vessel launched in 1886 in Scotland. Around the corner on Pier 45, you can take an audio tour of the U.S.S. *Pampanito,* a restored World War II long-range submarine.

There are more ships to explore, and exhibits featuring boatbuilding and tools, old photographs, and detailed displays. You may also see riggers working high aloft on the masts of ships and shipwrights using traditional skills and tools. For newcomers to San Francisco, it's a pleasant surprise to discover this fascinating, high-quality national park plunked down in the dross of touristy Fisherman's Wharf.

TOURING TIPS A guided tour of each ship is offered daily, based on ranger availability; stop by or call the day before for a schedule. Your ticket is good for five days.

OTHER THINGS TO DO NEARBY More naval history and lore is on display in the art deco building housing the San Francisco Maritime Museum (at the foot of Polk Street). Aquatic Park is the perfect place for a breather after the stresses of exploring Fisherman's Wharf. You can also follow the Golden Gate Promenade past the museum all the way to the Golden Gate Bridge. If the line isn't long at the cable-car stop, go for it. Almost directly across the street is Ghirardelli Square, a boutique mall where you can give your credit cards a workout.

San Francisco Museum of Modern Art

APPEAL BY AGE	PRESCHOOL ★	GRADE SCHOOL ★★	TEENS ★★★
YOUNG ADULTS ★★★	OVER 30 ★★★★		SENIORS ★★★★★

151 Third Street, San Francisco; south of Market Street below Union Square, between Mission and Howard streets (adjacent to Yerba Buena Gardens and across from Moscone Convention Center);
☎ **415-357-4000; www.sfmoma.org**

Type of attraction Modern and contemporary art from the museum's permanent collection of 15,000 works and temporary shows. Self-guided and guided tours. **Admission** $12.50 for adults, $8 for seniors, $7 for students, free for children ages 12 and under (with an adult); half-price admission on Thursday, 6–9 p.m.; free on the first Tuesday of the month. **Hours** Friday–Tuesday, 11 a.m.–5:45 p.m.; Thursday, 11 a.m.–8:45 p.m. Closed Wednesday and July Fourth, Thanksgiving, Christmas, and New Year's Day. **When to go** Anytime. **Special comments** Free 45-minute gallery tours are offered daily, starting at 11:30 a.m. and about every hour thereafter. **Author's rating** World-class modern art in a magnificent gallery that's a work of art itself. ★★★★. **How much time to allow** 2 hours to get the gist of the place, but art buffs should figure on half a day, easily.

DESCRIPTION AND COMMENTS This modern-art emporium is just what you'd expect in San Francisco, an international center of the avant garde. Physically stunning and fairly new, the museum is designed to let the Bay Area's fabled light flood the four gallery levels. Blond hardwood on a springy dance-floor base makes it easy on the feet. A central skylight bathes the piazza-inspired atrium in natural light; from above, you can watch other gallery visitors walk across a white metal bridge that spans the four levels below. Simply breathtaking.

TOURING TIPS Take a free 45-minute tour; the first is offered at 11:30 a.m. and skips around to various galleries, whetting your appetite and revealing the museum's layout. It usually starts on level two, where the permanent collection features works by Henri Matisse, one of the first modern artists to use color as an expression of emotion. In other rooms you'll see works by masters such as Pablo Picasso and Georges Braque. After viewing the art on level two, take the elevator to level five, which features changing exhibits from artists of the 1990s. Bring an open mind and be ready to have some fun. You'll find more outrageous art on level four (walk across the white bridge and down the stairs) and a small photo gallery on level three.

The museum shop on the ground level is huge and has a great selection of postcards (none, alas, of the Golden Gate Bridge or Chinatown), among other things. Caffe Museo (☎ 415-357-4500) opens an hour before the museum and offers a good selection of reasonably priced items.

OTHER THINGS TO DO NEARBY Yerba Buena Gardens, with an art gallery and attractive grounds, is across the street. Market Street, with a wide selection of restaurants, is a block and a half away. The Cartoon Art Museum is nearby on Mission Street. Metreon, an entertainment complex with theaters, shopping, and more, is at Fourth and Howard streets.

kids San Francisco Zoo

APPEAL BY AGE	PRESCHOOL ★★★★★	GRADE SCHOOL ★★★★★	TEENS ★★★★
YOUNG ADULTS ★★★★		OVER 30 ★★★	SENIORS ★★★

Sloat Boulevard at 47th Street; in southwest San Francisco near Great Highway and the Pacific Coast (a vehicles-only entrance is on the Great Highway); ☎ 415-753-7080; www.sfzoo.org

Type of attraction At 66 acres and growing, the largest zoo in northern California. A self-guided tour. **Admission** For nonresidents of San Francisco: $11 adults, $8 children ages 12–17 and seniors, $5 children ages 3–11, free for children ages 2 and under. For residents of San Francisco: $9 adults, $4.50 children ages 12–17 and seniors, $2.50 children ages 3–11, free for children ages 2 and under. Free on the first Wednesday of the month. **Hours** Daily, 10 a.m.–5 p.m. The Children's Zoo is open Monday–Friday, 11 a.m.–4 p.m.; Saturday and Sunday (and daily in the summer), 10:30 a.m.–4:30 p.m. **When to go** In nice weather. Also, animals are more active early in the day and late in the afternoon. **Special comments** Most animals are in unenclosed exhibits that are open to the elements; bring an umbrella if rain is expected. **Author's rating** An older zoo that's nice but not spectacular. Most animals are in natural habitats behind moats. ★★★½. **How much time to allow** 2 hours to half a day.

DESCRIPTION AND COMMENTS This venerable animal park, which opened in 1929, is making a comeback after the 1989 earthquake (it damaged a few exhibits). Millions of dollars have been spent on innovative exhibits such as the Primate Discovery Center; a recently passed San Francisco bond issue paves the way for more renovations and repairs. Unlike most older zoos, the majority of the 1,000-plus animals are housed in naturalistic enclosures behind moats, and visitors can see the exotic wildlife hanging from trees, roaming through fields, and frequently snoozing in high grass.

The zoo's major exhibits include Gorilla World, one of the largest naturalistic gorilla habitats in the world; visitors can get close-up views of the huge primates from strategically placed viewing areas. This is also one of only a handful of zoos in the United States with koalas. Penguin Island features a colony of more than 50 Magellanic penguins frolicking in a 200-foot pool (black tie required). Another recent addition is the Feline Conservation Center, a 20,000-square-foot sanctuary where rare and endangered cats such as snow, black, and Persian leopards are bred and studied; and the lemur forest, where you can watch 20 or so of these endangered primates leaping away. At the Children's Zoo, youngsters can pet and feed barnyard animals such as goats, sheep, chickens, donkeys, and even a llama. Be careful, though: if this South American cousin of the camel starts to smile, he may be about to spit.

TOURING TIPS   The San Francisco Zoo Zebra Train no longer runs. The Little Puffer Steam Train (an actual steam locomotive built in 1904 and brought to the zoo in 1923) has been reintroduced to the public. Boarding is located across from the Polar Bears, adjacent to the Zoo Terrace Café. The locomotive will take passengers along a one-third mile route past the blackbuck, sea lions, bears, and lower lake. Each ride lasts about six minutes and is $2. Children under age 3 ride for free.

The Leaping Lemur is the best lunch spot. The café provides indoor seating for visitors to escape the ocean breezes and fog that come from being so close to the ocean.

The Lion House does feedings at 2 p.m., and the penguins are fed at 3 p.m. except Thursday, when they chow at 2:30 p.m. Summers at the zoo allow the opportunity to sit in on the Meet the Keeper talks. Please call ahead to get the updated seasonal schedule.

OTHER THINGS TO DO NEARBY   Breathe salt air and feel sand between your toes at nearby Ocean Beach, four miles long and always windy and wavy. But don't plan on a frolic in the surf; the water is always dangerous, even when it looks calm. To the south is Fort Funston ("Fort Fun" to the natives), where you'll find easy hiking trails, great views of the ocean and the seaside terrain, and hang gliders taking advantage of the area's high winds. To the north along Ocean Beach is Golden Gate Park, with some of San Francisco's best museums, trails, gardens, monuments, the Japanese Tea Garden, and a Dutch windmill. Across from the entrance to the San Francisco Zoo is the Carousel Diner, a hot-dog stand out of the 1950s; looming over the parking lot is an oversized representation of a dog clad in a chef's hat. Fans of Bill Griffith's "Zippy the Pinhead" comic strip will instantly recognize this fine example of suburban kitsch.

Strybing Arboretum and Botanical Gardens

APPEAL BY AGE   PRESCHOOL ★★★   GRADE SCHOOL ★★   TEENS ★★
YOUNG   ADULTS ★★★   OVER   30 ★★★   SENIORS   ★★★★

Ninth Avenue at Lincoln Way, Golden Gate Park, San Francisco;
☎ **415-661-1316; www.strybing.org**

Type of attraction A botanical garden featuring more than 7,500 plant species on 70 acres. Guided and self-guided tours. **Admission** Free. **Hours** Monday–Thursday, 8 a.m.–4:30 p.m.; Saturday, Sunday, and holidays, 10 a.m.–5 p.m. **When to go** When it's not raining or extremely windy. The California Native Garden is spectacular from early March to late April. **Special comments** Free docent tours are offered daily at 1:30 p.m.; no tours on major holidays. No bicycles, roller skates, skateboards, Frisbees, active sports, barbecues, or pets are allowed in the park. **Author's rating** Blissfully peaceful and beautiful; a chance to further appreciate San Francisco's Mediterranean climate. ★★★. **How much time to allow** 1–2 hours.

DESCRIPTION AND COMMENTS Manicured grounds, paved paths, benches, ponds, and towering trees that absorb most of the nearby traffic sounds are the hallmarks of this world-class botanical garden in Golden Gate Park, which opened in 1940. San Francisco's unusual climate allows an astounding range of plant life to flourish in the 17 gardens, grouped in three major collections: Mediterranean Climate, Temperate Climate, and Montane Tropic.

TOURING TIPS The garden has a north entrance near the Japanese Tea Garden and a main entrance on Martin Luther King Jr. Drive near Lincoln Boulevard. Unless you have a specific interest in, say, the plant life found in New World cloud forests, just wander around in a clockwise or counterclockwise direction, and eventually you'll see everything. The Strybing Bookstore offers botany and horticulture books, cards, gift items, and maps for self-guided tours of the garden and other nearby attractions (such as the Marin Headlands). Hard-core gardeners may want to check out the Helen Crocker Russell Library of Horticulture, the largest of its kind in California; it's open daily (except major holidays), 10 a.m. to 4 p.m. The store and library are located near the main entrance.

OTHER THINGS TO DO NEARBY The Japanese Tea Garden is close to the north entrance of the garden. The California Academy of Sciences across the Music Concourse is very popular with families. If it's a nice day, drive or walk to Stow Lake and rent a rowboat ($13 an hour). Hungry? You'll also find a snack bar at Stow Lake.

Wax Museum at Fisherman's Wharf

APPEAL BY AGE   PRESCHOOL ★★★   GRADE SCHOOL ★★★★   TEENS ★★★½
YOUNG   ADULTS ★★   OVER   30 ★★   SENIORS   ★★

Fisherman's Wharf (145 Jefferson Street, San Francisco);
☎ **800-439-4305; www.waxmuseum.com**

Type of attraction Nearly 250 wax figures, ranging from the historical (Elizabeth Taylor as Cleopatra) to Hollywood (uh, Elizabeth Taylor as Cleopatra). A self-guided tour. **Admission** $12.95 for adults, $10.95 for seniors, and $6.95 for children ages 4–11. On our visit, $3 off coupons were available in giveaway tourist guidebooks and on the museum's Web site. **Hours** Monday–Friday, 10 a.m.–9 p.m.; Saturday and Sunday, 9 a.m.–9 p.m. Open every day of the year. **When to go** Anytime. **Special comments** Located in the strip shopping center with all the tacky T-shirt shops and overpriced gift shops that face Fisherman's Wharf. **Author's rating** This has nothing to do with San Francisco. ★. **How much time to allow** 1 hour.

DESCRIPTION AND COMMENTS Recently reopened after a multimillion dollar renovation, your reviewer's hopes ran high that the Wax Museum would emphasize San Francisco's rich visual history–the Gold Rush, the Earthquake and Great Fire, Dashiell Hammett gumshoeing in the 1920s and 1930s, the Beat Era, Haight-Ashbury and the Summer of Love, the dot-com boom/bust, the Quake of 1989. Yet what we get is just another cheesy tourist attraction that could be plopped down on any rundown boardwalk in any ocean resort in America–and with nary a reference to the City by the Bay. Inside the emphasis is on Hollywood (*Titanic*, Robin Williams, and an uncomfortable-looking Woody Allen), the historical (FDR, Winston Churchill, George W. Bush, John Major, but no Tony Blair), the religious (these attractions always feature the Last Supper), and the gruesome (Boris Karloff as Frankenstein and lots of implements of torture). You've been warned.

TOURING TIPS Don't go. But if you're tugged inside by an insistent adolescent, don't miss a chance to shove the little monster into the electric chair, which administers a (visual) jolt. Kids love it.

OTHER THINGS TO DO NEARBY Fisherman's Wharf isn't all crummy, overpriced tourist rip-offs. The San Francisco Maritime National Historical Park–Hyde Street Pier and the San Francisco Maritime Museum are both worthwhile touring options. Visit Alcatraz (which may require advance reservations) or take a boat tour of San Francisco Bay. Or rent a bike and ride the Golden Gate Promenade on a windy, three-and-a-half mile stretch along the bay to Fort Point and the Golden Gate Bridge. Ghirardelli Square and the Cannery are both only a credit card's throw away and feature plenty of restaurants and shops.

Wells Fargo History Museum

APPEAL BY AGE	PRESCHOOL ★★★	GRADE SCHOOL ★★★	TEENS ★★★
YOUNG ADULTS ★★		OVER 30 ★★	SENIORS ★★

420 Montgomery Street (Financial District), San Francisco;
☎ **415-396-2619; www.wellsfargohistory.com/museums**

Type of attraction A museum displaying artifacts and memorabilia of the American West and Wells Fargo, the banking and express firm founded in San Francisco in 1852. A self-guided tour. **Admission** Free. **Hours** Monday–Friday, 9 a.m.– 5 p.m. Closed weekends and bank holidays. **When to go** Anytime. **Special comments** One set of stairs up to the mezzanine. **Author's rating** This small, attractive museum is chock-full of authentic items that make the old West come alive; ★★½. **How much time to allow** 30 minutes to 1 hour.

DESCRIPTION AND COMMENTS A real, century-old stagecoach is the main attraction of this museum run by the Wells Fargo Bank, a firm famous for operating the Pony Express and a stagecoach empire throughout the western United States in the late 19th century. Other displays include mining tools, an incredibly complicated harness worn by the horses that pulled the stagecoaches, gold, money, treasure boxes, old postal envelopes, and photographs of the 1906 San Francisco earthquake and fire. While not worth a special trip, this bright and attractive space is a nice fill-in spot while you're exploring the Financial District, especially if you've got kids in tow.

TOURING TIPS Don't miss the mezzanine level, where you can climb inside a stagecoach compartment and listen to a taped presentation. The real thing, on the main level below, is strictly hands-off.

OTHER THINGS TO DO NEARBY To stay with the Old West and Gold Rush themes, have lunch at nearby Tadich Grill, established 1849.

Yerba Buena Gardens/Center for the Arts

APPEAL BY AGE	PRESCHOOL ★★	GRADE SCHOOL ★★	TEENS ★★
YOUNG ADULTS ★★		OVER 30 ★★	SENIORS ★★★

701 Mission Street, San Francisco; at Third Street south of Union Square in the SoMa District; ☎ 415-978-2700 (administration); ☎ 415-978-ARTS (ticket office); www.yerbabuenaarts.org

Type of attraction A cultural complex of grass and art, an art gallery, a theater, a memorial to Martin Luther King Jr., cafés, ice skating, and bowling. A self-guided tour. Admission Gallery: $6 for adults, $3 for students and seniors. Free for center members, gardens are free. Hours Gallery and theater hours are Tuesday, Wednesday, Friday, Saturday, and Sunday, noon–5 p.m.; first Thursday of the month, noon–8 p.m. Gardens are open daily, sunrise–10 p.m. When to go Anytime for the art gallery; in nice weather for the outdoor gardens. Special comments A nice side trip—and a place to relax. Author's rating Of more interest to San Franciscans than to most visitors, who must take potluck on Yerba Buena's constantly changing schedule of exhibitions, shows, concerts, lectures, films, and videos; ★★. How much time to allow 1 hour for the gallery and as long as you care to linger in the 5.5-acre gardens.

DESCRIPTION AND COMMENTS Yerba Buena is a nonprofit arts complex in the up-and-coming SoMa neighborhood. It features two buildings (a two-level art gallery and a theater) and a park with an outdoor stage, two cafés, the Butterfly Garden, a redwood grove, sculptures, a waterfall, and a memorial to Dr. Martin Luther King Jr. The small gallery features temporary art exhibits that change about every two and a half months; on our visit there was a display of modern and avant-garde paintings and multimedia art—very San Francisco and a lot of fun.

TOURING TIPS Stop in the gallery and pick up a current copy of the *Center for the Arts* newsletter, which gives a complete description of events at Yerba Buena. If the exhibit looks interesting, tour the gallery. Don't miss

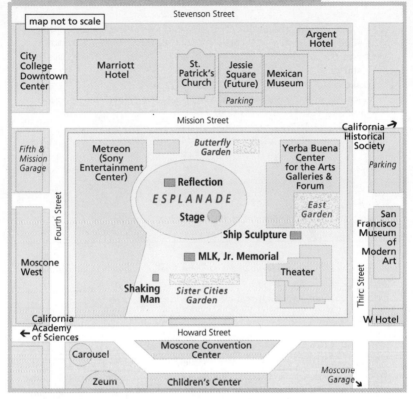

yerba buena gardens and environs

map not to scale

Stevenson Street

City College Downtown Center

Marriott Hotel

St. Patrick's Church

Jessie Square (Future)

Mexican Museum

Argent Hotel

Parking

Mission Street

California → Historical Society

Fifth & Mission Garage

Metreon (Sony Entertainment Center)

Butterfly Garden

Reflection

ESPLANADE

Stage

Yerba Buena Center for the Arts Galleries & Forum

East Garden

Parking

San Francisco Museum of Modern Art

Fourth Street

Ship Sculpture

Moscone West

MLK, Jr. Memorial

Theater

Third Street

Shaking Man

Sister Cities Garden

California Academy of Sciences

W Hotel

Howard Street

Carousel

Moscone Convention Center

Moscone Garage ↘

Zeum

Children's Center

the Martin Luther King Jr. Memorial and its 22-foot-high, 50 foot-wide waterfall. Free (with admission) walk-in gallery tours are offered on the second Saturday of the month at 1 p.m.

OTHER THINGS TO DO NEARBY   The San Francisco Museum of Modern Art is across Third Street and the Cartoon Art Museum is nearby on Mission Street. Metreon, an entertainment complex featuring theaters, shopping and more, is at Fourth and Howard streets. The area is surrounded by dozens of restaurants.

PART SEVEN

DINING *and* RESTAURANTS

THE VOLUPTUOUS PLEASURES OF SAN FRANCISCO'S table still ring with the echoes of the Barbary Coast. People have been writing of memorable dining here since Mark Twain sojourned in the city and wrote of its charms in the 1860s. More than ever, people in San Francisco consider restaurants and the culinary arts one of the most important topics of discussion. And the chefs and their patrons concern themselves with both the end result and the entire process—from the origin and freshness of the ingredients, to the utensils with which they are prepared, to diners' and servers' states of mind. There is a personal quality to gastronomy in the city. Chefs adapt the lessons learned in European kitchens to the dictates of locally grown foodstuffs and further incorporate the diverse cultural influences of the region.

Perhaps unique to the city is the possibility of genuinely friendly service. The best San Francisco restaurants are not stuffy or formal and will not treat you with condescension. Most are happy to hear about unsatisfactory service or a dish that was improperly prepared. Unlike New York, San Francisco has few of the imposing, intimidating, ghastly expensive Taj Mahals whose raison d'être has been obscured by interests other than the table. And as for Los Angeles . . . well, San Francisco eats L.A.'s lunch!

This is the capital of the three-star restaurant. Diners want the best in food and service and the best in price. And they want no snooty waiters. Even the four- and five-star restaurants are short on pretense and long on service. The common person is king here; he (or she) just happens to have a discriminating palate.

Whence came this egalitarian attitude? The Old West—with its frontier meritocracy, lusty democracy, and demand for good vittles—is newest here. You still find the legacies of Spanish missionaries and ranchers, Chinese railroad workers, Italian vintners, and nouveau riche gold miners seeking to mirror European splendor. Mix in

Japanese, Vietnamese, and Russian immigration. Add the organic and sustainable agriculture movement, local growers' experimentation with artisan crops such as Japanese persimmons, kiwis, habanero peppers, and heirloom varieties of fruits and vegetables; and the blossoming of boutique wineries, cheesemakers, and game farms. Put these with a skepticism of high-falutin' New York ways, and you have the makings of the culinary revolution that began in the 1970s. Creative chefs are drawn to the area because of the year-round availability of superior produce and the relative sophistication of native palates and tastes, along with diners' senses of humor and commitment to a casual brand of elegance.

There's a restaurant to suit any occasion, appetite, or budget. There's also likely to be a very good, even great, place to dine within walking distance of anywhere you might be. San Francisco is known, after all, as the "walking city." A brisk walk through the cool tang of a San Francisco fog is one of the best appetizers the city has to offer. And it's free.

TOURIST PLACES

IN THE RESTAURANT PROFILES THAT MAKE UP this section, you may notice that a few well-known or highly visible restaurants are missing. This is not an oversight. The following restaurants may come to your attention, but in our opinion they're not as worthwhile as other comparable options.

- **Sinbad's** *Seafood* Pier 2, Embarcadero Street; ☎ 415-781-2555
- **Scoma's** *Seafood* Pier 47, Fisherman's Wharf; ☎ 415-771-4383; 588 Bridgeway, Sausalito; ☎ 415-332-9551
- On **Fishermen's Wharf,** those food stands that sell white clam chowder in a hollowed out sourdough loaf.
- **Empress of China** *Pan Chinese* 838 Grant Avenue; ☎ 415-434-1345
- **Lori's** *"Fabulous 50s Diner"* 500 Sutter Street, ☎ 415-981-1950; 149 Powell Street, ☎ 415-677-9999; 336 Mason Street, ☎ 415-392-8646

THE RESTAURANTS

OUR FAVORITE SAN FRANCISCO RESTAURANTS

WE HAVE DEVELOPED DETAILED PROFILES FOR THE best and most interesting restaurants (in our opinion) in town. Each profile features an easily scanned heading that allows you, in just a second, to check out the restaurant's name, cuisine, star rating, cost, quality rating, and value rating.

CUISINE This is actually less straightforward than it sounds. A couple of years ago, for example, "pan-Asian" restaurants were generally serving what was then generally described as "fusion" food—Asian ingredients with European techniques, or vice versa. Since then, there has been a pan-Asian explosion in the area, but nearly all specialize in what would be street food back home: noodles, skewers, dumplings, and soups. Once-general categories have become subdivided—French into bistro fare and even Provençal; "new continental" into regional American and "eclectic"—while others have broadened and fused: Middle Eastern and Provençal into Mediterranean, Spanish, and South American into nuevo Latino, and so on. In these cases, we have generally used the broader terms (i.e., "French"), but sometimes added a parenthetical phrase to give a clearer idea of the fare. Again, though, experimentation and "fusion" is growing more common, so don't hold us, or the chefs, to a strict style.

OVERALL RATING The overall rating encompasses the entire dining experience, including style, service, and ambience in addition to the taste, presentation, and quality of the food. Five stars is the highest rating possible and connotes the best of everything. Four-star restaurants are exceptional and three-star restaurants are well above average. Two-star restaurants are good. One star is used to indicate an average restaurant that demonstrates an unusual capability in some area of specialization—for example, an otherwise unmemorable place that has great barbecue chicken.

COST The expense description provides a comparative sense of how much a complete meal will cost. A complete meal for our purposes consists of an entree with vegetable or side dish and choice of soup or salad. Appetizers, desserts, drinks, and tips are excluded.

Inexpensive	$14 and less per person
Moderate	$15–$25 per person
Expensive	$26–$40 per person
Very Expensive	More than $40 per person

A NOTE ON MENUS AND PRICES The better restaurants in The City and around the bay change their menus at least seasonally. Others change it monthly or weekly or even daily. Or with what's available at the market, or with the chef's whim. Anything we tell you is on the menu today might not be there tomorrow. And of course, prices will fluctuate with the menu changes. But not a lot, and they go down as well as up. Just don't be surprised if things aren't quite the same when you get there.

QUALITY RATING The food quality is rated on a scale of ★–★★★★★, with ★★★★★ being the best rating attainable. It is based expressly on the taste, freshness of ingredients, preparation, presentation, and creativity of food served. There is no consideration of price. If you are a person who wants the best food available, and cost is not an issue, you need look no further than the quality ratings.

VALUE RATING If, on the other hand, you are looking for both quality and value, then you should check the value rating. The value ratings are defined as follows:

San Francisco Restaurants by Neighborhood

NAME	CUISINE	OVERALL RATING
CHINATOWN		
The Carnelian Room	New American	★★★★
Palio D'Asti	Italian	★★★★
Sam Woh	Chinese	★½
Yuet Lee	Chinese	★★½
CIVIC CENTER		
Harris' Restaurant	Steak	★★★★½
House of Prime Rib	American	★★★½
Jardiniere	California	★★★★★
Max's Opera Café	Deli/Barbecue	★½
Millennium	Vegetarian	★★★½
Momi Toby's Revolution Café	Eclectic	★★
Ruth's Chris Steak House	Steak House	★★½
Swan Oyster Depot	Seafood	★★
Tommy's Joynt	American	★★
UNION SQUARE		
Asia de Cuba	Chino-Latino	★★★★
B44	Spanish	★★★
Café de la Presse	French Basque	★★★
Campton Place	French	★★★★★
Cortez	Mediterranean	★★★½
E&O Trading Company	Southeast Asian	★★★
Farallon	Mediterranean/Seafood	★★★★★
First Crush	Californian	★★★
Fleur de Lys	French	★★★★
Grand Café	Mediterranean	★★★½
John's Grill	Steak House	★★★
Kuleto's	Californian/Italian	★★★½
Le Colonial	French/Vietnamese	★★★½
Lefty O'Doul's	Hof Brau	★★½
Masa's	French	★★★★★
Original Joe's	American/Italian	★★
Pacific	Californian	★★★★
Plouf	French	★★
Ponzu	Contemporary Asian	★★★★½
Scala's Bistro	Italian/French	★★★½

NAME	CUISINE	OVERALL RATING
FINANCIAL DISTRICT		
Cafe Tiramisu	Italian	★★★
Il Fornaio	Italian	★★★½
Kokkari Estiatorio	Greek	★★★
MacArthur Park	American	★★★
Tadich Grill	American	★★★
Tommy Toy's	Chinese	★★★½
Yank Sing	Chinese	★★★
MARINA DISTRICT		
Ana Mandara	Vietnamese	★★★★
The Brazen Head	Continental	★★★
The Buena Vista Café	American	★
Greens	Vegetarian	★★★★
Izzy's Steak and Chop House	Steak House	★★★
McCormick & Kuleto's	Seafood	★★★
Perry's	American	★★
Zarzuela	Spanish	★★★
NORTH BEACH		
A. Sabella's Restaurant	Italian	★★★
Café Pescatore	Italian/Seafood	★★★
Calzones	Italian	★★
Enrico's	Californian/ Mediterranean	★★★
Fog City Diner	American	★★★
Helmand	Afghan	★★★
Moose's	Californian	★★★★
Piperade's	West Coast Basque	★★★
The Stinking Rose	Italian	★★★
Trattoria Pinocchio	Italian	★★★½
SOMA/MISSION DISTRICT		
Acme Chop House	Steak House	★★★★
Bambuddha Lounge	Pan Asian	★★★
Bistro Clovis	French	★★
Boulevard	American/French	★★★½
Buzz 9	California	★★★
The Cosmopolitan Restaurant	New American	★★★
Dusit	Thai	★★½

San Francisco Restaurants by Neighborhood (continued)

NAME	CUISINE	OVERALL RATING
SOMA/MISSION DISTRICT (CONTINUED)		
El Nuevo Fruitlandia	Puerto Rican	★★½
Fringale	French	★★★★
Hawthorne Lane	Californian	★★★★
Louie's Bar and Grill	Bar and Grill	★★
Lulu	French	★★★½
Luna Park	American	★★
Oola	California Fresh	★★★½
Paragon	New American	★★
Red's Java House	Dive	★
Shanghai 1930	Chinese	★★★
Sheraton Palace Garden Court	New American	★★★★
South Park Café	French	★★★
Thirstybear	Spanish	★★★
Ti Couz	Crêperie	★★
Town's End Restaurant and Bakery	New American	★★★
Tu Lan	Vietnamese	★½
Watergate	French/Asian	★★★★
Zuni Café and Grill	Italian	★★★

★★★★★	Exceptional value, a real bargain
★★★★	Good value
★★★	Fair value, you get exactly what you pay for
★★	Somewhat overpriced
★	Significantly overpriced

PAYMENT We've listed the type of payment accepted at each restaurant using the following code: AE equals American Express (Optima), CB equals Carte Blanche, D equals Discover, DC equals Diners Club, MC equals MasterCard, and V equals VISA.

WHO'S INCLUDED Restaurants in San Francisco open and close at an alarming rate. So, for the most part, we have tried to confine our list to establishments with a proven track record over a fairly long period of time. The exceptions here are the newer offspring of the demi-gods of the culinary world—these places are destined to last, at least until our next update. Newer or changed establishments that demonstrate staying power and consistency will be profiled in subsequent editions. Also, the list is highly selective. Noninclusion of a particular place does not

NAME	CUISINE	OVERALL RATING
RICHMOND/SUNSET DISTRICT		
Aziza	Moroccan	★★★½
Beach Chalet	American	★★★½
Clement Street Bar and Grill	New American	★★★
Clementine	French	★★★★
PJ's Oyster Bed	Seafood	★★★
Straits Café	Singaporean	★★★★
Thanh Long	Vietnamese	★★★
TIBURON/SAUSALITO		
Ondine	Californian	★★★★
OAKLAND		
Baywolf	Mediterranean	★★★★½
Le Cheval	Vietnamese	★★★★
Oliveto	Italian	★★★★
SAN FRANCISCO INTERNATIONAL AIRPORT		
West Bay Café	Californian	★★★

necessarily indicate that the restaurant is not good, but only that it was not ranked among the best in its genre. Detailed profiles of individual restaurants follow in alphabetical order at the end of this chapter.

MORE RECOMMENDATIONS

The Best Bagels

- **Marin Bagel Company** 1560 Fourth Street, San Rafael; ☎ 415-457-8127
- **Noah's New York Bagels** Bon Air Center, Greenbrae; ☎ 415-925-9971

The Best Beer Lists

- **Duke of Edinburgh** 10801 North Wolf Road, Cupertino; ☎ 408-446-3853
- **Mayflower Inn** 1533 Fourth Street, San Rafael; ☎ 415-456-1011
- **The Pelican Inn** 10 Pacific Way, Muir Beach; ☎ 415-383-6000
- **Tommy's Joynt** 1101 Geary Boulevard, San Francisco; ☎ 415-775-4216

The Best Burgers

- **Bubba's** 566 San Anselmo Avenue, San Anselmo; ☎ 415-459-6862

The Best San Francisco Restaurants

TYPE AND NAME	OVERALL RATING	COST	QUALITY RATING	VALUE RATING
AFGHAN				
Helmand	★★★	Inexp	★★★★	★★★★★
AMERICAN				
Boulevard	★★★½	Exp	★★★★	★★★★½
Beach Chalet	★★★½	Mod	★★★★	★★★★
House of Prime Rib	★★★½	Exp	★★★★	★★★★
MacArthur Park	★★★	Mod	★★★★½	★★★★
Tadich Grill	★★★	Mod	★★★★	★★★★★
Fog City Diner	★★★	Mod	★★★★	★★★★
Tommy's Joynt	★★	Inexp	★★★½	★★★★★
Luna Park	★★	Mod	★★★½	★★★★
Original Joe's	★★	Inexp	★★★½	★★★★
Perry's	★★	Inexp	★★★½	★★★
The Buena Vista Café	★	Inexp	★★★½	★★★
BAR AND GRILL				
Louie's Bar & Grill	★★	Inexp	★★★½	★★★★
CALIFORNIAN				
Jardiniere	★★★★★	Exp	★★★★★	★★★★½
Waterfront Upstairs	★★★★½	Exp	★★★★★	★★★★★
Moose's	★★★★	Mod	★★★★½	★★★★½
Pacific	★★★★	Exp	★★★★½	★★★★
Hawthorne Lane	★★★★	Exp	★★★½	★★★★
Café Majestic	★★★½	Exp	★★★★	★★★★
Kuleto's	★★★½	Mod	★★★★	★★★★
Oola	★★★½	Mod	★★★	★★★★
Buzz 9	★★★	Mod	★★★★	★★★★
Enrico's	★★★	Mod	★★★★	★★★★
West Bay Café	★★★	Mod	★★★★	★★★★
First Crush	★★★	Mod	★★★½	★★★★
MC2	★★★	Mod	★★★½	★★★★
CHINESE				
Tommy Toy's	★★★½	Mod	★★★★	★★★★
Yank Sing	★★★	Inexp	★★★½	★★★★
Shanghai 1930	★★★	Exp	★★★	★★★★
Yuet Lee	★★½	Inexp/Mod	★★★½	★★★★★

TYPE AND NAME	OVERALL RATING	COST	QUALITY RATING	VALUE RATING
CHINESE (CONTINUED)				
Sam Woh	★½	Inexp	★★★	★★★★
CHINO-LATINO				
Asia de Cuba	★★★★	Exp	★★★★½	★★★★★
CONTEMPORARY ASIAN				
Ponzu	★★★★½	Mod/Exp	★★★★★	★★★★
CONTINENTAL				
The Brazen Head	★★★	Mod	★★★½	★★★★★
CRÊPERIE				
Ti Couz	★★★	Inexp	★★★	★★★★
DELI/BARBECUE				
Max's Opera Café	★¼	Mod	★★★	★★★★
DIVE				
Red's Java House	★	Inexp	★★★	★★★★★
ECLECTIC				
Momi Toby's Revolution Café	★★	Inexp	★★★½	★★★
FRENCH				
Campton Place	★★★★★	Exp	★★★★★	★★★★★
Masa's	★★★★★	Exp	★★★★★	★★★★★
Fleur de Lys	★★★★	Exp	★★★★★	★★★★
Fringale	★★★★	Mod	★★★★½	★★★★★
Watergate	★★★★	Mod	★★★★½	★★★★★
Clementine	★★★★	Exp	★★★★½	★★★★
Lulu	★★★½	Mod	★★★★	★★★★
South Park Café	★★★	Mod	★★★★	★★★★★
Café de la Presse	★★★	Mod	★★★★	★★★★
Bistro Clovis	★★	Mod	★★★½	★★★★
Plouf	★★	Mod	★★★	★★★
FRENCH/VIETNAMESE				
Le Colonial	★★★½	Exp	★★★★	★★★
GREEK				
Kokkari Estiatorio	★★★	Exp	★★★★½	★★★★

The Best San Francisco Restaurants (continued)

TYPE AND NAME	OVERALL RATING	COST	QUALITY RATING	VALUE RATING
HOF BRAU				
Lefty O'Doul's	★★½	Inexp	★★★½	★★★★
ITALIAN				
Palio d'Asti	★★★★	Exp	★★★★★	★★★★★
Oliveto	★★★★	Exp	★★★★	★★★★
Scala's Bistro	★★★½	Exp	★★★★	★★★★
Il Fornaio	★★★½	Mod	★★½	★★★★
Trattoria Pinocchio	★★★½	Mod	★★★★½	★★★★★
A. Sabella's Restaurant	★★★	Mod/Exp	★★★★	★★★★
Zuni Café and Grill	★★★	Mod	★★★★	★★★★
Café Pescatore	★★★	Mod	★★★½	★★★★
The Stinking Rose	★★★	Mod	★★★½	★★★★
Cafe Tiramisu	★★★	Mod	★★★	★★★
Calzones	★★	Mod	★★½	★★★
MEDITERRANEAN				
Farallon	★★★★★	Exp	★★★★★	★★★★★
Baywolf	★★★★½	Exp	★★★★½	★★★★½
Grand Café	★★★½	Exp	★★★★½	★★★★
Cortez	★★★½	Mod	★★★★	★★★
MOROCCAN				
Aziza	★★★½	Mod	★★★	★★★★
NEW AMERICAN				
The Dining Room at the Ritz-Carlton	★★★★★	Exp	★★★★★	★★★★
The Carnelian Room	★★★★	Exp	★★★★½	★★★★
Sheraton Palace Garden Court	★★★★	Exp	★★★★½	★★★★
Town's End Restaurant	★★★	Mod	★★★★	★★★★
Clement Street Bar and Grill	★★★	Mod	★★★½	★★★
The Cosmopolitan Restaurant	★★★	Mod/Exp	★★★	★★★★
Paragon	★★	Mod	★★★½	★★★
PAN ASIAN				
Bambuddha Lounge	★★★	Mod	★★★½	★★★★½
PUERTO RICAN				
El Nuevo Fruitlandia	★★½	Inexp	★★★½	★★★★

TYPE AND NAME	OVERALL RATING	COST	QUALITY RATING	VALUE RATING
SEAFOOD				
PJ's Oyster Bed	★★★	Mod	★★★★	★★★★
McCormick & Kuleto's	★★★	Mod	★★★	★★★
Swan Oyster Depot	★★	Inexp	★★★½	★★★★★
SINGAPOREAN				
Straits Café	★★★★	Mod	★★★★½	★★★★★
SOUTHEAST ASIAN				
E&O Trading Company	★★★	Exp	★★★★	★★★★
SPANISH				
Zarzuela	★★★	Mod	★★★★	★★★★★
B44	★★★	Mod	★★★★	★★★★
Thirstybear	★★★	Mod	★★★½	★★★★
STEAK HOUSE				
Harris' Restaurant	★★★★½	Exp	★★★★★	★★★★½
Acme Chop House	★★★★	Exp	★★★★★	★★★★
NV Restaurant & Lounge	★★★★	Mod	★★★★	★★★★½
Izzy's Steak and Chop House	★★★	Mod	★★★★	★★★★★
John's Grill	★★★	Mod	★★★½	★★★★★
Ruth's Chris Steak	★★½	Mod	★★★½	★★★★
THAI				
Dusit	★★½	Inexp	★★★½	★★★★
VEGETARIAN				
Greens	★★★★	Mod	★★★★	★★★★
Millennium	★★★½	Mod	★★★★½	★★★★
VIETNAMESE				
Ana Mandara	★★★★	Mod/Exp	★★★★½	★★★★
Le Cheval	★★★★	Mod	★★★★	★★★★
Thanh Long	★★★	Inexp/Mod	★★★★	★★★★
Hung Yen	★★½	Inexp	★★★	★★★★
Tu Lan	★½	Inexp	★★★	★★★★★
WEST COAST BASQUE				
Piperade's	★★★	Mod	★★★★	★★★★

dining around town

1. A. Sabella's Restaurant
2. Acme Chop House
3. Ana Mandara
4. Bambuddha Lounge
5. Beach Chalet
6. Bistro Clovis
7. Boulevard
8. The Brazen Head
9. The Buena Vista Café
10. Buzz 9
11. Café Majestic
12. Café Pescatore
13. Clement Street Bar and Grill
14. Clementine
15. The Cosmopolitan Restaurant
16. Dusit
17. El Nuevo Fruitlandia
18. Fog City Diner
19. Fringale
20. Greens
21. House of Prime Rib
22. Izzy's Steak and Chop House
23. Jardiniere
24. Lulu
25. Luna Park Kitchen and Cocktails
26. MacArthur Park
27. Max's Opera Café
28. Millennium
29. Momi Toby's Revolution Café
30. Paragon
31. Perry's
32. Piperade's
33. PJ's Oyster Bed
34. Red's Java House
35. Ruth's Chris Steak House
36. Shanghai 1930
37. Strait's Café
38. South Park Café
39. Swan Oyster Depot
40. Than Long
41. Thirstybear
42. Ti Couz
43. Tommy's Joynt
44. Town's End Restaurant and Bakery
45. Tu Lan
46. Zarzuela
47. Zuni Café and Grill

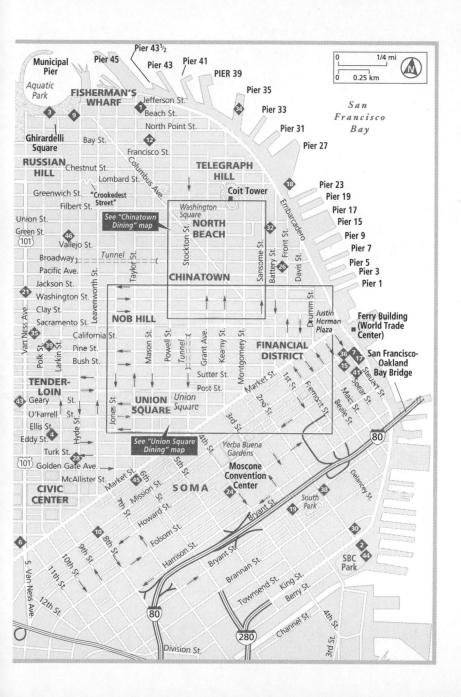

Municipal Pier

Pier 45

Pier 43½

Pier 43

Pier 41

PIER 39

Pier 35

Pier 33

Pier 31

Pier 27

Aquatic Park

FISHERMAN'S WHARF

Jefferson St.

Beach St.

North Point St.

San Francisco Bay

Ghirardelli Square

Bay St.

Francisco St.

RUSSIAN HILL

Chestnut St.

Lombard St.

TELEGRAPH HILL

Coit Tower

Pier 23

Pier 19

Greenwich St.

"Crookedest Street"

Washington Square

Pier 17

Pier 15

Filbert St.

Union St.

Green St.

See "Chinatown Dining" map

NORTH BEACH

Pier 9

Pier 7

101

Vallejo St.

Broadway

Tunnel

Pier 5

Pier 3

Pacific Ave.

Jackson St.

CHINATOWN

Pier 1

Washington St.

Clay St.

Sacramento St.

NOB HILL

Justin Herman Plaza

Ferry Building (World Trade Center)

California St.

Pine St.

Bush St.

FINANCIAL DISTRICT

San Francisco–Oakland Bay Bridge

TENDER-LOIN

Geary   St.

O'Farrell   St.

Ellis St

Eddy St.

Sutter St.

Post St.

UNION SQUARE

Union Square

Turk St.

101 Golden Gate Ave.

McAllister St.

See "Union Square Dining" map

Yerba Buena Gardens

Moscone Convention Center

80

CIVIC CENTER

Market St.

Mission St.

SOMA

Howard St.

South Park

Folsom St.

Harrison St.

Bryant St.

SBC Park

Brannan St.

Townsend St.

King St.

Berry St.

80

280

Channel St.

Division St.

0   1/4 mi

0   0.25 km

union square dining

BART/Muni
M BART/Muni
Cable Car
One Way

1/10 mile
0
100 meters
0

The Embarcadero

Steuart St.
Spear St.
Main St.
Howard St.

29

BART/Muni
Embarcadero
Station M

Beale St.

Drumm St.

Davis St.

Washington St.

Fremont St.

Transbay
Transit
Terminal

Clay St.

Embarcadero
Center

Front St.

1st St.

Natoma St.

Mission St.

15

Jackson St.

Battery St.

Sansome St.

Clay St.

Sacramento St.

FINANCIAL
DISTRICT

26

Market St.

12

Stevenson St.

14

Minna St.

2nd St.

Transamerica
Pyramid

Montgomery St.

California St.

Kearny St.

BART/Muni
Montgomery
St. Station M

New Montgomery St.

Third St.

25

13

Yerba Buena
Gardens

Columbus Ave.

21

Kearny St.

22 2

Claude Ln.

Crocker
Galleria

CHINATOWN

Grant Ave.

Pine St.

Bush St.

Sutter St.

Grant Ave.

3

1

Compton Pl.

Maiden La.

4

Market St.

Fourth St.

Stockton St.

Stockton Tunnel

19

Stockton St.

24

UNION
SQUARE

Macy's

BART/Muni
Powell St.
Station

9

Powell St.

Powell St.

5

16

8

18

Jackson St.

Washington St.

Sacramento St.

California St.

Mason St.

Pine St.

Bush St.

Sutter St.

Mason St.

Post St.

21

UNION
SQUARE

Geary St.

1

O'Farrell St.

Ellis St.

20

NOB
HILL

Grace
Cathedral

Huntington
Park

28

Clay St.

Taylor St.

Taylor St.

17

23

6

Cosmo Pl.

10

7

Jones St.

Jones St.

1. Asia de Cuba
2. B-44
3. Café de
   la Presse
4. Campton Place
5. Compass Rose
6. Cortez
7. E&O Trading
   Company
8. Farallon
9. First Crush
10. Fleur de Lys
11. Grand Café
12. Harpoon Loui's
13. Hawthorne
    Lane
14. John's Grill
15. Kokkari
    Estiatorio
16. Kuleto's
17. Le Colonial
18. Lefty O'Doul's
19. Masa's
20. Original Joe's
21. Pacific
    Restaurant
22. Plouf
23. Ponzu
24. Scala's Bistro
25. Sheraton Palace
    Garden Court
26. Tadich Grill
27. Tommy Toy's
28. Watergate
29. Yank Sing

chinatown dining

1. Calzones
2. The Carnelian Room
3. Enrico's
4. Helmland
5. Moose's
6. Palio D'Asti
7. Sam Woh
8. The Stinking Rose
9. Trattoria Pinocchio
10. Yuet Lee

- **Flippers** 482 Hayes Street, San Francisco; ☎ 415-552-8880
- **Louie's Bar & Grill** 55 Stevenson Street, San Francisco; ☎ 415-543-3540
- **Kirk's** 1330 Sunnyvale-Saratoga Road, Cupertino; ☎ 408-446-2988
- **Perry's** 1944 Union Street, San Francisco; ☎ 415-922-9022
- **Rockridge Café** 5492 College Avenue, Oakland; ☎ 510-653-1567

The Best Business Dining

- **The Carnelian Room** 555 California Street, 52nd floor, San Francisco; ☎ 415-433-7500
- **The Duck Club** 100 El Camino Real, Menlo Park; ☎ 650-322-1234
- **Rue de Main** 22622 Main Street, Hayward; ☎ 510-537-0812
- **Tadich Grill** 240 California Street, San Francisco; ☎ 415-391-1849

The Best Coffee

- **The Dipsea Café** 200 Shoreline Highway, Mill Valley; ☎ 415-381-0298

The Best Desserts

- **Campton Place Restaurant** 340 Stockton Street, San Francisco; ☎ 415-955-5555
- **Masa's** 648 Bush Street, San Francisco; ☎ 415-989-7154

The Best Dining and Dancing

- **Horizons** 558 Bridgeway, First Floor, Sausalito; ☎ 415-331-3232

The Best Martinis

- **Buckeye Roadhouse** 15 Shoreline Highway, Mill Valley; ☎ 415-331-2600
- **House of Prime Rib** 1906 Van Ness, San Francisco; ☎ 415-885-4605
- **No Name Bar** 757 Bridgeway, Sausalito; ☎ 415-332-1392

The Best Oyster Bars

- **LuLu** 816 Folsom Street, San Francisco; ☎ 415-495-5775
- **PJ's Oyster Bed** 737 Irving Street, San Francisco; ☎ 415-566-7775
- **Swan Oyster Depot** 1517 Polk Street, San Francisco; ☎ 415-673-1101

The Best Pizza

- **Benissimo Ristorante** 18 Tamalpais Drive, Corte Madera; ☎ 415-927-2316
- **Frankie Johnnie & Luigi Too** 939 West El Camino Real, Mountain View; ☎ 650-967-5384
- **Milano Pizza** 1 Blackfield Drive, Tiburon; ☎ 415-388-9100
- **Mulberry Street Pizzeria** 101 Smith Ranch Road, San Rafael; ☎ 415-472-7272
- **Salute** 706 Third Street, San Rafael; ☎ 415-453-7596

The Best Seafood

- **The Fish Market** 3150 El Camino Real, Palo Alto; ☎ 650-493-9188
- **Rooney's Café and Grill** 38 Main Street, Tiburon; ☎ 415-435-1911
- **Sam's Anchor Café** 27 Main Street, Tiburon; ☎ 415-435-4527
- **Tadich Grill** 240 California Street, San Francisco; ☎ 415-391-1849

The Best Sunday Brunches

- **Buckeye Roadhouse** 15 Shoreline Highway, Mill Valley; ☎ 415-331-2600
- **Sheraton Palace Garden Court** 2 New Montgomery Street, San Francisco; ☎ 415-546-5010
- **The Station House Café** 11180 Shoreline Highway, Point Reyes Station; ☎ 415-663-1515

The Best Sushi Bars

- **Robata Grill** 591 Redwood Highway, Mill Valley; ☎ 415-381-8400
- **Yoshi's** 510 Embarcadero West, Oakland; ☎ 510-238-9200

The Best Wee Hours Service

- **Marin Joe's** 1585 Casa Buena Drive, Corte Madera; ☎ 415-924-2081
- **Max's Opera Café** 601 Van Ness Avenue, San Francisco; ☎ 415-771-7300
- **Sam Woh** 813 Washington Street, San Francisco; ☎ 415-982-0596
- **Yuet Lee** 1300 Stockton Street, San Francisco; ☎ 415-982-6020

The Best Wine Bars

- **El Paseo** 17 Throckmorton Avenue, Mill Valley; ☎ 415-388-0741
- **Manka's Inverness Lodge** 30 Calendar Way at Argyle, Inverness; ☎ 415-669-1034
- **The Mountain Home Inn** 810 Panoramic Highway, Mill Valley; ☎ 415-381-9000
- **Rue de Main** 22622 Main Street, Hayward; ☎ 510-537-0812

▌ RESTAURANT PROFILES

Acme Chop House ★ ★ ★ ★

STEAK HOUSE	EXPENSIVE	QUALITY ★ ★ ★ ★ ★	VALUE ★ ★ ★ ★

24 Willie Mays Plaza, SoMa/Mission; ☎ 415-644-0240; www.acmechophouse.com

Reservations Recommended. **When to go** Anytime. **Entree range** $18–$39. **Payment** All major credit cards. **Service rating** ★★★★. **Friendliness rating** ★★★★. **Parking** Street, lot. **Bar** Full service. **Wine selection** Short but good. **Dress** Casual. **Disabled access** Yes. **Customers** Locals, baseball fans. **Hours** Tuesday and Wednesday, 11 a.m.–2:30 p.m. and 5:30–9 p.m.; Thursday and Friday, 11 a.m.–2:30 p.m. and 5:30–10 p.m.; Saturday, 5:30–10 p.m.; Sunday, 5:30–9 p.m.; closed Monday.

SETTING AND ATMOSPHERE A big, roomy space with high ceiling. Almost barn-like, but plush. Locals often crowd the bar, which also includes a raw bar full of oysters, sushi, mussels, and the like. It's a great place for a snack. The main dining area looks into the sprawling open kitchen, providing patrons with excellent dinner theater.

HOUSE SPECIALTIES MEAT! Organically raised for the most part. Grassfed beef steaks are more flavorful that grain fed, and have a texture that many prefer. Pork chops are monstrous, thick, and juicy. Roasts are done to perfection. And all meat dishes are served with your choice of sauce, such as béarnaise or green peppercorn. Duck, chicken, and catch of the day are also offered. Most preparations are simple but draw out all the flavorful possibilities of the meat.

OTHER RECOMMENDATIONS Side dishes at Acme are pure comfort food. Creamed spinach is made with fresh spinach and real cream. Mashed potatoes are a buttery treat that you could eat as a main course. Mac 'n' cheese will make you feel like a kid again. It just doesn't get any better.

SUMMARY AND COMMENTS This place was a hit from the moment the doors opened, and you'll quickly see why. Portions are huge, and you'll want to try more than one side dish, so a party of two might consider ordering a salad, three or four sides, and then split one main course. It's located at the ballpark, so you'll need reservations on game days.

A. Sabella's Restaurant ★ ★ ★

| ITALIAN | MODERATE/EXPENSIVE | QUALITY ★★★★ | VALUE ★★★★ |

2766 Taylor Street at Jefferson, 3rd Floor (private elevator), North Beach; ☎ 415-771-6775; www.asabellas.com

Reservations Recommended. **When to go** Lunch, dinner. **Entree range** $13–$57. **Payment** All major credit cards. **Service rating** ★★★. **Friendliness rating** ★★★★. **Parking** Street and 3-hour validated parking at 350 Beach Street. **Bar** Full service. **Wine selection** Extensive and excellent. **Dress** Casual, business. **Disabled access** Yes. **Customers** Tourists, locals, businesspeople. **Hours** Daily, 5–9:45 p.m.

SETTING AND ATMOSPHERE The Fisherman's Wharf area often equates with "tourist trap" today, and many visitors and locals try to avoid it. There still sits, however, between the tawdry shops and weird museums, the true wharf of a working fleet and fine seafood restaurants. A. Sabella's, more than 100 years old, is one those treasures. A third-floor location lifts the hungry traveler above the tourist mania, and the floor plan, open and unobstructed, offers each table a spectacular view of the Bay and the Golden Gate Bridge through large, curved windows. Plan a sunset dinner or, as often happens in San Francisco, a view of the famous fog rolling through the Gate. A cozy bar opens to the left of the dining room, offering an alternate vista of San Francisco's steep hills.

HOUSE SPECIALTIES Fresh seafood prepared and presented so that the flavors of the sea are brought out to their best. The seasonally changing menu includes: a variety of Dungeness classics including crab Louie and crab cake; mixed seafood risotto; gargan elli with fish, calamari, clams, and mussels; sautéed petrale; steamed Maine lobster; Monterey Bay red abalone. Three huge saltwater tanks for live Dungeness crab, abalone, and Maine lobster are maintained year-round, guaranteeing freshness and availability.

OTHER RECOMMENDATIONS Pasta, meats, desserts; orecchiette with artichoke, shiitake, and tomato; lamb chops; the classic chocolate profiteroles. A child-friendly menu for those ages 12 and under is also available.

SUMMARY AND COMMENTS Antone and Lauren Sabella carry on their family's tradition of offering to their guests warm Sicilian hospitality combined with the freshest delicacies of the sea. Brave the carny atmosphere of the waterfront and you'll find that at A. Sabella's, the old wharf is alive and well.

Ana Mandara ★ ★ ★ ★

MODERN VIETNAMESE   MODERATE/EXPENSIVE   QUALITY ★ ★ ★ ★ ½   VALUE ★ ★ ★ ★

891 Beach Street, San Francisco, Marina District; ☎ 415-771-6800; www.anamandara.com

Reservations Recommended. **When to go** Anytime. **Entree range** $18–$32. **Payment** All major credit cards. **Service rating** ★ ★ ★ ★. **Friendliness rating** ★ ★ ★ ★. **Parking** Valet or one-and-a-half-hour free at Ghirardelli Square. **Bar** Full service. **Wine selection** Excellent. **Dress** Casually elegant. **Disabled access** Yes. **Customers** Locals, tourists, and celebs. **Hours** Monday–Thursday, 11:30 a.m.–2 p.m. and 5:30–9:30 p.m.; Friday, 11:30 a.m.– 2 p.m. and 5:30–10:30 p.m.; Saturday, 5:30–10:30 p.m.; Sunday, 5:30–9:30 p.m.

SETTING AND ATMOSPHERE Exotic and inviting. Ana Mandara means "beautiful refuge," and it is. It's a luxury just to step inside the expansive main dining room filled with Asian art and antiques, fountains, a grand staircase, and theatrical lighting, the latter befitting a restaurant owned by actor Don Johnson. The brick building is historic, once serving as the old generator room for the Ghirardelli chocolate factory. So designers had to work with the cavernous space, adding smaller nooks on a floor-level faux balcony trimmed with bamboo window shades that look out over the main dining room. The brass-railed staircase leads up to the second-floor Cham bar. Palm trees and full-grown ficus reach up to the ceiling. With all this grandeur, the feel is surprising comfortable. Black-and-white family photos grace one wall—relatives of executive Chef Khai Duong. And several of his family members work in the restaurant, providing gracious service and sage menu suggestions.

HOUSE SPECIALTIES Classic Vietnamese dishes with a French touch. Chef Duong grew up in Vietnam and received his formal training at Le Cordon Bleu, resulting in delightful taste combinations. Seared foie gras with truffle oil and fresh mango. Grilled rack of lamb with a Vietnamese cinnamon–star anise rub and a spicy tamarind sauce. The entree portions are quite large to encourage sharing, but you may not want to. The traditional claypot fish is a favorite, a spicy caramelized sauce over seared basa on a bed of snappy snowpeas. You must have some starters and sides. Yummy garlic noodles. The tender steamed dumplings with shrimp and chicken are a nice balance to the crispy lobster ravioli with mango and coconut sauce. None too spicy, but subtle, never drowning the flavor of the food.

OTHER RECOMMENDATIONS Have a cocktail before dinner from the inventive bartenders in the Cham bar. One recent creation is the Fukien Mist, a sweet sensation of lychee-fruit liqueur with gin, a hint of lemon juice, and some grenadine to give it a rosy tone. It will give you a rosy tone, as well. To finish off the meal, try the mango spring rolls or the banana boat dessert, a twist on the classic fried banana, but a little lighter in a delicious, thick caramel sauce with candied walnuts.

SUMMARY AND COMMENTS Atmosphere is everything here—glamour and grace. There is live jazz in the Cham Bar Thursday, Friday, and Saturday nights. They take out the tables and chairs in the main dining room and turn it into a dance floor, catering to a well-dressed, mature crowd in their 30s and 40s. Though on touristy Fisherman's Wharf, lots of locals come to this refuge for special occasions—at least half a dozen weddings are held here every year. And the tourists who do make the find go back home and tell everyone about it.

Asia de Cuba ★ ★ ★ ★

CHINO-LATINO	EXPENSIVE	QUALITY ★★★★½	VALUE ★★★★★

Clift Hotel, 495 Geary Street, Union Square; ☎ 415-929-2300; www.clifthotel.com

Reservations Recommended. **When to go** All day and night. **Entree range** $22–$56. **Payment** All major credit cards. **Service rating** ★★★★. **Friendliness rating** ★★★. **Parking** Valet. **Bar** Full service. **Wine selection** Excellent. **Dress** Casually elegant. **Disabled access** Yes. **Customers** Local swells and wide-eyed tourists. **Hours** Sunday–Wednesday, 7–11 a.m., 11:30 a.m.–2:30 p.m., and 5:30–10:30 p.m.; Thursday–Saturday, 7–11 a.m., 11:30 a.m.–2:30 p.m., and 5:30 p.m.–midnight.

SETTING AND ATMOSPHERE Something San Francisco does best: In-your-face elegance backed up by unimpeachable quality and imbued with frontier egalitarianism. You can come here in a tux or sleek strapless gown; you can come here in a sweater or sport coat. It's dark and velvety and trimmed in redwood and held up by huge columns. Plush booths occupy the corners, tables are lined up by the walls, and a T-shaped bar in the center of the room is good for eating or just drinking.

HOUSE SPECIALTIES The cuisine is based on the Chino-Latino cookery of Chinese restaurants in pre-Castro Havana. Many Chinese emigrated to Miami, where they continued to prepare dishes that were recognizably of the Chinese school, yet doused with strictly local ingredients and cooking practices that give the finished product a unique and delicious character. Appetizers include Tunapica, a spicy tartare with currants, almonds, and soy-lime vinaigrette; oxtail spring rolls; lobster potstickers; and crab cakes with shiitake mushrooms. Signature entrees include coriander-encrusted flat-iron steak with bonito mash; Chino-Latino Peking duck; and Hunan whole crispy fish.

OTHER RECOMMENDATIONS Entrees are huge and meant to be shared family style. But the side dishes are just as interesting and could be made into meals. Try stir-fried coconut rice, plantain fried rice, or black-bean croquettes.

SUMMARY AND COMMENTS You might start with a drink in the adjacent Redwood Room bar. Formerly it was a sedate place, but a renovation and the opening of Asia de Cuba have made it a must-have-a-drink place for tourists and locals alike. At any rate, come here hungry and in no hurry. This is a superb place for lingering and malingering.

Aziza ★ ★ ★ ½

MOROCCAN	MODERATE	QUALITY ★ ★ ★	VALUE ★ ★ ★ ★

5800 Geary Boulevard, Richmond District; ☎ 415-752-2222; aziza-sf.com

Reservations Recommended. **When to go** Dinner. **Entree range** $16–$23. **Payment** All major credit cards. **Service rating** ★ ★ ★ ★. **Friendliness rating** ★ ★ ★ ★. **Parking** Valet ($8 weekdays, $10 weekends), street. **Bar** Full service. **Wine selection** Good. **Dress** Business, casual. **Disabled access** Yes. **Customers** Locals from all over town. **Hours** Wednesday–Monday, 5:30–10:30 p.m.; closed Tuesday

SETTING AND ATMOSPHERE San Francisco has intriguing restaurants throughout its many neighborhoods, and Aziza, located in the Geary, is one of them. Exquisite Moroccan food prepared with local organic produce and free-range meat, game, and poultry from local farms and ranches awaits those who leave the well-trampled gourmet path. The traditional Bedouin tent style of most Moroccan restaurants has been replaced with intimate booths and elegant hand-carved tables. Spanish tiles cover bits and pieces of the walls, and brightly decorated arches give the three-room restaurant a mysterious, intimate air. Color is used lavishly throughout the rooms—watermelon, deep blues, tangerine, and saffron add to the dining excitement. A small cave-like bar seeped in dark blue plaster and dimly lit by Moorish lanterns is popular for its specialty drinks.

HOUSE SPECIALTIES Moroccan food with a light touch and delicate flavor. For starters, try a vegan soup of organic green lentils, lemony tomato broth, and cilantro-oil drizzle or medjool date-and-sesame-crusted goat cheese with zaatar croutons. Entrees: Chicken Basteeya baked phyllo dough pie with braised saffron chicken, spiced almonds, powdered sugar, cinnamon, and saffron; grilled rosemary lamb with steamed saffron couscous; black cod clay pot baked in Spanish saffron sauce with parslied little farm potatoes and green olives; Moroccan spiced prawn tagine on a bed of fresh herbed vegetable ragout.

OTHER RECOMMENDATIONS For a full tour of the flavors and textures presented in the menu, try the $45 tasting menu. A culinary bang for the buck! Sample the sweets, particularly the French almond cake with spiced huckleberries and cinnamon stick ice cream.

SUMMARY AND COMMENTS A trip to "the outback" of San Francisco is well rewarded at Aziza. Its superb cooking style combining traditional and modern influences will quickly change diners' perceptions of Moroccan cuisine as heavy and overcooked. The friendly and knowledgeable waitstaff rounds off a marvelous dining experience.

B44　★ ★ ★

| SPANISH CATALONIAN | MODERATE | QUALITY ★ ★ ★ ★ | VALUE ★ ★ ★ ★ |

44 BeldenPlace, Union Square; ☎ 415-986-6287; www.b44sf.com

Reservations Recommended. **When to go** Anytime. **Entree range** $15–$30. **Payment** AE, MC, V. **Service rating** ★★★. **Friendliness rating** ★★★★. **Parking** Street. **Bar** Full service. **Wine selection** Excellent. **Dress** Casual. **Disabled access** Yes. **Customers** Local Bohemians and Europeans. **Hours** Monday–Thursday, 11:30 a.m.–11 p.m.; Friday, 11:30 a.m.–10:30 p.m.; Saturday, 5–10:30 p.m.; Sunday, 4–9 p.m.

SETTING AND ATMOSPHERE If it weren't for the fog, you might think you were in Barcelona. Most of the staff are Spanish; the food and wine are Iberian; the television in the restroom plays videos of Spanish scenes. Only the weather and the well-made martinis at the full-service bar proclaim that you're in The City.

HOUSE SPECIALTIES Arroz negra is a signature dish of Catalonia and of this restaurant. It's like paella, a rice casserole, but flavored and dyed with the ink of squids. Now don't turn the page! This stuff is music in your mouth, a common dish in Spain, and you should try it. If that doesn't float your boat, try lamb chops in a sauce based on aged sherry vinegar; roasted monkfish with clams and fingerling potatoes; or the dish of grilled veggies known as "escalivada." Yum!

OTHER RECOMMENDATIONS Creamy Spanish desserts such as crema catalana, and lovely things made with chocolate by the people who brought chocolate from the Old World to the New.

SUMMARY AND COMMENTS Chef Daniel Olivella has spent his adult life pleasing the crowd, both as a chef and as a jazz musician. His current gig is bringing the genuine Spanish article to San Francisco. No cloying sangria, no bland, overcooked paella, and no fake Spanish ham. Nothing but the real thing. Including the wine list with a good selection of sherry and manzanilla.

Bambuddha Lounge　★ ★ ★

| PAN ASIAN | MODERATE | QUALITY ★ ★ ★ ½ | VALUE ★ ★ ★ ★ ½ |

601 Eddy Street, Phoenix Motel, near SoMa; ☎ 415-885-5088; www.bambuddhalounge.com

Reservations Accepted. **When to go** Late. **Entree range** $8–$24. **Payment** All major credit cards. **Service rating** ★★★★. **Friendliness rating** ★★★★. **Parking** Street, lot for motel guests. **Bar** Full service. **Wine selection** Excellent. **Dress** Business. **Disabled access** Good. **Customers** Locals, tourists. **Hours** Monday–Thursday, 6–10 p.m.; Friday and Saturday, 6–10:30 p.m.

SETTING AND ATMOSPHERE Located in the famous Phoenix Motel, known as the city's "rock 'n' roll" motel for its wild décor and attraction of traveling rock musicians. This restaurant is ultramodern and uber-hip, yet welcomes a very broad-based clientele. Hanging lamps cast a low red-gold light, and polished black reflecting walls amplify the effect. The fireplace crackles cheerily as the well-dressed crowd table-hops and schmoozes, keeping up a house-party atmosphere. On Friday and Saturday, the adjoining lounge teems with party-minded people as the DJ spins.

HOUSE SPECIALTIES "Pan Asian" is something purists tend to run away from, and not without cause. But here it works, partly because most dishes are skillfully seasoned, rarely venturing into the land of bland. So why not sally forth into five-spice duck with coconut pancake studded with chile and crushed peanuts, drizzled with hoisin lime sauce; seared scallops with grilled watermelon, papaya salad, and basil syrup; skirt steak in a sweet soy and mirin sauce with garlic pea shoots; Malaysian "lollipop" lamb chops served with a cooling cucumber sambal.

OTHER RECOMMENDATIONS A very thoughtful wine list. It's heavy on the European, especially German, whites, which tend to go especially well with spicy fare.

SUMMARY AND COMMENTS Because so many musicians on tour stay in the motel, they often end up in the Bambuddha before or after their gigs. Though dinner service here ends at 10:30 p.m. on weekends, it still can turn into an all-night party. If you dine here with a party of up to four, call ahead and request the table next to the fireplace.

Baywolf ★ ★ ★ ★ ½

MEDITERRANEAN	EXPENSIVE	QUALITY ★★★★½	VALUE ★★★ ½

3853 Piedmont Avenue, Oakland; ☎ 510-655-6004; www.baywolf.com

Reservations Recommended. When to go Anytime. Entree range $18–$27. Payment All major credit cards. Service rating ★★★. Friendliness rating ★★★. Parking Street. Bar Beer, wine. Wine selection Very good. Dress Casual. Disabled access Yes. Customers Locals, accidental tourists. Hours Monday–Thursday, 11:30 a.m.–2 p.m. and 6–9 p.m.; Friday, 11:30 a.m.–2 p.m. and 5:30–9:30 p.m.; Saturday, 5:30–9:30 p.m.; Sunday, 5:30–9 p.m.

SETTING AND ATMOSPHERE This handsome old converted house offers a collection of small, cozy dining areas decorated to feel like a French farmhouse, with all its welcoming warmth. Here is some of the most intimate dining in town. The place is fronted by a large veranda where the regulars like to dine alfresco. In contrast to the sedate interior, the atmosphere outside is more festive.

HOUSE SPECIALTIES The menu changes every month, or sometimes with availability or chef's inspiration. Fortnightly offerings usually feature some particular region of the Mediterranean: Spain, Greece, Italy, South of France, etc. On occasion, the menu will migrate to New Orleans or the American Southwest, maybe even to North Africa, but it always returns to its roots in the Middle Sea. Past offerings have included braised lamb shanks with polenta; buckwheat crêpes with smoked trout; grilled swordfish with couscous; a very richly flavored grilled duck with chutney; horseradish mashed potatoes good enough to make a meal of.

OTHER RECOMMENDATIONS Seasonal produce is a real specialty here. Whatever is available in the farmers markets is what to look for. They do especially wonderful things with tomatoes. And anything incorporating an artisanal cheese is worth trying.

SUMMARY AND COMMENTS Call ahead to ask for parking advice. There is plenty to be had, but you have to know where to find it. In its 30 years of operation, Baywolf has earned a very loyal clientele of very demanding people. Many local business people come here for lunch almost every day. The owners began life in academia and literature, but their devotion to the culinary art led them to follow the path to Baywolf. You can still see the exactitude of the academic and the passion of the man of letters in their work.

Beach Chalet ★ ★ ★ ½

AMERICAN BISTRO AND BREWPUB   MODERATE   QUALITY ★★★★   VALUE ★★★★

1000 Great Highway, Richmond/Sunset District; ☎ 415-386-8439; www.beachchalet.com

Reservations Recommended. **When to go** Sundown. **Entree range** $16–$30. **Payment** MC, V. **Service rating** ★★★. **Friendliness rating** ★★★. **Parking** Free lot. **Bar** Full service. **Wine selection** Fair. **Dress** Casual. **Disabled access** Yes. **Customers** Locals and tourists in the know. **Hours** Monday–Thursday, 9 a.m–10 p.m.; Friday, 9 a.m.– 11 p.m.; Saturday, 10 a.m.–11 p.m.; Sunday, 2–10 p.m.; brunch: Saturday and Sunday, 9 a.m.–2 p.m.

SETTING AND ATMOSPHERE Built in 1925 as a tea house, the large, historic building sits hard by Ocean Beach at the western end of Golden Gate Park. In the 1930s, WPA artists executed a series of murals depicting life in The City, and their artwork is the first thing you'll see upon entering the ground floor. Upstairs it's big, boisterous, and beery—a bubble and hubbub as people enjoy the food, drink, each other, and the stunning view of the Pacific Ocean at sunset.

HOUSE SPECIALTIES For breakfast, try eggs Benedict or buttermilk pancakes. For lunch you'll see soup, salad, sandwiches, and entrees like seafood linguini, fish and chips, and roast chicken. Dinner features a catch of the day, New York steak, pork loin with fig compote, grilled vegetables, and pasta. A special children's menu is available for $6.50.

OTHER RECOMMENDATIONS Beers and ales. Nearly a dozen house brews from light to stout. You can also have a tour of the brewery if you ask. There is also a decent, though short, wine list featuring California vintages, as well as a full bar. Live music on Tuesday, Thursday, and Friday nights.

SUMMARY AND COMMENTS There are cozy corners for couples, plenty of space for families, and areas that can be screened off for private parties. This is a good place for a business lunch or dinner. The staff is well versed in the house beers and able to offer sound advice on matching them with food. There is occasional live music, and that makes this a good place to spend the whole evening. Call ahead.

Bistro Clovis ★ ★

FRENCH · **MODERATE** · **QUALITY** ★ ★ ★ ½ · **VALUE** ★ ★ ★ ★

1596 Market Street, SoMa; ☎ 415-864-0231

Reservations Accepted. **When to go** Anytime. **Entree range** $13–$21. **Payment** MC, V. **Service rating** ★ ★ ★. **Friendliness rating** ★ ★ ★. **Parking** Street. **Bar** Beer, wine. **Wine selection** Good. **Dress** Casual. **Disabled access** Yes. **Customers** Locals, businesspeople. **Hours** Tuesday–Sunday, 11:30 a.m.–2:30 p.m. and 5:30–11 p.m.; closed Monday.

HOUSE SPECIALTIES A large blackboard displays a wide variety of daily bistro fare. Hot potato salad with herring; lamb salad with sun-dried tomatoes; smoked salmon in white wine sauce; jumbo prawns with avocado and whatever is fresh in the market that day.

OTHER RECOMMENDATIONS Beef bourguignonne, veal stew, and a delightful range of appetizers and desserts.

SUMMARY AND COMMENTS Traditional, simply prepared, well-presented French bistro food. Come here for dinner after work; it's accessible from much of the city. Relax, enjoy a glass of good wine, and dine in peace.

Boulevard ★ ★ ★ ½

AMERICAN/FRENCH · **EXPENSIVE** · **QUALITY** ★ ★ ★ ★ · **VALUE** ★ ★ ★ ★ ½

1 Mission Street, SoMa; ☎ 415-543-6084; www.boulevardrestaurant.com

Reservations Recommended. **When to go** Anytime. **Entree range** Lunch, $18–$22; dinner, $29–$39. **Payment** AE, CB, D, DC, MC, V. **Service rating** ★ ★ ★. **Friendliness rating** ★ ★ ★. **Parking** Valet, metered street. **Bar** Full service, fresh squeezed juices. **Wine selection** Extensive. **Dress** Fashionable/business. **Disabled access** Adequate (elevator to restrooms). **Customers** Businesspeople and well-heeled young clientele, tourists, and families. **Hours** Monday–Thursday, 11:30 a.m.–2 p.m. and 5:30–10 p.m.; Friday, 11:30 a.m.–2 p.m. and 5:30–10:30 p.m.; Saturday, 5:30–10:30 p.m.; Sunday, 5:30–10 p.m.

SETTING AND ATMOSPHERE Dramatic, dark, Belle Epoque interior. Velvet curtains, artisan ironwork, and art nouveau light fixtures of hand-blown glass recall the French style of the Audiffred Building in which the restaurant is housed. Striking details include a domed roof of pale bricks and a peacock mosaic design on the floor of the bar.

HOUSE SPECIALTIES Chef Nancy Oakes takes great care in searching out the best ingredients for seasonal appetizers such as Heirloom Tomato Salad, as well as perennial favorites like Dungeness crab cakes, and roasted pork tenderloin with pork sausage and fava bean relish. Entrees include several seafood options and a variety of meats. The main dishes always have innovative flavorings from vegetables and spices, but are not laden with sauce. The dessert menu changes seasonally and often features fruit and chocolate treats. Be sure to try the caramel bottom vanilla brûlée when available.

OTHER RECOMMENDATIONS The wine list is impressive and the waitstaff well informed, so don't hesitate to try a suggested glass to pair with your dish. You won't feel rushed here, so consider enjoying a drink from the excellent bar as you peruse the ample menu, and don't forget to save room for the fresh desserts, especially house sorbets and ice creams.

SUMMARY AND COMMENTS The experience of eating in this bustling restaurant is surprisingly relaxed. You can gaze out of large windows onto the Embarcadero and the Bay Bridge. The open kitchen also gives an entertaining view of the cooks working the grill and wood-fired oven. The feel here is at once cosmopolitan and comfortable as the crew goes about their work with professionalism and friendliness. To top it all off, the food is wonderful.

The Brazen Head ★ ★ ★

CONTINENTAL	MODERATE	QUALITY ★★★½	VALUE ★★★★★

3166 Buchanan Street at Greenwich Avenue, Marina District;
☎ **415-921-7600; www.brazenheadsf.com**

Reservations Not accepted. **When to go** Before 8 p.m. and after 10 p.m. **Entree range** $14–$25. **Payment** No credit cards; ATM nearby; accepts debit cards and cash only. **Service rating** ★★. **Friendliness rating** ★★★. **Parking** Street. **Bar** Full service. **Wine selection** Good. **Dress** Casual. **Disabled access** None. **Customers** Locals, other restaurant workers, writers. **Hours** Daily, 5 p.m.–1 a.m.

SETTING AND ATMOSPHERE Except for the lack of trophy animal heads, this place has the look and feel of a rich, cozy, European hunting lodge. All is deep and dark; polished hardwood and brass trim. Antique etchings and photographs cover the walls. A loyal patronage returns regularly, and one sometimes gets the feeling of being in the television bar Cheers. No credit cards or checks are accepted, but there is an ATM next to the restrooms.

HOUSE SPECIALTIES Meat! (And fish.) As befits the hunting lodge atmosphere, grills and roasts of lamb, beef, and pork. Also veal piccata, sautéed prawns, chicken, burgers, and a daily pasta dish. All entrees include vegetable of the day and potato or rice. Pepper steak is the chef's signature dish.

OTHER RECOMMENDATIONS A good selection of salads and appetizers, such as crab cakes, oysters, and roasted garlic; mixed greens, shrimp, and Caesar salads.

SUMMARY AND COMMENTS Situated on a street corner not far from the Golden Gate Bridge. The cheery lights of this place beckon through the San Francisco fog like a warm cabin in a cold wood. There is often a wait for a table, but you can join the locals and regulars at the bar for a convivial drink.

The Buena Vista Café ★

AMERICAN DINER	INEXPENSIVE	QUALITY ★★½	VALUE ★★★

2765 Hyde Street (at Beach), Marina District; ☎ **415-474-5044;**
www.thebuenavista.com

Reservations Not accepted. **When to go** Anytime. **Entree range** $9–$16. **Payment** AE, CD, MC, V. **Service rating** ★. **Friendliness rating** ★★. **Parking** Lot and metered street. **Bar** Full service. **Wine selection** Limited. **Dress** Sporty. **Disabled access** None. **Customers** Tourists. **Hours** Monday–Friday, 9 a.m.–9:30 p.m.; Saturday and Sunday, 8 a.m.–9:30 p.m.; bar open till 2 a.m. nightly.

SETTING AND ATMOSPHERE The Buena Vista is more than 100 years old and is situated across the street from The Cannery and the Hyde and Powell cable car turnaround. Communal tables of chunky brown wood and yellowing walls don't deter hoards of tourists who enjoy lively rounds of drinking at the bar and the excellent views of Alcatraz Island, the Golden Gate Bridge, and the Bay.

HOUSE SPECIALTIES Tourists flock to the Buena Vista not only to visit one of the oldest restaurants in San Francisco, but also to experience "the best Irish coffee in the world." According to the restaurant's lore, the boozy beverage was perfected by one-time owner Jack Koeppler and travel writer Stanton Deleplane in 1952. The Irish coffee is indeed delicious and takes the edge off the sore feet and cold fingers of tourists who have spent the day hiking through the fog. San Francisco's misty landscape is at its most romantic after a generous shot of Irish whiskey.

OTHER RECOMMENDATIONS Souvenirs are on the menu here and The Buena Vista gift shop sells everything from cocktail napkins to fleece vests emblazoned with the restaurant's logo. The food is standard pub fare with offerings like cheddar burgers and club sandwiches and nightly specials such as corned beef and cabbage. Chicken tenders and grilled cheese are available on the children's menu. Breakfast is served all day long. At day's end, The Buena Vista is the ideal place for a nightcap, and since it is open late you can go there after the theater or even after a night of clubbing; but keep in mind the kitchen closes at 9:30 p.m.

SUMMARY AND COMMENTS The Buena Vista seems to bask in the memory of its own good old days, but the bustling crowds of today are convivial. A trip to San Francisco is truly complete after a historic gaze at the bay and an Irish coffee here.

Buzz 9 ★★★

CALIFORNIAN	MODERATE	QUALITY ★★★★	VALUE ★★★★

139 Eighth Street, SoMa; ☎ **415-255-8783; www.buzz9.com**

Reservations Accepted. **When to go** Anytime. **Entree range** $10–$18. **Payment** All major credit cards. **Service rating** ★★★. **Friendliness rating** ★★★★. **Parking** Street. **Bar** Full service. **Wine selection** Very good. **Dress** Casual to trendy. **Disabled access** Yes. **Customers** Locals, hipsters, and artists. **Hours** Monday–Wednesday, 11 a.m.–10 p.m.; Thursday–Saturday, 11 a.m.–midnight; Sunday, 11 a.m.–3 p.m.

SETTING AND ATMOSPHERE In what was at one time a Prohibition-era speakeasy, this charming little joint still keeps a feeling of something "gay" in the old-time sense of the word. When it's at perfect pitch, you think maybe, just maybe, people will actually start to dance the tango on the tabletops. Hardwood floors bespeak its age, the artwork on the walls bespeaks its status as a favorite haunt of local artists and writers (the successful ones, that is), and its comfortable banquettes and magazine rack proclaim it as a place where regulars like to come just to spend time.

HOUSE SPECIALTIES This is an only-in-San Francisco menu. The owner is a South African of Czech descent serving California cuisine with a dash of French and Cal-Mex just to keep it lively. Lime and cumin chicken skewers is a tangy starting dish, and the house-made chips served with guacamole are like nothing you buy in a bag. Pan-roasted chicken with a crispy polenta cake might be the signature dish. The chicken is always flavorful and juicy. Whole-grain mustard and caper sauce brings out the best in grilled salmon.

OTHER RECOMMENDATIONS Pasta dishes are unusually good, and most can be served vegetarian. If you're after some simple comfort food, the burgers are great, the quesadillas satisfying, and the onion soup a perfect antidote to the local weather.

SUMMARY AND COMMENTS While local literati and artsy types tend to congregate here, it's never staid or snooty, and neither is it edgy or tragically hip. This is a good place to kick off a night of SoMa clubbing or for a late dinner after a performance at the nearby Great American Music Hall. The basement houses a popular bar and lounge where DJs spin on weekends and a very mixed crowd likes to party.

Café de la Presse ★ ★ ★

| FRENCH/BASQUE | MODERATE | QUALITY ★★★★ | VALUE ★★★★ |

469 Bush Street, near Union Square; ☎ 415-249-0900;
www.cafedelapresse.com

Reservations Accepted. **When to go** Anytime. **Entree range** $13–$24. **Payment** All major credit cards. **Service rating** ★★★. **Friendliness rating** ★★★. **Parking** Street. **Bar** Full service. **Wine selection** Excellent. **Dress** Business casual. **Disabled access** Yes. **Customers** Local suits and downtown tourists. **Hours** Daily, 7 a.m.–11 p.m.

SETTING AND ATMOSPHERE It looks like it was designed and built in Paris and then shipped entire to San Francisco. Billed as "a European accent on the plate and in the air," it's a quiet haven popular with stockbroker types, and you can often tell how the market is doing just by their composure. The wall of windows gives you a good view of the street and all its passersby. Dark wood is warm and comforting, and the framed mirrors gracing the walls give it just a bit of whimsy.

HOUSE SPECIALTIES Croque Monsieur is good for lunch; duck with potato croquettes is great for dinner; and veal Marengo anytime. Anything from the sea is good, and people travel across town for onion soup gratinée.

OTHER RECOMMENDATIONS A fine burger and fries; croissant pudding.

SUMMARY AND COMMENTS The staff is very knowledgeable about both food and wine, and you can rely on their advice. Be advised that not only is the food delicious, but the portions are large and on the heavy side. If you don't want to carry away a doggie bag, you might consider sharing a single entree.

Café Pescatore ★ ★ ★

ITALIAN/SEAFOOD	MODERATE	QUALITY ★ ★ ★ ½	VALUE ★ ★ ★ ★

**2455 Mason Street, North Beach; ☎ 415-561-1111;
www.cafepescatore.com**

Reservations Accepted. **When to go** Sundown. **Entree range** $14–$25. **Payment** All major credit cards. **Service rating** ★ ★ ★. **Friendliness rating** ★ ★ ★. **Parking** Street. **Bar** Full service. **Wine selection** Good. **Dress** Casual. **Disabled access** Yes. **Customers** Tourists and neighborhood regulars. **Hours** Monday–Friday, 7–10:30 a.m. and 11:30 a.m.–10 p.m.; Saturday and Sunday, 7–10 a.m., 10 a.m.–2 p.m. (brunch), and 2–10 p.m.

SETTING AND ATMOSPHERE There are a lot of places in the Fisherman's Wharf area that appeal to the casual tourist who might not give due consideration to dining. But Pescatore is not among them. Step in and you can tell immediately that the feel is old San Francisco. Creamy walls, wood trim, tile floors, and molding at the ceiling, as well as a full bar in the center of the room all speak "The City" in unambiguous terms. Call it "wharf bistro" décor with old-timey pix, models of boats hanging from the ceiling, and all warmly lit. It's a comfort station in the fog.

HOUSE SPECIALTIES All the usual suspects in an old fisherman's eatery. You can start with classic clam chowder or roasted tomato soup. Salads and antipasti, even pizza and bruschetta. Move on to linguini con vongole; crab-stuffed ravioli; oven-roasted sea bass. For the meat eater, order a grilled rib eye or a seared chicken breast with mushrooms and Marsala sauce.

OTHER RECOMMENDATIONS Cioppino is The City's signature dish, and purists say that it can only be made with the local Dungeness crab. But here they violate the rule and make it year-round from Alaskan king crab.

SUMMARY AND COMMENTS This is also a good place to drink—not to party and dance and get wild and loud—but to drink calmly, coolly, leisurely, as you gaze out the large picture windows. So it is fitting that the house offers a wide range of wines, liquors, and cordials. Enjoy a grappa, a single-malt scotch, or even a special espresso drink as you watch through the windows as the local folk negotiate the gathering fog.

Cafe Tiramisu ★ ★ ★

ITALIAN	MODERATE	QUALITY ★ ★ ★	VALUE ★ ★ ★

**28 Belden Place, Financial District; ☎ 415-421-7044;
www.cafetiramisu.com**

Reservations Recommended, especially for outdoor seating. **When to go** Lunch or dinner. **Entree range** $15–$32. **Payment** All major credit cards. **Service rating**

★★★. **Friendliness rating** ★★½. **Parking** Street. **Bar** Full service. **Wine selection** Vast. **Dress** Casual. **Disabled access** Yes. **Customers** Repeat locals, businesspeople, tourists. **Hours** Monday–Thursday, 11:30 a.m.–3 p.m. and 5–10 p.m.; Friday, 11:30 a.m.–3 p.m. and 5–10:30 p.m.; Saturday, 5–10:30 p.m.; closed Sunday.

SETTING AND ATMOSPHERE A mini trip to Europe, before you even get to the restaurant. On the brief, block-long Belden Place, between Bush and Pine in the city's financial district, Cafe Tiramisu is clustered with several other fine restaurants, most with European flair—Cafe Bastille, Plouf, B44, Cafe 52, Brindisi—all with hosts on the sidewalk wooing passersby with tempting menus. There's also Sam's Grill, one of the oldest restaurants in the city, in business since 1867 and here since 1946. Plus there's a mod bar called Voda, great for an after-dinner drink. This one-time alley became a dining destination in the early 1990s. And now, near the mammoth Bank of America building, bright umbrellas shade outdoor tables. Strings of white lights dangle above, for an ever-starry sky. Tables nudge each other, and so do diners' knees. Outside Tiramisu, the warm hum of chatter blends with the clinking of plates, as energetic waiters nearly sprint from kitchen to table at this always-busy spot. Guests come in a variety of ages, and attire is anything from jeans and casual shirts to sport coats and even a tie here and there.

HOUSE SPECIALTIES The menu keeps close to Mother Italia with such elegant pasta dishes as linguini with spicy clam sauce and sliced zucchini and the lobster-and-crab ravioli with lobster bisque. Venture into the seafood and meat dishes, too. Other items to try are the monkfish with roasted tomatoes and cauliflower; pork chops with berry chutney and a potato cucumber salad; veal scaloppini with a lemon-caper sauce over spinach.

OTHER RECOMMENDATIONS Got wine? You'll get it here. The wine list is so long it has a table of contents, all in a bound leather volume heavy enough to make a fine door stop. Pages 6–10 are Italian whites, and 11–28 are Italian reds. And that's only about half the book. It's a little overwhelming, so feel free to ask for help. The by-the-glass list is more maneuverable at only one page. And don't forget dessert, particularly the restaurant's namesake tiramisu—creamy, boozy, fluffy, and certainly uplifting, especially with a good cup of coffee. Other rich finds are the rum bittersweet chocolate cake with roasted banana ice cream, apple torte with pine nuts and raisins, or the chocolate caramel torte with raspberry coulis.

SUMMARY AND COMMENTS The cafe truly offers three dining experiences in one, depending on your location. The coveted outside tables are festive, noisy, and fun, barring rain. Heaters fend off the chill. Inside on the first floor, it's still intimate, still pleasantly noisy, but more traditional and very Italy, with fresco murals of Pompeii and other Roman ruins. Downstairs there are tables tucked in the wine cellar, hidden in soft light. Feels like you're getting away with something.

Calzones ★ ★

| ITALIAN | MODERATE | QUALITY | ★★½ | VALUE | ★★★ |

**430 Columbus Avenue, North Beach; ☎ 415-397-3600;
www.calzonesf.com**

Reservations Accepted. **When to go** Anytime. **Entree range** $12–$24; prix fixe $19.95–$29.95. **Payment** All major credit cards. **Service rating** ★★★★. **Friendliness rating** ★★★. **Parking** Street, nearby lots. **Bar** Full service. **Wine selection** Limited, with a $9 corkage fee. **Dress** Informal. **Disabled access** Yes. **Customers** Locals, tourists. **Hours** Daily, 11 a.m.–1 a.m.

SETTING AND ATMOSPHERE Cool old North Beach 1960s décor: black-tiled walls, lots of brightly colored glass bottles; Italian cheeses, salamis, garlic hanging everywhere; chandeliers. Seating indoors and out, at one of the cute mosaic tables. A bustling little place with a great location in the heart of North Beach supported by a friendly and attentive staff. Small wood-fired brick oven faces the main dining area.

HOUSE SPECIALTIES Naturally there is lasagna, Gnocchi Genoese, ravioli, also many pasta dishes, pizza, roasted chicken, seared lamb loin, and filet mignon.

OTHER RECOMMENDATIONS Italian pot stickers filled with sausage, mushrooms, garlic, and ginger; excellent table bread and desserts.

SUMMARY AND COMMENTS You'll love the wide windows where you can watch the whole world parade by. The food is served on unusually shaped, long oblong platters, and that makes it a little difficult to balance everything on a small round table. Portions were more than ample, but the quality is uneven. The vegetable-infused patate puree served as a side dish with the entrees is bland. And the gumbo tastes more like minestrone with some seafood thrown in. Better to stick with the delicious appetizers and then splurge on the Chocolate truffle mousse cake. And watch the action on Columbus.

Campton Place Restaurant ★ ★ ★ ★ ★

COUNTRY FRENCH	EXPENSIVE	QUALITY ★★★★★	VALUE ★★★★★

**340 Stockton Street, 1st Floor, Union Square; ☎ 415-955-5555;
www.camptonplace.com**

Reservations Recommended. **When to go** Anytime. **Entree range** Breakfast $5–25; lunch 2, 3, and 4 courses, $34–$49; dinner 3 and 4 course, $78–$88; tasting menu, $135. **Payment** All major credit cards. **Service rating** ★★★★★. **Friendliness rating** ★★★★. **Parking** Valet, $9. **Bar** Full service. **Wine selection** Excellent. **Dress** Wear a tie; dressy. **Disabled access** Yes. **Customers** Business people, tourists, the demanding. **Hours** Monday–Thursday, 7–10:30 a.m., 11:30 a.m.–2 p.m., and 5:30–9:30 p.m.; Friday, 7–10:30 a.m., 11:30 a.m.–2 p.m., and 5:30–10 p.m.; Saturday, noon–2 p.m. (brunch) and 5:30–10 p.m.; Sunday, 8–11 a.m., 11 a.m.–2 p.m. (brunch), and 5:30–9:30 p.m.

SETTING AND ATMOSPHERE In the top-end Campton Place hotel, this room is formal but not fussy. Tieless men won't be turned away, but they'll wish they'd worn a tie. Décor is modern, clean, and spare compared to most luxurious establishments. It's a study in serenity, full of flowers and soothing artworks. An elegant setting for a breakfast of corned beef hash and poached eggs.

HOUSE SPECIALTIES Breakfast is famous here, with all of the traditional favorites, including corn muffins that are light as a cloud. For dinner, try duck with orange blossom honey; catch of the day prepared simply and garnished with aromatic fried rosemary or other herbs; creative dishes like foie gras with crispy oxtail bonbon and truffle vinaigrette. And presentations are as artful as origami.

OTHER RECOMMENDATIONS Rely on the sommelier to match wines from the extensive list. For dessert, try chocolate pastilla with orange guajillo confit.

SUMMARY AND COMMENTS In the hotel of the same name. This is a temple to the muse of American cooking in a city famous for its foreign culinary establishments. Excellent American fare prepared to the most rigorous European standards without the emphasis on fancy sauces. Mark Twain would have written glowingly of it. It's expensive, right down to the drinks in the bar, but nothing's overpriced. Quality is king, and you get what you pay for.

The Carnelian Room ★ ★ ★ ★

NEW AMERICAN	EXPENSIVE	QUALITY ★★★★½	VALUE ★★★★

555 California Street, Chinatown; ☎ **415-433-7500;**
www.carnelianroom.com

Reservations Recommended. **When to go** Sunset, brunch, or any other time. **Entree range** Sunday brunch, $40; prix fixe dinner, $45; entrees, $20 children, $28–$50 adults. **Payment** All major credit cards. **Service rating** ★★½. **Friendliness rating** ★★½. **Parking** Pay-lots and garages; street. **Bar** Full service. **Wine selection** Excellent. **Dress** Business attire. **Disabled access** Good. **Customers** Tourists, businesspeople, locals. **Hours** Daily, 6–9:30 p.m.; Sunday brunch, 10 a.m.–2 p.m.

SETTING AND ATMOSPHERE High above the city on the 52nd floor of the Bank of America Building, the Carnelian Room is a private banker's club by day, and it looks it, with high ceilings, dark wood paneling, soft carpet, and upholstered chairs. But the main decorations are breathtaking wraparound views of San Francisco, the bay, the fog, and the hills beyond. The main dining room is the most formal; there's a lounge with equally stunning views and limited food service.

HOUSE SPECIALTIES Sonoma foie gras; crispy-skin king salmon; tableside Caesar salad; roasted rack of lamb; oven-roasted sea scallops; Maine lobster; black-peppered prime rib.

OTHER RECOMMENDATIONS Prix fixe, three-course dinner; chocolate crème brûlée.

SUMMARY AND COMMENTS Restaurant trends may come and go, but nothing quite equals the glamour of an expensive dinner high in the sky, with a view of the surrounding world twinkling below through an evanescent veil of fog. The Bank of America's high-speed elevator has an unnerving rumble as it zooms to the top, but in the bar and dining room, luxury and peace prevail. Service is impeccable if a bit stiff, and the food is fine, though not wildly adventuresome. The prices are, of course, a bit steep. Appetizers and drinks or coffee and desserts in the more intimate lounge are an excellent way to enjoy the amenities for less money.

Clementine ★ ★ ★ ★

FRENCH	EXPENSIVE	QUALITY ★ ★ ★ ★ ½	VALUE ★ ★ ★ ★

126 Clement Street (between Second and Third avenues), near Richmond; ☎ 415-387-0408;

Reservations Accepted. **When to go** Anytime. **Entree range** $16–$22. **Payment** MC, V. **Service rating** ★★★. **Friendliness rating** ★★★. **Parking** Street. **Bar** Full service. **Wine selection** Mostly French. **Dress** Casual chic. **Disabled access** Good. **Customers** Neighborhood dwellers, French expatriates. **Hours** Tuesday–Sunday, 5:30–10:30 p.m.

SETTING AND ATMOSPHERE Clementine is a relaxed neighborhood spot. The dining room looks as if it were imported from a little French town. Peach walls are hung with oil paintings and copper pans. Mirrors and soft lighting create a spacious yet cozy effect. Even when the restaurant gets busy, you feel a sense of privacy.

HOUSE SPECIALTIES The menu continues the authentic French approach. Appetizers include a salad of magret de cannard (smoked duck breast), seared foie gras with a port reduction sauce, and escargots. A fresh pea soup garnished simply with fresh chives is delicious. Main dishes, such as rack of lamb with gratin Dauphinois (scalloped potatoes), are well executed. Coquille Saint-Jacques (scallops) are perfectly cooked and paired with savoy cabbage braised in mussel juice for a light, interesting dish. Confit of duck, quail, and a veal chop are among the typical French offerings.

OTHER RECOMMENDATIONS This is one of the few places in town where you can find traditional French desserts such as île flottante (meringue) or a colonel (sorbet and vodka). The pain perdu (French toast) in caramel sauce served with hazelnut ice cream is heavenly. You may also finish your meal with a cheese plate. The predominantly French wine list is not long, but reflects interesting selections. The restaurant's wine buyer favors lesser-known wines as a way of getting higher quality at a lower cost.

SUMMARY AND COMMENTS Clementine is a small neighborhood restaurant with food the caliber of a downtown hot spot. Service is attentive and the overall experience pleasant. This is a good place to keep in mind for smaller parties who like to talk and enjoy a leisurely meal.

Clement Street Bar and Grill ★ ★ ★

NEW AMERICAN	MODERATE	QUALITY ★ ★ ★ ½	VALUE ★ ★ ★

708 Clement Street, Richmond; ☎ 415-386-2200

Reservations Recommended. **When to go** Anytime. **Entree range** Brunch and lunch, $8–$14; dinner, $12–$20. **Payment** All major credit cards. **Service rating** ★★★. **Friendliness rating** ★★★½. **Parking** Street, metered during the day. **Bar** Full service. **Wine selection** Fair. **Dress** Casual. **Disabled access** Good. **Customers**

Locals, businesspeople. **Hours** Tuesday–Thursday, 11:30 a.m.–2:30 p.m. and 5:30–10 p.m.; Friday and Saturday, 11:30 a.m.–2:30 p.m. and 5–10:30 p.m.; Sunday, 4:30–9:30 p.m.; Saturday and Sunday brunch, 10:30 a.m.–2:30 p.m.; Monday, closed.

SETTING AND ATMOSPHERE From the entrance, Clement Street Bar and Grill seems dim, narrow, and dominated by the bar, but there's a roomy rear dining area with an impressive brick fireplace and a ship's cabin atmosphere. It's simply furnished with dark carpet, varnished plywood benches, and captain's chairs, but the cut-glass candleholders and white tablecloths add a touch of ceremony; coat hooks at the entry lend a genial neighborhood mood. No smoking is allowed despite the barroom atmosphere.

HOUSE SPECIALTIES Daily specials may include roasted garlic with crostini; roasted red pepper filled with three cheeses, herbs, and pine nuts over spinach salad; wild mushroom tortellini; grilled fish specials; veal scaloppine with wild mushrooms. Vegetarian offerings include grilled portobello mushroom with warm spinach and hazelnuts; grilled and roasted vegetables; wild mushroom tortellini with roma tomatoes, garlic, herbs, and white wine.

OTHER RECOMMENDATIONS Salads, sandwiches, and burgers.

SUMMARY AND COMMENTS Step in and enter the 1930s. Talk discreetly with private eyes, mysterious ladies, and intriguing gentlemen, while the trio plays Gershwin. Indulge your fantasies. This place is rich; better if you are, too, or willing to act and feel like it.

Cortez ★ ★ ★ ½

MEDITERRANEAN	MODERATE	QUALITY ★ ★ ★ ★	VALUE ★ ★ ★

**550 Geary Street, Union Square; ☎ 415-292-6360;
www.cortezrestaurant.com**

Reservations Recommended. **When to go** Anytime. **Entree range** $10–$17. **Payment** All major credit cards. **Service rating** ★ ★ ★. **Friendliness rating** ★ ★ ★. **Parking** Street. **Bar** Full service. **Wine selection** Good. **Dress** Casual. **Disabled access** Yes. **Customers** Locals, tourists. **Hours** Daily, 5:30–10:30 p.m.; bar open 5 p.m.–1 a.m.

SETTING AND ATMOSPHERE It's mod-elegant. Hip, but not painfully so. Situated off the lobby of the Hotel Adagio in the theater district, Cortez is aglow with dots of color. Bold illuminated panels on white walls send a nifty nod to Mondrian. Big orb ceiling lamps in red, blue, and yellow cast a tender glow. They dangle mid-air like mobiles or swirling atoms. It's Calder meets Oppenheimer. Whimsical overhead, serious style and good taste below. Even the tableware has visual interest, with modern-art butter dishes and bags o' bread—small burlap sacks replace boring bowls. Local sophisticates, out-of-towners, and hotel guests merge in casual elegance. A 30-something base. It's a little noisy, but in a good way.

HOUSE SPECIALTIES Small plates that make for big variety. Plan on two to three per person. Husband-and-wife chefs Quinn and Karen Hatfield fuse clever combinations such as glazed Long Island duck breast with gingered green beans, roasted cherries, and sunchoke puree. Seasonings and sauces serve as transparencies for the food, enhancing rather than overpowering. Try the roasted organic beets in balsamic shallot vinaigrette and Point Reyes blue cheese, perked up with some tasty bites of candied walnuts. Or the slow-roasted—for 36 hours—Berkshire pork belly with crispy herbed spaetzle, carrot coriander puree, and ginger-balsamic butter. Pork so tender you could cut it with a noodle.

OTHER RECOMMENDATIONS Have a refreshing cucumber gimlet cocktail before dinner; Sky vodka infused with cool cukes. It's like drinking a trip to the spa. And when you're ready for dessert, check out some surprise taste sensations. The yummy gooey warm chocolate peanut butter truffle cake comes with a small scoop of salted caramel ice cream with a scattering of nuts. Sweet and salty all at once, like a handful of Cracker Jacks. Or experience the white corn ice cream that complements a baked lemon custard tartlet. Each dessert comes with a recommendation for a shot of liqueur.

SUMMARY AND COMMENTS Experiment. Share. That's the idea of the small plates. There's a long and lovely wine list, bottles or by the glass. And don't be afraid to ask for suggestions. It's a savvy staff.

The Cosmopolitan Restaurant ★ ★ ★

NEW AMERICAN   MODERATE/EXPENSIVE   QUALITY ★★★   VALUE ★★★★

121 Spear Street, SoMa; ☎ 415-543-4001;
www.thecosmopolitancafe.com

Reservations Recommended. **When to go** Anytime. **Entree range** lunch, $17–$30; dinner, $18–$32. **Payment** AE, DC, MC, V. **Service rating** ★★½. **Friendliness rating** ★★★. **Parking** Valet at dinner, lot, metered street. **Bar** Full service. **Wine selection** Good. **Dress** Business casual. **Disabled access** Good. **Customers** Businesspeople, tourists. **Hours** Monday–Wednesday, 11:30 a.m.–9:30 p.m.; Thursday and Friday, 11:30 a.m.–10 p.m.; Saturday, 5:30–10 p.m.; closed Sunday.

SETTING AND ATMOSPHERE The Cosmopolitan Restaurant has two large bars, one upstairs with a television for watching sports and a separate menu of appetizers and one below in the main dining room. Lots of dark wood paneling, trendy light fixtures, patterned carpet, and a huge portrait of a couple's embrace give the restaurant a young, if somewhat generic, feel. Booths and oversized chairs keep diners comfortable.

HOUSE SPECIALTIES Chef Steven Levine creates "inspiration trio," appetizers and dessert plates in which he uses one ingredient in three different ways. These allow ingredients in season to shine and make beautiful presentations. Look out for crisp calamari and artichoke, and creative soups on the appetizer menu. High-quality meats such as sautéed sea scallops and Niman Ranch lamb pot roast form the basis for large entrees. Seafood is paired with vegetables in season. Similarly, desserts show off seasonal fruit and are charming. A plate of baked-to-order chocolate-chunk cookies comes out with an adorable mini-milkshake.

OTHER RECOMMENDATIONS A diversity of ingredients come together here to make California and New American dishes. Crusts of falafel and semolina replace plain breading. Chiles, soybeans, and arugula-walnut pesto give standard preparations a new twist. The breadth of the menu here is surprisingly wide. It is easy to overload your palate with too many flavors, so order carefully. Look out for some quality California wine choices.

SUMMARY AND COMMENTS Part sports bar and after-work hangout for young professionals, part California comfort food spot with a complex menu, The Cosmopolitan Restaurant is doing a lot all at once. The Levines, a husband and wife team, and their friendly staff aim to please, but some very nice details, such as top-quality ingredients, a selection of artisan cheeses, and fine wine miss their due attention amid all the bustle. Still a fine place to keep in mind for good food in a casual setting.

Dusit ★ ★ ½

THAI	INEXPENSIVE	QUALITY ★★★½	VALUE ★★★★

3221 Mission Street, Mission District; ☎ 415-826-4639

Reservations Accepted. When to go Anytime. Entree range $8–$14. Payment All major credit cards. Service rating ★★½. Friendliness rating ★★. Parking Street. Bar Beer, wine. Wine selection House. Dress Casual. Disabled access Limited. Customers Locals. Hours Monday, Wednesday–Friday, 11:30 a.m.–2:30 p.m. and 5–10 p.m.; Saturday and Sunday, 5–10 p.m.; closed Tuesday.

SETTING AND ATMOSPHERE A small place in an ordinary neighborhood. Nothing remarkable to look at, but it's clean and well lit, and it has just a touch of class. This is a temple of Thai cuisine, and the votaries of this muse are happily at work pleasing anyone who walks in.

HOUSE SPECIALTIES Most of the items you would expect on a Thai menu, but better than usual, especially considering the price. Orchid duck boned and sautéed with ginger, mushrooms, tomatoes, pineapple, and onions; garlic prawn with black pepper and veggies; sautéed squid with bamboo, chile, and basil; chicken salad with sweet-spicy dressing.

OTHER RECOMMENDATIONS Good fried noodles. Vegetarian dinners.

SUMMARY AND COMMENTS Lunchtime prices are somewhat lower, although the food is just as good and plentiful. But even at dinner it's downright cheap. For quality and quantity, this place is at the top of the list. It's worth a trip across town to dine well at low prices in a pleasant, undemanding environment.

E & O Trading Company ★ ★ ★

SOUTHEAST ASIAN	EXPENSIVE	QUALITY ★★★★	VALUE ★★★★

314 Sutter Street, near Union Square; ☎ 415-693-0303; www.eotrading.com

Reservations Highly recommended. When to go Weeknights. Entree range $13–$27. Payment All major credit cards. Service rating ★★★. Friendliness rating ★★. Parking Valet after 6 p.m. or Sutter Stockton Garage next door. Bar

Full service. **Wine selection** Good. **Dress** Casual to business. **Disabled access** Yes. **Customers** After-work crowd, tourists. **Hours** Monday–Thursday, 11:30 a.m.– 10 p.m.; Friday and Saturday, 11:30 a.m.–11 p.m.; Sunday, 5–9:30 p.m.

SETTING AND ATMOSPHERE Bustling energy comes in from Union Square like the tradewinds, halting right at the foot of the 35-foot Dragon Bar. Following an age-old love story of Theodore Bailey and his escapades, the three-story craft brewery and Pan Asian grill was designed for the downstairs to give the feel of a trading post and the mezzanine to be the meeting house of refined merchants. And that it does, with its framed botanical pictures on ivory walls with palm-leaf fans.

HOUSE SPECIALTIES Signature Indonesian corn fritters with chile soy dipping sauce; ginger mushroom tower with marinated portobello mushrooms with ginger and sweet soy dipping sauce; Thai-style fried jasmine rice with peas, egg, green onion, and chiles.

OTHER RECOMMENDATIONS Indo peanut chicken satay marinated in sweet soy, garlic, and spices; ahi tartare mixed with lemon grass, chiles, cilantro, green onion, and sesame oil; smoked pork with crispy taro strips, scallions, lettuce, Hoisin and Sriracha sauces. Choosing whether to have beer or wine with dinner might be a toughie. The beers are excellent and crafted in-house with seasonal selections. The wines are also good, and the waitstaff is exceptionally knowledgeable and adept at making suggestions that complement your meal.

ENTERTAINMENT AND AMENITIES Live jazz trio on Sunday and Monday evenings. Live classical guitar music on Tuesday evenings.

SUMMARY AND COMMENTS The menu is a combination of Asian cuisines inspired by Indonesia, Vietnam, Thailand, Malaysia, and East India. To make the most of the experience, have fun ordering a table full of small plates, salads, and satays. Whether upstairs or downstairs, this is a great place to people-watch and let yourself get sucked into the décor, feeling transported overseas. The plate presentations are equally as imaginative and impressive as the interior designed by Paul Ma.

El Nuevo Fruitlandia ★ ★ ½

PUERTO RICAN/CUBAN	INEXPENSIVE	QUALITY ★★★½	VALUE ★★★★

3077 24th Street, Mission District; ☎ 415-648-2958

Reservations Recommended on weekends. **When to go** Anytime. **Entree range** $12–$16. **Payment** MC, V. **Service rating** ★★★. **Friendliness rating** ★★★. **Parking** Street. **Bar** Beer, wine. **Wine selection** House. **Dress** Casual. **Disabled access** Yes. **Customers** Locals. **Hours** Tuesday–Friday, 11:30 a.m.–3 p.m. and 5–9 p.m.; Saturday and Sunday, noon–10 p.m.

SETTING AND ATMOSPHERE Unadorned, uncomplicated, unpretentious, and small. But it's friendly and comfortable, and the staff will treat you well.

HOUSE SPECIALTIES Roast pork with rice and yucca; a variety of plantains; chicken in green sauce; shredded beef with peppers; Puerto Rican dumplings; shrimp in garlic sauce.

OTHER RECOMMENDATIONS Batidos de frutas, thick fruit shakes, or smoothies.
SUMMARY AND COMMENTS This is a good place for a lunch that will stay with you the rest of the day and into the evening. If you're planning nocturnal activities and won't be able to sit down to a leisurely dinner, fortify yourself here first. Que rico!

Enrico's ★ ★ ★

CALIFORNIAN/MEDITERRANEAN   MODERATE   QUALITY ★★★★   VALUE ★★★★

504 Broadway, North Beach; ☎ 415-982-6223;
www.enricossidewalkcafe.com

Reservations Accepted. **When to go** Anytime. **Entree range** $16–$30. **Payment** AE, MC, V. **Service rating** ★★★. **Friendliness rating** ★★. **Parking** Lot; valet, $10 (valet begins at 5:30 p.m.). **Bar** Full service. **Wine selection** Very good. **Dress** Casual, business. **Disabled access** Yes. **Customers** Eclectic. **Hours** Sunday–Thursday, 11:30 a.m.–11 p.m.; Friday and Saturday, 11:30 a.m.–midnight.

SETTING AND ATMOSPHERE A social gathering place as much as an eatery. Booths line the walls; woodwork and plants throughout. One of the more popular bars in North Beach. Between the entry and the sidewalk is an outdoor dining and lounge area. Excellent for people-watching.

HOUSE SPECIALTIES Pizza, pasta, grilled seafood, and steak; casseroles and stews; Spanish-style paella; duck confit with sausage, baked beans, and bacon; roasted clams.

OTHER RECOMMENDATIONS Pizza with wild mushrooms.

SUMMARY AND COMMENTS A San Francisco landmark and tradition. Many local writers have used it as a writing studio or general hangout. The young man or woman studiously scribbling away while quaffing black coffee may be someone whose work you'll be reading soon. Enrico's devotees will argue to the death that Irish coffee was invented here. Every night, patrons ensconce themselves in the outdoor lounge and fend off the San Francisco fog with this warm and cheering draught. Who cares where it was invented? This is the place to drink it.

Farallon ★ ★ ★ ★ ★

MEDITERRANEAN SEAFOOD   EXPENSIVE   QUALITY ★★★★★   VALUE ★★★★★

450 Post Street off Union Square; ☎ 415-956-6969;
www.farallonrestaurant.com

Reservations As far in advance as possible. **When to go** Lunch and dinner. **Entree range** $34–$39. **Payment** All major credit cards. **Service rating** ★★★★. **Friendliness rating** ★★★★. **Parking** Street or various lots close by. **Bar** Full service. **Wine selection** Excellent. **Dress** Business, dressy. **Disabled access** Yes. **Customers** Locals, tourists, businesspeople. **Hours** Tuesday–Thursday, 11:30 a.m.–2:30 p.m. and 5:30 p.m.–10:30 p.m.; Friday and Saturday, 11:30 a.m.–2:30 p.m. and 5:30 p.m.–11 p.m.; Sunday, 5–10 p.m.; Monday, 5:30–10 p.m.

SETTING AND ATMOSPHERE A total sensory experience. Farallon's décor is an imaginative seascape done with fine art and whimsy. The entrance and bar area are a kelp-and-seaweed forest of stylized bronze plants wrapped around glowing light columns that rise to the ceiling. Multi-colored blown-glass jellyfish lamps hang at various levels, quietly lighting the sand-colored walls. A bronze seaweed staircase curves up to an intimate balcony overlooking the entrance area. The restaurant swirls like the tide out toward the main dining area, passing a recessed bar overhung with suggestions of fossilized whalebones, flowing by a scooped-out section of rounded booths and whorled columns. The mosaic floor continues to rise gently to the central dining room, a place reminiscent of some ancient sea cave. It's dominated by a curved mosaic ceiling and the huge, fantastical sea anemone lamps hanging from it. Diners are seated in deep, comfortable booths or rounded tables all dressed in snowy napery and elegant table settings. Dinner here needs to be long and slow!

HOUSE SPECIALTIES Seafood superbly cooked and imaginatively presented. Try iced shellfish indulgence: a dish full of surprises and meant to be shared; roasted mahimahi with arugula pistou; pan-roasted black mussels with pommes frites, arugula, and roasted shallot crème fraîche; shellfish bisque with chives.

OTHER RECOMMENDATIONS The chef's Coastal Cuisine Dinner: an opulent three-course meal at $45 per person served nightly until 6:30 p.m. The meat dishes: red wine–braised veal cheeks or roasted double-cut pork chop with butternut squash gratin. Every dessert, especially the chocolate mud pie with peppermint ice cream.

SUMMARY AND COMMENTS Farallon is a very popular place. Come early, before the appreciative crowds sweep in to savor the incredible décor, fine food, and superb service.

First Crush ★ ★ ★

CALIFORNIAN	MODERATE	QUALITY ★ ★ ★ ½	VALUE ★ ★ ★ ★

101 Cyril Magnin Street, Union Square; ☎ 415-982-7874; www.firstcrush.com

Reservations Accepted. When to go Anytime. Entree range $16–$27. Payment All major credit cards. Service rating ★ ★ ★. Friendliness rating ★ ★ ★. Parking Street. Bar Full service. Wine selection Huge. Dress Business casual. Disabled access Yes. Customers 20–30-something locals. Hours Sunday–Wednesday, 5–11 p.m.; Thursday–Saturday, 5 p.m.–midnight.

SETTING AND ATMOSPHERE Situated on a corner with lots of picture windows, this place offers a splendid view of San Francisco walking by. The L-shaped dining room has what appear to be church pews (cushioned) running along the walls, and comfy booths in the corners. Despite the windows on the world of San Francisco, it maintains a cozy cavelike atmosphere.

HOUSE SPECIALTIES Reflecting the tapas trend, First Crush offers about 11 "small dishes" that are super for sharing as appetizers, or for constructing a complete dinner of 6–8 courses. The menu is categorized by source. "From the garden" includes wild mushroom and roasted vegetable risotto. "From the sea" offers seared ahi tuna and horseradish crusted salmon. "From the land" provides such things as grilled rack of lamb on braised fava beans and asparagus. "From the pasture" offers superb cheeses.

OTHER RECOMMENDATIONS There are also about ten full-size entrees available every night.

SUMMARY AND COMMENTS So many selections from the menu, and 325(!) from the wine list make it almost a daunting task to dine here. But come in, sit down, close your eyes, and just point to places on the menu. You can't go wrong. And it's one of the best of the few places downtown for a late-night nosh.

Fleur de Lys ★ ★ ★ ★

| FRENCH | EXPENSIVE | QUALITY ★ ★ ★ ★ ★ | VALUE ★ ★ ★ ★ |

777 Sutter Street, Union Square; ☎ 415-673-7779; www.fleurdelyssf.com

Reservations Accepted. When to go Anytime. Entree range 3-, 4-, or 5-course dinner, $70–$88; vegetarian, $70; with an additional $65 for wine pairings. Payment All major credit cards. Service rating ★★★★. Friendliness rating ★★★★. Parking Valet, $10. Bar Full service. Wine selection Excellent. Dress Dressy. Disabled access Yes. Customers Locals, tourists. Hours Monday–Thursday, 6–9:30 p.m.; Friday and Saturday, 5:30–10:30 p.m.; Sunday, closed.

SETTING AND ATMOSPHERE The interior, designed to resemble the inside of a silken tent, recalls a movie set for the story of a sheik or a medieval joust. Lots of mirrors and cubbyholes; a very busy décor that can entertain the eye throughout the meal. But it's never too much. It's exotic, colorful, entertaining, yet not distracting. All the soft surfaces help to maintain low noise level, but this is also a place where thoughtful patrons come come to dine in a serene atmosphere. While many places in the city have terrifically high noise levels, you can actually have a quiet conversation here.

HOUSE SPECIALTIES Many seafood selections: sea scallops with truffle bread pudding; braised Alaskan halibut; pistachio-crusted salmon; sea bass with black mussels; marinated venison loin with sautéed pineapple julienne; a duo of veal tenderloin and braised veal shank. A reasonably priced wine list, considering the venue.

OTHER RECOMMENDATIONS The Menu Gourmand, offering a fixed selection of appetizer, fish, entree, and dessert; or the larger Menu Prestige. Both help contain costs in an expensive restaurant.

SUMMARY AND COMMENTS One of the best, most fun restaurants in town. The service is attentive and formal, yet, like the décor, it's never too much. The food presentations are always pleasing, showcasing the natural colors and textures of the food; nothing is too sculpted or contrived. It's easy to spend three hours at dinner here, and that's exactly what you should do. It's well worth a splurge.

Fog City Diner ★ ★ ★

AMERICAN	MODERATE	QUALITY ★★★★	VALUE ★★★★

**1300 Battery Street, North Beach; ☎ 415-982-2000;
www.fogcitydiner.com**

Reservations Recommended. **When to go** Off hours if possible. **Entree range** lunch, $10–$20; dinner, $12–$28. **Payment** All major credit cards. **Service rating** ★★★. **Friendliness rating** ★★★. **Parking** Street. **Bar** Full service. **Wine selection** Good. **Dress** Casual. **Disabled access** Yes. **Customers** Locals, tourists. **Hours** Monday–Thursday, 11 a.m.–10 p.m.; Friday, 11 a.m.–11 p.m.; Saturday, 10:30 a.m.–11 p.m.; Sunday, 10:30 a.m.–9 p.m.; Saturday and Sunday brunch, 10:30 a.m.–3 p.m.

SETTING AND ATMOSPHERE The Fog City experience starts from a block away. The streamliner-styled cafe, ablaze with neon, shimmers through the fog like the ghost of a lost dining car. An art deco interior, dark wood paneling, comfy leather booths with etched class dividers, and low lighting provide the relaxed atmosphere necessary for comfort-food dining. About the booths and tables are brass name plaques of regulars past and present who have graced Fog City over its history.

HOUSE SPECIALTIES "There is nothing so American as the diner," states Fog City's menu, and there's never been a diner quite like this one. Yes, you can find your shakes, burgers, and fries, but the hungry diner just in from wandering The City can also choose from The Large Plates: Dungeness crab cioppino with prawns and local fish; macaroni and gouda cheese with Hobb's ham and English peas. If portion size is important, look to The Small Plates: grilled quail with pancetta and sweet peas; seared halibut with crab hollandaise; ahi tuna tartare with jalapeño, mint, and cilantro. A specialty of the house is the combination bread plate: jalapeño corn sticks, sourdough loaf with leek and basil butter, and cheddar biscuits. Coupled with a glass of wine, it's a hardy snack, indeed.

OTHER RECOMMENDATIONS The raw oyster bar and the banana bread pudding.

SUMMARY AND COMMENTS The generous booth size offers diners a chance to get together with friends or family for the pleasure of great comfort food and time together. It's a popular place, so make reservations or come during off hours. Singles and couples can enjoy dining at the convivial bar.

Fringale ★ ★ ★ ★

FRENCH BASQUE	MODERATE	QUALITY ★★★★½	VALUE ★★★★★

570 Fourth Street, SoMa; ☎ 415-543-0573; www.fringalerestaurant.com

Reservations Recommended. **When to go** Lunch and dinner. **Entree range** $16–$24. **Payment** AE, MC, V. **Service rating** ★★★★. **Friendliness rating** ★★★★. **Parking** Street. **Bar** Full service. **Wine selection** Limited but good. **Dress** Business casual. **Disabled access** Yes. **Customers** Locals, businesspeople, tourists. **Hours** Tuesday–Thursday, 11:30 a.m.–3 p.m. and 5:30–10 p.m.; Friday, 11:30 a.m.–3 p.m. and 5:30–10:30 p.m.; Saturday, 5:30–10:30 p.m.; closed Sunday.

SETTING AND ATMOSPHERE After 15 years, Fringale has settled comfortably into this corner of SoMa, creating the warm ambience of a southern French bistro; a respite from the frenetic energy of Fourth Street. Chefs Gerald Hirigoyen and Jean-Marie Legendre, together with their superb staff, provide a convivial, relaxed atmosphere that has succeeded in building up a cadre of regulars, one of whom often shares his wine with fellow diners.

HOUSE SPECIALTIES   Modern interpretations drawn from the rich culinary history of French-Basque fare: duck leg confit with green lentils; sautéed prosciutto and sheep's milk cheese terrine; steamed mussels with marinated chopped tomatoes and coriander; New York Angus steak with red-wine butter and pomme frites; marinated, roasted rack of lamb with potato gratin.

OTHER RECOMMENDATIONS   Pork tenderloin confit with cabbage, onion, and apple marmalade; all desserts, but especially the sorbet du jour, an intense palate cleanser, and the exquisite bittersweet chocolate truffles.

SUMMARY AND COMMENTS   Embraced by the friendliest of staffs, surrounded by décor both casual and elegant, and comfortably seated, the diner gradually relaxes into the bistro mood. Chefs Hirigoyan and Legendre have created a taste of the south of France here in the south of Market.

Grand Café ★ ★ ★ ½

MEDITERRANEAN	EXPENSIVE	QUALITY ★★★★½	VALUE ★★★★

501 Geary Street, Union Square; ☎ 415-292-0101;
www.grandcafe-sf.com

Reservations Accepted. **When to go** Anytime. **Entree range** Lunch $12–$20; dinner $19–$28. **Payment** All major credit cards. **Service rating** ★★★★. **Friendliness rating** ★★★. **Parking** Street, nearby lots. **Bar** Full service. **Wine selection** Extensive. **Dress** Evening casual. **Disabled access** Yes. **Customers** Locals, tourists. **Hours** Monday–Thursday, 7–10:30 a.m., 11:30 a.m.–2:30 p.m., and 5:30–10 p.m.; Friday, 7–10:30 a.m., 11:30 a.m.–2:30 p.m., and 5:30–11 p.m.; Saturday, 8 a.m.–2:30 p.m. (brunch) and 5:30–11 p.m.; Sunday, 9 a.m.–2:30 p.m. (brunch) and 5:30–11 p.m.

SETTING AND ATMOSPHERE   Originally a hotel ballroom, and a very elegant one. Everything is marble, brasswork, and wood. Huge columns support the high chandelier ceiling. There is always a lot of hubbub and goings on here. Tourists gawk at the splendor, regulars table-hop, everybody eats and drinks well.

HOUSE SPECIALTIES   It's a Mediterranean-inspired menu with a good balance of meat, fish, and fowl. For lunch, start with a salad of hearts of romaine and move on to sautéed salmon with lentils, or try the croque monsieur on house-baked sour-cream bread. For dinner, consider a starter of Prince Edward Island mussels steamed in white wine, torchon of foie gras, or chef Paul Arenstam's signature dish: wild-mushroom tart with black truffle sabayon. Follow with sautéed skate wing with braised cabbage; proscuitto-wrapped pork with brussels sprouts; pan-roasted venison with oxtail potato galette. Selections change seasonally, so be prepared to dine according to local offerings from Mother Nature, not to what's coming in from Chile.

OTHER RECOMMENDATIONS Side dishes can make a meal. Mashed potatoes that are good enough to have for dessert, sautéed summer beans with garlic pommes frites, steamed spinach with roasted garlic.

SUMMARY AND COMMENTS This is a good place to dress up. It's very fancy without being snooty. It opens with a large and comfy cocktail lounge, but it's a very popular watering hole and sometimes, simply impossible to find space. Have a drink at your table. Being a block from the Geary Theater, this is a good place before or after a show.

Greens ★★★★

VEGETARIAN   MODERATE   QUALITY ★★★★   VALUE ★★★★

Building A, Fort Mason Center (Marina Boulevard and Buchanan), Marina District; ☎ 415-771-6222; www.greensrestaurant.com

Reservations Required. When to go Lunch. Entree range $16–$23. Payment AE, MC, V. Service rating ★★★. Friendliness rating ★★★. Parking Lot. Bar Beer, wine. Wine selection Very good. Dress Casual. Disabled access Yes. Customers All walks of life. Hours Tuesday–Saturday, noon–2:30 p.m. and 5:30–9 p.m.; Monday, 5:30–9 p.m. (Saturday, prix fixe only, $48); Sunday brunch, 10:30 a.m.–2 p.m.

SETTING AND ATMOSPHERE Full view of the Golden Gate Bridge bordered by the southern promontories of Marin County. Large and airy; the restaurant was formerly an enclosed pier. Polished wood floors, lovely paintings on the walls, and comfortable lounging area. Serene atmosphere.

HOUSE SPECIALTIES The menu changes with the seasons, but you might be treated to mesquite grilled winter vegetables; salad of watercress and escarole, fresh pea ravioli with saffron butter; masa harina pastry filled with butternut squash, potatoes, tomatoes, grilled onions, and cheddar cheese.

OTHER RECOMMENDATIONS Chocolate hazelnut mousse cake.

SUMMARY AND COMMENTS No health food, no hippie food, no orange and parsley garnish, but the finest in vegetarian cuisine. This is not a PC restaurant; no one is on a crusade here. Its reason for being is the best of dining without meat. When it opened 20 years ago, this was the only restaurant of its kind. Some people are saying that it's not keeping up with the new competition. It's still good, though not quite great. And it still has what is arguably the best Sunday brunch in town.

Harris' Restaurant ★★★★ ½

STEAK   EXPENSIVE   QUALITY ★★★★★   VALUE ★★★★½

2100 Van Ness Avenue, Civic Center; ☎ 415-673-1888; www.harrisrestaurant.com

Reservations Recommended. When to go Anytime. Entree range $22–$42. Payment All major credit cards. Service rating ★★★★★. Friendliness rating ★★★★. Parking Valet ($7). Bar Full service. Wine selection Excellent. Dress Casually elegant. Disabled access Yes. Customers Locals, tourists, regulars. Hours Sunday–Thursday, 5:30–10:30 p.m.; Friday and Saturday, 5:30–11 p.m.

SETTING AND ATMOSPHERE Elegant old San Francisco charm with dark wood paneling the color of rich chocolate, 17-foot beamed ceilings, and large brass chandeliers. It opened in 1984, but never feels stodgy or outdated thanks to a lively, stylish menu and an energetic staff. Pastoral murals of cows grazing along the banks of Kings River in central California, painted by local artist Barnaby Conrad, grace the walls. The bar is dark and alluring, with a fine jazz trio Thursday through Saturday nights. In the dining room, conversation hums nicely, not noisily. It's a generally older and affluent crowd of diners, whose experience has clearly taught them the right place to get the beef.

HOUSE SPECIALTIES Well, beef. In all shapes and one size—big. Here, they believe in bounty. There are chicken and seafood dishes too, but really the beef is the thing. And if it is possible to fall in love with a steak, this is where it will happen. Harris' uses a 21-day dry-aging process for its Midwestern corn-fed beef, which produces tender and succulent cuts of meat. Check out the slabs hanging in the famous display window out front as you're waiting for your table. Then start with the famous house-smoked salmon appetizer, fresh oysters on the half shell with three dipping sauces, or the traditional onion soup. Get some classic side dishes of sautéed mushrooms, creamed spinach, or crisp green beans. Then prepare for the best beef ever—the filet mignon Rossini, with grilled Sonoma foie gras and black truffle and cabernet sauce. As thick as it is wide—practically round—and the texture, like slicing through velvet. Or have the Porterhouse and exclaim, "Now that's a steak!"

OTHER RECOMMENDATIONS This is the time, the place, and the mood for a classic martini. Try the King Eider Martini: Duckhorn Winery's King Eider dry vermouth with Grey Goose vodka and a swirl of lemon in Harris' traditional barrel presentation—basically a double martini, but in a single glass so the remainder is kept frosty in a little bottle in a mini wooden barrel of ice. The wine list is long and diverse, both in geography and style, with an emphasis on Napa and Sonoma. And while steak houses are usually not known for their desserts, Harris' is the exception. The peach-blueberry crisp is so good you'll be scraping every last crumb of crisp off the edges of the ramekin.

SUMMARY AND COMMENTS This old-style but upscale spot is a refreshing change from so many too-mod, too-trendy scenes. It's elegant yet comfy. A highly professional staff, very familiar with the restaurant's offerings. Many have been there for years, so trust them for recommendations. You will be leaving with a doggie bag.

Hawthorne Lane ★ ★ ★ ★

| CALIFORNIAN | EXPENSIVE | QUALITY ★★★½ | VALUE ★★★★ |

22 Hawthorne Street, SoMa; ☎ 415-777-9779; www.hawthornelane.com

Reservations Recommended. When to go Anytime. Entree range lunch, $13–$23; dinner, $14–$36. Payment All major credit cards. Service rating ★★★★. Friendliness rating ★★★. Parking Street, valet ($8, lunch; $10, dinner). Bar Full service. Wine selection Excellent, $25 corkage fee. Dress Business. Disabled access Yes.

Customers Demanding locals with cash. **Hours** Monday–Thursday, 11:30 a.m.–1:30 p.m. and 5:30–9 p.m.; Friday, 11:30 a.m.–1:30 p.m. and 5:30–10 p.m.; Saturday, 5:30–10 p.m.; Sunday, 5:30–9 p.m.; closed on some holidays.

SETTING AND ATMOSPHERE This is arguably one of the most gorgeous restaurants in The City. It's like dining in a museum of fine art. The layout is sleek and modern with clean lines, lots of warm wood, huge floral arrangements, and soft, comfy booths that you can sink into and not want to leave. Beautiful paintings grace the walls, and even the dishes are works of art. It enriches the experience if you contemplate them before eating from them.

HOUSE SPECIALTIES Start with house breads, a basket of which will be delivered to your table upon arrival. They are varied and delicious, pretty and whimsical, and the scent of the sweet butter is seductive. And that's just the bread and butter! Signature dishes include duck roasted in a Chinese inspired–style with green onion buns; grilled pork chop with caramelized onions and apples.

OTHER RECOMMENDATIONS The menu changes with the seasons, and chef Bridget Batson was raised on a farm, so she is keenly attuned to vegetables and fruits at their times of harvest. Watch especially for seasonal soups and salads. She is especially fond of peas and other legumes, and she will seduce you with them.

SUMMARY AND COMMENTS In keeping with the décor, the dishes at Hawthorne Lane are beautiful to look at. This is truly food as art. And while the menu is very diverse, it is not confused. Everything fits nicely together. Never worry that one dish will conflict with another. Order what you will and feel free to share with your tablemates. You'll all be enriched.

Helmand ★ ★ ★

AFGHAN	INEXPENSIVE	QUALITY ★ ★ ★ ★	VALUE ★ ★ ★ ★ ★

430 Broadway, North Beach; ☎ 415-362-0641

Reservations Accepted. **When to go** Anytime. **Entree range** $10–$17. **Payment** AE, MC, V. **Service rating** ★★★★. **Friendliness rating** ★★★. **Parking** 468 Broadway; valet $6 on weekdays and $10 on weekends. **Bar** Full service. **Wine selection** Fair. **Dress** Casual. **Disabled access** Yes. **Customers** Locals, businesspeople, tourists. **Hours** Sunday–Thursday, 5:30–10 p.m.; Friday and Saturday, 5:30–11 p.m.

SETTING AND ATMOSPHERE Helmand is named for a river in Afghanistan. Rooms are decorated in classical Persian simplicity, and the tables are set with Western, though not stuffy, formality. Beautiful Persian rugs are everywhere; walls are hung with Afghan portraits. Afghan strings and flutes play softly in the background.

HOUSE SPECIALTIES Afghan food is heavily influenced by neighbors India and Persia. It's based on flat breads and rice, fresh vegetables, and lamb and chicken cooked in mild spice mixtures. Tomatoes or yogurt are common bases for sauces. Dishes include rack of lamb with Persian spices; chicken sautéed with yellow split peas; potatoes and garbanzo beans in vinaigrette with cilantro; meat pies flavored with onion; leek-filled ravioli.

OTHER RECOMMENDATIONS A good number of meatless dishes and salads. The baked fresh pumpkin with yogurt sauce is music in your mouth. Order two!

SUMMARY AND COMMENTS This is a good family restaurant, and as such it's a bellwether for the changing neighborhood, which was once the heart of the city's topless district. The low prices and the generous portions make this one of the best restaurant deals in town. And it's the only Afghan restaurant in town—it's crowded on weekends.

House of Prime Rib ★ ★ ★ ½

AMERICAN	EXPENSIVE	QUALITY ★★★★	VALUE ★★★★

1906 Van Ness Avenue, Civic Center; ☎ 415-885-4605

Reservations Strongly advised. When to go Dinner only. Entree range $28–$35. Payment AE, MC, V. Service rating ★★★. Friendliness rating ★★★½. Parking Valet, $9. Bar Full service. Wine selection Good. Dress Business, dressy. Disabled access Yes. Customers Locals, businesspeople, tourists. Hours Monday–Thursday, 5:30–10 p.m.; Friday, 5–10 p.m.; Saturday, 4:30–10 p.m.; Sunday, 4–10 p.m.

SETTING AND ATMOSPHERE Plush. Large, comfortable rooms with booths and alcoves; tables set with heavy napery. A mirrored bar with hardwood floor and fireplace in the lounge. Wall adorned with murals and heavy draperies. The lounge has a fireplace that is delicious to sit by in the cooler weather and sip a well-made martini.

HOUSE SPECIALTIES Prime rib, of course. You can have it thick cut or "English cut"—several thinner slices that some people say brings out more flavor. The jury is out on this, but either taste is accommodated here. Baked or mashed potato; creamed spinach; generous tossed salad.

OTHER RECOMMENDATIONS Fresh catch of the day for the occasional patron who prefers not to have red meat. A good children's menu for $9.45.

SUMMARY AND COMMENTS One of the older restaurants in town and a temple to red meat. It would be hard to find more civilized surroundings for indulging in that most primitive of appetites. The meat is wheeled to your table on a silver steam cart, and the great haunch is displayed to you in all its glory. "Thick cut, madam? English cut, sir?" It can make you proud to be a carnivore.

Il Fornaio ★ ★ ★ ½

ITALIAN	MODERATE	QUALITY ★★½	VALUE ★★★★

1265 Battery Street, Financial District; ☎ 415-986-0100; www.ilfornaio.com

Reservations Recommended. When to go Anytime. Entree range Lunch, $10–$18; dinner, $16–$30. Payment AE, MC, V. Service rating ★★★★. Friendliness rating ★★★★. Parking Valet, metered street. Bar Full service. Wine selection Good. Dress Business casual. Disabled access Good. Customers Local, tourists. Hours Monday–Thursday, 11:30 a.m.–10 p.m.; Friday, 11:30 a.m.–11 p.m.; Saturday, 9 a.m.–11 p.m.; Sunday, 9 a.m.–5 p.m.

SETTING AND ATMOSPHERE   Il Fornaio is set in a corner of Levi Plaza adjacent to one of the most beautiful fountains in San Francisco. Diners can enjoy the cascading waters from the sheltered outdoor patio or from the spacious, high-ceilinged dining room accented in dark wood and white marble. Large mural-like paintings cover the walls, bringing to mind a Venetian villa. A convivial atmosphere reigns among the patrons—lively but not loud. Those wishing to sit in the inner dining room can observe the chefs and bakers at work in the open kitchen. If you arrive early, have a drink at the long, curving, black-and-white marble bar—a sensuous experience in itself.

HOUSE SPECIALTIES   The antipasta dishes are simple but large enough to share: try duck lasagna with artichokes and butternut squash pasta, and calamaretti fritti or baby squid lightly floured and deep fried, served with spicy tomato-basil Sicilian olive oil. A large variety of house-made pastas are available, as well as Italian specialties from the wood-fired rotisserie and mesquite grill: pollo Toscano with Petaluma chicken; anatra alla Perugina with Petaluma duck; and scaloppini al Carciofi with local veal tenderloin. All entrees served with a variety of potatoes and vegetables.

OTHER RECOMMENDATIONS   A special menu featuring dishes from various regions of Italy is offered monthly. Also try the thin-crust pizzas with house-made marinara sauce and real mozzarella baked in the wood-fired oven. And the full-service deli and delicious bakery are great for building picnic lunches in the nearby park.

SUMMARY AND COMMENTS   Il Fornaio meets its goal of providing the diner with authentic Italian food made with the freshest and best products available. The waitstaff is friendly and knowledgeable and round off a fine dining experience.

Izzy's Steak and Chop House   ★ ★ ★

STEAK HOUSE	MODERATE	QUALITY ★★★★	VALUE ★★★★★

3345 Steiner Street, Marina District; ☎ 415-563-0487

Reservations Accepted. **When to go** Anytime. **Entree range** $10–$24. **Payment** All major credit cards. **Service rating** ★★★. **Friendliness rating** ★★★. **Parking** Street; lot. **Bar** Full service. **Wine selection** Good. **Dress** Casual. **Disabled access** Yes. **Customers** Locals, businesspeople, tourists. **Hours** Monday–Saturday, 5:30–10 p.m.; Sunday, 5–10 p.m.

SETTING AND ATMOSPHERE   A modernized version of an old-time steak house. Sometimes fills to overflowing with locals who come for beef, booze, and merriment. You'll see a lot of back slapping, glad handing, laughing, and carrying on here. In the bar, where patrons are in no particular hurry, the generations mix as the big drinks flow.

HOUSE SPECIALTIES   Aged Black Angus beef served in he-man portions: New York steak; pepper steak; Cajun-style blackened steak; untampered with, unalloyed steak.

OTHER RECOMMENDATIONS   Creamed spinach. Huge and tasty desserts.

SUMMARY AND COMMENTS Many of the patrons are regulars who live in the neighborhood and know each other. When they meet here, it's party time. Don't come for quiet, and don't come overdressed. Come hungry and happy. On Fridays and Saturdays they can't accommodate parties of more than eight.

Jardiniere ★ ★ ★ ★ ★

CALIFORNIAN	EXPENSIVE	QUALITY ★ ★ ★ ★ ★	VALUE ★ ★ ★ ★ ½

300 Grove Street, Civic Center; ☎ 415-861-5555; www.jardiniere.com

Reservations Recommended. When to go Anytime. Entree range $19–$41; 6-course tasting menu $79. Payment All major credit cards. Service rating ★★★★. Friendliness rating ★★★. Parking Street. Bar Full service. Wine selection Short but good. Dress Casual. Disabled access Yes. Customers Locals, tourists. Hours Sunday–Wednesday, 5–10:30 p.m.; Thursday–Saturday, 5–11:30 p.m.

SETTING AND ATMOSPHERE If décor were food you could get fat in this place. In a city full of gorgeous restaurants, this is one of the most gorgeous. Designed by Pat Kuleto, California's most famous restaurant designer, this is over-the-top elegance. But it's in that uniquely San Francisco style that doesn't intimidate. Its sense of frontier egalitarianism says "come one, come all." On the ground floor, the circular bar is the first thing you see, and above it the bar-sized opening in the floor of the second level, and above that the enormous ceiling light. All is plush, with deep carpet and heavy draperies, dark chocolatey woodwork, and heavy furniture.

HOUSE SPECIALTIES A very innovative California-style menu. Where else could you find chestnut spaetzle to support your pork tenderloin with caramelized parsnips? And this is one of the few restaurants brave enough to offer Brussels sprouts. In most restaurants, people won't order them, but at Jardiniere people can't imagine not liking something. Things such as Alaskan sablefish with escarole, smoked bacon, gala apples, and fingerling potatoes; warm bread salad with baby artichokes and marinated Crescenza cheese.

OTHER RECOMMENDATIONS Lamb dishes are especially good here, and you may be offered a plate of lamb in two or three ways such as roast or sausage. Desserts, like warm chocolate cake, take a backseat to none.

SUMMARY AND COMMENTS About a five-minute walk from the opera house, symphony hall, and Herbst Theater, Jardiniere is a great choice for dinner and a show. But it's also the perfect restaurant for lingering. The atmosphere is seductive, and the pampering is good. Upstairs, a live jazz duo plays at just the right volume and tempo. This is one of the most civilized and civilizing places you could hope to find. Definitely worth a splurge.

John's Grill ★ ★ ★

STEAK HOUSE	MODERATE	QUALITY ★ ★ ★ ½	VALUE ★ ★ ★ ★ ★

63 Ellis Street, Union Square; ☎ 415-986-3274; www.johnsgrill.com

Reservations Accepted. When to go Anytime. Entree range Lunch, $12–27; dinner, $20–45. Payment AE, D, DC, MC, V. Service rating ★★★. Friendliness rating ★★★. **Parking** Street, lot. **Bar** Full service. **Wine selection** Good. **Dress** Casual, business. **Disabled access** No. **Customers** Locals, businesspeople, tourists. **Hours** Monday–Saturday, 11 a.m.–10 p.m.; Sunday, 5–10 p.m.

SETTING AND ATMOSPHERE Dark wood and brass trim; the 1930s at their best. You're transported to another (many would say better) San Francisco. Sepia photographs of celebs and local potentates cover the west wall. Deep and narrow with booths and small tables; the general feeling is one of cozy intimacy.

HOUSE SPECIALTIES Steaks, chops, and seafood. Dungeness crab cakes (a must at any historic place in the city); fried oysters; Sam Spade's lamb chops; broiled swordfish with a Dijon mushroom sauce; a giant porterhouse steak; broiled calf livers; chicken Jerusalem.

OTHER RECOMMENDATIONS Variety of salads; clam chowder; oysters Wellington.

SUMMARY AND COMMENTS "Spade went to John's Grill, asked the waiter to hurry his order of chops, baked potato, sliced tomatoes . . . and was smoking a cigarette with his coffee when . . . " Open since 1908, this landmark restaurant was the setting for Dashiell Hammett's novel *The Maltese Falcon*. To dine or drink martinis here is to imbibe the history and literature of the city.

Kokkari Estiatorio ★★★

GREEK	EXPENSIVE	QUALITY ★★★★½	VALUE ★★★★

200 Jackson Street (at Front), Financial District; ☎ 415-981-0983; www.kokkari.com

Reservations Recommended. **When to go** Anytime. **Entree range** Lunch, $15–$26; dinner, $19–$35. **Payment** AE, D, DC, MC, V. **Service rating** ★★★. **Friendliness rating** ★★★. **Parking** Valet at dinner $8, metered street, lots. **Bar** Full service. **Wine selection** Extensive. **Dress** Fashionable, business, or semiformal attire. **Disabled access** Reasonable (elevator to restrooms). **Customers** Well-heeled crowd of locals and tourists. **Hours** Monday–Thursday, 11:30 a.m.–2:30 p.m. and 5:30–10 p.m.; Friday, 11:30 a.m.–2:30 p.m. and 5:30–11 p.m.; Saturday, 5–11 p.m.; bar menu, daily, 2:30–5:30 p.m.

SETTING AND ATMOSPHERE Kokkari has a dramatic setting with a number of unique details such as huge wood-shuttered windows and an enormous fireplace. Everything, from the chairs to the water glasses, is oversized. The dark and elegant space envelops and transports you to a far-off place more elegant than Athens.

HOUSE SPECIALTIES Traditional Greek dishes are put in their best light through thoughtful preparation and good ingredients. Lamb shanks and chops brought in from a Texas ranch have diners raving. Seafood offerings such as roasted grouper steak and a grilled swordfish are simply but beautifully prepared. A plateful of Greek spreads makes a mouthwatering appetizer with tzatziki so rich that it is hard to believe it was made with yogurt alone; and don't forget the hot grilled pita bread.

OTHER RECOMMENDATIONS You can't go wrong when ordering at this restaurant, so don't be afraid to try something different. The chefs at Kokkari have respect for tradition but also know how to innovate. A bowl of risotto with herbed feta and fava beans uses Greek staples in the style of California cuisine. A roasted quail with poached figs and quail jus demonstrates similar inspiration. Desserts such as yogurt sorbet and walnut and honey baklava lift up the palate at the end of a long meal.

SUMMARY AND COMMENTS   Kokkari has a grand and lavish feel befitting a special occasion. Two separate rooms are available for private events, and the main dining rooms, while not packed, feel somehow communal. Its the perfect setting for a clan-like family celebration. The food here is fit for kings but retains its connection to the earth. A truly outstanding dining experience.

Kuleto's ★ ★ ★ ½

CALIFORNIAN/ITALIAN	MODERATE	QUALITY ★★★★	VALUE ★★★★

221 Powell Street, Union Square; ☎ 415-397-7720; www.kuletos.com

Reservations Recommended. **When to go** Anytime. **Entree range** $14–$25. **Payment** All major credit cards. **Service rating** ★★★. **Friendliness rating** ★★★★. **Parking** Street. **Bar** Full service. **Wine selection** Good. **Dress** Smart/casual. **Disabled access** Yes. **Customers** Tourists and local regulars. **Hours** Monday–Friday, 7 a.m.–11 p.m.; Saturday and Sunday, 8 a.m.–11 p.m.

SETTING AND ATMOSPHERE   Enter through the adjacent wine bar with its hardwood floor, marble table tops, and friendly staff. Here in a corner of the lobby of the elegant Villa Florence hotel, ask for the advice of the bar staff on how to begin your wine and dine experience. After a glass of something sparkling, amble over to the main restaurant. High vaulted ceilings, Italian marble floors, wrought iron and copper railings backed by dark wood and warm lighting provide a gleeful combination of old San Francisco elegance and Italian verve and vitality.

HOUSE SPECIALTIES   Contemporary Italian cuisine with a concentration on fresh Californian ingredients. Excellent house-made pastas, traditional Italian salads with balsamic vinegar, mesquite-grilled fresh fish, and flavorful meats. All baked goods, pastries, and desserts are prepared daily in-house.

OTHER RECOMMENDATIONS   Desserts are outstanding. Crisp cannoli pastry shells filled with mascarpone cream and toasted pistachios; warm peach-and-blackberry cobbler with house-made vanilla gelato; lime-champagne zabaglione with fresh seasonal berries; tiramisu, espresso, and rum-soaked ladyfingers with mascarpone cream.

SUMMARY AND COMMENTS   This is a warm and festive place, always full of happy, convivial people looking for a good meal and a good time. Tourists and locals alike find their way here, and they usually find their way back.

La Toque ★ ★ ★ ★ ½

FRENCH/CALIFORNIAN	EXPENSIVE	QUALITY ★★★★★	VALUE ★★★★½

1140 Rutherford Cross Road, Rutherford; ☎ 707-963-9770; www.latoque.com

Reservations Required. **When to go** Dinner. **Entree range** A fixed-price tasting menu averages $100 per person. **Payment** All major credit cards. **Service rating** ★★★★★. **Friendliness rating** ★★★★. **Parking** Lot. **Bar** Wine only. **Wine selection** Excellent. **Dress** Business or business casual. **Disabled access** Yes. **Customers** Locals and tourists in the know. **Hours** Wednesday–Sunday, first seating at 5:30 p.m., second seating at 8:30 p.m.

SETTING AND ATMOSPHERE Walk into rustic Wine Country elegance. The room has the feel of a small, country-style cathedral with its high, airy spaces and oculus window at the fore. But it's stripped down to the bare essentials of light, shadow, quiet color, and the soft, easy tone of conversation. Background music is surprisingly hip for such a temple to gastronomy, ranging from soft jazz to 1960s rock, yet it's at such low volume it never screams for your attention.

HOUSE SPECIALTIES The menu changes weekly and sometimes with the chef's whim or inspiration, but it always relies on fresh, seasonal ingredients produced, raised, or caught as close to home as possible. In the California Cuisine ideal, you get the genuine taste of the region, not things imported, frozen, or canned or foreign to the native soil. Smooth soups are a frequent item, and the chef makes especially good use of oils and herbs. It's always a fixed-price menu, offering two choices for each of five courses, plus an optional sixth course at an extra charge.

OTHER RECOMMENDATIONS The sommelier is a master of the extensive wine list, and you should rely on him for advice in choosing your wines. With each night's menu, he composes a suggested pairing for each course and this accompanies your menu. At about $62 per person, this is the "cheap" way to go.

SUMMARY AND COMMENTS The locals are very loyal and regular customers. You should reserve a table as far in advance as you can.

Le Cheval ★★★★

VIETNAMESE	MODERATE	QUALITY ★★★★	VALUE ★★★★

1007 Clay Street, Oakland; ☎ 510-763-8495; www.lecheval.com

Reservations Recommended. **When to go** Anytime. **Entree range** Tapas, $4–$9; entrées, $9–$16. **Payment** All major credit cards. **Service rating** ★★★. **Friendliness rating** ★★½. **Parking** Street. **Bar** Full service. **Wine selection** Good. **Dress** Casual. **Disabled access** Good. **Customers** Locals and politicians of all stripes. **Hours** Monday–Saturday, 11 a.m.–9:30 p.m.; Sunday, 5–9:30 p.m.

SETTING AND ATMOSPHERE Elegant without being overwhelming. It's a large venue with three contiguous, different sizes spaces, including the bar. The décor might be called colonial, it might be called classical Vietnamese. There is a lot of polished wood and big round tables for family-style meals. Vietnamese hangings and artworks dot the rather generous landscape. And the place is always crowded and festive and full of hubbub and buzz.

HOUSE SPECIALTIES All the usual suspects of any good Vietnamese restaurant, plus a few rarely seen outside Vietnam. Appetizers include the standard deep fried imperial rolls, as well as the fresh spring rolls filled with shrimp and rice vermicelli. A dish of three roasted quail seems straight out of the last emperor's kitchens. Firepot soups are bubbling cauldrons brought to the table into which diners add their own meat, fish and fowl and enjoy together. Bo 7 Mon is a Vietnamese party favorite, being seven small dishes of beef, each prepared in a different way.

OTHER RECOMMENDATIONS　Vegetarians are easily satisfied with a range of tofu dishes, as well as piles of fresh vegetables cooked to perfection. Try the pea sprouts with garlic. Claypot dishes, both meat and vegetable, are especially rich and savory, have been long simmered in traditional sauces and served in the pot.

ENTERTAINMENT AND AMENITIES　Spotting local politicos, including Oakland mayor and former California governor Jerry Brown.

SUMMARY AND COMMENTS　Le Cheval was an instant hit when it opened in 1985 and it has never sagged or flagged or lost any of its popularity. Efficient servers continue to rush savory and aromatic dishes to crowds of happy diners. The bar tenders know how to shake a proper martini. It might just be one of the best reasons to come to downtown Oakland at night. And it's even worth a trip across the Bay.

Le Colonial ★ ★ ★ ½

| FRENCH/VIETNAMESE | EXPENSIVE | QUALITY ★★★★ | VALUE ★★★ |

20 Cosmo Place (between Taylor and Jones, Sutter and Post), Union Square; ☎ 415-931-3600; www.lecolonialsf.com

Reservations Recommended. **When to go** Anytime. **Entree range** $20–$38. **Payment** All major credit cards. **Service rating** ★★★★. **Friendliness rating** ★★★★. **Parking** Valet, $6 for first hour, $2 each 30 additional minutes. **Bar** Full service. **Wine selection** Very good. **Dress** Casually elegant, no athletic wear. **Disabled access** Yes. **Customers** Trendy locals in the know. **Hours** Sunday–Wednesday, 5:30–10 p.m.; Thursday–Saturday, 5:30–11 p.m.

SETTING AND ATMOSPHERE　Rattan couches and chairs, wooden shutters, ceiling fans, and palm fronds transport you back to a bygone time of colonial enterprise. This 1920s-themed two-tiered French-Vietnamese restaurant certainly does more than serve fine food; between the tropical décor and savory tastes you might well forget you're in San Francisco. Downstairs is the more formal dining area. Upstairs, hipsters enjoy the trendy watering hole where jazz can be heard on Friday and Saturday nights starting at 10 p.m.

HOUSE SPECIALTIES　Most dishes, particularly the appetizers, are for sharing. The crispy spring rolls with shrimp, pork, and chili fish sauce come highly recommended. Many enjoy the seared pot stickers and so should you. They're filled with scallops, ginger, and herbs served with a citrus sauce. Dinner entrees: steamed sea bass wrapped in a banana leaf with shiitake mushrooms, ginger, and scallions is a favorite.

OTHER RECOMMENDATIONS　There's a fine selection of Scotch and lots of tropical concoctions. Smoke on the patio downstairs or upstairs on the outdoor veranda. Other civil establishments in The City only offer the sidewalk.

SUMMARY AND COMMENTS Le Colonial is a good place to relax and take in the social scene of San Francisco. There is plenty to contemplate: Asian-inspired dishes prepared with local ingredients; an urban and cosmopolitan crowd; the sounds of many languages; and the teasing aroma of a varied cuisine. Period photographs from Vietnam grace the walls. The Orient, Europe, and California meet here for a gracious time.

Lefty O'Doul's ★ ★ ½

HOF BRAU	INEXPENSIVE	QUALITY ★★★½	VALUE ★★★★

333 Geary Street, Union Square; ☎ 415-982-8900; www.leftyodouls.biz

Reservations Not accepted. **When to go** Anytime. **Entree range** $7–$12. **Payment** MC, V. **Service rating** ★★. **Friendliness rating** ★★★. **Parking** Street. **Bar** Full service. **Wine selection** House. **Dress** Casual. **Disabled access** Limited. **Customers** Locals, businesspeople. **Hours** Daily, 7 a.m.–2 a.m.; breakfast served daily from 7–11 a.m.; lunch and dinner from 11 a.m.–midnight; bar open until 2 a.m.

SETTING AND ATMOSPHERE A rather gritty sports bar with a steam table and a baby grand piano. Directly across the street from the elegant Michael Mina in the Saint Francis Hotel, Lefty's seems to have been put there deliberately to add counterpoint to the high-toned hostelry and its expensive watering hole.

HOUSE SPECIALTIES All the usual roasts: beef, turkey, ham. Dinner plates, hot open-faced sandwiches. Polish sausage, corned beef and cabbage, soup, salad, and daily specials. Omelettes and pancakes for breakfast.

SUMMARY AND COMMENTS Named for the baseball player, this is a neighborhood institution full of regulars and hungry shoppers. It's big and cavernous, yet it maintains an air of cozy familiarity. It's also considered neutral ground by warring factions. When the San Francisco 49ers won their first Super Bowl, there was pandemonium in the streets and a huge police presence. The celebrations went on long into the night, exhausting cops, revelers, and paddy-wagon drivers. Between skirmishes, both sides could be seen recuperating at adjacent tables in Lefty's.

Louie's Bar & Grill ★ ★

BAR AND GRILL	INEXPENSIVE	QUALITY ★★★½	VALUE ★★★★

55 Stevenson Street, SoMa; ☎ 415-543-3540; www.sflouies.com

Reservations Accepted. **When to go** Lunch. **Entree range** $8–$15. **Payment** AE, D, MC, V. **Service rating** ★★. **Friendliness rating** ★★★★. **Parking** Street. **Bar** Full service. **Wine selection** House. **Dress** Casual. **Disabled access** Yes. **Customers** Locals, businesspeople. **Hours** Monday–Friday, 11 a.m.–10 p.m.; Saturday and Sunday, closed.

SETTING AND ATMOSPHERE A neighborhood tavern in an old brick building. Old photos of old stars and local sports figures and a big oil painting of a leggy nude cover the walls. Pretty much a male hangout, but ladies are welcome.

HOUSE SPECIALTIES Hamburgers and big schooners of draught beer; fried fish of the day; pasta; salads. The menu changes daily, but you can get on the mailing list and learn of advance changes if you want to be a regular. Everything is cooked to order.

OTHER RECOMMENDATIONS The Blue Plate Special.

SUMMARY AND COMMENTS Louie's Bar & Grill is a neighborhood place that considers itself part of the community. After the Loma Prieta earthquake of 1989, Louie's fed locals on the street. Service can be slow, so don't go when you're pressed for time.

Lulu ★ ★ ★ ½

RUSTIC FRENCH/PROVENÇAL   MODERATE   QUALITY ★★★★   VALUE ★★★★

816 Folsom Street, SoMa; ☎ 415-495-5775; www.restaurantlulu.com

Reservations Recommended. **When to go** Anytime. **Entree range** $15–$30. **Payment** AE, DC, MC, V. **Service rating** ★★★. **Friendliness rating** ★★★. **Parking** Valet, $10. **Bar** Full service. **Wine selection** Extensive. **Dress** Fashionably casual. **Disabled access** Good. **Customers** Locals, businesspeople, some tourists. **Hours** Sunday–Thursday, 11:30 a.m.–10 p.m.; Friday and Saturday, 11:30 a.m.–11 p.m.

SETTING AND ATMOSPHERE Towering ceilings, skylights, and statuesque floral arrangements all add to the wide-open feeling of space within this environment. The muted tones of the walls are offset by a vibrant wall mural, which complements the bustling and festive ambience of this place. Family-style dining: massive portions served on gorgeous blue and yellow crockery just perfect for sharing.

HOUSE SPECIALTIES Changing seasonal menu, nightly rotisserie specials. Predominantly Mediterranean influenced dishes: delicious fritto misto with aïoli and Parmesan; squab with roasted apples; a very dramatic serving of iron skillet roasted mussels; incredibly moist pork loin with fennel; fresh halibut with mushrooms, fava beans, and spring onions. The vegetable side dishes are not to be missed. The olive-oil mashed potatoes and piquant broccoli rabe are particular standouts.

OTHER RECOMMENDATIONS The restaurant is making an effort to put more of an emphasis on wine here, now pouring more than 70 different wines by the glass as well as ample choices for dessert. But the bar itself is also worth note, serving a martini prepared perfectly to instructions as well as an interesting liqueur-laced machiotto.

SUMMARY AND COMMENTS It's great to see that the nature of service has improved radically since previous visits. The noise level is a bit daunting at first, but the knowledgeable and helpful staff put one almost immediately at ease. Lulu is a class act from start to finish.

Luna Park ★ ★

AMERICAN   MODERATE   QUALITY ★★★½   VALUE ★★★★

694 Valencia Street, Mission District; ☎ 415-553-8584; www.lunaparksf.com

Reservations Recommended. **When to go** Lunch and dinner. **Entree range** Lunch, $13–$17; dinner, $15–$26. **Payment** AE, DC, MC, V. **Service rating** ★★★. **Friendliness rating** ★★★. **Bar** Full service. **Wine selection** Good. **Dress** Very casual. **Disabled access** Good. **Customers** Locals. **Hours** Monday–Thursday, 11:30 a.m.–2:30 p.m. and 5:30–10:30 p.m.; Friday, 11:30 a.m.–2:30 p.m. and 5:30–11:30 p.m.; Saturday, 11:30 a.m.–3 p.m. (brunch) and 5:30–11:30 p.m.; Sunday, 11:30 a.m.–3 p.m. (brunch) and 5:30–10 p.m.

SETTING AND ATMOSPHERE The Mission District has long been known for down-to-earth restaurants with reasonable prices, and Luna carries on the tradition. A small storefront entrance opens onto an airy rectangular space made cool and inviting by its dark maroon walls. Deep booths line the walls and surround a small central dining area, while colorful crystal chandeliers run the length of the room. The open kitchen bustles with activity and emanates warmth and good smells. A bar extends along one side, providing the neighborhood with a pleasant gathering place.

HOUSE SPECIALTIES Comfort food with patrician taste is what Luna is all about: marinated Hawaiian tuna "poke" with fried wonton chips; pork cutlet stuffed with mushrooms and Gruyère cheese combined with mashed potatoes, string beans, and apple-cranberry sauce; grilled chicken with butternut squash and hazelnut honey.

OTHER RECOMMENDATIONS Desserts made to cure the blues, especially: bananas Foster with banana ice cream and s'mores you make at the table—molten marshmallow and bittersweet chocolate served with house graham cookies.

SUMMARY AND COMMENTS Since Luna is a popular spot, noise can be a big problem. Come early to avoid it or be ready to jump into the bedlam. Management is presently looking into sound abatement devices, but as of this writing, it's still pretty loud.

MacArthur Park ★ ★ ★

AMERICAN	MODERATE	QUALITY ★★★★½	VALUE ★★★★

607 Front Street, Financial District; ☎ 415-398-5700; www.macpark.com

Reservations Recommended. **When to go** Anytime. **Entree range** Lunch, $12–$19; dinner, $12–$38. **Payment** All major credit cards. **Service rating** ★★★. **Friendliness rating** ★★. **Parking** Valet, street, nearby private garages. **Bar** Full service. **Wine selection** Good. **Dress** Casual. **Disabled access** Good. **Customers** Locals, businesspeople. **Hours** Monday–Thursday, 11 a.m.–10 p.m.; Friday, 11 a.m.–11 p.m.; Saturday, 5–10 p.m.; Sunday, 4:30–10 p.m.

SETTING AND ATMOSPHERE Upscale brick and timber loftlike setting with modern Americana art. In the heart of Jackson Square and just down the street from Levi's Plaza, this restaurant has made its home from an old Barbary Coast warehouse built in the early 1900s. There are two upfront bar sections, two dining areas, and an outside patio.

HOUSE SPECIALTIES Upscale barbecue and American comfort food. Grilled beef tenderloin medallions with melted gorgonzola cheese; griddled corn and crab cakes with Maryland-style tartar sauce; dry aged New York steak with onion strings and spinach; famous baby-back ribs with cole slaw and garlic mashed potatoes; grilled pasilla peppers filled with three cheeses and served with salsa cruda; signature tamarind flavored barbecue sauce.

OTHER RECOMMENDATIONS Great bar and wine list featuring microbrew beers on tap, American whiskey, and a good wine list showcasing Zinfandel. One of the best happy hours in town, offering free appetizer with the purchase of a drink.

SUMMARY AND COMMENTS Experienced chef Melissa Miller is masterful at balancing a classic menu with a regular crowd. If everyone but one person in your party wants barbecue, have no fear, there are many menu options for all. This is where you come when you want homestyle cooking but don't want to do it yourself. After work, or in between shopping, eat in or take home with their great take-out menu. Delivery is available through Waiters on Wheels or Dine-One-One, and excellent for football season.

Masa's ★ ★ ★ ★ ★

FRENCH	EXPENSIVE	QUALITY ★ ★ ★ ★ ★	VALUE ★ ★ ★ ★ ★

648 Bush Street, Union Square; ☎ 415-989-7154;
www.masasrestaurant.com

Reservations Required. **When to go** Anytime. **Entree range** Prix fixe, $79–$120. **Payment** All major credit cards. **Service rating** ★★★★★. **Friendliness rating** ★★★★. **Parking** Valet, $12. **Bar** Full service. **Wine selection** Excellent. **Dress** Formal. **Disabled access** Yes. **Customers** Locals, tourists. **Hours** Tuesday–Saturday, 5:30–9:30 p.m.; Sunday and Monday, closed.

SETTING AND ATMOSPHERE It ain't cheap, and it don't look it. But it's never intimidating. How a place can be so grand and yet not be stuffy, pretentious, or snobby is hard to fathom, but there you have it. The staff is not concerned with impressing or looking down on their patrons, but with seeing that they get the superb gastronomic experience they pay so dearly for.

HOUSE SPECIALTIES A unique blend of French and California turned out in an elegant fashion that no other restaurant could imitate even if it tried. It's the result of the Japanese founder's 30 years in French kitchens, honing his style and making his mark. The rather short menu may begin with kadota and black mission figs in a balsamic-fennel oil or housemade foie gras with spinach. Entrees include yellowfin tuna with yuzu-wasabi crème fraîche; rib eye with German butterball potatoes and sweet white corn; Thai snapper with mashed crescent potatoes and tomato marmalade.

OTHER RECOMMENDATIONS Desserts are worth the trip if you have a sweet tooth. Chocolate and almond meringues with coconut milk sherbert.

SUMMARY AND COMMENTS This is often said to be a New York restaurant located in San Francisco. That might be saying a little too much for New York. It is without a doubt one of the best restaurants in the city and, indeed, in the state. It could also be the most expensive, especially if you have wine with your meal. And the corkage fee is $30! But if you're swimming in money or content to eat humble fare for a week or two after, it's worth a blow-out splurge.

Max's Opera Café ★ ½

DELI/BARBECUE	MODERATE	QUALITY ★★★	VALUE ★★★★

601 Van Ness Avenue, Civic Center; ☎ 415-771-7300;
www.maxsworld.com

Reservations Not accepted. **When to go** Before or after the show. **Entree range** $12–$25. **Payment** All major credit cards. **Service rating** ★★. **Friendliness rating** ★★★. **Parking** Street. **Bar** Full service. **Wine selection** Limited but good. **Dress** Casual to dressy. **Disabled access** Yes. **Customers** Theatergoers, tourists, locals. **Hours** Sunday–Tuesday, 11:30 a.m.–10 p.m.; Wednesday and Thursday, 11:30 a.m.–11 p.m.; Friday and Saturday, 11:30 a.m.–11:30 p.m.

SETTING AND ATMOSPHERE New York deli cum piano bar and cocktail lounge with barbecue on the side. Spacious and well-lit, with high ceilings and a large window onto the streets and city hall. Though it's a broad space, it has lots of nooks, booths, and intimate corners.

HOUSE SPECIALTIES Big deli sandwiches; barbecue with unique sauces, some with subtle hints of Asian spices; pasta with wild mushrooms; pastrami and corned beef (ask for it easy on the lean). Take-out available.

OTHER RECOMMENDATIONS Desserts and salads.

SUMMARY AND COMMENTS Located near the War Memorial Opera House, Herbst Theater, and Davies Symphony Hall, this is an ideal spot for a pre-theater dinner. Service is generally quick and efficient with no fluff or folderol; they know you've got tickets to the show. Parking can actually be had on the street now and then.

McCormick & Kuleto's ★★★

SEAFOOD	MODERATE	QUALITY ★★★	VALUE ★★★

900 North Point Street (in Ghirardelli Square), Marina District;
☎415-929-1730; www.mccormickandschmicks.com

Reservations Recommended. **When to go** Anytime. **Entree range** $18–$26. **Payment** All major credit cards. **Service rating** ★★★. **Friendliness rating** ★★★. **Parking** Validated at Ghirardelli garage. **Bar** Full service. **Wine selection** Extensive. **Dress** Casual to dressy. **Disabled access** Yes. **Customers** Tourists and businesspeople. **Hours** Sunday–Thursday 11:30 a.m.–10 p.m.; Friday and Saturday, 11:30 a.m.–11 p.m.

SETTING AND ATMOSPHERE Great views of the Bay through big plate-glass windows make you feel small. Tables and booths, tiered and facing the waterfront, take full advantage of sunsets flaming over Mount Tamalpais, turning the Bay to diamonds. Or the traditional puffs of fog curling past the Golden Gate. With the water just outside lapping against the shores of Aquatic Park and historic tall ships bobbing at neighboring Hyde Street Pier, it's easy to pretend you're on board a ship. Dark mahogany beams and brass accents add to this mood, as if in an elegant stateroom. Unusual bathtub-sized-and-shaped stained-glass light fixtures cast a romantic glow when the exterior light fades, and the sparkles of ferry boats, Tiburon, Alcatraz, and the East Bay emerge outside.

HOUSE SPECIALTIES A fresh seafood menu that just won't quit. Literally. It's in perpetual motion, reprinted twice daily to keep up with the latest delivery of fresh fish and shellfish from local waters and all over the globe—Atlantic salmon from New Brunswick, Canada; Dungeness crab from Bodega Bay; halibut from Sitka, Alaska; ahi tuna from Hawaii. At the top of the menu is the list of the days's offerings, often 30 or more. You can have them simply grilled with lemon or try one of the specialty preparations. Either way, plan to spend many minutes in the decision-making process.

OTHER RECOMMENDATIONS Perhaps skip the ubiquitous chowder, which can be a little salty, and opt for one of the creative appetizers. The lobster-and-shrimp spring rolls arrive with an enticing aroma and a spicy cashew dipping sauce, plus a surprise of sweet corn kernels inside. For an entree, the tilapia from San Jose, Costa Rica is cashew-crusted with a Jamaican hot-rum butter and delicious. Some yummy desserts include the banana toffee cream pie; it's not just your run-of-the-bakery banana-cream pie. This one comes with fresh sliced banana chunks as a thick, sweet blanket on top, all draped in a delicious caramel sauce. The truffle cake is so dense, no light could possibly escape its surface. It's almost chewy, in a good way. A cross between cake and fudge.

SUMMARY AND COMMENTS Abundance is the theme here, with wide selections on every front. The wine list is extensive too, emphasizing California chardonnays. The bar menu rivals it in length, with 14 tequilas, 21 vodkas, 23 single-malt scotches, and much more. Try the restaurant's signature drink, the Kuleto Coffee: Kahlua, Cointreau, and coffee served in a caramelized Bacardi 151 and sugar-rimmed glass. There is also an abundance of diners at this busy place. The crowd is a combo of fleece-and-jeans tourists and business diners. Some cluster in the bar, decorated with fishing lures and giant lobster claws. The bar, that is, not the crowd.

Millennium ★ ★ ★ ½

VEGETARIAN/VEGAN	MODERATE	QUALITY ★★★★½	VALUE ★★★★

**580 Geary Street, Civic Center; ☎ 415-345-3900;
www.millenniumrestaurant.com**

Reservations Recommended. **When to go** Dinner. **Entree range** $18.95–$21.95. **Payment** AE, MC, V. **Service rating** ★★★. **Friendliness rating** ★★★½. **Parking** Valet parking $11 for 3 hours; street and nearby parking garages. **Bar** Full service. **Wine selection** Well chosen. **Dress** Casual. **Disabled access** Yes. **Customers** Locals. **Hours** Sunday–Thursday, 5:30–9:30 p.m.; Friday and Saturday 5:30–10 p.m.

SETTING AND ATMOSPHERE In the ground floor of the Savoy Hotel and just off the lobby. Hung with gauzy drapes and low lit, with a popular bar where singles, couples, and tourists alike gather, this is a place where you might find love with a perfect stranger.

HOUSE SPECIALTIES Some of the best vegan dining to be had anywhere. The dedicated carnivore can feast sumptuously at Millennium and not even realize that he's just had a meatless, dairyless meal. The vegan diet would be a lot more popular if all the cooks came from here. Signature dish is called black bean mole torte. No words do it justice. It's not too sweet or spicy, and it doesn't taste Mexican despite the tortillas. If you eat nothing else in San Francisco besides the famous sourdough bread, eat this.

OTHER RECOMMENDATIONS Butternut squash raw-violi: layers of marinated Portobello mushroom, pepper and olive picadillo, lemon-sage almond cheese, avocado sun-dried tomato salad, and Meyer lemon cream; cornmeal-crusted oyster mushrooms with Asian pear salad, roasted garlic aioli, and kumquat-Thai chile jam. The Chef's tasting menu and wine paring, a culinary adventure!

SUMMARY AND COMMENTS An eclectic menu informed by classic cooking techniques makes Millennium one of San Francisco's treasures. The kitchen makes no compromise in the pursuit of the gourmet dining experience. It labors to extract the last measure of value and character from all of the foods at its disposal, making even the simplest root or leafy green come alive on your palate. The dishes are vibrant with flavor, aroma, and varying textures and colors. A feast for all the senses.

Momi Toby's Revolution Café ★ ★

ECLECTIC	INEXPENSIVE	QUALITY ★★★½	VALUE ★★★

528 Laguna Street, Civic Center; ☎ 415-626-1508

Reservations Not accepted. **When to go** Anytime. **Entree range** $5–$8. **Payment** Cash. **Service rating** ★★. **Friendliness rating** ★★★. **Parking** Street. **Bar** Beer, wine. **Wine selection** House. **Dress** Casual. **Disabled access** No. **Customers** Neighborhood. **Hours** Monday–Friday, 7:30 a.m.–10 p.m.; Saturday and Sunday, 8 a.m.–10 p.m.

SETTING AND ATMOSPHERE This renovation of a 100-year-old bakery is reminiscent of a Berlin cafe, right down to the lamps and the bar. Dark-paneled walls and hardwood floors abound and create a comfortable atmosphere for long conversations over coffee, lunch, or dinner.

HOUSE SPECIALTIES Along with the usual coffee-shop fare, try enchilada pie, meatless pesto lasagna, taqueria-style burritos, or Caesar salad. It seems at first glance that this is a menu that can't make up its mind, but it all hangs together nicely.

SUMMARY AND COMMENTS This is not just a restaurant, it's a local hangout. The regulars are very regular, and people come often just to relax, linger over coffee, meet friends, and feel at home.

Moose's ★ ★ ★ ★

CALIFORNIAN	MODERATE	QUALITY ★★★★½	VALUE ★★★★½

1652 Stockton Street, North Beach; ☎ 415-989-7800; www.mooses.com

Reservations Accepted. **When to go** After the theater. **Entree range** $15–$30; prix fixe $29.95 plus an additional $15 for wine pairing. **Payment** All major credit cards. **Service rating** ★★★★. **Friendliness rating** ★★★★. **Parking** Street, valet $6–$9. **Bar** Full service. **Wine selection** Excellent. **Dress** Business. **Disabled access** Good. **Customers** Locals, tourists. **Hours** Monday–Wednesday, 5:30–10:30 p.m.; Thursday, 11:30 a.m.–2:30 p.m. and 5:30–10:30 p.m.; Friday and Saturday, 5:30–11 p.m.; Sunday, 10 a.m.–2:30 p.m. (brunch) and 5–10 p.m.

SETTING AND ATMOSPHERE Classic San Francisco egalitarian elegance. A fancy festive atmosphere and a staff that performs with aplomb. They are knowledgeable but unpretentious, helpful but not obsequious. Even the sommelier is a regular guy, and he aims to please. You know you're in a place dedicated to the enjoyment of a good dinner when you see table tents with the polite request to turn off your cell phone, please.

HOUSE SPECIALTIES A hard-to-pigeonhole mix of Italian, French, and Californian. Pizza, pasta, and Caesar salad; lamb chops and roasted chicken; smoked meats and crab cakes; mashed potatoes and gravy. It changes seasonally, and when the Dungeness crabs are running, this is the best place in town for San Francisco's signature dish: cioppino (cho PEEN oh).

OTHER RECOMMENDATIONS Organic garden greens are regularly served, as is prosciutto with Mission figs. House smoked pork loin is always worth trying. And vegetarian selections are always good.

SUMMARY AND COMMENTS The warmth and conviviality of Moose's is the most sure antidote to a night of San Francisco's fog. There is piano jazz nightly from 8 to 11 p.m. Every dish is prepared with the utmost love and care and professionalism. In the open kitchen, where skillful hands are the most valuable tools in the shop, you can watch superior workers practicing their art. The wine list is impressive and contains many unique or hard-to-find wines. This is a place that will accommodate almost any budget. You can have a small pizza and a beer while watching a game on TV in the bar for about ten bucks, or you can max out your gold card if you want to in the dining room, or anything in between. This place is so emblematic of the city that if you don't visit Moose's at least once, you just haven't been to San Francisco.

NV Restaurant & Lounge ★ ★ ★ ★

STEAK HOUSE	MODERATE	QUALITY ★★★★	VALUE ★★★★½

1106 First Street, Napa; ☎ 707-265-6400

Reservations Recommended. **When to go** Anytime. **Entree range** $21–$30. **Payment** All major credit cards. **Service rating** ★★★★½. **Friendliness rating** ★★★★½. **Parking** Street, lot. **Bar** Full service. **Wine selection** Excellent. **Dress** Casually elegant. **Disabled access** Yes. **Customers** Locals and accidental tourists. **Hours** Monday–Saturday, 5–10 p.m.

SETTING AND ATMOSPHERE Being located on deep First Street gives this place a feel of being in some hidden grotto or secluded glen. The blond hardwood interior is warm and welcoming (as are the staff). The colorful paintings hanging on the walls are in unconventional shapes that tease and please the eye without being outright distracting. You can take a table mid-room, or you can relax on one of the banquettes that line two of the walls, where you'll sit beneath the oversized sconces.

HOUSE SPECIALTIES As with any California cuisine restaurant, the menu is "ingredient driven."All ingredients are locally produced and used in their season, so obviously the menu changes a lot. And the chef is pleased to run a "backdoor kitchen." He is open to any producer of superior ingredients, no matter how small or obscure, to come to the door and offer them for sale or trade. Having been in high-end food and drink retailing, the chef knows how to locate and reach out to such producers. And patrons reap the benefits. Recent offerings have included mussels done three ways—steamed, baked, and rolled in pancetta), pork belly with baby apples, and herb-crusted lamb loin. A signature dish is a superb beef short rib with carrots and onions. It's comfort food as art.

OTHER RECOMMENDATIONS Desserts are always special, and you could almost make a meal on them. Poached pear sable is music in your mouth. Lemon goat-cheese cake makes a delightful twist on the usual product. But for true creativity, and true knowledge of ingredients and how they can work together, do try the seared Sonoma foie gras with sautéed apples and pears, drizzled with chocolate mole. The mole is more spicy than sweet, making this a truly memorable dish.

SUMMARY AND COMMENTS This is a good place to linger, so come early if you can. And after dinner on weekend nights you can repair to the bar for drinks or a flight of wines and enjoy the soft jazz or other musical offerings.

Oliveto Restaurant ★ ★ ★ ★

ITALIAN	EXPENSIVE	QUALITY ★ ★ ★ ★	VALUE ★ ★ ★ ★

5655 College Avenue, Oakland; ☎ 510-547-5356; www.oliveto.com

Reservations Recommended. **When to go** Anytime. **Entree range** $14–$29. **Payment** All major credit cards. **Service rating** ★★★. **Friendliness rating** ★★★. **Parking** Street. **Bar** Full service. **Wine selection** Extensive. **Dress** Casual. **Disabled access** Yes. **Customers** Locals, frequent visitors. **Hours** Monday, 11:30 a.m.–2 p.m. and 5:30–9 p.m.; Tuesday and Wednesday, 11:30 a.m.–2 p.m. and 5:30–9:30 p.m.; Thursday and Friday, 11:30 a.m.–2 p.m. and 5:30–10 p.m.; Saturday, 5:30–10 p.m.; Sunday, 5–9 p.m.

SETTING AND ATMOSPHERE The Tuscan villa comes alive with hand-rubbed walls and limestone bar, elegant but simple, never showy. A fine contrast to the richness and variety of the cuisine. Oliveto is built on two levels, with the main dining room upstairs, where sits the limestone countertop, good for dining or enjoying a glass of wine. Downstairs is the smaller "cafe" with its wood-burning pizza oven and full bar. Also, there is sidewalk dining during the day in fine weather. And this is all situated next to the famous Market Hall, where some of the best fresh food and produce in the state are sold.

HOUSE SPECIALTIES Come here for the rustic cookery of northern Italy. No spaghetti and meatballs here. And if there is ravioli, it's likely two will make a meal and will be stuffed with something like butternut squash. The menu changes often, but you may encounter Tuscan bread soup;

chicken cooked under a brick; pan-roasted halibut with artichokes; some kind of squab preparation, even a pigeon salad.

OTHER RECOMMENDATIONS Bold chefs are tired of the tyranny of politically correct nutritionists who rail against the use of fat in the diet. We need some fat, after all. So when you see pork belly featured here, go for it. You won't regret it.

SUMMARY AND COMMENTS The upstairs kitchen is open to view from the limestone counter and the staff are an inspiration to watch as you dine there. The staff are especially well informed about the menu items, and can tell in intimate detail how dishes are made and how they taste. Rely on them. You would also do well to rely on them for suggestions for pairing food to wine, as well as their good selection of craft beer.

Oola ★ ★ ★ ½

CALIFORNIA FRESH	MODERATE	QUALITY ★★★	VALUE ★★★★

860 Folsom Street, SoMa; ☎ 415-995-2061; www. oola-sf.com

Reservations Recommended. **When to go** Dinner. **Entree range** $10–$32. **Payment** Major credit cards except D. **Service rating** ★★★★. **Friendliness rating** ★★★★. **Parking** Street lot and valet, $10. **Bar** Full service. **Wine selection** Comprehensive. **Dress** Business casual. **Disabled access** Yes. **Customers** Local tourists. **Hours** Sunday and Monday, 6 p.m.–midnight; Tuesday–Saturday, 6 p.m.–1 a.m.

SETTING AND ATMOSPHERE Popular SoMa dining spot, especially with the late-dinner crowd. Oola reflects the industrial neighborhood, with its sleek minimal design. Large light fixtures are hung in different lengths from the beamed ceiling, and exposed brick walls are soften by warm wood and beige stone accents. An intimate atmosphere is achieved by the low lighting, comfortable booths, and gauzy drapery fluttering above. A mezzanine, set apart by a blue glass partition, seems ideal for a romantic late-night rendezvous.

HOUSE SPECIALTIES The menu ranges from the basics, all-natural Creek Stone Farms hamburger and baby back ribs to upscale items: potato wrapped day boat scallops with shaved truffles, chicken and foie gras ravioli, and roasted local halibut with heirloom-tomato bread salad.

OTHER RECOMMENDATIONS Kumamoto and Malpeque oysters served with mignonette and cocktail sauce on the half shell and port-glazed foie gras torchon entice the appetite. And to complete the journey, the hazelnut chocolate croissant bread pudding.

SUMMARY AND COMMENTS The total design of Oola works to relax diners and prepare them for a tasty meal, and the well-trained and friendly staff add their part. A refuge from the "hard streets" of South of Market!

Original Joe's ★ ★

AMERICAN/ITALIAN	INEXPENSIVE	QUALITY ★★★½	VALUE ★★★★

144 Taylor Street, Union Square; ☎ 415-775-4877

Reservations Recommended. **When to go** Anytime. **Entree range** $8–$22. **Payment** All major credit cards. **Service rating** ★★. **Friendliness rating** ★★★.

Parking Lot; $2 dollar credit with dinner. **Bar** Full service. **Wine selection** Fair. **Dress** Casual. **Disabled access** Yes. **Customers** Locals, tourists, regulars. **Hours** Daily, 10:30 a.m.–12:30 a.m.

SETTING AND ATMOSPHERE This is the original Original Joe's. It's one of the oldest places in the neighborhood, and many will say it looks like it. Most of the staff seem to date from the same year of its founding. The menu, décor, and patrons never seem to change, either. Red plastic booths and a long bar and counter overlooking the kitchen; low lights and some plants. A certain hominess prevails, perhaps born of old familiarity.

HOUSE SPECIALTIES Italian meat and potatoes. Joe's buys whole sides of beef and then ages and cuts them in-house. From these come the monster steaks and hamburgers that the regulars eat in quantity. Also, overcooked pasta with superior sauce; thick-cut french fries; corned beef and cabbage; prime rib.

SUMMARY AND COMMENTS This place has been here for decades. Dine here once and you'll know why. The familiarity, conviviality, and family-style welcoming attitude are rare in the restaurant business. Trendy places come and go. But Joe's stays forever. The neighborhood has gone down in recent years, so you should park in the lot or nearby on the street. Unlike the OJ's in San José, the bar here serves up a hefty drink in a friendly atmosphere.

Pacific ★ ★ ★ ★

CONTEMPORARY CALIFORNIAN   EXPENSIVE   QUALITY ★★★★½   VALUE ★★★★½

500 Post Street, third floor of the Pan Pacific Hotel, Union Square;
☎ **415-929-2087**

Reservations Recommended. **When to go** Anytime. **Entree range** $17–$40; prix fixe, $60 plus an additional $29 for wine pairing. **Payment** All major credit cards, personal checks. **Service rating** ★★★★. **Friendliness rating** ★★★★. **Parking** Valet parking. **Bar** Full service. **Wine selection** Very good. **Dress** Casual. **Disabled access** Yes. **Customers** Tourists and local regulars. **Hours** Monday–Friday, 6:30–11 a.m., 11:30 a.m.–2:30 p.m., and 5:30–9:30 p.m.; Saturday, 7–11:30 a.m. and 5:30–10 p.m.; Sunday, 7–11:30 a.m. and 5:30–9:30 p.m.

SETTING AND ATMOSPHERE This is not a place to people-watch but a place to dine in splendid isolation. Take a lover here on a special evening, or take a table or two with friends and relish the great food and quiet setting. A spacious outlay of tables contributes to a sense of calm. You certainly don't feel like you're in a hotel. The dining area is graciously tiered and divided from the courtyard with low glass walls and four trees. There's a roaring fireplace, a fine antidote to a foggy evening. Four larger-than-life bronze figures by Elbert Weinberg pose gracefully around a fountain. First glance: The spirit of Matisse's painting Dance has taken flight from the canvas.

HOUSE SPECIALTIES The menu changes frequently, but always showcases a sumptuous collection of dishes from the Pacific Rim. For starters, you might be offered a pan-fried Dungeness crab cake or an asparagus salad with a warm pancetta vinaigrette. Try the wild striped bass with chanterelles, caramelized garlic, fingerling potatoes, and the seared diver scallops with white corn, cuitlacoche fritter, and summer truffle sauce. The crème brûlée is the most popular dessert, but the roasted banana-cream pie with rum anglaise is a close second.

OTHER RECOMMENDATIONS The Pacific caters to the theater-going crowd so it's not surprising to find an excellent selection of wines by the glass and a delicious choice of appetizers. A five-course tasting menu is available. You have the option of a paired beverage for each course, a choice of appetizers and entrees.

SUMMARY AND COMMENTS The Pacific is one of the area's top culinary destination points and definitely the hardest-working hotel restaurant in town. The menu is comprised of seasonally inspired dishes. Seafood is their specialty. Live entertainment Friday and Saturday from 5:30 to 9:30 p.m.

Palio d'Asti ★ ★ ★ ★

| ITALIAN | EXPENSIVE | QUALITY ★★★★★ | VALUE ★★★★★ |

640 Sacramento Street, Chinatown; ☎ 415-395-9800; www.paliodasti.com

Reservations Recommended. When to go Lunch, dinner. Entree range $16–$33; tasting menu, $70. Payment AE, D, MC, V. Service rating ★★★★. Friendliness rating ★★★★. Parking Street. Bar Wine bar and full bar. Wine selection Excellent and extensive. Dress Casual, business. Disabled access Yes. Customers Locals, business people. Hours Monday–Friday, 11:30 a.m., with the last seating for lunch at 2:30 p.m.; Enoteca della Douja, from 5 p.m.; and 5:30 p.m. to last seating at 9 p.m.

SETTING AND ATMOSPHERE Rough concrete pillars, set at odd angles in the dining room of this 1905 building, disappear into the lofty ceiling, leaving the impression that one has entered the streets of medieval Italy. Brilliant banners in the colorful designs of the Palio, the ancient bareback horse race celebrating the harvest in Italy, are suspended overhead. Vast gray reaches of wall are softened by sound absorbing cloth panels, a dropped ceiling, and warmed by the extensive use of dark woods and glowing brass fixtures. Comfortable banquettes and strategically placed tables round off this pleasant ambience. The glass-enclosed kitchen provides patrons with an intriguing view of kitchen activities.

HOUSE SPECIALTIES Italian, specializing in the Piemonte and Toscana regions of Italy. The restaurant has always been known for wonderful house pastas and risottos using the freshest and most authentic Italian products. The menu changes often, providing the diner with such delicacies as: potato and Parmigiano dumplings with beef, veal, and pork melted in red wine sauce; house almond-and-fontina-filled ravioli in broth with spinach and white truffle oil; grilled rare ahi tuna steak with cauliflower, green olives, capers, and garum; sautéed milk-fed veal served piemontese-style with glazed wild mushrooms and sorrel.

OTHER RECOMMENDATIONS The wine bar at the front of the restaurant, Enoteca della Douja, named after the famous wine competition that takes place in Asti each September. Here, 30 wines, mostly Italian, are available by the glass or by the 2.5-ounce taste. During the week it is also an "enoteca," or place where people can meet to share small plates of regional dishes.

SUMMARY AND COMMENTS Palio d'Asti is a true ristorante Piemontese, known for its great pastas, risotto, and freshest and most authentic Italian products. Its wine bar, Enoteca della Douja, is one of the City's foremost gathering places for savvy foodies and society folks. Being located in the financial district gives it the advantage of relatively easy street parking after hours.

Paragon ★ ★

NEW AMERICAN	MODERATE	QUALITY ★ ★ ★ ½	VALUE ★ ★ ★

701 Second Street (at Townsend), SoMa; ☎ 415-537-9020; www.paragonrestaurant.com

Reservations Recommended (especially for pre-game meals). **When to go** Anytime. **Entree range** $12–$20. **Payment** AE, D, MC, V. **Service rating** ★ ★ ½. **Friendliness rating** ★ ★ ★. **Parking** Complimentary with validation at lunch; street. **Bar** Full service. **Wine selection** Small, California focus. **Dress** Casual. **Disabled access** Good. **Customers** Game-goers headed to Pac Bell Park, young business types. **Hours** Monday–Thursday, 11:30 a.m.–2:30 p.m. and 5:30–10 p.m.; Friday, 11:30 a.m.–2:30 p.m. and 5:30–11 p.m.; Saturday, 5:30–11 p.m. If there is a crowd, they keep the kitchen running all night.

SETTING AND ATMOSPHERE Located just a block away from Pac Bell Park, Paragon is a lively young spot. High ceilings, chrome, and mirrors create an industrial chic ambience. A large cherrywood bar is the heart of this large restaurant. A partially open kitchen and a private room can be found towards the back of the house. Jazz plays over the din of conversation that the acoustics of the space encourage.

HOUSE SPECIALTIES French brasserie meets American pub in this restaurant where duck confit with lentils might share the table with a gourmet bacon cheeseburger. Dishes often include seasonal and Mediterranean accents as well. Try the spring pea and mint raviolis with goat cheese; seared sea bass with summer bean ragout and cilantro; housemade wild boar sausage with sweet and spicy mustards. Big entrees like grilled double-cut pork chop and roasted chicken are sure to tide you over through every inning of the baseball game.

OTHER RECOMMENDATIONS Paragon could be described as a drinker's restaurant with a food lover's taste. The bar boasts more than 50 varieties of vodka, and 18 wines, mostly California vintages, are available by the glass. In addition to French aperitifs including Lillet, Paragon offers classic American cocktails and a menu of house specialty drinks. All of these drinks pair nicely with rich appetizers such as wild mushroom tart and buttery mussels.

SUMMARY AND COMMENTS Paragon's proximity to Pac Bell Park makes its pace unique. On game nights, huge crowds have come and gone from the restaurant by 7 p.m. The atmosphere transforms from clamorous to calm and you find yourself enjoying a quiet dinner spot.

Perry's ★★

AMERICAN	INEXPENSIVE	QUALITY ★★★½	VALUE ★★★

1944 Union Street, Marina District; ☎ 415-922-9022

Reservations Accepted. **When to go** Anytime. **Entree range** $16–$27. **Payment** All major credit cards. **Service rating** ★★★. **Friendliness rating** ★★★. **Parking** Street. **Bar** Full service. **Wine selection** Fair. **Dress** Casual. **Disabled access** Yes. **Customers** Locals, businesspeople, singles. **Hours** Sunday–Thursday, 9 a.m.–11 p.m.; Friday and Saturday, 9 a.m.–midnight; Saturday and Sunday brunch, 9 a.m.–3 p.m.

SETTING AND ATMOSPHERE Sports bar, singles meeting place, business rendezvous, bar and grill; a pleasant American bistro. Congenial long bar surrounded by checker-clothed tables on a bare wood floor. Wide windows overlook fashionable Union Street, and the back has a pleasant patio for quieter dining.

HOUSE SPECIALTIES Burgers; shoestring fries; meatloaf; grilled ahi tuna; London broil; chicken fajitas; grilled double chicken breast; New York steak; linguine with clams.

OTHER RECOMMENDATIONS Apple Brown Betty.

SUMMARY AND COMMENTS This bar has always been a great place to meet friends or strangers. Go for a cocktail before or a cordial after dinner, or a late snack after dancing.

Piperade's ★★★

WEST COAST BASQUE	MODERATE	QUALITY ★★★★	VALUE ★★★★

1015 Battery Street, North Beach; ☎ 415-391-2555; www.piperade.com

Reservations Recommended. **When to go** Lunch, dinner. **Entree range** $18–$25. **Payment** All major credit cards. **Service rating** ★★★. **Friendliness rating** ★★★. **Parking** Street. **Bar** Full service. **Wine selection** Extensive, excellent. **Dress** Casual, business. **Disabled access** Yes. **Customers** Locals, businesspeople. **Hours** Monday–Friday, 11:30 a.m.–3 p.m. and 5:30–10:30 p.m.; Saturday, 5:30–10:30 p.m.

SETTING AND ATMOSPHERE Entering Piperade's from the brick and steel of the Battery Street warehouse area is a comforting experience. Reminiscent of the Basque men's dining clubs of San Sebastian, you're surrounded by warm wood paneling; a low, exposed beamed ceiling; soft lighting; and a sense of conviviality. The bar runs the length of the main dining area, its mirrored back wall adding depth to this small bistro. The bar gives those waiting a chance to observe and lust after the hardy and innovative Basque cuisine on its way to table.

HOUSE SPECIALTIES Basque in essence, which means comfort food deluxe. The menu is divided into small plates, big plates, and Basque classics.

The chilled mussel and bread salad with red wine vinaigrette or the piquillo peppers stuffed with goat cheese, pine nuts, and golden raisins are small plates large on taste. For big appetites, try steamed Pacific snapper with spinach and fried garlic vinaigrette or the classic Veal stew "axoa" braised with peppers.

OTHER RECOMMENDATIONS Whatever you do, order the Gascon fries, and for dessert choose the turron mousse cake with roasted almonds.

SUMMARY AND COMMENTS Basque food is hardy and savory and needs time to be enjoyed thoroughly. Piperade's brings you this experience but not quite at peak hours. It is a San Francisco favorite and can be very crowded. To take advantage of the friendly and knowledgeable staff and fully enjoy the delicious food, go early or at off hours.

PJ's Oyster Bed ★ ★ ★

SEAFOOD	MODERATE	QUALITY ★ ★ ★ ★	VALUE ★ ★ ★ ★

737 Irving Street, Sunset; ☎ 415-566-7775; www.pjsoysterbed.com

Reservations Recommended. **When to go** Anytime. **Entree range** $12–$25. **Payment** All major credit cards. **Service rating** ★★★. **Friendliness rating** ★★★½. **Parking** Street. **Bar** Beer, wine. **Wine selection** Adequate. **Dress** Casual. **Disabled access** Yes. **Customers** Locals, occasional tourists. **Hours** Sunday–Thursday, 11:30 a.m.–3 p.m. and 5–10 p.m.; Friday and Saturday, 11:30 a.m.–3 p.m. and 5–11 p.m.

SETTING AND ATMOSPHERE Casual, comfortable atmosphere; always intriguing counter seating and table service. Locals would keep this place going if it never saw another tourist. So you'll always find it full of regulars. And it's a bit off the tourist track, so you won't see many out-of-towners. It's a good place to dine with San Franciscans in their native habitat.

HOUSE SPECIALTIES Wide selection of oyster dishes and many Cajun specialties. New Orleans–style gumbo.

OTHER RECOMMENDATIONS Try the alligator. It's good.

SUMMARY AND COMMENTS With its "distinctive" weather, this has always been a hot-bowl-of-soup kind of town, and PJ's clam chowder fills the bill for a respite from those chilling winds and damp fogs. It's best to come here by car or taxi; it's a long bus ride from downtown.

Plouf ★ ★

FRENCH	MODERATE	QUALITY ★ ★ ★	VALUE ★ ★ ★

40 Belden Place (between Bush and Pine), Union Square;
☎ 415-986-6491; www.ploufsf.com

Reservations Accepted. **When to go** Anytime. **Entree range** $14–$24. **Payment** AE, MC, V. **Service rating** ★★. **Friendliness rating** ★★. **Parking** Metered street, neighborhood lots. **Bar** Full service. **Wine selection** Extensive; $17 corkage fee. **Dress** Casual. **Disabled access** Good. **Customers** Young clientele, businesspeople. **Hours** Monday–Thursday, 11:30 a.m.–3 p.m. and 5:30–10 p.m., Friday, 11:30 a.m.–3 p.m. and 5:30–11 p.m.; Saturday, 5:30 p.m.–11 p.m.; closed Sunday.

SETTING AND ATMOSPHERE Plouf has an oceanic theme. Huge trophy fish hang from the walls and the old-fashioned white tile floor and high pressed-tin ceiling with skylights give the restaurant a spacious feel. Cafe-style tables are somewhat close together, but the folding chairs are more comfortable than they appear. The mood here is bustling and young, as friendly staff maneuver hot crocks of mussels amid the crowd. A functional fireplace adds a cozy touch on cold nights, and when it is warm enough, the outdoor patio fills up like a Parisian cafe.

HOUSE SPECIALTIES Mussels, mussels, and more mussels. Any diner who has traveled in France will appreciate the authenticity of the menu. Moulles Mariniere, Provençal, and Bretonne recall the offerings of every French mussel bistro. The seafood doesn't stop with the mussels, though. Plouf features several fish entrees daily and also has oysters on the half shell, calamari, prawns, and scallops on the appetizer menu. If anyone in your party is averse to seafood, they can still enjoy some French fare in the form of a leek tart with Roquefort cheese or classic dinners such as roasted chicken with Moroccan spiced potatoes.

OTHER RECOMMENDATIONS The offerings from the bar are impressive. In addition to the large wine list, aperitifs, champagne, and after-dinner liqueurs bring the European drinking sensibility to the American table. Why not enjoy a relaxed drink before you even order?

SUMMARY AND COMMENTS Plouf is a good spot to know about if you are working or shopping downtown and need a place to eat or have a drink. The weekday lunch is a good value. The French staff is upbeat and hardworking and the Belden Place location, adjacent to Café Bastille and a few other casual but trendy eateries that also occupy sidewalk space, gives Plouf a distinctly European feel.

Ponzu ★ ★ ★ ★ ½

CONTEMPORARY ASIAN	MODERATE/EXPENSIVE	QUALITY ★ ★ ★ ★
VALUE ★ ★ ★ ★ ★		

**401 Taylor Street, Union Square; ☎ 415-775-7979;
www.ponzurestaurant.com**

Reservations Recommended. **When to go** Anytime. **Entree range** $18–32. **Payment** All major credit cards. **Service rating** ★ ★ ★ ★. **Friendliness rating** ★ ★ ★ ★. **Parking** Validated parking. **Bar** Full service. **Wine selection** Very good. **Dress** Casually elegant, no athletic wear. **Disabled access** Yes. **Customers** Locals in the know. **Hours** Monday–Thursday, 7–10 a.m. and 5–10 p.m.; Friday, 7–10 a.m. and 5–11 p.m.; Saturday, 8–11 a.m. and 5–11 p.m.; Sunday, 8–11 a.m. and 5–10 p.m. Bar open 4:30 p.m.–midnight.

SETTING AND ATMOSPHERE Hip and edgy décor softened with a wonderful touch of feng shui: low undulated walls, artful light fixtures, a circular ceiling pattern repeated on the floor, lots of curves, and soft velvet-covered seats. Festive and youthful atmosphere, particularly after the middle of the week. Lots of space and plenty of romantic nooks for an evening with someone special.

HOUSE SPECIALTIES Traditional Asian techniques and cooking styles combined with local ingredients cannot be done better. The menu consists of meticulously crafted Thai, Malaysian, Japanese, Chinese, Korean, and Vietnamese dishes. But this is not fusion food. Nothing is muddled together. For starters, try the chile-salt fried calamari with a garlic dipping sauce as well as the garlic-fried roti bread with pear chutney and cucumber raita. Among the entrees, lamb tenderloin with mixed squash and tomato chutney; and spicy Korean pork chop with mung bean pancakes are extraordinary.

OTHER RECOMMENDATIONS Ponzu has happy hours twice nightly from 5 to 7 p.m. and again from 10 p.m. to midnight. Lots of theatergoing folks can be found here and the actors hang out during the second happy hour. Lots of wonderful finger food to share. Try the specialty cocktails. They're served with swizzle sticks, umbrellas, and other playful garnishes and are as exotic as their names suggest: Buddha's Passion, Spiritual Sparkler.

SUMMARY AND COMMENTS This is one of the best deals in town, a great bang for your buck. There's a seasonal twist to the menu but it basically stays the same. The mood shifts over the course of the evening. The darker, the sexier, and so it goes as the evening wears on. It's best to valet park. The neighborhood, though vastly improved, is still a little raw. The restrooms may be the coolest in the City.

Red's Java House ★

DIVE	INEXPENSIVE	QUALITY ★ ★ ★	VALUE ★ ★ ★ ★ ★

Pier 30, SoMa; ☎ 415-777-5626

Reservations No way. When to go Daytime. Entree range $4–$7. Payment Cash. Service rating ★. Friendliness rating ★. Parking Street. Bar Beer. Wine selection None. Dress Work clothes. Disabled access No. Customers Locals, workers. Hours Monday and Tuesday, 6 a.m.–4 p.m.; Wednesday–Friday, 6 a.m.–8 p.m.; Saturday, 9 a.m.–8 p.m.; Sunday, 9 a.m.–3 p.m.

SETTING AND ATMOSPHERE It's little more than a shack on the waterfront, a place where dock workers once took a hearty breakfast and lunch. The city's waterfront glory days are long passed, but Red's just won't go away. The chief attraction here is the view. In front you can see the East Bay and the Bay Bridge. Behind you is the bulk of the city. Red's history is documented in scores of black-and-white photos of people and patrons from the waterfront. All else is tacky and tattered—that's just how the patrons like it.

HOUSE SPECIALTIES Double burgers; double hot dogs; deviled-egg sandwiches.

OTHER RECOMMENDATIONS What many will argue is a great cup of coffee.

SUMMARY AND COMMENTS A generous burger and a long-neck beer in a place that also serves up huge plates of nostalgia, and for only five bucks. Who could complain? Down to your last dollar? Eat here.

Ruth's Chris Steak House ★ ★ ½

STEAK HOUSE	MODERATE	QUALITY ★★★½	VALUE ★★★★

1601 Van Ness Avenue, Civic Center; ☎ 415-673-0557;
www.ruthschris.com

Reservations Strongly advised. **When to go** Anytime. **Entree range** $17–$34.95 (á la carte). **Payment** All major credit cards. **Service rating** ★★★. **Friendliness rating** ★★★. **Parking** Street; valet, $8. **Bar** Full service. **Wine selection** Good. **Dress** Casual. **Disabled access** Yes. **Customers** Locals, tourists. **Hours** Monday–Thursday, 5–10 p.m.; Friday and Saturday, 5–10:30 p.m.; Sunday, 4:30–9:30 p.m.

SETTING AND ATMOSPHERE A proper-looking steak house in the best tradition. The dark wood suggests a cattle ranch, and the well-set, clean tables tell you you're in a place of serious eating. Any doubts are dispelled by the black-and-white-clad waiters, who look like real pros.

HOUSE SPECIALTIES Serious steak. It's all from the Midwest, where beef is something more than mere food. Corn-fed, aged USDA prime is what you'll get here. It makes up the top 2% of market beef; you'll taste the difference.

OTHER RECOMMENDATIONS Barbecued shrimp; lamb chops; seared ahi tuna; chicken; shellfish. Creamed spinach; potatoes au gratin; shoestring potatoes.

SUMMARY AND COMMENTS The menu defines what rare means—as well as the other grades of doneness—and the cooks are good about it. You'll get what you order. Portions are big and may look daunting, but they're so good that they seem to disappear.

Sam Woh ★ ½

CHINESE	INEXPENSIVE	QUALITY ★★★	VALUE ★★★★

813 Washington Street, Chinatown; ☎ 415-982-0596

Reservations Not accepted. **When to go** Lunch. **Entree range** $5–$10. **Payment** Cash. **Service rating** ★. **Friendliness rating** ★. **Parking** Street. **Bar** None. **Wine selection** None. **Dress** Casual. **Disabled access** Adequate. **Customers** Locals, businesspeople. **Hours** Monday–Saturday, 11 a.m.–3 a.m.; Sunday, 12:30–9:30 p.m.

SETTING AND ATMOSPHERE Hole-in-the-wall rabbit warren. Three floors of deep, narrow rooms with a cramped feeling, especially during the lunchtime squeeze. Even when you're alone in the place you feel the need for elbow room. And the décor? There is no décor.

HOUSE SPECIALTIES All the usual suspects in a Chinese restaurant. Chow mein with a variety of additions; crisp fried noodles; sautéed shellfish; won ton soup; fried rice.

OTHER RECOMMENDATIONS More of the same.

SUMMARY AND COMMENTS The motto hangs from the wall: "No credit card, no fortune cookie, just damn good food!" It's not quite a dive, but almost. And it's one of the most popular places in the neighborhood. Of its kind, it might be the most popular place in town. The staff is singularly intolerant, demanding, disputatious, and sometimes downright rude. "You! Move over. Somebody else gotta sit down, too." That's how you get seated when it's very crowded, as it is daily at noon. Lingering too long after lunch? "You! Whatsamatta you? People waiting. You go!" Somehow it's not insulting. Somehow that's just the way they say howdy. There is no wine or beer, but the package store just across the street will sell you a cold one or a bottle of jug wine and wrap it in a brown paper bag for you to take into the restaurant. They know the drill, and they're quick about it. You hungry now? You go!

Scala's Bistro ★ ★ ★ ½

ITALIAN/FRENCH	EXPENSIVE	QUALITY ★★★★	VALUE ★★★★

**432 Powell Street, Union Square; ☎ 415-395-8555;
www.scalasbistro.com**

Reservations Accepted. **When to go** Anytime. **Entree range** $14–$30. **Payment** All major credit cards. **Service rating** ★★★★. **Friendliness rating** ★★★. **Parking** Street, nearby lots; valet $11. **Bar** Full service. **Wine selection** Extensive. **Dress** Evening casual. **Disabled access** Yes. **Customers** Locals, tourists. **Hours** Monday–Friday, 7–10:30 a.m., 11 a.m.–4 p.m. and 5:15 p.m.–midnight; Saturday and Sunday, 8–10:30 a.m., 11 a.m.–4 p.m. and 5:15 p.m.–midnight.

SETTING AND ATMOSPHERE Located in the historic Sir Francis Drake hotel. Walking into this place feels like walking into an older, more colorful and vibrant San Francisco. It's very much alive. Rows of wood and leather booths sit beneath mural-painted walls, and large windows give a sweeping view of the street and all its pageant flowing by.

HOUSE SPECIALTIES A mix of regional Italian, country French, and California. The menu changes often, but grilled double-cut pork chop with fingerling potatoes, artichokes, and roasted garlic is a signature dish and can be counted on, as is seared salmon filet with buttermilk mashed potatoes. For pasta, the best is linguine with clams.

OTHER RECOMMENDATIONS A superb cheese board for dessert. Or if you're a real cheese head, make it your main course. The house baked breads go very well with it.

SUMMARY AND COMMENTS It's not often that we can recommend a hotel restaurant, but it's not often that a place like Scala's comes along. While this is one of the best places in town for meats and seafood, the chef is very adept at putting together a vegetarian meal. You just have to ask.

Shanghai 1930 ★ ★ ★

CHINESE	MODERATE	QUALITY ★★★	VALUE ★★★★

133 Steuart Street, SoMa; ☎ 415-896-5600; www.shanghai1930.com

Reservations Accepted. **When to go** Anytime. **Entree range** $12–$36. **Payment** All major credit cards. **Service rating** ★★★. **Friendliness rating** ★★★. **Parking** Valet, $10; street. **Bar** Full service. **Wine selection** Varied, with many California wines. **Dress** Business. **Disabled access** No. **Customers** Locals, tourists. **Hours**

Monday–Thursday, 11 a.m.–2 p.m. and 5:30–10 p.m.; Friday, 11 a.m.–2 p.m. and 5:30–11 p.m.; Saturday, 5:30–11 p.m.; closed Sunday.

SETTING AND ATMOSPHERE Another theme restaurant from SF restaurateur George Chin, this one evoking the glamorous, indulgent, and romantic Shanghai of the 1930s. The gorgeous blue art deco–style bar evokes the feel of an elegant opium den and has been used as a set for the television series "Nash Bridges." Comfortable booths line both sides of the main room and a large room at the rear is available for groups.

HOUSE SPECIALTIES The seasonal menu is divided into familiar categories but with unusual combinations and flavorings. Signature selections cover the popular mainstays that are unlikely to threaten yet still include a creative twist, such as fish on a vine, a fillet of whole fish shaped to resemble a cluster of grapes; minced duck in lettuce petals or braised five-spice pork shank with pea shoots. On the more exotic side, try beggar's chicken (24-hour notice needed) or glazed pork belly in red wine lees.

OTHER RECOMMENDATIONS Go for contrasts and the unusual. Try the tea-smoked squab served with a sour plum sauce and lotus buns.

SUMMARY AND COMMENTS Out-of-town guests searching for a taste of the elegance they've seen in Zhiang Ximou movies will feel as though they have arrived on the set as they descend the stairs into this subterranean restaurant. The atmosphere could only be improved if everyone wore white smoking jackets or slinky satin dresses. Live jazz on Thursday, Friday, and Saturday evenings.

Sheraton Palace Garden Court ★ ★ ★ ★

| NEW AMERICAN | EXPENSIVE | QUALITY ★★★★½ | VALUE ★★★★ |

Market Street at New Montgomery Street #2, SoMa; ☎ 415-546-5010; www.gardencourt-restaurant.com

Reservations Recommended. When to go Anytime. Entree range $17–$27. Payment All major credit cards. Service rating ★★★½. Friendliness rating ★★½. Parking Hotel garage. Bar Full service. Wine selection Excellent. Dress Informal, dressy. Disabled access Good. Customers Tourists, businesspeople, locals. Hours Monday–Friday, 6:30–11 a.m. and 11:30 a.m.–2 p.m.; Saturday, 6:30 a.m.–10:30 a.m., 11:30 a.m.–2 p.m., and 2–4 p.m. (tea); Sunday, 6:30–9:30 a.m. and 10 a.m.–2 p.m. (brunch)

SETTING AND ATMOSPHERE The Sheraton Garden Court may be the most gorgeously rococo room in San Francisco, with its 40-foot atrium ceiling and copious lead crystal chandeliers dwarfing the baby grand. The room is softly carpeted, with plush sofas in the lounge. This is as grand as it gets.

HOUSE SPECIALTIES Breakfast or Sunday brunch buffet; Japanese breakfast; sautéed dover sole with dried pineapple pilaf and toasted almonds; warm calamari salad.

OTHER RECOMMENDATIONS Tenderloin of beef and shrimp with braised truffle potatoes; chicken breast with corn posole polenta.

SUMMARY AND COMMENTS Opulent, plush, hushed, and halcyon; if you've recently won the lottery, the Garden Court's grandeur will no doubt satisfy your need to pamper yourself. You're definitely paying for the atmosphere and deferential service; the food, while meticulously prepared and admirably presented, is among the highest-priced in the city and can be equaled in quality elsewhere for considerably less. But hey, it isn't just about the food, it's the total experience. At the least, stop in for a drink on the way to somewhere else. The afternoon teas, topping off with a champagne tea for $24–$42, are a luxurious treat.

South Park Café ★ ★ ★

FRENCH	MODERATE	QUALITY ★ ★ ★ ★	VALUE ★ ★ ★ ★ ★

108 South Park Boulevard, SoMa; ☎ 415-495-7275; www.southparkcafesf.com

Reservations Recommended. **When to go** Anytime. **Entree range** Lunch, $8.50–$15; dinner, $13–$19, 3-course prix fixe, $29.95. **Payment** All major credit cards. **Service rating** ★ ★ ★ ½. **Friendliness rating** ★ ★ ★ ½. **Parking** Street. **Bar** Full service. **Wine selection** Limited but good. **Dress** Casual, informal. **Disabled access** Good. **Customers** Locals, businesspeople, tourists. **Hours** Monday–Friday, 8–11:30 a.m. (pastries and coffee), 11:30 a.m.–2:30 p.m., and 5:30–10 p.m.; Saturday, 5:30–10 p.m.; closed Sunday.

SETTING AND ATMOSPHERE South Park Café's enchanting location on historic South Park Boulevard creates a pared-down neighborhood bistro ambience: affable clamor and bustle with relatively bright lighting. It's a very romantic street but not a romantic restaurant.

HOUSE SPECIALTIES Dinners include grilled hangar steak with a red wine sauce; slow roasted lamb; braised vegetable couscous with lemon mint yogurt.

OTHER RECOMMENDATIONS Nightly specials, including desserts. apple cake with geranium ice cream and Calvados crème anglaise.

SUMMARY AND COMMENTS South Park's minimalist approach arrived as a forerunner antidote to the more flamboyant and expensive dinner houses of the 1980s. Heralding the gentrification of quaint South Park Boulevard, the original affluent section of old San Francisco then down at the heels in an industrial neighborhood, South Park offered a small, well-executed bistro menu served in a simple setting for shockingly low prices. Others have followed, spiffing up the neighborhood and spawning a whole movement. And being near the new Pacbell Park, this is a good spot for dinner before or after a ballgame or concert.

The Stinking Rose ★ ★ ★

ITALIAN	MODERATE	QUALITY ★ ★ ★ ½	VALUE ★ ★ ★ ★

325 Columbus Avenue, North Beach; ☎ 415-781-7673; www.thestinkingrose.com

Reservations Recommended. **When to go** Anytime. **Entree range** $14–$35. **Payment** All major credit cards. **Service rating** ★ ★ ★. **Friendliness rating** ★ ★. **Parking** Street. **Bar** Full service. **Wine selection** Short but good. **Dress** Casual. **Disabled access** Yes. **Customers** Locals, tourists. **Hours** Daily, 11 a.m.–11 p.m.

SETTING AND ATMOSPHERE The main room is a mix of murals, a Rube Goldberg garlic factory, and toy trains. Garlic braids hang from the ceiling, photos of celebrities smile from the walls, and understatement is nowhere in sight. A second room is strewn with plain wooden tables and festooned with straw-wrapped Chianti fiasci. All is exuberant without being overpowering, rather like the aroma of cooked garlic.

HOUSE SPECIALTIES "Garlic seasoned with food." The mostly Italian menu is comprised of well-made pastas and seafood laden with garlic. The garlic is usually cooked long and slow to mellow it, so you won't step out of here a bane to vampires, but people will know where you've been. Weekly specials include meat loaf with garlic mashed potatoes and garlic-encrusted baby back ribs.

OTHER RECOMMENDATIONS Forty-clove chicken, pork chops with sweet garlic relish and apples, braised rabbit, vegetarian dishes. Specially marked items can be made without the pungent lily on request.

SUMMARY AND COMMENTS One-and-a-half tons of garlic and 12,000 mints a month! This is a fun place, one that takes itself not too seriously but not too lightly either. It's dedicated to gustatory enjoyment. The bar is a popular place to meet. Regulars will often come in just for a drink and a deep breath or two. At Candlestick Park, you can buy the Stinking Rose's 40-clove chicken sandwich.

Straits Café ★ ★ ★ ★

SINGAPOREAN	MODERATE	QUALITY ★★★★½	VALUE ★★★★★

3300 Geary Boulevard, Richmond; ☎ 415-668-1783; www.straitsrestaurants.com

Reservations Accepted. **When to go** Anytime. **Entree range** $10–$27. **Payment** All major credit cards. **Service rating** ★★★★. **Friendliness rating** ★★★★. **Parking** Street; No valet parking. **Bar** Full service. **Wine selection** Limited. **Dress** Casual. **Disabled access** Yes. **Customers** Trendy locals. **Hours** Monday–Thursday, noon–2:30 p.m. and 5:30–10 p.m.; Friday and Saturday, noon–11 p.m.; Sunday, noon–10 p.m.

SETTING AND ATMOSPHERE Chris Yeo, the owner/chef, has worked magic in the smallest of spaces. The playful décor evokes a Singaporean street scene, with pastel-colored facades, balconies, shutters, even clotheslines. Subtle lighting. Busy with people of every ethnicity.

HOUSE SPECIALTIES Singaporean cookery blends the best of Indonesian, Chinese, Malay, Indian, and Nonya cuisines (the latter a result of the marriages between Chinese men and Malay women generations ago). Dishes are designed to be shared. Start with the roti prata, a grilled Indian bread served with a subtle curry dipping sauce. Another house specialty is the seafood curry with mussels, prawns, and calamari in a rich yellow curry with eggplant; and the salmon covered with puréed chili, lemongrass, garlic, and onion wrapped in a banana leaf and grilled.

OTHER RECOMMENDATIONS The bartender specializes in a long list of tropical concoctions and a variety of infused drinks: pineapple, mango, ginger, and apple. The recommended Navarro white wine admirably complements many of the dishes on the menu.

SUMMARY AND COMMENTS A great place for superbly tasty, beautifully presented food in an intimate setting. This is still a neighborhood restaurant: affordable, cozy, and filled with regulars. Straits Café is San Francisco's first, and only, authentic Singaporean restaurant.

Swan Oyster Depot ★ ★

OYSTER BAR	INEXPENSIVE	QUALITY ★★★½	VALUE ★★★★★

1517 Polk Street, Civic Center; ☎ 415-673-1101

Reservations Not accepted. **When to go** Lunch. **Entree range** $15–$25. **Payment** Cash. **Service rating** ★★★. **Friendliness rating** ★★★. **Parking** Street. Bar Beer, wine. **Wine selection** House. **Dress** Casual. **Disabled access** No. **Customers** Locals. **Hours** Monday–Saturday, 8 a.m.–5:30 p.m.; closed Sunday.

SETTING AND ATMOSPHERE Really a fishmonger's, this little gem boasts a long marble bar where you sit on ancient stools feasting on the freshest seafood in town. It's an old-time San Francisco neighborhood joint.

HOUSE SPECIALTIES Raw oysters; shellfish cocktails; seafood salads.

OTHER RECOMMENDATIONS New England clam chowder with sourdough bread.

SUMMARY AND COMMENTS Friendly family members of this Polk Street business entertain you with continuous conversation while they shuck, peel, and crack your order of shellfish. One of the few places in town that still serves old-fashioned oyster crackers.

Tadich Grill ★ ★ ★

AMERICAN	MODERATE	QUALITY ★★★★	VALUE ★★★★★

240 California Street, Financial District; ☎ 415-391-1849

Reservations Not accepted. **When to go** Anytime. **Entree range** $15–$25. **Payment** MC, V. **Service rating** ★★★. **Friendliness rating** ★★½. **Parking** Street. Bar Full service. **Wine selection** Good. **Dress** Casual, business. **Disabled access** Yes. **Customers** Locals, businesspeople, tourists, day-trippers. **Hours** Monday–Friday, 11 a.m.–9 p.m.; Saturday, 11:30 a.m.–9 p.m.

SETTING AND ATMOSPHERE The oldest restaurant in the city; founded in 1849 and still operated by the same family. It's brightly lit, but the heavily draped tables and curtained booths give a warm ambience (if you're lucky enough to get a table or booth). Otherwise, a seat at the long marble counter affords delightful glimpses into the open kitchen.

HOUSE SPECIALTIES Seafood. Or anything else you want grilled. Tadich is a place for plain cooking, no fancy sauces or tarted-up presentations. Straightforward and honest Yankee fare. This is one of the few places that still serves the gold rush specialty Hangtown Fry, basically a frittata of oysters and bacon.

OTHER RECOMMENDATIONS Good bar to help you through the long wait for seating.

SUMMARY AND COMMENTS A culinary, cultural treasure. Quite possibly built over the sunken ships of the gold rush. Step into Tadich and partake of the city's rich gastronomic history. It's best to come here early or late, as the place is jammed most of the time. And order conservatively; portions are heavy.

Thanh Long ★ ★ ★

VIETNAMESE	INEXPENSIVE/MODERATE	QUALITY ★ ★ ★ ★	VALUE ★ ★ ★ ★

4101 Judah Street at 46th Avenue, Sunset; ☎ **415-665-1146;**
www.anfamily.com

Reservations Recommended on weekends. **When to go** Weeknights. **Entree range** $10–$30. **Payment** All major credit cards. **Service rating** ★ ★ ★. **Friendliness rating** ★ ★ ★ ★. **Parking** Street, valet. **Bar** Beer, wine. **Wine selection** House. **Dress** Casual, informal. **Disabled access** Good. **Customers** Locals, businesspeople, tourists. **Hours** Tuesday–Thursday and Sunday, 4:30–10 p.m.; Friday and Saturday, 4:30–11 p.m.; closed Monday.

SETTING AND ATMOSPHERE Operated by the An family for more than 25 years, Thanh Long's dining room is done in shades of muted green, with one room wallpapered with tropical flowers. Simple but pleasant. Not that anyone really notices; the food's the star here. Thanh Long is close to the beach and a neighborhood favorite, so it can get crowded on warm-weather weekends.

HOUSE SPECIALTIES Whole roasted crab with garlic and lemon butter or sweet-and-sour sauce is the house's signature dish, and people come from all over town for it; soft rice-paper shrimp rolls; crab cheese puffs; chicken and prawn egg noodles; salmon in a ginger sauce served with squash and asparagus; squid stuffed with pork and mushrooms; lemongrass chicken; broiled red snapper.

SUMMARY AND COMMENTS Thanh Long's soft, green ambience provides a cool backdrop for the vibrant, flame-colored platters of whole crabs emerging from the kitchen. Crab is the main event here, and everyone orders it in one form or another; some say it's the best to be had in a town famous for its crab purveyors. The shrimp rolls are also excellent, as is the grilled pork, beef, and squid. Thanh Long is a good dinner stop after a day at the beach, but make reservations in advance to avoid a wait. If you're staying downtown, come by car or taxi; it's a long bus ride.

Thirstybear ★ ★ ★

SPANISH	MODERATE	QUALITY ★ ★ ★ ½	VALUE ★ ★ ★ ★

661 Howard Street, SoMa; ☎ **415-974-0905; www.thirstybear.com**

Reservations Recommended. **When to go** Anytime. **Entree range** Tapas, $5–$10; entrees, $13–$20. **Payment** All major credit cards. **Service rating** ★ ★ ★ ★. **Friendliness rating** ★ ★ ★. **Parking** Self-parking at the Moscone Parking Garage on Third. **Bar** Full service but specializes in house-brewed beers. **Wine selection** Good. **Dress** Casual. **Disabled access** Good. **Customers** Businesspeople and late-20 to 30-somethings. **Hours** Monday–Thursday, 11:30 a.m.–2:30

p.m. and 4:30–10 p.m.; Friday, 11:30 a.m.–2:30 p.m. and 4:30 p.m.–midnight; Saturday, noon–3 p.m. and 4:30 p.m.–midnight; Sunday, 5–10 p.m.

SETTING AND ATMOSPHERE High energy bounces off the walls and lofty timber-beamed ceilings in this brewpub cum Spanish cookery. The modern wall art and showcased stainless steel brewery equipment is balanced by the weathered brick walls typical of SoMa buildings. If the noise level in the front bar area can make it hard to hear conversations, venture upstairs, where there are pool tables and often banquets. Let the desserts overwhelm you instead of the crowd.

HOUSE SPECIALTIES A long list of both hot and cold tapas (small plates) that can be snack, appetizer, or by ordering a few, a whole meal. Cold tapas include the staples of the Spanish bar such as Boquerones, sardines marinated in a garlicky vinaigrette, or a tempting red snapper cevice with poblano peppers and lime. For a red meat fix, try the bite-sized pieces of grilled flank steak. Follow it all with classic desserts like a velvety flan, a warm apple crisp, or a Spanish-inspired, orange-almond bread pudding.

OTHER RECOMMENDATIONS It's easy to fill up on a mixture of cold and hot tapas, but leave room for the amazing entrees. The rioja wine–braised short ribs are a huge favorite with regulars. Duck breast with lentils is richly flavored and satisfying. Try the Paella Valenciana, prepared in a cazuela with squid, shrimp, and mussels and named after the town in Spain where paella originated. Do not miss the patatas bravas, deep fried cubes of potato served with spicy romesco sauce.

This is one of the best microbreweries in the city, so do try the seasonal beers in addition to the favorite standbys like the IPA.

ENTERTAINMENT AND AMENITIES Frequent live music from klezmer to jazz. Upstairs available for banquets and parties.

SUMMARY AND COMMENTS More than just an after-work hangout for good beer and gossip, the Thirstybear is a fantastic place to bring out-of-town visitors to dinner. Its popularity seems to be focused on the beer and tapas, while kudos should be shifted to the kitchen and its dedication to preserving the flavors of Spain. The chef trains each new waiter for three days to learn the details plate by plate. In addition, the chef returns to Spain at least once a year to study the cuisine and expand the menus.

Ti Couz ★★

CRÊPERIE	INEXPENSIVE	QUALITY ★★★	VALUE ★★★★

3108 16th Street, Mission District; ☎ 415-252-7373

Reservations Not accepted. **When to go** Before or after a movie. **Entree range** $6–$14. **Payment** MC, V. **Service rating** ★★. **Friendliness rating** ★★★. **Parking** Street. **Bar** Full bar. **Wine selection** Adequate. **Dress** Casual. **Disabled access** Yes. **Customers** Locals, moviegoers. **Hours** Monday and Friday, 11 a.m.–11 p.m.; Tuesday–Thursday, 5–11 p.m.; Saturday and Sunday, 10 a.m.–11 p.m.

SETTING AND ATMOSPHERE Clean, bright, polished blue and white. Simple décor befitting the simple yet good fare. Located across from the Roxie

Theater, it's often peopled by a boisterous and friendly mob of film fans and bookstore denizens.

HOUSE SPECIALTIES Crêpes, crêpes, and more crêpes. Crêpes of every description and possible filling. Sweet crêpes, savory crêpes, plain and fancy crêpes. Fillings include seasonal fruits and butter or chocolate; mushrooms with sauce; seafood with sauce; cheese and crème fraîche.

OTHER RECOMMENDATIONS A pretty good selection of beers.

SUMMARY AND COMMENTS It's quick and good, and the surroundings are undemanding of the discriminating diner. And that's meant in the nicest way. You don't have to put on the dog or your best clothes to have a good feed here.

Tommy Toy's ★ ★ ★ ½

CHINESE	MODERATE	QUALITY ★★★★	VALUE ★★★★½

655 Montgomery Street, Financial District; ☎ 415-397-4888; www.tommytoys.com

Reservations Recommended. When to go Anytime. Entree range $11–$30. Payment All major credit cards. Service rating ★★★★. Friendliness rating ★★★. Parking Street; valet, $5 (dinner only). Bar Full service. Wine selection Good. Dress Business; jacket and tie required for dinner. Disabled access Yes. Customers Locals, tourists. Hours Monday–Friday, 11:30 a.m.–2:30 p.m. and 5:30–9:30 p.m.; Saturday and Sunday, 5:30–9:30 p.m.

SETTING AND ATMOSPHERE The pedestrian entrance to Tommy's belies the magnificent setting that awaits the patron inside. The décor was fashioned after the 19th-century sitting room of the Empress Dowager and is a tapestry of etched glass panels, carved wooden archways, silvered mirrors, silk draperies, and ancient Chinese artifacts.

HOUSE SPECIALTIES According to Toy, there are only two great cuisines: Chinese and French. His chef prepares dishes that combine the best features of both traditions. Or as he puts it, "Chinese with a soupçon of French. Try the minced squab imperial served in lettuce cups, seafood bisque chinoise with yellow chives, and Chinese angelhair-crystal noodles.

OTHER RECOMMENDATIONS Reading the menu is its own special delight. It presents unusual but delicious combinations: smoked black cod with camphorwood and tea leaves served with chives, string beans, and wood ear mushrooms; vanilla prawns with fresh melon and raisins; and deep-fried tenderloin of pork with Chinese fruits in cassia nectar. If you have a huge appetite, especially for meat, fish and fowl, the Signature Dinner is a great value at $57.50

SUMMARY AND COMMENTS Prix fixe lunches are offered, averaging about $18 per person depending on the season and selections. It's best to put yourself in the very capable hands of the gracious and knowledgeable staff for your dining selections. They know all the items on the menu, what goes best with what and can prepare a fine evening of culinary delights for you and your guests. Do start the evening at Tommy's intimate and cozy bar. Just sitting in its tranquil atmosphere melts the day's tensions away.

Tommy's Joynt ★ ★

AMERICAN	INEXPENSIVE	QUALITY ★ ★ ★ ½	VALUE ★ ★ ★ ★ ★

**1101 Geary Boulevard, Civic Center; ☎ 415-775-4216;
www.tommysjoynt.com**

Reservations Not accepted. **When to go** Anytime. **Entree range** $5–$8. **Payment** Cash. **Service rating** ★ ★. **Friendliness rating** ★ ★. **Parking** Lot. **Bar** Full service. **Wine selection** Fair. **Dress** Casual. **Disabled access** Poor. **Customers** Everybody. **Hours** Daily, 11 a.m.–1:45 a.m.

SETTING AND ATMOSPHERE Crowded, noisy, crazy place with everything conceivable on the walls and ceiling. If you've ever lost anything, you might well find it here.

HOUSE SPECIALTIES Hof brau and deli; you can also find what roams on the range: genuine buffalo stew and, as an added treat, buffalo sandwich. Also famous for their pastrami and corned beef. The Irish come here on St. Patrick's day.

OTHER RECOMMENDATIONS Cheesecake, one of the best collection of imported beers in the city.

ENTERTAINMENT AND AMENITIES The décor.

SUMMARY AND COMMENTS This is one of the older places in the city to survive the earthquake of 1906. Don't come here to relax—come for the beer, buffalo, and fun.

Town's End Restaurant and Bakery ★ ★ ★

NEW AMERICAN	MODERATE	QUALITY ★ ★ ★ ★	VALUE ★ ★ ★ ★

2 Townsend Street, Building 4, SoMa; ☎ 415-512-0749

Reservations Recommended. **When to go** Anytime. **Entree range** Breakfast or brunch, $6–$10; lunch, $10–$14; dinner, $12–$20. **Payment** AE, MC, V. **Service rating** ★ ★ ★. **Friendliness rating** ★ ★ ★ ½. **Parking** Street, metered during day. **Bar** Beer, wine. **Wine selection** Limited but good. **Dress** Casual, informal. **Disabled access** Good. **Customers** Locals, businesspeople, tourists. **Hours** Tuesday–Thursday, 7:30–11 a.m., 11:30 a.m.–2:30 p.m., and 5–9 p.m.; Friday and Saturday, 7:30–11 a.m., 11:30 a.m.–2:30 p.m., and 5–10 p.m.; Saturday and Sunday brunch, 8 a.m.–2:30 p.m.

SETTING AND ATMOSPHERE Located at the breezy vanguard of the tony South Beach Marina Apartments on the Embarcadero south of the Bay Bridge, Town's End doesn't exactly command a view, but it feels as if it does, with its azure trompe l'oeil mural, glass walls, and the bridge twinkling in the distance to the north. The long, narrow dining area has an airy feel, an open kitchen, and a Zen approach to flower arrangement.

HOUSE SPECIALTIES Baskets of house-baked breads; homemade pastas, and house-smoked red trout and salmon. Niçoise salad; grilled salmon with corn and tomatillo relish; curried lamb stew with pecan-currant couscous; grilled chicken marinated in garlic, lemon, and lime with organic greens, pears, Roquefort, and walnuts. Lemon meringue pie with raspberry sauce; white chocolate Napoleon; raspberry brown butter tartlet.

OTHER RECOMMENDATIONS Brunch: fritatta scamorza with smoked mozzarella; wild mushrooms, sun-dried tomatoes and fresh herbs; Dungeness crab cakes with red peppers and green onions; Swedish oatmeal pancakes with pears and almonds.

SUMMARY AND COMMENTS Town's End is another SoMa venue with moderate prices and a tasty, freshly prepared menu. The fresh breads, pastries, and pastas are outstanding, but the salads and grilled offerings are good, too. Town's End's sauces are its major failing; they frequently do not equal the expertise of the pastas. Still, the unusual waterfront location, with neighboring gardens and parks, offers an idyll away from but still within the boundaries of city life. All wines on the small list are offered by the glass. The bakery section, with a few small tables, is open all day for coffee and pastry.

Trattoria Pinocchio ★ ★ ★ ½

ITALIAN	MODERATE	QUALITY ★★★★½	VALUE ★★★★★

**401 Columbus Avenue, North Beach; ☎ 415-392-1472;
www.trattoriapinocchio.com**

Reservations Accepted. When to go Anytime. Entree range $9–$24. Payment All major credit cards. Service rating ★★★★. Friendliness rating ★★★★. Parking No valet. Bar Full service. Wine selection Limited but good. Dress Casual. Disabled access Yes. Customers Tourists, locals. Hours Sunday–Thursday, 11:30 a.m.–11 p.m.; Friday–Saturday, 11:30 a.m.–midnight.

SETTING AND ATMOSPHERE Traditionally a trattoria is a notch below a ristorante in décor. Not so here. A sleek marble bar runs nearly the length of the restaurant. And a marble counter wraps around the open kitchen, affording views of the skilled staff. But there's still the la familia feel to the place, as if everyone knows everyone. Almost all the staff is Italian, very professional, and friendly.

HOUSE SPECIALTIES "Tomatoes, basil, and garlic, that's Italian, it's very simple," explains Elena Fabbri, the Tuscan-born chef of Pinocchio. The portobello is her signature dish. The cioppino—mussels, clams, calamari, fresh fish, and prawns in a tomato-garlic sauce—is also a favorite as is the carpaccio prepared the traditional way: hand-cut and pounded into paper-thin slices. Recommended entrees: scaloppine piccata or veal sautéed with a white wine and caper sauce. And perhaps the only dish with a sauce, the delicious grilled filet mignon, whole peppercorns, demi-glace sauce served with grilled asparagus and ciabatta bread. The bread absorbs the tasty flavors and the dish goes very well with a wonderful red wine: Montepulciano d'Abruzzo.

OTHER RECOMMENDATIONS Pizza. Desserts are always changing, but you might be offered crème brûlée, poached pear with chocolate, or tiramisu.

SUMMARY AND COMMENTS If you're on a walkabout, this is great place for a respite. The windows stretch from floor to ceiling and provide a great opportunity to sit and soak up the ambience of North Beach. There are also plenty of outdoor tables, all heated for the inevitable chilly evening.

Tu Lan ★ ½

VIETNAMESE	INEXPENSIVE	QUALITY ★★★	VALUE ★★★★★

8 Sixth Street, SoMa; ☎ 415-626-0927

ReservationsNot accepted. **When to go**Anytime. **Entree range**$5–$12. **Payment** Cash. **Service rating**★★. **Friendliness rating**★★. **Parking**Street. **Bar**Beer, wine. **Wine selection**House. **Dress**Casual. **Disabled access**No. **Customers**Locals, businesspeople. **Hours**Monday–Saturday, 11 a.m.–9 p.m.; closed Sunday.

SETTING AND ATMOSPHERE A scruffy, old, downtown diner with no friends. Old wooden floors, a long Formica counter, and rickety wooden tables and chairs, none which have four legs of the same length.

HOUSE SPECIALTIES Some really outstanding Vietnamese fare, considering the price. Hot and spicy soup dotted with pineapple bits; pounded shrimp wrapped on sugarcane sticks and broiled; spring rolls; imperial rolls; ginger fish or chicken; pork shish kebab; lemon beef salad.

OTHER RECOMMENDATIONS Curry potatoes are aromatic and delicious.

SUMMARY AND COMMENTS You can't miss Tu Lan. It's the tacky place on the corner with all the newspaper and magazine reviews taped on the window. There is only one reason to come here: to get what is, for the money, one of the best Vietnamese meals you can find outside of Saigon. It's located in what has been for a long time a tough and seedy neighborhood. The local denizens will likely be hanging out along your route, but if you walk by quickly they won't bite.

Watergate ★★★★

FRENCH/ASIAN	MODERATE	QUALITY ★★★★½	VALUE ★★★★★

1177 California Street, Mission District; ☎ 415-474-2000;
www.watergaterestaurant.com

Reservations Accepted. **When to go** Anytime. **Entree range** Prix fixe menu $19–$33. **Payment** AE, MC, V. **Service rating**★★★. **Friendliness rating**★★★. **Parking**Street. **Bar**Beer, wine. **Wine selection**Excellent. **Dress**Casual. **Disabled access** Yes. **Customers** Locals, tourists. **Hours** Sunday–Thursday, 5:30–10 p.m.; Friday and Saturday, 5:30–11 p.m.

SETTING AND ATMOSPHERE Elegant dark wood wainscoting contrasting with creamy walls. Wide windows opening out into the warm Mission evening. Gorgeous framed mirrors and geometric, semicubist mosaics on the wall give this place an air of the 1920s. Beautiful brocade chairs, linen tablecloths.

HOUSE SPECIALTIES Interesting pairings of traditional French sauces with many unusual Asian ingredients; unusual salads; wonderful soft-shell crab, daikon and tomato salad, hazelnuts, mustard sauce; sautéed foie gras, grapes, verjuice sauce; black Mission figs filled with brie, prosciutto, veal sauce; salmon carpaccio, avocado salad, tobikko, basil oil. Seasonal menu changes daily.

OTHER RECOMMENDATIONS The desserts are lovely (especially the Napoleons); definitely sample one of the many after-dinner teas served in charming one-of-a-kind purple clay teapots.

SUMMARY AND COMMENTS A wonderfully refined and understated place without the snootiness associated with an establishment of this caliber. The presentation and colors of the prepared dishes is exceptional, as well the as freshness of the ingredients. Wonderfully unique cuisine in an unexpected environment: directly in the heart of burrito heaven: the Mission.

West Bay Café ★ ★ ★

CALIFORNIAN	MODERATE	QUALITY ★★★★	VALUE ★★★★

1177 Airport Boulevard, Burlingame, San Francisco International Airport; ☎ **650-373-7038; www.sfocp.com**

Reservations Accepted. When to go Anytime. Entree range $8–$20. Payment All major credit cards. Service rating ★★★. Friendliness rating ★★★½. Parking Hotel lot. Bar Full service. Wine selection Short but good. Dress Casual. Disabled access Yes. Customers Locals, frequent flyers. Hours Daily, 6 a.m.–10 p.m.

SETTING AND ATMOSPHERE A roomy open space with soft lighting welcomes the weary traveler. Earth tones and pecan-colored woodwork form a backdrop for large pictures of grapevines overlooking cozy booths. This is a place to decompress when you have battled the traffic to the airport, or to have that farewell dinner before boarding your flight home next morning (if you're staying in the adjoining hotel).

HOUSE SPECIALTIES It's basically a California cuisine kitchen. The chef (a graduate of the Culinary Institute of America) takes what's available locally and in season and interferes with it as little as possible. Soups are superb, with clam chowder and tomato bisque among the best. Herbed lamb chops are the chef's signature dish, but we love the seafood and sausage stew enough to make a special trip for it. Pan-roasted basil chicken is moist and tender and herby, and there is always a vegan or vegetarian plate available. It changes daily.

OTHER RECOMMENDATIONS Crab cakes are superior, served with avocado salad. Desserts are made fresh daily in house. Try the chocolate molten cake drenched with grappa, cranberries, and topped with pecan butter ice cream.

SUMMARY AND COMMENTS It's a rare thing when we recommend a hotel restaurant. Such places tend to rely on their "captive audience" and so fall short of the mark. We are always happy to report exceptions to the rule. Only two miles south of SFO, it's an oasis in an otherwise gastronomic desert.

Yank Sing ★ ★ ★

CHINESE	INEXPENSIVE	QUALITY ★★★½	VALUE ★★★★

101 Spear Street (located at One Rincon Center), Financial District; ☎ **415-957-9300; www.yanksing.com** **49 Stevenson Street;** ☎ **415-541-4949; www.yanksing.com**

Reservations Accepted. When to go Lunch. Entree range $7–$12 (à la carte). Payment All major credit cards. Service rating ★★½. Friendliness rating ★★½. Parking Street. Bar Beer, wine. Wine selection House. Dress Casual. Disabled access Yes. **Customers** Locals, businesspeople. **Hours** 101 Spear: Monday–Friday, 11 a.m.–3 p.m.; Saturday and Sunday, 10 a.m.–4 p.m.; 49 Stevenson: Daily, 11 a.m.–3 p.m.

SETTING AND ATMOSPHERE A modernly furnished restaurant; white tablecloths and impeccable service make it a step above the usual dim sum house. A class act for simple fare.

HOUSE SPECIALTIES Dim sum and yet more dim sum constantly issuing forth fresh from the kitchen. Choose barbecued pork buns; shrimp moons; and silver-wrapped chicken wheeled out on trolleys.

OTHER RECOMMENDATIONS Small portions of Peking duck. A wide variety of vegetarian dim sum, including pea leaves; sautéed eggplant and mustard greens; chrysanthemum blossom tea.

SUMMARY AND COMMENTS Selections are cooked with less fat than usual. Yuppies love it here; they can stuff themselves without having to spend any extra time at the gym.

Yuet Lee ★ ★ ½

| CHINESE | INEXPENSIVE/MODERATE | QUALITY ★ ★ ★ ½ | VALUE ★ ★ ★ ★ ★ |

1300 Stockton Street, Chinatown; ☎ 415-982-6020

Reservations Not accepted. **When to go** Anytime. **Entree range** $7–$15. **Payment** Cash only. **Service rating** ★★★. **Friendliness rating** ★★★. **Parking** Street, public pay lots. **Bar** Beer, wine. **Wine selection** House. **Dress** Casual. **Disabled access** Good. **Customers** Locals, businesspeople, tourists. **Hours** Wednesday–Monday, 11 a.m.–3 a.m.; closed Tuesday.

SETTING AND ATMOSPHERE Nondescript, clangorous, Formica-tabled seafood and noodle shop on a busy corner in north Chinatown; fresh seafood tanks, chartreuse-framed windows, and an open kitchen with flying cleavers.

HOUSE SPECIALTIES Fresh seafood specialties: seasonal lobster; pepper-and-salt prawns; crab with ginger and onion; fresh boiled geoduck or razor clams; steelhead fillet with greens; sautéed fresh and dried squid. Clay pots: salted fish with diced chicken and bean cake; roast pork, bean cake, and shrimp sauce; oyster and roast pork with ginger and onion. Roast squab; braised chicken with abalone; fresh New Zealand mussels with black-bean sauce; steamed live rock cod with ham and shredded black mushrooms. Also, a vast assortment of noodles and noodle soups: wontons and dumplings; braised noodles with beef stew; Amoy- or Singapore-style rice sticks.

OTHER RECOMMENDATIONS Rice soups or plates; roast duck.

SUMMARY AND COMMENTS There are basically two kinds of people in the world: those who believe salvation can be found in a bowl of Chinese noodles and those who do not. If you are among the former, you will not care about Yuet Lee's fluorescent lighting, linoleum floors, and slam-bang service. You will forsake soft music and cloth napkins and candlelight. You will know that each vessel of glistening dumplings swimming in broth perfumed by star anise and ginger and scattered with emerald scallions contains all the mysteries of the universe. You will want to taste every item on the menu; stay until closing time at 3 a.m. just to watch the fragrant platters come steaming from the kitchen, yea, verily, to become one with the noodles and the fish.

Zarzuela ★ ★ ★

SPANISH	MODERATE	QUALITY ★★★★	VALUE ★★★★★

2000 Hyde Street, Marina District; ☎ 415-346-0800

Reservations Not accepted. When to go Anytime. Entree range Tapas, $4–$9; entrees, $12–$17. Payment MC, V. Service rating ★★★★. Friendliness rating ★★★★. Parking Street. Bar Beer, wine. Wine selection Limited but good. Dress Casual. Disabled access Good. Customers Locals, tourists. Hours Tuesday–Thursday, 5:30–10 p.m.; Friday and Saturday, 5:30–10:30 p.m.

SETTING AND ATMOSPHERE Disarming warmth beckons as piquant aromas of garlic and seafood waft over the sidewalk. Modest appointment inside; tawny walls and tile floors, beamed ceilings and arched windows, hand-painted dishes on the walls, and the music of soft guitars. The nuances of Spanish culture and charm softly beguile.

HOUSE SPECIALTIES Thirty-eight types of tapas. Mussels or clams with white wine and garlic; paella; grilled shrimp; poached octopus with potatoes and paprika; snails baked on croutons; grilled scallops and chard with red pepper sauce; Spanish sausage with wine; cold roast veal with olives; grilled vegetables; rolled eggplant with goat cheese. Entrees include Zarzuela, a Catalan seafood stew; pork tenderloin in raisin and pine nut sauce; paella; loin of lamb in thyme and red wine.

OTHER RECOMMENDATIONS Sangria; gazpacho; romaine salad with roasted garlic; caramel flan; Alicante Muscatel dessert wine.

SUMMARY AND COMMENTS Oranges and olives, garlic and olives, red wine and sherries; Spanish cuisine presents a provocative departure from French and Italian in its colorful little tapas plates and the substantial offerings issuing forth from Zarzuela's kitchen. Dishes are as refined as they are close to the earth. Prices are as soothing as the ambience, and a small group of diners can sample a wide assortment of dishes without having to run to the ATM. Darkly sweet and spicy sangria is poured into large goblets. Zarzuela is a quintessential neighborhood restaurant: low-key, low-priced, and welcoming.

Zuni Café and Grill ★ ★ ★

ITALIAN	MODERATE	QUALITY ★★★★	VALUE ★★★★

1658 Market Street, Mission District; ☎ 415-552-2522

Reservations Accepted. When to go Anytime. Entree range $17–$24. Payment AE, MC, V. Service rating ★★★. Friendliness rating ★★★. Parking Street. Bar Full service. Wine selection Superior. Dress Casual, business. Disabled access Yes. Customers Locals, businesspeople, tourists. Hours Tuesday–Saturday, 11:30 a.m.–midnight; Sunday, 11 a.m.–11 p.m.

SETTING AND ATMOSPHERE Lots of bustle. A happy and exuberant place full of people coming and going, eating and enjoying, at all hours of the day and into the night. There's a long copper bar just right for bellying up and holding forth to all who will listen and an excellent view of busy Market Street.

HOUSE SPECIALTIES The menu changes daily, and only the best stuff is purchased for Zuni. Rib-eye steak; roast chicken; grilled tuna; braised cod; pasta dishes; any soup; vegetable fritters.

OTHER RECOMMENDATIONS Regularly available hamburgers and pizza. Fans of the Zuni say that it offers the best burger and fries in town.

SUMMARY AND COMMENTS This place concentrates on perfecting the simple. The kitchen team will mine a single ingredient or recipe for the most it can give while still retaining its essential character. An example is the use of Meyer lemons. They are grown almost exclusively in the backyards of East Bay homes and are sweeter and more aromatic than other lemons. The Meyer is to lemons what the truffle is to mushrooms.

PART EIGHT

ENTERTAINMENT and NIGHTLIFE

PERFORMING ARTS

WHILE SAN FRANCISCO HAS TO FIGHT OFF a reputation for provincialism when it comes to the arts, it's the only city on the West Coast to boast its own professional symphony, ballet, and opera companies. They benefit from the thriving support of the city's upper crust, who wine and dine their way through glittering fund-raisers. Other hallmarks of the San Francisco cultural milieu include free summer music concerts and a burgeoning theater scene.

CLASSICAL MUSIC

Louise M. Davies Symphony Hall (201 Van Ness Avenue at Grove Street; ☎ 415-864-6000) is the permanent home of the **San Francisco Symphony**. Musical Director Michael Tilson Thomas and many of the world's best-known soloists and guest conductors offer a year-round season of classical music, as well as occasional performances by offbeat musical and touring groups. The cheapest seats are generally around $20. Call about the availability of standby tickets on the day of a concert; they sometimes cost less than $30; visit **www.sfsymphony.org.**

A night at the opera in San Francisco is no small affair. The newly renovated **War Memorial Opera House** in the Civic Center District is an opulent venue for the **San Francisco Opera Association,** which has received rave reviews since the building opened in 1932. The San Francisco Opera consistently wins critical acclaim for operatic warhorses as well as obscure Russian opuses that other companies prefer not to tackle.

With its considerable international weight, the San Francisco Opera pulls in heavy hitters such as Placido Domingo, Marilyn Horne, Joan Sutherland, and others. The three-month main season starts at the beginning of September, and opening night is one of the main social events on the West Coast. Tickets start at more than $35, but standing room costs considerably less. For ticket and schedule information, call ☎ 415-864-3330; or visit **www.sfopera.com.**

BALLET

THE **San Francisco Ballet** ALSO CALLS THE WAR MEMORIAL Opera House home. The oldest and third-largest ballet company in the United States has a four-month season from February to May. The San Francisco Ballet was the first company in the country to perform *The Nutcracker* as a Christmas event (and still does each December) and offers consistently excellent productions of full-length neoclassical and contemporary ballets. Tickets range from $8 to $199. For ticket and schedule information, call ☎ 415-865-2000; or visit **www.sfballet.org.**

SUMMER CLASSICAL MUSIC FESTIVALS

THE **Stern Grove Festival** IS ONE OF THE NATION'S OLDEST (since 1938) free summer music festivals. The festival presents ten outdoor concerts on Sunday afternoons from June through August at the sylvan **Sigmund Stern Grove** in San Francisco. Performances include the San Francisco Ballet, Symphony, and Opera, as well as a diverse mix of blues, jazz, popular, and world music. Come early with a blanket to this magnificent, eucalyptus-lined grove. For schedule information, call ☎ 415-252-6252; or visit **www.sterngrove.org.**

Midsummer Mozart presents a summer season of the works of Mozart in many venues around the Bay Area. The **Festival Orchestra** is conducted by George Cleve and features well-known soloists. Chamber concerts are presented on the first Saturday of the month during the year at the Legion of Honor. Tickets range from $20 to $50. For schedule and ticket information, call ☎ 415-627-9141; or visit **www.midsummermozart.org.**

THEATER

THE MAJORITY OF SAN FRANCISCO'S THEATERS congregate downtown around the Theater District, just west of Union Square. The **American Conservatory Theater** (ACT) is the Bay Area's leading theater group, offering celebrated classics and new works on the stage of the **Geary Theater** (450 Geary Boulevard at Mason Street). Celebrated thespians to appear in ACT productions include Olympia Dukakis, John Turturro, and Annette Bening. The season runs from September through July, and tickets range from $12 to $65. For more information, call the box office at ☎ 415-749-2ACT; or visit **www.act-sfbay.org.**

Three downtown theaters concentrate on Broadway productions; call ☎ 415-551-2000 for schedule and ticket information; or visit **www.shnsf.com.** The **Curran Theatre** (445 Geary Street at Taylor

Street) sometimes tackles the bigger shows such as Andrew Lloyd Webber's *The Phantom of the Opera* under the direction of its original London production team; the show ran for five years. Presently, the Curran is hosting the Best of Broadway series featuring famous musicals. The **Golden Gate Theatre** (1 Taylor Street at Market Street), built in 1922, is often described as an Art Deco palace. The ornate **Orpheum Theatre** (1192 Market at Eighth Street), a city historical monument, presents a variety of traveling musical productions.

After the ACT, **Magic Theatre** in Fort Mason is one of the city's busiest companies—and consistently rated the most exciting. The company specializes in the works of contemporary playwrights and emerging talent; Sam Shepard traditionally premiered his new plays here. For schedule and ticket information, call ☎ 415-441-8822; or visit **www.magictheatre.org.**

In the heart of San Francisco, the **Yerba Buena Center for the Arts** presents art and art education in a lovely location. Attractions include award-winning theater groups, film and video presentations, and museum and gallery exhibitions. The center is located at 701 Mission Street across from the Moscone Convention Center in SoMa. For ticket information, call ☎ 415-978-ARTS; or visit **www.ybca.org.**

TICKET AGENCIES

Mr. Ticket (2065 VAN NESS AVENUE) IS THE BAY AREA'S largest ticket agency offering premium seating for sports, concerts, and theater productions at market prices. Major credit cards are accepted, and delivery is available. For more information, call ☎ 415-775-3031 from San Francisco or ☎ 800-424-7328 outside the area; or visit their Web site at **www.mrticket.com.**

Tickets.com offers tickets for theater, sports, concerts, and other Bay Area events through their Web site. A service charge is added to the ticket price.

TIX Bay Area sells half-price, day-of-performance tickets for selected theater, dance, and music events (cash only), as well as full-price, advance-sale tickets for local performing events (by credit card). A service charge is added to ticket prices. TIX is located on the western side of Union Square on Powell Street. Call ☎ 415-433-7827 for information; or visit **www.tixbayarea.com.**

▌▌ SAN FRANCISCO NIGHTLIFE

YOU'VE JUST LANDED IN ONE OF THE BEST nightlife cities in the Western world. Do you want to dance—free-form, rhumba, tango, or swing? Dressed in formal, leather, or naked (well, almost)? Do you want to drink microbrews with local Bohemians, shoot darts with the Irish, sing off-key with tourists, or prowl a singles meat market where hormones are as thick as San Francisco fog? Do you want fancy, not so fancy, or downright dirty? Straight, gay, bi, all of the above, or just confused? San Francisco opens its Golden Gate to you.

Any style, taste, gender, or orientation can be found here, but one of the most important trends in San Francisco nightlife and culture is the "retro" scene. Choose your decade: 1940s big-band elegance, 1950s swing, even 1960s groove (1970s disco rarely rears its blow-dried head). Take a trip to a vintage clothing store or just come as you are. Step into a retro club and through the portals of time. The bouncer is dressed in a zoot suit or bears a faint resemblance to Elvis. The bartender is shaking martinis, there's a cigarette girl making her rounds, the dance floor is full of jitterbugs, and the only way you can tell that the girl in the 1940s hairdo and the cashmere sweater isn't Rosie the Riveter is by the ring in her nose. Retro does not preclude piercings and tattoos.

A related aspect of this scene, permeating all nightlife culture, is the return of "cocktail nation." Skillful mixologists are now almost as highly regarded as the DJs who mix the music. Gone, mercifully, are the days when a club-hopper ordered just a glass of white wine or some crazy brain-food drink, or a slam-dunk to a cheap drunk. The martini in classic form and many variations, along with its cousin the Cosmopolitan, are among the most popular drinks.

Along with this return to "Happy Days" is a sense of elegance and a restoration of polite behavior. In a retro club, and even in a not-so-retro club, it is not considered chic, progressive, or relevant to talk with a loud or foul mouth, energetically condemn the establishment, or dress like a slob to show one's lemming-like individualism. San Francisco, always a more civilized place than most, is these days even more civilized.

The city is also one of the most important musical centers of the nation. All kinds of jazz, rock, punk, acid, and even orchestral music have been incubated here. The only thing you won't find here is country/western music. You'll have to head south to San Jose for line dancing and cowboy hats. Virtually every neighborhood in the city has a variety of music venues, so common and plentiful that they're taken for granted.

Some practical considerations: Most of the clubs listed are located in a contiguous swath running from North Beach (quaint, excellent views, less fog) through the Union Square area (uptown, elegant) to the SoMa and Mission Districts (leading edge, alternative). And since San Francisco is a small city, clubs are not far apart. If you don't find one to be your cup of tea, just check out its neighbors. In North Beach, all you have to do is walk along Broadway, peering down the side streets as you go. At Union Square, just stand on a corner and point yourself in any direction. In the SoMa and Mission districts, the greatest concentration of clubs is on Folsom Street, between Seventh and Eleventh streets. It's a good idea to go by foot or taxi. Driving under the influence is a serious offense here, and the cops will frequently set up drunk-driver checks on the main streets.

unofficial **TIP**
Go to the clubs by foot or taxi. The cops will frequently set up drunk-driver checks on the main streets.

A good way to see the city by night without having to drive is to travel with **3 Babes & a Bus.** Every Saturday and sometimes on Friday, for $35, Rishi, CC, and Jaz will load you and yours onto a party bus with a highly mixed and totally unpredictable crowd of revelers and take you on a nocturnal tour of the city, stopping at three or four of the more popular clubs. You won't have to pay cover charges, you get priority admittance, and you leave the driving and often impossible parking to them. This is also a good way to meet other revelers. Gentlemen should be advised that bachelorette parties are frequent patrons of the 3 Babes. In fact, women usually make up the majority of patrons. You must be 21 with a valid ID; jeans and tennis shoes are a no-no. Pickup is at Ruby Skye (see below) at 9:30 p.m., with drop-off around 1:30 a.m. (☎ 800-414-0158 or visit **www.threebabes.com**).

Another kind of movable feast is **Mr. Rick's Martini Club.** If you like vintage clothing, a touch of elegance, swing and ballroom dancing, and convivial dining with like-minded people, this is for you. Martini Club events happen at a different location every month or so. Cover charge is about $30 per person and includes the martini of your choice. The fixed-price dinner also usually runs about $32. The best big bands and swing ensembles play these gigs, and some very fine dancers and eager beginners fill the floor. Get the schedule from Laurie Gordon at ☎ 415-566-2545; or check out the Web site at **www.martinimusic.com/clubhome.htm.**

Up-to-the-minute club information is listed in the *San Francisco Bay Guardian* (**www.sfbg.com**) and *San Francisco Weekly,* (**www.sfweekly.com**), free weekly newspapers available at any newsstand. It is illegal to smoke in any restaurant, and in any bar not owner-operated. Most Californians are nonsmokers and support the law. And if you call a bar and ask if they are in comportment with the law they will likely say "yes." The truth, however, is often a bit more, shall we say, smoky. A few establishments are in open defiance and have become havens for smokers. And some have been heavily fined for it. You will know as soon as you enter them which ones don't comply. And it's easy to tell which ones are in conformity, as they will have a small crowd of patrons standing outside lighting up.

Ever since the gold rush of 1848, San Francisco has been a city of revels. Many locals live for it. Some make it an art form. People from Los Angeles and Seattle fly in for it. And now you're in the middle of it. Tip a dollar per drink, pace yourself, and don't forget your trench coat.

San Francisco Nightclubs by Neighborhood

NAME	DESCRIPTION
CHINATOWN	
Li Po	Bar
Tonga Room	Tropical island bar
Top O' the Mark	Rooftop lounge and dance floor
CIVIC CENTER	
Fillmore	Rock and roll ballroom
Great American Music Hall	Rock concert hall
Jade Bar	Asian chic cocktail lounge
Noc Noc	Cave bar
UNION SQUARE	
Biscuits & Blues	Blues supper club
Gold Dust Lounge	Barbary Coast saloon
Harry Denton's Starlight Room	Rooftop dance club
The Plush Room	Cabaret and cocktail lounge
The Red Room	Retro cocktail lounge
Ruby Skye	Swank nightclub
FINANCIAL DISTRICT	
Bubble Lounge	Champagne bar
NORTH BEACH	
Bimbo's 365 Club	Classic big-band nightclub
Impala	Restaurant and nightclub
Pier 23	Jazz bar and restaurant
Tosca's	Opera bar
SOMA/MISSION DISTRICT	
Amira	Middle Eastern coffee house
The Café	Gay and lesbian club
Café du Nord	Dance club
The Elbo Room	Neighborhood pub cum dance club
Harvey's	Gay bar
Make-Out Room	Neo-Bohemian hipster bar
Martunis	Cocktail lounge as art
RICHMOND/SUNSET DISTRICT	
Club Deluxe	Retro hot spot
Plough and the Stars	Irish pub

NIGHTCLUB PROFILES

Amira Restaurant

MIDDLE EASTERN COFFEE HOUSE

590 Valencia Street, SoMa/Mission District; ☎ **415-621-6213;**
www.amiraistanbul.com

Cover None. **Minimum** None. **Mixed drinks** None. **Wine** $3.50. **Beer** $3.50.
Dress Casual. **Specials** Middle Eastern music. **Food available** Sandwiches, salads,
soups, Turkish and Greek snacks and desserts. **Hours** Tuesday and Thursday,
5 p.m.–1 a.m.; Wednesday, 5–11 p.m.; Friday and Saturday, 5 p.m.–midnight.

WHO GOES THERE   The quiet, the tired, the bleary-eyed club-hopper.

WHAT GOES ON   A recovery room in the night scene of the Mission District. A
   chance to decompress with a delicious cup of rich, black, steamy Turkish
   coffee and a bite to eat. People come here to wind down after an
   evening's revels or just to catch their breath in the midst of an all-nighter.

SETTING AND ATMOSPHERE   Arabian Nights setting; a golden glow in the foggy
   San Francisco evening. Low tables, stools, throw pillows, brass artifacts,
   and the smell of coffee and rose water.

IF YOU GO   On belly dancing nights, you'll need reservations after 8:30 p.m.

Bimbo's 365 Club

CLASSIC BIG-BAND NIGHTCLUB

1025 Columbus Avenue, North Beach; ☎ **415-474-0365;**
www.bimbos365club.com

Cover Varies according to show. **Minimum** 2 drinks. **Mixed drinks** $4.50 and up.
Wine $4–$8. **Beer** $3–$4. **Dress** Varies. **Food available** None. **Hours** Shows usually begin at 8 p.m., with doors open 1 hour before

WHO GOES THERE   Very mixed crowd.

WHAT GOES ON   A wide range of musical entertainment from lounge to jazz
   to rock and soul. The big draws these days are retro nights, when guys
   and dolls wear zoot suits, circle skirts, tuxedos, and full-length gowns.
   The Preservation Hall Jazz Orchestra or Mr. Rick's martini band might
   play after Work That Skirt gives free dance lessons. Tap and bubble
   dancers often round out the program.

SETTING AND ATMOSPHERE   Beautifully restored, 1940s-style nightclub with a
   large stage and dance floor, roving photographer and cigarette girl, and
   the famous Dolphina, the nude lady in a giant fishbowl. Put on your
   black and white and step into another, better time.

IF YOU GO   Call for information and reservations.

Biscuits & Blues

BLUES SUPPER CLUB

401 Mason Street, Theater District; ☎ **415-292-2583;**
www.biscuitsandblues.com

san francisco after dark

Nightclubs
1. Amira
2. Bimbo's 365 Club
3. Biscuits & Blues
4. Blue Lamp
5. Bruno's Cafe
6. The Café
7. Café du Nord
8. Club Deluxe
9. The Elbo Room
10. Fillmore
11. Gold Dust Lounge
12. Great American Music Hall
13. Harry Denton's Starlight Room
14. Harvey's
15. Li Po
16. Make-Out Room
17. Martunis
18. Noc Noc
19. Pier 23
20. Plough and the Stars
21. The Plush Room
22. The Red Room
23. Tonga Room
24. Top O' the Mark
25. Tosca's

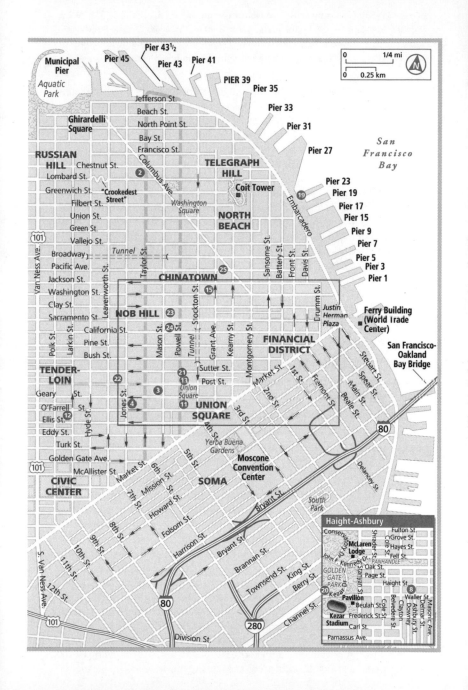

Municipal Pier
Aquatic Park
Ghirardelli Square
Pier 45
Pier 43½
Pier 43
Pier 41
PIER 39
Pier 35
Pier 33
Pier 31
Pier 27

Jefferson St.
Beach St.
North Point St.
Bay St.
Francisco St.

RUSSIAN HILL
Chestnut St.
Lombard St.
Greenwich St.
Filbert St.
Union St.
Green St.
Vallejo St.
"Crookedest Street"
Columbus Ave.
Washington Square

TELEGRAPH HILL
Coit Tower
NORTH BEACH

San Francisco Bay

Pier 23
Pier 19
Pier 17
Pier 15
Pier 9
Pier 7
Pier 5
Pier 3
Pier 1

Broadway
Pacific Ave.
Jackson St.
Washington St.
Clay St.
Sacramento St.
Tunnel
Van Ness Ave.
Leavenworth St.
Taylor St.
CHINATOWN
NOB HILL
California St.
Pine St.
Bush St.
Mason St.
Powell St.
Tunnel
Stockton St.
Grant Ave.
Kearny St.
Montgomery St.
Sansome St.
Battery St.
Front St.
Davis St.
Drumm St.
Embarcadero
Justin Herman Plaza

FINANCIAL DISTRICT

Ferry Building (World Trade Center)

San Francisco–Oakland Bay Bridge

TENDER-LOIN
Geary St.
O'Farrell St.
Ellis St.
Eddy St.
Turk St.
Golden Gate Ave.
McAllister St.
Polk St.
Larkin St.
Hyde St.
Jones St.
Sutter St.
Post St.
Union Square
UNION SQUARE
Market St.
1st St.
2nd St.
3rd St.
Fremont St.
Beale St.
Main St.
Spear St.
Steuart St.

CIVIC CENTER
SOMA
Yerba Buena Gardens
Moscone Convention Center
Mission St.
Market St.
4th St.
5th St.
6th St.
7th St.
8th St.
9th St.
10th St.
11th St.
12th St.
S. Van Ness Ave.
Howard St.
Folsom St.
Harrison St.
Bryant St.
Brannan St.
Townsend St.
King St.
Berry St.
Channel St.
Division St.
South Park
Delancey St.

0   1/4 mi
0   0.25 km

Haight-Ashbury
Conservatory
McLaren Lodge
GOLDEN GATE PARK
John F. Kennedy Dr.
Kezar Dr.
Stanyan St.
Shrader St.
Cole St.
PANHANDLE
Pavilion
Beulah St.
Kezar Stadium
Frederick St.
Carl St.
Parnassus Ave.
Fulton St.
Grove St.
Hayes St.
Fell St.
Oak St.
Page St.
Haight St.
Clayton St.
Belvedere St.
Cole St.
Ashbury St.
Downey St.
Delmar St.
Waller St.
Masonic Ave.

Cover $5–$30 (varies by artist). **Minimum** None. **Mixed drinks** $3.50–$8. **Wine** Bottles, $14–$28; $6–$8 by the glass. **Beer** $3.50–4.75. **Dress** Casual. **Food available** Full menu. **Hours** Tuesday–Saturday, 7 p.m.–1 a.m. (depending on length of show); Sunday and Monday, 7 p.m.–midnight (depending on length of show)

WHO GOES THERE Eclectic crowd of blues lovers.

WHAT GOES ON Dedication to the preservation of the blues. Eat Southern country cooking and listen raptly and politely to some great and some not-so-great practitioners of this uniquely American musical form. In recent months, other musical forms have been featured as well: rockabilly, funk, and swing are among the more popular. Call for the current acts.

SETTING AND ATMOSPHERE The club is located in the type of basement venue that was first a necessity, then a statement, and now the norm for jazz, blues, and other non-mainstream types of music clubs. It's close, cramped, and intimate, with some splashes of modern art, and candles on tables arranged in a horseshoe shape around the stage and small dance floor. Movie actor Danny Glover is part owner and his culinary background is reflected in a menu featuring fried chicken and biscuits (quite good), hush puppies (not quite so good), deep-fried dill pickles (you be the judge), and black-eyed peas. Some good beers, a short wine list, and a fine collection of single-malt scotch.

IF YOU GO The kitchen can be glacially slow until food service stops at about 10 p.m. People start dancing at about the same time.

Bubble Lounge

CHAMPAGNE BAR

714 Montgomery Street, Financial District; ☎ **415 434-4204;**
www.bubblelounge.com

Cover None. **Minimum** None. **Mixed drinks** $4 and up. **Wine** $6 and up. **Beer** $4–$6. **Dress** Casually elegant. **Food available** Appetizers, oyster bar. **Hours** Monday, 5:30 p.m.–1 a.m.; Tuesday–Saturday, 6:30 p.m.–2 a.m.; closed in winter.

WHO GOES THERE Locals who love sparkling wines and sparkling conversation.

WHAT GOES ON No staid wine bar this is. It's more like a mirthful cocktail party, as sparkling as the wines it specializes in. People come here to escape loud music, the press of crowds, and the frenetic experience that city nightlife can become. Yet they don't want to be bored. It's popular as an after-work tipple place, then picks up again in mid-evening, and goes on all night with champagne corks popping every few minutes.

SETTING AND ATMOSPHERE An elegant (but not pretentious) salon, with draperies hanging from the walls, settees and couches as well as easy chairs and coffee tables placed strategically about. Plenty of standing room remains for clustering and table hopping. The staff go to great lengths to maintain the civilized atmosphere, and a dress code is strictly enforced. "A neat overall appearance is sought, and the following clothing items will not be accepted: sneakers, gym or workout garments, sandals, baseball caps, military or combat fatigues, and swimwear." And gentlemen are required to remove their hats upon entering.

IF YOU GO Go early if you want to sit at the bar.

The Café

GAY AND LESBIAN

2369 Market Street at Castro Street, SoMa/Mission District;
☎ **415-861-3846;**

Cover None. Minimum None. Mixed drinks $3.50. Wine $2.50–$4.75. Beer $1.25–$3. Dress Everything from jeans to drag. Food available None. Hours Daily, 3 p.m.–2 a.m.

WHO GOES THERE Women seeking women, men seeking men.

WHAT GOES ON The question is, what doesn't go on? Originally set up by women to be one of the premier lesbian social centers, The Café has become extremely popular among gay male fun-seekers. Mostly a dance house for high-energy techno music, but there's a pool table for variety.

SETTING AND ATMOSPHERE A dark, neon-lit, coed dance club that overlooks the Castro. It's hot and hopping in here, but there's an outdoor balcony where you can take a breather. Don't bother coming if you don't want to be checked out; this is definitely a spot where you'll be hit on, unless you're obviously straight. The drinks are cheap, and the staff is friendly.

IF YOU GO You better not care about second-hand smoke, or PDA (public displays of affection) for that matter. On weekends it's nearly impossible to get in, so start early. And don't worry about taking the time to go to the bank; there's an ATM in the back by the bar.

Café Du Nord

DANCE CLUB

2170 Market Street, SoMa/Mission District;
☎ **415-861-5016; www.cafedunord.com**

Cover Varies; no cover before 8 p.m. Minimum None. Mixed drinks $4–$9. Wine $3.50–$6.50. Beer $3.75–$4.50. Dress Dress to impress. Food available American continental with European flair; Thursday–Saturday, 7–11 p.m., entrées, $13.50–$16. Hours Sunday–Tuesday, 6 p.m.–2 a.m.; Thursday–Saturday, 4 p.m.– 2 a.m.; dinner served Wednesday–Saturday, 6:30–11 p.m.

WHO GOES THERE 20- to 30-something hipsters.

WHAT GOES ON A mix of music and dance. Tuesday nights usually feature live jazz, while Saturdays often showcase a live rock band. Some nights have DJs instead of live bands and are aimed at the Gen-Xers, with the crowd leaning to the gothic younger side. Check out the club's Web site for updated show schedules.

SETTING AND ATMOSPHERE If you get past the weekend line, you'll walk downstairs to this basement cabaret that used to be a 1920s speakeasy. There are oil paintings alongside black-and-white photos dimly lit by converted gaslamps. Experienced swing and salsa dancers inspire you to take lessons. If the scene is too fast for you, escape back past the bar to cuddle up with a love interest on an antique couch. The polished hardwood floors and trim complement the well-dressed hipsters and specialty liquors. If you're not here on a date, it's quite possible you could leave with one.

IF YOU GO The place doesn't start jumpin' until around 10 p.m., so if you're not into loud rock bands or scary 1980s DJ music, come early for a pint or a whiskey and cuddle up on a couch with your honey at one of the most seductive lounges in town.

Club Deluxe

RETRO HOT SPOT

1509–1511 Haight Street, Richmond/Sunset District; ☎ 415-552-6949; www.clubdeluxesf.com

Cover $3–$5. **Minimum** None. **Mixed drinks** $3.50–$8. **Wine** $3–$5. **Beer** $3–$5. **Dress** Vintage. **Food available** None. **Hours** Monday–Friday, 6 p.m.–2 a.m.; Saturday, 2 p.m.–2 a.m.; Sunday, 2 p.m.–2 a.m.

WHO GOES THERE Gen-X retro hipsters, Haight Street locals.

WHAT GOES ON Sipping cocktails, lounging like a lizard, and looking cool.

SETTING AND ATMOSPHERE A step back from the 1960s world of Haight-Ashbury to the hip, art deco 1940s. Smooth leather booths and slick Formica tables accessorize the suspenders, skirts, suits, and 'dos of the impressively retro room and ultimate retro crowd. Quality local jazz and swing bands play Wednesday through Sunday after 9 p.m. ATM inside.

IF YOU GO Known among locals to have the best Bloody Mary in town. Parking, like everything else, can sometimes be crazy on Haight Street. Try a few blocks up from the strip or take the 6, 7, 33, or 43 Muni bus.

The Elbo Room

NEIGHBORHOOD PUB CUM DANCE CLUB

647 Valencia Street, SoMa/Mission District; ☎ 415-552-7788; www.elbo.com

Cover $5–$10. **Minimum** None. **Mixed drinks** $4. **Wine** $4–$8. **Beer** $3.50 and up. **Dress** Casual. **Specials** Drink specials nightly. **Food available** None. **Hours** Daily, 5 p.m.–2 a.m.

WHO GOES THERE Local Bohemians.

WHAT GOES ON In the large bar downstairs, neighborhood regulars drink beer, shoot pool, and schmooze. One expects to see Archie Bunker in his younger days. Upstairs, soul funk and Latin musicians play for a very discriminating crowd of music aficionados and polished dancers (beginners are welcome, too). On nights with no live music, talented DJs work the sounds.

SETTING AND ATMOSPHERE Look at it with one eye and you'd call it "working class." Look at it with the other eye and you might call it "Bohemian."

Either way it's unpretentious, and unventilated as well. People here don't mind sweating.

IF YOU GO Don't go tired or hungry.

Fillmore

ROCK AND ROLL BALLROOM

**1805 Geary Boulevard (at Fillmore Street), Civic Center;
☎ 415-346-6000; www.thefillmore.com**

Cover $9 and up. Minimum None. Mixed drinks $3.75–$6.75. Wine $3.75–$5.25. Beer $3.50–$4.75. Dress Varies. Food available American cuisine upstairs amid a selection of infamous vintage psychedelic concert posters. Hours Doors usually open at 7 p.m. or 8 p.m.; show starts an hour later

WHO GOES THERE Those looking to see a great band or needing a nostalgia fix.

WHAT GOES ON "Return to the sixties" parties, big-name and on-the-rise rock concerts, formal sit-down dinners. This rock-and-roll landmark continues to put out the San Francisco sound that made it famous in the 1960s.

SETTING AND ATMOSPHERE Distinct San Francisco soul still lives and breathes direct from the Fillmore. The place that birthed the Grateful Dead, Janis Joplin, and Santana still gives the leg up to climbing, young, quality bands. This hall features the largest collection of historic concert posters on view in the world. A few tables and chairs are in the balconies off to the sides.

IF YOU GO You can always find a listing of upcoming events in the Sunday "pink pages." Tickets are on sale at tickets.com (subject to a service charge) and on show nights 7:30–10 p.m. Advance tickets are on sale at the Fillmore box office Sunday, 10 a.m.–4 p.m. only, with a limit of six tickets per person. The hall is available to rent for parties or events and holds 1,200.

Gold Dust Lounge

A LIVE BAND IN A FESTIVE AND FROLICSOME SAN FRANCISCO CLASSIC SALOON

247 Powell Street, Union Square; ☎ 415-397-1695

Cover None. Minimum None. Mixed drinks $3.75. Wine $3.75–$5. Beer $3.75–$5. Dress Anything goes. Specials None. Food available None. Hours Daily, 6 p.m.–2 a.m.

WHO GOES THERE Mixed crowd of tourists and local regulars.

WHAT GOES ON A variety of musical acts in a bawdy and gaudy San Francisco classic saloon est. 1933. As the place is centrally located and the sound of its rollicking good times spills onto the street, tourists from all over the world and the United States find themselves in here. There's no room to dance, but people do it anyway.

SETTING AND ATMOSPHERE It's deep and narrow and often tightly packed so it's hard not to get friendly with the people next to you. A lot of rich wood, brass and gilt, and paintings of early 20th-century nymphs and satyrs cavorting in what were once considered risque postures. This is the San Francisco of old-movies fame.

IF YOU GO Brush up on your foreign-language skills; you may have a chance to use them. And be prepared to sing along with the band.

Great American Music Hall

ROCK CONCERT HALL

859 O'Farrell Street (at Polk and Larkin), Civic Center;
☎ **415-885-0750; www.musichallsf.com**

Cover $10 and up. **Minimum** None. **Mixed drinks** $3–$4. **Wine** $3–$5. **Beer** $2.75–$3.50. **Dress** Casual to impressive. **Food available** Assorted appetizers, finger food. **Hours** Vary.

WHO GOES THERE Music enthusiasts of all types.

WHAT GOES ON A variety of nationally or internationally recognized music shows ranging from local bands on their way up to Latin ensembles, folk, country, and even jazz.

SETTING AND ATMOSPHERE The fact that this turn-of-the-20th-century bordello theater has been preserved is one of the things that makes San Francisco so special. The gold rococo balcony, wood floors, high fresco ceiling, and marble columns make it a timeless classic. For your favorite bands, come early and scream away Beatlemania-style up front by the stage.

IF YOU GO The hall is available to rent for events and parties of up to 600. Be on the lookout for a touch of the dangerous and the lewd; next door is the famous Mitchell Brothers' O'Farrell Theatre, described by Hunter S. Thompson as "the Carnegie Hall of public sex in America."

Harry Denton's Starlight Room

ROOFTOP DANCE CLUB

450 Powell Street, Union Square; ☎ **415-395-8595;**
www.harrydenton.com

Cover $5–$10. **Minimum** None. **Mixed drinks** $7 and up. **Wine** $7–$20. **Beer** $4–$5. **Dress** Dressy. **Specials** Happy hour Monday–Friday, 5–8 p.m. **Food available** Hors d'oeuvres, raw bar. **Hours** Daily, 6 p.m.–2 a.m.

WHO GOES THERE A well-dressed mixed crowd.

WHAT GOES ON Party, party, party! Dance to a wide variety of music, heavy on rock and retro. Cocktail culture asserts itself in style. Socialites, yuppies, tourists, other club owners, the odd Bohemian stuffed into a jacket and tie, and Harry Denton himself (no dancing on the bar unless accompanied by Harry) are drawn to the Starlight Room like moths to a flame; they all party and dance to the collection of local bands' repertoires, which runs the gamut from the 1940s to the 1990s.

SETTING AND ATMOSPHERE Exuberantly elegant décor and staff on the top floor of the Sir Francis Drake hotel. At the bar, the sound of the cocktail shaker never stops. Through the big picture windows the stars twinkle, and overhead, yes, that's you looking into the mirrored ceiling. The atmosphere is thick and heady, the crowd is at capacity, and there is so much energy that it will be a long time before you sleep again.

IF YOU GO Reservations are highly recommended. Go early or late, unless you're a party animal. Make sure you have a supply of one- and five-dollar bills for tipping the waiters and bartenders and the coat-check girl. Call for information on entertainment and private parties.

Harvey's

GAY BAR

500 Castro Street, SoMa/Mission District; ☎ 415-431-4278

Cover None. Minimum None. Mixed drinks $5 and up. Wine $5–$6. Beer $4–$7. Dress Casual. Food available Appetizers, burgers, salads, chicken dishes. Hours Monday–Friday, 11 a.m.–midnight; Saturday and Sunday, 9 p.m.–2 a.m.

WHO GOES THERE Locals, gay pilgrims, and straight looky-loos.

WHAT GOES ON A hard core of locals use it as their neighborhood pub and tourists of any persuasion come to pay homage or gawk. Named after Harvey Milk, the assassinated gay city supervisor, this was once a place where members of the local gay community came to relax and take pride. Everybody gets along.

SETTING AND ATMOSPHERE Like a Hard Rock Café with a gay theme. Lots of media and sports memorabilia tacked to the walls. It's just a neighborhood good-time bar. A gay "Cheers." Sundays occasionally feature drag shows.

IF YOU GO Be cool.

Impala

RESTAURANT AND NIGHTCLUB

501 Broadway, North Beach; ☎ 415-982-5299

Cover None. Minimum None. Mixed drinks $5.50 and up. Wine $8–$10. Tequila $8 and up. (tequila sampler: 4–6 tastes for $60). Dress Trendy casual. Food available Full restaurant. Specials Taco Tuesdays. Hours Daily, 5 p.m.–2 a.m.; restaurant closes at 11 p.m.

WHO GOES THERE 20-somethings, early 30s trendy crowd.

WHAT GOES ON Hot nightclub scene in the North Beach strip-club area, a location that at first blush sounds a bit dubious but is really the utmost of trendy and the current place to be. Impala offers two bars—one on street level, one below—with pounding techno-salsa DJ music and dancing for a 20s-to-30-something ultrahip crowd, some young professionals just off work, some out for a night on the town. There's not only nightlife but a fine Latin fusion restaurant to boot, serving up creative takes on traditional dishes, such as roasted vegetable and goat-cheese empanadas, or exploring new ground with a smoky ahi tuna dressed in salsa verde and pumpkin seeds—all on a menu designed by Chef Kerry Simon. The premium tequila selection is extensive, with at least 64 options listed alphabetically, from Amate to Tres Generaciones. Try the sampler, four to six tequilas for $60.

SETTING AND ATMOSPHERE Upstairs, it's dark and glamorous, with a rustic edge. Rough-hewn wooden tables dot the dining area, heavy wooden beams crisscross the ceiling with the glitz of mirrors in between. Gauzy fabric in reds and purples drape from columns. The upper bar is separated from the dining tables only by some ceiling-to-floor wrought-iron bars, so it can get a little loud. But by then it's time to head downstairs to the basement lounge and do some serious, sophisticated partying. A line can develop quickly after 10 p.m., so if you're in, you're in like Flynn. Here, reds rule, with plush and modern red velvet chairs and glass-top tables with red feathers inside. Even the restrooms are swanky, with black tile, dramatic lighting, and baskets of hairspray and lotions for the ladies.

IF YOU GO To dine easily, go early. To party, go late. That's when the scene heats up. In the restaurant, note the waitstaff is possibly hired more on looks than service, but that's not necessarily a bad thing. Make a reservation for bottle service in the lower-level lounge, and ask about private parties.

Jade Bar

ASIAN CHIC COCKTAIL LOUNGE

650 Gough Street, Civic Center; ☎ 415-869-1900; www.jadebar.com

Cover None. Minimum None. Mixed drinks $6 and up. Wine $6 and up. Beer $5 and up. Dress Smart. Food available Appetizers. Hours Monday–Saturday, 5 p.m.–2 a.m.

WHO GOES THERE Stylish locals, visitors in the know.

WHAT GOES ON With Herbst Theater, the Opera House, and the symphony hall nearby, as well as some fine restaurants, a lot of smart-looking people stop in for a pre-show or pre-dinner drink. And then maybe an after-show/dinner drink and some schmoozing in a rather serene setting that invites conversation.

SETTING AND ATMOSPHERE Ultra hip (but not tragically), relying a lot on polished hardwoods. Arranged in three levels connected by beautiful hardwood staircases and strewn with plush chairs and lined with banquettes. The 20-foot water cascade and the koi pond make an ideal focus for contemplating one of the house signature cocktails.

IF YOU GO Arrive at dinner/show time to avoid crowds.

Li Po

BAR

916 Grant Avenue, Chinatown; ☎ 415-982-0072

Cover None. Minimum None. Mixed drinks $3.50. Wine $4 and up. Beer $3. Dress Casual. Specials Li Po Special Snifter, $6. Food available None. Hours Daily, 2 p.m.–2 a.m.

WHO GOES THERE Locals in the know and accidental tourists.

WHAT GOES ON Drinking in the dark. Pinball on a "Creature of the Black Lagoon" machine. Low conversations in the nooks and crannies of an ancient labyrinthine structure. A few Chinese-speaking Chinese and a lot of hip folks from North Beach speaking English.

SETTING AND ATMOSPHERE Dark and cavernous. Like a subterranean Chinese shrine to money and Miller Genuine Draft. The main room is dominated by a Chinese deity and currency from around the world tacked to the wall. Chinese lanterns and brewing-company neon leap out at you. If you've ever been a sailor in old Hong Kong, you'll feel nostalgic. If you've seen the movie *Suzy Wong,* you'll feel like you just stepped onto the set. It's a cliché with drinks.

IF YOU GO It's so garish and in such bad taste that it will charm you from the moment you enter.

Make-Out Room

NEO-BOHEMIAN HIPSTER BAR

**3225 22nd Street (near Mission Street), SoMa/Mission District;
☎ 415-647-2888; www.makeoutroom.com**

Cover $6–$10. Minimum None. Mixed drinks $4.50 and up. Wine $3.50–$8. Beer $3.75 and up. Dress Casual. Food available None, but you can bring it in. Hours Daily, 6 p.m.–2 a.m.

WHO GOES THERE Gen-Xers looking for alternatives.

WHAT GOES ON Nightly entertainment. The main attraction is escaping from the usual shoulder-to-shoulder, ear-shattering trauma that is the delight of so many club-hoppers. You can shoot pool and you won't get a cue in the gut when you turn around. You can enjoy a microbrew or a cocktail at the bar or a booth or table and feel that you're in a happening place, but it won't overwhelm.

SETTING AND ATMOSPHERE This place is cavernous. It looks almost like a high-school gym decorated for a dance. The big space, high ceiling, and darkness sprinkled with colored lights feel outdoorsy, especially when the doors are open and the fog rolls in.

IF YOU GO Be cool. Relax. Enjoy. Pssst: people don't really make out here.

Martuni's

COCKTAIL LOUNGE AS ART

4 Valencia Street, SoMa/Mission District; ☎ 415-241-0205

Cover None. Minimum None. Mixed drinks $6. Wine $5–$8. Beer $3.50–$4.75. Dress Evening casual. Food available None. Hours Daily, 4 p.m.–2 a.m.

WHO GOES THERE Mixed crowd of gay and straight.

WHAT GOES ON A variety of cool jazz and other lounge music accompanied by the cheerful clinking of cocktail glasses. Music might be a trio or a solo at the varnished mahogany piano bar. Classic cocktails and new inventions are served up large, with a smile. If you sit at the piano, you might be asked to sing.

SETTING AND ATMOSPHERE It might have been called the Black Room, a Yin to the Red Room's Yang. It's dark in here. And the heavy drapes, thick carpet, and indirect lighting make it more so. Even when you come in at night, you have to let your eyes adjust. But it gives you the sense of being far away in some cozy, friendly getaway where all the strangers are just friends you haven't met.

IF YOU GO Don't go on an empty stomach. The drinks are huge, and you'll be bombed before you know it.

Noc Noc

CAVE BAR

557 Haight Street (at Fillmore and Steiner streets), Civic Center;
☎ **415-861-5811**

Cover None. **Minimum** None. **Mixed drinks** None. **Wine** $3.25 and up. **Beer** $3.25–$4.75. **Specials** Sake: $3, small; $5, large. **Dress** Casual. **Special comments** Alternative happy hour daily , 5–7 p.m. **Food available** Bar snacks. **Hours** Daily, 5 p.m.–2 a.m.

WHO GOES THERE Gen-Xers, 30-something locals.

WHAT GOES ON Gen-Xers come here to be mellow and avoid those who care to see and be seen. Perfect post-date spot for the tragically hip and alternative.

SETTING AND ATMOSPHERE The Stone Age meets *The Road Warrior*. A small cave den littered with hieroglyphics, metal levers, bombs, and airplane wings. Scattered large throw pillows and pit booths are great for intimate chatting. A cozy escape from the harried lower-Haight scene.

IF YOU GO Great locations for a crawl. The Toronado, known by beer connoisseurs for its wide selection on draft and bottled, is just a few doors down. Also a stone's throw away are the British hangout Mad Dog in the Fog, Midtown, and Nickie's BBQ. These bars specialize in beer; you'll have to go elsewhere if you want a decent cocktail. The ATM inside is an added bonus.

Pier 23

JAZZ BAR/RESTAURANT

Pier 23, between Green Street and Battery Street, North Beach;
☎ **415-362-5125; www.pier23cafe.com**

Cover $5, Friday–Sunday. **Minimum** None. **Mixed drinks** $4.50. **Wine** $3.50–$8. **Beer** $3.50–$4.75. **Dress** Casual. **Food available** Meat and potatoes, seafood. **Hours** Monday–Saturday, 11:30–2 a.m.; Sunday, 11:30 a.m.–11 p.m.

WHO GOES THERE Locals, sailors, and jazz aficionados.

WHAT GOES ON In the afternoons you can sit at the beaten copper bar, drink, and watch the parade of watercraft on the bay. In the evenings, dine and listen to popular local jazz bands of all kinds.

SETTING AND ATMOSPHERE An airy waterfront version of a smoky, late-night jazz basement. It's an old-time dockside cafe with a concrete floor; the pier in the back serves as a patio and a place for the fireboats to tie up. A cheery place with lots of regulars.

IF YOU GO The bands play inside, where there's limited seating for dinner, so many dine outside on the pier and listen to the music being piped out. If you do this, remember the highly changeable San Francisco weather and bring a coat. Bartenders can be surly, so bring your patience, too.

Plough and the Stars

IRISH PUB

116 Clement Street, between Second and Third, Richmond/Sunset District; ☎ **415-751-1122**

Cover $5 on weekends. Minimum None. Mixed drinks $3.75 and up. Wine $3.50–$5. Beer $3.50–$4. Dress Casual. Specials Happy hour, weekdays, 4–7 p.m. Food available Cheese and crackers during Friday happy hour. Hours Monday, 4 p.m.–2 a.m.; Tuesday–Thursday, 2 p.m.–2 a.m.; Friday–Sunday, noon–2 a.m.

WHO GOES THERE Irish gents and lasses, Richmond-area locals.

WHAT GOES ON Home of traditional Irish music in the Bay Area; good local bands play nightly after 9:30 p.m. Pool, darts, and chewing the fat with the regulars.

SETTING AND ATMOSPHERE Accents are thick, and so is the Guinness. No one comes here just once, so make yourself comfortable at the long wooden tables or pull up a stool and chat with the regulars at the bar. It's easy to forget you're in San Francisco, not Ireland, amid the acoustic ballads beneath the Irish Republic flag. It's sometimes hard to have an intimate conversation when everyone is clapping their hands to the music.

IF YOU GO Feel free to do the Irish crawl. Though Plough and the Stars is known among locals to have the best Guinness in town, there's a plethora of Irish hangouts just a jig away, including the Bitter End, Ireland 32s, Pat O'Shea's, and the Front Room.

The Plush Room

CABARET AND COCKTAIL LOUNGE

940 Sutter Street (between Levenworth and Hyde) in the York Hotel, Union Square; ☎ **415-885-6800; www.plushroom.com**

Cover $20–$35, for shows. Minimum 2 drinks. Mixed drinks $6.50–$10.50. Wine $6.50–$7.50. Beer $4.50. Dress Gussied-up, rhinestones and silk. Specials Changing jazz and cabaret performances. Food available None. Hours Monday–Saturday, 5 p.m.–2 a.m.

WHO GOES THERE Older gay men, tourists, some locals.

WHAT GOES ON Lounge acts. Sultry cabaret singers and jazz music. Old time talents include Rita Moreno and Paula West.

SETTING AND ATMOSPHERE A San Francisco nightlife tradition lives on in the Plush Room of the York Hotel. The stained glass ceiling from the early 1900s reinforces the old-fashioned style. Reams of red velour and generic hotel carpeting and furniture sound a note of tacky schmaltz, but it somehow makes the place feel more authentic. Fresh flowers atop the baby grand add a touch of genuine elegance, and when the lights go down and the star glimmers before you, you're transported to a world of splendor.

IF YOU GO Love a cabaret. Service can be slow and drinks weak, but if you appreciate the tawdry antics and true skill involved in a lounge act, this is the spot for you.

The Red Room

RETRO COCKTAIL LOUNGE

827 Sutter Street, Union Square; ☎ 415-346-7666

Cover None. **Minimum** None. **Mixed drinks** $5–$8. **Wine** $6–$8. **Beer** $3.50–$4.75. **Dress** Dressy. **Food available** None. **Hours** Monday–Saturday, 5 p.m.–2 a.m.; Sunday, 7 p.m.–2 a.m.

WHO GOES THERE Hipsters in their 20s and 30s.

WHAT GOES ON Young yuppies who are too cool to cop to the term come to this oh-so-hip location to advance the cause of cocktail culture. Aside from the décor, nothing distracts the patrons from themselves and their long-stemmed glasses.

SETTING AND ATMOSPHERE Red. Crimson. Vermillion. Sanguine. Longer wavelengths of the visible light spectrum. It's red, by God, red! The ceiling, the floor, the wallpaper, the drapes. Even the lights are red, though you should read nothing into that. The place is small and smoky, with a horseshoe bar commanded by an Amazon and her assistant; they slosh out a variety of martinis into cocktail glasses the size of bull horns.

IF YOU GO Go early. The terminally hip tend to crowd this place so much in the evening that a doorman has to ask guests to form a line; they're allowed in only after a reverential wait. But don't let this deter you. Before the hordes of hip descend, it's a great place for a predinner cocktail. All that red is somehow soothing when accompanied by a well-made martini.

Ruby Skye

SWANK NIGHTCLUB

420 Mason Street, Union Square; ☎ 415-693-0777; www.rubyskye.com;

Cover $15. **Minimum** None. **Mixed drinks** $5 and up. **Wine** $6 and up. **Beer** $5. **Dress** Impressive. **Food available** Catering for private parties. **Hours** Thursday–Saturday, 9 p.m.–3 a.m.

WHO GOES THERE Well-dressed locals, informed tourists.

WHAT GOES ON Dancing to world-class DJs and live acts by people who are "grown up, make money, and dress nice," according to the owner. A lot of flirting, a lot of quiet conversations in private booths or VIP rooms, and a lot of very good times. Well-catered private parties on off nights.

SETTING AND ATMOSPHERE Originally a theater built in the 19th century and said to have served as a house of discreet assignations. The designers have made the most of the original décor while bringing it up to date with the

latest in sound and lighting. Four large main rooms give the place a spacious feel even when the dance floors are jammed, which is often.
IF YOU GO Dress to the nines.

Tonga Room

TROPICAL ISLAND BAR

950 Mason Street in the Fairmont Hotel, Chinatown; ☎ 415-772-5278; www.tongaroom.com

Cover $7. Minimum 1 drink. Mixed drinks Tropical cocktail specials. $8.50–$25. Wine $6 and up. Beer $4 and up. Dress Evening casual to dressy. Specials Live music; happy hour, weekdays 5–7 p.m. Food available Yes. Hours Sunday–Thursday, 6 p.m.–midnight; Friday and Saturday, 5 p.m.–1 a.m.

WHO GOES THERE Nob Hill locals, tourists, and happy hour crowd.

WHAT GOES ON A wide mix of people come to drink the island cocktails and swoon to their sweetheart beneath straw huts and palm trees, but most just wait for the periodic man-made thunderstorms.

SETTING AND ATMOSPHERE A tropical island oasis in the Fairmont Hotel atop Nob Hill. Watch a live band on a moated island while sipping an umbrella-clad drink from a coconut. The South Seas décor is more of an upscale tiki lounge than a seaman's dive.

IF YOU GO Don't miss the $7 all-you-can-eat weekday buffet from 5 to 7 p.m (with a one-drink minimum). It's easy to make a meal out of potstickers, barbecue spareribs, teriyaki drumsticks, veggies and dip, a cheese plate, egg rolls, and more. Watch out for the Scorpion. It's the most expensive drink on the menu for a reason.

Top o' the Mark

ROOFTOP LOUNGE AND DANCE FLOOR

999 California Street, 19th floor, Chinatown; ☎ 415-616-6916; www.san-francisco.intercontinental.com

Cover Weeknights, $8; weekends, $10. Minimum None. Mixed drinks $7 and up. Wine $6 and up. Beer $5 and up. Dress Smart casual to dressy. Specials The view at sunset. Food available Finger foods, elegant hors d'oeuvres, 3-course prix fixe on Thursday, Friday, and Saturday, $39. Hours Opens daily at 3 p.m.

WHO GOES THERE Well-dressed 30s and up, tourists, and regulars.

WHAT GOES ON Dancing, romancing, schmoozing, and boozing. Musical offerings include in-house pianists, cool jazz combos, and retro groups. People come here for swing and ballroom dancing, sunset cocktails, business talks, romantic assignations, and conspiracies.

SETTING AND ATMOSPHERE Understated elegance on the most romantic rooftop in town, on top of the Mark Hopkins hotel, on top of Nob Hill. The elevated dance floor is in the center of the room and surrounded by plush seating along the huge windows that give a near 360° view of the city. Despite the price and the sophistication, it's never intimidating, always welcoming, almost homey.

IF YOU GO Valet parking is $23. Take a taxi or the California line cable car and get off right at the Mark. No minors are allowed after 8:30 p.m.

Tosca Cafe

OPERA BAR

242 Columbus Avenue, North Beach; ☎ 415-391-1244

Cover None. **Minimum** None. **Mixed drinks** $3.50–$3.75. **Wine** $4–$6. **Beer** $2.50–$3.50. **Dress** Come as you are **Specials** Irish coffee, house cappuccino. **Food available** None. **Hours** 5 p.m.–2 a.m.

WHO GOES THERE Mostly locals, 30-something and up.

WHAT GOES ON Conversation and playing the jukebox. It's the only jukebox in town with many selections from the world of opera. A lot of locals, including a few celebs, camp out here. In the back is an invitation-only pool room said to be a fave of Sam Shepard and Francis Ford Coppola.

SETTING AND ATMOSPHERE A big place for a bar. All wood with red uphol-stered booths and a long bar on which sit dozens of Irish coffee glasses already charged with whiskey, sugar, and cream, waiting to be filled with hot coffee.

IF YOU GO Afternoon to early evening is best, especially when the fog rolls in. At night the thunderous base notes of the disco in the basement can be felt through the floor.

PART NINE

SHOPPING

IN THE GOLD-RUSH DAYS OF MINERS, SOLDIERS, sailors, and scoundrels, folks used to come into the city of San Francisco to shop. The city has long since been eclipsed by Los Angeles as a West Coast center of consumer excess, but it still has unmatched treasures. It's still a frontier town, although today the frontiers are different; multimedia and technology, global commerce, and artistic innovation are some of the new territories.

There's been a new gold rush, of course: computers, multimedia, and e-commerce have made San Francisco and nearby Silicon Valley one of the most expensive places to live—and shop—in the country. Since the dot bomb, the tech rush has simmered down, but, undeniably, some new money has been created—very new money. The infusion of money and youth (and moneyed youth) has ratcheted up the quality of the shopping (they gotta spend it somewhere)—and the prices along with it.

Rest assured that San Francisco's merchants still know how to separate fools from their gold. Shopping here is about more than getting the goods; it's about the neighborhood. And shopping in these distinct neighborhoods (they even have their own "microclimates") is a good way to glimpse the city's kaleidoscope of cultures.

Real San Franciscans wouldn't be caught dead in a mall or a superstore for something they can find at a neighborhood place for less. Those shopping venues are peopled more often by the "bridge and tunnel" crowd, folks from neighboring cities who come to SF to shop, dine, and party. Supporting small businesses and local artists and craftspeople who sell their wares is a matter of civic pride, a way of voting with the wallet, a mix of economic necessity, political conscientiousness, and style. The locals don't say "I'm going shopping." (How suburban!) They say, "I'm going to the Haight (or the Castro or Cow Hollow or the Mission)." They have a thing for shops with personality. The neighborhoods here are notorious for banning

unofficial **TIP**
Catch some of the best shopping values (and best people-watching) at the annual spring and summer street fairs thrown by the city's major neighborhoods. The biggies are the Union Street Festival (June) and the Haight (June), Castro, and Folsom Street fairs (October and September).

chains from their enclaves and supporting mom-and-pop operations (even if the mom and pop in question are a pair of 20-something mom-and-mom entrepreneurs).

Here's a look at San Francisco shopping, with an eye on the specialties (and peculiarities) of the Bay Area—its fixations on food, wine, recycled and earth-friendly merchandise, and, of course, sex, drugs, and rock and roll. This is the birthplace of such stylish hometown enterprises as Levi Strauss, Gap, Banana Republic, Old Navy, Esprit, Williams-Sonoma, and Bebe. It's also the hothouse of trends; the continuing craze for tattooing and piercing was born here.

If you want some shopping guidance, consider a shopping tour such as **Shopper Stopper Escorted Tours** (☎ 707-829-1597). You might also check online at the San Francisco Web sites—**CitySearch San Francisco** (**www.citysearch7.com**) and the more hip **www.sfstation.com**—both of which are continually updated with up-to-the-minute information on new shops or new tours on offer.

unofficial **TIP**
Hunting for bargains? Pick up Sally Socolich's definitive *Bargain Hunting in the Bay Area* (published by Chronicle Books), which maps out discount shopping in the city and surrounding areas.

Combined with a stop at one of the area's almost ridiculously plentiful cafes, window-shopping is as satisfying as shelling out the cash. When you go home (if you do), you can take back something more than a loaf of airport gift-shop sourdough, a Hard Rock Cafe T-shirt, and a case of Rice-A-Roni.

TOP SHOPPING NEIGHBORHOODS

UNION SQUARE

WHILE THE WORD EPICENTER SHOULD NOT BE thrown around too casually in this town, Union Square is indeed the epicenter of shopping. While not exactly a neighborhood, Union Square is the closest the city comes to a downtown, at least in terms of shopping. There's an enormous underground public parking lot beneath the 2.6-acre green park at the center of the square; the park is peopled with chess players, street artists and musicians, street characters, and bustling shoppers from around the world.

Framing this colorful square are the main shopping streets (Stockton Street, Powell Street, Geary Street, and Post Street) and the city's densest concentration of major department stores, tony boutiques, restaurants and cafes, big hotels, and corner flower stands.

Moving clockwise from the Saint Francis Hotel on Powell Street, you'll find the following: **Disney Store** (400 Post Street at Powell Street; ☎ 415-391-6866), **Borders Books and Music** (400 Post Street; ☎ 415-399-1633), **Saks Fifth Avenue** (384 Post Street; ☎ 415-986-4300), **Tiffany & Co.** (350 Post Street at Union Square; ☎ 415-781-7000), and **Neiman Marcus** (150 Stockton Street at Geary Boulevard; ☎ 415-362-3900), which each year sends the city's most spectacular Christmas tree soaring to the top of its stained-glass dome. A megalithic **Macy's** (170 O'Farrell Street at Stockton Street; ☎ 415-397-3333), which took over the building vacated by the sadly folded San Francisco institution I. Magnin & Co., recently underwent a handsome renovation. Sprawling over three city blocks, it includes a new **Wolfgang Puck Express,** where you can nosh on made-to-order pastas, salads, entrées, and sushi; **Boudin's Bakery,** where you can get clam chowder in a sourdough bread bowl; for dessert there's **The Cheesecake Factory** on the top floor, sweets with a view; and fresh-squeezed smoothies and soups at **Jamba Juice.**

During the computer boom, the Union Square district saw a burst of new growth, including Sony's state-of-the-art **Metreon Center** (101 Fourth Street at Mission Street; ☎ 415-369-6000), a sleek, high-style, high-tech shopping and entertainment complex, which landed upon downtown like the Retail Mothership.

Like elsewhere in the country, chain stores are moving into San Francisco, robbing the Union Square shopping zone of some of its legendary exclusivity. The square has been recently colonized by the theme park–like megastores, the shopping equivalents of Planet Hollywood and Hard Rock Cafe. The newest is the **Levi's Superstore** (300 Post Street at Stockton Street; ☎ 415-501-0100) a four-story retail entertainment hybrid which features clothing-customization services such as 3D body scanning, laser etching, hand painting, and fabric ornamentation and embroidery.

Not far away (and giving Levi run for its money) is **House of Blue Jeans** (979 Market Street; ☎ 415-252-2929). Not just Levi's. They claim to have the largest selection in town. As well as shirts, jackets, T-shirts, and accessories. And they can ship your purchase home for you. Other Union Square superstores include **Niketown** (278 Post Street; ☎ 415-392-6453), **Disney Store,** and **Virgin Records** (2 Stockton Street at Market Street; ☎ 415-397-4525). The newest twist on the megastore is the in-store DJ—everyone's got one now—including **Levi's, Virgin,** and **Diesel** (101 Post Street at Kearny Street; ☎ 415-982-7077), where you can shop the four-story oasis of uncasually priced casual gear and denim while grinding your teeth and snapping your fingers to the tweakiest techno in town. The dozens of tony boutiques on the side streets offer shopping with an international feel and "if you have to ask . . ." prices: **Gucci** (200 Stockton Street; ☎ 415-392-2808), **Hermes** (125 Grant Avenue; ☎ 415-391-7200), **Louis Vuitton** (233 Geary Street; ☎ 415-391-6200), and **Cartier** (231 Post Street between Grant and Stockton streets; ☎ 415-397-3180). And for something not quite expected, **The Whisky Shop** (360 Sutter Street; ☎ 415-989-1030; www.whiskyshopusa.com) is THE place to shop for single-malt scotch, as well as other things Scottish such as kilts and tartans. **Burberry** (225 Post Street; ☎ 415-392-2200) is the inventor of the trench coat, designed in 1914 for wear by British army officers. Nowadays Burberry produces an extensive range of apparel and accessories for both men and women.

Tangential to the square is Maiden Lane, a narrow, car-free alley that once housed ladies of the evening. Now the quaint street features pricey shops and restaurants, including a three-floor **Chanel** (155 Maiden Lane between Grant and Stockton streets; ☎ 415-981-1550), the Paris-based **Christofle Silversmiths** (140 Grant Avenue at Post Street; ☎ 415-399-1931), and an outpost of Seattle's **Sur La Table** (77 Maiden Lane between Grant and Kearny streets; ☎ 415-732-7900), a gourmet kitchenware boutique.

Also in the Union Square area are a handful of San Francisco–based stores, including 150-year-old **Shreve & Co. Jewelers** (200 Post Street at Grant Street; ☎ 415-421-2600) and the equally venerable **Gumps** (135 Post Street between Kearny and Grant streets; ☎ 415-982-1616), one of the world's most beautiful and unusual department stores. Gumps features china, crystal, Asian art treasures, antiques, and one-of-a-kind objects and furniture.

These old-timers are balanced out by fresh-faced young merchandisers near Union Square like fun and funky **Urban Outfitters** (80 Powell Street; ☎ 415-989-1515), the **Williams-Sonoma** flagship store (340 Post Street; ☎ 415-362-9450), **Crate & Barrel** (55 Stockton Street at O'Farrell; ☎ 415-986-4000), and the vast khaki-and-cream expanses of the **Banana Republic** flagship store (256 Grant Ave. at Sutter Street; ☎ 415-788-3087).

San Francisco–based **Gap** boasts a sleek, stark, three-story flagship store at Union Square, which also houses siblings **Gap Kids** and **Baby Gap** (890 Market Street at Powell Street; ☎ 415-788-5909) right next to the tourist-choked cable-car turnaround on Market Street. Across the street is the even more recently-opened three-story flagship store of Gap's kid-sister store **Old Navy** (801 Market Street at Fourth Street; ☎ 415-344-0375). Across Market Street from the cable-car turnaround is the **San Francisco Shopping Centre** (865 Market Street at Fifth; ☎ 415-495-5656; www.sanfranciscocentre.com), a multilevel enclosed urban mall anchored by **Nordstrom** (☎ 415-243-8500) with its five-floor spiral escalator, and a "mall-esque" array of shops including **Abercrombie & Fitch** for sporting attire (☎ 415-284-9276) and its competitive clone **American Eagle Outfitters**

(☎ 415-543-4550). For hardcore outdoor gear, check out nearby **North Face** (180 Post Street; ☎ 415-433-3223), a place for high-quality outdoor and adventure gear.

PACIFIC HEIGHTS/COW HOLLOW/MARINA

THE CITY'S SECOND-LARGEST UPSCALE SHOPPING ZONE covers three linked neighborhoods: the five blocks of Fillmore Street between Geary Boulevard and Jackson Street, the six-block stretch of Union Street from Gough to Steiner streets (also known as Cow Hollow because it evolved from grazing pasture to browsing nirvana), and the seven blocks of Chestnut Street known as the Marina District. **Chadwick's of London** (2068 Chestnut Street; ☎ 415-775-3423) carries fine cotton-and-lace lingerie. **SMASH** (2030 Chestnut Street; ☎ 415 673-4736) is known for its decadent selection of shoes. And **Marina Sol Eyewear** (2128 Chestnut Street; ☎ 415-749-0383) will put the coolest shades on your eyes. The beautifully preserved Victorian and Edwardian homes of Union Street, many of which survived the 1906 earthquake, now house hip, upscale, yuppie boutiques and cafes and offer some of the city's best window-shopping. Check out **Tate & Kennedy** for a wide range of personal luxuries and great gifts (2042 Union Street; ☎ 415-474-8283). At **UKO** (2070 Union Street; ☎ 415-563-0330), you'll find women's and men's apparel that is best described as casually elegant.

Fillmore has evolved from a run-down area into a gauntlet of chic boutiques and restaurants. **Gallery of Jewels** (2115 Fillmore Street; ☎ 877-566-9725) offers beautiful hand-crafted adornment. And **Plumpjack Wines** (3201 Fillmore Street; ☎ 415-346-9870) is *the* place for both California and foreign wines.

CHINATOWN

MORE CAR CHASES ARE FILMED IN CHINATOWN THAN in any other neighborhood of this cinematic city. A visit to this famous, fascinating district—home to more than 200,000 Chinese Americans (the Chinese community is second in size only to New York's Chinatown)—begins at the large, ornate gateway at the intersection of Grant and Bush streets, just above Union Square. You'll encounter otherworldly vegetables, live animals, exotic spices, herbs, ivory, jade, pearls, and other prizes amid the Oriental kitsch. Shops like **Dragon House** (455 Grant Avenue; ☎ 415-421-3693) and the **China Trade Center** (838 Grant Street between Clay and Washington streets; ☎ 415-837-1509), which is a three-floor mini-mall, typify tourist trinket market of Chinatown, and minimize the jostling. Watch Chinese make fortune cookies at **Golden Gate Fortune Cookie**

unofficial **TIP**
Don't even think of driving in Chinatown. You'd miss all the sights, sounds, tastes, and smells of the bustling streets. And for a real Chinese shopping experience, prowl the alleys and side streets.

(56 Ross Alley; ☎ 415-781-3956). If you want to take home some really superior tea (not the stuff you find every day at the supermarket), visit **Ten Ren Tea Company** (949 Grant Street; ☎ 415-362-0656). And to really go native, stroll along the food markets on Stockton Street, one block west of Grant.

Bordering Chinatown is the formerly Italian neighborhood known as North Beach, the main stomping grounds of the Beat poets and artists who made **City Lights Bookstore** (261 Columbus Avenue at Broadway; ☎ 415-362-8193) and **Caffe Trieste** (609 Vallejo Street; ☎ 415-982-2605) their home. You'll find hours of browsing potential on the streets bordering Washington Square Park, and the plentiful Italian cafes and pastry shops alone are a shopping experience. For music lovers, especially for vintage vinyl, run to 101 Music (1414 Grant Street; ☎ 415-392-6369). 45s and LPs cram the shelves, along with some CDs and cassettes.

JAPANTOWN

SUNDAY IS THE BUSIEST SHOPPING DAY IN Japantown, and the five-acre enclosed mall **Japan Center** (1737 Post Street; ☎ 415-922-6776) is its heart. The shops and boutiques contain everything from antique kimonos and scrolls to ultramodern furniture and electronics. Favorite shops for Westerners are **Kinokuniya Stationery and Gifts** (1581 Webster Street at Post Street; ☎ 415-567-8901), with its fascinating array of intricate notecards and writing implements, and **Kinokinuya Book Store** (1581 Webster Street at Post Street; ☎ 415-567-7625), which has a vast assortment of books and magazines in Japanese and English. The complex also includes the **AMC Kabuki 8 Cinemas** (1881 Post Street; ☎ 415-931-9800) and the recently renovated **Kabuki Springs and Spa** (1750 Geary Boulevard; ☎ 415-922-6002), a Japanese spa where you can steam, soak, and sigh away a hard day's shop.

HAYES VALLEY

COLONEL THOMAS HAYES PROBABLY WOULDN'T recognize the urban "valley" that bears his name. It's more like the Valley of the Interior Decorators: distressed-furniture boutiques, art-deco specialty shops, and other retro-contemporary brokers line this relatively small shopping district between the Castro and Civic Center, along with dozens of tiny boutiques that look like settings for photo shoots for *Wallpaper* magazine. Good bets include **Azalea Boutique** (411 Hayes Street; ☎ 415-861-9888), offering an eclectic mix of apparel and accessories for both men and women, stuff that bucks the mass-production lock-step, and a nail bar for a bit of pampering; **Wishbone** (601 Irving at Seventh Avenue; ☎ 415-242-5540), an eccentric tchochke shop; and **Lava9** (542 Hayes Street; ☎ 415-552-6468), your place for needs in leather jackets and bags—not the whips-and-chains kind, but elegant and fashionable.

THE HAIGHT

HIP AND HIPPIE—THAT'S THE ESSENCE OF THE Haight today. To many visitors and residents, the time warp known as Haight Street is still synonymous with hippies. Even though the famous corner of Haight and Ashbury streets is now bounded by a **Ben & Jerry's** and a **Gap,** and even though music and fashion have passed through punk and techno, the Haight has managed to hang onto its 1960s reputation. A mishmash of head shops, secondhand stores, record and book shops, and the city's most alternative shopping experiences line Haight Street from Masonic to Stanyan streets.

Although the novelty of flower power has faded, today's progressive subcultures add a changing style to the Haight. You'll still find clusters of head shops, packs of grungy panhandling teens, and other historical artifacts like the Red Vic Theater, Haight-Ashbury Free Clinic, and **Bound Together Anarchist Bookstore** (1369 Haight Street between Central and Masonic streets; ☎ 415-431-8355), but now the Haight offers a fusion of old and new.

Some of the street's colorful landmarks include **Positively Haight Street** (1400 Haight Street; ☎ 415-252-8747), which has all things hippie and Summer of Lovey. T-shirts, tie-dyes, baggy pants, everything you need for a retro trip back to the 1960s.; **Planet Weavers** (1573 Haight Street at Clayton Street; ☎ 415-864-4415), a Toys 'R Us for fans of new age, world music, and multiculturalism in general, filled with candles, drums, and fountains; and **Bound Together,** the truly anarchist bookstore previously mentioned.

SOUTH OF MARKET

OTHERWISE KNOWN AS SOMA, THE SPRAWLING, industrial warehouse–filled South of Market area, with clusters of outlet and discount stores, is a focal point for bargain hunters. An enormous Costco (450 Tenth Street; ☎ 415-626-4388), dominates an entire city block; other discount stores include **Bed Bath & Beyond, Trader Joe's, Yerba Buena Square,** and **Burlington Coat Factory.** Because the nightclub scene also thrives in SoMa, there's a host of leather and fetish stores and other purveyors of "underground" attire and accessories, including **Stormy Leather** (1158 Howard Street; ☎ 415-626-1672).

THE CASTRO

IN THE SUNNY, PREDOMINANTLY GAY AND LESBIAN neighborhood known as the Castro, you never know what you'll see. A controversy once erupted over a bookstore's window display, which featured an anatomically correct porn star; many other gift stores, including the aptly-named and in-your-face shop Erotic Art, continue to make window-shopping in the Castro an eye-popping, NC-17, at-your-own-risk experience.

A self-sufficient village, the Castro has become the equivalent of an island resort overrun with pricey boutiques offering gifts, trendy clothing, coffee, burritos, more coffee, more burritos, and fruit juice. Don't-miss shops include the neoclassic **Cliff's Variety** hardware store (479 Castro at 18th Street; ☎ 415-431-5365), sort of *Mayberry R.F.D.* circa 2021, and **Under One Roof** (549 Castro Street at 19th Street; ☎ 415-503-2300), a lovely, imaginative, upscale gift boutique staffed entirely by volunteers—all profits are divided among more than 35 AIDS organizations in the area.

BERKELEY

IN THE REPUBLIC OF BERKELEY THERE IS ONE STREET that maintains a pretty good balance between indie and mainstream. **Fourth Street** manages to appeal to the newfound yuppiness of the surrounding neighborhood while keeping in tune with the hippie vibe that has marked Berkeley as the brainchild of creative innovation. Whether you are looking for a gift for someone else or looking to indulge yourself you can find almost anything here. It's niche shopping at its best. You can walk away with hard-to-find CDs or books from **Hear Music** (1809 Fourth Street; ☎ 510-204-9595) or **Cody's Books,** which has two locations; one on Fourth Street (☎ 510-559-9500) and the other on Telegraph Avenue (☎ 510-845-7852). There are plenty of shoe stores and hipster Euro-style boutiques, also. How 'bout walking away with some garbage? **Urban Ore** on Seventh Street at Ashby (☎ 510-841-7283) sells for reuse over 3,500 tons of "garbage" retrieved from the Berkeley garbage pits. As you would expect from Berkeley, even the stores do their share to maintain a balanced environment. One-of-a-kind finds are what lure Berkeleyites—the home remodeler, the collector, the musician, etc.—here year after year. Berkeley is also where you will find one of the most beautiful grocery stores ever. **Berkeley Bowl** (2020 Oregon Street; ☎ 510-843-6929) boasts the largest produce (mostly organic) section in all of Northern California. Come to select food or come to take pictures! Its international section is a one-stop shop for everything—wasabi, pickled ginger, and seaweed paper.

Another shopping enclave is Telegraph Avenue, which runs directly toward the Berkeley campus. Through all the tie-dye and hippie craftsmanship on sale on the streets, you will discover unique book and music stores, shoe stores, pastry shops, and, if you are lucky, a group of singing Hare Krishnas. **Annapurna** (2416 Telegraph Avenue; ☎ 510-841-6187) is the oldest, and possibly the last, "Head Shop." If you can brave the parking challenges, you will be excited by the unique shopping opportunities here. It's a day well spent!

THE MALLS

DESPITE WHAT YOU MAY HAVE SEEN IN MOVIES like *Clueless* and *Valley Girl,* malls no longer define the California shopping experience (and anyway, that was Southern California). The Bay Area is almost actively anti-mall (as well as anti-Wal-Mart), and neighborhood shopping is de rigueur. But if you must mall it, there are several not unattractive options.

kids The latest un-mall is Sony Corporation's retail and entertainment megaplex called **Metreon** (101 Fourth Street at Mission Street; ☎ 415-369-6000; **www.metreon.com**), which architects and shoppers are hailing as the wave of the future. Featuring 15 state-of-the-art movie theaters and an eight-story IMAX auditorium, plus a high-tech arcade and restaurants that go way beyond the term "food court," the shops include **Sony Style, Chronicle Books,** plus the ubiquitous **Starbucks.**

Built in 1988 to house Nordstrom, the downtown **San Francisco Shopping Centre** (865 Market Street at Fifth Street; ☎ 415-495-5656; **www.sanfranciscocentre.com**) boasts more than 100 different merchants, including **Kenneth Cole, J. Crew, Ann Taylor, Abercrombie & Fitch,** and **Victoria's Secret.** Shoppers wind their way up curved escalators designed by Mitsubishi through four floors of shops; connection to the Powell Street BART and Muni terminal makes getting there easy.

Too fancy to be called a mall, the seriously stylin' **Crocker Galleria** (50 Post Street at Kearny Street; ☎ 415-393-1505; **www.shopatgalleria .com**) in the heart of the downtown Financial District was fashioned after the Galleria Vittorio Emanuele in Milan. The galleria offers 50 shops, restaurants, and services, including **Versace** and **Ralph Lauren** boutiques and a charming rooftop park. Parking is free on Saturday with a $10 purchase (which, in a place that sells $50 undershirts, should take about ten seconds).

By the waterfront is the monumental **Embarcadero Center** (Clay Street between Battery Street and Justin Herman Plaza; ☎ 415-772-0500; **www.embarcaderocenter .com**), a complex of four office towers housing two levels of restaurants, movie theaters, and shops, including **Ann Taylor, Banana Republic, Gap, Crabtree and Evelyn, Pottery Barn,** and **Sam Goody,** plus a few interesting local boutiques like **L'Occitane,** an aromatherapy bath and skin-care shop, and **Kidi Niki,** which offers children's clothing.

The **Stanford Shopping Center** (610 El Camino Real, Palo Alto; ☎ 650-617-8585; **www.stanford shop.com**), which is owned by Stanford University, offers the most concentrated upscale retail experience in the area, with **Bloomingdale's, Neiman Marcus, Macy's, Nordstrom, Tiffany & Co., Smith & Hawken,** and **Crate & Barrel.** San Francisco's only genuine enclosed mall in the city

unofficial **TIP**
The SoMa District is full of big game for bargain hunters. Check out **Yerba Buena Square,** an urban outlet mall (899 Howard Street at Fifth) anchored by a **Burlington Coat Factory Warehouse** and **The Shoe Pavilion.** Not so far away is the **Six Sixty Factory Outlet Center** (660 Third Street at Townsend Street), with bargains on many name brands.

limits is **Stonestown Galleria** (3251 20th Avenue at Winston Street; ☎ 415-759-2626; **www.stonestowngalleria.com**) in the outer Sunset District. The mall includes a substantial 120 shops anchored by **Nordstrom, Macy's, Pottery Barn, Eddie Bauer,** and **Williams-Sonoma.**

SPECIALTY SHOPS

ALTERNATIVE SHOPPING

SAN FRANCISCO SPECIALIZES IN ECCENTRICS AND subcultures (this is, after all, a city with a church—Saint John Coltrane African Orthodox Church—devoted to jazz music; **www.coltranechurch.org**). Body modification through tatooing and body-piercing is one souvenir that keeps on giving. If you decide to get a new perforation while you're here, get something cool to put in it. For body jewelry and other accessories, visit **Anubis** (1525 Haight Street at Ashbury; ☎ 415-431-2218). **Cold Steel Piercing & Tatooing** (1783 Haight Street; ☎ 415-933-7233) is perhaps the most upscale place of its kind. The artful displays and furnishings give it a museum-like feel.

The Beats go on, and so do the hippies, at least in the memories and imaginations of most visitors. For Beat memorabilia, **City Lights Bookstore** (261 Columbus Avenue at Broadway; ☎ 415-362-8193) in North Beach is un-Beat-able; a window-shopping stroll through the Haight District will turn up all sorts of flashbacks, from head shops to vintage rock-concert poster peddlers.

 Kids love the **Sanrio** flagship store (865 Market Street; ☎ 415-495-3056) of Hello Kitty and her cloyingly cute chums. **Gamescape** (333 Divisadero Street at Oak Street; ☎ 415-621-4263) specializes in games for all ages. For pure whimsy the **Chinatown Kite Shop** (717 Grant Street; ☎ 415-989-5182) is the place for your inner child.

Wig Factory (3020 Mission Street between Army and Precita streets; ☎ 415-282-4939) displays the city's most outlandish collection of wigs (and in San Francisco, that's really saying something). **Botanica Yoruba** (998 Valencia Street; ☎ 415-826-4967) offers candles, potions, herbs, and incantations for every need or desire—sort of a "Pagans 'R Us." One of the most unusual and off-the-beaten-path shops in town, **Paxton Gate** (824 Valencia Street; ☎ 415-824-1872) may be the world's most bizarre gardening store, as evidenced by its displays of eerie air plants, mounted bugs and butterflies, and stuffed and costumed mice.

Extreme Sports

San Francisco has hosted the X-games and that's no coincidence. The city is full of adrenaline-inducing jumps, trails, surf, rock, and slopes. No place is proper gear more mandatory than this playground of a city.

Despite appearances, it ain't cheap being a skatepunk. What with the skater duds, shoes, customized boards, wheels, and magazines, you gotta keep up. At **DLX** (1831 Market Street at Octavia Street; ☎ 415-626-5588) they've got it all. Same goes for snowboarding, another accessory-intensive sport: **SFO** (618 Shrader Street at Haight Street; ☎ 415-386-1666) is the sweet spot for boots, boards, and bundle-up wear. Gear-head heaven for any sport is located in either **Sports Basement** (In The Presidio at 610 Mason Street; ☎ 415-437-0100); or **Lombardi Sports** (1600 Jackson Street; ☎ 415-771-0600). Both places offer helpful and knowledgeable service, and floors are divided by activity. For rock climbing you can visit either of the multi-purpose stores mentioned above or head to **Mission Cliffs** (2295 Harrison Street at 19th Street; ☎ 415-550-0515). They have all the necessary gear, including helmets, harnesses, climbing shoes, ropes, biners, etc.

ANTIQUES

SAN FRANCISCANS ARE IN LOVE WITH HISTORY, and the antiques stores are stocked with everything from ultrapricey traditional pieces and 1950s kitschware to last month's fads.

In the area once known as the Barbary Coast, Jackson Square, San Francisco's first designated historic district (it was the only group of downtown buildings to survive the 1906 earthquake and fire), has fittingly become the city's official antiques district. Bounded by Jackson, Washington, Montgomery, and Sansome streets, the square, which showcases its pieces like small museums, houses about two dozen dealers, such as **Argentum—The Leopard's Head** (72 Jackson Street near Sansome Street; ☎ 415-296-7757) with 16th through 19th century silver; and **Daniel Stein Antiques** for traditional English and Continental furniture (458 Jackson Street near Montgomery Street; ☎ 415-956-5620; **www.danielsteinantiques.com**).

Grand Central Station Antiques (333 Ninth Street at Folsom; ☎ 415-252-8155) is like a classic jumble sale, with two floors of fun finds.

Perhaps the most pleasurable antiques shopping is on Russian Hill at **Russian Hill Antiques** (2200 Polk Street at Vallejo Street; ☎ 415-441-5561). If Early American seems a bit too drab for your taste, head to **Retrospect Custom Furniture** (1649 Market Street; ☎ 415-863-7414). It's all about retro here—from the 1940s, 1950s, and 1960s.

BARGAINS/THRIFT

ALTHOUGH SHOPPING IN SAN FRANCISCO MAY NOT be the way of life or contact sport it is in Los Angeles or New York, the locals are nevertheless competitive about what they get. And how they get it. If you compliment a San Franciscan about his new computer bag or her little black dress, be prepared to hear the tale of how cheap it was at a thrift store (or at a sidewalk sale). The more obscure the source and the lower the price, the better. Never underestimate the talent it takes to emerge from **Community Thrift** with something cheap that you'll actually use or wear! In San Francisco, people try on and toss off new personas the way other folks change underwear. Previously owned and recycled everything—from clothes to records to kitchenware—is big business. Nostalgia cycles seem to speed up in this town and Bohemian, artist-friendly neighborhoods like the Haight and the upper Mission have particularly high concentrations of vintage and thrift stores, but you can go on a bargain bender even in snooty Pacific Heights.

American Rag (1305 Van Ness Avenue at Sutter Street; ☎ 415-441-0537) has the largest and trendiest selection of retro rags in town, but the prices don't really qualify as thrift. (They also offer new designer goods.) Gargoyles guard the carnival-like exterior of the Haight's **Wasteland** (1660 Haight Street at Clayton Street; ☎ 415-863-3150), and if you can bear the famously loud and obnoxious music, you'll be rewarded with great finds. **Community Thrift** is a veritable second-hand department store (623 Valencia Street; ☎ 415-861-4910) where you can specify which of more than 200 charities you want your purchase to benefit. Other old faithfuls include **Crossroads Trading Co.** (1901 Fillmore Street; ☎ 415-775-8885; or 2123 Market Street near Church Street; ☎ 415-626-8989) and **Buffalo Exchange** (1555 Haight Street between Clayton and Ashbury streets; ☎ 415-431-7733). The enormous **Goodwill** store (1580 Mission Street at South Van Ness Avenue; ☎ 415-575-2240) is as brightly lit as any grocery store, and it's always chock-full of new and old trash and treasure.

unofficial **TIP**
Near the holidays, in early November, and in May before Mother's Day, the merchants of the **Gift Center** (888 Brannan Street at Eighth; ☎ 415-861-7733) offer their samples and over-stock on six levels of the building. It's like the world's biggest garage sale. And you can have a nice lunch or a drink at the **Pavilion Café and Deli,** which also houses the popular **Peet's Coffee** (☎ 415-552-8555).

For a highbrow rummage-sale experience, try the Pacific Heights version. Rich folks unload their castoffs at the **Next-to-New Shop** (2226 Fillmore Street between Sacramento and Clay streets; ☎ 415-567-1628), which gets its goods from the Junior League of San Francisco, and at **Repeat Performance Thrift Shop** (2436 Fillmore Street between Jackson and Washington streets; ☎ 415-563-3123), which benefits the San Francisco Symphony.

Secondhand shopping isn't confined to clothing. The trend for recycled merchandise extends to books, CDs, records, and even cookware. **Cookin'** (339 Divisadero Street near Haight Street; ☎ 415-861-1854) is like your grandmother's attic, filled with classic kitchen gadgets, dishware, cookbooks, and anything else the gourmet in you might desire.

BOOKS AND MAGAZINES

SINCE MANY COME TO SAN FRANCISCO TO BE writers, artists, and musicians (or just to be near them), the city has an unusually well-read population and plenty of well-stocked and personable bookstores. The big guys are here, of course—including **Borders Books & Music** (400 Post Street at Powell Street; ☎ 415-399-0522), a superstore with four stories of books, music, and videos, and **B&N** (well, if we have to spell it out for you—**Barnes and Noble**) at 2550 Taylor Street; ☎ 415-292-6762.

But as is the case with other shoppers in San Francisco, book enthusiasts are loyal to their neighborhood booksellers. One of the city's favorite bookstores, **A Clean Well-Lighted Place for Books** (Opera Plaza, 601 Van Ness Avenue at Golden Gate; ☎ 415-441-6670), offers frequent readings, book signings, and bountiful sale and remainder tables. You'll find (or stumble over) more than a million used books, records, and magazines in the overstuffed **McDonald's Bookshop** (48 Turk Street near Market Street; ☎ 415-673-2235), affectionately known as "A Dirty, Poorly Lit Place for Books." **A Different Light** is a remarkably well-stocked gay and lesbian bookstore that functions as a de facto community center (489 Castro Street at 18th; ☎ 415-431-0891). Beat headquarters and the publishing home and hangout of Jack Kerouac and Allen Ginsberg, **City Lights Booksellers & Publishers** (261 Columbus Avenue between Pacific Street and Broadway; ☎ 415-362-8193) is probably San Francisco's best-known bookstore. You still may find founder-poet Lawrence Ferlinghetti hanging around.

Magazine lovers should check in at **Harold's International Newsstand** (454 Geary Boulevard between Mason and Taylor streets; ☎ 415-441-2665). **Naked Eye News and Video** (607 Haight Street; ☎ 415-864-2985) specializes in culture rags and 'zines—the more obscure, the better. **The Magazine** (920 Larkin Street; ☎ 415-441-7737) is one of many strangely wonderful shops in town; it's where all those old magazines you threw away wind up, and its obsessively catalogued gay and straight porn section is a miracle of modern library science. Or something.

For the best used bookstore, it's a tie between Russian Hill's **Acorn Books** (1436 Polk Street at California Street; ☎ 415-563-1736) and Richmond's bewildering, maze-like **Green Apple Books** (506 Clement Street at Sixth; ☎ 415-387-2272). Bookstores cater to almost every specialized taste. Find books from an African-American perspective at **Marcus Books** (1712 Fillmore Street; ☎ 415-346-4222). **William Stout Architectural Books** (804 Montgomery Street at Jackson Street; ☎ 415-391-6757) is one of the best of its kind in the country. **Fields Book Store** (1419 Polk Street between Pine and California streets; ☎ 415-673-2027) seriously specializes in spiritual and New Age books. **The Limelight** (1803 Market Street; ☎ 415-864-2265) is stocked with books on film, TV, acting, and its main attraction, unbound sometimes-yet-to-be-published screenplays. Check out **Socialist Action Bookstore** (298 Valencia; ☎ 415-821-0459), where you'll find books by such renegades as Che Guevara and Malcolm X. Travelers can map out their lives at **Get Lost Travel Books Maps & Gear** (1825 Market Street at Pearl Street; ☎ 415-437-0529).

CLOTHING

SAN FRANCISCANS TAKE PRIDE IN DEFINING themselves by what they are not—as in, not L.A. and not N.Y. A (sometimes ostentatious) lack of ostentation defines Northern California style. Sure, San Francisco may be less image conscious and clothes crazy than, say, Los Angeles; but as low key and (sophisticatedly, sensibly) dressed down as San Franciscans are, they like to look good. Fortunately, there are plenty of places to dress up (or down).

For women, **Union Square** is the hot spot for shopping, offering all the famous fashion names in boutiques and department stores. Union Street, in its ten-block shopping area, has more than 40 clothing boutiques, from trendy to traditional, including San Francisco–based **Bebe** (2095 Union Street; ☎ 415-563-2323), which has classic-to-trashy suiting for the chic and slim contemporary woman, and **Girlfriends** (1824 Union Street; ☎ 415-673-9544), whose distinctive logo items have become coveted souvenirs. For the unpredictable San Francisco weather, layering is essential. Stop at **Three Bags Full** (2181 Union Street at Fillmore; ☎ 415-567-5753) for hand-knit sweaters and sportswear. At **Carol Doda's Champagne and Lace** (1850 Union Street; ☎ 415-776-6900) in a picturesque Union Street alley, San Francisco's famous former stripper sells lingerie and bodywear for women of every size. **Canyon Beachwear** (1728 Union Street; ☎ 415-885-5070) is San Francisco's only women's specialty swimwear shop.

Behind the Post Office (1510 Haight Street; ☎ 415-861-2507) is known for its shabby-chic style made by top local designers. You won't have the problem of duplicates at a party if you shop at this store. Sizes run small so you gotta like them tight-fitted. If you want to sport true 1940s patterns with today's chic infused in the fabric, check out **Manifesto** (514 Octavia Street; ☎ 415-431-4778). Combining the appeal of those sit-and-gossip hair salons, the owner of **Brown Eyed Girl** (2999 Washington Street; ☎ 415-409-0214) opened her boutique in a quaint Victorian home to welcome women inside not just for shopping but for an intimate getaway. Shopping as an experience! You can find evening dresses to just the right everyday purse here. Europe meets Asia for a trendy funk infusion at **Ab Fits** (1519 Grant Avenue; ☎ 415-982-5726). Service is excellent here, especially when it comes to finding the proper fit in jeans, which is the lure for many jeans seekers. Whether you are going to trendy nightspots or looking for a chic outfit to teach the third grade, a city favorite amongst females is **Ambiance,** with two locations: one on 1458 Haight Street (☎ 415-552-5095) and the other on Union Street (☎ 415-923-9797). The store on Union Street is said to be the friendliest around.

Look sharp, men. San Francisco's snazzy former Mayor Willie Brown is friendly with the equally dandyish proprietor of **Wilkes Bashford** (375 Sutter Street between Grant and Stockton streets; ☎ 415-986-4380), who keeps Brown in fedoras and tailored suits in an opulent atmosphere; Don Johnson shops here, too. For more traditional men's clothing, **Cable Car Clothiers** (200 Bush Street at Sansome; ☎ 415-397-4740) is a good bet for the jacket-and-tie set. On the other side of the couture coin, **Saks Fifth Avenue Men's Store** (384 Powell and Post streets; ☎ 415-986-4300) stocks gear by Versace, Gaultier, and Dolce & Gabbana. For nightlifers, **Daljeets** (1773 Haight Street at Cole; ☎ 415-752-5610) has off-the-wall clothes for street and club wear, and the clothing and underwear shop **Rolo** (2351 Market Street near Castro Street; ☎ 415-431-4545) is so up-to-date it's futuristic.

Shoes

We won't mention the infamous political leader's wife who had enough shoes to probably circle the earth if placed toe-to-heel, but if you can sympathize with her cause and want to go home with some marvelous magic slippers, San Francisco will be a foot-pleaser. Aside from the great selections at top department stores like Macy's or Nordstrom, there are some quaint shoe stores like **Smash Shoes** (2030 Chestnut Street; ☎ 415-673-4736) that redefine that little black shoe. For a bit of Marcia Brady in your wardrobe with an urban slant, one of the most popular fashions for feet is this Haight favorite—**Shoe Biz** (1446 Haight Street; ☎ 415-864-0990). The selection will please club kids and even conservative classic dressers with a bit of a funky edge.

Retro Clothing

San Francisco is a nexus of the retro-swing craze, and what with Lindy-hoppin' hotspots like Club Deluxe and others, some people here make living in the past a full-fledged way of life. Vintage clothing is big business, and while these shops are no bargain, you can find the real deal. **Held Over** (1543 Haight Street; ☎ 415-864-0818) has one of the best collections of formalwear, leather jackets, and trousers in crazy patterns. La Rosa Vintage (1711 Haight Street; ☎ 415-668-3744) has enough vintage shoes to satisfy even Imelda Marcos. Also, embroidered blouses, lounge-lizard wear, and lots of men's hats. This is a high-class operation and you'll never feel like you're in a secondhand store.

CREATIVITY AND THE DECORATIVE ARTS

SAN FRANCISCO IS KNOWN FOR ITS CREATIVITY and free spirit. Start beautifying your life with a stop at **FLAX** (1699 Market Street at Valencia Street; ☎ 415-552-2355), a distinctive arts-supply superstore with paints and paper, furniture, lighting, framing, wrapping paper, and unusual jewelry and toys.

You can actually rent a painting (with an option to buy) from the **San Francisco Museum of Modern Artists Gallery** (Building A, Fort Mason Center at Buchanan Street and Marina Boulevard; ☎ 415-441-4777). The gallery's goal is to give exposure to new artists, and if you decide the work looks good over your couch, half of the rental fee goes toward the purchase price.

FLOWERS AND PLANTS

THE BAY AREA IS ONE OF THE NATION'S PREMIER flower-growing areas, and the city is abloom with talented florists like the Castro's avant-garde **Ixia** (2331 Market Street between Noe and Castro streets; ☎ 415-431-3134), creating wildly abstract, attention-grabbing bouquets. You can make your own arrangements after a visit to the **San Francisco Flower Mart** (640 Brannan Street at Sixth Street; ☎ 415-392-7944), which fills an entire city block with blooms and branches. Some parts of the market are accessible only to professionals with badges, but several outlets offer fresh and unusual flowers, plants, and paraphernalia at budget prices. And for flowers on the fly just walk around Union Square. You'll see small florists on every other corner. If you want an arrangement to last longer, **Coast Wholesale Florist** (149 Morris Street in the Flower Market; ☎ 415-781- 8533) is a warehouse with dried versions of nearly every plant on earth.

unofficial **TIP**
One of the best flower deals in the city is the green-and-white tent that is **Rincon Flowers** (corner of Spear and Mission streets). Every Friday they run a half-off special.

FOOD

PERHAPS BECAUSE SAN FRANCISCO IS THE home of California cuisine, restaurant dining has become one of the city's most popular participatory sports, and locals watch the trades and power plays of big-name chefs the way they watch their quarterbacks and stock options. Many of the city's foodies, known for their sophisticated tastes and obsession with fresh local ingredients, will tell you they live here because it's so near the source of wonderful produce. And with Napa Valley and Sonoma wine country so close, almost everyone knows something about wine.

A few food specialty stores, including an outpost of Seattle's **Sur La Table** (77 Maiden Lane; ☎ 415-732-7900), can be found in Union Square. In North Beach, you can't go wrong at many of the Italian bakeries and delis; start at the century-old deli **Molinari's** for first courses (373 Columbus Avenue at Vallejo Street; ☎ 415-421-2337). In Chinatown, **The Wok Shop** (718 Grant Street between Sacramento and Clay streets; ☎ 415-989-3797) specializes in everything you need for cooking Chinese cuisine, including cookbooks. And for the perfect end to the meal, **Golden Gate Fortune Cookie Company** (56 Ross Alley off Jackson Street; ☎ 415-781-3956) makes traditional fortunes, as well those with customized messages to order. **Joseph Schmidt Confections** (3489 16th Street; ☎ 415-861-8682) is the city's premier (and quite imaginative) chocolatier, especially famed for its chocolate sculptures. Bring back your souvenirs in chocolate.

Even something as mundane as grocery shopping can provide a California experience at places like **Real Food Company** (2140 Polk Street between Vallejo Street and Broadway; ☎ 415-673-7420); **Whole**

Foods (1765 California Street; ☎ 415-674-0500), a gourmet megastore where museum-quality carrots, tomatoes, and peppers are displayed as if this were the Produce Prado; and **Rainbow Grocery Cooperative** (1745 Folsom at Division Street; ☎ 415-863-0621), a crunchier, co-op version of Whole Foods, with pierced, tattooed staffers ringing up your bulk food items. **Trader Joe's** (555 Ninth Street at Bryant Street; ☎ 415-863-1292) has become a favorite for its discount gourmet snacks, health foods, and fresh juices, and a great selection of wines and beers.

Coffee is still the craze in hyper-caffeinated San Francisco, and you can find a cafe selling java and whole beans on almost every corner. Originally from Berkeley, **Peet's Coffee and Tea** (2139 Polk Street; ☎ 415-474-1871) was the inspiration for the creators of Starbuck's. The aroma of fresh-roasted coffee in the blocks around **Graffeo** (735 Columbus near Filbert Street; ☎ 415-986-2420), a beloved hometown roastery and wholesale distributor in North Beach, is one of the signature scents (and tastes) of San Francisco. To steep yourself in Chinese culture and gastronomica, take a walking/shopping/eating tour of Chinatown with the City's most renowned tour guide Shirley Fong-Torres. She'll take you to the best places for Chinese kitchen equipment, as well as foods, spices, and medicinal herbs. You'll see fortune cookies being made, perhaps a cooking demonstration, and best of all you'll have lunch with Shirley. Her operation is known as **Wok Wiz** and offers both tours and classes (☎ 415-981-8989; shirley@wokwiz.com). Make a stop at **Mitchell's Ice Cream** (688 San Jose Avenue; ☎ 415-648-2300), unarguably the best ice cream in the city—proven by the lines of tongue-lapping wannabes with their number in hand, anxiously waiting. You'll find the traditional flavors like vanilla, chocolate, yeah, yeah, yeah, but it's the unusual flavors that put Mitchell's on the map. Try mango, langka (a tart melon), macapuno (meaty coconut), or our favorite Cinnamon Snap. You can pick up pints and enjoy it all week.

Another distinctive San Francisco shopping experience is an early morning visit to one of the weekly farmers' markets. On Wednesday and Sunday at **United Nations Plaza** (Market Street between Grove and Fulton streets, near the Civic Center), the **Heart of the City Farmers' Market** (1182 Market Street at Eighth Street; ☎ 415-558-9455) replaces the panhandlers with dozens of booths featuring fresh-from-the-farm fruits, vegetables, and flowers. Saturday mornings used to be the day for the outdoor market across the Embarcadero from the Ferry Building. But no more. Now it's every day, all day, and even into the night, inside the newly refurbished Ferry Building. Not only is this a grand place to come for fresh produce, but also bakery goods and ready-to-eat foods. At the time of writing it has just opened and not all tenants are in place yet. But look for a fish market and restaurant or two to be added soon. Chinatown's open produce markets, which have the feel of exotic farmers' markets, are open every day. Look for them on Stockton Street running the length of Chinatown.

Plump Jack Wines (3201 Fillmore Street at Greenwich Avenue; ☎ 415-346-9870) in the Marina is a companion store to Plumpjack Café, and it's one of the best places in San Francisco to find impressive and obscure labels. Free delivery is available anywhere in the city. The name says it all—the **Napa Valley Winery Exchange** (415 Taylor Street between Geary Boulevard and O'Farrell Street; ☎ 415-771-2887; **www.nvwe.com**) is a wine boutique specializing in hard-to-find vintages and labels from nearby Napa. They ship. Other good spots for California wines are **D&M Liquors** in Pacific Heights (2200 Fillmore Street at Sacramento Street; ☎ 415-346-1325) and **Wine Club** (953 Harrison Street; ☎ 800-966-7835), which sells wine from jug to connoisseur at just above wholesale prices. The Wine Club boasts the largest selection of Burgundy and Bourdeaux wines west of the Mississippi. For spirits of another sort, head to the Financial District for a visit to **John Walker & Co. Wine and Spirits** (175 Sutter Street between Montgomery and Kearny streets; ☎ 415-986-2707), the city's oldest specialty and import liquor merchant.

INSIDER SHOPS

Cliff's Variety (479 CASTRO STREET BETWEEN 18TH and Market streets; ☎ 415-431-5365), with its friendly, small-town feel, everything-but-the-kitchen-sink stock, and outlandish seasonal window displays, has become a Castro institution. If you're stumped about a gift, turn the problem over to the staff at **Dandelion** (55 Potrero Avenue at Alameda Street; ☎ 415-436-9500), which celebrates "the home and sharing great things with friends" in 40 mini-departments on two floors. **See's Candies** is an old-fashioned candy shop—the kind where people behind the counter give you a free sample if you buy something and sometimes even if you don't. Stores are located throughout the city (☎ 800-347-7337).

And if you need something at any hour, there's a good chance you'll find it (or something that will do until the shops open) at one of the city's all-purpose 24-hour stores, including **Safeway** (2020 Market Street at Church Street; ☎ 415-861-7660) and **Walgreen's** (498 Castro Street at 18th; ☎ 415-861-6276).

KIDS

KIDS WILL GET A KICK OUT OF A VISIT TO THE **Basic Brown Bear Factory** (2801 Leavenworth Street, second floor; ☎ 415-409-2806), where they can watch a bear-making demonstration and pick out their own cuddly pal. Pacific Heights and the Marina are the spots for the stroller set; **Dottie Doolittle** (3680 Sacramento Street between Locust and Spruce streets; ☎ 415-563-3244), **Jonathan-Kaye by Country Living** (3548 Sacramento Street between Laurel and Locust streets;

☎ 415-563-0773), and **Mudpie** (1694 Union Street; ☎ 415-771-9262) are just a few of the upscale kidswear boutiques for label-savvy Pacific Heights tots.

As a major metropolis, San Francisco has its **Toys 'R Us** (☎ 415-931-8896), of course, but the hometown toybox of choice is **Jeffrey's Toys** downtown (685 Market Streetat Third Street; ☎ 415-243-8697), with a great comic book collection, and a center for all things *Star Wars.* Just try to extricate your offspring from the first-in-the-world, hands-on **Sony Playstation Store,** at Metreon (150 Fourth Street at Mission; ☎ 415-369-6000).

MUSEUM SHOPS

SAN FRANCISCO IS RICH WITH MUSEUMS, AND THE gift shops are full of take-home treasures. Consider the shops your own team of personal shoppers. The **California Historical Society** (678 Mission Street at Fourth; ☎ 415-357-1848) has beautiful graphics of California's parks. There are three museums in Golden Gate Park, each with its own unique shop. The **Legion of Honor** (Golden Gate Park; ☎ 415-750-3642), sells books and objects related to recent shows. The internationally famous **Exploratorium** (3601 Lyon Street next to the Palace of Fine Arts; ☎ 415-561-0390) is an interactive science museum, and its gift shop is full of intriguing science kits and games for children of all ages. The **San Francisco Museum of Modern Art** (151 Third Street; ☎ 415-357-4035) is a San Francisco landmark, and its innovative museum store has racked up high sales.

MUSIC

THE BIRTHPLACE OF ACID ROCK, A HOTBED OF JAZZ, and a historically culture-craving town full of classical music buffs and operaholics, San Francisco is rich in record stores. There are two **Tower Records** locations (Castro: 2280 Market at Noe Street, ☎ 415-621-0588; and Columbus Avenue and Bay Street; ☎ 415-885-0500). The **Virgin Megastore** (2 Stockton Street at Market Street; ☎ 415-397-4525) has three sprawling, noisy floors of CDs, DVDs, books, magazines, a cafe, and its own DJ. It's a good place to listen before you buy, and the import section is tops.

The used-records scene is a way of life. The biggest used-records game in town is **Amoeba** (1855 Haight Street; ☎ 415-831-1200), which operates a superstore in a former Haight Street bowling alley. Other places to search for that Holy Grail–like CD or record: **Streetlight** (3979 24th Street between Sanchez and Noe streets; ☎ 415-282-3550) and **Recycled Records** (1377 Haight Street at Masonic Street; ☎ 415-626-4075). Vinyl lives on at **Grooves** (1797 Market Street at Elgin Park; ☎ 415-436-9933) and **Medium Rare Music** (2310 Market Street near Castro Street; ☎ 415-255-RARE), which specializes in all sorts of campy old platters.

Then there's the new and the next. San Francisco has a thriving dance culture and techno scene, and the hippest kids shop where the local DJs get their discs: **Spundae Reckords + CDs** (678 Haight Street; ☎ 415-575-1580) is where the DJs shop, and you'll likely see a few foraging. It's a great place for the latest house mixes on 12-inch singles, and some CDs are available, too.

PLEASURE CHEST: SEXY SHOPPING

WITH ITS (WELL-DESERVED) ANYTHING-GOES reputation, San Francisco is synonymous with sex. Here's where to get your sensual supplies. **Good Vibrations** (603 Valencia Street between 23rd and 24th; ☎ 415-522-5640) is a friendly, nonfurtive store that's been women-owned and operated for 20 years; it sells sex supplies, books, and videos. Check out the vibrator museum. Often voted "best place to buy drag" in local alternative weeklies, **Piedmont Boutique** (1452 Haight Street; ☎ 415-864-8075) is a glitzy showgirl shop, but most of the showgirls are guys. Piedmont has been dressing strippers and drag queens for 33 years. **Foxy Lady Boutique** (2644 Mission Street between 22nd and 23rd; ☎ 415-285-4980) has wigs, gowns, lingerie, accessories, and shoes and boots up to size 16.

Stormy Leather (1158 Howard Street between Seventh and Eighth; ☎ 415-626-1672) specializes in leather and vinyl fetish wear for women. **Leather Etc.** (1201 Folsom Street; ☎ 415-864-7558; www.leatheretc.com) features PVC lingerie, a wide selection of Goth clothing and acres of leather. You're gonna look good when you leave here. **Madame S. Fetish Boutique** (385 Eighth Street; ☎ 415-863-9447) maintains a safe, secure environment where nobody get whipped without permission. Come here for corsets, literature, latex, and leather.

TOURISTARAMA

IF YOU ABSOLUTELY MUST GO HOME WITH AN Alcatraz shot glass, miniature cable car, or "fog dome," all this tourist merchandise and more (mind-bogglingly more) is conveniently concentrated in the boardwalk-like waterfront area known as **Fisherman's Wharf.** Shopping for nonessentials and unnecessary items is plentiful at the wharf's street vendors, as well as at Pier 39. **Ghirardelli Square** (900 North Point; ☎ 415-775-5500), with its clusters of 70 specialty shops surrounding the delightfully old-fashioned **Ghirardelli Chocolate Manufactory and Soda Fountain** (☎ 415-781-2601), and the **Cannery** (2801 Leavenworth Street near Hyde Street; ☎ 415-771-3112) is where you can take a breather from shopping with the live entertainment in the courtyard. One place that stands out is **Golden Gate Bridge Shop** (at the bridge toll plaza on the San Francisco side of the bridge; ☎ 415-923-2331), where you can purchase authentic pieces of cable and rivets from the Golden Gate Bridge. You can also pick up an original Lombard Street brick from the City Store in Pier 39. The store is run by homeless and formerly homeless folk in cooperation with a nonprofit organization and the city.

We've Got What You Need: The Bests

BEST SHOPPING STREETS Chestnut Street in the Marina or Union Street in Cow Hollow; upper and lower Fillmore Street; The Haight district

BEST TRINKET SHOP Golden Gate Bridge Shop (☎ 415-923-2331)

BEST PLACE TO BUY A GIFT "FROM SAN FRANCISCO" Mark Reuben Gallery (900 North Point; ☎ 415-543-5433) and the City Store at Pier 39

BEST SHOPS FOR THE NIECES AND NEPHEWS Exploratorium (at Marina Boulevard and Lyon Street; ☎ 415-561-0390); Gamescape (333 Divisadero Street; ☎ 415-621-4263)

BEST DRESSING ROOM Saks Fifth Avenue (384 Post Street; ☎ 415-986-4300)

BEST USED-BOOK STORE Green Apple Books (506 Clement Street; ☎ 415-387-2272)

PART TEN

EXERCISE *and* RECREATION

IN SAN FRANCISCO, SIMPLY GOING FROM your hotel to your car or out to brunch can be more exercise than most people get in a week. The city is a giant playground equipped with natural jungle gyms—paved hills, zigzagging steps, and giant green spaces expansive enough to fly a kite or even paraglide. Those who live here know what treasures await. And instead of replacing their clutch every month or so, they opt to foot it, bike it, climb it, pedal it, and public-transport it, which can require a whole new level of flexibility and balance during those sardined rides. So as the *Unofficial Guide* sets out to do, we want to empower you with the insider scoop—to do as the locals do but with a newcomer perspective!

THE GREAT INDOORS

FITNESS CENTERS AND AEROBICS

THE GYMS IN SAN FRANCISCO UNDERSTAND the conditioning demanded by the city's fitness freaks. Whether they are training for marathons or bike races or the popular Escape from Alcatraz swim, the gyms provide equipment and classes that can get any glute, tri, bi, quad, or calf pumped up. Hours for most gyms are similar—from 5:30 to 6 a.m. to about 8 p.m. A popular place for biker-shorts-clad, fitness-sophisticate Marina types is the heart-thumping, music-blaring **Gorilla Sports** (2324 Chestnut Street, ☎ 415-292-8470; 2330 Polk Street, ☎ 415-292-5444; **www.gorillasports.com**). The gym's two locations offer a free three-day trial pass. Their classes are pretty extensive, incorporating yoga, Pilates, kickboxing, and traditional aerobics.

    Club One, www.clubone.com, has seven locations with free weights, Nautilus, aerobic equipment, Jacuzzis, steam rooms, aerobics classes, and certified fitness trainers. Locations are Citigroup Center (1 Sansome Street; ☎ 415-399-1010), Yerba Buena (350 Third Street;

☎ 415-512-1010), Embarcadero Center (2 Embarcadero Center; ☎ 415-788-1010), Civic Center (450 Golden Gate Avenue; ☎ 415-876-1010), Fillmore Center (1455 Fillmore Street; ☎ 415-749-1010), and Nob Hill (Fairmont Hotel, 950 California Street; ☎ 415-834-1010). The daily rate is $15 with a member, $20 without.

24-Hour Fitness, www.24hourfitness.com, is a favorite of locals. Their color-coded machines, depending on which part of the body you want to work, is a convenient way to a self-guided workout. Although some feel that the gyms are too bare-bones and a bit grungy, the locations are convenient—seven in all, including 100 California Street (☎ 415-434-5080) and 1200 Van Ness Avenue (☎ 415-776-2200). The daily rate for each facility is $15.

Why not the Y? The **YMCAs, www.ymcasf.org,** in San Francisco are not bleach-smelling, family-infested, cinder-blocked gyms. They are clean and surprisingly effective facilities. The YMCA at the Embarcadero (169 Steuart Street; ☎ 415-957-9622) is a favorite for its huge swimming pool (five 25-meter lanes), excellent views, and low-key clientele. Cardio equipment, located in two adjoining rooms, includes 18 treadmills and 14 Netpulse Internet-equipped stationary bikes. Keep track of your workouts electronically with the FitLinxx system. The deck on the fifth floor is a hot-spot for sun worshippers. Daily rate is $15.

At the two locations of **Pinnacle Fitness, www.pinnaclefitness.com,** guests can swim at indoor pools after working out on Cybex weight-training gear or free weights; both locations have steam rooms (1 Post Street, ☎ 415-781-6400; and 345 Spear Street in the Hills Plaza on the Embarcadero, ☎ 415-495-1939). The daily fee is $15.

HOTELS FOR HEAVY SWEATERS

ARE YOU ARE THE TYPE WHO LUGS AROUND A portable ab machine purchased off some infomercial featuring Suzanne Somers and, while vacationing or attending business in San Francisco, is anxious about keeping the heart rate and metabolism on schedule? Most of the larger downtown hotels have excellent fitness centers on the premises, including the **Ritz-Carlton,** the **St. Francis,** and the **Nikko.** The Nikko comes with quite an extensive gym and swimming pool, which are available for a per day fee of $6, or can be included in a package deal. The **Grand Hyatt, Sheraton Palace, Beresford, Diva, Donatello, Juliana, Cartwright,** and the **Hilton** hotels struck a deal with Pinnacle Fitness Centers allowing guests to work out at any Pinnacle facility for only $10. The **Nob Hill Lambourne** on Pine Street is for the most exercise-obsessed. A stationary bike, treadmill, or rowing machine come in each room, and the hotel offers yoga equipment for guest use. Call ☎ 415-433-2287; **www.nobhilllambourne.com.**

SPAS

Whether you are looking for a back massage, acupuncture, manicure and pedicure, tanning, facial, or even a communal bath, San Francisco has plenty of offerings. **Kabuki Springs & Spa** (Japan Center, 1750 Geary Street at Fillmore; ☎ 415-922-6000; **www.kabuki springs.com**) offers traditional Japanese communal baths. Don't knock it until you've tried it. You can take a cold plunge and then soak in hot baths while you polish your skin with sea salts. Your skin will feel cleansed and buffed. No hanky panky goes on here— although bathing suits are optional, except on Tuesday, when they are enforced. The baths are open for women only on Sunday, Wednesday, and Friday, and to men only on Monday, Thursday, and Saturday. Tuesday is co-ed (thus the bathing suit mandate.) If bathing isn't your forte, the spa also offers 18 different spa treatment rooms, including acupuncture. Appointments are necessary. One neighborhood novelty for the last 20 years or so is Noe Valley's **Elisa's Beauty & Health Spa** (4028 24th Street; ☎ 415-821-6727; **www.elisasbeauty. citysearch.com**). Elisa's has indoor and outdoor hot tubs and saunas and is pretty laid back—usually you can just show up. Also offered are wraps of every kind, facials, waxing, and a variety of massages. Specials run quite often, so be sure to call. One of the best places in the city is the chichi **Spa Radiance** (3011 Fillmore Street; ☎ 415-346-6281). If you are prepared to feel like a shrink-wrapped piece of meat and pay big bucks for it, then this is the place. Everything from body wraps to specialized facials is offered, as well as Endermologie, a rub-down treatment for cellulite.

CLIMBING

IF YOU'VE EVER DREAMED OF CLINGING TO A wall or ceiling like Spider-Man, **Mission Cliffs** (2295 Harrison Street at 19th Street; ☎ 415-550-0515; **www.touchstoneclimbing.com**), the Bay Area's premier indoor-climbing haven, has more square clingage than even the original superhero could handle. With more than 14,000 square feet of climbing terrain and walls exceeding 50 feet high, it is the best preparation if you plan to take advantage of real rock in nearby climbing haven Yosemite or other national parks. Mission Cliffs is a must-try if you have never climbed, and a perfect way to confront that fear of heights once and for all! The gym also has a complete weight room, locker rooms, showers, and sauna. It's open seven days a week until 10 p.m. You will have to pass a belay test, which will cost $20, but once certified you can come and climb till your fingers cramp. For nonmembers, the weekday price after 3 p.m. and on weekends is $18; before 3 p.m. and for kids ages 6 to 17 it's $8. You can rent all the necessary gear for $5. If you'd like to see what Mission Cliffs looks like, take a virtual tour at their Web site.

DANCING

Metronome Dance Center (1830 17th Street, ☎ 415-252-9000) is the city's premier venue for ballroom and swing dance. It is open seven days and nights a week. Lessons for groups, couples, and singles are offered throughout the day and into the early evening. There are lessons every night, with dances on Friday and Saturday nights, including, swing, salsa, ballroom and tango. **Emeryville's Allegro Ballroom** (5855 Christie Avenue, Emeryville; ☎ 510-655-2888; **www.allegroballroom.com**) hosts salsa on Sunday, taught by one charismatic Garry Johnson and Isabelle Rodriguez. There are two afternoon classes, and a party in the evening is included in your $12 fee. If either salsa or Sunday isn't your speed, try Argentinean tango on Tuesday.

ICE SKATING AND BOWLING

THE NEW **Yerba Buena Ice Skating and Bowling Center** provides public skating and bowling as well as lessons. The center is located at 750 Folsom Street (☎ 415-820-3532; **www.skatebowl.com**).

OUTDOORS, NATURALLY!

WALKING: FUN CITY RAMBLES

IMAGINE THIS. AN OLD DUTCH WINDMILL TO THE right, and as you pass, the trees clear with the lightest of ocean breezes, revealing Ocean Beach. Continuing this walk through **Golden Gate Park** you come to Fort Funston, where you can perch yourself on a dizzying cliff that overlooks the crashing waves below. And what is this? Is it a bird, a plane . . . ? It's a hang glider swooping and sailing the wind's current just in front of you over the waves. Just an ordinary walk in San Francisco! Whether you prefer simple rambles or full-blown hikes, there are tons of opportunities in San Francisco. It would be a sin to leave the walking shoes at home.

San Francisco's premier rambling destination is the **Golden Gate Promenade,** a three-and-a-half-mile paved footpath that starts in Fort Mason (just west of Fisherman's Wharf) and ends at the famous bridge of the same name. As the trail follows the shoreline along San Francisco Bay, it passes through Marina Green, the Yacht Harbor, Crissy Field, and the Presidio; it ends at Fort Point (a Civil War–era brick fortress). Along the way are picnic areas, restrooms, restaurants, beaches, drinking water, fishing piers, quiet stretches of shoreline, and breathtaking views, not to mention excellent photo ops of Alcatraz. To lengthen the walk, hike the Coastal Trail along the Pacific coast to Cliff House.

unofficial **TIP**
Temperatures can change rapidly along the shoreline of the Coasta Trail, and wind is often strong; bring a jacket or sweater.

Visitors can begin a stroll in South Beach Harbor on the northeast side of the city facing Oakland. Start at Pier 40 and walk north along the promenade past the new marina, new apartment complexes, and South Beach Park, where artists sometimes set up their easels on the lawn beneath the colossal red-and-silver Mark di Suvero sculpture "Sea

Change." It's a place where picnickers and dog-walkers gather to watch the boats. As you walk north, the Bay Bridge soon arches above; curving along the sidewalk for nearly half a mile is a ribbon of glass blocks lit with fiber-optic cable and set in concrete; some of it is raised for use as benches or tables. This public art is a nice place to relax and watch the bay and the parade of joggers, skaters, and strollers.

In the northwest corner of the city, the 1,480-acre **Presidio** has 11 miles of trails in a variety of landscapes, including coastal bluffs, forested hills, and historic architectural settings (such as the old army buildings on the main post). You can pick up a trail map at the visitor center, open from 9 a.m. to 5 p.m. daily (☎ 415-561-4323). Golden Gate Park features miles of walking, multipurpose bicycle, and bridle paths. Probably the best place for walkers is Strybing Arboretum near the Japanese Tea Garden, part of the San Francisco Botanical Garden. The beauty and tranquility of the many gardens inside the 70-acre arboretum and its manicured lawns are unsurpassed.

Only about 30 minutes outside of the city, another not-to-be-missed walk is through the towering redwoods of **Muir Woods National Monument** (☎ 415-388-2596). Paved trails wander through the forest of giant trees, and information signs guide your experience. Located on the south side of Mount Tamalpais, 12 miles north of San Francisco, the park is open daily from 8 a.m. to sunset. It can get crowded on weekends. Admission is $3. (For more information, see Part Six, Sightseeing, Tours, and Attractions.)

HIKING

THE MARIN HEADLANDS Hiking paradise exists just over the Golden Gate Bridge in the **Marin Headlands,** close in distance and time but many moods apart. Within 15 minutes of leaving the city you are in total solitude, with hiking trails of varying difficulty intersecting all around you. A lovely stretch of the California Coastal Trail, a 1,200-mile trail that stretches the entire length (an ongoing effort) of the California coast (and hugging the Pacific the entire way), travels through the Headlands. You can meet up with it for day hikes or pack along with the tent and sleeping bag and find shelter for a weekend hike. This section is also part of the Bay Area Ridge Trail, so don't get confused. The trail is used by hikers, bikers, and equestrians. The approach is different for each user but all meet up at the trail at a junction called Five Corners. The trailhead for hikers starts at the northwest portal of the Golden Gate Bridge.

MOUNT TAMALPAIS is another favorite. Although the hikes are shadowed by the world-class fat-tire trails, there are still top-notch hiking trails for all levels with views and gorgeous scenery. Or if mountains and altitude have you panting for breath already, try hikes along **Muir Beach or Stinson Beach.** It is much easier to hike downhill! Stinson stretches beneath steep coastal bluffs (the ones you would be hiking up if choosing Mt. Tamalpais option) with vistas out to sea. **Olema Valley** is for the more advanced hiker as the trails are long and steep, ascending to ridgetops for breathtaking ocean views. Some trails connect the Valley to **Point Reyes National Seashore,** more than 70,000 acres of pristine coast land. Point Reyes has more than 147 miles of trails and four designated backcountry camping areas. This is a pre- ferred hiking destination because of the diversity of trail levels, well-maintained campsites, and the almost-certain chance of seeing northern fur seals, sea lions, and herds of tule elk. You can moonlight on the Point during summer months. What better than hiking under a full moon? You can get a naturalist guide for your nocturnal hike by calling Point Reyes Field Seminars at ☎ 415-663-1200. Muir Woods also hosts evening hikes every full moon. There is nothing more special than to look up at the towering trees illuminated by the moon. No planning necessary. Just come with a flashlight and meet at the Muir Woods Visitor Center at 7 p.m. sharp. For information, call ☎ 415-388-2596.

unofficial **TIP**
The weather in the Golden Gate National Recreation Area varies hourly. Fog and winds are usually at their most fierce closer to the bridge. Bring a fleece, plenty of water, and al- ways wear wool socks for foot ventilation. Depend- ing on the length of your hike, boots or Teva sandals are sufficient.

Listing all the trails and hiking opportunities within the Headlands and beyond would need a book of its own. Space is limited here, unfortu- nately. But if the Grizzly Adams in you desires more, there are tons of other hikes in the Head- lands and the best resource for trail maps and lodging information is the Golden Gate Na- tional Recreation Area, which begins where the Pacific Ocean meets San Francisco Bay. All in all, it is the largest urban national park in the world, a whopping 76,500 acres of land and water that includes 28 miles of wild coastline. You can get information by calling ☎ 415-556-0560; brows- ing **www.nps.gov/goga;** or writing Golden Gate National Recreation Area, Fort Mason, Building 201, San Francisco, CA 94123-0022. Inquire about their new hiking property, Phleger Estate.

 ONLY IN SAN FRANCISCO
Step Right Up

In no other city will you find more stairs outside, and in the most innovative and creative city in the country you shouldn't be surprised to find them used as stairways to buns of steel. Here is a breakdown of some of our favorite urban climbs.

The Greenwich Steps (East)
WHERE Bottom, on Sansome and Greenwich Streets; Top, Telegraph Hill Place at Greenwich Street
COUNTDOWN TO HEAVEN OR HELL 387 steps
Perched along the precariously steep slopes of Telegraph Hill and set among what seems to resemble gardens in Tuscany, this stairway is chock

full of camera-toting tourists gawking at the view. Sights along the climb include the art deco apartment house at 1360 Montgomery Street that was the façade used in the Humphrey Bogart/Lauren Bacall flick, *Dark Passage*; the doggie park on Montgomery Street, and the romantic quaint restaurant Julius' Castle.

Lyon Steps

WHERE Bottom, Green Street at Lyon; Top, Broadway at Lyon Street
COUNTDOWN TO HEAVEN OR HELL 291 steps; for the best views, the top 166
A meat market of sorts—and a fashion show. Bring your best work-out duds and don't forget the makeup. Business cards a necessity.

Pemberton Steps

WHERE Bottom, Clayton Street at Pemberton Place (look for a hidden sign on the right); Top, Pemberton Place and Crown Terrace
COUNTDOWN TO HEAVEN OR HELL 204 seemingly endless stairs
A very low-key, relaxed, and shaded atmosphere with daisies and rhododendrons with a view of Mount Diablo in the distance.

Bench Warming

It may not be the most effective for calorie burning or physical recreation, but for many, sitting on a good bench and people-watching is recreation enough. San Francisco has some darn good benches. Consider it a mental exercise to feel the burn of a city and its people in motion. Along the **Marina Green** off of Marina Boulevard, east of Crissy Field, offers the best benches for watching the city's yuppie set jog, walk Fido, or Rollerblade. There are kite fliers, groups of friends playing volleyball, and the obvious perk of views of Alcatraz, the bay, the Headlands, and the Golden Gate Bridge. Nearby, the **Palace of Fine Arts** is also home to some fine benches. Wedding parties are usually dispatched here in droves for photo ops—always a fun sight. And at sunset, the Palace lights up and is almost as dramatic as Rockefeller's Christmas Tree. Whether or not you play golf, you will appreciate the benches at the 13th hole of **Lincoln Park Golf Course,** which you can reach after a beautiful drive through the Presidio. It's one of the most beautiful panoramic vistas of downtown San Francisco anywhere. Across the bridge in **Tiburon,** while you wait for the ferry to Angel Island or for the return trip to San Francisco, the benches that line the waterfront are great for watching walkers, dogs, boats, rolling fog, and the cityscape on the horizon.

ISLANDS IN THE BAY

AT 4:30 P.M., THE LAST FERRY FLOATS OUT FROM **Angel Island State Park,** smack dab in the middle of San Francisco Bay. Why do you need to know this? Because if you are looking for your own private heaven, Angel Island is just that. No cars to wind gears into your slumbering dreams, just endless hiking trails, camping facilities, and a perch at the top with fine, fine views (as you noticed there is no shortage of fine views in this city.) It's the perfect place for a remote retreat. You never feel totally alone, though. The evenings are illuminated by lights from the city and the Golden Gate Bridge, and during day-hikes, it seems as if the entire bay area has its energetic glow wrapped around you. There are nine campsites complete with picnic areas, food lockers, pit toilet, and grills. Reservations are required and cost $14 per night, plus $6.75 reservation fee. A good option for accessing the island is ferry from Pier 43 in San Francisco ($12) or Tiburon ($5). The price includes the state park entrance fee. The boat drops you at Perimeter Trailhead, which takes you around the island on clearly marked and well-maintained trails. Along the trail are opportunities for bike rentals ($12 to $25 per day depending on style of bike), new tram tours ($5 per person), kayak rentals ($20 for two hours), and eating at the Cove Café. Open daily April through October, and Thursday through Monday in March and early November. Closed in winter. For recorded information, call ☎ 415-435-1915; or look at **www.angelisland.org.**

Prisoners once dreamed of "walking." And now the place that barred them from freedom, **Alcatraz Island,** is an evolving ecological preserve—and a great walking destination. The absence of four-footed predators has made the island a haven for birds, as well as thriving populations of crabs, seastars, and other marine animals living in tide pools. Visitors can see this on the **Agave Trail,** which follows the islands' shoreline. The trail is part of a bird sanctuary and is open from September through February. Ferries to Alcatraz leave from Pier 41 at Fisherman's Wharf; make reservations in advance. For information and ticket purchases, call ☎ 415-705-5555. You can also order tickets online at **www.telesales.com.**

RUNNING

THERE ARE ENOUGH RUNNING OPPORTUNITIES in San Francisco to satisfy the Forrest Gump in all of us. You'll see plenty of runners on the sidewalks downtown. But for visitors who would rather avoid traffic, large crowds, and stoplights, there are plenty of other options. Flat but usually windy, the four-mile **Golden Gate Promenade** offers runners a paved and scenic route for a workout, not to mention a friendly camaraderie among other runners; the round trip from Fort Mason to the Golden Gate Bridge is seven miles. Not that you have to stop at the landmark span; you can run across the bridge on its pedestrian walkway to the challenging **Marin Headlands** or continue along the Pacific coast on the **Coastal Trail.** The Coastal Trail (this is a section of the California Costal Trail; see above) is a scenic 9.2-mile run that will lead you through the posh neighborhood of Seacliff, China Beach, Land's End, and the Cliff House near Ocean Beach.

If the hills of the Headlands seem too challenging for you, after the bridge turn right toward Sausalito—it's about a 9-mile run from Aquatic

Park on the Promenade. The run is refreshingly downhill, and if you are exhausted you can take the ferry back from Sausalito to Fisherman's Wharf.

Usually less windy, Golden Gate Park has plenty of paved roads and miles of pedestrian, bike, and bridle paths on rolling terrain; the main drag, Kennedy Drive, is closed to traffic on Sundays. On the east side of the city in South Beach, a promenade heads north along the shoreline toward the Bay Bridge; it's a favorite destination for joggers and runners.

ROAD BICYCLING AND IN-LINE SKATING

IN DOWNTOWN SAN FRANCISCO, MOST FOLKS will want to leave bicycling and in-line skating to bike messengers and street-savvy natives. Yet skinny-tire cyclists and skaters don't need to go far to find some excellent places to spin the cranks or skate the black ice. The **Golden Gate Promenade** starts in Fort Mason (just west of Fisherman's Wharf) and follows the bay shore for three and a half miles to the bridge of the same name (which has a pedestrian and bike lane). The scenery from the bridge is spectacular, but winds are usually strong enough to push you over. Across the bridge in **Marin County** at the end of the Vista Point parking lot is a bike lane that parallels US 101 and then turns off to Alexander Avenue through Sausalito.

For a more recreational bike run than those in the Headlands and closer to home, **The Presidio** has 14 miles of paved roads, open to cyclists and in-line skaters, that weave through groves of trees and wind past military housing. Because most of the old military post's roads were laid out in horse-and-buggy days, all grades are easy to moderate. **Golden Gate Park** has seven and a half miles of designated designated paved trails for bikes that extend from the tip of the Panhandle through Golden Gate Park to Lake Merced. In addition, some roads (such as Kennedy Drive, the main drag) are closed to car traffic on Sundays; it's heaven for San Francisco in-line skaters.

With its three bicycle lanes, the flat, three-mile sidewalk along **Ocean Beach** (Great Highway) provides a great workout and can be incorporated into a longer tour of the Sunset District. Ride south on the Great Highway for two miles past the San Francisco Zoo to Skyline Boulevard and turn right onto Lake Merced Boulevard; then ride for five miles around the lake and nearby golf course.

unofficial **TIP**
Although most folks drive or take a tour bus, a more exhilarating way to get to the summit of **Twin Peaks** and its stupendous view is to run or walk. Routes include the back roads from the University of California Medical Center or either of the two main roads that lead to the top. The best time is early morning when the city is quiet and the air is crisp; just make sure you pick a morning that's not fog bound.

unofficial **TIP**
The hills on the Marin side of the Golden Gate run are killer— affectionately called the Rambo run by those who frequent it! Be prepared. Temperatures also increase on this side as well, so hydration is important.

For another variation along the Pacific shoreline, ride north along the Great Highway from Lake Merced toward Cliff House. Just before you get there, gear down for a 200-foot ascent. Then veer right onto Point Lobos Avenue and turn right onto 43rd Avenue. Then it's all downhill to Golden Gate Park; enter at Chain of Lakes Drive East, which takes you back to Kennedy Drive. Turn right and continue west to the Great Highway, which takes you back to Lake Merced.

A San Francisco classic for the thin-tire set is a 19-mile loop ride across the Golden Gate Bridge to Sausalito and Tiburon that returns you to San Francisco on a ferry. The ride can start at the parking lot at the south end of the bridge or at Fisherman's Wharf; after the one-and-a-half-mile bridge crossing, descend into Sausalito on Alexander Avenue, ride into Tiburon, and catch the ferry to Fisherman's Wharf. Check with a local bike shop for turn-by-turn directions and a map; it's also a good idea to check the ferry schedule by calling the Red and White Fleet at ☎ 800-229-2784.

Biking Wine Country

One way to avoid drinking and driving but still feel a buzz is to bike it! Napa is way too street-crowded for such an excursion, so instead head to calmer pastures in Sonoma County, specifically the nice, flat, wide Dry Creek Valley. Healdsburg is the starting point. Leave your car here—a convenient place to return to and eat, or hang in the park. Dry Creek Road starts at Healdsburg Avenue and you can stay on it until you are too tired or too hammered. Wineries line the road all the way to the turnoff at Lambert Bridge Road, which loops you around to West Dry Creek Road for a total trip distance of 14 miles.

For Extreme Eyes Only!

This guide wouldn't be called *Unofficial* if it didn't include the Everest of in-line skating ops. The so-called **6 Parnassus Ski Lift** that runs up and down the Ninth and Tenth Avenue "slopes," was first made famous by intrepid and lunatic skateboarders who first discovered the great hill. The procedure: take the bus at Ninth Avenue and Judah, and don't forget that transfer ticket, because it is what gets you back up the hill over and over for the next two hours. The hill is long, steep, and will have you close to breaking the sound barrier in no time! You don't want to forget the helmet, knee pads, and wrist guards for this run. If you prefer fancy footwork, try **Hubba Hideout,** at Maritime Plaza at Battery Street. Stairs and handrails and hills, oh my!

Renting Bikes and In-Line Skates

Bike and skate rentals are widely available throughout San Francisco; some shops also provide guided tours. **Bay City Bike** at the Cannery in Fisherman's Wharf (☎ 415-346-2453; **www.baycitybike.com**) rents 21-speed hybrid (city) bikes starting at $7 an hour and $25 a day;

helmet, rear rack and bag, lock, maps, tour info, and water bottles are included. They also offer a guided tour for four or more people across the Golden Gate Bridge to Sausalito and a return to San Francisco by ferry for $35 (cost varies based on group size).

Blazing Saddles rents computer-equipped bikes for self-guided tours of San Francisco, the Marin Headlands, Muir Woods, and Mount Tamalpais. Mountain bike rentals start at $7 an hour or $28 a day, and they offer even lower rates for multiday rentals. Also available for rent are road bikes, city bikes, tandems, kids' bikes, and car racks. The shop is at 1095 Columbus Avenue (at Francisco); call ☎ 415-202-8888; or visit **www.blazingsaddles.com.** There is also a satellite store at Fisherman's Wharf, which makes it convenient to rent and then hop over to Angel Island or Tiburon.

In Golden Gate Park, **Wheel Fun Rental** rents in-line skates starting at $6 an hour and bikes at $5 an hour; the shop, located at Stow Lake (closed Wednesdays and rainy days) also rents tandem bikes and pedal-powered surreys. For more information, call ☎ 415-668-6699.

At Angel Island State Park in San Francisco Bay, **Angel Island Company** rents 21-speed mountain bikes for exploring traffic-free roads and paths on the island. Basic rentals start at $10 an hour or $30 a day and include a helmet. Open daily May through October, and weekends only in November and March; closed December through February. For more information, call ☎ 415-897-0715 or visit **www.angelisland.com**; for ferry schedules from Pier 43 in Fisherman's Wharf, call ☎ 800-229-2784.

MOUNTAIN BIKING

WHILE FAT-TIRE MOUNTAIN BIKES ARE FINE for riding on San Francisco's streets and paved trails, off-road aficionados who prefer the feel of dirt between their knobbies should look farther afield, but not too far. Across the Golden Gate Bridge lies Marin County, where popular myth says mountain biking was invented 20 years ago.

The cradle of mountain biking civilization is reputed to be Mount Tamalpais. It's so popular a destination among fat-tire fanatics that the sport has been banned from single-track trails, and cops with radar guns give out tickets to cyclists who exceed 15 miles an hour on the fire roads. The most popular route is technically easy, but aerobically demanding—Old Railroad Grade to the historic West Point Inn (where, incidentally, you can stop over a stack of pancakes) and the East Peak. There are lots of scenic spots along the way, and the reward is a breathtaking (not that you'll have much breath left), 360-degree view of San Francisco Bay. And, as they say, it's all downhill from here. Once you reach the top there is a snack bar with hot dogs and bagels and cream cheese. (Not advertised, reserved for those in the know, are the frozen fruit bars. Ask for them.) You could even choose to make a weekend out of it and stay overnight at the West Point Inn.

To reach the Old Railroad Grade (an unpaved fire road), load your bike onto your car and take US 101 north across the Bay Bridge to the Tiburon Boulevard/East Blithedale Avenue exit. Then turn left, heading under US 101 and west onto East Blithedale Avenue. Take East Blithedale as it turns into West Blithedale Avenue and go past an intersection with Eldridge Road. About a mile later, Old Railroad Grade branches off to the right over a wooden bridge. Park as close to this bridge as you can. Unload your bike and ride across the bridge.

If you are new to the sport and want to earn bragging rights for having survived fat-tire trails in California, try Crystal Springs Reservoir, in the South Bay. The heart barely pumps and the adrenaline stays at a minimum on the flat wooded path that starts at the gate just off the Highway 92 West Exit. The path circles the reservoir, eventually depositing you at the dam where another trail heading to Skyline Boulevard intersects. Your only obstacles are joggers and trees.

The all-inclusive combo recreational/sightseeing haven is of course Angel Island. Again, take the ferry from Fisherman's Wharf or Tiburon to get there; bikes are permitted on the ferry for free except from Tiburon, where they charge you $1. You can also rent one on the island (see above), but rentals are cheaper on the mainland. There are about eight miles of easy, unpaved fire roads to explore, and the scenery is terrific, especially from the upper fire road. Alas, mountain bikes are not permitted on trails on the island and ferry service is limited to weekends in the winter.

BEACHES

FOR ALL YOU *BAYWATCH* WANNABES, THE BAD news is that it's usually too chilly to put on those teeny-weenie bikinis and lather up on the beach. The Pacific is frigid—just dip your toes in and see—and the unpredictable fog causes lines at most area tanning salons. But just because the Bay Area beaches aren't perfect for sunbathing or swimming doesn't eliminate them altogether. Most are Hollywood-perfect, with cliffs breathing down over quiet coves, and each beach creates a unique vibe appreciated by natives and remembered by visitors. To highlight these unique uses and features, we've compiled a rather unofficial survey of what's offered at the beaches by the bay.

BEST CONTEMPLATIVE CURRENTS Muir Beach in Marin County off Highway 1 (west of Highway 101, take the Stinson Beach/Mill Valley exit) with its pristine sand and quaint cove surrounded by towering cliffs, is the best beach to bring a copy of *Conversations with God* or your journal. It's quiet and just an all-around good beach.

unofficial **TIP**
The water at Ocean Beach is treacherous even when it looks calm, so use extreme caution if wading or swimming.

BIGGEST WAVES Ocean Beach is the best place to watch surfers who come for the picture-perfect pipes. The Great Highway, which runs parallel to Ocean Beach's four miles (the longest beach in the Bay Area), is sometimes closed due to the too-close-for-car-comfort crashing waves.

MOST ROMANTIC BEACH Drake's Beach along Point Reyes National Seashore, off Highway 1, with its sheltered beach, towering white cliffs, and fine sand, is one of the most romantic. The drive to get there is all part of the seduction.

BEST BEACH TO RE-CREATE SCENES FROM "BEACH BLANKET BINGO" Even the road getting there—along Highway 1 off of 101—is good for a party. Put the top down on the car and wind over narrow cliff clinging roads down to the lively, friend-gathering **Stinson Beach.**

BEST BIRTHDAY SUIT BEACH North Baker Beach is the most popular naked spot in the city. The sand is clean and the parking lot safe. Temps are chilly though . . . so beware. Also, nudity is not permitted at the south end of the beach. The beach is located at Lincoln Boulevard and Bowley Street, near 25th Avenue. Honorable mentions include: **Fort Funston,** off of Great Highway north of Skyline Boulevard; and **Lands End** on the western edge of the city (popular with gay men), just above Cliff House on the Great Highway.

BEST BEACH FOR THE LITTLE ONES The stretch of **China Beach** is small enough to keep an eye on them and all facilities, including picnic tables, and the restrooms are spotless. (Would you expect anything less in the Seacliff neighborhood?) You can also walk up Seacliff Avenue past the mauve house flying the flag with the blue wolf on it—that's where Robin Williams lives.

BEST BEACH FOR FIDO If you couldn't stomach leaving the dog at the kennel, the beach along **Crissy Field** at the end of the Marina Green is small but it is one huge frolicking playground for the pups. Let 'em loose and sit back and enjoy the wind and kite surfers circling the pillars of the Golden Gate Bridge. (Don't forget the plastic gloves to de-poop the beach of your doggy's droppings.)

SEA KAYAKING

THE CURRENTS IN THE BAY ARE QUITE TOUGH TO maneuver but despite this, kayakers come from all over to slide their sleek craft—a stable, covered boat similar to a canoe but propelled by a double-bladed paddle—into the waters off San Francisco. **Sea Trek Ocean Kayaking Center** offers tours for novices around Angel Island, Sausalito, and Point Reyes. A novice can glide out from Sausolito's Schoonamaker Point marina and join seals, pelicans, and even the

unofficial **TIP**
Many beaches around San Francisco allow nudity, with the interesting caveats that you don't touch anybody and nobody complains. (If you equate nudity with sex, keep in mind that in the Golden Gate National Recreation Area, where many of the nude beaches are located, public sex is a federal offense.) Other negatives to lounging in the buff at San Francisco beaches include cool temperatures, fog, wind, rocky beaches with little or no sand, and gawkers. In addition, many of the beaches are difficult to reach, requiring long walks on narrow, steep paths lined with poison oak.

occasional whale in Richardson Bay. Rentals for single kayaks: $15 an hour; double kayaks are $25 an hour. Wetsuits, paddle jackets, spray skirts, paddles, pumps, and paddle floats are included with rentals. Call ☎ 415-488-1000 for more information or visit **www.seatrek kayak.com.** To check on tide conditions, look up **www.tidesonline. nos.noaa.gov** before heading out.

Blue Waters Kayaking in Marin County offers instruction, rentals, and tours in Point Reyes and Tomales Bay; no experience is necessary for some tour packages. They offer a half-day morning tour from 9 a.m. to noon for $68; $88 for their "Day on the Bay" tour. An all-day introductory kayaking course is $89. Sea kayak rentals start at $30 for two hours and $45 for four hours. Double kayaks start at $50 for two hours and $65 for four hours. For reservations and more information, call ☎ 415-669-2600; **www.bwkayak.com.**

ROCK CLIMBING

IF YOU HAVE ALREADY TRIED THE PLASTIC HOLDS of an indoor climbing gym and want to test your skill on real granite, there is no better destination than the Bay Area. **Yosemite** is *the* climbing destination and it is only about a three-hour drive away! Closer still is **Red Rock Beach,** south of Stinson Beach off of Highway 1 at mile post 11.43. Mickey's, as locals call it, is a demanding rock with a dazzling ocean view. Its face rises and falls, with 55 feet of cracks and crevices. You just may want to look down here—nudists populate the beach below. Because the Pacific pounds below, access to most of its face depends on tides. Safety check: the rock isn't appropriate for beginners, and tides control access to most of its face (so check **www.tides online.nos.noaa.gov** before heading up). Skilled climbers only.

Climbers of all levels can head to a more controlled environment at Mission Cliffs, the Bay Area's indoor climbing gym (see page 363).

HANG GLIDING

WITH ITS PERSISTENT COASTAL WINDS, San Francisco is an excellent place to go hang gliding. The **San Francisco Hang Gliding Center** specializes in tandem hang-gliding flights. You can see some of Northern California's most beautiful terrain, ☎ 510-528-2300; **www.sfhanggliding.com**). The basic tandem flight is about $300. Simply call to arrange a meeting spot at the launch—usually Mount Tamalpais. From there you glide to the north end of Stinson Beach. If you'd rather just watch, head for Fort Funston south of Ocean Beach, where hang gliders launch off 200-foot cliffs and soar on coastal breezes.

unofficial **TIP**
There are benches atop the cliffs at Fort Funston that are perfect for observing. Be careful not to enter the launch and landing zone. Pilots are pretty adamant about it.

SAILING

SAN FRANCISCO BAY, ONE OF THE LARGEST AND most beautiful harbors in the world, is also a major yachting center, although sailing on the bay is challenging even for the most experienced sailor. Certified skippers can charter anything from day sailors to luxury yachts and sail past all the landmarks that make the bay so famous. Don't know a spinnaker from a jib? You can also learn how to sail while you're on vacation in San Francisco.

Cass' Marina charters day sailors that accommodate up to six people, starting at $162 a day on weekdays; each boat is equipped with toilet facilities and life vests. Cruising boats for large daytime outings or overnight charters start at $365 a day; weekend, five-day, and weekly rates are also available. Cass' offers a full complement of instructional courses for beginners to advanced sailors. A basic keel-boat certification course with 29 hours of instruction is $795; completion qualifies you to bare-boat (no crew) charter a cruising sailboat. Private instruction is available for about $289 for three hours on weekdays (for one or two people), and $326 on weekends. Cass' Marina is located at 1702 Bridgeway at Napa Street in Sausalito (across the bay from San Francisco); ☎ 415-332-6789; **www.cassmarina.com** for more information.

Also in Sausalito is **Atlantis Yacht Charters,** where you can charter 30-foot and longer yachts. Bareboat charters start at $295 a day for an Ericson 30 that sleeps four; a Nordic 44 goes for $600 a day midweek and sleeps seven adults. Skippered charters start at $400 for three hours midweek; the price includes captain, yacht, and fuel. For more information, call ☎ 800-65-YACHT; or visit **www.yachtcharter.com.**

WINDSURFING AND KITESURFING

GOOD COASTAL WINDS MAKE SAN FRANCISCO one of the top spots in the country for windsurfing, and the increasingly popular kitesurfing, where riders are lifted out of the water by, yep, you guessed it, one big kite. The premier location in the city is **Crissy Field,** where experienced board sailors frolic on wind and waves.

GOLF

SAN FRANCISCO HAS TWO MUNICIPAL GOLF courses that are open to the public. **Golden Gate Park Course** (47th Avenue and Fulton Street; ☎ 415-751-8987) is a small nine-hole course covering 1,357 yards. It is open every day, 6:30 a.m. until dusk. **Lincoln Park Golf Course** (34th Avenue and Clement Street; ☎ 415-750-4653) offers 18 holes and covers 5,081 yards. The oldest course in the city, it offers beautiful views and fairways—just stop and check out what's in front of you at the 13th hole! It is open every day, 6:30 a.m. until dusk. Green fees are $ 31 during the week and $36 on weekends and holidays. In Berkeley, the Tilden

Park Golf Course (Grizzly Peak Boulevard and Shasta Road; ☎ 510-848-7373) offers the best deals in town. It's easy and cheap to get in 18 holes before dark—it's a $23 weekday/$29 weekend twilight rate. If you consider yourself more of a morning golfer—how does the $16 early-bird rate sound to you?

TENNIS

MORE THAN 132 TENNIS COURTS ARE OPERATED throughout the city by the San Francisco Recreation and Parks Department. All are available free on a first-come, first-served basis, with the exception of 21 courts in **Golden Gate Park,** where a fee is charged and reservations must be made in advance for weekend play. The courts are located off Kennedy Drive opposite the conservatory; individual and group lessons are available.

To make weekend reservations at a court in Golden Gate Park, call ☎ 415-753-7001 on the preceding Wednesday evening between 4 and 6 p.m., the preceding Thursday between 9:15 a.m. and 5 p.m., or the preceding Friday between 9:15 and 11:30 a.m. (Call Wednesday evening to avoid disappointment.) The nonresident court fee is $8 for a 90-minute play period. For more information and the locations of other courts around San Francisco, call the parks department at ☎ 415-753-7001; or visit **www.parks.sfgov.org.**

FISHING

DEEP-SEA FISHING CHARTER BOATS LEAVE Fisherman's Wharf daily, depending on weather and season. Catches in the Pacific waters beyond the Golden Gate include salmon, halibut, and striped bass. Licenses (required), rods, and tackle are available on board; plan for wind and some rough seas, and bring motion-sickness preventatives and warm clothing. *Miss Farallones,* a 50-foot charter boat, sets out on sportfishing expeditions from Fisherman's Wharf most days and can carry up to 38 passengers. For rates and more information, call ☎ 925-689-0900; **www.sfsportfishing.com.**

Freshwater fishing is available at **Lake Merced,** south of downtown where Skyline Boulevard meets the Great Highway at the Pacific coast. Large trout and some catfish and bass are stocked in the 360-acre lake, which is open year-round. Anglers must purchase a $9.70 one-day fishing license and pay a $5 access fee. Rowboats are available to rent for $12 an hour. Paddleboats, which can hold up to four people, rent for $15 an hour. They no longer rent electric boats. You can also fish from the bank of the lake, which stocks trophy trout of two pounds and more. For more information, call parks and recreation at ☎ 415-831-2700.

NATURE VIEWING

Whale-Watching

Each year gray whales embark on one of the longest migrations of any mammal, and the coast near San Francisco is one of the best places to observe these giants during their 6,000-mile journey between their Arctic feeding grounds and Baja, California. The nonprofit **Oceanic Society** offers naturalist-led expeditions year-round to observe the whales as well as nature cruises to the Farallon Islands, stark granite cliffs 27 miles from the Golden Gate that teem with marine life.

Gray-whale cruises depart from San Francisco at 9:30 a.m. on selected dates from December to May and last six hours, returning to the dock at 4 p.m. Rates for adults start at $78; bring your own lunch and beverages. The expedition transports guests under the Golden Gate Bridge and north along the Marin coast to search for gray whales off the Bolinas and Point Reyes areas.

Farallon Islands nature cruises depart at 8:30 a.m. on selected dates from June through November and last eight hours. Rates for adults start at $88; bring your own lunch and beverages. The cruise sails under the Golden Gate Bridge and goes west to the Farallon Islands, where a quarter-million seabirds nest and visible marine mammals include California sea lions, Steller's sea lions, northern elephant seals, harbor seals, and possibly humpback and blue whales. A not so visible resident is the Great White-this is the largest breeding ground in the world for them, after all!

All cruises are aboard a Coast Guard–certified, fully insured motor vessel with an open observation deck, indoor salon, and a passenger capacity of 37. Off-street parking is available at the harbor at Fort Mason. Youths ages 15 and under must be accompanied by an adult, and children ages 10 and under aren't permitted on the boat. Reservations are required; call ☎ 800-326-7491 or 415-474-3385 for a schedule, and make reservations at least two weeks in advance (although it's possible to get aboard at the last minute if there are cancellations). Look up **www.oceanic-society.org** for more information.

> *unofficial* **TIP**
> If you're going on a gray-whale cruise, bring rain gear and warm clothing; the cruises depart rain or shine. Don't forget binoculars, a camera with a telephoto lens, sunscreen, and motion-sickness medicine. More advice: bring crackers to nibble and ginger ale to sip to help avoid queasiness on the cruise. If you are taking seasickness medication, be sure to take it before you depart—unfortunately, once the sickness starts, it's too late.

California Sea Lions and Seals

OK, it may not be the most pristine of scenes but the California Sea Lions that bark, clap, and flop over the floating piers at Pier 39 near Fisherman's Wharf are certainly worth a trip. Otherwise, you can usually spot them popping up for air at any point along the bay. **The Marine Mammal Center** in Fort Cronkite near Rodeo Lagoon in the Marin Headlands, ☎ 415-289-7325, is where you can go to see marine biologists nurse ailing and orphaned California sea lions and seals back to health. You can watch pups being bottle-fed and ask questions about them as well as the whales found in these waters. A great place for the family.

Zebra?

Yes, zebras, as well as giraffes, lemurs, several cats, and other exotic game can be found at **Safari West Wildlife Preserve and Tent Camp** (3115 Porter Creek Road, Santa Rosa; ☎ 707-579-2551; **safariwest@ safariwest.com**). The sanctuary is one of a few in North America that sets out to protect these endangered species through breeding, education, and research. It is home to more than 400 mammals and birds. In fact, two species of bird—the white-naped crane and the Indian hornbill—are currently registered with the international Species Survival Program.

To go on "safari," you will need to make reservation. Tours run at 9 a.m., 1 p.m., and 4 p.m. in the summer season, and 10 a.m. and 2 p.m. the remainder of the year. The tours, consisting of both driving and walking portions, last two-and-a-half hours and are guided by a naturalist. Prices for adults are $60, and for children under 14 years, $28. The adventurous can choose to make a weekend out of it and rent one of the tents for $225 per night per couple, two-night minimum (in summer). If the thought of a wild cat creeping up on you in the middle of the night makes the hairs on your arms stand up, you can stay in a cottage for $350 per night. The price includes four adults and a two-night minimum. It's great to do this with a group.

Bird-watching

Point Reyes National Seashore is probably the premier place to bring the binoculars and spot birds like California quail, Anna's and Allen's, hummingbirds, Nuttall's woodpecker, Pacific-slope flycatcher, Hutton's vireo, chestnut-backed chickadee, oak titmouse, pygmy nuthatch, wrentit, and California towhee. Seabirds such as red-throated and Pacific loons and brown pelicans are also primary residents of this bird haven. You can head on a self-guided tour if you are an experienced bird peeper, or for tour information call ☎ 415-454-5100. The park service offers a beginning birding tour once a month on Sundays, as well as guided tours to the lighthouse on Saturday, Sunday, and Monday at 12:30 p.m. Alcatraz Island is also becoming quite a bird sanctuary. Black-crowned night heron is one of many bird species that nest on Alcatraz. For guided tours, call ☎ 415-705-5555.

SPECTATOR SPORTS

BY AND LARGE, SAN FRANCISCANS ARE SPORTS enthusiasts—not just in participatory activities such as running, biking, and tennis. In fact, Bay Area fans' dedication to their professional sports teams can verge on the obsessive. The professional sports scene in the Bay Area includes football, baseball, basketball, and horse racing.

PRO TEAMS

Baseball

The National League **San Francisco Giants** play home games at the new SBC Park, located at 24 Willie Mays Plaza in the China Basin area, south of Market Street. The season starts in April and goes through October. Tickets are available through **tickets.com.**

The American League **Oakland Athletics,** the 1989 world champs, play at the sunnier McAfee Coliseum across the bay (take the Hegenberger Road exit off I-880). The stadium seats 34,000 baseball fans and is served by BART's Coliseum station. Tickets to home games are available from the coliseum box office or by phone from **tickets.com.**

Football

The San Francisco 49ers, five-time Super Bowl champs, play home games at Monster Park Sundays from August through December. They're best known for their intelligence, speed, and grace. Good luck getting tickets, though. The games sell out early in the season, but sometimes select tickets are available; call the box office at ☎ 415-656-4900. If you're willing to pay an inflated price, tickets may be available from ticket agents before game days and from scalpers at the gate; expect to pay up to $100 for a seat. Talk to your hotel concierge or stop by City Box Office (14 Kearny Street; ☎ 415-392-4400). Muni operates special express buses to the park, located about eight miles south of downtown, from Market Street on game days; call ☎ 415-673-6864 for more information.

Also, the Bay Area has two pro football teams again. Across the bay are the 49ers' arch enemy the **Oakland Raiders,** who returned to Oakland from Los Angeles in 1995 after abandoning the city for sunny Southern California 13 years before. Known as blue-collar heroes, the team charges country-club prices; expect to pay at least $60 for a ticket. Home games are played at the McAfee Coliseum off I-880. For tickets information, call ☎ 800-949-2626.

Basketball

The Bay Area's NBA team is the **Golden State Warriors,** who play in the newly renovated Oakland Arena across the bay. The season runs from November through April; most games start at 7:30 p.m. The arena is located at the Hegenberger Road Exit off I-880, south of downtown Oakland. For tickets, go to **tickets.com** or **www.gs-warriors.com.**

If you aren't so interested in spending half your vacation money on courtside tickets, consider heading to the San Francisco Bay Area ProCity Summer Basketball League. It's free, but the talent is top notch. Top pro and former collegiate players gather in Kezar Pavilion from mid-June through mid-August to stay on top of their game. You can get your hoop thrills at 755 Stanyan Street; **www.sanfrancisco proam.com.**

HORSE RACING

THE BAY AREA IS HOME TO TWO HORSE-RACING tracks. **Scenic Golden Gate Fields,** located in the East Bay off Gilman Street (off I-80 in Albany, ten miles northeast of San Francisco), features thoroughbred racing from February through May and August through October. For post times and more information, call ☎ 510-559-7300; or visit **www.goldengatefields.com.**

The racing closest to San Francisco is at **Bay Meadows,** south of San Francisco in San Mateo (on US 101 at the Hillsdale exit). The thoroughbred track hosts races Wednesday through Sunday during January and February, May and June, and October through December. It's one of the oldest, busiest, and most beautiful ovals in California. For more information and post times, call ☎ 650-574-7223; or visit **www.baymeadows.com.**

AMATEUR SPORTS

LOCAL COLLEGE GRIDIRON ACTION IS PROVIDED by the **University of California Golden Bears,** who play at Memorial Stadium across the bay in Berkeley. For game times and ticket information, call ☎ 800-GO-BEARS or visit **www.calbears.com;** tickets are usually available on game day. From November to March, the Bears men's basketball squad plays at the new $40 million Haas pavilion, which opened on campus in 1999.

The **University of San Francisco Dons** men's basketball team provides on-the-court excitement from November to March at the War Memorial Gymnasium on campus (2335 Golden Gate Avenue). Games start at 7 p.m.; for tickets and schedules, call ☎ 415-422-6USF or visit **tickets.com.**

EVENTS FOR THE OUTDOOR ENTHUSIAST

CONTACT THE VISITORS AND CONVENTIONS BUREAU for up-to-date information regarding these events and possible participation. ☎ 415-391-2000; **www.sfvisitor.org.**

ESCAPE FROM ALCATRAZ TRIATHALON Amateur and professional athletes make the one-and-a-half-mile swim from a chartered ferry in the Bay between the City and Alcatraz Island. The race continues with an 18-mile bike ride. The finish is under the Golden Gate Bridge. For more information, call ☎ 831-373-0678 or visit **www.tri california.com/alcatraz/2006/index.htm.**

BAY TO BREAKERS FOOT RACE Not quite for the competitive at heart, although serious runners do compete. Most come dressed in costume or not (clothes optional) and bring everything including the kitchen sink and kegs of beer. Anyone can participate in this annual spring ritual, usually held in May. For more information, call ☎ 415-359-2800 or visit **www.baytobreakers.com.**

SAN FRANCISCO MARATHON For the big guns who can handle the 26.2-mile course, and even for those who want to participate in half of that in the Split the Distance Marathon, Half Marathon, or 5K Fun Run—all on the same day, usually in July each year. The course takes in the "best of San Francisco," offering a scenic loop. For more information, including how to register, check out the Web site at **www.runsfm.com** or call ☎ 800-698-8699.

ACCOMMODATIONS INDEX

AAA hotel ratings, 49
Accommodations Express, 41
Acqua Hotel (Marin County), 59, 62
Airport, San Francisco
    Best Western Grosvenor Hotel, 62
    Doubletree Hotel, 66
    hotel comparisons, 59
    Hyatt Regency, 59, 73
    Marriott, 59, 79
    Red Roof Inn, 59, 79
    Sheraton Gateway Hotel, 81
    Travelodge, 59, 83
    Vagabond Inn Airport, 59, 83
    Westin Hotel, 59, 84
Amenities, room ratings and, 46–51
Andrews Hotel (Union Square), 50, 55, 61, 62
Archbishop's Mansion (Civic Center), 50, 52,
    61–62
Argent Hotel San Francisco (SoMa/Mission
    District), 51, 52, 63, 88
Auberge du Soleil (Wine Country), 60, 63
Automobile/travel clubs, room discounts from, 39

Bed and Breakfast
    Blue Violet Mansion (Napa), 168
    Bordeaux House (Yountville), 169
    Castillo Inn (Castro District), 37
    Cedar Gables Inn (Napa), 60–61, 64, 169
    Edward II Inn and Suites (Castro District), 37
    Hayes Valley Inn (Civic Center), 37
    House O'Chicks (Castro District), 37
    The Napa Inn Bed and Breakfast (Napa), 168
    Red Victorian Bed, Breakfast, and Art Center,
        36–37
    Web sites for finding, 38, 175
Beresford Arms (Union Square), 50, 54, 63, 366
Berkeley, Calif.
    Claremont Resort, 64

Doubletree Hotel Berkeley Marina, 66
    hotel comparisons, 59
    Hotel Durant, 70
"Best of" lists
    by neighborhood, 50–51
    outside San Francisco, 59
    in San Francisco, 52–55, 60–61
    in Wine Country, 60–61
Best Western
    Grosvenor Hotel (Airport), 59, 62
    Sonoma Valley Inn (Wine Country), 60, 62
    toll-free numbers, 45
Blue Violet Mansion (Napa), 168
Bordeaux House (Yountville), 169
Buena Vista Motor Inn (Marina District), 51, 54,
    60, 62

Calistoga Spa Hot Springs (Napa Valley),
    174, 180
Campton Place Hotel (Union Square),
    50, 52, 63
Cartwright Hotel (Union Square), 50, 54,
    63, 366
Casa Madrona (Marin County), 59, 63
Castillo Inn (Castro District), 37
Castle in the Clouds (Yountville), 169
Castro District, B&B's in, 37
Cathedral Hill Hotel, 50, 52, 60, 64
Cedar Gables Inn (Napa), 60–61, 64, 169
Central Reservations Service, 41
Civic Center area
    Archbishop's Mansion, 50, 52, 61–62
    Cathedral Hill Hotel, 64
    Hayes Valley Inn, 37
    Hotel Carlton, 50, 52, 60, 69
    Hotel Majestic, 50, 52, 60, 71
    Inn at the Opera, 36, 50, 52, 61, 72
    Jackson Court, The, 50, 52, 61, 73

Civic Center area *(continued)*
Phoenix Hotel, 50, 54, 61, 77
Queen Anne Hotel, 50, 54, 61, 78
Claremont Resort (Berkeley), 59, 64
Clift Hotel (Union Square), 50, 52, 65
Comfort Inn
Comfort Inn by the Bay, 51, 55, 65
toll-free numbers, 45
Commodore Hotel, The (Union Square), 50, 53, 61, 65
Cost comparisons, hotel, 41–51
Courtyard by Marriott
Fisherman's Wharf, 51, 54, 64
toll-free numbers, 45
Cow Hollow Motor Inn and Suites (Marina District), 51, 55, 61, 64
Credit cards, avoiding theft of, 124–28
Crime, avoiding, 124–28
Crowne Plaza Union Square, 50, 54, 64

Days Inn
Days Inn at the Beach (Richmond/Sunset District), 51, 55, 65
Fisherman's Wharf, 51, 55, 65
toll-free numbers, 45
Discounted room rates, 39–42
Donatello, The (Union Square), 50, 53, 65, 366
Doubletree Hotels
Berkeley Marina, 66
San Francisco Airport, 59, 66
toll-free numbers, 45
Dr. Wilkinson's Hot Springs Resort (Napa Valley), 60–61, 66, 174, 180

Econo Lodge, toll-free numbers, 45
Edward II Inn and Suites (Castro District), 37, 51, 54, 61, 67
El Bonita Motel (Wine Country), 60–61, 67
El Dorado Hotel (Wine Country), 60–61, 67
El Pueblo Inn (Wine Country), 60–61, 66
Embassy Suites
Embassy Suites Hotel (Marin County), 59, 66
Embassy Suites San Francisco (Airport), 59, 66
toll-free numbers, 45
Encore, 40
Entertainment Publications, 40
Exercise and Recreation, hotels catering to, 366
Fairmont Hotel (Nob Hill), 36, 51, 52, 67, 102
Financial District
Hotel Vitale, 51, 52, 72
Hyatt Regency San Francisco, 51, 53, 73
Mandarin Oriental, 51, 52, 75
Fisherman's Wharf. *See* North Beach
Fitzgerald Hotel (Union Square), 50, 53, 60, 67
Four Seasons Hotel (SoMa/Mission District), 51, 52, 67

Frequent flyer/mileage clubs, 39

Galleria Park Hotel (Union Square), 50, 53, 68, 88
Gays and Lesbians
finding accommodations, 27
information resources for, 27–28
properties catering to, 37
Grand Hyatt San Francisco (Union Square), 50, 53, 68, 366
Grant Plaza (Union Square), 50, 55, 60, 68
Gratuities. *See* Tipping for services
Great American Traveler, 40

Haight-Ashbury District
Red Victorian Bed, Breakfast, and Art Center, 36–37
Half-Price Programs, discounts from, 40–41
Hampton Inn, toll-free numbers, 45
Handlery Union Square Hotel (Union Square), 50, 55, 69
Harbor Court Hotel (SoMa/Mission District), 51, 53, 69
Harvest Inn (Saint Helena), 170
Harvest Inn (Wine Country), 60, 69
Hayes Valley Inn (Civic Center), 37
Health spas
Calistoga Spa Hot Springs (Napa Valley), 174, 180
Dr. Wilkinson's Hot Springs Resort (Napa Valley), 174, 180
Elisa's Beauty & Health Spa (Noe Valley), 367
Hideaway Cottages (Napa Valley), 180
Kabuki Springs and Spa (Japantown), 348, 367
Spa Radiance, 367
Hideaway Cottages (Napa Valley), 180
Hilton Hotels
fitness facilities, 366
Hilton San Francisco, 50, 53, 68
Oakland Airport, 77
toll-free numbers, 45
Holiday Inn, toll-free numbers, 45
Hotel, choosing a
See also hotel by name
comparing cost, 51–55
comparing ratings, 52–55, 59–61
discounted rates, 39–43
information resources for, 35
maps for, 56–58
money-saving tips on, 38
by neighborhood, 50–51
room ratings & rankings, 46–51
using this guide for, 7, 38
Hotel & Travel Index, 41
Hotel Adagio (Union Square), 50, 53, 68
Hotel Beresford (Union Square), 50, 55, 68

Hotel Bijou (Union Square), 36, 50, 53, 69
Hotel Carlton (Civic Center), 50, 52, 60, 69
Hotel del Sol (Marina District), 51, 54, 60
Hotel Diva (Union Square), 36, 50, 52, 60, 70, 366
Hotel Drisco (Richmond/Sunset District), 51,
    53, 70
Hotel Durant (Berkeley), 70
Hotel Majestic (Civic Center), 50, 52, 60, 71
Hotel Milano (SoMa/Mission District), 51, 53, 71
Hotel Monaco (Union Square), 36, 50, 52, 71
Hotel Nikko (Union Square), 50, 52, 70, 366
Hotel Palomar (SoMa/Mission District), 51, 52,
    70
Hotel Reservations Network, 41
Hotel Rex (Union Square), 50, 53, 70
Hotel St. Helena (Wine Country), 60, 71
Hotel Triton (Union Square), 36, 50, 53, 71
Hotel Union Square (Union Square), 50, 53, 60,
    71
Hotel Vintage Court (Union Square), 50, 55, 72
Hotel Vitale (Financial District), 51, 52, 72
House O'Chicks (Castro District), 37
Howard Johnson, toll-free numbers, 45
Huntington Hotel (Nob Hill District), 51, 52,
    72, 102
Hyatt Hotels
    Fisherman's Wharf, 51, 53, 73
    Grand Hyatt San Francisco (Union Square),
        50, 53, 68, 366
    Hyatt Regency San Francisco (Airport), 59, 73
    Hyatt Regency San Francisco (Financial
        District), 51, 53, 73
    toll-free numbers, 45

Inn Above Tide (Marin County), 59, 72
Inn at Southbridge (Wine Country), 60, 72
Inn at the Opera (Civic Center), 36, 50, 52, 61, 72
Inn at Union Square, 50, 54, 73
Internet. See Web sites
ITC-50, 40

Jackson Court, The (Civic Center), 50, 52, 61, 73
John Muir Inn (Wine Country), 60, 73

Kensington Park Hotel (Union Square), 50, 53,
    60, 74
King George Hotel (Union Square), 50, 55, 74

La Quinta Inn Oakland Airport (Oakland), 59, 74
Laurel Inn (Richmond/Sunset District), 51, 54, 75
Liquor sales, 124

MacArthur Place (Sonoma Valley), 180
Mandarin Oriental (Financial District), 51, 52, 75
Maps
    hotel location, 56–58

Official San Francisco Street and Transit Map, 123
Marin County
    Acqua Hotel, 62
    Casa Madrona, 63
    hotel comparisons, 59
    Inn Above Tide, 59, 72
    Mill Valley Inn, 59, 75
    Villa Inn, 59, 82
Marina District
    Buena Vista Motor Inn, 51, 54, 60, 62
    Comfort Inn by the Bay, 51, 65
    Cow Hollow Motor Inn and Suites, 51, 55,
        61, 64
    Days Inn Fisherman's Wharf, 51, 65
    Edward II Inn and Suites, 51, 67
    Hotel del Sol, 51, 54, 60
    Marina Motel, 51, 55, 75
    Motel Capri, 51, 55, 61, 75
    Pacific Heights Inn, 51, 55, 60, 76
    Star Motel, 51, 55, 81
    Super 8 Motel, 51, 55, 81
    Town House Motel, 51, 55, 82
    Travelodge by the Bay, 51, 55, 82
    Travelodge Golden Gate, 51, 55, 82
    Union Street Inn, 51, 53, 83
Marina Motel (Marina District), 51, 55, 75
Mark Hopkins Inter-Continental (Nob Hill
    District), 51, 53, 74, 102, 341–42
Marriott Hotels
    Fisherman's Wharf, 51, 54, 74
    Napa Valley Marriott Hotel (Wine Country),
        60–61
    Oakland City Center, 59, 76
    San Francisco Marriott (Airport), 59, 79
Marriott Hotels (continued)
    San Francisco Marriott (SoMa/Mission
        District), 51, 53, 79, 88, 110, 155
    toll-free numbers, 45
Maxwell Hotel (Union Square), 50, 54, 74
Mill Valley Inn (Marin County), 59, 75
Mission District. See SoMa/Mission District
Miyako Hotel (Civic Center), 50, 54, 61, 78
Mobil hotel ratings, 49
Money-saving tips, 38, 90
Monticello Inn (Union Square), 50, 54, 75
Moscone Center (Civic Center), 86–88
Motel Capri (Marina District), 51, 55, 61, 75
Mount View (Wine Country), 60–61, 76

Napa Valley
    Blue Violet Mansion, 168
    Bordeaux House, 169
    Calistoga Spa Hot Springs, 174, 180
    Castle in the Clouds, 169
    Cedar Gables Inn, 60–61, 64, 169
    Dr. Wilkinson's Hot Springs Resort, 174, 180

Napa Valley *(continued)*
  Harvest Inn, 170
  Hideaway Cottages, 180
  The Inn at Southbridge, 170
  The Napa Inn Bed and Breakfast, 168
  Napa Valley Lodge, 60, 76
  Napa Valley Marriott Hotel, 60–61, 76
  Napa Valley Railway Inn, 60–61, 77
  The Pink Mansion, 170
  Safari West Wildlife Preserve and Tent Camp,
    170
  Silver Rose Resort Winery, 170
  Villagio Inn & Spa, 169
Neighborhoods
  area maps of, 56–58
  hotels listed by, 50–51
Nob Hill Lambourne (Union Square), 36, 50,
  52, 61, 77, 90, 366
Nob Hill/Russian Hill District
  Fairmont Hotel, 36, 51, 52, 67, 102
  Huntington Hotel, 51, 52, 72, 102
  Mark Hopkins Inter-Continental, 51, 53, 74,
    102, 341–42
North Beach
  Courtyard by Marriott, 51, 64
  Hyatt Fisherman's Wharf, 51, 53, 73
  Marriott Fisherman's Wharf, 51, 54, 74
  Radisson Fisherman's Wharf, 51, 55, 78
  Sheraton Fisherman's Wharf, 51, 53, 80

Oakland, Calif.
  hotel comparisons, 59
  La Quinta Inn Airport, 59, 74
  Marriott City Center, 59, 76
  Oakland Airport Hilton, 77
  Waterfront Plaza Hotel, 59, 83
Official San Francisco Street and Transit Map, 123

Pacific Heights Inn (Marina District), 51, 55, 60, 76
Package Vacations, 42–44
Pan Pacific Hotel (Union Square), 50, 52, 76
Parc Fifty Five (Union Square), 50, 53, 61, 79
Parking
  city regulations, 130–32
  disabled access, 122–23
  hotel, 43, 129–30
  valet tipping, 120–21
Petite Auberge (Union Square), 50, 54, 77
Pets, traveling with, 37
Phoenix Hotel (Civic Center), 50, 54, 61, 77
Point Reyes National Seashore, 189
Prescott Hotel (Union Square), 50, 52, 61, 77
Privilege Card International, 40

Quality. *See* Service and quality
Quality Inn, toll-free numbers, 45

Queen Anne Hotel (Civic Center), 50, 54, 61, 78
Quickbook, 42

Rack rates, 41, 51, 88
Radisson Hotels
  Fisherman's Wharf, 51, 55, 78
  Miyako Hotel (Civic Center), 50, 54, 61, 78
  toll-free numbers, 45
Ramada Inn, toll-free numbers, 45
Rancho Caymus (Wine Country), 60, 79
Rates, room
  convention, 88–90
  cost comparisons, 41–51
  discounts for, 39–42
  location, location, location, 35
  money-saving tips on, 38, 90
Rating & ranking, hotel
  Airport hotels, 59
  outside San Francisco, 59
  rooms, 46–51
  San Francisco hotels, 51–58
Red Roof Inn San Francisco (Airport), 59, 79
Red Victorian Bed, Breakfast, and Art Center
  (Haight-Ashbury District), 36–37
Renaissance Hotels and Resorts
  Parc Fifty Five (Union Square), 50, 53, 61, 79
  Stanford Court Hotel (Nob Hill), 51, 52,
    61, 78
  toll-free numbers, 45
Rental cars, 43
Reservation Services, 41–42, 175
Reservations, making your own, 44–46
Richmond/Sunset District
  Days Inn at the Beach, 51, 65
  Hotel Drisco, 51, 53, 70
  Laurel Inn, 51, 54, 75
  Seal Rock Inn, 51, 54, 61, 80
  Stanyan Park Hotel, 51, 54, 61, 81
Ritz-Carlton
  fitness facilities, 366
  Half Moon Bay (South Bay), 59, 78
  Nob Hill, 51, 52
  toll-free numbers, 45
Room rates. *See* Rates, room
Room service, money-saving tips on, 38

Safari West Wildlife Preserve and Tent Camp
  (Calistoga), 170, 382
Safety & security, 47
San Francisco Reservations, 42
Savoy Hotel (Union Square), 50, 54, 61, 79
Seal Rock Inn (Richmond/Sunset District), 51,
  54, 61, 80
Seniors, discounted rates for, 39
Serrano Hotel (Union Square), 50, 53, 80
Service and quality

information resources for, 35–36
room ratings & rankings, 46–51
tipping for, 120–21
Sheraton Hotels
Fisherman's Wharf, 51, 53, 80
Sheraton Gateway Hotel (Airport), 59, 81
Sheraton Palace Hotel (SoMa/Mission
District), 51, 53, 81, 88, 366
toll-free numbers, 45
Silver Rose Resort Winery (Calistoga), 170
Silverado Country Club and Resort (Wine
Country), 60–61, 81
Sir Francis Drake Hotel (Union Square), 50, 53, 80
Smoking regulations, 124
SoMa/Mission District
Argent Hotel San Francisco, 51, 52, 63, 88
Four Seasons Hotel, 51, 53, 60, 67
Hotel Milano, 51, 53, 71
Hotel Palomar, 51, 52, 70
San Francisco Marriott, 51, 53, 79, 88, 110, 155
Sheraton Palace Hotel, 51, 53, 81, 88, 366
W Hotel San Francisco, 83
Sonoma Valley
Best Western Sonoma Valley Inn, 62
The Fairmont Sonoma Mission Inn, 180
The Lodge at Sonoma, 180
MacArthur Place, 180
Sonoma Creek Inn, 180
Sonoma Hotel, 60–61, 80
Sonoma Mission Inn and Spa, 60, 80
Sonoma Valley Inn, 60
South Bay, 59, 78
Stanford Court Hotel (Nob Hill), 51, 52, 61, 78
Stanyan Park Hotel (Richmond/Sunset District),
51, 54, 61, 81
Star Motel (Marina District), 51, 55, 81
Sunset District. See Richmond/Sunset District
Super 8 Motel (Marina District), 51, 55, 81

Taxes, hotel sales, 124
Taxi cabs. See Transportation
The Fairmont Sonoma Mission Inn (Sonoma
Valley), 180
The Inn at Southbridge (Saint Helena), 170
The Lodge at Sonoma (Sonoma Valley), 180
The Napa Inn Bed and Breakfast (Napa), 168
The Pink Mansion (Calistoga), 170
Theft, room security from, 47
Tipping for services, 120–21
Toll-free telephone numbers
Half-Price Programs, 40
hotel and motel chain, 45
Reservation Services, 41–42
Town House Motel (Marina District), 51, 55, 82
Transportation
Alameda/Oakland Ferry, 95–96

AMTRAK, 96
avoiding crime, 126–27
BART, 21, 92, 94–95
cabs and shuttles, 93–95, 137–38
disabled access, 122–23
Official San Francisco Street and Transit Map, 123
Paratransit Taxi Service, 123
tipping for service, 120–21
Travel agents, 39–44
Travelodge
San Francisco Airport North, 59, 83
Travelodge by the Bay (Marina District), 51, 55,
82
Travelodge Golden Gate (Marina District), 51,
55, 82

Union Square
Andrews Hotel, 50, 55, 61, 62
area map of, 58
Beresford Arms, 50, 63, 366
Campton Place Hotel, 50, 52, 63
Cartwright Hotel, 50, 54, 63, 366
Clift Hotel, 50, 52, 65
Commodore Hotel, The, 50, 53, 61, 65
Crowne Plaza, 50, 54, 64
Donatello, The, 50, 53, 65, 366
Fitzgerald Hotel, 50, 67
Galleria Park Hotel, 50, 53, 68, 88
Grand Hyatt San Francisco, 50, 68, 366
Grant Plaza, 50, 55, 60, 68
Handlery Union Square Hotel, 50, 55, 69
Hilton San Francisco, 50, 53, 68
Hotel Adagio, 50, 53, 68
Hotel Beresford, 50, 55, 68
Hotel Bijou, 36, 50, 53, 69
Hotel Diva, 36, 50, 52, 60, 70, 366
Hotel Monaco, 36, 50, 52, 71
Hotel Nikko, 50, 52, 70, 366
Hotel Rex, 50, 53, 70
Hotel Triton, 36, 50, 53, 71
Hotel Union Square, 50, 53, 60, 71
Hotel Vintage Court, 50, 55, 72
Inn at Union Square, 50, 54, 73
Kensington Park Hotel, 50, 53, 60, 74
King George Hotel, 50, 55, 74
Maxwell Hotel, 50, 54, 74
Monticello Inn, 50, 54, 75
Nob Hill Lambourne, 36, 50, 52, 61, 77, 90,
366
Pan Pacific Hotel, 50, 52, 76
Petite Auberge, 50, 54, 77
Prescott Hotel, 50, 52, 61, 77
Savoy Hotel, 50, 54, 61, 79
Serrano Hotel, 50, 53, 80
Sir Francis Drake Hotel, 50, 53, 80
Villa Florence, 50, 54, 82

Union Square *(continued)*
Warwick Regis Hotel, 50, 53, 61, 83
Westin St. Francis, 35, 51, 52, 84, 366
White Swan Inn, 51, 84
Union Street Inn (Marina District), 51, 53, 83
Unofficial Guides
defining, 3–5
room ratings & rankings, 46–51
sharing your comments, 7, 53–55

Vacation Packages, 42–44
Vagabond Inn Airport (SFO), 59, 83
Villa Florence (Union Square), 50, 54, 82
Villa Inn (Marin County), 59, 82
Villagio Inn & Spa (Yountville), 169
Vintage Inn (Wine Country), 60, 82

W Hotel San Francisco (SoMa/Mission
District), 51, 52, 83
Warwick Regis Hotel (Union Square), 50, 53,
61, 83
Waterfront Plaza Hotel (Oakland), 59, 83
Web sites
for discounted room rates, 39–42
for finding B&B's, 38

Reservation Services, 41–42
Wine Country, 175, 181
Westin Hotels
Westin Hotel San Francisco (Airport), 59, 84
Westin St. Francis (Union Square), 36, 51, 52,
84, 366
White Swan Inn (Union Square), 51, 52, 61, 84
Wine Country. *See also* Napa Valley;
Sonoma Valley
Auberge du Soleil, 63
El Bonita Motel, 67
El Dorado Hotel, 67
El Pueblo Inn, 66
Harbor Court Hotel, 51, 53, 69
Harvest Inn, 60, 69
hotel comparisons, 60–61
Hotel St. Helena, 60, 71
Inn at Southbridge, 60, 72
John Muir Inn, 60, 73
Mount View Hotel, 60–61, 76
Rancho Caymus, 60, 79
Silverado Country Club and Resort, 60–61,
81
Vintage Inn, 60, 82
Wyndham, toll-free numbers, 45

RESTAURANT INDEX

A. Sabella's Restaurant (North Beach), 239, 252–53
Acme Chop House (SoMa District), 239, 251–52
Airport (SFO), West Bay Café, 241, 316
American Market Café (Napa), 172
Ana Mandara (Marina District), 239, 253–54
Angle Island, Cove Café, 151
Asia de Cuba (Union Square), 238, 254–55
Aziza (Richmond/Sunset District), 241, 255–56

B44 (Union Square), 238, 256
Bambuddha Lounge (SoMa District), 239, 256–57
Barney's Hamburgers, 155
Bay Wolf (Oakland), 186
Baywolf (Oakland), 241, 257–58
Beach Chalet (Richmond/Sunset District), 241, 258–59
Berkeley, Calif.
    Bette's Oceanview Diner, 148
    Millennium Restaurant, 149
    Viks Distributors Inc., 148
"Best of" lists
    for Bagels, 241
    for Beer, 241
    for Burgers, 241, 250
    for Business Dining, 250
    for Coffee, 250
    by cuisine, 242–45
    for Desserts, 250
    for Martinis, 250
    by neighborhood, 238–41
    for Oyster Bars, 250
    for Pizza, 250
    for Seafood, 251
    for Sunday Brunch, 251
    for Sushi Bars, 251
    for Wee Hours Service, 251
    for Wine Bars, 251

Bette's Oceanview Diner (Berkeley), 148
Bistro Clovis (SoMa District), 239, 259
Bottom of Hill (Potrero Hill), 109
Boulevard (SoMa District), 239
Brannan's Grill (Calistoga), 170
The Brazen Head (Marina District), 239, 260
Brix Restaurant (Yountville), 169
The Buena Vista Café (Marina District), 239
Buzz 9 (SoMa District), 239, 261–62

Café de la Presse (Union Square), 238, 262–63
Café Flore (Castro District), 108
Café For All Seasons (Sunset District), 117
Café Pescatore (North Beach), 239, 263
Cafe Tiramisu (Financial District), 239, 263–64
Caffe Trieste (North Beach), 149, 348
Calzones (North Beach), 239, 264–65
Campton Place Restaurant (Union Square), 238, 265–66
The Carnelian Room (Chinatown), 238, 266–67
Castro District
    Café Flore, 108
    Firewood Café, 108
    Red Dora's Bearded Lady Dyke Café, 108
Cheesecake Factory (Union Square), 345
Children, traveling with, 155
Chinatown
    The Carnelian Room, 238, 266–67
    Empress of China, 236
    Hang Ah Tea Room, 100
    Palio D'Asti, 238, 298–99
    Sam Woh, 238, 304–05
    Ton Kiang Restaurant, 150
    Yuet Lee, 238, 317–18
Civic Center
    Harris' Restaurant, 238, 277–78
    House of Prime Rib, 238, 280

Civic Center (continued)
    Jardiniere, 238, 282
    Max's Opera Café, 238, 291
    Millennium, 238, 292–93
    Momi Toby's Revolution Café, 238, 293
    Ruth's Chris Steak House, 238, 304
    Swan Oyster Depot, 238, 309
    Tommy's Joynt, 238, 313
Clement Street Bar and Grill (Richmond/Sunset
    District), 241, 267–68
Clementine (Richmond/Sunset District), 241, 267
Copia, the American Institute for Wine Food and
    the Arts (Napa), 172
Cortez (Union Square), 238, 268–69
The Cosmopolitan Restaurant (SoMa District),
    239, 269–70
Cove Café (Angel Island), 151
Credit cards, avoiding theft of, 124–28
Crime, avoiding, 124–28
Cuisine, "best of" list for, 242–45

Doce Lunas (Sonoma Valley), 179
Dusit (Mission District), 239, 270

E&O Trading Company (Union Square), 238,
    270–71
Ebisu Sushi (Sunset District), 150
El Nuevo Fruitlandia (Mission District), 240,
    271–72
Ella's Restaurant, 150
Empress of China (Chinatown), 236
Enrico's (North Beach), 239, 272

Farallon (Union Square), 238, 272–73
Financial District
    Cafe Tiramisu, 239, 263–64
    Il Fornaio, 239, 280–81
    Kokkari Estiatorio, 239, 283–84
    MacArthur Park, 239, 289–90
    Tadich Grill, 232, 239, 309–10
    Tommy Toy's, 312
    Tommys Toy's, 239
    Yank Sing, 239, 316–17
Firewood Café (Castro District), 108
First Crush (Union Square), 238, 273–74
Fleur de Lys (Union Square), 238, 274
Fog City Diner (North Beach), 239, 275
French Laundry (Yountville), 169
Fringale (SoMa District), 240, 275–76

The Garden Terrace (SoMa District), 155
Grand Café (Union Square), 238, 276–77
Gratuities. See Tipping for service
Greens (Marina District), 239, 277

Hang Ah Tea Room (Chinatown), 100
Hard Rock Café (Fisherman's Wharf), 155

Harris' Restaurant (Civic Center), 238, 277–78
Hawthorne Lane (SoMa District), 240, 278–79
Helmland (North Beach), 239, 279–80
The House (Sunset District), 117
House of Prime Rib (Civic Cen(ter)), 238, 280

Il Fornaio (Financial District), 239, 280–81
Information resources, 121–22
Izzy's Steak and Chop House (Marina District),
    239, 281–82

Jardiniere (Civic Center), 238, 282
Johnny Rockets (Marina District), 155
John's Grill (Union Square), 238, 282–83
Julia's Kitchen (Napa), 168, 172

Kokkari Estiatorio (Financial District), 239, 283–84
Kuleto's (Union Square), 238, 284

La Taqueria (Mission District), 150
La Toque (Saint Helena), 169, 284–85
Le Cheval (Oakland), 241, 285–86
Le Colonial (Union Square), 238, 286–87
Lefty O'Doul's (Union Square), 149, 238, 287
Lilo Lounge (Potrero Hill), 109
Louie's Bar and Grill (SoMa District), 240,
    287–88
Lulu (SoMa District), 240, 288
Luna Park (Mission District), 240, 288–89

MacArthur Park (Financial District), 239, 289–90
Maps
    Chinatown dining, 249
    dining around town, 246–47
    Union Square dining, 248
Marina District
    Ana Mandara, 239, 253–54
    The Brazen Head, 149, 239, 260
    The Buena Vista Café, 239, 261
    Greens, 239, 277
    Izzy's Steak and Chop House, 239, 281–82
    Johnny Rockets, 155
    McCormick & Kuleto's, 239, 291–92
    Perry's, 239, 300
    Scoma's, 236
    Sinbad's, 236
    Zarzuela, 239, 318
Martini House (Saint Helena), 169
Masa's (Union Square), 238, 290
Max's Opera Café (Civic Center), 238, 291
McCormick & Kuleto's (Marina District), 239,
    291–92
Mel's Drive-In, 155
Millennium (Civic Center), 238, 292–93
Millennium Restaurant (Berkeley), 149
Mission District
    Dusit, 239, 270

El Nuevo Fruitlandia, 240, 271–72
La Taqueria, 150
Luna Park, 240, 288–89
Ti Couz, 240, 311–12
Watergate, 240, 315–16
Zuni Café and Grill, 240, 318–19
Mitchell's Ice Cream, 149
Momi Toby's Revolution Café (Civic Center), 238, 293
Money-saving tips, 38
Moose's (North Beach), 239, 293–94
Moscone Center (SoMa District), 86–88
Mrs. Field's Cookies, 155
Museum of Modern Art Café (Civic Center), 88

Napa Valley
    American Market Café, 172
    Brannan's Grill, 170
    Brix Restaurant, 169
    Calistoga Inn, 170
    The French Laundry, 169
    Julia's Kitchen, 168, 172
    La Toque, 169
    Martini House, 169
    NV Restaurant, 168, 294–95
    Wine Garden Restaurant, 169
    Wine Spectator Greystone Restaurant, 169
    Wine Train, 174–75. See also Wine Country
Neighborhood, "best of" restaurants by, 238–41
No Name Bar (Sausalito), 181
North Beach
    A. Sabella's Restaurant, 239, 252–53
    Café Pescatore, 239, 263
    Caffe Trieste, 149, 348
    Calzones, 239, 264–65
    Enrico's, 239, 272
    Fog City Diner, 239, 275
    Helmand, 239
    Helmland, 279–80
    Moose's, 239, 293–94
    Piperade's, 239, 300–301
    The Stinking Rose, 239, 307–08
    Trattoria Pinocchio, 239, 314
NV Restaurant (Napa), 168, 294–95

Oakland
    Baywolf, 186, 241, 257–58
    Le Cheval, 241, 285–86
    Oliveto, 241
    Oliveto Restaurant, 295–96
Oliveto Restaurant (Oakland), 241, 295–96
Ondine (Tiburon/Sausalito), 241
Oola (SoMa District), 240, 296
Original Joe's (Union Square), 238, 296–97

Pacific (Union Square), 238, 297–98
Pacific Union Club (Nob Hill District), 101

Palio D'Asti (Chinatown), 238, 298–99
Paragon (SoMa District), 240, 299–300
Perry's (Marina District), 239, 300
Piperade's (North Beach), 239, 300–301
PJ's Oyster Bed (Richmond/Sunset District), 241, 301
Plouf (Union Square), 238, 301–02
Point Reyes National Seashore, 189
Ponzu (Union Square), 238, 302–03
Potereo Hill
    Bottom of Hill, 109
    Lilo Lounge, 109
    Thanya & Salee, 109

Ratings. See "Best of" ratings
Recommendations, understand UG ratings and, 236–37, 240
Red Dora's Bearded Lady Dyke Café (Castro District), 108
Red's Java House (SoMa District), 240, 303–04
Restaurants, using this guide for, 5–6
Richmond/Sunset District
    Aziza, 241, 255–56
    Beach Chalet, 241, 258–59
    Café For All Seasons, 117
    Clement Street Bar and Grill, 241, 267–68
    Clementine, 241, 267
    Ebisu Sushi, 150
    The House, 117
    PJ's Oyster Bed, 241, 301
    Strait's Café, 241, 308–09
    Thanh Long, 241, 310
    Ruth's Chris Steak House (Civic Center), 238, 304

Saddles Steakhouse (Sonoma Valley), 179
Saffron (Sonoma Valley), 180
Sam Woh (Chinatown), 238, 304–05
Sam's Anchor Cafe (Tiburon), 152
San Francisco Magazine, 122
Scala's Bistro (Union Square), 238, 305
Scenic views
    Top o' the Mark, 102, 341–42
    View Lounge, 110
Scoma's (Marina District), 236
Sears Fine Foods Restaurant (Union Square), 150
Service and quality
    "best of" by neighborhood, 238–41
    tipping for, 120–21
Shanghai 1930 (SoMa District), 240, 305–06
Sheraton Palace Garden Court (SoMa District), 240, 306–07
Sinbad's (Marina District), 236
SoMa District
    Acme Chop House, 239, 251–52
    Bambuddha Lounge, 239, 256–57
    Bistro Clovis, 239, 259
    Boulevard, 239, 259–60

SoMa District *(continued)*
Buzz 9, 239, 261–62
The Cosmopolitan Restaurant, 239, 269–70
Fringale, 240, 275–76
The Garden Terrace, 155
Hawthorne Lane, 240, 278–79
Louie's Bar and Grill, 240, 287–88
Lulu, 240, 288
Moscone Center, 86–88
Oola, 240, 296
Paragon, 240, 299–300
Red's Java House, 240, 303–04
Shanghai 1930, 240, 305–06
Sheraton Palace Garden Court, 240, 306–07
South Park Café, 240, 307
Thirstybear, 240, 310–11
Town's End Restaurant and Bakery, 240, 313–14
Tu Lan, 240, 315
Yerba Buena Center, 86, 88
Sonoma Valley. *See* Wine Country
South Park Café (SoMa District), 240, 307
The Stinking Rose (North Beach), 239, 307–08
Strait's Café (Richmond/Sunset District), 241,
    308–09
Sunset District. *See* Richmond/Sunset District
Swan Oyster Depot (Civic Center), 238, 309

Tadich Grill (Financial District), 232, 239, 309–10
Taxes on food service, 124
Thanh Long (Richmond/Sunset District), 241, 310
Thanya *&* Salee (Potrero Hill), 109
Thirstybear (SoMa District), 240, 310–11
Ti Couz (Mission District), 240, 311–12
Tiburon/Sausalito
Ondine, 241
Sam's Anchor Cafe, 152
Tipping for service, 120–21
Tommy Toy's (Financial District), 239, 312
Tommy's Joynt (Civic Center), 238, 313
Ton Kiang Restaurant (Chinatown), 150
Top o' the Mark, 102, 341–42
Town's End Restaurant and Bakery (SoMa
    District), 240, 313–14
Trattoria Pinocchio (North Beach), 239, 314
Tu Lan (SoMa District), 240, 315

Union Square
Asia de Cuba, 238, 254–55
B44, 238, 256
Boudin's Bakery, 345

Café de la Presse, 238, 262–63
Campton Place Restaurant, 238, 265–66
Cheesecake Factory, 345
Cortez, 238, 267–68
E*&*O Trading Company, 238, 270–71
Farallon, 238, 272–73
First Crush, 238, 273–74
Fleur de Lys, 238, 274
Grand Café, 238, 276–77
Jamba Juice, 345
John's Grill, 238, 282–83
Kuleto's, 238, 284
Le Colonial, 238, 286–87
Lefty O'Doul's, 149, 238, 287
Masa's, 238, 290
Original Joe's, 238, 296–97
Pacific, 238, 297–98
Plouf, 238, 301–02
Ponzu, 238, 302–03
Scala's Bistro, 238, 305
Sears Fine Foods Restaurant, 150
Wolfgang Puck Express, 345
Unofficial Guides
"best of" by cuisine, 242–45
"best of" by neighborhood, 238–41
how to use, 3–5, 236–37, 240
sharing your comments, 7

Viks Distributors Inc. (Berkeley), 148

Watergate (Mission District), 240, 315–16
West Bay Café (SFO), 241, 316
Where San Francisco, 121
Wine Country. *See also* Napa Valley
Doce Lunas (Kenwood), 179
La Toque (Saint Helena), 169, 284–85
Saddles Steakhouse (Sonoma), 179
Saffron (Glen Ellen), 180
Wine Garden Restaurant (Yountville), 169
Wine Spectator Greystone Restaurant
    (Saint Helena), 169
Wolfgang Puck Express (Union Square), 345

Yank Sing (Financial District), 239, 316–17
Yerba Buena Center (SoMa District), 86, 88
Yuet Lee (Chinatown), 238, 317–18

Zarzuela (Marina District), 239, 318
Zuni Café and Grill (Mission District), 240,
    318–19

SUBJECT INDEX

Accommodations. *See* Accommodations Index
African-American community
    Afro Solo Arts Festival, 32
    Black Panthers and, 21
    Fort Mason and, 2
    Lorraine Hansberry Theatre (Union Square), 103
    Martin Luther King Celebration, 29
AIDS, 21–22, 26–27, 108, 350
AIDS Memorial Chapel, 28
Airports
    Oakland International Airport (OAK), 92, 95
    porter/skycap tipping, 120
    San Francisco International Airport (SFO),
        92–93
Alcatraz Island
    avoiding crowds at, 24
    Escape From Alcatraz Triathalon, 384
    as federal prison, 19
    outdoor exercise on, 372
    scenic views of, 160
    tours of, 89, 98
Alcohol. *See* Liquor
American Conservatory Theatre (Union Square),
    103, 322
Americans with Disabilities Act, 122–23
AMTRAK, 96
Amusement Parks
    Monterey Bay Aquarium, 156
    Paramount's Great America, 156
    Six Flags Marine World, 156
Angel Island State Park, 98, 144, 151, 184,
    371–72, 375
Año Nuevo State Reserve, 191
Aquarium of the Bay, 105
Aquatic Park, 160
Art. *See also* Attractions, UG list of top; Museums
    Asian Art Museum (Civic Center), 201–2
    Berkeley Art Museum, 187
    city calendar of events, 29–34

information resources for, 121–22
Mission Street murals, 109
Museum of Modern Art (SFMOMA), 2, 86, 110
Palace of Fine Arts, 104, 371
Palace of the Legion of Honor, 112, 154, 361
San Francisco Art Institute, 85, 102
San Francisco Arts Monthly, 122
Asian Art Museum (Civic Center), 100
Asian community, 29–34
Attractions
    avoiding crowds at, 24–25
    for children, 153–57
    free admission to, 157
    for gays and lesbians, 28
    Napa Valley, 172–74
    parks and recreational areas, 98
    secret staircases, 159–60
    Sonoma Valley, 177–79
    using this guide for, 5–6
    Victorian homes, 2, 104–5, 114, 145
Attractions, UG list for kids. *See also* Art; Museums
    Aquarium of the Bay (North Beach), 200–201
    Cliff House (Richmond/Sunset District), 208–9
    Exploratorium (Marina District), 222–23
    Ghirardelli Choclate Manufactory and Soda
        Fountain (Marina District), 211–12
    Hyde Street Pier (Marina District), 105,
        226–27
    Lawrence Hall of Science (Berkeley), 159, 187,
        213–14
    Palace of Fine Arts (Marina District), 222–23
    Phoebe A. Hearst Museum of Anthropology
        (Berkeley), 223–24
    Ripley's Believe It or Not! Museum (North
        Beach), 224–25
    San Francisco Craft and Folk Art Museum
        (Marina District), 225
    San Francisco Maritime Museum (Marina
        District), 225–26

Attractions, UG list for kids. *(continued)*
San Francisco Maritime National Historical
Park (Marina District), 226–27
San Francisco Zoo (Richmond/Sunset District),
228–29
Attractions, UG list of top, 198–99
Alcatraz Island (North Beach), 193, 196–97, 200
Asian Art Museum (Civic Center), 201–2
Berkeley Art Museum, 202
Berkeley Rose Gardens, 203
Cable Car Barn and Museum (Chinatown),
135–36, 153, 203–4
California Academy of Sciences (SoMa
District), 204
California Historical Society (SoMa) District, 204
California Palace of the Legion of Honor
(Richmond/Sunset District), 204–6, 361
Cartoon Art Museum (SoMa District), 206
Castro Theatre (Mission District), 206–7
Center for the Arts (SoMa District), 232–33
City Lights Bookstore (North Beach), 20, 107,
207–8
Coit Tower (North Beach), 209–10
de Young Memorial Museum (Golden Gate
Park), 210
Fort Point National Historic Site (Presidio),
210–11
Haas-Lilienthal House (Civic Center), 212
Japanese Tea Garden (Richmond/Sunset
District), 212–13
Marin French Cheese Company, 214–15
Marine Mammal Center, 215–16
Mexican Museum (Mission District), 216
Mission Dolores (Mission District), 216–17
Mount Tamalpais-East Peak (Marin County),
217–18
Muir Woods National Monument (Marin
County), 98, 142–43, 185, 191, 218–19
Museum of Money of the American West (Fi-
nancial District), 219–20
Museum of Opthalmology (North Beach), 220
Neptune Society Columbarium
(Richmond/Sunset District), 220–21
Oakland Museum of California, 221–22
Pacific Film Archive (Berkeley), 202
San Francisco Museum of Modern Art
(SFMOMA), 227–28
Strybing Arboretum and Botanical Gardens
(Richmond/Sunset District), 230
Wax Museum at Fisherman's Wharf, 230–31
Wells Fargo History Museum (Financial
District), 231–32
Yerba Buena Gardens (SoMa District), 232–33
Automobiles. *See also* Parking; Transportation
avoiding rush-hour traffic, 24–25, 130
curb your wheels on hills, 131–32
drinking and driving, 325
getting around by, 91–92, 117–20, 129–30
hotel parking, 43
International Auto Show, 34
pedestrian safety, 138
rental agencies, 89, 93, 130

Ballet
Fort Mason and, 2
San Francisco Ballet, 34, 322
Stern Grove Festival, 322
Ballroom dancing, 325. *See also* Dancing
Barbary Coast District, 18
Bay Area Rapid Transit (BART)
Berkeley service, 188
construction of, 21
disabled access, 123
getting around by, 94–95, 135
Market Street service, 118–19
Mission District service, 108
Moscone Center service, 88
Oakland service, 186–87
SFO service, 92
The Bay Area Reporter, 122
Bay Bridge, 19, 117
Bay City Guide, 122
Bay to Breakers Race, 28, 31, 384–85
Beaches
"Best of" list, 376–77
child friendly, 154
getting to, 111–12
Berkeley, Calif.
Children's Science Museum, 159
Convention and Visitors Bureau, 96
Lawrence Hall of Science, 159, 187, 213–14
protest movement, 20–21, 187
shopping, 350
things to do in, 187–88
Bernal Heights, 29, 139
"Best of" lists. *See also* Accommodations Index;
Dining and Restaurants Index
for attractions, 198–99
for exercise and recreation, 89
for nightclubs, 326
for shopping, 363
using this guide for, 5
Big Basin Redwoods State Park, 191
Biking/Bicycle rental. *See also* Mountain biking
Angel Island, 151, 184, 375
Blazing Saddles, 151–52, 375
The Headlands, 184–85
Napa Valley, 173
for outdoor exercise, 373–75
Sonoma Valley, 178
Wine Country, 374
Bird-watching, 382
Books, events and bookstores
Bound Together Anarchist Bookstore
(Haight-Ashbury), 349
city calendar of, 30

City Lights Bookstore (North Beach), 20, 107, 207–8, 348
A Different Light Bookshop (Castro Street), 28, 355
Kinokinuya Book Store (Japantown), 348
San Francisco Public Library, 100
shopping for, 354–55
Buses, 133–34. See also Public transportation
Business travel
corporate rates, 39
local services to support, 87–88
Moscone Center and, 86–87
use of this guide for, 5, 85–86

Cable cars
Bell-Ringing Competition, 32
Cable Car Barn and Museum, 135–36, 153, 203–4
getting around by, 88, 135–37
history of, 101
Moscone Center service to, 86
Muni passports for, 133, 157
Pacific heights, 104
sound like a native on, 121
Union Square, 102
Calendar of events and festivals, 29–34
California Academy of Sciences, 114
California Gold Rush, 14–7
California Historical Society, 86, 160, 361
California Republic, independence and, 14
California Road Conditions, 130
The Cannery (Fisherman's Wharf), 105
Carjacking, 127
Carmel-by-the-Sea, 190, 192
Castro Street
city gay history and, 26
gay events on, 28
gay neighborhoods at, 28–29
getting around, 108
shopping, 349–50
summer street fair, 344
walking tours, 145
Cautions. See Safety and security
Children. See also Attractions, UG list for kids
beaches for, 376–77
Children's Fairyland (Oakland), 156, 186
Napa Valley, 172–73
shopping with, 351–52, 360–61
Six Flags Marine World, 156
Sonoma Valley, 178
traveling with, 153–56
Chinatown
August Moon Festival, 32
Chinese New Year, 29, 100
cultural diversity and, 2
getting around, 99–100, 117–20
nightclubs in, 326
walking tours, 145

Churches
Buddhist Church of San Francisco (Japantown), 116
Church of St. Peter and Paul (North Beach), 107
Grace Cathedral (Nob Hill District), 102
St. Mary's Cathedral (Japantown), 116, 145
Cinco De Mayo Celebration, 31
City Lights Bookstore (North Beach), 20, 107, 207–8, 348
CityPass, 156–57
Civic Center District
Asian Art Museum, 201–2
getting around, 100–101
Haas-Lilienthal House, 212
nightclubs in, 326
War Memorial Opera House, 321–22
Cliff House (Ocean Beach), 112, 159
Climate
clothing for the, 23–24
look like a native, 121
planning for the, 1–2, 370
Wine Country tours and, 166
winter road conditions, 130
Coit Tower (North Beach), 19, 107, 158–59
Contemporary art venues, 2
Convention and Visitors Bureaus, 25, 96, 133, 145
Credit cards, avoiding theft of, 124–28
Crime, avoiding, 124–28
Crowds, avoiding, 5
Cultural identity, neighborhood, 2
Curran Theatre (Union Square), 103, 322

Dancing. See also Nightclub profiles
ballroom, 325
Emeryville's Allegro Ballroom, 368
Metronome Dance Center, 367
Day trips. See also Tours
beyond the Bay area, 191–92
East Bay, 185–87
Marin County, 181–85
self-guided city, 145–52
south of San Francisco, 190–91
Wine Country, 161–67
de Young Memorial Museum (Golden Gate Park), 114
A Different Light Bookshop (Castro Street), 28, 355
Disabled access, 122–23, 131
Dolores Park (Noe Valley), 109
Dry cleaning, 89

Earthquakes
of 1906, 17–8
of 1989, 21–22
cable car operations and, 136
Marina District and, 103
Market Street and, 119
San Andreas Fault, 97

East Bay, 117, 185–88. *See also* Berkeley, Calif.;
     Oakland, Calif.
Emergency 911 service, 125
Entertainment and Nightlife. *See also* Nightclub
     profiles
   AMC Kabuki 8, 155
   business traveler, 90
   Club Fugazi *Beach Blank Babylon,* 146–47
   Condor Club (North Beach), 107
   etiquette and behavior, 324
   information resources for, 121–22, 325
   Metreon and IMAX theatre, 86, 110, 155, 351
   San Francisco Magazine, 122
   SoMa District, 110
   tipping for service, 326
   using this guide for, 5–6
Events and festivals
   Castro Street fair, 344
   city calendar of, 29–34
   Folsom Street fair, 344
   gay and lesbian community, 28
   Haight Street Fair, 31, 114, 344
   Independent Film Festival, 116
   summer classical music, 322
   Union Street Festival, 344
Exercise and Recreation. *See also* Accommodations
     Index; Biking/Bicycle rental; Kayaking; Races;
     Rock climbing; Windsurfing and kitesurfing
   aerobics and fitness centers, 365–66
   Mission Cliffs, 89, 155
   Napa Valley, 173–74
   Pacific Rod and Gun Club, 89
   for runners, 372–73
   secret staircases for, 159–60, 370–71
   Yerba Buena Ice Skating and Bowling Center,
     368
Exploratorium science museum, 104, 154, 361

Ferry boats
   Alameda/Oakland Ferry, 95–96
   Alcatraz Island, 105
   to Angel Island, 98, 144, 184
   getting around by, 137
   to Six Flags Marine World, 156
   Tiburon/Sausalito, 181–83
Festivals. *See* Events and festivals
Film and movies
   calendar of festivals, 29–34
   San Francisco Movie Map, 160
   San Francisco-themed, 160–61
Financial District
   1980's development of, 21, 99
   getting around, 103, 117–20
   nightclubs in, 326
Fire Department assistance, 125
Fisherman's Wharf. *See also* Marina District
   avoiding crowds at, 24
   Bay sightseeing cruises, 137, 181–83

deep-sea fishing charters, 380
   getting around, 105
   look like a native at, 121
   map of, 106
Fishing/deep-sea fishing, 380
Fitness facilities, 365–66. *See also* Exercise and
     Recreation
Flower and garden
   city calendar of shows, 29–34
   San Francisco Botanical Garden, 369
   shopping for, 358
Fly-Away Vacations, 44
Fort Funston, 112, 154, 368, 377
Fort Mason
   art venues, 2
   Golden Gate Promenade and, 139
   scenic view from, 160
   things to do at, 104, 122
   in World War II, 19
Fort Point National Historic Site, 104, 111, 158, 368

Galleries. *See* Art; Museums
Gay and Lesbian community
   The Café (SoMa/Mission District), 331
   Castro District, 108
   city history of, 21, 26–27
   information resources for, 27–28
   neighborhoods catering to, 28–29
   Noe Valley, 109
Geary Theatre (Union Square), 322
Ghirardelli Square, 121
Golden Gate Bridge
   construction of, 19
   history of, 111
   pedestrian walkway, 159
   scenic view of, 158
Golden Gate National Recreation Area, 21, 98,
     184–85
Golden Gate Park
   biking, 373–75
   Children's Playground, 154
   de Young Memorial Museum, 210
   getting to, 120
   golf and tennis, 379–80
   for outdoor exercise, 368
   things to do in, 112–14
Golden Gate Promenade, 104–5, 119, 138–39,
     154, 368, 372
Golden Gate Theatre, 323
Golden State Warriors, 383
Golf
   Golden Gate Park Course, 379
   Lincoln Park Golf Course, 371, 379
   Presidential Putting Greens, 89
   Tilden Park Golf Course (Berkeley), 379–80
Grace Cathedral (Nob Hill District), 102
Gray Whale Cove State Beach, 190
Great Highway, 120, 151–52

Greenwich Steps (Telegraph Hill), 108

Haight-Ashbury District
  getting around, 114–15
  Haight Street Fair, 31
  psychedelic 1960's and, 20
  shopping, 349
  walking tours, 145
Half Moon Bay, Calif., 190
Hallidie Plaza, 25
Handicap access, 122–23
Hang gliding, 154, 378
Hayes Valley, 29, 348
Health spas. See Accommodations Index
History, people in San Francisco
  Anza, Juan Bautista de, 12
  Ayala, Juan Manuel de, 12
  Bidwell, John, 14
  Bogart, Humphrey, 108
  Cabrillo, Juan, 12
  Cleaver, Eldridge, 21
  Coit, Lillie Hitchcock, 107
  Didion, Joan, 101
  DiMaggio, Joe, 107
  Drake, Francis, 12, 98, 188
  Feinstein, Diane, 21
  Ferlinghetti, Lawrence, 20, 207–8, 355
  Fremont, John C., 14
  Ginsberg, Allen, 20, 355
  Hallidie, Andrew, 16
  Hearst, George, 16
  Hearst, Patty, 21
  Kerouac, Jack, 19–20, 107, 207, 355
  Marshall, James, 14
  Meese, Edwin, 20
  Milk, Harvey, 21, 26, 100, 108
  Monroe, Marilyn, 107
  Montez, Lola, 15
  Moscone, George, 21, 26, 100
  Newton, Huey, 21
  Portola, Gaspar de, 12
  Queen Elizabeth I, 12
  Reagan, Ronald, 20
  Seale, Bobby, 21
  Sutro, Adolf, 16
  Vizcaino, Sebastian, 12
  White, Dan, 21, 26, 100
History, San Francisco
  exploration and settlement, 11–4
  gold and silver discovery, 14–7
  1906 Earthquake, 17–8
  1930's and Great Depression, 18–9
  1940's and post-War period, 19–20
  1960's psychedelic era, 20
  1970's and 1980's, 21–22
  1990's dot.com boom, 22
  racism in, 17, 21
Homeless population, 128

Horse racing, 384
Horseback riding, Wine Country, 173, 178
Hot-air ballooning and airplane rides, 143,
    173–74, 179
Hotels, choosing. See Accommodations Index
Human Rights Campaign Action Center, 108
Hyde Street Pier, 105, 226–27

Information resources. See also Maps; Web sites
  entertainment and nightlife, 325
  gay and lesbian, 27–29, 122
  Joie de Vivre Hospitality, 158
  maps and brochures, 96
  newspapers and magazines, 121–22
  planning your visit, 25
  ticket agencies, 323
  Wine Country, 175, 181
In-line skating, 373–75
Irish-American community, 30
Italian-American culture
  Fort Mason and, 2
  North Beach and, 105–7
  parade and festival, 33

Japanese Consulate (Japantown), 116
Japanese Tea Garden (Golden Gate Park), 114,
    145, 369
Japantown
  AMC Kabuki 8, 155, 348
  Cherry Blossom Festival, 30
  getting around, 115–16
  Japan Center, 116, 348
  Nihonmachi Street Fair, 32
  shopping, 348
Jazz and blues festivals, calendar of, 29–34
Jewish Film Festival, 32
Jewish Museum, 86

Kayaking. See also Exercise and Recreation
  Angel Island, 184
  Napa Valley, 173
  Sausalito, 152
  Sea Trek Ocean Kayaking Center, 377–78

Lake Tahoe, 192
Lands End, 111–12, 377
Lighthouses
  Pigeon Point, 190
  Point Bonita, 185
  Point Reyes, 98, 188
Lincoln Park, 154, 371
Liquor
  drinking and driving, 325
  hours for sales of, 124
  nightclub behavior and, 324
  shopping for, 360
  The Whiskey Shop (Union Square), 346
Lombard Street, 143, 155

Lorraine Hansberry Theatre (Union Square), 103
Los Angeles, Calif., 117
Louise M. Davis Symphony Hall (Civic Center),
    100, 321

Magic Theatre (Fort Mason), 104, 323
Maps
    Attractions around Town, 194–95
    Civic Center, 101
    Fisherman's Wharf, 106
    Golden Gate National Recreation Area, 196–97
    Golden Gate Park, 113
    Haight-Ashbury District, 115
    Marin County, 182
    nightclubs, 328–29
    Official San Francisco Street and Transit Map, 123,
        133
    San Francisco Movie Map, 160
    San Francisco neighborhoods, 8–9
    where to get, 96, 121–22
    Wine Country, 162
    Yerba Buena Gardens (SoMa District), 233
Marin County, 19, 96, 117, 123, 181–85. *See also*
    Muir Woods National Monument
Marin Headlands, 98, 151, 159, 184–85, 369–70,
    372
Marina District, 103–5, 347. *See also* Fisherman's
    Wharf
Marina Green, 154, 371
Marine Mammal Center, 381
Marine's Memorial theatre (Union Square), 103
Maritime Museum (Fisherman's Wharf), 105
Market Street, 118–19
Medical emergency assistance, 125
Mendocino, Calif., 117, 192
Mexican culture
    Cinco De Mayo Celebration, 31
    Fort Mason and, 2
    Mission District and, 108–9
Mexican Museum, 2, 86
Mission Cliffs, 89, 155, 367
Mission District
    art venues, 2
    city gay history and, 26
    gay safety in, 29
    getting around, 108–9, 117–20
    Great Earthquake and, 18
    Mission Cultural Center, 109
    nightclubs in, 326
Mission Dolores (Nuestra Señora de Dolores),
    12–13, 108
Mission Santa Clara, 13
Money-saving tips
    CityPass and ticket books, 156–57
    free admission to attractions, 157
    half-price theatre tickets, 103
    Muni Passports, 133, 157

Rincon Flowers, 358
    ticket agencies, 323
Monterey, Calif., 117, 192
Moscone Center (SoMa District), 86–88, 110
Mount Tamalpais, 98, 152, 158, 184–85, 369–70
Mountain biking, 375–76. *See also* Biking/
    Bicycle rental
Muir Woods National Monument (Marin
    County), 98, 142–143, 185, 191, 218–19, 369
Muni Metro, 88, 123, 133–35. *See also* Public
    transportation
Muni Passports, 133, 157
Museums. *See also* Art; Attractions, UG list of top
    Asian Art Museum, 100
    Berkeley Art Museum, 187
    Cable Car Barn and Museum, 135–36, 153,
        203–4
    Cartoon Art Museum, 86
    Children's Science Museum (Berkeley), 159
    Exploratorium, 104, 154
    free admission, 157
    Golden Gate Park, 114
    Jewish Museum, 86
    list of, 157
    Maritime Museum, 105
    Mexican Museum, 86
    Oakland Museum of California, 186
    Palace of the Legion of Honor, 112, 154,
        204–06, 361
    San Francisco Museum of Modern Art
        (SFMOMA), 2, 86, 110, 357
    The Sharpsteen Museum (Calistoga), 172–73
    shopping at, 361
    Silverado Museum (Saint Helena), 173
    Sonoma Valley, 177–79
    Wax Museum, 105
    Wells Fargo History Museum, 103
Music festivals and stores
    calendar of, 29–34
    Midsummer Mozart, 322
    Palace of the Legion of Honor, 204–06
    shopping, 361–62
    Stern Grove Festival, 322

Napa Valley
    American Safari Cruises, 175
    attractions, 172–73
    Conference and Visitors Bureau, 175
    dining and lodging, 168–70
    exercise and recreation, 173–74
    getting to, 117, 170
    health spas, 174
    history of wine in, 167–68
    list of wineries, 170–71
    Napa Valley Winery Exchange, 360
    shopping, 174
    Wine Train, 174–75

National Coalition for the Homeless, 128
National Park Service. *See also* Parks
 Fort Point National Historic Site, 104
 Golden Gate National Recreation Area, 21, 98
 Hyde Street Pier, 105
 Muir Woods National Monument (Marin County), 98, 142–43, 185, 191, 218–19, 369
 Point Reyes National Seashore, 98, 188–89, 370
 Presidio and Fort Point, 110–11
 San Francisco National Military Cemetery, 111
 Yosemite National Park, 117, 191–92
National Public Radio, 122
Native Americans, 11–13, 30, 108
Neighborhoods.
  See also specific neighborhood by name
 Beaches and Lands End, 111–12
 Castro Street, 108
 Chinatown, 99–100
 Civic Center, 100–101
 cultural identity in, 2
 etiquette and behavior, 324
 Financial District, 99
 Fisherman's Wharf, 105
 gay and lesbian, 28–9
 Golden Gate Park, 112–14
 Haight-Ashbury District, 114–15
 Japantown, 115–16
 Marina District/Pacific Heights, 103–5
 Mission District, 108–9
 Nob Hill/Russian Hill, 101–2
 North Beach, 105–7
 parking access in, 131
 Potrero Hill, 109–10
 Presidio, Fort Point and the Golden Gate Bridge, 110–11
 SoMa (South of Market) District, 110
 special features of, 5
 Telegraph Hill, 107–8
 Tenderloin District, 100–101
 Twin Peaks, 116–17
 Union Square, 102–3
Nightclub profiles. *See also* Entertainment and Nightlife
 Amira Restaurant (SoMa/Mission District), 327
 Bimbo's 365 Club (North Beach), 327
 Biscuits & Blues (Union Square), 327, 330
 Bubble Lounge (Financial District), 330–31
 The Café (SoMa/Mission District), 331
 Café Du Nord (SoMa/Mission District), 331–32
 Club Deluxe (Richmond/Sunset District), 332
 The Elbo Room (SoMa/Mission District), 332–33
 Fillmore (Civic Center), 333
 Gold Dust Lounge (Union Square), 333–34
 Great American Music Hall (Civic Center), 334
 Harry Denton's Starlight Room (Union Square), 334–35

Harvey's (SoMa/Mission District), 335
Impala (North Beach), 335–36
Jade Bar (Civic Center), 336
Li Po (Chinatown), 336–37
Make-Out Room (SoMa/Mission District), 337
Martuni's (SoMa/Mission District), 337–38
Noc Noc (Civic Center), 338
Pier 23 (North Beach), 338–39
Plough and the Stars (Richmond/Sunset District), 339
Plush Room (Union Square), 339–40
The Red Room (Union Square), 340
Ruby Skye (Union Square), 340–41
Tonga Room (Chinatown), 341
Top o' the Mark (Chinatown), 102, 341–42
Tosco Cafe (North Beach), 342
911 emergency service, 125
Nob Hill/Russian Hill District, 101–2, 117–20
Noe Valley, 29, 109
North Beach
 Beat Generation of, 19
 City Lights Bookstore, 20, 107, 207–8
 getting around, 105–7
 nightclubs in, 326
 North Beach Festival, 31
 walking tours, 145
Nude beaches, 98, 190, 377

Oakland, Calif., things to do in, 186–87
Oakland Athletics, 383
Oakland International Airport (OAK), 92, 95
Oakland Raiders, 383
Oceanic Society, 381
Official San Francisco Street and Transit Map, 123
Olema Valley, 370
Opera
 Fort Mason and, 2
 San Francisco Opera Association, 321–22
 Stern Grove Festival, 322
 War Memorial Opera House, 100, 321
Orpheum Theatre, 323

Pacific Heights, 29, 103–5, 347
Package Vacations, 42–44
Palace of Fine Arts (Marina District), 104, 371
Palace of the Legion of Honor (Lands End), 111–12, 154, 204–6, 361
Panama Pacific International Exhibition of 1915, 18, 104, 222
Parades and events, city calendar of, 28–34
Paratransit Taxi Service, 123
Parking. *See also* Automobiles
 at Berkeley, 187
 city regulations, 130–32
 curb your wheels on hills, 131–32
 disabled access, 122–23
 hotel, 43, 129–30

Moscone Center, 88
valet tipping, 120
Parks. *See also* Amusement Parks; National Park
Service
Angel Island State Park, 98, 144, 151, 184,
371–72, 375
Año Nuevo State Reserve, 191
Aquatic Park, 139, 160
Bale Grist Mill State Historical Park
(Napa Valley), 172
Big Basin Redwoods State Park, 191
Crissy Field, 104, 139, 377
Dolores Park, 109, 159
Fort Mason, 139, 160
Golden Gate Park, 112–14, 120, 154
Gray Whale Cove State Beach, 190
Half Moon Bay State Beach, 190
Huntington Park (Nob Hill District), 102
Jack London State Historic Park (Sonoma
Valley), 178
Lincoln Park, 154, 371
Marina Green, 139, 154, 371
People's Park (Berkeley), 187
The Presidio, 154
Sonoma State Historical Park (Sonoma Valley),
178
Sutro Heights Park, 159
Wilder Ranch State Park, 191
Performance Arts. *See* Ballet; Opera; Symphony
Petaluma, Calif., 117
Pets, traveling with, 377
Pickpocketing, 127–28
Pigeon Point Lighthouse, 190
Point Bonita Lighthouse, 185
Point Reyes Lighthouse, 98, 188
Point Reyes National Seashore, 98, 188–89, 370,
377, 382
Police assistance, 125
Potrero Hill, getting around, 109–10
Precautions. *See* Safety and security
Presidio, Fort Point and the Golden Gate Bridge,
110–11, 132, 138–39, 154, 369
Professional Sports, 155–56, 382–84
Public transportation, 117, 133–38. *See also* Bay
Area Rapid Transit (BART); Muni Metro

Races. *See also* Exercise and Recreation
Across the Bay 12K Race, 30
Bay to Breakers Race, 28, 31, 384–85
Escape From Alcatraz Triathalon, 384
San Francisco Marathon, 385
Radio stations, 122
Recommendations, using this guide for, 3–5
Rental cars. *See* Automobiles
Restaurants. *See also* Dining and Restaurant Index
Richmond/Sunset District, 19, 326
Ripley's Believe It or Not, 105
Ripoffs and scams, 127–28

Rock climbing
Mission Cliffs indoor, 89, 155, 367
Red Rock Beach, 378
Yosemite National Park, 378
Rush-hour traffic, avoiding, 24–25, 130
Russian Hill. *See* Nob Hill/Russian Hill District

Safety and security
airport, 93
avoiding crime, 124–28
cable car operations, 136–37
curb your wheels on hills, 131–32
earthquake, 97
gay bashing, 29
pedestrian, 138
winter driving, 130
Sailing, 156, 379
San Andreas Fault, 97. *See also* Earthquakes
San Diego, Calif., 117
San Francisco 49ers, 383
San Francisco Art Institute, 85, 102
San Francisco Arts Monthly, 122
San Francisco Bay Guardian, 121, 325
San Francisco Botanical Garden, 369
San Francisco Chronicle, 121
San Francisco City Hall, 100–101
San Francisco Flower Mart, 358
San Francisco Friends of the Library, 144
San Francisco Giants, 383
San Francisco International Airport (SFO), 92–93
San Francisco Magazine, 122
San Francisco Marathon, 385
San Francisco Municipal Railway (Muni), 133
San Francisco Museum of Modern Art
(SFMOMA), 2, 86, 110, 357, 361
San Francisco National Military Cemetery, 111
San Francisco Opera Association, 321–22
San Francisco Public Library, 100
San Francisco State University, 85
San Francisco Stock Exchange, 17
San Francisco Symphony, 321
San Francisco Weekly, 325
San Francisco Zoo, 112, 117, 120
San Jose, Calif., 13, 117
Santa Barbara, Calif., 117
Santa Cruz, Calif., 117, 190, 192
Santa Cruz Mountains, 98
Santa Rosa, Calif., 117
Scenic views, guide to city, 158–60
Sea Kayaking. *See* Kayaking
Seal Rocks (Ocean Beach), 112, 159
Secret staircases, 159–60
SF Weekly, 121
Shopping
with children, 155, 351–52, 360–61
Chinatown, 347–48
Cow Hollow, 347
Crocker Galleria, 351

Embarcadero Center, 351
escorted tours, 344
Hayes Valley, 348
Marine District, 347
Metreon, 351
Moscone Center, 86
Napa Valley, 174
Pacific Heights, 347
sales taxes on purchases, 124
San Francisco Shopping Centre, 351
souvenir, 362
Specialty Shops, 352–62
Stanford Shopping Center, 351
Stonestown Galleria, 112, 351
Union Square, 102, 344–47
Sierra Nevada Mountains, 117
Sightseeing, using this guide for, 5–6
Sigmund Stern Grove, 322
Silicon Valley, 22, 85, 117
Six Flags Marine World, 156
Smoking regulations, 124, 325
SoMa (South of Market) District
    art venues in, 2
    dot.com boom and, 22
    gay neighborhoods in, 28–29
    getting around, 110, 117–20
    Moscone Center, 86–88
    nightclubs in, 326
    shopping, 349
Sonoma Valley
    attractions, 177–78
    dining and lodging, 179–81
    exercise and recreation, 178–79
    getting to, 117
    list of wineries, 176–77
    shopping, 179
Sports. See also Exercise and Recreation
    and chilren's amusements, 156
    college and amateur, 384
    professional, 155, 382–84
    shopping for, 352–53
    World Series of 1989, 21–22
St. Patrick's Day Parade, 30
Stairway Walks in San Francisco (Wilderness Press),
    159–60
State Office Building, 100
Street fairs, city calendar of, 28–34
Street Sheet, 122
Streetcars. See Muni Metro;
    Public transportation
Strybing Arboretum, 114, 369
"Summer of Love" of 1967, 20, 36–37, 145
Sutro Baths (Ocean Beach), 112
Sutro Heights Park, 159
Sutter's Mill, 14
Symphony
    Festival Orchestra, 322
    Fort Mason and, 2

Louise M. Davis Symphony Hall, 100, 321
Stern Grove Festival, 322

Taxi cabs. See Transportation
Telegraph Hill, 107–8, 158–59
Telephone area codes, 123–24
Tenderloin District, 29, 100–101
Tennis facilities, 380
Theatres and performance arts. See also Ballet;
    Opera; Symphony
    AMC Kabuki 8, 155
    American Conservatory Theatre (ACT), 103,
        322
    Castro Theatre, 108
    Club Fugazi Beach Blank Babylon, 146–47
    Curran Theatre, 322
    Geary Theatre, 322
    Golden Gate Theatre, 323
    Kabuki Comples, 116
    Magic Theatre, 104, 323
    Metreon and IMAX theatre, 86, 110, 155, 351
    Oakland Paramount Theatre, 186
    Orpheum Theatre, 323
    Theatre Rhinoceros, 28
    ticket agencies, 323
    Union Square, 103
    Yerba Buena Center, 323
Tiburon/Sausalito, 117, 152, 181–83
Tipping for service, 120–21, 326
Tour operators
    All About Chinatown, 145
    Angel Island Ferry, 98, 144, 184
    Blue & Gold Fleet, 143
    City Guides, 144
    Friends of Recreation & Parks, 145
    Gray Line, 141–43
    Haight-Ashbury Flower Power, 145
    Helen's Walk Tour, 145
    Quality Tours, 143
    Red & White Fleet, 143
    San Francisco Helicopter Tours and Charters,
        144
    San Francisco Seaplane Tours, 144
    Tower Tours, 143
    Victorian Home Walk, 145
Tours. See also Day trips
    air, 144
    Alcatraz Island, 105
    Angel Island, 151
    Bay sightseeing cruises, 137, 143–44
    bicycle, 374–75
    Cruisin' the Castro Tour, 28, 108
    Golden Gate Promenade, 104–5, 119
    gray-whale cruises, 381
    Joie de Vivre Hospitality, 158
    kayaking, 378
    Mission Street, 109
    motor coach, 141–43

Tours. *(continued)*
nightclub, 325
planning your itinerary, 145–53
Point Reyes Field Seminars, 370
shopping, 344
trolley, 102–3
Twin Peaks, 116
walking, 144–45
Wine Country, 174–75
Traffic, avoiding
pedestrian safety and, 138
rush hour, 24–25, 130
using this guide for, 5
Transamerica Pyramid, 21, 103
Transportation. *See also* Automobiles; Bay Area
Rapid Transit (BART); Muni Metro; Parking
Alameda/Oakland Ferry, 95–96
AMTRAK, 96
avoiding crime, 126–27
bridges, streets and highways, 117–19
cable cars, 86, 88
cabs and shuttles, 93, 137–38
disabled access, 122–23
Official San Francisco Street and Transit Map, 123
Paratransit Taxi Service, 123
San Francisco International Airport (SFO),
92–94
Treasure Island, 158
Twin Peaks, 116–17, 158, 160

U. S. Mint, 16
Union Square
area map of, 58
getting around, 102–3
nightclubs in, 326
shopping, 344–47, 356
walking tours, 145
University of California
Berkeley, 20–21, 85, 187
Golden Bears football, 384
Hastings College of Law, 85
Medical Center, 85
University of San Francisco, 85, 384
Unofficial Guides
defining, 3–5
list of top attractions, 198–99
sharing your comments, 7, 53–55

Vacation Packages, 42–44
Veterans Auditorium Building, 100
Victorian homes
city heritage of, 2
Haight-Ashbury, 114
Pacific heights, 104–5
walking tours, 145
Virginia City, Calif., 17

Walking, getting around by, 138–39, 145–53,
159–60
Walking tours. *See* Day trips; Tours
War Memorial Opera House, 321–22
Washington Square (North Beach), 107
Wax Museum (Fisherman's Wharf), 105
Web sites
for city events and festivals, 29–34
for gay and lesbian resources, 27–28
Moscone Center, 90
newspapers and magazine, 121–22
for planning your visit, 25
for professional sports, 383–84
ticket agency, 323
tour operator, 142–45
tourist information, 96, 158
Wine Country, 175, 181
Welcome Aboard, 123
Wells Fargo History Museum (Financial District),
103
"West Coast Live" radio show, 122
Whale watching, 98, 152, 188, 380–81.
See also Wildlife
Wheelchair access, 122–23, 131
Where San Francisco, 121
Wilder Ranch State Park, 191
Wildlife. *See also* Whale watching
Año Nuevo State Reserve, 191
Golden Gate National Recreation Area, 185
Golden Gate Park Bison Paddock, 114
Marine Mammal Center, 381
Point Reyes National Seashore, 98, 188–89
Safari West Wildlife Preserve and Tent Camp,
170, 382
San Francisco Zoo, 112, 117
Seal Rocks, 112
Six Flags Marine World, 156
Windsurfing and kitesurfing, 151, 379
Wine Country. *See also* Napa Valley;
Sonoma Valley
avoiding crowds in, 24
biking, 374
choosing the Valley, 163–64
Conference and Visitors Bureau, 96
getting to, 167
guided bus tours, 143, 164
map of, 162
self-guided day tours, 161–64
shipping wine home, 167, 360
when to go, 166
winery guided tours, 165

Yerba Buena, 13, 15
Yerba Buena Center for the Arts, 86, 88, 323
Yosemite National Park, 117, 143